2011-11-08

Dear Paul,
Thanks for leaving me to the Center.
Best wishes,

Longitudinal Data Analysis
for the Behavioral Sciences
Using R

To Leslie and Mike

Longitudinal Data Analysis
for the Behavioral Sciences
Using R

Jeffrey D. Long
University of Iowa

⑤SAGE

Los Angeles | London | New Delhi
Singapore | Washington DC

SAGE

Los Angeles | London | New Delhi
Singapore | Washington DC

FOR INFORMATION:

SAGE Publications, Inc.
2455 Teller Road
Thousand Oaks, California 91320
E-mail: order@sagepub.com

SAGE Publications Ltd.
1 Oliver's Yard
55 City Road
London EC1Y 1SP
United Kingdom

SAGE Publications India Pvt. Ltd.
B 1/I 1 Mohan Cooperative Industrial Area
Mathura Road, New Delhi 110 044
India

SAGE Publications Asia-Pacific Pte. Ltd.
33 Pekin Street #02-01
Far East Square
Singapore 048763

Acquisitions Editor: Vicki Knight
Associate Editor: Lauren Habib
Editorial Assistant: Kalie Koscielak
Production Editor: Brittany Bauhaus
Copy Editor: Gillian Dickens
Typesetter: C&M Digitals (P) Ltd.
Proofreader: Christina West
Cover Designer: Bryan Fishman
Marketing Manager: Helen Salmon
Permissions Editor: Adele Hutchinson

Copyright © 2012 by SAGE Publications, Inc.

All rights reserved. No part of this book may be reproduced or utilized in any form or by any means, electronic or mechanical, including photocopying, recording, or by any information storage and retrieval system, without permission in writing from the publisher.

Printed in the United States of America

Library of Congress Cataloging-in-Publication Data

Long, Jeffrey D., 1964-

Longitudinal data analysis for the behavioral sciences using R / Jeffrey D. Long.

p. cm.
Includes bibliographical references and index.

ISBN 978-1-4129-8268-9 (cloth)

1. Social sciences—Research. 2. Longitudinal method. 3. Mathematical statistics—Data processing. 4. R (Computer program language) I. Title.

H62.L64 2012
300.285'5133—dc23   2011019184

This book is printed on acid-free paper.

11 12 13 14 15 10 9 8 7 6 5 4 3 2 1

Brief Contents

About the Author	xv
Preface	xvii
1 Introduction	1
2 Brief Introduction to R	33
3 Data Structures and Longitudinal Analysis	63
4 Graphing Longitudinal Data	105
5 Introduction to Linear Mixed Effects Regression	147
6 Overview of Maximum Likelihood Estimation	191
7 Multimodel Inference and Akaike's Information Criterion	227
8 Likelihood Ratio Test	285
9 Selecting Time Predictors	321
10 Selecting Random Effects	357
11 Extending Linear Mixed Effects Regression	405
12 Modeling Nonlinear Change	443
13 Advanced Topics	489
Appendix: Soft Introduction to Matrix Algebra	515
References	525
Author Index	535
Subject Index	539

Detailed Contents

About the Author		xv
Preface		xvii

1 Introduction — 1
- 1.1 Statistical Computing — 3
- 1.2 Preliminary Issues — 3
  - 1.2.1 Means Versus Correlations — 3
  - 1.2.2 Measurement Issues — 7
  - 1.2.3 Response Variable Assumptions — 8
- 1.3 Conceptual Overview of Linear Mixed Effects Regression — 8
  - 1.3.1 Goals of Inference — 9
  - 1.3.2 Random Effects — 13
  - 1.3.3 How Important Are Random Effects? — 18
- 1.4 Traditional Approaches — 19
- 1.5 MPLS Data Set — 21
- 1.6 Statistical Strategy — 23
- 1.7 LMER and Multimodel Inference — 27
  - 1.7.1 Statistical Hypotheses — 27
- 1.8 Overview of the Remainder of the Book — 32

2 Brief Introduction to R — 33
- 2.1 Obtaining and Installing R — 34
- 2.2 Functions and Packages — 35
- 2.3 Essential Syntax — 36
  - 2.3.1 Prompt Versus Script Files — 36
  - 2.3.2 Input and Output Appearance in This Book — 36
  - 2.3.3 Quitting R — 37
  - 2.3.4 Terminating a Process — 37
  - 2.3.5 Basic Calculations — 38
  - 2.3.6 Objects — 38
  - 2.3.7 Concatenation — 39
  - 2.3.8 Statistical Functions — 40
- 2.4 Data Types — 41
  - 2.4.1 Missing Values — 43
- 2.5 Matrices, Data Frames, and Lists — 44
  - 2.5.1 Vector — 44
  - 2.5.2 Matrix — 45
  - 2.5.3 Data Frame — 45
  - 2.5.4 List — 46

2.6	Indexing		49
	2.6.1	Matrix and Data Frame	49
	2.6.2	Vector	50
	2.6.3	List	51
	2.6.4	Sorting	52
	2.6.5	Recoding	52
	2.6.6	Saving Objects	53
	2.6.7	Loading and Listing Objects	53
2.7	User-Defined Functions		54
2.8	Repetitive Operations		55
	2.8.1	`rdply()`	55
	2.8.2	`for()` Loop	57
2.9	Linear Regression		59
2.10	Getting Help		61
2.11	Summary of Functions		61

3 Data Structures and Longitudinal Analysis — 63

3.1	Longitudinal Data Structures		63
	3.1.1	Wide Format	64
	3.1.2	Long Format	64
3.2	Reading an External File		65
	3.2.1	Reading a Text File With `read.table()`	65
	3.2.2	Displaying the Data Frame	68
	3.2.3	Converting and Recoding Variables	70
3.3	Basic Statistics for Wide-Format Data		72
	3.3.1	Means, Variances, and Correlations	73
	3.3.2	Missing Data Statistics	74
	3.3.3	Conditioning on Static Predictors	75
3.4	Reshaping Data		76
	3.4.1	Wide to Long Format	76
	3.4.2	Long to Wide Format	79
3.5	Basic Statistics for Long-Format Data		80
	3.5.1	Means, Variances, and Correlations	80
	3.5.2	Missing Data Statistics	82
	3.5.3	Conditioning on Static Predictors	82
3.6	Data Structures and Balance on Time		84
3.7	Missing Data in LMER Analysis		85
	3.7.1	Retain or Omit Missing Data Rows?	88
3.8	Missing Data Concepts		89
	3.8.1	Missing Completely at Random	90
	3.8.2	Missing at Random	91
	3.8.3	Not Missing at Random	92
	3.8.4	Missing Data Mechanisms and Statistical Analysis	93
	3.8.5	Missing Data Simulation	94
	3.8.6	LMER Analysis	97

		3.9	Extensions to More Complex Data Structures*	100
		3.9.1	Multiple Dynamic Variables*	100
		3.9.2	Unbalanced Data*	102

4 Graphing Longitudinal Data — 105

4.1	Graphing and Statistical Strategy	105
4.2	Graphing With `ggplot2`	106
	4.2.1 Graph Components	107
	4.2.2 Layering	107
4.3	Graphing Individual-Level Curves	109
	4.3.1 Superimposed Individual Curves	109
	4.3.2 Facet Plots of Individual Curves	112
	4.3.3 Selecting Subsets	113
	4.3.4 Graphing Fitted Curves	115
4.4	Graphing Group-Level Curves	122
	4.4.1 Curve of the Means	123
	4.4.2 Graphing Fitted Curves	126
	4.4.3 Graphing Individual-Level and Group-Level Curves	129
4.5	Conditioning on Static Predictors	130
	4.5.1 Categorical Static Predictors	132
	4.5.2 Quantitative Static Predictors	139
4.6	Customizing Graphs*	143
	4.6.1 Customizing Axes*	143
	4.6.2 Customizing Facets*	144
	4.6.3 Customizing the Legend*	144
4.7	Summary of `ggplot2` Components	145

5 Introduction to Linear Mixed Effects Regression — 147

5.1	Traditional Regression and the Linear Model	148
5.2	Regression Examples	150
	5.2.1 Single Quantitative Predictor	150
	5.2.2 Analysis of Covariance	154
	5.2.3 Interaction Model	158
5.3	Linear Mixed Effects Regression	160
	5.3.1 LMER as a Multilevel Model	163
	5.3.2 Random Effects as Errors	167
	5.3.3 Assumptions Regarding Random Effects and Random Error	168
	5.3.4 Random Effects and Correlated Observations	169
5.4	Estimating the LMER Model	170
	5.4.1 Time as a Predictor	170
	5.4.2 Anchoring the Intercept	175
5.5	LMER With Static Predictors	177
	5.5.1 Intercept Effects	177

		5.5.2	Slope and Intercept Effects	178
		5.5.3	Initial Status as a Static Predictor	179
		5.5.4	Extensions to More Complex Models	180
		5.5.5	Summary of `lmer()` Syntax	181
	5.6	Additional Details of LMER*		181
		5.6.1	General Form of the LMER Model*	182
		5.6.2	Variance-Covariance Matrix Among Repeated Measures*	184
		5.6.3	Importance of Random Effects*	186
		5.6.4	Working With Matrices in `R`*	187

6 Overview of Maximum Likelihood Estimation — 191

	6.1	Conceptual Overview		192
	6.2	Maximum Likelihood and LM		194
		6.2.1	Several Unknown Parameters	202
		6.2.2	Exhaustive Search and Numerical Methods	204
		6.2.3	Restricted Maximum Likelihood	207
		6.2.4	Extracting the Log-Likelihood and the Deviance	208
		6.2.5	Comparing Models	208
	6.3	Maximum Likelihood and LMER		212
		6.3.1	LMER Deviance Function	214
		6.3.2	ML Standard Errors	216
		6.3.3	Additional SE Details	220
		6.3.4	Default `lmer()` Output	222
		6.3.5	Assumptions Regarding Missing Data	223
	6.4	Additional Details of ML for LMER*		224

7 Multimodel Inference and Akaike's Information Criterion — 227

	7.1	Objects of Inference		228
	7.2	Statistical Strategy		232
	7.3	AIC and Predictive Accuracy		235
		7.3.1	Extension to LMER	243
		7.3.2	AIC Corrected	245
	7.4	AICc and Effect Size		246
		7.4.1	Delta	246
		7.4.2	Weight of Evidence	248
		7.4.3	Evidence Ratio	252
	7.5	AICc and Multimodel Inference		254
		7.5.1	Contrast With NHST	255
	7.6	Example of Multimodel Analysis		260
		7.6.1	Guidelines for Model Formulation	260
		7.6.2	Example Set of Models	261
		7.6.3	Bar Graphs of Results	264
		7.6.4	Interpretation of Global Results	265

		7.6.5	Details of Models	268
		7.6.6	Comments Regarding the Multimodel Approach	273
		7.6.7	Post Hoc Models	273
	7.7	Example Write-up		275
	7.8	Parametric Bootstrap of the Evidence Ratio*		277
		7.8.1	Performing the Parametric Bootstrap*	278
		7.8.2	Caveats Regarding the Parametric Bootstrap*	282
	7.9	Bayesian Information Criterion*		282
8	**Likelihood Ratio Test**			**285**
	8.1	Why Use the Likelihood Ratio Test?		286
	8.2	Fisher and Neyman-Pearson		288
	8.3	Evaluation of Two Nested Models		291
		8.3.1	Calibrating p-Values Based on Predictive Accuracy	295
	8.4	Approaches to Testing Multiple Models		301
	8.5	Step-Up Approach		302
		8.5.1	Order of Testing	306
		8.5.2	Comments on the Step-Up Approach	307
	8.6	Top-Down Approach		307
	8.7	Comparison of Approaches		310
	8.8	Parametric Bootstrap*		312
		8.8.1	Comments on the Parametric Bootstrap*	315
	8.9	Planning a Study*		316
		8.9.1	Comment on the Procedure*	320
9	**Selecting Time Predictors**			**321**
	9.1	Selection of Time Transformations		322
	9.2	Group-Level Selection of Time Transformations		325
	9.3	Multimodel Inference		326
		9.3.1	Analysis Without Static Predictors	327
		9.3.2	Analysis With Static Predictors	329
	9.4	Likelihood Ratio Test		333
		9.4.1	Analysis Without Static Predictors	333
		9.4.2	Analysis With Static Predictors	335
	9.5	Cautions Concerning Group-Level Selection		335
	9.6	Subject-Level Selection of Time Transformations		336
		9.6.1	Level 1 Polynomial Model	336
		9.6.2	Missing Data	337
		9.6.3	Subject-Level Fits	338
		9.6.4	Pooled Measures of Fit	346
		9.6.5	Clustering of Subject Curves*	350

10 Selecting Random Effects — 357
- 10.1 Automatic Selection of Random Effects — 358
- 10.2 Random Effects and Variance Components — 359
  - 10.2.1 Restricted Maximum Likelihood — 361
  - 10.2.2 Random Effects and Correlated Data — 363
- 10.3 Descriptive Methods — 371
  - 10.3.1 OLS Estimates — 372
  - 10.3.2 Examining Residuals — 376
  - 10.3.3 Residuals and Normality — 382
- 10.4 Inferential Methods — 383
  - 10.4.1 Likelihood Ratio Test — 383
  - 10.4.2 AICc — 393
- 10.5 Variance Components and Static Predictors — 394
- 10.6 Predicted Random Effects — 394
  - 10.6.1 Evaluating the Normality Assumption — 397
  - 10.6.2 Predicted Values for an Individual — 399

11 Extending Linear Mixed Effects Regression — 405
- 11.1 Graphing Fitted Curves — 405
- 11.2 Static Predictors With Multiple Levels — 409
  - 11.2.1 Evaluating Sets of Dummy Variables — 415
  - 11.2.2 Evaluating Individual Dummy Variables — 416
- 11.3 Interactions Among Static Predictors — 420
  - 11.3.1 Static Predictor Interactions With `lmer()` — 422
  - 11.3.2 Interpreting Interactions — 424
  - 11.3.3 Nonlinear Static Predictor Effects — 426
- 11.4 Indexes of Absolute Effect Size in LMER — 427
  - 11.4.1 Alternative Indexes — 429
- 11.5 Additional Transformations — 433
  - 11.5.1 Time Units and Variances — 434
  - 11.5.2 Transforming for Standardized Change — 437
  - 11.5.3 Standardizing and Compositing — 439

12 Modeling Nonlinear Change — 443
- 12.1 Data Set and Analysis Strategy — 444
- 12.2 Global Versus Local Models — 448
- 12.3 Polynomials — 449
  - 12.3.1 Mean-Corrected Polynomials — 454
  - 12.3.2 Orthogonal Polynomials — 454
  - 12.3.3 The `poly()` Function — 455
  - 12.3.4 Polynomial Example — 459
- 12.4 Alternatives to Polynomials — 460
- 12.5 Trigonometric Functions — 461
- 12.6 Fractional Polynomials — 466
  - 12.6.1 First-Order Fractional Polynomials — 467
  - 12.6.2 Second-Order Fractional Polynomials — 471

		12.6.3 Static Predictors	474
		12.6.4 Caveats Regarding the Use of Fractional Polynomials	475
	12.7	Spline Models	478
		12.7.1 Linear Spline Models	479
		12.7.2 Higher Order Regression Splines	485
	12.8	Additional Details*	486
		12.8.1 Computing Orthogonal Polynomials*	486
		12.8.2 General Form of Fractional Polynomials*	488

13 Advanced Topics   489

	13.1	Dynamic Predictors	490
		13.1.1 Dynamic Predictor as a Single Effect	493
		13.1.2 Dynamic Predictor With a Time Variable	496
	13.2	Multiple Response Variables	500
		13.2.1 Reading and Mathematics	500
		13.2.2 Analyzing Two Responses With `lmer()`	501
	13.3	Additional Levels of Nesting	507
		13.3.1 Three-Level Model	508
		13.3.2 Static Predictors in Three-Level Models	513

Appendix: Soft Introduction to Matrix Algebra   515

A.1	Matrices	515
A.2	Transpose	517
A.3	Matrix Addition	518
A.4	Multiplication of a Matrix by a Scalar	518
A.5	Matrix Multiplication	518
A.6	Determinant	520
A.7	Inverse	521
A.8	Matrix Algebra and R Functions	523

References   525

Author Index   535

Subject Index   539

---

*Denotes optional section

About the Author

Jeffrey D. Long, PhD, is Professor of Psychiatry in the Carver College of Medicine at the University of Iowa. He is also the Head Statistician for Neurobiological Predictors of Huntington's Disease (PREDICT-HD), a longitudinal National Institutes of Health–funded study of early detection of Huntington's disease. His undergraduate degree is from the University of California at Los Angeles, and his doctoral degree is from the University of Southern California in the area of quantitative psychology.

Preface

This book is the culmination of years of teaching a graduate course in longitudinal methods for the behavioral sciences. The graduate course was targeted to applied researchers in various disciplines. These included business administration, developmental psychology, child psychology, clinical psychology, communication disorders, cognitive psychology, curriculum and instruction, educational policy and administration, educational psychology, family social science, health services research, industrial relations, kinesiology, mass communication, natural resources sciences and management, public policy, school psychology, special education, social psychology, and sociology.

The major piece of feedback from the course was that the students did not just want to learn *why* particular models are appropriate for longitudinal data; they also wanted to learn *how* to estimate the models and interpret the output. In response to this feedback, details about computer software and data preparation were incorporated into the body of the course. The result was that the students were better equipped to analyze their own data after leaving the class.

Providing details of software means, of course, that at least one software program needed to be adopted. Several software packages were tried over the years, which spurred additional feedback. Most of the feedback was related to the diversity of the research areas of the students, as the list above illustrates. Many of the larger units that housed the students' programs did not provide free access to the commercial software that was being used in the course. Furthermore, a number of people went on to work in organizations that could not afford to purchase the software. It was apparent that a low-cost or no-cost solution would benefit the students. The result was the adoption of the R computer program for the course.

Readers with knowledge of the statistical sciences will be well acquainted with R, but those in the behavioral sciences might be completely unfamiliar with the software. R is a freely available system for statistical computation and graphics (Hornik, 2010). The `base` package or system is maintained by a core team of developers (R Development Core Team, 2010). There are add-on packages available for a wide variety of analysis needs, including longitudinal data analysis. Many of the packages are developed by internationally recognized authorities. Additional details are provided in Chapter 2.

Based on experiences in the course, the goal was to write a book that interweaves R computer examples with the narrative. There are many fine books that do this, the most relevant being Bates (2011) and Pinheiro and Bates (2000). There are a number of differences between the current text and those just cited.

- The focus of this book is exclusively on longitudinal data, rather than the general topic of correlated data.
- Much of the mathematical detail is omitted or appears in optional sections.
- The examples and narrative focus on the behavioral sciences.

Given the diversity of subject matter in the behavioral sciences (see the list above), another motivating factor was to focus on a good general-purpose model for longitudinal data analysis. The result is that only random effects models are discussed in the text. Using the terminology of Bates (2005), the focus is on *linear mixed effects regression* (LMER). There are many alternatives to LMER for longitudinal and correlated data. An accessible introduction can be found in Fitzmaurice, Laird, and Ware (2004).

A final motivation for writing this text was to emphasize the benefits of using Akaike's information criterion (AIC) for evaluating a set of models (Akaike, 1973, 1974, 1981). A strong impetus for the AIC is provided in the writings of Kenneth Burnham and David Anderson (Anderson, 2008; Anderson & Burnham, 2002; Anderson, Burnham, Gould, & Cherry, 2001; Anderson, Burnham, & Thompson, 2000; Burnham & Anderson, 2002, 2004), as well as Malcolm Forster and Elliott Sober (Forster, 1999, 2000, 2002; Forster & Sober, 1994, 2004, 2011; Sober, 2002, 2006). The multimodel inference of Burnham and Anderson is a good alternative to evaluating models with traditional hypothesis testing, especially for the observational data discussed in this book.

Features of This Book

The intention was to create a text that can be used as a stand-alone guide to longitudinal data analysis. It is assumed the reader has familiarity with traditional multiple regression, including the specification and interpretation of predictor interactions. This is important, as LMER is presented as an extension of multiple regression. Familiarity with R is also helpful, but not essential. Chapter 2 presents basic syntax for those who have never used the software, although some readers might want to consult additional introductory resources, such as Hogan (2010).

To aid the reader in planning a roadmap for further reading, an overview of the remaining chapters is presented below. A typical graduate course on longitudinal data analysis would cover Chapters 1 to 8. Material in other chapters would be assigned or recommended based on the needs of the audience. If this book is used as a supplement, an instructor may be more judicious in the selection of the material. Depending on the interest of the reader, then, certain chapters may be skipped or skimmed.

Many chapters have optional sections at the end that contain information at a higher level than in the earlier sections. These sections are denoted with an asterisk (*) next to their title. This material is intended for readers who want more technical details.

It is suggested that all readers attempt the material in the optional sections, but it is not compulsory for a working knowledge of longitudinal data analysis. For certain optional sections, basic knowledge of matrix algebra is helpful. A soft introduction to matrix algebra is presented in the Appendix.

The following is a brief synopsis of each chapter.

- Chapter 1 is an introduction and overview. Preliminary issues related to the analysis of longitudinal data in the behavioral sciences are discussed. There is a conceptual introduction to LMER that includes a thumbnail sketch of random effects and their importance in accounting for dependency due to repeated measures. Specifics of the Minneapolis School District (MPLS) data set are presented, which form the basis for all the examples in the book. The basics of multimodel inference are considered along with an example.
- Chapter 2 provides an introduction to R. The reader is introduced to the basics of the program in the hope of providing a foundation for the analyses discussed in the remainder of the book. Some basic syntax is presented, along with concepts important for typical operations.
- Chapter 3 discusses data structures and the relation to longitudinal analysis. LMER analysis requires the data set to be in a particular format that is not the traditional format. The chapter provides practical illustrations for reshaping data. Missing data and missing data concepts are very important in longitudinal data analysis. The latter part of the chapter provides a guide to the treatment of missing data in applied longitudinal analysis.
- Chapter 4 presents graphical methods for longitudinal data. Graphing can be an important part of longitudinal data analysis. Use of the ggplot2 package is featured. The chapter covers construction of many additional types of graphs of interest to applied researchers. The last portion of the chapter covers customization for fine-tuning.
- Chapter 5 reviews topics in traditional regression, including single-predictor models and multiple-predictor models. Models with quantitative predictors, categorical predictors, and interactions are considered. The lm() function is presented for estimating traditional regression models. LMER is introduced as an extension of traditional regression appropriate for longitudinal data analysis. Analogous problems as modeled with traditional regression are set up with LMER. Algebraic details of the LMER models are discussed, including fixed effects, random effects, and random error. The lmer() function from the lme4 package is introduced, which is used for estimation. For the interested reader, more technical material underlying LMER is provided in optional sections.
- Chapter 6 provides an overview of maximum likelihood estimation. Basic concepts underlying the inferential methods covered in the book are presented. These include methods of estimation, global measures of fit, and statistical tests. Particulars of the default output of lmer()

are explained, with an emphasis on conceptual understanding. A brief overview of model comparison is also presented.
- Chapter 7 provides an extensive introduction to the AIC and multimodel inference. Several philosophical issues regarding model selection in the context of longitudinal data analysis are covered. Interpretation of the AIC as a measure of predictive accuracy is stressed, along with a variant of the AIC appropriate for small samples. Several types of AIC scalings are discussed, with the goal of quantifying relative effect size. An extensive example of multimodel inference is presented, including a mock write-up of the results. For the interested reader, a parametric bootstrap method for multimodel inference is provided in an optional section.
- Chapter 8 focuses on hypothesis testing using the likelihood ratio test (LRT). Foundational issues are discussed, and the distinction is drawn between the two dominant frameworks of traditional testing. Comparison of two nested LMER models is illustrated using the `anova()` function. Calibration of the LRT p-value based on differences in the AIC is presented, mainly as an aid to interpreting the former. Approaches to using the LRT for evaluating a set of more than two models are discussed. For the interested reader, the parametric bootstrap alternative to the LRT is provided in an optional section. There is also an optional section covering a parametric bootstrap method for estimating required sample size when planning a study.
- Chapter 9 addresses the topic of selecting time predictors for adequately modeling change. Descriptive and inferential methods are discussed, targeted at the subject and group levels. Advantages and disadvantages of the approaches are contrasted. For the interested reader, a clustering method for suggesting the shape of the change curve is provided in an optional section.
- Chapter 10 deals with the selection of random effects. Descriptive and inferential methods are presented, with bootstrap methods emphasized for the latter. Computation of random effects scores based on a fitted LMER model is discussed. The evaluation of statistical assumptions (e.g., normality) based on realized random effects scores is also covered.
- Chapter 11 extends certain topics in LMER analysis presented in earlier chapters. These topics include graphing fitted curves, categorical static predictors with multiple levels, and interactions among static predictors. Indexes of absolute (as opposed to relative) global effect size measures are presented. Practical issues pertaining to time units, standardization, and compositing are also discussed.
- Chapter 12 focuses on the modeling of nonlinear trends using transformations of the time predictor. Topics include correlated and orthogonal polynomials, trigonometric functions, fractional polynomials, smoothers, and splines. Emphasis is on applying the transformations with the `lmer()` function.

- Chapter 13 covers three advanced topics: dynamic predictors models, multiple-response variable models, and additional levels of nesting. The discussion is practical, with emphasis on appropriate data structures and `lmer()` syntax for estimating the models.

Book Website

There is a website for the book at http://www.sagepub.com/long. The website has the data sets used in the book, along with all the R syntax.

Acknowledgments

Thanks to Dave Heistad and Chi-Keung Chan of the Minneapolis School District for allowing the use of the data for the book. Thanks to Sage's editor Vicki Knight, who was helpful and supportive throughout the writing process. Several previously anonymous reviewers provided very useful feedback on an earlier version of the manuscript:

- Jochen Albrecht, Hunter College, CUNY
- William Anderson, School of Operations Research and Information Engineering and Department of Statistical Science, Cornell University
- Arny L. Blanchard, Institute of Marine Science, University of Alaska, Fairbanks
- Fuxia Cheng, Illinois State University
- Jonathan N. Katz, California Institute of Technology
- Murlidharan Nair, Indiana University, South Bend
- Cheryl A. Terrance, University of North Dakota
- Tian Siva Tian, University of Houston
- Corey S. Sparks, University of Texas at San Antonio
- Toshiyuki Yuasa, University of Houston

A special thanks to the many researchers, programmers, and statisticians who contribute to the larger scientific community through their tireless work related to R. These people include the following: the R Development Core Team; Douglas Bates, author of `lme4`; Hadley Wickham, author of `ggplot2` and `plyr`; Marc Mazerolle, author of `AICcmodavg`; Christophe Genolini, author of `kml`; Fabian Scheipl, author of `RLRsim`; and Torsten Hothorn, Frank Bretz, Peter Westfall, Richard Heiberger, and Andre Schuetzenmeister, authors of `multcomp`.

Finally, this book was written using freely available software. The text editor GNU Emacs (version 23.2) was used with the Emacs Speaks Statistics (ESS) software (version 5.13) for running R (Rossini et al., 2010; Stallman, 2010). The bundled distribution for Windows is available for download from Vincent Goulet's website at http://vgoulet.act.ulaval.ca/en/emacs/. Typesetting was accomplished using the TEX document preparation system of the MikTEX (version 2.8) distribution for Windows (Schenk, 2009). Friedrich Leisch is the author of the Sweave program that was used for mixing the text, R code, and output, in the TeX document (Leisch, 2002). Frank Harrell's Sweave template (Sweavel.sty) was used for the formatting of R input and output, which is available at http://biostat.mc.vanderbilt.edu/wiki/Main/SweaveTemplate.

Introduction 1

This book is intended to be a practical guide for the analysis of longitudinal behavioral data. Longitudinal data consist of repeated measures collected on the same subjects over time. Such data are collected by researchers in psychology, education, organization studies, public policy, and related fields. A variety of substantive research questions are addressed with longitudinal data, including how student achievement changes over time, how psychopathology develops, and how intra-group conflict evolves.

There are practical issues associated with longitudinal data collection that impact analysis. Longitudinal data are a special case of repeated measures data, with duration or time constituting the dimension over which the measurements are collected. In contrast to repeated measurements across experimental conditions, the time dimension does not allow the order of presentation to be randomized or counterbalanced. Consequently, longitudinal data have characteristics that require a flexible statistical model for analysis. Some of the traditional methods, such as repeated measures analysis of variance (RM-ANOVA), are not as flexible as the more modern methods discussed in this book.

A common feature of longitudinal data is that the variance of the response variable tends to change over time. It is common in behavioral studies for individuals to change at different rates, leading to increasing or decreasing dispersion as the study progresses. It seems important, then, to choose a statistical model that allows for fanning-out or squeezing-in of the data points over time.

Another feature of longitudinal data is the tendency of observations more closely spaced to have a higher correlation than observations more distantly spaced. One reason for this phenomenon is the presence of intervening factors that affect responses, such as life events of the subjects. When the repeated measurements are closely spaced, intervening factors are expected to change little and have a relatively small influence. This results in a relatively high correlation for response variable scores at adjacent time points. When the repeated measurement are not closely spaced, the intervening factors have a greater chance of influencing responses, leading to decreased correlations.

The timing of the observations, then, has an influence on the correlations. Measurement times are usually determined by the content under study. However, available resources or happenstance might also play a role. The frequency of observations is usually set by the researcher to be sensitive to "real" change in the response variable. Observations too closely spaced might not allow for the observation of phenomena that take time to manifest. On the other hand, observations too distantly spaced may miss important intervening landmarks of change or development. It follows that the researcher should think carefully about the intervals of measurement, and whether they should be a matter of seconds, minutes, days, months, or years.

A complication in having a relatively long duration between repeated measurements is an increased potential for missing data. As time elapses, subjects can grow weary of being measured, or they can have significant life events, such as changes in employment status or marital status. Such events can precipitate dropout from the study. When a subject drops out, they might not re-enter the study and they might not be replaced. Study resources are usually not allocated for replacement subjects that can result in severely staggered start times. This is especially so when the dropout is late in a study that spans a relatively long period of time, such as several years.

From an applied data analysis perspective, it is desirable to have a statistical method that can accommodate missing data and adequately account for the typical pattern of variances and correlations among the repeated measures. One method that addresses both issues is *linear mixed effects regression* (LMER), which is the primary analysis tool discussed in this book. (LMER is pronounced as "el-mer".)

In addition to providing an appropriate statistical model for longitudinal data, LMER allows for the examination of predictors of change, sometimes referred to as covariates of change. In behavioral science analysis, the term *covariate* is closely associated with a control variable used in the analysis of covariance (ANCOVA). Here the term is used more broadly and refers to any type of regression predictor.

Predictors of change are vital when a researcher wants to know about conditional change, or change that varies according to the values of one or more covariates. For example, a researcher might want to know if change in reading achievement is conditional on gender. Such an analysis involves an examination of the reading achievement trajectory of males to determine if it is substantially different than the trajectory of females. In another example, a researcher might want to examine if trajectories of externalizing behavior (e.g., aggression) vary based on the quality of parenting. Individuals with relatively low quality of parenting might have higher levels and higher rates of growth than individuals with relatively high quality. Research questions such as these are common in behavioral research, and LMER is well suited for addressing them.

1.1 Statistical Computing

Statistical computing is broadly defined as any use of a computer program for manipulating and analyzing data. Consistent with the practical goals of this book, statistical computing is discussed in detail. Rather than relegate computer examples to the end of chapters or a remote website, the approach is to interweave the examples within the narrative of the book. In future chapters, statistical concepts will be presented immediately followed by illustrations of how the related analysis can be carried out.

A single data set is used throughout much of the book, presented in table form later in this chapter, and also available on the book website. The intention is that the reader can duplicate what is seen in the book, perhaps in a dynamic fashion by having the book and computer side-by-side. This will help the reader to gain insights into both the statistical methods and statistical computing.

True to the title of this book, the freely available R program (R Development Core Team, 2010) is used for all computer examples. Among other features, R has the advantage of accessibility. Anyone with an Internet connection has access to this very powerful program for statistical computing and graphics. There are free add-on packages for manipulating, graphing, and analyzing longitudinal data that are among the best available in any statistical computing program.

Though R is widely used in the statistical sciences, it is not as widespread in the behavioral sciences. For this reason, it is assumed the reader has never used the program, and a primer on R is provided in Chapter 2. Rather than attempt to pack all the relevant concepts into the primer, many statistical computing concepts and methods are presented as the occasion warrants in later chapters.

1.2 Preliminary Issues

Every discipline provides a specific context for data analysis. In the analysis of longitudinal behavioral data, there are particular preliminary issues that are important to ponder prior to the data analysis, or even prior to data collection. Consideration of these preliminary issues can help a researcher determine what type of statistical analysis is appropriate for their data. A survey of these issues also helps provide an indication of the extent to which the data lend themselves to drawing valid inferences. If certain data conditions are met, then this can increase the likelihood of drawing sound conclusions from a LMER analysis.

1.2.1 MEANS VERSUS CORRELATIONS

The primary focus of this book is examining change in the quantity (or level) of a response variable repeatedly measured over time. It is assumed the researcher has obtained repeated measurements on several individuals, and the primary goal of the analysis is to examine aggregate change. Throughout this text, aggregate change will be indexed by the arithmetic mean. Thus, mean change will be the focus of analysis.

In addition to means, correlations between pairs of time points are informative. Correlations indicate the strength of dependency of the response over time. The correlation matrix among all the time points is useful as an indication of the extent of dependency, and how this dependency is related to the spacing of observations. In many longitudinal data sets, observations more closely spaced have a higher correlation than observations more distantly spaced. When considering longitudinal data analysis, it is advantageous to use a model that accounts for such a pattern. As will be explained later, LMER is one such model.

Correlations are standardized covariances, and the diagonal of a correlation matrix consists of 1s. Sometimes in longitudinal analysis, covariances among the time points rather than correlations are discussed. Similar information about strength of dependency can be obtained with the covariance matrix, but it has the advantage that the diagonal elements are variances. Thus, the covariance matrix allows examination of change in variability over time in addition to between-time dependency.

Mean change might not be an obvious touchstone for some researchers, as there are many instances in the behavioral sciences when correlations rather than means are used in longitudinal analysis (e.g., Burt, Obradović, Long, & Masten, 2008; Masten et al., 2005). It seems valuable then, to highlight the types of information represented by means and correlations, and how this relates to the study of change.

A correlation cannot be used to make inferences about absolute — as opposed to relative — change in quantity. Correlations are based on standard scores (or z-scores) that have a mean value of 0. When computed for each time point, z-scores guarantee a constant mean of 0 over time, precluding meaningful examination of change in quantity or level.

When an analysis uses correlations and excludes means, the focus is not on the change in quantity, but on the change in relative position of subjects over time. Between-time correlations largely index changes in rank order of individuals. For this reason, the between-time correlation is known as a *stability coefficient* (McDonald, 1999, chap. 5). The extent of stability is reflected in the value of the coefficient, with higher values indicating greater persistence of rank-order over time.

The mean and correlation difference is illustrated with the made-up achievement data that appear in Figure 1.1. Each graph depicts achievement scores (y), measured at two time points for the same cohort of individuals. For each subject, the two repeated measures scores are connected by a line. The lines are called *growth curves* or *change curves*. In this book, these terms will be used to refer either to lines connecting observed scores, as in Figure 1.1, or lines connecting fitted or predicted scores, as discussed in later chapters.

1.2 Preliminary Issues

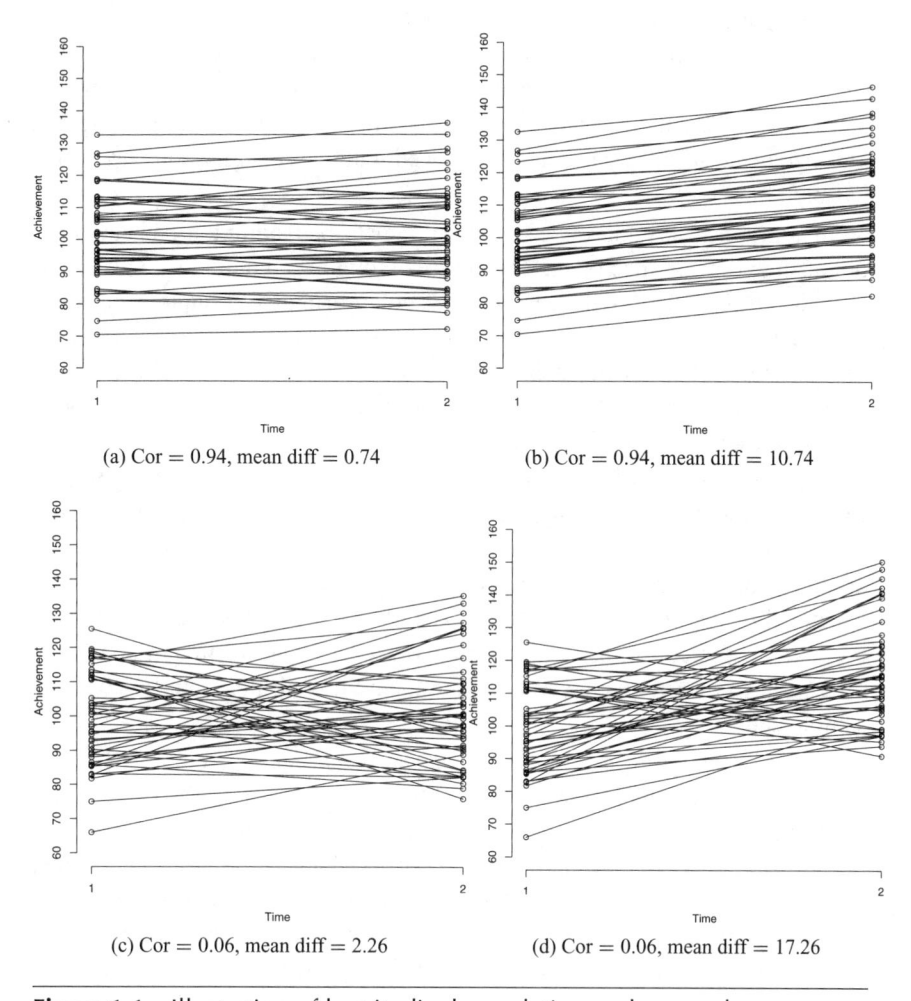

Figure 1.1 Illustration of longitudinal correlation and mean change.

(a) Cor = 0.94, mean diff = 0.74
(b) Cor = 0.94, mean diff = 10.74
(c) Cor = 0.06, mean diff = 2.26
(d) Cor = 0.06, mean diff = 17.26

The extent of the crossing lines is related to the strength of the stability coefficient, which is Pearson's correlation coefficient (*cor*) computed between the time points. The graphs in the first row show relatively few crossing lines, which indicates little rank order change and high stability. This is reflected in a high correlation, $cor = 0.94$. The graphs in the second row show extensive crossing of lines, which indicates low stability and a correlation that is close to 0, $cor = 0.06$.

A comparison of the left and right columns in Figure 1.1 illustrate that mean change is indifferent to the between-time correlation. For the graphs in a row of the figure, the correlations are identical, but the mean difference, mean diff = $\bar{y}_2 - \bar{y}_1$, is quite different. Figure 1.1a in the upper left has mean diff = 0.74, whereas Figure 1.1b in the upper right has mean diff = 10.74. The graphs in the bottom row, Figures 1.1c and 1.1d, show a greater contrast in mean difference for the same between-time correlation.

The right-hand graphs (Figures 1.1b and 1.1d) were created by starting with the left-hand graphs (Figures 1.1a and 1.1c) and adding a constant to each score at the second time point. A value of 10 was added for the top graphs and a value of 15 for the bottom graphs. Any value can be added, showing that any size of mean difference can be induced without changing the correlation between time points.

In addition to leaving the correlation undisturbed, adding a constant does not change the variance or the covariance among the time points. This shows that, like the correlation, the covariance is not informative about mean change. Though the covariances among the time points cannot be used to directly study mean change, it is shown later that they are important in an indirect sense. The covariances are used in computing the standard errors (SEs) of parameter estimates that directly index mean change.

What accounts for the crossing lines in Figure 1.1? One factor is variability in individual rate of change; people increase or decrease at different rates. Another factor is random measurement error. The scores from the instrument are not reliable, which causes inconsistent measurement over time. A statistical model is required to sort out the impact of these two influences. The LMER models considered in this book can be used to estimate the magnitude of the variability in rate of change and measurement unreliability from longitudinal sample data.

It is informative to examine both mean change and correlations (covariances) in a longitudinal analysis. As mentioned, some longitudinal analyses in the behavioral sciences involve only correlations. The focus on correlations may be due to particular characteristics of the data, or the research design. One reason for considering correlations rather than means is to accommodate the switching of measures over the course of data collection. Measures are typically switched because subjects outgrow them. If the span of the data collection crosses landmark developmental thresholds, this can render the use of the same instrument developmentally inappropriate.

As an example of development inappropriateness, consider the longitudinal measurement of externalizing behavior. Externalizing behavior is an outward display of a person's negative reaction to their environment, such as aggression or hyperactivity. The tracking of externalizing behaviors over time can be important in examining the development of psychopathology (Klimes-Dougan et al., 2010).

Suppose the goal is to assess the aggression of subjects who are tracked from 5 to 30 years old. For 5-year-olds, aggression might be defined as the frequency at which the subject bites others while interacting on the playground. This seems to be a perfectly valid measure of aggression for young children, but it may be completely invalid for 30-year-olds. Assuming a normative sample, biting and playgrounds seem to have no relevance for indexing externalizing behavior in adults. A different item should probably be used at some point, such as the ability of the subjects to get along with their boss at work. This idea generalizes to instruments made up of several items. The point is that researchers should ponder the appropriateness of their measures for indexing the same construct over time. This is especially pertinent if the observation period spans several years.

Switching instruments precludes a valid analysis of change in level, unless considerable ancillary work is accomplished prior to the analysis. The problem is that the instrument switch is confounded with change, making it difficult to draw unambiguous conclusions. Suppose a childhood externalizing behaviors measure is switched for an adult version over the course of the longitudinal study, when the subjects turn 18. Imagine that the means of the childhood instrument are relatively small in value, but the means of the adult instrument are relatively large. How is one to assess if this is an instance of true development, or an artifact of switching instruments?

When instruments are switched over time, it is possible to study mean change, provided some type of *vertical equating* is used (Kolen & Brennan, 2004). In contrast to z-scores, vertical equating sets different instruments on a common scale, but the mean can change over time. Therefore, under certain assumptions, scores on the common scale can be validly used to track changes in the quantity of the construct. A potential complication is that proper equating typically requires a large sample size and knowledge of test theory, especially *item response theory* (IRT; McDonald, 1999, chap. 12). These requirements can be onerous for applied researchers. In addition, there is the drawback that substantial resources may be expended on an issue that is tangential to the major thrust of the research.

1.2.2 MEASUREMENT ISSUES

When the same instrument is used over the course of a longitudinal study, there still may be questions as to whether change in quantity can be validly studied. As mentioned, items of instruments can change their meaning as subjects age. For this reason, it cannot always be taken for granted that the same instrument will measure the same construct(s) as a study progresses (Long, Herring, Brekke, Test, & Greenberg, 2007).

It is possible to conduct empirical checks on the consistent measurement of a construct over time. These checks are typically based on longitudinal IRT models (Muthén & Christoffersson, 1981). Evidence of longitudinal validity is provided in the form of invariance of measurement parameters over time (e.g., difficulty and discrimination). Similar to equating, longitudinal validity analysis typically constitutes a preliminary or stand-alone analysis based on a large number of subjects. For examples of longitudinal validity analysis, see Long et al. (2007), Obradović, Pardini, Long, and Loeber (2007), Pitts, West, and Tein (1996), and Vandenberg and Lance (2000).

In addition to consistency in measurement, the analysis of mean change requires that the construct in question be measured in an absolute sense. Certain physical constructs, such as height, meet this criterion. The height of a single subject is determined in reference to an objective distance scale, for example, a meter stick. An individual's height is not influenced by the measurement of other subjects, at least not explicitly.

In contrast to physical constructs, there are certain behavioral constructs that have only a relative determination. This occurs when a construct is measured by assigning ratings for a subject based on their relative standing to other subjects. An example is when a teacher assigns a Likert rating to a student for social cooperation (sometimes called citizenship) relative to other students in a classroom.

Such ratings are difficult to interpret in an absolute sense, as they are affected by changes in the composition of the class. If students are added or removed from the class, it is plausible the assigned social cooperation for a given student could change, even though the student's true (unknown) absolute level remains unchanged. A student initially rated as relatively uncooperative might improve in ranking if uncooperative students happen to be added to the class. A student rated as relatively affable might be downgraded if some apple-polishers come into the class. Due to this problem, relative scores appear to be an inadequate basis for studying mean change.

1.2.3 RESPONSE VARIABLE ASSUMPTIONS

In light of the above discussion, it is assumed throughout that the repeatedly measured response variable constitutes a valid foundation for making inferences about mean change. The researcher should carefully consider this assumption before commencing with an analysis. In the material to follow, variances, covariances, and correlations will be considered, but they will not have as high a priority as means. A proper model for the covariance matrix, for example, is required for proper inferences about mean change, but ultimate interest is in the nature of the change over time.

It is also assumed throughout that the response variable is quantitative or continuous. A quantitative variable has numbers that represent amounts of things. This is in contrast to categorical variables whose values denote different categories of membership, or count variables that record the frequency of an event. A generalized type of LMER can be used for the case of categorical and count response variables; for an introduction, see Fitzmaurice et al. (2004), chap. 10. Though the response is always considered to be quantitative in this book, the predictors can be quantitative, categorical, or a combination. Additional detail is provided below and in future chapters.

1.3 Conceptual Overview of Linear Mixed Effects Regression

The method of analysis featured in this book is LMER. The focus of LMER is mean change over time, but it also allows for the examination of

1.3 Conceptual Overview of Linear Mixed Effects Regression

Table 1.1 Components of linear mixed effects regression.

Component	Description	Level of Effect	Symbol
Fixed effects	Regression coefficients	Group	β
Random effects	Individual deviations from fixed effects	Individual	b
Random error	Regression error term	Individual	ε

individual variability in change. Furthermore, LMER incorporates a random error term that accounts for measurement unreliability. Components of the LMER model for longitudinal data are presented in Table 1.1. The symbols in the last column are used in the algebraic formulas presented in future chapters.

LMER can be viewed as an extension of traditional multiple regression. The extension is made by introducing individual-level terms to the regression model that index variability among the subjects. These terms are known as *random effects*. The random effects are in contrast to the *fixed effects*, which are similar to the traditional regression coefficients. Fixed effects are constant among individuals and index group-level change. It is the mix of fixed and random effects that is the genesis of the term *linear mixed effects regression*. Random effects vary among individuals and index deviations from the group. In the context of longitudinal models, the random effects reflect variation among individual change curves.

The basic ideas of LMER can be illustrated with the small data set of Table 1.2. The four subjects depicted in the table are from a larger data set to be presented later in this chapter. The data are in *long format*, meaning the blocks of data for the subjects are stacked one atop another and separated by horizontal lines in the table. Chapter 3 provides a discussion of how traditionally structured data can be converted into long format. For the moment, the data are simply presented this way.

There are five columns in the table, with the first being the subject identifier or subject variable, `subid`.[1] The response variable measured over time is reading achievement (`read`) in the second column. The third column has the grade at which reading achievement is measured (`grade`), and the predictor variables, gender (`gen`) and attendance proportion (`att`), are in the last two columns. The variable `grade` is considered to be a *time predictor*, as it is an index of duration. That is, `grade` is a proxy for annual measurement.

1.3.1 GOALS OF INFERENCE

The general goal of regression analysis is to account for the variability of the response variable. In the case of longitudinal data there are two types of response variability, *within-subjects* and *between-subjects*. Within-subjects variability is represented by row-to-row change for individual subjects in

---
[1] The convention used throughout this book is that a variable name in an actual data set appears in `typewriter font`.

Table 1.2 Data of four subjects in long format.

subid	read	grade	gen	att
1	172	5.00	F	0.94
1	185	6.00	F	0.94
1	179	7.00	F	0.94
1	194	8.00	F	0.94
3	191	5.00	M	0.97
3	199	6.00	M	0.97
3	203	7.00	M	0.97
3	215	8.00	M	0.97
5	207	5.00	F	0.85
5	213	6.00	F	0.85
5	212	7.00	F	0.85
5	213	8.00	F	0.85
7	199	5.00	M	0.97
7	208	6.00	M	0.97
7	213	7.00	M	0.97
7	218	8.00	M	0.97

Table 1.2. Between-subjects variability is represented by block-to-block change, with the blocks being demarcated by the horizontal lines in the table.

Within-subjects variability is due to changes in the response variable over time, that is, variability among the repeated measures. Within each block of Table 1.2, it can be seen that `read` changes over time for each subject. This row-to-row change indicates that within-subjects variability does exit for the response variable.

Between-subject variability is variation due to individual differences. This variability is evident when subjects differ on some characteristic that is not measured over time. For example, Table 1.2 shows that subjects vary in terms of their gender and attendance proportion. This block-to-block change indicates between-subjects variability does exist for the predictor variables.

Accounting for the types of variability constitutes two goals of inference in LMER. These goals are accomplished by the use of different types of predictors. The predictor variables in Table 1.2 account for the different types of variability based on whether their scores change over time. Any predictor that changes over time accounts for within-subjects variability, and any predictor that is constant over time – but not constant among subjects – accounts for between-subjects variability.

From Table 1.2, it can be seen that `grade` accounts for within-subject variability, whereas `gen` and `att` account for between-subject variability. Within-subject predictors are known as time-varying predictors or *dynamic predictors*. A special case of a dynamic predictor is a time predictor mentioned above. Dynamic predictors need not be time predictors as when, for example, math scores are collected over time and used to predict reading

1.3 Conceptual Overview of Linear Mixed Effects Regression

scores. Models for dynamic predictors other than time predictors are discussed in Chapter 13.

Between-subject predictors are known as time-invariant predictors or *static predictors*. Static predictors have their scores repeated for the duration of time (see the last two columns of Table 1.2).

As explained in Chapter 5, when the dynamic predictor is a time predictor like grade, the regression analysis involves the fitting of a curve for the response variable over time. Such curves are traditionally known as growth curves, but the term change curves is preferred as not all responses accumulate over time. In many instances, the response goes up or down over time, as when depression scores increase and then decrease, or vice versa.

The values of grade are consecutive integers, indicating the regression of read on grade results in fitting a linear change curve. A straight line is fit to the scatter of points defined by the two variables. The regression line consists of the fitted values of read, which can be interpreted as predicted mean values for the fixed values of grade. Therefore, the regression of a longitudinal response variable on a time predictor focuses on the trend of the means, or the *mean trend* over time.

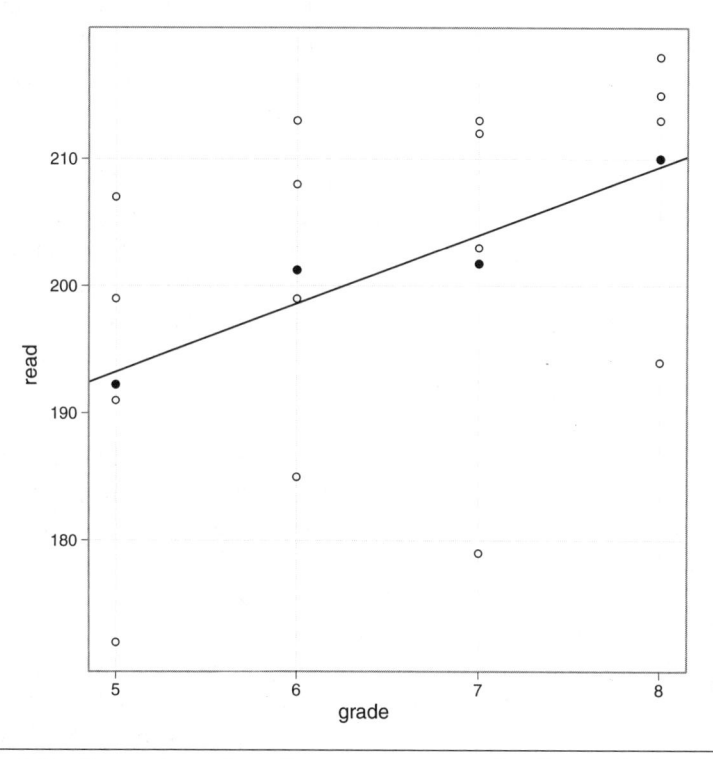

Figure 1.2 Regression of reading scores on grade. Open circles are the individual data points, filled circles are the means, and the solid line is the regression line.

A graph of read by grade for the Table 1.2 data is shown in Figure 1.2. The open circles are the individual read scores for the fixed values of grade, and the filled circles are the means. The regression line shows that the means tend to increase over time.

For purposes of illustration, the regression line in Figure 1.2 was produced using traditional regression methods. Traditional regression is wrong for this situation because there are repeated measures. In a moment, a more appropriate analysis using LMER is presented. Additional details of the contrast between traditional regression and LMER are provided in Chapter 5.

For a number of data sets, a linear time variable does not adequately account for the within-subjects variability. In such cases, transformations of the original time variable can be substituted and/or added to the regression equation to account for nonlinear change. It is common to include power transformations of the time variable, for example, $grade^2$, in order to add bends to the change curve. Transformations of the time predictor for modeling nonlinear change are discussed beginning in Chapter 3, but the most extensive material appears in Chapter 12.

In some cases, the only variables collected by the researcher are the response variable (e.g., read) and the time predictor (e.g., grade). The emphasis is on accounting for the within-subjects variability, or the change over time. The analysis typically involves trying different time predictor transformations to account for nonlinear trends. Or, if a linear trend is apparent, the focus is on the estimation of the change curve parameters and statistical inference for the fixed effects. Between-subjects variability can also be examined in this case. This provides an assessment of the correspondence of individual subjects' regression lines with the overall regression line, as discussed below.

In other analyses (almost all?), the researcher collects data on static predictors, in addition to the response and the time predictor. The focus is on both within-subjects change and between-subjects differences in that change. As shown in Chapter 5, when the static predictors are considered in combination with the time predictors, between-subjects differences in change curves can be examined in a regression equation.

For example, one can study whether reading achievement change curves are different for gender groups, or whether change curves differ by levels of attendance proportion. This is accomplished by including time predictors and static predictors as single predictors and as interactions. Interactions in this context are product terms among the predictors. The mathematical details are deferred until Chapter 5.

Consider Figure 1.3 that shows the means and regression lines by gender group. Males start a bit higher than females and increase at a faster rate. In terms of the sample regression lines, there is a difference in intercepts meaning a difference in starting points,[2] and a difference in slopes. Here the effects are assessed based on a graph of the sample data; inferences can also be based on LMER, as discussed below. (Figure 1.3 might seem counter-intuitive, as females usually are better readers at these grades. Keep in mind the sample size is very small, and gender could be confounded with one of the variables discussed later.)

---

[2] It is assumed here that the intercept is anchored at the first time point; see Chapter 5 for details.

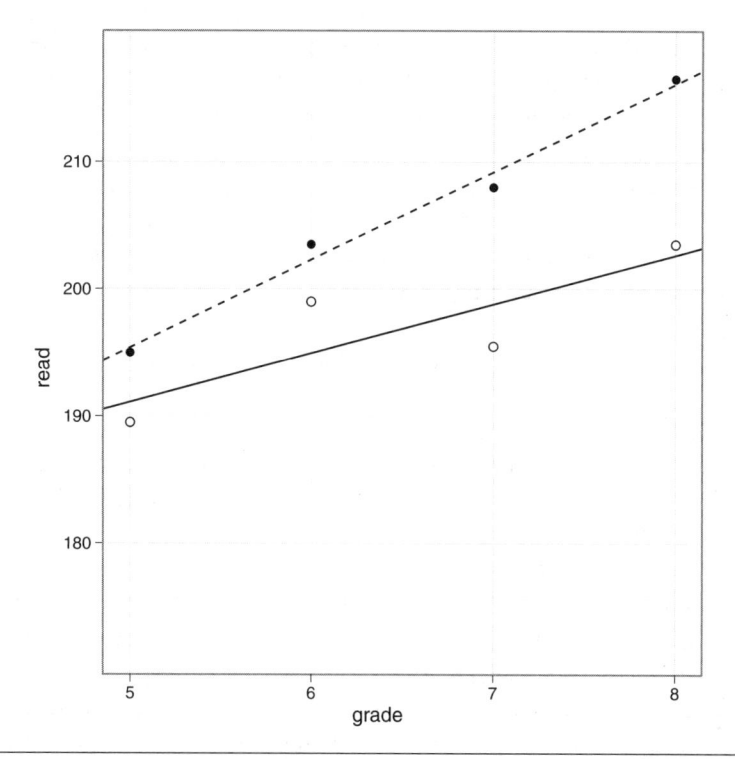

1.3 Conceptual Overview of Linear Mixed Effects Regression

Figure 1.3 Regression lines and means of gender groups. Open circles are for females and filled circles are for males.

When the static predictor is a categorical variable like gender, then the change curves in question are mean trends for the groups. This concept generalizes to the case of quantitative static predictors like attendance proportion, for which the levels of the predictor may be considered as strata. In such a case, mean trends are considered for each stratum, at least in principle.

1.3.2 RANDOM EFFECTS

The regression lines in the examples above were computed using traditional regression methods, and this is pause for concern. Traditional regression does not correctly associate a subject with its repeated measures, and no distinction is made between dynamic and static predictors. Thus, when traditional regression is used with the Table 1.2 data, the variance of the response is not properly partitioned into its within-subjects and between-subjects portions. This is important, as valid SEs, among other things, are predicated on such partitioning.

Moreover, since the blocks of Table 1.2 are ignored, every row is treated as a unique subject. This leads to incorrect bookkeeping, meaning that important quantities, such as degrees of freedom (df), cannot possibly be correct. The typical assumption of independence of observations is certainly violated, which casts doubt on the validity of any inferential results. Clearly, traditional regression is inappropriate for analyzing longitudinal data.

In contrast to traditional regression, LMER does associate subjects with their repeated measures. This is accomplished by introducing random effects in the regression equation. Random effects summarize individual change. The proper bookkeeping provided by the random effects means that LMER is a better basis for inference with longitudinal data than traditional regression. LMER recognizes the distinction between dynamic and static predictors, so that the response variance is partitioned into within-subjects and between-subjects portions. Such partitioning provides more accurate SEs, among other things.

In Figures 1.2 and 1.3, group-level curves were considered that summarized the reading/grade relationship for all the subjects. To provide a conceptual understanding of random effects, it is useful to consider individual change curves. Figure 1.4a shows the observed points for the four individuals in the example data set, along with their fitted regression lines. There is one panel per subject, and the subject identifier is in the panel title (subid). For simplicity, linear change is considered, but the concepts to be discussed also generalize to nonlinear change.

Random effects are useful for modeling and examining individual variation in change. As the graph in Figure 1.4a reveals, there is variability among the subjects in terms of their intercepts, or where the regression lines begin. Subject 1 starts relatively low, whereas Subject 5 starts relatively high. There is also variability among their slopes, or variability in the slant of their regression lines. Subject 5 has a relatively shallow slope, being the closest to a horizontal line of the bunch. The other individuals have lines with greater slants rising from lower left to upper right.

The first key to understanding random effects is that each subject in Figure 1.4a has their own intercept and slope. Though these intercepts and slopes are unobserved random variables in LMER, they can be computed based on sample data as discussed in Chapter 10. A crude method inferior to those discussed in Chapter 10, is to compute the intercepts and slopes using ordinary least squares (OLS) of traditional regression. Since OLS is assumed to be familiar to the reader, it is used here for purposes of illustration. The OLS equations for the sample intercept and slope are the following,

$$\text{slope} = \hat{\beta}_1^* = \frac{\sum(y-\bar{y})(x-\bar{x})}{\sum(x-\bar{x})^2}, \qquad (1.3.1)$$
$$\text{inter} = \hat{\beta}_0^* = \bar{y} - (\hat{\beta}_1^*)(\bar{x}).$$

The asterisk (*) is used to denote that the formulas are for a *single subject*. Additional details about the notation are provided in Chapter 5. Since the formulas of Equation 1.3.1 apply to an individual, the summation ($\sum$) is over the repeated measures for the individual (not over subjects).

As an example of the calculations, consider Table 1.3 that shows the relevant quantities for Subject 1. The data in the x and y columns are from the

1.3 Conceptual Overview of Linear Mixed Effects Regression

Table 1.3 Slope and intercept calculations for subject 1.

time	y	x	$(y - \bar{y})$	$(x - \bar{x})$	$(y - \bar{y})(x - \bar{x})$	$(x - \bar{x})^2$
1	172	5	−10.50	−1.50	15.75	2.25
2	185	6	2.50	−0.50	−1.25	0.25
3	179	7	−3.50	0.50	−1.75	0.25
4	194	8	11.50	1.50	17.25	2.25
Sum	730	26	0	0	30	5

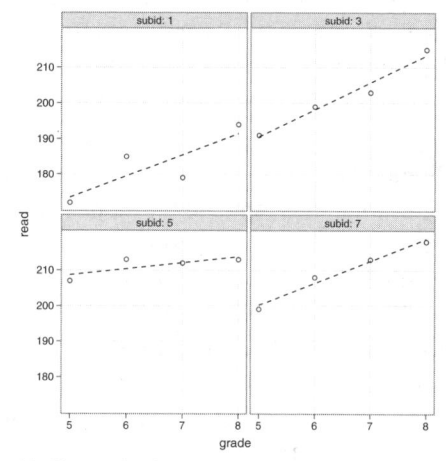

(a) Observed points (circles) and fitted regression lines (dashed).

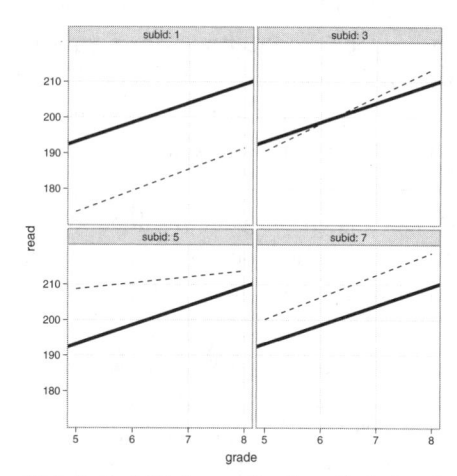

(b) Individual fitted regression lines (dashed) and group fitted line (solid).

Figure 1.4 Illustration of random effects based on four subjects.

first block in Table 1.2. From Table 1.3, it should be clear that $\bar{y} = \frac{730}{4} = 182.50$, $\bar{x} = \frac{26}{4} = 6.50$, slope $= \hat{\beta}_1^* = \frac{30}{5} = 6$, and inter $= \hat{\beta}_0^* = 182.50 - (6)(6.50) = 143.50$.

Table 1.4 lists the intercept and slope for each subject computed with the OLS formulas of Equation 1.3.1. The last row of the table lists the group-level intercept and slope, which is computed by regressing `read` on `grade` for the entire sample. The regression using all the subjects need not be performed, as the group-level quantities are the mean of the individual values.

The second key to understanding random effects is that an individual's intercept and slope are expressed in relation to the group intercept and slope. The concept is illustrated in Figure 1.4b that depicts the individual regression lines along with the group regression line. The solid group regression line is the same in each panel, illustrating that a group-level effect is constant among individuals. The dashed individual lines are particular to the subjects, illustrating individual variability. *Random effects are represented by the deviation of the individual regression lines from the group regression line.*

In the case of Figure 1.4b, there are two components of the regression lines that are of interest: the intercept and the slope. As will be see in future chapters, it is not compulsory to include every possible random effect in the model. The first random effect, which is a *random intercept*, is the difference between an individual's intercept and the group intercept. As can be seen in Figure 1.4b, Subject 1 has a negative value for their random intercept, as the person's curve starts (and continues) at a lower point than the group curve. Subject 3 also has a negative value, but it is much closer to 0 than Subject 1. Subjects 5 and 7 have positive random intercept values, as their curves start at a higher point than the group curve.

The second random effect is a *random slope*, which indicates the discrepancy of an individual's slope from the group slope. Subject 1 has an individual curve that is almost parallel with the group curve. This results in a random slope that is near to 0. The person's rate of change is almost the same as the group rate of change — there is almost no deviation from the group trend. A similar situation applies for Subject 7.

The slope for Subject 3 is greater than the slope for the group. This means the random slope for Subject 3 will be a positive value. In contrast, the slope for Subject 5 is lower than the group slope indicating a negative random slope value.

For this simple example, crude types of random effects are computed by subtracting out the respective group values from the individual scores; a better method is described in Chapter 10. The random intercept of Subject 1, for example, is $143.50 - 166.38 = -22.88$, and the random slope is $6.00 - 5.38 = 0.63$. The random effects scores are listed in the `inter-M` and `slope-M` columns. The notation of the variable labels indicates that the individual scores are mean-corrected.

In this example, the group intercept and group slope are the means of the respective individual estimates. Thus, subtracting out the group component is equivalent to mean-correcting the individual intercept and slope scores. In LMER, the random effects are the mean-corrected scores, `inter-M` and `slope-M`. However, interest is usually in the variances and covariances of

1.3 Conceptual Overview of Linear Mixed Effects Regression

the random effects, which are the same whether the mean-corrected or mean-uncorrected versions are used.

As discussed in future chapters, a key assumption for inference in LMER is that the subjects have been randomly sampled from a population. Under this assumption, the scores in the rows of Table 1.4 are independent. The random sampling assumption is the genesis of the term, *random effects*. In addition to independence, inference in LMER is often predicated on the joint normality of the random effects, an assumption made throughout this book.

Table 1.4 Intercepts and slopes of four subjects, mean uncorrected and mean corrected versions, and two static predictors.

subid	inter	slope	inter-M	slope-M	gen	att
1	143.50	6.00	−22.88	0.63	F	0.94
3	152.60	7.60	−13.77	2.22	M	0.97
5	200.20	1.70	33.83	−3.68	F	0.85
7	169.20	6.20	2.82	0.83	M	0.97
Mean	166.38	5.38	0	0		

Many of the conceptual aspects of LMER can be gleaned from a comparison of Table 1.4 and Table 1.2. The random effects act to reduce the dimension of the original regression problem by summarizing change over time. The random effects scores represent a collapsing over the time dimension that yields the traditional one-row-per-subject data set of Table 1.4. Assuming random sampling, the rows of Table 1.4 are independent, which is in contrast to the dependency among the rows in Table 1.2.

In collapsing over the time dimension, there is an inevitable loss of information about the response scores. As depicted in Figure 1.4a, there is scatter of the observed points about an individual's regression line. This scatter is *within-subject error*. The error is assumed to be random, so it is also known as the random error previously mentioned. The error variance computed among all the subjects is the *within-subjects error variance*. The within-subjects error variance is considered to be a result of measurement unreliability. Typical of regression models, the assumption is made that the within-subjects error is normally distributed, with a mean equal to 0 and a constant variance; see Chapter 5.

Having collapsed over the within-subjects time dimension, attention now turns to differences between individuals, or put another way, between-subjects variability. Table 1.4 shows there is variability in random intercepts and in random slopes. Subjects start at different levels, and they change over time at different rates. The variability can be quantified by computing the variance of the intercepts and the variance of the slopes. The variance does not change under subtraction of a constant, so it does not matter if `inter` and `slope` are used, or `inter-M` and `slope-M`.

One might also want to compute the covariance or correlation between the random effects, as this indicates how the two are related. In this example, the correlation between the random effects is $cor = -0.87$, indicating that those who start lower have a faster rate of change than those who start higher. This is illustrated in Figure 1.4b. Subject 3 starts at a lower point than the group curve, but increases at a faster rate. Conversely, Subject 5 starts at a higher point than the group curve, but increases at a slower rate.

When there are no static predictors, between-subjects effects are represented by the variance-covariance matrix among the random effects. When there are static predictors, as in the example of gender and attendance, then an additional set of between-subjects effects can be addressed. The random intercepts and random slopes can be regressed on the static predictors to learn about between-subject differences in change. Gender and/or attendance might account for variance in the random intercepts and/or slopes. To the extent this is the case, either the starting point (intercept), or rate of change (slope), or both, can be predicted from the static predictors. These types of static predictor effects are often of prime interest in LMER analysis.

As a conceptual example, consider the correlation between `att` and `inter`, and then `att` and `slope`. Using information from the table, it can be shown that $cor(\texttt{att}, \texttt{inter}) = -0.79$, and $cor(\texttt{att}, \texttt{slope}) = 0.97$. The negative correlation with the intercept indicates that those with lower attendance proportions tend to have higher starting points (intercepts), and those with higher attendance proportions tend to have lower starting points. The positive correlation with the slopes indicates that those with lower attendance proportions tend to have lower rates of linear change, and those with higher attendance proportions tend to have higher rates of linear change. In later chapters, methods of inferences for such effects are discussed.

1.3.3 HOW IMPORTANT ARE RANDOM EFFECTS?

Having introduced random effects as a crucial feature for the proper analysis of longitudinal data, it may seem strange to ask about their importance. Random effects are certainly important for analyzing longitudinal data, as they provide a proper accounting of the repeated measures. Furthermore, the random effects account for the dependency due to repeated measures, which is crucial for a proper longitudinal model. The demonstration of the random effects in this role is relatively complicated, requiring the development of some preliminary material. Details are provided in Chapters 5 and 6.

Despite the importance of random effects, the primary objects of inference in the majority of behavioral science applications are the fixed effects. Recall the fixed effects are the group-level regression coefficients, which are in the last row of Table 1.4. Similar to traditional regression, applied researchers are usually interested in summarizing among subjects, meaning the group-level fixed effects are of prime interest.

With the above in mind, one view of LMER is as a fixed effects model with an error term appropriate for longitudinal data; or more simply, a regression model with a correlated error term (Verbeke & Molenberghs, 2000, chap. 3). As shown in Chapter 5, the random effects can be considered as part of a composite error term. In this view, the variances and covariances of the random effects are largely treated as "nuisance" parameters. They are a necessary consequence of including random effects, but they are the handmaiden of the fixed effects used primarily to account for the dependency due to repeated measures.

Though the random effects per se are rarely a concern, their variances and covariances (or correlations) are of interest, especially when one wants to know about individual variability in change. Output from LMER analysis provides estimates of the variances and correlations among the random effects. The interpretation of these estimates are discussed in future chapters.

Based on what appears to be the typical priority of applied researchers, LMER will mainly be treated as a fixed effects model with correlated errors induced by including random effects. Not all readers will appreciate this emphasis, but this approach seems to reflect the primary interest of most applied researchers.

There are practical advantages of focusing on fixed effects. As discussed in Chapter 7, model building is much simpler when the number of random effects is determined before the fixed effects are considered. Things can be quite involved when both random and fixed effects are simultaneously selected in the same analysis. Among other problems, statistical tests for inclusion of random effects are not standard and require special consideration; see Chapter 10.

Such problems hold the possibility that undue time and resources will be expended on effects that are not of primary interest. In many instances, graphs of the data can be used to suggest a reasonable number of random effects. Graphing procedures are covered in Chapters 3, 9, and 10. Informal methods are stressed for the selection of the random effects, but formal inferential methods are also discussed.

1.4 Traditional Approaches

The use of LMER in behavioral science analysis is relatively new. Until recently, longitudinal data were analyzed with traditional approaches such as RM-ANOVA, and repeated measures multivariate analysis of variance (RM-MANOVA). In this book, the traditional approaches are not discussed in detail because they have particular features that make them less attractive for applied longitudinal analysis than LMER. It is worthwhile to highlight some of these features, so as to be clear why a growing number of applied researchers are turning to LMER.

From an applied research perspective, the Achilles heal of the traditional methods is the inability to accommodate missing data. Traditional methods require the data set to be complete, and subjects who have any amount of missing data are mercilessly omitted. For the situation in which there is a small amount of missing data per subject, but a moderate number of subjects in this predicament, *df* can be small relative to the number of original subjects.

Many applied researchers are not comfortable with this potentially large loss of information. The result is a turn to alternative methods that allow subjects with incomplete data to be included in the analysis.

In most computer realizations of RM-ANOVA and RM-MANOVA, the statistical program fits a series of orthogonal polynomials to the data; see Chapter 12. The number of polynomials fit is one less than the number of time points. In most cases, there is no user control over this fitting. When the number of time points is large, say greater than four, high order polynomials are fit regardless if they are useful or interpretable. For the applied researcher analyzing 10 time points, an all-too-often occurrence is to find a single statistically significant high order polynomial, such as the 8th. Rarely is such an effect hypothesized, and there seems to be scant direction as to how such a finding should be interpreted. A statistical consultant might comment that an 8th order polynomial is "wavy," but this is probably not much help to the researcher. It would be better for the researcher to specify only the effects of interest, which is possible with LMER.

Another issue with RM-ANOVA and RM-MANOVA is they represent two extremes. On the one hand is RM-ANOVA, whose basic inferential methods rely on the assumption that the rate of change for all the subjects is constant. This scenario seems overly restrictive for much longitudinal data, as individual variability in rate of change appears to be the rule rather than the exception; see Figure 1.1. A constant rate of change is plausible when the presentation of repeated measures is counterbalanced. Thus, RM-ANOVA seems most appropriate for experimental designs, in which the repeated measures are conditions that subjects endure, rather than time points at which behavior is observed. This is why the history of the traditional approaches is closely associated with randomized experimental designs (Keppel, 1991, chap. 15).

At the other extreme is RM-MANOVA, which relaxes the requirement of constant rate of change for all subjects. However, the model, in effect, provides a unique correlation or covariance parameter for each pair of time points. This means the number of covariance components expands with the number of time points, potentially resulting in a large number of parameters. When there are more than two time points, the number of covariance components can be greater than the number of change curve parameters. As discussed above, the correlations among the repeated measures are important, but they are of relatively minor interest in comparison to mean change over time. Therefore, RM-MANOVA devotes an undue number of parameters to an aspect of the model that is largely ignored in the results. In the LMER models considered later, adequate accounting of the correlation among the repeated measures is accomplished with fewer parameters.

The advantages of LMER over the traditional methods are summarized in the following list.

- *LMER can accommodate missing data.* Subjects who have response data for at least one time point can be included in the analysis. However,

valid inference under these conditions is predicated on assumptions regarding the mechanism that caused the missingness; see Chapter 3.
- *LMER provides control over the number and nature of terms used to model change over time.* Regardless the number of time points, the researcher can fit a low order polynomial, or fit other types of curves that directly address research questions; see Chapter 12.
- *LMER is very flexible regarding the structure of the data.* Timing of observations can vary among subjects, and the distance between adjacent time points need not be equal.
- *Finally, LMER allows for various types of predictors.* Predictors can be dynamic and/or static, quantitative and/or categorical.

The above features are attractive for the analysis of longitudinal behavioral data. LMER provides the flexibility to cover a multitude of empirical data structures. The remainder of the book focuses on LMER, though passing reference is sometimes made to RM-ANOVA/MANOVA to point out similarities of the models where they exist.

1.5 MPLS Data Set

For the majority of the examples in this book, a single data set will be used. The data appear in Table 1.6 and are also available on the book website. A missing value is coded as -99. A relatively small data set of $N = 22$ is considered because it is manageable. The reader can print the data set to the computer screen, or to a single sheet of paper. For the reader just becoming familiar with the R computer program, the ability to see the entire data set is beneficial. Results of data manipulations can be readily seen, which facilitates understanding of the workings of particular functions. There is benefit in using the same data set for different illustrations, such as graphing and data analysis. The continuity reduces the need to comprehend new substantive issues along with new statistical issues that can arise when data sets are switched.

The data in Table 1.6 are taken from a much larger data set collected by the Minneapolis Public School District (MPLS) in Minnesota (USA), and deidentified for the purposes of secondary data analysis. The data were collected in part because of district efforts to comply with recent federal accountability requirements, namely Title X of the No Child Left Behind Act of 2001 (2002). Data collection began with the 2004–2005 school year, and the larger data set has $N = 16561$ students.

The variables in Table 1.6 are reading achievement scores from grades 5 through 8 (read.5-read.8), risk group (risk), gender (gen), ethnicity (eth), English language learner status (ell), special education services (sped), and attendance proportion (att). The reading scores constitute the repeatedly measured response variable that is referred to as read. All variables other than read and grade are static predictors. A limited description of the variables is provided below; additional details are found in Obradović et al. (2009).

The reading achievement scores are from the reading portion of the Northwest Achievement Levels Tests (NALT; Northwest Evaluation Association, 2003). The NALT is a multiple-choice adaptive assessment of academic achievement. NALT raw scores are converted to vertically-equated scaled scores based on IRT models (see Kolen & Brennan, 2004). In principle, the scaling provides a valid basis for using NALT scores to study change in level over time. NALT administration was in the fall for all students, so that `grade` represents a yearly measurement.

The risk group variable constitutes classification of individuals based on the MPLS assessment of homeless and highly mobile (HHM) status and poverty status (POV). HHM status is defined by a family living in inadequate and/or transitional conditions, such as on the street, in a shelter, or doubled up with relatives. Individuals are classified as HHM if they meet the district definition at any time over the course of the study.

POV is defined by student eligibility for free or reduced-price meals based on federal standards. A person is classified in the POV group if they qualify for free or reduced lunch at least once over the course of the study, but at no time qualify as HHM. All those in the HHM group qualify for free or reduced lunch, and thus, are also a special case of POV. Individuals are classified as advantaged (ADV) if they do not qualify for classification in the other two categories. As indicated below and in future chapters, the HHM and POV groups will often be combined and designated as the disadvantaged (DADV) group.

As for the other static predictors, gender is coded as F = female and M = male. English language learner status is coded as 0 = is not a learner and 1 = is a learner, and special education services is coded as N = not receiving and Y = receiving. Attendance proportion is the average number of days attended by a student divided by the number of days enrolled for the duration of the data collection. Ethnicity is coded as Afr = African American, His = Hispanic, and Whi = White (W). For some examples, the first two ethnicity groups will be combined and designated as the non-White (NW) group.

The static predictors in Table 1.6 can be classified as categorical or quantitative variables based on their level of measurement (Long, Feng, & Cliff, 2003). Categorical variables denote membership in different groups (or classes) and can use numbers, letters, or names. When numbers are used, they do not represent amounts of things, but different categories of membership. All the static predictors, except for attendance proportion, are categorical. Quantitative variables use only numbers, and the numbers stand for amounts of things. Attendance proportion is the sole quantitative predictor. It is possible to have categories with a natural ordering, such as 1 = low, 2 = medium, and 3 = high. A variable like this might be classified as ordinal or ordered categorical. Ordinal variables are sometimes treated as quantitative if there are many categories (e.g., ten), or treated as categorical if there are few categories (e.g., three).

A point of clarification should be mentioned regarding dynamic and static variables. It is possible for a dynamic variable to have constant values over time, such as when a subject has the same reading score at each time point. Such an event is unlikely, but the possibility nonetheless does exist. The distinction between static and dynamic variables is that the researcher fixes the values of static variables, but does not fix the values of dynamic variables. Dynamic variables can be treated as static if the researcher chooses. For example, the baseline value of a variable can be repeated for each time point, or the average over all the time points can be repeated. The latter approach was taken in computing attendance proportion in Table 1.6. A related discussion is found in Section 5.5.3.

The decision to treat a predictor as dynamic or static depends on such things as the research questions, the nature of the variable, and the study design. In the MPLS study, the yearly variation in attendance was judged by district officials to not be particularly important due to unreliability of reporting. Thus, the researchers chose to represent an overall level for each subject.

It must be emphasized that though analysis with the larger data set is no trifling matter, the Table 1.6 data set should be considered a toy. Serious issues regarding academic achievement are discussed below and in future chapters. *Analysis with the Table 1.6 data set should not be taken as a serious attempt to address these deep issues.* It is perhaps a bitter reality of applied research that small data sets have limited information, and this precludes addressing certain types of research questions. For example, perusal of the ethnicity variable (`eth`) in Table 1.6 reveals that only one subject is Hispanic (`His`). We certainly would not want to make ethnic group comparisons based on a single case.

On a related note, LMER models can have relatively many parameters when there are numerous static predictors. Each static predictor can have an intercept and slope effect, and possibly more, when the change curve is nonlinear (see Chapters 5 and 12). Though relatively complex models will be considered for pedagogical purposes, such models can be unstable when the sample size is small. Results based on the sample data set of Table 1.6 should not be used to make definitive assessments regarding the plausibility of the estimated models.

1.6 Statistical Strategy

Applied data analysis consists of more than statistical concepts and formulas. There is always an underlying philosophy of the data analysis, referred to as the *statistical strategy* (Hand, 1996; Mallows, 1998). Unfortunately, in much applied data analysis, statistical strategy for an analysis is not explicitly stated. All too often, data analysis is guided by convention and intuition. The justification for using particular approaches and/or analysis steps is left vague, or swept under the rug altogether.

Statistical strategy should be made explicit, so that the consumer of one's results will be clear about the justification, rationale, and viewpoint of the statistical methods used, even if there is disagreement. To this end, the statistical strategy of this book will emphasize what is known as an *information-theoretic* approach to statistical analysis. For model evaluation, focus will be on the use of a global statistical fit measure known as *Akaike's Information Criterion* (AIC), due to the statistician Hirotugu Akaike (Akaike, 1973, 1974, 1981). (Akaike is roughly pronounced as "ah-kah-ee-kay.")

Why is the AIC emphasized? The evaluation of statistical evidence obtained from sample data is considered to be a primary goal of applied analysis. The AIC provides a clear measure of such evidence. Once AIC values are determined for a set of fitted models, clear evidential statements can be made regarding the plausibility of the models and the scientific hypotheses they represent. A limited example is provided below, with a more extensive example provided in Chapter 7.

The AIC can be use to rank-order models in terms of their plausibility, and the probability of a particular model can be determined, given some conditions. Meaningful statements regarding differences in the plausibility of the models can also be made. The best fitting model, for example, might be slightly more plausible than the next best model, or much more plausible.

An emphasis on the AIC means a deemphasis on traditional methods, such as *null hypothesis statistical testing* (NHST), with its reliance on the p-value. This does not imply that NHST is wrong. NHST is a sound and perfectly appropriate method for certain purposes, such as evaluating evidence from randomized controlled experiments. However, for the case of regression models with observational data – the primary domain of this book – the AIC provides a clearer representation and evaluation of statistical evidence. In the dominant traditional interpretation, p-values do not indicate effect size (Goodman, 1999). Thus, they cannot be used to rank-order a set of regression models in terms of their plausibility. Rank-ordering and effects size are fundamental to the scientific enterprise. Thus, the AIC is preferred to NHST in most applications considered in this book. Additional points are discussed in Chapters 7 and 8.

The use of the AIC is closely associated with an approach to data analysis know as *multimodel inference* (Burnham & Anderson, 2002, 2004; Anderson, 2008). Multimodel inference has three main aspects.

1. A set containing two or more candidate models (e.g., regression models) is formulated prior to the data analysis.

2. The AIC is used to evaluate the models in terms of relative fit and plausibility.

3. Limited results are presented for all the models in the set, such as the AIC values, and detailed results are presented only for the best fitting model(s).

An advantage of multimodel inference is that it stresses careful and deliberate thought prior to the analysis. This is probably a reaffirmation of what many

1.6 Statistical Strategy

researchers already do, but it speaks to the merits of planned analysis rather than data-driven analysis. It has long been documented that data-driven analysis, sometimes called *exploratory analysis*, is highly vulnerable to errors of inference (Chatfield, 1995; Faraway, 1992; Freedman, 1983; Lovell, 1983).

Sample data contain *information* about the phenomenon under study, and its compliment, *non-information* (Anderson, 2008, chap.1). Researchers are concerned with correctly winnowing information from non-information, as the former is the enduring part of the sample data. The enduring part of the sample data is instructive about the mechanisms underlying the content of interest.

It has long been argued that the best strategy for data analysis is to carefully formulate several scientific hypotheses prior to the analysis (Chamberlain, 1890; Feyerabend, 1968; Peirce, 1903; Platt, 1964). These hypotheses, known as *working hypotheses*, are formulated based on theory, expert knowledge, the extent literature, and interaction with colleagues. The working hypotheses are the embodiment of the underlying processes that give rise to the information in the sample data. Statistical models, such as regression models, represent the hypotheses and are estimated based on the sample data. The estimation is sometimes referred to as *fitting the model to the data*.

When scientific hypotheses are carefully and pain-stakingly formulated, it is reasonable that the information from the sample – as opposed to the non-information – is being drawn upon to validate the associated models. If one model has better fit than another, it is thought that the associated hypothesis is a better representation of the processes that generated the information.

Exploratory analysis involves little or no extra-data knowledge to guide it. As a result, exploratory analysis is extremely prone to conflating information and non-information. The statistical models are suggested by the data, meaning they are suggested by information *and* non-information. This phenomenon is referred to as *overfitting* the data. Because non-information is a potentially blatant influence in exploratory analysis, the hypotheses generated from data-driven models are misleading. They are potentially poor representations of the true underlying mechanisms that generated the information in the sample.

Multimodel inference is desirable because it emphasizes confirmatory research. Though it is acknowledged that both confirmatory and exploratory analysis are needed, the former is to be preferred. This partisan stance is motivated by the fact that exploratory analysis is vulnerable to misuse. Given the speed and ease of modern computers, there is a temptation to devote considerable time to sifting the data with statistical procedures. In many cases, time is probably better spent sifting the available literature on the substantive topic of interest. Statistical computing should never be substituted for careful thought about the variables in the analysis, nor as a substitute for formulating sensible scientific hypotheses and statistical models.

The purpose of exploratory analysis is to generate scientific hypotheses for future research. For this reason, exploratory analysis should be based only on graphical and descriptive methods. Exploratory analysis should not be based on inferential methods like *p*-values, hypothesis tests, or confidence intervals (Tukey, 1977). To this end, an entire chapter is devoted to graphing longitudinal data (Chapter 3), and descriptive methods are discussed throughout the book, especially in Chapters 9 and 10.

Output from LMER analysis qualifies as descriptive information, and its use can be important in exploratory analysis. However, when LMER is used for exploratory analysis, the output should not be used to generate *p*-values for hypothesis testing because of the problem of overfitting. As discussed in Chapter 6, the R package that will be used for longitudinal data analysis is very desirable in this regard, as only descriptive statistics are printed in much of the default output. It has been repeatedly demonstrated that given a sufficiently thorough search through the data, a seemingly meaningful pattern can always be found, even when the variables are randomly generated with a computer (Miller, 2002, chap. 1). Iterative procedures, in which multiple models are fit with different numbers of variables based on statistical tests, are especially prone to spurious results (Freedman, 1983).

There is a certain sympathy for researchers who want to "let the data speak," but it is important to remember that the data always speak a combination of truth and lies, or in statistics speak, information and non-information. The first line of defense against letting non-information drive the selection of models is to bring theory, previous research, experience, and expert opinion to bare on the problem prior to the analysis. The second line of defense is to be extremely cautious with analyses that are not pre-planned.

Another advantage of multimodel inference is that the results are more realistic than with traditional methods. A single final model is not presented as if it is the true model, or even an adequate model. Rather, a "bouquet of models" (Tukey, 1995) is considered in any one analysis, with some models – the better fitting ones – more sweet smelling than others. The bouquet provides an indication of the relative plausibility of the scientific hypotheses the models represent. Based on sample evidence, some models are expected to die off and be discarded, whereas other models are born and added to the bouquet for further consideration. Details of multimodel inference are discussed in Chapter 7, and a thumbnail sketch is provided later in this chapter.

Lest some readers have become nervous by the last few paragraphs, rest assured that NHST is thoroughly treated in Chapters 6 and 8, emphasizing a test procedure known as the *likelihood ratio test* (LRT). Though multimodel inference is preferred, it is acknowledged that NHST is compulsory in a number of quarters. In the hope that researchers will transition from NHST to multimodel inference, the LRT is related to the AIC in Chapter 8. The relation not withstanding, the LRT may be used for traditional testing without reference to information theory. In addition to the analytic LRT, parametric bootstrap approaches are also discussed that are applicable for a wider number of testing situations.

Finally, the statistical inference discussed in this book is based on classical or frequentist principles, as opposed to other schools of thought, such as

Bayesian statistics. The frequentist approach is based on the idea of repeatable research procedures (Fisher, 1991, p.14). Sample data are assumed to come from a hypothetical infinite population and are generated by the repeated research procedures in question (Sprott, 2000, chap.1). This concept forms the basis of inference using the predictive accuracy underlying the AIC (see Chapter 7), and the method of maximum likelihood (ML) underlying the LRT (see Chapters 6 and 8).

1.7 LMER and Multimodel Inference

Having introduced LMER, the AIC, and multimodel inference, a limited analysis example is provided using the MPLS data set. A more extensive analysis is provided in Chapter 7. To keep things simple, examination is restricted to questions regarding risk group differences in reading achievement over time. More complex research questions are examined in the remainder of the book.

Details of LMER, parameter estimation, and multimodel inference are provided in future chapters. Here a conceptual thumbnail sketch of the important issues is provided. The hope is that the example will motivate exploration of the remaining chapters.

1.7.1 STATISTICAL HYPOTHESES

Several longitudinal studies have reported initial and on-going differences in reading achievement among socioeconomically advantaged and disadvantaged groups (Arnold & Doctoroff, 2003; Chatterji, 2006; Eamon, 2002; McLoyd, 1998; Pungello, Kupersmidt, Burchinal, & Patterson, 1996). Advantaged students generally have higher achievement scores than disadvantaged students, with an important issue being the extent and duration of the achievement gap. There is conflicting evidence regarding the persistence of an early achievement gap into latter grades. Depending on the historical epoch, and relevant factors like school-based interventions, early differences might remain stable over time (Applebee & Langer, 2006), or narrow or widen (Caro, McDonald, & Willms, 2009; Dearing, Kreider, Simkins, & Weiss, 2006).

The research findings suggest several LMER models that might be fit to the sample data. For this example, the single static predictor of risk is considered. Due to the small sample size of the MPLS data set, the dichotomous version of risk will be used, consisting of the DADV group, and the ADV group. Recall the disadvantaged students are classified as such if they meet eligibility for free or reduced-price meals based on federal standards. All HHM students are eligible for this aid, and thus, are absorbed into the disadvantaged group. The advantaged students have high enough family incomes to disqualify them for disadvantaged status. There is considerable controversy regarding whether free and reduced lunch is a valid indicator of disadvantage due to poverty, but this consideration is beyond the scope of this example (see e.g., Harwell & LeBeau, 2010).

The single time predictor is grade, which is considered to be an essential part of every model. Based on a voluminous research literature (Shin, Davison, & Long, 2009), there is a strong expectation that reading achievement will increase over time regardless of risk. Given the relatively short grade span (5–8), the increase is expected to be linear, as this is consistent with similar studies (Ding, Davison, & Petersen, 2005). Therefore, all models considered will be linear growth models and include grade as the sole time predictor.

Assuming linear change and two risk groups, there are four main models one might consider for LMER analysis. The mathematical details of LMER are delayed until Chapter 5. Here a heuristic approach is presented using graphs to convey the essence of the models.

Graphical illustrations of the four LMER models are shown in Figure 1.5. Model A in Figure 1.5a depicts the situation in which the DADV and ADV change curves are identical. There is no intercept difference or slope difference among the groups. The advantaged and disadvantaged lines are atop one another, giving the appearance of only one curve in the graph. It follows that this is a model with no achievement gap.

Model B in Figure 1.5b depicts an intercept difference. This is a stable achievement gap model. The change curves increase over time, but they are parallel. The DADV curve starts at a lower point on the horizontal axis than the ADV curve, and the difference endures over time.

Figure 1.5c shows Model C has a slope difference, but not an intercept difference. This is a model that has no initial achievement gap, but one develops over time. The groups begin at the same value, but the ADV group increases at a faster rate than the DADV group.

Finally, Model D in Figure 1.5d depicts both an intercept difference and a slope difference. This is a changing achievement gap model, with the gap narrowing over time. The ADV group starts at a higher value than the DADV group, but the DAVD group increases at a faster rate. Another possibility for a changing-gap model is that the gap widens over time, that is, the group curves increasingly diverge as time elapses.

Multimodel inference begins with a set of working hypotheses. The statistical models discussed in future chapters are considered as representatives of these working hypotheses. The distinction between a working hypothesis and its representative statistical model is usually blurred. The consequence is that the representative is often referred to as a *statistical hypothesis*. One tenet of multimodel inference is that each statistical hypothesis should have a sound scientific justification. The intention here is to reinforce the good practice of carefully thinking about theoretical issues before examining the data. Consequently, based on the brief sketch of the extent literature provided above, two of the models in Figure 1.5 are not plausible, Model A and Model C. As mentioned, an initial achievement gap has been consistently found over many studies spanning many years of research. Model A and C do not have an early achievement gap, and thus, are not scientifically justified.

The omission of unjustifiable hypotheses is in contrast to the traditional approach of NHST. NHST often involves an unrealistic *null hypothesis*, such

1.7 LMER and Multimodel Inference

as Model A or C. Usually a justifiable hypothesis or *alternative hypothesis*, like Model B or D, is tested against the null hypothesis. When the data are used to evaluate the hypotheses, it is no surprise that the justifiable hypothesis is usually chosen over the unjustifiable hypothesis. For this reason, the use of NHST has been criticized when used with a meaningless null hypothesis, as the results are not helpful in evaluating the alternative hypothesis of interest (Cohen, 1994; Hubbard & Lindsay, 2008; Meehl, 1978, 1997; Tukey, 1991).

In contrast, multimodel inference considers only alternative hypotheses. In the case of the models represented in Figure 1.5, only Model B and D are considered justifiable, and thus, are the two alternative models of interest. The set of models for the analysis, then, consists of Model B and Model D. Model B represents an enduring achievement gap model with an intercept difference. Model D represents a changing achievement gap model with intercept and slope differences. In an actual analysis, it is common to consider many more than two alternative models.

The graphs of Figure 1.5b and Figure 1.5d illustrate the fixed effects portion of the models. The details of the random effects portion will be discussed in future chapters. Suffice it to say, the two models will both have two random effects: random intercepts and random slopes. Recall this means the models allow for individual variation in starting points, and individual variation in rates of change over time. These two types of variation are typically modeled in an actual analysis (Cnaan, Laird, & Slasor, 1997; Ware, 1985).

In the results below, focus is on the fixed effects, as these are usually the objects of interest for applied researchers. Information about the variability of the random effects is also provided, but such information is usually not emphasized. Furthermore, the focus is on the static risk predictor effects rather than grade, as both models (B and D) have linear change curves.

Table 1.5 summarizes the two alternative models and provides statistical evidence based on the fit to the MPLS data set. In future chapters, parameter estimation and the computation of the AIC will be discussed in detail. For the moment, the AIC values and related information are simply listed, having been obtained from fitting the models to the data. Given the small sample size of this example, a variant of the AIC should be used that is appropriate for small samples. This variant is presented in Chapter 7.

Table 1.5 Set of two models for multimodel inference.

Model	Description	AIC	Weight
B	Risk group intercept difference	563.89	0.71
D	Risk group intercept and slope differences	565.70	0.29

A smaller AIC value indicates better fit, and argues for greater plausibility of the model in question. As seen in Table 1.5, Model B has a smaller AIC than Model D, indicating that Model B is the more plausible of the two. Plausibility is a relative concept, and much more will be said about this in Chapter 7. For

(a) Model A: No differences (lines are atop one another).

(b) Model B: Intercept difference.

(c) Model C: Slope difference.

(d) Model D: Intercept and slope differences.

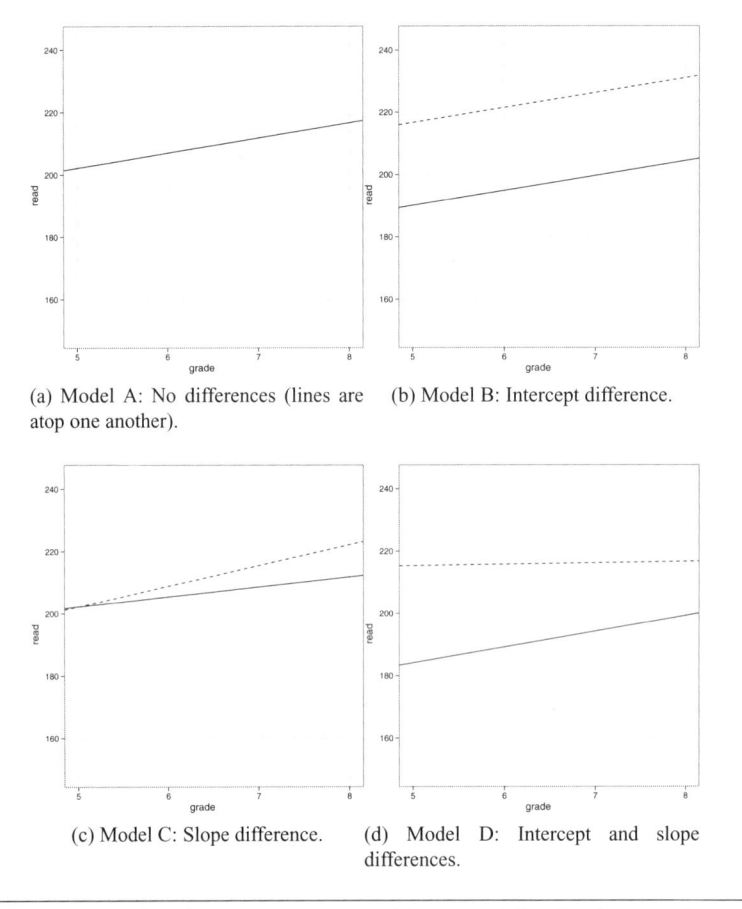

Figure 1.5 Graphical representations of four models of risk group intercept and slope differences. The dashed line is for the advantaged group and the solid line is for the disadvantaged group.

the moment, it is stressed that there is no statistical testing with the AIC. All that can be said is that a model with the smaller value is better fitting and more plausible than a model with a larger value.

An advantage of the AIC is that much can be said regarding relative fit and plausibility. It is possible to quantify the extent of the plausibility using probability statements. Along with the AIC, Table 1.5 lists the weight of evidence, which is a probability scaling of the AIC. The weights fall between 0 and 1 inclusive, and their sum is always 1. The weight of evidence is the probability of the model given the data, the model set, and inability to know the true model; see Chapter 7. In this case, the weight of Model B is approximately $2\frac{1}{2}$ times larger than the weight of Model D. The interpretation is that Model B is more plausible than Model D, but Model D probably cannot be completely ruled out. The basis for such statements is provided in Chapter 7.

In a write-up of the results, Table 1.5 would be included along with the interpretative statements of the last paragraphs. In addition, parameter

1.7 LMER and Multimodel Inference

Table 1.6 MPLS data set in wide format.

subid	read.5	read.6	read.7	read.8	risk	gen	eth	ell	sped	att
1	172	185	179	194	HHM	F	Afr	0	N	0.94
2	200	210	209	−99	HHM	F	Afr	0	N	0.91
3	191	199	203	215	HHM	M	Afr	0	N	0.97
4	200	195	194	−99	HHM	F	Afr	0	N	0.88
5	207	213	212	213	HHM	F	Afr	0	N	0.85
6	191	189	206	195	HHM	M	Afr	0	N	0.90
7	199	208	213	218	POV	M	Afr	1	N	0.97
8	191	194	194	−99	POV	F	His	1	Y	0.97
9	149	154	174	177	POV	F	Afr	0	Y	0.97
10	200	212	213	−99	POV	F	Afr	0	N	0.96
11	218	231	233	239	POV	F	Whi	0	N	0.98
12	228	232	248	246	POV	F	Whi	0	Y	0.96
13	228	236	228	239	ADV	F	Whi	0	N	0.99
14	199	210	225	235	ADV	M	Afr	1	N	0.99
15	218	223	236	−99	ADV	F	Whi	0	N	1.00
16	228	226	234	227	ADV	M	Whi	0	N	0.97
17	201	210	208	219	ADV	M	Whi	0	N	0.98
18	218	220	217	221	ADV	M	Whi	0	N	1.00
19	215	216	221	−99	ADV	F	Whi	0	N	0.96
20	204	215	219	214	ADV	F	Afr	0	N	0.95
21	237	241	243	−99	ADV	M	Whi	0	N	0.98
22	219	233	236	−99	ADV	F	Afr	0	N	0.96

estimates of the most plausible Model B, would also be presented. This is to provide additional detail important for comprehending the results, such as the estimated values of the intercepts, and the estimated rate of growth over time.

Details of obtaining parameter estimates are discussed in Chapters 5 and 6. For now, the parameter estimates obtained with the data are presented in the narrative, although usually a table of estimates is constructed. Beginning with the fixed effects estimates, the results indicate the ADV group had an estimated intercept of 192.78, with an estimated SE of 6.51. The intercept estimate indicates the estimated mean reading achievement for the ADV group at the fifth grade was 192.78. The DADV group had an estimated intercept 26.58 less than the ADV group, with a SE of 4.83 for the difference. The estimated rate of change for the two groups was 4.78, with a SE of 0.73. The slope estimate indicates the groups increased in their reading achievement at a mean annual rate of 4.78.

In terms of individual variability, the estimated variance of the random intercepts was 579.5, or a standard deviation (SD) of 24.07. Using the vertical axes in Figure 1.5 as a reference, this indicates relatively extensive individual variability in starting points. The estimated variance of the random slopes was 6.75 (SD = 2.6), illustrating there were individual differences in rate of change over time. The estimated correlation between the random intercepts and slopes was $cor = -0.9$. The correlation indicates those who started lower tended to have a faster increase over time, and those who started higher tended to have a slower increase over time. Estimates of SEs for the variances and correlation are not presented for reasons discussed in Chapter 5.

To summarize, Model B with a constant achievement gap had superior fit to Model D with a changing gap. The fit of Model B was approximately $2\frac{1}{2}$ times better. Estimated parameters for Model B were provided to illustrate the differences between the groups. The difference was such that the advantaged group started higher, but both groups had a constant rate of increase over time. In terms of the bouquet of models, Model B was definitely more fragrant than Model D. The weights of evidence indicate, however, that Model D was not entirely malodorous, and probably should not be completely discounted in future research.

1.8 Overview of the Remainder of the Book

The example of LMER and multimodel inference in the last section was conceptual. The intent of the remaining chapters is to fill in the details that were glossed over. This includes details of LMER, such as the algebraic formulas, and details regarding how the parameter estimates are obtained from sample data using R. Particulars of multimodel inference and NHST will be presented, illustrating among other things, how the values in Table 1.5 are obtained and interpreted.

An additional goal of the remaining chapters is to expand the repertoire, so that more complex analyses can also be handled. Examples of such analyses include models with multiple static predictors, and models with nonlinear change curves. For researchers who anticipate using exploratory analysis, descriptive and graphical methods will be covered.

Brief Introduction to R

2

The computer examples of this book all use the R program. This chapter is intended for readers who have never encountered R, or for readers who want a refresher on some basic topics. The programming topics discussed here provide necessary building blocks for more complex data manipulation and analysis presented in later chapters. Additional syntax will be presented in future chapters as the need arises.

According to the R FAQ, R is "a system for statistical computation and graphics" (Hornik, 2010). In its basic form, R consists of a `base` package for performing numerical calculations, looping and branching, and various types of statistical analysis. In addition to the `base` package, there are add-on packages written by users to perform all sorts of graphical and statistical analysis. A number of these add-on packages for longitudinal data analysis will be used in future chapters.

One benefit of R, as opposed to other programs popular in the behavioral sciences, is that it is free. R is licensed under the GNU General Public License to help ensure it remains free (Free Software Foundation, 2007). Overstating the advantages of using a freely available program is difficult. Free software means people with varied resources can use the program, as long as they have an Internet connection. It also implies greater freedom, as one is not constrained by the software choices of the larger entity of which they are a part, such as a business, an academic department, a research lab, and so on.

Another advantage of R is that it is syntax based. This means the user must supply the input to tell the computer what to do, rather than select menu options to accomplish tasks. This certainly is not exclusive to R, but it is nonetheless an advantage. The term *syntax*, or *code*, is used to refer to the input supplied by the user. The main advantage of a syntax-based program is reproducibility. The analyst can save the computer code as a *script file*, so that all the analyses in one session can be reproduced in a future session. Syntax also facilitates *analysis comprehension*, meaning there is a greater demand on the user to understand the analysis. In most contexts, one must have at least a working knowledge of a topic in order to successfully program in R. The structure of the syntax often provides insights into the nature of the statistical method in question, and insight into how its parameters are estimated.

Because R is a programming language, it is highly flexible and customizable. This means R can perform a wide number of tasks and analyses, with tailoring possible for the problem at hand. Accomplishing certain tasks does require an understanding of some programming skills, an introduction to which appears below.

When one hears complaints about R having "a steep learning curve," perhaps what is being referred to is the fact that knowledge of syntax and functions is necessary to use the program. Many of the functions are part of add-on packages that must be installed. R does not provide a self-contained, readily accessible list of functions, although an Internet search will reveal lists that have been compiled by users. Consequently, some who are new to R might feel frustrated by the "blank slate" nature of the program.

Two approaches are suggested for facilitating the learning of R. The first is to work through the primer provided in this chapter and possibly other available primers. The second is to use the help facilities in R described in Section 2.10. The help facilities can be used to acquaint the user with available functions and packages to solve specific problems, such as the analysis of longitudinal data.

2.1 Obtaining and Installing R

To download and install R, the computer must have a connection to the Internet. The latest version of R (2.12.2 as of this writing) is obtained from the *R Project for Statistical Computing* at http://www.r-project.org/. After navigating to the website, click on CRAN under Download, Packages on the left-hand side of the welcome screen. A server must be selected, called a *CRAN mirror*, in a preferable country of origin (e.g., United States). After selecting a server, the appropriate operating system for the computer must be chosen: Linux, MacOS, or Windows. For Linux and MacOS, there are directions at the top of the download page for installation. For Windows, the base package is downloaded and installed like any other executable file. On Windows machines, the user might need to have administrator privileges to successfully install and use the program. This problem can often be circumvented by installing R outside of the default Program Files directory (e.g., install in C:\R).

A FAQ for each operating system is available on the website, and it should be consulted in the event there are problems with downloading or installing the program. User-written help documents and videos can be obtained with a judicious Internet search.

2.2 Functions and Packages

The `base` package has an impressive variety of functions for manipulating, analyzing, and graphing data. For more specialized analysis, such as that involving longitudinal data, it is often advantageous to use one of the user-contributed add-on packages. These packages typically have specialized functions tailored for specific topics. Many of the add-on packages are written by world-leading authorities on the topic of interest.

Throughout this book, names of packages and functions appear in `typewriter font`. Functions will be written with trailing parentheses, as in `mean()`, to denote the fact that *arguments* must be supplied to the functions. The arguments constitute pieces of information that influence the workings of the function. For instance, many functions require an argument naming the variable to be analyzed and options for treating missing data. The following is an example of the `mean()` function with two arguments (arg. 1 and arg. 2) that will be explained below.

$$\underbrace{\text{mean}(\underbrace{x}_{\text{arg. 1}}, \underbrace{\text{na.rm} = \text{TRUE}}_{\text{arg. 2}})}_{\text{function}}$$

Add-on packages, beyond the `base` package, must be installed before they can be used. The easiest method of installing is within R. After invoking R, an add-on package can be installed by using menu options. For Windows computers, this is accomplished with the `Packages` menu option. Alternatively, the `install.packages()` function can be used at the prompt, or from a script file. The name of the package to be installed must be supplied in quotes, along with the quoted name of the repository (remote server) that houses the package. A list of repositories is provided on the *R Project for Statistical Computing* website.

As an example, consider installation of the add-on package `ggplot2`, useful for graphing longitudinal data. Assume the `base` package has been successfully installed and the R program has been invoked (started). The following syntax installs the `ggplot2` package from the repository at the University of California at Los Angeles (UCLA):

```
install.packages("ggplot2",repos = "http://cran.stat.ucla.edu/")
```

To be perfectly clear, the above syntax is typed at the prompt, >, in the R console window, which is the window that appears when R is first invoked. After typing the syntax, the Enter key is pressed to execute it. Alternatively, the syntax can be executed from a script file that is explained in a moment. After submitting the syntax, the console window will show some relatively cryptic messages, but the last line should indicate successful installation.

In addition to the `ggplot2` package, extensive use is made of `lme4` and `AICmodavg` in the following chapters. Additional packages will be mentioned as needed. Many primary packages link to, or depend on, other ancillary packages. These ancillary packages are usually automatically installed along with the primary package. For example, when the `ggplot2` package is installed, the `plyr` package for data manipulation and analysis is also automatically installed. To ensure that dependent packages are always installed, the additional argument `dependencies=TRUE` should be included in the `install.packages()` function.

Once a package is installed, its functions are not automatically made available. The `library()` or `require()` function must be used to load the package. If you want to use the functions in the `ggplot2` package, for example, type `require(ggplot2)` at the prompt, or execute the syntax from a script file. Ancillary packages are also made available when a primary package is loaded. The `require(ggplot2)` not only loads `ggplot2`, but also loads `plyr` and other related packages.

2.3 Essential Syntax

Every syntax-based computer program has its own conventions. The following sections outline concepts and syntax that are essential building blocks for the data manipulation and analysis covered later in this book.

2.3.1 PROMPT VERSUS SCRIPT FILES

One method of executing syntax is to type it at the prompt in the R console window and press the Enter key. Syntax can also be typed in a script file and executed in part or whole. R provides a script editor for creating script files that is accessed by the menu options. A whole host of free third-party script editors are also available.

The main advantage of the script file is that the contents can be saved. The script file is a record of the analyses you perform, and the file can be opened in future R sessions. The script file should be saved periodically using the appropriate menu options or key strokes. The script file is saved with the extension `*.r` or `*.R`.

The computer examples in this book depict the syntax as being typed and executed from the prompt in the console window. However, this is done for clarity of presentation, and it is suggested that a script file be routinely used.

2.3.2 INPUT AND OUTPUT APPEARANCE IN THIS BOOK

In this book, R syntax and output appear in `typewriter font`. In addition, input and output are shaded in gray. Syntax (input) is always preceded by the symbol >, which is the R prompt in the console window. When syntax runs over one line, a plus sign (+) appears at the beginning of any continuation lines. If the reader is copying syntax from the book, the plus sign should not be submitted as part of the syntax. Output is always boxed to distinguish it from syntax. Depending on the nature of the output, it might be indexed by numbers appearing in single brackets, for example, [1], or double brackets, [[2]]. The details of indexing are discussed later in this chapter.

In certain cases, it is desirable to discuss specific parts of multiline syntax or output. To facilitate this, line numbers will sometimes appear to the left of the syntax or output box. The following is an example; do not worry about the meaning of the syntax for the time being.

```
> summary(c(10, 5, 2))
```

```
1  Min.    1st Qu.  Median   Mean    3rd Qu.   Max.
2  2.000   3.500    5.000    5.667   7.500     10.000
```

Line 1 contains the headings of the columns. Line 2 contains the numerical output that will be explained later. The reader familiar with elementary statistics can probably determine the meaning of the statistics by the column headings (e.g., Min. is the minimum value).

2.3.3 QUITTING R

The R session is terminated by typing q() at the command prompt, running the syntax from the script file, or selecting the appropriate menu options (e.g., File, Exit on Windows machines). When quitting, there is a prompt to save the workspace image. The workspace image consists of the objects created in the session (see below), but *not* the syntax. The workspace is saved in a file that is only readable by R having the extension *.rdata or *.Rdata. Typically, important things like data sets and output are saved within the session, so the workspace image need not be saved when exiting.

2.3.4 TERMINATING A PROCESS

Sometimes a syntax mistake is made, and a process is initiated that is unintended on the part of the user. Other times a closing parenthesis or curly bracket (}) is omitted, and the user cannot return to the console prompt. In these situations, the Esc key (escape key) can be used on a Windows machine to terminate a process. This returns the cursor to the console prompt. The menu option Misc can also be used.

2.3.5 BASIC CALCULATIONS

A basic use of R is as a calculator. Using commands for addition (+), multiplication (*), division (/), exponents (^), and so on, all the typical operations available on handheld calculators can be performed. Suppose you want to carry out the calculations in the following equation:

$$(2+3)+(2\cdot 3)-\left(\frac{6}{3}\right)-3^2=0. \qquad (2.3.1)$$

The syntax for the operations is shown below. When the syntax is executed, the result is printed to the computer screen, which is the same as saying it is printed to the R console window.

```
> (2 + 3) + (2 * 3) - (6 / 3) - 3 ^ 2
```
```
[1] 0
```

The input and output above are similar to what appears when the syntax is executed from the R prompt. As shown above, syntax is preceded by the > symbol, and each line of syntax has its output immediately below, appearing in a box. Boxing is used to facilitate understanding in this text, but it is not used in the R program. The [1] preceding each output line is for indexing, conveying that there is only one line of output.

Basic calculations are often used within more complex operations. An advantage of R is that several things can be done "on the fly" by embedding simpler operations within more complex ones. Examples appear in later sections.

2.3.6 OBJECTS

R is an object-oriented program. Objects are named storage entities to which things such as numbers, words, or data sets are *assigned*. The assignment of things to objects requires use of the assignment operator, <-. The assignment operator is formed with the < and - keys. The required form is

object name ← thing to be assigned.

An example will help clarify the assignment concept. Suppose the result of simple addition is assigned to the object myresult.

```
> myresult <- 2 + 3
> myresult
```
```
[1] 5
```

The object stores the result of the operation, and its contents are displayed by typing the object name. This is an *implicit print*. An *explicit print* can be performed by using the print() function, as in print(myresult).

2.3 Essential Syntax

Explicit print is sometimes desirable, as additional arguments can be used to alter the output.

One of the powerful features of R is that after an object is created, it can be used in subsequent operations. As an illustration, consider the following.

```
> myresult * 2
```

```
[1] 10
```

In the example, `myresult` consists of a number, and it can be manipulated in the same way as using the number directly. In most of the analyses presented in future chapters, extensive use of objects is made.

Object names are arbitrary, but some conventions should be followed when naming. Names cannot begin with a number and should not have spaces. A period rather than an underscore (or other character) should be used for clarity, for instance, `my.result`. Objects should not have the same names as functions (see below), so names like `mean` or `sd` are to be avoided. In addition, R is case sensitive. You cannot type `Myresult` to display `myresult`, as the two names are interpreted as different objects.

Up to this point, objects have been proxies for numbers. The object-oriented approach is more impressive when one considers that an object can consist of complex things, such as a data set, or the output from a statistical analysis. An example of storing a data set as an object is presented in Section 2.5.3. In Section 2.9, the output of a statistical analysis is saved as an object.

2.3.7 CONCATENATION

A group or list of numbers, known as a vector, is assigned to an object using the concatenation function, `c()`. The following syntax assigns a vector of numbers to the object `mydat`.

```
> mydat <- c(2, 3, 1, 0, 3, 4)
> mydat
```

```
[1] 2 3 1 0 3 4
```

The commas are necessary separators for the numbers in the syntax, but the spaces are optional. Because the values in the vector are numbers, `mydat` is a *numeric vector*. The `mydat` object can be used in similar operations as an object consisting of a single number.

It is important to understand how R interprets the syntax when the object is a vector. Suppose `mydat` is multiplied by 2.

```
> mydat * 2
```

```
[1] 4 6 2 0 6 8
```

Comparison with the previous output shows that the original vector is multiplied by 2 on an element-by-element basis. That is, each element of mydat is multiplied by 2. Functions that are not element-wise are available for other types of operations on vectors. Some of these are shown in the Appendix, where an introduction to matrix algebra is presented. Additional functions are introduced as needed in the following chapters.

The concatenation operator can be used with nonnumeric data. For example, a vector of names rather than numbers is created below.

```
> mynames <- c("Carlos", "Marta", "Salome","Philip")
> mynames
```
```
[1] "Carlos" "Marta" "Salome" "Philip"
```

The quotes are necessary in c() for nonnumeric data, and the resulting object is a *character vector* or *string vector*. In printing the character vector, the quotes are removed by using an explicit print with the logical argument quote=FALSE, as in print(mynames, quote=FALSE).

R will return an error message if non-permissible operations are attempted with character vectors. For example, the following will produce an error message.

```
> mynames * 2
```

There are permissible operations with character vectors. As an example, two character vectors are concatenated to produce a new character vector using the paste() function.

```
> paste("grade.", as.character(5:8), sep = "")
```
```
[1] "grade.5" "grade.6" "grade.7" "grade.8"
```

As shown in the output, the as.character() function converts the numbers 5, 6, 7, 8 to characters and then concatenates each with grade. The sep= argument sets no separation space between the concatenated elements (the default is a single space).

2.3.8 STATISTICAL FUNCTIONS

The base package has a number of useful statistical functions. The statistical functions are usually used with vector objects, but they can also be used with other types of objects. Below are examples of some common statistical functions and the output they produce. Various statistics are computed for the mydat vector from the previous section.

```
> mydat                    # Display the data.
```
```
[1] 2 3 1 0 3 4
```

```
> mean(mydat)              # Mean.
```
```
[1] 2.166667
```
```
> sd(mydat)                # Standard deviation.
```
```
[1] 1.47196
```
```
> summary(mydat)           # Descriptive statistics.
```
```
   Min.   1st Qu.    Median      Mean   3rd Qu.      Max.
  0.000     1.250     2.500     2.167     3.000     4.000
```
```
> min(mydat); max(mydat)   # Minimum and maximum values.
```
```
[1] 0
```
```
[1] 4
```

The pound sign (#) is used for comments, allowing the input program to be annotated for increased comprehension. Everything following the pound sign to the end of the line will be ignored by the program. The last line of syntax uses a semicolon (;) to separate two functions. This convention must be followed if more than one function is used on a single line. As shown above, the output is stacked when the semicolon is used.

A number of additional statistical functions will be introduced in the following chapters. Many of these functions are specific to the package designed for particular purposes.

2.4 Data Types

There are different data types in R, and vectors of data are characterized by the data they contain. Data types are important to consider, as they have implications for data analysis. Two types have already been encountered: numeric data and character data.

A third data type is a *factor*. A factor variable represents a categorical variable, or grouping variable, that uses numbers to represent its categories or levels. Factor variables are created with the factor() function. One method of creating a factor variable is to first create a numeric vector and then associate character descriptors with each number. It is common for the factor vector to have few distinct values, perhaps two or three.

Suppose the goal is to create a factor variable of gender, with coding of male and female. First, a vector of 0s and 1s is created, and then 0 is associated with "male" and 1 is associated with "female." The following syntax accomplishes the task.

```
> myfac0 <- c(0, 1, 1, 0)
> myfac <- factor(myfac0, labels = c("Male", "Female"))
> myfac
```

```
[1] Male Female Female Male
Levels: Male Female
```

Line 1 of the output contains an index, [1], and then a listing of the factor vector contents. Line 2 of the output provides an exhaustive list of the category labels. In this instance, the exhaustive list is not needed, as the label categories are readily apparent from the listing of the factor vector contents. In other situations, the exhaustive list is helpful in understanding the details of the factor vector.

A function helpful for understanding output objects is the structure function, str(). The structure function provides a partial listing of vector contents and provides information about data type. Suppose that str() is used with myfac.

```
> str(myfac)
```

```
Factor w/ 2 levels "Male","Female": 1 2 2 1
```

The output indicates myfac is a factor variable with two levels, and the levels are coded as "Male" and "Female." The numbers on the right index the levels and are in the same order as the original values. The numeric levels are produced in this case by adding 1 to the original values of 0 and 1, yielding 1 and 2, respectively. Factor vectors are very useful when one wants to include a categorical variable in an analysis. Examples are shown in future chapters.

The str() function can be used with almost any output object. Consider its use with a numeric vector and a character vector.

```
> mynum <- c(1.5, 10, 8.467, 8)
> str(mynum)
```

```
num [1:4] 1.5 10 8.47 8
```

```
> mychar <- c("Carlos", "Marta", "Salome", "Philip")
> str(mychar)
```

```
chr [1:4] "Carlos" "Marta" "Salome" "Philip"
```

In the output, num stands for numeric and chr stands for character. The bracketed numbers, [1:4], refer to there being 1 through 4 elements in the vectors—more on this later.

2.4.1 MISSING VALUES

An important consideration with all data types is the coding of missing elements or missing values. In R, missing values are represented as NA, "not available." NA is used when an observation is not available, but a place holder is desired anyway. Consider an example of a numeric vector with the second element missing.

```
> mynum2 <- c(1.5, NA, 8.467, 8)
> mynum2
```

```
[1] 1.500   NA 8.467 8.000
```

In the concatenation function, NA is *not* quoted. The output shows the second element is not available, but a space (or location) is retained for it anyway.

In the NA example, why not skip over the missing value and simply assign c(1.5, 8.467, 8)? The answer is that it is often desirable to reserve a space for observations that were intended and not realized. Suppose the intention is to obtain scores from four subjects, but the second subject's score cannot be ascertained. For bookkeeping purposes, it is desirable to index the fact that there was an attempt to obtain scores from four subjects. The bookkeeping is especially important when observations are collected on many variables. Certain subjects may have missing values on some variables, but not others. It is confusing to have the data vectors contract and expand based on the missing data. Including missing data values allows a clear matching of the subjects with their data.

Missing values present issues for the use of R functions. All functions have a default method of treating missing data that can be changed with optional arguments. The default method for a function is found on the function's help page, as described later.

Some functions, such as summary(), will ignore missing data by default and compute descriptive statistics on the nonmissing values. Values other than NA are referred to as *available values*. In what follows, the summary() function is used on the numeric vector with a missing value.

```
> mynum2
```

```
[1] 1.500   NA 8.467 8.000
```

```
> summary(mynum2)
```

```
  Min.  1st Qu.  Median   Mean  3rd Qu.   Max.   NA's
 1.500    4.750   8.000  5.989    8.234  8.467  1.000
```

As the output shows, descriptive statistics are computed on the available values. The summary() function counts and displays the number of missing values in the NA's column.

Other functions, such as `mean()` and `sd()`, do not use available values by default. Consider what happens when `mean()` is applied to the vector with a missing value.

```
> mean(mynum2)
```
```
[1] NA
```

The result is a missing value. Although this default might appear inconvenient at first, it is useful for alerting the user to the presence of missing data. This is not crucial in the small example, but it can be with larger data vectors.

To have functions ignore missing values, one must include the logical argument `na.rm=TRUE`. A logical argument takes the value of `TRUE` or `FALSE`. The logical argument tells the function to remove the missing values and then compute the mean. Consider what happens when the optional syntax is used.

```
> mean(mynum2, na.rm = TRUE)
```
```
[1] 5.989
```

Now the mean of the available values is computed. In the chapters to follow, additional details regarding missing values and their treatment are discussed.

2.5 Matrices, Data Frames, and Lists

There are three main formats, or *data structures*, for the arrangement of data in R. These are a *matrix*, a *data frame*, and a *list*. A summary of the main features is shown in Table 2.1.

A matrix is a rectangular array for only one data type. A soft introduction to matrices is provided in the Appendix. A vector is a special case of a matrix that has only one column or one row. A data frame is similar to a matrix, but different columns (vectors) can have different data types. You cannot mix types of data in the same column. The use of NA in a numeric vector may appear to violate the same-column convention, but NA is *not* a character string in R.

An important characteristic of both a matrix and a data frame is that the columns are of the same length. A list is similar to a data frame, allowing different vectors to have different types of data, but the vectors need not be of the same length.

2.5.1 VECTOR

As seen above, a vector is constructed with the concatenation function. Suppose that the numeric and character vectors previously considered are once again created.

2.5 Matrices, Data Frames, and Lists

```
> mynum  <-  c(1.5, 10, 8.467, 8)
> mychar <- c("Carlos","Marta","Salome","Philip")
```

These vectors will be considered for calculations in the sections below.

2.5.2 MATRIX

A matrix can be made from the two vectors, `mynum` and `mychar`. As indicated in Table 2.1, a matrix must have columns (vectors) of equal length, and `mynum` and `mychar` meet this requirement. In addition, a matrix can only have one type of data. This is a problem because one vector is numeric and the other is character. In such situations, R will coerce the data to be of one type.

In the syntax below, the `matrix()` function is used to create a matrix. The concatenation function is used to list the two vectors that will be the columns of the `mymat` matrix. The argument `ncol=` specifies the number of columns of the matrix. The number of rows is determined from the `ncol=` argument and the data.

```
> mymat <- matrix(c(mynum, mychar), ncol = 2)  # Matrix with 2 columns.
> mymat
```

```
       [,1]       [,2]
[1,]  "1.5"     "Carlos"
[2,]  "10"      "Marta"
[3,]  "8.467"   "Salome"
[4,]  "8"       "Philip"
```

The output shows that each element of `mymat` is quoted. Quotes denote character data, illustrating that R forces the numeric vector to be a character vector in the matrix. The column and row brackets (e.g., `[1,]`) are used for indexing to be discussed in a moment. For now, it should be evident the matrix consists of two columns, each having four rows.

To gain further insight, the `str()` function is used with the matrix object.

```
> str(mymat)
```

```
chr [1:4, 1:2] "1.5" "10" "8.467" "8" "Carlos" "Marta" ...
```

The output reveals that `mymat` is a character matrix (`char`). A partial listing of the matrix elements is displayed, beginning with the first column.

2.5.3 DATA FRAME

A data frame is created using the `data.frame()` function. A data frame is also created with `read.table()`, which is used to read an external text file into R. The reading in of data is discussed in the next chapter.

Table 2.1 shows that a data frame has columns with equal numbers of rows, only the data types can differ. Consider a data frame created from the numeric and character vectors. Column labels, or variable names, are specified by using the equal sign (=).

```
> mydat <- data.frame(Char = mychar, Num = mynum)    # Data frame.
> mydat
```

```
     Char     Num
1   Carlos   1.500
2   Marta   10.000
3   Salome   8.467
4   Philip   8.000
```

As the syntax shows, `data.frame()` does not require the use of `c()`. The vector objects to be included are listed, separated by a comma.

The output illustrates some useful characteristics of data frames. The character vector and the numeric vector are displayed without quotes, indicating that different data types are associated with different columns. The headings of the columns are known as *column names*, which can be changed. The numbers to the extreme left of the vectors are *row names*, which also can be changed.

Consider the use of the `str()` function with the data frame object.

```
> str(mydat)
```

```
'data.frame': 4 obs. of 2 variables:
$ Char: Factor w/ 4 levels "Carlos","Marta",..: 1 2 4 3
$ Num : num 1.5 10 8.47 8
```

Line 1 of the output shows `mydat` is a data frame with four rows and two columns (two variables). Line 2 lists the first column name after the dollar sign ($) and reveals it is a factor variable. Both the category labels and the level numbers are listed. The `data.frame()` function converts a character vector to a factor vector by default. Character vectors are retained as such by using the logical argument `stringsAsFactors=FALSE`. Line 3 shows the second column is numeric (`num`) and lists its values.

2.5.4 LIST

A list is created using the `list()` function. Table 2.1 shows that a list can have different data types and different column lengths. To illustrate different column lengths, a list with three elements is created, the last element being a numeric vector with one row shorter than the others.

```
> mylist <- list(Char = mychar, Num4 = mynum, Num3 = c(1,2,3))    # List.
> mylist
```

2.5 Matrices, Data Frames, and Lists

```
$Char
[1] "Carlos"  "Marta"   "Salome"  "Philip"

$Num4
[1] 1.500 10.000  8.467  8.000

$Num3
[1] 1 2 3
```

The output for the `mylist` list object depicts the vectors in rows rather than columns. The character vector has quoted elements, whereas the numeric vectors do not, illustrating that mixed data types are allowed. The third vector is one element shorter than the first two, but all the vectors are displayed. The bracketing ([1]) is indexing, which is discussed in the next section.

Further insight is obtained by using the `str()` function on the list object.

```
> str(mylist)
```

```
1  List of 3
2  $ Char: chr [1:4] "Carlos" "Marta" "Salome" "Philip"
3  $ Num4: num [1:4] 1.5 10 8.47 8
4  $ Num3: num [1:3] 1 2 3
```

Line 1 indicates the `mylist` object is a list with three elements. Line 2 shows the first vector is a character vector (char). Lines 3 to 4 reveal the remaining two vectors are numeric and are of different lengths.

Table 2.1 Features of R data structures.

Structure	Data Type	Indexing	Column Lengths	Function
Vector	Single	[row] or [column]	Not applicable	c(), matrix()
Matrix	Single	[row, column]	Equal	matrix()
Data frame	Mixed	[row, column]	Equal	data.frame(), read.table()
List	Mixed	[[vector]] [row][a]	Unequal	list()

a. Assumes elements are vectors (see text).

2.5.4.1 WORKING WITH DATA FRAMES

The data frame will be the primary data structure in future chapters, so it is beneficial to mention some additional characteristics. First, the column names of a data frame are changed using the `colnames()` function. Second, a column (vector) is accessed or extracted by using the data frame object name followed by a dollar sign ($) and the column name. Consider an illustration.

```
> colnames(mydat)        # Shows the column names.
```
```
[1] "Char" "Num"
```

```
> colnames(mydat) ← c("Name","Score")   # Assigns new column names.
> mydat                                 # Implicit print.
```
```
    Name     Score
1   Carlos   1.500
2   Marta   10.000
3   Salome   8.467
4   Philip   8.000
```

```
> mydat$Name                    # Print first column (variable).
```
```
[1] Carlos Marta Salome Philip
Levels: Carlos Marta Philip Salome
```

```
> mydat$Score                   # Print second column (variable).
```
```
[1] 1.500 10.000 8.467 8.000
```

Small data frames with a limited number of rows and columns are easily created with the concatenation function, as shown above. Larger data frames are usually created by reading in a text file of the data set with the read.table() function. Discussion of read.table() is deferred to the next chapter.

An alternative to the dollar sign syntax for accessing variables is attach() and detach(). By including the data frame name in attach(), the variables of the data frame are made available directly by their names. The direct naming is ended by including the data frame name in detach(). Consider the following.

```
> attach(mydat)
> mean(Score)
```
```
[1] 6.99175
```

```
> sd(Score)
```
```
[1] 3.759513
```

```
> detach(mydat)
```

Since Score is a variable in the mydat data frame, it is accessed directly after executing attach(mydat). The access is ended by executing detach (mydat). Using mean(Score) outside of attach() and detach() returns an error. Any number of procedures can be performed between

2.6 Indexing

attach() and detach(), and above two were shown for brevity. It is always good to use detach() when finished with the data frame. This avoids the potential problem of similarly named variables in one data frame replacing (masking) variables in another data frame.

Another alternative is the with() function, which is similar to attach() and detach(), only it is used a single time. In the syntax below, with() is used to allow the variable names to appear in mean().

```
> with(mydat, mean(Score))
```
```
[1] 6.99175
```

```
> with(mydat, c(mean(Score), sd(Score)))
```
```
[1] 6.991750 3.759513
```

The second line of syntax uses c() to perform two tasks.

2.6 Indexing

Accessing and extracting individual elements of a vector, matrix, data frame, or list is accomplished using the indexing conventions of R. See Table 2.1 for a summary of syntax conventions.

2.6.1 MATRIX AND DATA FRAME

For a matrix and a data frame, each element has a location defined by the row and column where it resides. The row and column address is denoted by square brackets separated by a comma, [,]. For example, mymat[1,2] refers to the element in the first row and second column of the matrix object. Listing the object name and bracket indexes implicitly prints the element to the computer screen. Here are some examples.

```
> mymat              # Display all matrix elements.
```
```
       [,1]         [,2]
[1,]   "1.5"        "Carlos"
[2,]   "10"         "Marta"
[3,]   "8.467"      "Salome"
[4,]   "8"          "Philip"
```

```
> mymat[1,2]         # First row, second column.
```
```
[1] "Carlos"
```

```
> mydat              # Display all data frame elements.
```

```
    Name     Score
1   Carlos   1.500
2   Marta   10.000
3   Salome   8.467
4   Philip   8.000
```

```
> mydat[2,2]    # Second row, second column.
```

```
[1] 10
```

Several row and/or column elements can be indexed in various ways. Contiguous elements are indexed by a colon (:), and the concatenation function is used for noncontiguous elements. An entire row or column is denoted by a blank. Examples using these conventions are the following.

```
> mymat[1:2,2]      #First two rows of the second column.
```

```
[1] "Carlos" "Marta"
```

```
> mydat[1:2,1:2]    # First two rows, first two columns.
```

```
    Name     Score
1   Carlos   1.5
2   Marta   10.0
```

```
> mymat[c(1,3),1]   # First and third rows of the first column.
```

```
[1] "1.5" "8.467"
```

```
> mydat[ ,1]        # All rows of first column.
```

```
[1] Carlos Marta Salome Philip
Levels: Carlos Marta Philip Salome
```

```
> mydat[1, ]        # All columns of first row.
```

```
Name Score
1 Carlos 1.5
```

2.6.2 VECTOR

A vector is a matrix with only one column or one row. As a consequence, vector objects have a single index. Elements of a vector are referred to by a single entry in brackets. Consider the following.

```
> mynum <- c(1.5, 10, 8.467, 8)
> mynum[1]            # First element.
```

2.6 Indexing

```
[1] 1.5

> mynum[3]              # Third element.
[1] 8.467
```

The vector index is often used in output. Each output example above consists of a single row. The output indexing is particularly helpful when output wraps onto multiple lines.

2.6.3 LIST

Indexing for lists requires double square brackets, [[ ]]. The double brackets are used to access specific vectors. Single brackets are used in conjunction with double brackets to access elements of specific vectors. Consider these examples.

```
> mylist                # Print all list elements.
$Char
[1] "Carlos" "Marta"  "Salome" "Philip"

$Num4
[1]  1.500 10.000  8.467  8.000

$Num3
[1] 1 2 3

> mylist[[2]]           # Second vector.
[1]  1.500 10.000  8.467  8.000

> mylist[[2]][2]        # Second element of second vector.
[1] 10

> mylist[[3]]           # Third vector.
[1] 1 2 3

> mylist[[3]][1]        # First element of third vector.
[1] 1
```

In the examples here, the list elements are vectors, and the indexing represented in Table 2.1 applies. However, lists are general, and the individual elements can be almost anything like matrices, data frames, and statistical output. In these more complex situations, the double-bracket notation can be used to access a list element, but the single bracketing might require both a row and column, or single bracketing might not work at all.

2.6.4 SORTING

Indexing can be used to sort the rows of data. As discussed in future chapters, it is often desirable to sort the rows of a data frame by the subject identification number. Sorting of rows is accomplished by using the `order()` function in the row index of a data frame. The sort variable must be supplied to `order()`. Consider sorting the `mydat` data frame by `Score`.

```
> mydat                                           # Unsorted data frame.
     Name      Score
1    Carlos    1.500
2    Marta     10.000
3    Salome    8.467
4    Philip    8.000

> mydat2 ← mydat[order(mydat$Score), ]   # Sort data frame by Score.
> mydat2                                          # Sorted data frame.
     Name      Score
1    Carlos    1.500
4    Philip    8.000
3    Salome    8.467
2    Marta     10.000
```

The `order()` function appears in the row index, and the column index is left blank, indicating the intent to sort all the columns (variables). The sort variable, `Score`, must be attached to its data frame, `mydat`, using the dollar sign, so that R properly recognizes it. The sorted data are saved in a new data frame, `mydat2`. As shown here, it is recommended that data frame manipulations be saved to a new object in case of error.

2.6.5 RECODING

Indexes can be used to recode specific elements. Suppose the goal is to recode the second element in the second column of the `mydat2` object to NA. The following syntax accomplishes this goal.

```
> mydat2[2,2] ← NA                        # Recode a value to NA.
> mydat2
     Name      Score
1    Carlos    1.500
4    Philip    NA
3    Salome    8.467
2    Marta     10.000
```

2.6.6 SAVING OBJECTS

Objects are saved to file with the `save()` function. A single object or multiple objects can be saved in a single file. The saved file has the extension *.rdata or *.Rdata. The objects to be saved must be supplied along with the name and location of the Rdata file. Consider saving the `mynum` and `mydat` objects to a file on a Windows computer.

```
> save(mynum, mydat, file = "C:/Mine/myfile.Rdata")
```

The `mynum` vector and the `mydat` data frame are both saved to `myfile.Rdata`. Note the use of the forward slash (/), which can also be replaced by a double back slash (\\). Rdata files are only recognized by R. Text files can be written with the `write.table()` function discussed in the next chapter.

2.6.7 LOADING AND LISTING OBJECTS

A saved Rdata file is loaded into R using the `load()` function. The quoted file name and location must be supplied. Once the objects are loaded into computer memory, a listing of available objects is obtained with `ls()` or `objects()`. Any object can be deleted from memory—but not from the Rdata file—using `rm()`. To delete objects from a Rdata file, a new Rdata file is saved omitting the desired object(s).

In the syntax below, all objects from memory are deleted. Then the `myfile.Rdata` file saved above is loaded. After loading the file, the objects in active computer memory are listed. Finally, it is shown how an individual object is deleted from computer memory.

```
> rm(list = ls())      # Delete all objects from memory.
> ls()                 # No objects available.
```
```
character(0)
```
```
> load(file="C:/Mine/myfile.Rdata")
```
```
> objects()
```
```
[1] "mychar"  "mydat"  "mynum"
```
```
> rm(mynum)
> objects()
```
```
[1] "mychar"  "mydat"
```

2.7 User-Defined Functions

For situations encountered later in this book, it is desirable to define functions that are not part of the standard set in the `base` package, nor in the add-on packages. Such functions are known as *user-defined functions*. User-defined functions are commonly used to handle special tasks, such as bootstrap simulations in LMER analysis (see the optional sections of Chapters 7 and 8).

User-defined functions are created with `function()`. The contents of `function()` are assigned to an object, and then the object is used in a similar manner as the other functions discussed in this chapter.

As an illustration, consider defining a function for computing the sample mean. There is no need to write a function for the sample mean, as `mean()` already exists. But this task affords the opportunity to compare and check the results of the user-defined function against an existing function from the `base` package.

Suppose the `mynum` numerical vector is created again, and a function is written to compute the mean. The goal is to compute the sum of the elements of `mynum` and divide by the total number of elements or the length of the vector. The `sum()` and `length()` functions are used along with division, `/`, to accomplish the goal. Consider the following.

```
> mynum <- c(1.5, 10, 8.467, 8)
> mymean <- function() {sum(mynum) / length(mynum)}
```

The operations are enclosed in curly brackets, `{ }`, but this is optional. The parentheses of `function()` must be included, although they are empty in this example. The syntax indicates the function will compute the sum of `mynum` and divide by its length.

The above syntax defines the `mymean()` function. Now the function is used and checked against the result of `mean()`.

```
> mymean()
```
```
[1] 6.99175
```

```
> mean(mynum)
```
```
[1] 6.99175
```

As the output shows, the user-defined `mymean()` function yields the same result as the `mean()` function.

In its current state, `mymean()` will only work on the `mynum` vector. To apply the function to a vector other than `mynum`, a variable must be specified in the definition. Any character string will work as a variable, and here the simple alternative of x is used. By incorporating x into the syntax in the following manner, it is possible to apply mymean() to any vector.

```
> mymean <- function(x) {sum(x) / length(x)}
```

Now an argument must be passed to mymean() to replace x in the function definition. In this case, the argument is the name of the vector for which the mean is to be computed. This can be made explicit by using the optional argument x=.

```
> mymean(x = mynum)
```
```
[1] 6.99175
```

```
> mynum2 <- c(10, 8, 2, 0)
> mymean(mynum2)
```
```
[1] 5
```

As shown in the output, mymean() can now be used with any numeric vector. Missing data treatments are not programmed in mymean(), which is a reason to use mean(). In general, an existing function is preferred to a user-defined function. However, in later chapters, operations are encountered that are not encompassed in any existing functions. In such cases, a user-defined function is valuable.

2.8 Repetitive Operations

In later chapters, statistical procedures known as bootstrap methods will be discussed. Bootstrap methods require that the same statistical operations be repeated a large number of times. Repetitive operations can be carried out in a number of ways, but two methods are particularly useful. The first uses the rdply() function from the plyr package, written by Hadley Wickham (Wickham, 2009a). The second uses a for() loop, which is the R version of a loop structure common in general computer programming.

It is easiest to use rdply() in conjunction with a user-defined function, which is illustrated below. With a for() loop, the user-defined function is incorporated into the programming structure. For the novice programmer, rdply() is easier to use than a for() loop, as the conventions of the latter usually require some getting used to.

2.8.1 rdply()

Necessary arguments for rdply() are the number of repetitions (.n=) and the function or expression to be repeated (.expr=). In the example below, the expression will be a user-defined function, although standard functions can also be used. There is an optional progress bar that indicates the progression of the repetitions (see Chapter 7).

As an illustration of `rdply()`, suppose for each replication, $N = 10$ scores from a normal distribution are generated, and the mean is computed. This simulates the process of drawing a random sample from a known population and computing the sample mean each time. Such a simulation is common in introductory statistics courses to illustrate the sampling distribution of the mean.

The `rnorm()` function is used for generating data from a normal distribution. The arguments are the sample size (n=), the population mean (mean=), and the population SD (sd=). For this example, a population with $\mu = 100$ and $\sigma = 15$ is arbitrarily selected. For each sample, the mean is computed using `mean()`.

The function `mymean2` is defined to carry out the operations for each repetition. The function is executed twice below to illustrate that a different random sample is selected for each repetition.

```
> mymean2 <- function(){
+   mysamp <- rnorm(n = 10, mean = 100, sd = 15)
+   mean(mysamp)
+ }

> mymean2()
```
```
[1] 90.63217
```
```
> mymean2()
```
```
[1] 108.9655
```

Assume the goal is to repeat the `mymean2()` function 15 times. The goal can be accomplished by executing 15 different lines of the same syntax. This is time-consuming, and the resulting means are not stored in any convenient manner.

A better option is to use `rdply()`, which stores the output in a data frame object. The output object will record the repetition number and the resulting mean. Below, the syntax `require(ggplot2)` is used to load the `ggplot2` and `plyr` packages. The `set.seed()` function with the arbitrary value 111 is included, so that the results can be replicated by the reader. In practice, the `set.seed()` function is not used unless the results need to be replicated.

```
> require(ggplot2)
> set.seed(111)
> myresult <- rdply(.n = 15, .expr = mymean2())
> colnames(myresult) <- c("rep", "mean")
> myresult
```

2.8 Repetitive Operations

```
    rep       mean
1    1     99.42380
2    2    102.14509
3    3     89.36441
4    4    104.51982
5    5    107.68322
6    6    107.04305
7    7    103.34770
8    8     95.59829
9    9     98.98696
10  10     99.15023
11  11     99.65499
12  12    107.91997
13  13     96.24939
14  14    106.01613
15  15     91.50929
```

The output shows the replication number in the rep column and the sample mean in the mean column. Consistent with statistical theory (see, e.g., Howell, 2010, chap. 4), the means appear to vary about $\mu = 100$.

To gain additional insight, consider a simulation using 15 000 samples rather than 15. For each sample, the mean is computed and stored. After this is performed, the ggplot() function from the ggplot2 package is used to create a density graph of the means.

In the next chapter, the details of ggplot() are thoroughly discussed. The minimal elements required to create a density graph are shown below. The data= argument specifies the data frame, the aes() component defines the horizontal axis (x-axis) variable for the graph, and geom_density() draws the density curve. The ggplot() syntax is enclosed in parentheses, forcing the automatic printing of the graph. When the syntax is executed, the graph will appear in the R graph window. The menu options in this window allow for the copying and saving of the graph.

```
> myresult ← rdply(.n = 15000, .expr = mymean2())
> colnames(myresult) ← c("rep", "mean")
> (ggplot(data = myresult, aes(x = mean)) + geom_density())
```

The density graph is shown in Figure 2.1. The distribution is approximately centered about $\mu = 100$, and the shape is consistent with a normal distribution.

2.8.2 for() LOOP

For certain bootstrap applications discussed later in this book, it is necessary to have greater control than that afforded by rdply(). In such cases, an alternative method of executing repetitive operations is used, the for() loop.

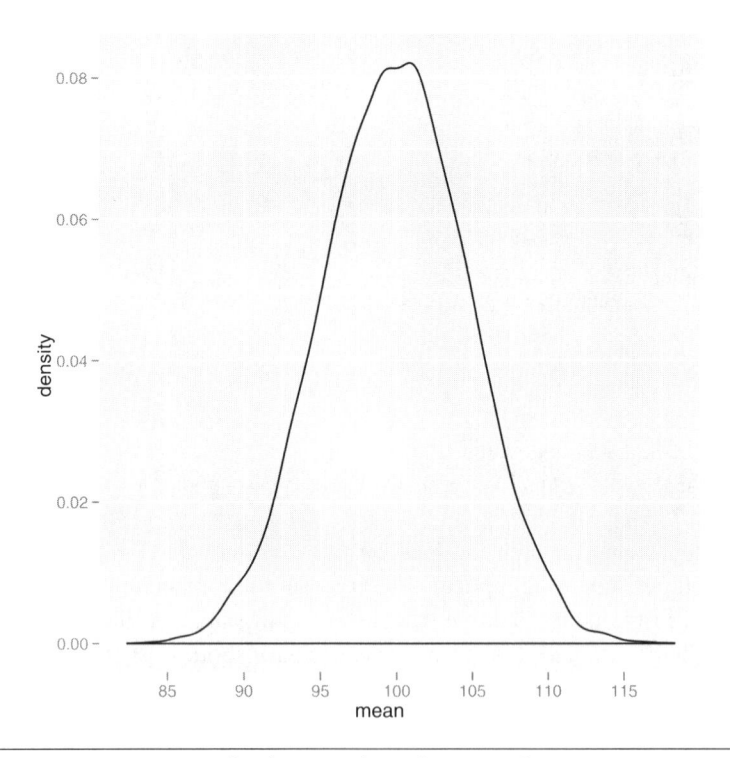

Figure 2.1 Density graph of means based on simulation.

The for() loop has the basic form,

for(replications){operations}.

The number and nature of the replications are defined in the parentheses, and the operations to be performed at each repetition are defined in the curly brackets. For this example, the operations are similar to the user-defined function considered above.

What makes the for() loop more difficult than rdply() for the novice programmer is that the details of the repetitions must be specified with some rather esoteric conventions. An example is for(i in 1:15), which will increment the i index by 1 starting at 1 and ending at 15 (i.e., 1, 2, 3, ..., 13, 14, 15). This will provide 15 repetitions for the operations defined in the curly brackets.

A second difficulty is that, in contrast to rdply(), one must define a storage data frame prior to the for() loop, and assign the results of the operations for each repetition. The assignment is performed using the indexes discussed earlier in this chapter.

To fix ideas, consider the repetition of the sample mean simulation that was first performed with rdply(). The following syntax performs 15 replications. For each one, a sample of $N = 10$ is generated from a normal distribution, the sample mean is computed, and the repetition number and sample mean are stored in the data frame `myresult`. A twist here is that `myresult` is defined prior to the `for()` loop with its elements set to `NA`. The missing values are replaced with the repetition number and the sample mean.

```
> myresult <- as.data.frame(matrix(NA,ncol= 2,nrow= 15))   # Define storage data frame.
> for(i in 1:15){                                          # Repetition details.
+       set.seed(i)                                        # Allows replication.
+       mysamp <- rnorm(n = 10, mean = 100, sd = 15)       # Generate sample data.
+       myresult[i,1] <- i                                 # Store repetition number.
+       myresult[i,2] <- mean(mysamp)                      # Store sample mean.
+       }
> colnames(myresult) <- c("rep", "mean")
> myresult
     rep       mean
1      1  101.98304
2      2  103.16727
3      3   98.99296
4      4  108.49794
5      5   98.81723
6      6  101.58037
7      7  101.55963
8      8   93.26021
9      9   96.71472
10    10   92.64015
11    11   96.54906
12    12   92.99179
13    13  109.00081
14    14  111.31309
15    15  102.67989
```

The output is the same form as that of `rdply()`, with the repetition number in the first column and the sample mean in the second column. The values of the means are different than in the `rdply()` example because `set.seed()` is used within the loop.

2.9 Linear Regression

Having discussed some basics of R programming, a more advanced example is included as a harbinger of things to come. Without much detail, a short traditional regression analysis is presented using made-up data. A more thorough treatment of traditional regression is given in Chapter 5.

Consider the two-predictor regression equation:

$$y = \beta_0 + \beta_1(x_1) + \beta_2(x_2) + \varepsilon, \tag{2.9.1}$$

where y is the response variable, x_1 and x_2 are the predictors, β_0 is the intercept, β_1 and β_2 are the regression coefficients (regression weights), and ε is a random error term.

The regression coefficients are estimated using the lm() function. Traditional regression is a special case of the *linear model* (LM), which explains the lm() abbreviation. The lm() function requires the names of the variables and replaces the equal sign in Equation 2.9.1 with a tilde (~).

In the syntax below, a sample size of $N = 20$ is generated for a response variable and two predictors. The set.seed() function is used so that the same random data can be generated by the reader in order to reproduce the example. The rnorm() function is used to generate the variables according to a normal distribution with $\mu = 100$ and $\sigma = 15$.

After generating the data, the parameters are estimated with lm(), and the output is saved as the object lm.out. The summary() function is used on the output object to display pertinent information.

```
> set.seed(123)                               # Allows reproduction of results.
> y <- rnorm(n = 20, mean = 100, sd = 15)     # Generate variables.
> x1 <- rnorm(n = 20, mean = 100, sd = 15)
> x2 <- rnorm(n = 20, mean = 100, sd = 15)
> lm.out <- lm(y ~ x1 + x2)                   #Estimate model and save output.
> summary(lm.out)                             # Display output.
```

```
1  Call:
2  lm(formula = y ~ x1 + x2)
3
4  Residuals:
5   Min    1Q  Median   3Q    Max
6  -15.887 -10.287 -1.550 9.395 20.044
7
8  Coefficients:
9              Estimate Std. Error t value Pr(>|t|)
10 (Intercept) 120.72000  28.30410   4.265  0.000523 ***
11 x1            0.05128   0.19302   0.266  0.793673
12 x2           -0.23315   0.21167  -1.101  0.286035
13 ---
14 Signif. codes:  0 '***' 0.001 '**' 0.01 '*' 0.05 '.' 0.1 ' ' 1
15
16 Residual standard error: 12.58 on 17 degrees of freedom
17 Multiple R-squared: 0.06826,  Adjusted R-squared: -0.04136
18 F-statistic: 0.6227 on 2 and 17 DF,  p-value: 0.5483
```

Lines 1 to 2 show the syntax that was used. Lines 4 to 6 show descriptive statistics for the residuals. Lines 8 to 14 show information about the intercept and regression coefficients: the estimated values, SEs, *t*-ratios, and *p*-values. This information is provided for the intercept on line 10, for x_1 on line 11, and for x_2 on line 12. Line 14 provides a key for interpreting the symbols attached to the *p*-values (e.g., *). Lines 16 to 18 show information about omnibus fit: the residual standard error (line 16), R^2 and adjusted R^2 (line 17), and the omnibus *F*-test (line 18).

Additional details of the lm() output are provided in Chapter 5. For the moment, it is stressed that the output of a statistical function can be saved as an object, and additional functions can act on the saved object. The advantages of these features are illustrated throughout the book.

2.10 Getting Help

There are a number of methods for obtaining help with R. If the name of the function for which one wants help is known, then typing a question mark (?) and the name of the function at the prompt will display its help page. For example, ?mean will display the help page for the mean() function. The help page shows the syntax conventions for the function including optional arguments. Most helpful to new users are the examples that appear at the bottom of the help page.

For packages of known name, the help() function can be used. Typing, for example, help(package=lme4) at the prompt will display the functions available in the lme4 package, supporting material, and technical specifications, if applicable.

The above two help functions require a user to know the name of the function or package for which they are requesting help. There is a potential for frustration, as one might feel there is an expectation to know what one does not know! To ease frustration, a topical search is recommended, as this only requires keywords for the topic of interest, for example, "standard deviation." A topical search is conducted with the RSiteSearch() function in the package of the same name. The function uses the search engine at http://search.r-project.org (the search engine can be used directly with a Web browser). A quoted topic must be supplied for the function, and the computer must be connected to the Internet.

Assume one wants help on the general topic of random effects. After submitting require(RSiteSearch), the syntax below will open a Web browser with listings that contain the quoted string:

RSiteSearch("random effects").

Without any options, the RSiteSearch() function displays help pages that contain the quoted string. Articles in the *R-help mailing list* can also be searched by adding the option, restrict=''Rhelp02a''. R manuals can be searched by using the option restrict=''docs''. The results can also be sorted; see ?RSiteSearch for more details.

2.11 Summary of Functions

A summary of the functions discussed in this chapter appears in Table 2.2. The functions are loosely grouped based on general-purpose categories. In addition to a brief description of each function, one or two key arguments are provided. The arguments may be optional depending on the function. For a more extensive list of options, the help page for the function should be consulted. In the remaining chapters, additional functions and arguments are presented as the need arises.

Table 2.2 List of R functions.

Function	Description	Arguments
Administrative		
q()	Quit	
ls(), objects()	List active objects	pattern=
rm()	Remove active objects	list=ls()
help()	Help for topic or package	package=
?	Help for a topic	
RSiteSearch()	Topical Internet search	restrict=
install.packages()	Install add-on packages	repos=
library(), require()	Load an installed package	
Statistical		
mean()	Mean	na.rm=
sd()	Standard deviation	na.rm=
summary()	Basic statistics	digits=
min(), max()	Minimum and maximum	na.rm=
sum()	Sum	na.rm=
length()	Length of a vector	
set.seed()	Set random number seed	
rnorm()	Generate normal data	n=, mean=, sd=
lm()	Linear regression	y~x, data=
Data Structure		
c()	Concatenation	
matrix()	Create matrix	nrow=, ncol=
data.frame()	Create data frame	var.name=
list()	Create a list	vector.name=
colnames()	Access data frame variable names	
rownames()	Access data frame row names	
factor()	Create factor variable	labels=
str()	Structure	digits.d=
order()	Sorting	decreasing=
read.table()	Read external text file	file=
Printing		
print()	Explicit print	quote=
Accessing Variables		
attach(), detach()	Use data frame variable names directly	
with()	Use data frame variable names directly	
Saving and Retrieving		
save()	Save objects in Rdata file	file=
load()	Load Rdata file	file=
Programming		
function()	User-defined functions	x
rdply()	Repetitive execution	.n=, .expr=
for()	Programming loop	

Data Structures and Longitudinal Analysis 3

In Chapter 1, the MPLS data set was introduced, with the response variable consisting of reading achievement collected over four grades. In Section 1.7, the rationale for a LMER analysis of reading differences by risk group was sketched, with specific candidate models that might be fit to the data.

To perform a LMER analysis, the data frame must have a particular structure or format. This format is different from the conventional setup familiar to applied researchers. In this chapter, the specifics of data structures are discussed, and it is shown how the conventional format can be converted into a format acceptable for analysis with LMER. Along the way, a number of ancillary issues are discussed, such as the reading in of an external data file and computation of basic statistics.

An important issue related to data structure is missing data. A missing value is defined as an observation that was intended to be collected by the researcher, but was not. The handling of missing values has direct implications for LMER analysis. Strategies for the treatment of missing values depend on the reasons for the missingness. An overview of missing data concepts is presented, along with a discussion of implications for the structuring of the data set.

3.1 Longitudinal Data Structures

Data structure refers to how the data are arrayed. Chapter 1 contains instances of two types of longitudinal data structures. Table 1.2 shows a data structure in *long format*, with stacked individual subject data. Table 1.6 shows a data structure in *wide format*, with a row corresponding to a subject and a column corresponding to a variable.

3.1.1 WIDE FORMAT

Wide format is the standard structure, and it is sometimes referred to as a *subjects-by-variables* format or *multivariate* format. Wide format has the characteristic that data collected at different time points appear in multiple columns. In Table 1.6, the reading scores appear in four columns, read.5 to read.8, reflecting the repeated measures aspect of the reading variable. A static variable, such as attendance (att), occupies only a single column because it is measured at a single occasion (or is treated as such).

The repeated measures are distinguished from static variables by their multiple column labels. For the restructuring to be discussed in a moment, it is preferable to follow some conventions for the naming of the repeated measures column labels. As shown in Table 1.6, the repeated measures column labels are a concatenation of the variable name and the grade at which the measurement is collected, separated by a period. It is important not to have spaces in the column names and to use a period rather than another character like an underscore. See Chapter 2 for additional naming conventions.

The wide format is necessary for traditional analysis with methods such as RM-ANOVA and RM-MANOVA. As discussed in Chapter 1, a problem with these methods is that no missing data are allowed. If the Table 1.6 data are used for traditional analysis, the participants with missing data (coded −99) are excluded. This seems rather drastic, as most subjects with missing data codes have only one missing value.

3.1.2 LONG FORMAT

LMER analysis requires the data structure to be long format. The main feature of long format is that the repeated measures of the subjects appear vertically and are stacked one atop another. Long format is sometimes referred to as *univariate* format because the response variable occupies a single column. The time metric is explicit in long format, appearing as a time predictor in its own column. Static variables appear in additional columns with their values repeated for the duration of time because their values do not change over time.

To illustrate how data are reshaped from wide to long format, consider the first subject in Table 1.6. Consistent with concepts developed in Chapter 2, the row of data for an individual subject is referred to as the subject's row vector. From Table 1.6, it can be seen that the row vector for the first subject is 1, 172, 185, 179, 194, HHM, F, Afr, 0, N, 0.94.

As a starting point, consider taking the repeated reading scores of the first subject, 172, 185, 179, 194, and arraying them in a column with four rows. Converting from row to column or vice versa is known as *transposing* (see the Appendix). After transposing the response data, the same is done for all the other variables, and they are listed in separate columns. For the static predictors, the values are repeated for the duration of the repeated measures.

Table 3.1 shows the long-format data structure for the first subject. The table illustrates the following key features.

- There are multiple rows of data for a single subject.
- For each subject, the response variable, time predictor, and other dynamic variables have values that typically vary among the rows.
- For each subject, the static variable scores are constant among the rows, as they do not change over time, or are treated as such.

Table 3.1 Data of first subject from Table 1.6 arrayed in long format.

subid	read	grade	risk	gen	eth	ell	sped	att
1	172	5	HHM	F	Afr	0	N	0.94
1	185	6	HHM	F	Afr	0	N	0.94
1	179	7	HHM	F	Afr	0	N	0.94
1	194	8	HHM	F	Afr	0	N	0.94

Suppose the second subject's row vector from Table 1.6 is arrayed in the same way as the first subject's data in Table 3.1. Then the same is done for the remaining subjects. Stacking all of the subjects' individual long data structures yields the long format.

A depiction of the long-format data set is shown in Table 3.2. The number of rows in the long format is much greater than in the wide format. For this reason, only the information for the subjects at the top and bottom of the data set is shown. Usually it is not possible to display the entire long-format data set on a computer screen. The topic of displaying subsets of the data is discussed below.

The `reshape()` function can be used to reshape a wide format to a long format and vice versa. Before considering `reshape()`, the topic of reading in external data sets to R is discussed.

3.2 Reading an External File

Large data sets are usually not created in R, but rather in computer programs that feature a graphical spreadsheet. A graphical spreadsheet consists of a grid of cells that is friendly for data entry. R does offer a spreadsheet-like editor, although it is not available on all platforms; see `?dataentry`. An external data set made in a spreadsheet computer program can be read into R using functions designed for such.

3.2.1 READING A TEXT FILE WITH `read.table()`

An external file is read into R using the `read.table()` function. The primary requirement of the function is that the external file be saved as a

Table 3.2 Long-format data structure.

subid	read	grade	risk	gen	eth	ell	sped	att
1	172	5	HHM	F	Afr	0	N	0.94
1	185	6	HHM	F	Afr	0	N	0.94
1	179	7	HHM	F	Afr	0	N	0.94
1	194	8	HHM	F	Afr	0	N	0.94
2	200	5	HHM	F	Afr	0	N	0.91
2	210	6	HHM	F	Afr	0	N	0.91
2	209	7	HHM	F	Afr	0	N	0.91
2	–99	8	HHM	F	Afr	0	N	0.91
3	191	5	HHM	M	Afr	0	N	0.97
3	199	6	HHM	M	Afr	0	N	0.97
3	203	7	HHM	M	Afr	0	N	0.97
3	215	8	HHM	M	Afr	0	N	0.97
⋮	⋮	⋮	⋮	⋮	⋮	⋮	⋮	⋮
20	204	5	ADV	F	Afr	0	N	0.95
20	215	6	ADV	F	Afr	0	N	0.95
20	219	7	ADV	F	Afr	0	N	0.95
20	214	8	ADV	F	Afr	0	N	0.95
21	237	5	ADV	M	Whi	0	N	0.98
21	241	6	ADV	M	Whi	0	N	0.98
21	243	7	ADV	M	Whi	0	N	0.98
21	–99	8	ADV	M	Whi	0	N	0.98
22	219	5	ADV	F	Afr	0	N	0.96
22	233	6	ADV	F	Afr	0	N	0.96
22	236	7	ADV	F	Afr	0	N	0.96
22	–99	8	ADV	F	Afr	0	N	0.96

text file, sometimes called an ASCII file. Two types of text files are considered, *space delimited* and *comma delimited*. Space delimited means that white space separates the columns of data, and comma delimited means that a comma (,) separates the columns of data.

Space-delimited and comma-delimited text files are usually saved within a spreadsheet program with a Save-as menu option. If possible, the column headings appearing in the original computer program should also be saved in the text file. The column headings must appear in the first row with the same formatting as the data (space delimiting or comma delimiting).

Table 3.3 shows an example of a space-delimited text file and a comma-delimited text file. For brevity, only subid and the reading variables are shown for the first four subjects. The variable labels appear at the top of each file in the same format as the data.

To avoid pitfalls when reading in data, it is suggested that spaces or underscores (_) not be used in the variable names. Furthermore, the naming conventions for the repeated measures columns previously mentioned should be used. The data can be numeric or character, as shown in Table 3.2, but there should be no spaces or underscores in character values. A character variable with values such as "tall boy" and "short boy" should be entered as tall.boy and short.boy. If spaces are compulsory, then a comma-delimited file should be used.

3.2 Reading an External File

Table 3.3 Text file examples.

		Space delimited		
subid	read.5	read.6	read.7	read.8
1	172	185	179	194
2	200	210	209	–99
3	191	199	203	215
4	200	195	194	–99

Comma delimited

subid,read.5,read.6,read.7,read.8
1,172,185,179,194
2,200,210,209,-99
3,191,199,203,215
4,200,195,194,-99

Suppose the goal is to read in the wide format MPLS data of Table 1.6, which is saved as the space-delimited text file `MPLSdata.txt`. A comma-delimited file can also be read in using some optional arguments, as explained below. Three pieces of information must be supplied to `read.table()`.

1. The file name and location

2. An indication of whether the column names (variables names) are included in the first row of the file

3. An indication of whether there are missing data values and how they are coded

In this example, the text file resides in the file directory `C:\Mine`. The variable names appear at the top of the file, and missing values are represented by −99, similar to what is shown in the top portion of Table 3.3. The following syntax applies to Windows-based computers.

```
> MPLS <- read.table("C:\\Mine\\MPLSdata.txt", header = TRUE, na.strings = "-99")
```

The `read.table()` function reads the file from the location indicated and assigns it to the data frame object `MPLS`. The file location is specified by double backward slashes (`\\`) rather than the usual single backward slash, and a single forward slash (`/`) can also be used. The argument, `header=TRUE`, indicates the column names are in the text file, also space delimited. If the column names are not included, then `header=FALSE` is used, or the argument is omitted.

The argument `na.strings="-99"` indicates that missing values are coded as −99 in the text file. If there are no missing values, the argument can be omitted. In the text file, missing values are denoted with numbers or characters, and multiple missing value codes are allowed. All missing values are transformed to `NA` when using `read.table()`. Multiple missing value codes are included in `na.strings=` using the concatenation function. For example, if missing values are coded as −99 and −88 in the text file, then `na.strings=c("-99","-88")` is used. Characters can also be used for missing values. If a missing value is denoted with a period, then the argument is `na.strings="."`.

On a Windows computer, a pop-up menu for selecting the text file is invoked by replacing the quoted string in `read.table()` with the argument `file.choose()`. The replacement for the example is shown below.

```
> MPLS <- read.table(file.choose(), header = TRUE, na.strings = "-99")
```

After selecting the file from the pop-up window, the quoted string of the file location and name will be substituted in place of `file.choose()`. The text file will be assigned to the MPLS data frame.

Comma-delimited files are read by including the argument `sep=","` in `read.table()`. An alternative is to use `read.csv()`, which makes the inclusion of `sep=","` unnecessary. If the text file `MPLSdata.txt` is comma delimited rather than space delimited, then the following syntax is used for each read method.

```
> MPLS <- read.table("C:\\Mine\\MPLSdata.txt",header = TRUE,na.strings = "-99",sep= ",")
> MPLS <- read.csv("C:\\Mine\\MPLSdata.txt", header = TRUE, na.strings = "-99")
```

Delimiters other than spaces or commas are also possible; see `?read.table`. Files created in a number of other computer programs can be directly read in using functions from the `foreign` package; see `help(package=foreign)`.

3.2.2 DISPLAYING THE DATA FRAME

An indication of successful reading in of the data set is the lack of warning or error messages in the R console window. R operates on a "no news is good news" policy in that the prompt is returned in the console window upon successful execution.

The lack of error messages does not ensure correct reading in of the data. It only ensures that the R checking procedures did not detect any problems. To verify correct reading in of the data, a portion of the data frame should be displayed on the computer screen, and basic descriptive statistics should be computed for each variable. This is also helpful for understanding the nature of the variables and to correct any data entry errors.

3.2 Reading an External File

There are four main ways of displaying the data frame, or portions of the data frame, on the computer screen.

- The entire data frame is displayed by typing the object name (e.g., MPLS) and pressing Enter. This method is not particularly useful with large data sets because the data go flying by. Furthermore, if there are many variables, the data columns are wrapped, making things difficult to sort out.
- The first few rows of the data frame are displayed using the head() function—for example, head(MPLS).
- The last few rows of the data frame are displayed using the tail() function—for example, tail(MPLS).
- Any portion of the data frame is displayed using row and column indexing with brackets ([,]), as discussed in Chapter 2. MPLS[1:2, 1:2] prints the first two rows and first two columns of the data frame. MPLS[1:5,] prints the first five rows and all the columns, and MPLS[,1:5] prints all the rows and the first five columns.

Here are illustrations using the last three methods above.

```
> head(MPLS)
```

	subid	read.5	read.6	read.7	read.8	risk	gen	eth	ell	sped	att
1	1	172	185	179	194	HHM	F	Afr	0	N	0.94
2	2	200	210	209	NA	HHM	F	Afr	0	N	0.91
3	3	191	199	203	215	HHM	M	Afr	0	N	0.97
4	4	200	195	194	NA	HHM	F	Afr	0	N	0.88
5	5	207	213	212	213	HHM	F	Afr	0	N	0.85
6	bhar-5191	189	206	195	HHM	M	Afr	0	N	0.90}

```
> tail(MPLS)
```

	subid	read.5	read.6	read.7	read.8	risk	gen	eth	ell	sped	att
17	17	201	210	208	219	ADV	M	Whi	0	N	0.98
18	18	218	220	217	221	ADV	M	Whi	0	N	1.00
19	19	215	216	221	NA	ADV	F	Whi	0	N	0.96
20	20	204	215	219	214	ADV	F	Afr	0	N	0.95
21	21	237	241	243	NA	ADV	M	Whi	0	N	0.98
22	22	219	233	236	NA	ADV	F	Afr	0	N	0.96

```
> MPLS[1:2,1:2]
```

	subid	read.5
1	1	172
2	2	200

```
> MPLS[1:5, ]
```

	subid	read.5	read.6	read.7	read.8	risk	gen	eth	ell	sped	att
1	1	172	185	179	194	HHM	F	Afr	0	N	0.94
2	2	200	210	209	NA	HHM	F	Afr	0	N	0.91
3	3	191	199	203	215	HHM	M	Afr	0	N	0.97
4	4	200	195	194	NA	HHM	F	Afr	0	N	0.88
5	5	207	213	212	213	HHM	F	Afr	0	N	0.85

Another useful function is `str()`, which was introduced in Chapter 2. Recall that this function provides information about the structure of the object and the variables. Consider the following.

```
> str(MPLS)
```

```
'data.frame':   22 obs. of  11 variables:
 $ subid : int  1 2 3 4 5 6 7 8 9 10 ...
 $ read.5: int  172 200 191 200 207 191 199 191 149 200 ...
 $ read.6: int  185 210 199 195 213 189 208 194 154 212 ...
 $ read.7: int  179 209 203 194 212 206 213 194 174 213 ...
 $ read.8: int  194 NA 215 NA 213 195 218 NA 177 NA ...
 $ risk  : Factor w/ 3 levels "ADV","HHM","POV": 2 2 2 2 2 3 3 3 3 ...
 $ gen   : Factor w/ 2 levels "F","M": 1 1 2 1 1 2 2 1 1 1 ...
 $ eth   : Factor w/ 3 levels "Afr","His","Whi": 1 1 1 1 1 1 1 2 1 1 ...
 $ ell   : int  0 0 0 0 0 0 1 0 0 ...
 $ sped  : Factor w/ 2 levels "N","Y": 1 1 1 1 1 1 1 2 2 1 ...
 $ att   : num  0.94 0.91 0.97 0.88 0.85 0.9 0.97 0.97 0.97 0.96 ...
```

Line 1 of the output indicates the object MPLS is a data frame, which as previously discussed, is a rectangular data set with all columns of equal length. A data frame allows variables with a mix of data types, such as numeric, character, and factor.

Line 1 of the output also shows there are 22 total observations, meaning 22 total rows. There are 11 variables, meaning 11 columns of data. The remaining lines of output, lines 2 to 12, show the names of the variables and their type, which in this case is `int` = integer, `num` = numeric, and `Factor` = factor. After each variable name and type, there is a partial listing of the data values. The dollar sign ($) means that a variable is accessed by listing the data frame name, the dollar sign, and then the variable name (see Chapter 2).

3.2.3 CONVERTING AND RECODING VARIABLES

In certain instances, it is desirable to convert a variable from one type to another. A case in point is provided by the `ell` variable. Line 10 of the output above shows that `ell` is an integer variable, and lines 7, 8, 9, and 11 show that all the other categorical variables are represented as factor variables.

The default representation of categorical variables is determined by the nature of their values in the text file. As seen in Table 1.6, the values of `ell` are numbers—0 = no, 1 = yes—whereas the values of all the other categorical variables are characters. The `read.table()` function automatically saves variables with character values as factor variables.

3.2 Reading an External File

A numeric variable is converted to a factor variable with the `factor()` function. This is preferable so that variables such as `ell` will not be mistaken for quantitative variables. Suppose the goal is to create the new factor variable, `ell2`, from the existing `ell` variable. The syntax below accomplishes the task.

```
> MPLS$ell2 <- factor(MPLS$ell, levels = c(0, 1),labels = c("No","Yes"))
> str(MPLS)
```

```
'data.frame':   22 obs. of  12 variables:
 $ subid  : int  1 2 3 4 5 6 7 8 9 10 ...
 $ read.5 : int  172 200 191 200 207 191 199 191 149 200 ...
 $ read.6 : int  185 210 199 195 213 189 208 194 154 212 ...
 $ read.7 : int  179 209 203 194 212 206 213 194 174 213 ...
 $ read.8 : int  194 NA 215 NA 213 195 218 NA 177 NA ...
 $ risk   : Factor w/ 3 levels "ADV","HHM","POV": 2 2 2 2 2 3 3 3 3 ...
 $ gen    : Factor w/ 2 levels "F","M": 1 1 2 1 1 2 2 1 1 1 ...
 $ eth    : Factor w/ 3 levels "Afr","His","Whi": 1 1 1 1 1 1 1 2 1 1 ...
 $ ell    : int  0 0 0 0 0 0 1 1 0 0 ...
 $ sped   : Factor w/ 2 levels "N","Y": 1 1 1 1 1 1 1 2 2 1 ...
 $ att    : num  0.94 0.91 0.97 0.88 0.85 0.9 0.97 0.97 0.97 0.96 ...
 $ ell2   : Factor w/ 2 levels "No","Yes": 1 1 1 1 1 1 2 2 1 1 ...
```

In the `factor()` syntax, the numeric values are listed with the optional argument, `levels=`. The corresponding labels are assigned with the `labels=` argument. The internal numeric representation consists of 1 and 2, as seen in the last line of the `str()` output above.

A new factor variable can be created based on recoding an existing factor variable. Suppose the objective is to create a dichotomous factor variable for risk. The HHM and POV groups are coded as DADV, and the ADV group keeps its code. The syntax below accomplishes this task using indexing for a vector (see Chapter 2).

```
> MPLS$riskC[MPLS$risk== "HHM"] <- "DADV" # Note "==" rather than "=".
> MPLS$riskC[MPLS$risk == "POV"] <- "DADV"
> MPLS$riskC[MPLS$risk == "ADV"] <- "ADV"
> MPLS$risk2 <- factor(MPLS$riskC)
> str(MPLS)
```

```
'data.frame':   22 obs. of  14 variables:
 $ subid  : int  1 2 3 4 5 6 7 8 9 10 ...
 $ read.5 : int  172 200 191 200 207 191 199 191 149 200 ...
 $ read.6 : int  185 210 199 195 213 189 208 194 154 212 ...
 $ read.7 : int  179 209 203 194 212 206 213 194 174 213 ...
 $ read.8 : int  194 NA 215 NA 213 195 218 NA 177 NA ...
 $ risk   : Factor w/ 3 levels "ADV","HHM","POV": 2 2 2 2 2 3 3 3 3 ...
 $ gen    : Factor w/ 2 levels "F","M": 1 1 2 1 1 2 2 1 1 1 ...
 $ eth    : Factor w/ 3 levels "Afr","His","Whi": 1 1 1 1 1 1 1 2 1 1 ...
 $ ell    : int  0 0 0 0 0 0 1 1 0 0 ...
 $ sped   : Factor w/ 2 levels "N","Y": 1 1 1 1 1 1 1 2 2 1 ...
 $ att    : num  0.94 0.91 0.97 0.88 0.85 0.9 0.97 0.97 0.97 0.96 ...
 $ ell2   : Factor w/ 2 levels "No","Yes": 1 1 1 1 1 1 2 2 1 1 ...
 $ riskC  : chr  "DADV" "DADV" "DADV" "DADV" ...
 $ risk2  : Factor w/ 2 levels "ADV","DADV": 2 2 2 2 2 2 2 2 2 2 ...
```

The first three lines of syntax create the character variable, `risk0`, with the categories `DADV` and `ADV`. Notice that "equal to" is represented by two symbols, `==`. After creating the character variable `riskC`, it is converted to the factor variable, `risk2`. The `str()` output shows the nature of the new variables.

3.3 Basic Statistics for Wide-Format Data

Having read in a wide-format data set in the last section, interest now turns to computing some basic descriptive statistics. A function that should be routinely used after reading in a data file is `summary()`. The `summary()` output is useful for examining cursory distributional information, identifying potential outliers and/or extreme values, erroneous values, and missing value codes. The function is applied to the entire data frame as illustrated below.

```
> summary(MPLS)
```

```
      subid              read.5              read.6              read.7
Min.   : 1.00      Min.   :149.0      Min.   :154.0      Min.   :174.0
1st Qu.: 6.25      1st Qu.:199.0      1st Qu.:201.2      1st Qu.:206.5
Median :11.50      Median :202.5      Median :212.5      Median :215.0
Mean   :11.50      Mean   :205.1      Mean   :211.5      Mean   :215.7
3rd Qu.:16.75      3rd Qu.:218.0      3rd Qu.:225.2      3rd Qu.:231.8
Max.   :22.00      Max.   :237.0      Max.   :241.0      Max.   :248.0

     read.8           risk        gen           eth              ell               sped
Min.   :177.0      ADV:10      F:14      Afr:12      Min.   :0.0000         N:19
1st Qu.:213.2      HHM: 6      M: 8      His: 1      1st Qu.:0.0000         Y: 3
Median :218.5      POV: 6                Whi: 9      Median :0.0000
Mean   :218.0                                        Mean   :0.1364
3rd Qu.:233.0                                        3rd Qu.:0.0000
Max.   :246.0                                        Max.   :1.0000
NA's   :  8.0
      att              ell2              riskC                   risk2
Min.   :0.8500     No :19       Length:22               ADV :10
1st Qu.:0.9525     Yes: 3       Class :character        DADV:12
Median :0.9700                  Mode  :character
Mean   :0.9564
3rd Qu.:0.9800
Max.   :1.0000
```

As seen in the output, when a variable is numeric, such as `read.5`, `summary()` computes the minimum and maximum values, the mean, and the quartiles. With factor variables, such as `gen`, a frequency table is produced, showing a tally of the number of subjects at each level or in each group. For character variables, `summary()` does not compute a frequency

3.3 Basic Statistics for Wide-Format Data

table and only reports the length and type of variable. This is seen in the output for `riskC`. A frequency table for a character variable such as `riskC` can be produced using `summary(as.factor(MPLS$riskC))`, or more simply with `table(MPLS$riskC)`.

For numeric and factor variables, missing values are tallied and attached to the end of the usual `summary()` output. This is seen in the output for `read.8`.

3.3.1 MEANS, VARIANCES, AND CORRELATIONS

Descriptive statistics for the repeated measures can be computed and displayed on the computer screen or saved as an output object. To compute means and SDs, the `mean()` and `sd()` functions can be used by supplying the repeated measures columns of the data frame. As shown in Chapter 2, missing values must be removed, or the result will be a missing value.

Below the means and SDs of the repeated measures are computed, saved, and then displayed.

```
> mymeans <- mean(MPLS[ ,2:5], na.rm = TRUE)
> mymeans
```

```
  read.5    read.6    read.7    read.8
205.1364  211.4545  215.6818  218.0000
```

```
> mysds <- sd(MPLS[ ,2:5], na.rm = TRUE)
> mysds
```

```
  read.5    read.6    read.7    read.8
19.99356  20.06116  19.44562  19.37881
```

The output shows that the means increase over time, but not at a constant rate. The difference between the first two means is greater than the difference between the last two means, indicating a deceleration over the latter grades. The SDs show a slight tendency to decrease over time.

Depending on the analysis strategy, the descriptive statistics might be used to suggest particular aspects of a statistical model, especially when the strategy is exploratory. There was some discussion of analysis strategy in Chapter 1, and this will be revisited in Chapters 7 and 8.

On a very cursory level, the means suggest fitting a nonlinear change curve model that allows for the deceleration over time. Caution must be exercised, however, as the statistics provide limited information; more extensive analysis is warranted. Furthermore, there are missing values at Grade 8, and the validity of inferences with missing values depends on certain assumptions, which are discussed later in this chapter.

Information about the dependency among the repeated measures is obtained by computing correlations and/or covariances. Correlations are computed with the cor() function, and covariances are computed with the cov() function. Similar to the previous functions, an optional argument is used when there are missing values. Otherwise, the result will be a missing value. Below, the argument use="complete.obs" is used to perform listwise deletion for the missing data. Pairwise deletion is specified as use="pairwise.complete.obs"; see ?cor.

```
> cor(MPLS[ ,2:5], use = "complete.obs")
```

	read.5	read.6	read.7	read.8
read.5	1.0000000	0.9756825	0.9283549	0.8825860
read.6	0.9756825	1.0000000	0.9130901	0.9287729
read.7	0.9283549	0.9130901	1.0000000	0.9227732
read.8	0.8825860	0.9287729	0.9227732	1.0000000

```
> cov(MPLS[ ,2:5], use = "complete.obs")
```

	read.5	read.6	read.7	read.8
read.5	502.8626	481.9451	421.0714	383.5385
read.6	481.9451	485.2088	406.8132	396.4615
read.7	421.0714	406.8132	409.1044	361.6923
read.8	383.5385	396.4615	361.6923	375.5385

Both matrices indicate a *decay pattern*, with scores closely spaced having a higher dependency than scores more distantly spaced. For instance, the correlation between read.5 and read.6 is higher than the correlation between read.5 and read.8.

3.3.2 MISSING DATA STATISTICS

In addition to means and SDs for the response, it is desirable to compute basic statistics for missing data. The proportion of missing values is computed at each time point using the logical function is.na(). This function returns TRUE when a value is missing and FALSE otherwise. The sum of a vector of these logicals yields the number of missing values, and the mean yields the proportion of missing values. The reason the sum and mean can be computed is that there is an internal coding of TRUE = 1 and FALSE = 0.

In the following syntax, is.na() is used within the colMeans() function to compute the proportion of missing values for the repeated measures. The colMeans() function computes the mean of each column of data.

```
> mymiss <- colMeans(is.na(MPLS[ ,2:5]))
> mymiss
```

read.5	read.6	read.7	read.8
0.0000000	0.0000000	0.0000000	0.3636364

The output shows there are no missing data for the first three time points. The fourth time point has approximately 36% of the values missing.

3.3.3 CONDITIONING ON STATIC PREDICTORS

When static predictor effects are of interest, it is useful to compute descriptive statistics conditioning on their values. This is easiest to do when the static predictors are categorical because they have defined levels or groups.

The values of quantitative static predictors usually need to be grouped using a median split (two groups), or a quartile split (four groups). There is a debate about whether quantitative variables should be discretized (grouped) for statistical analysis (Gelman & Park, 2008; McClelland & Irwin, 2003). The opinion here is that grouping is fine for computing descriptive statistics and graphs. However, for inferential analysis, the original continuous form of the variable should be used, unless there is a compelling reason not to.

Statistics conditional on static predictors are computed with the ddply() function of the plyr package. The repeated measures columns of the data frame must be supplied (.data=), along with the conditioning variable(s) (.variables=.()). The name of the statistical function (.fun=) also must be included, along with any pertinent optional arguments, such as na.rm=TRUE. Prefixes such as .variables= are optional but helpful to include. It is very important to remember that a period (.) precedes the parentheses of the conditioning variables—for example, .variables=.(MPLS $risk). In the following syntax, the means of the reading scores are computed by risk group.

```
> myrisk <- ddply(.data = MPLS[ ,2:5], .variables = .(MPLS$risk),
+                 .fun = mean, na.rm = TRUE)
> myrisk
  MPLS$risk  read.5    read.6  read.7    read.8
1       ADV   216.7  223.0000   226.7  225.8333
2       HHM   193.5  198.5000   200.5  204.2500
3       POV   197.5  205.1667   212.5  220.0000
```

The first column in the output lists the group, and the remaining columns list the mean reading scores. The row numbered as 1 in the output shows the means for the ADV group, line 2 shows the output for the HHM group, and line 3 shows the output for the POV group. It can be verified that at each time point, the mean of the ADV group is larger than that of the POV group, which is larger than that of the HHM group. These group differences are expected, as discussed in Chapter 1. The preliminary results will be followed up in future chapters.

As a second example, consider computing the mean of the reading scores at each time point based on a median split of attendance proportion (att). A dummy variable is created using the ifelse() function, with a value of 1 assigned if the att score is above the median and 0 otherwise. The dummy variable is then used in the ddply() function.

```
> msplit <- ifelse(test = MPLS$att>median(MPLS$att),yes = 1,no = 0)
> msplit
```

```
[1] 0 0 0 0 0 0 0 0 0 1 0 1 1 1 0 1 1 0 0 1 0
```

```
> ddply(.data = MPLS[ ,2:5], .variables = .(msplit), .fun = mean, na.rm = TRUE)
  msplit read.5   read.6   read.7 read.8
1      0  199.6 205.4000 210.3333  211.0
2      1  217.0 224.4286 227.1429  230.6
```

The msplit column indexes the split group. The mean for each grade by split group is shown in the remaining columns, read.5 to read.8. As seen in the output, the above-median group has a larger mean value than the other group at each time point.

3.4 Reshaping Data

The most common data structure is wide format because its subjects-by-variables arrangement is convenient for entering and organizing data. For analyzing longitudinal data with LMER, the long format is required. Long format is also convenient for graphing longitudinal data, which is discussed in the next chapter.

3.4.1 WIDE TO LONG FORMAT

Wide format is converted, or reshaped, to long format with the reshape() function. Previously, the wide-format MPLS data set was read into R and saved as the data frame MPLS. Now the goal is to reshape the data to long format.

Several pieces of information must be supplied to the reshape() function when going from wide to long format. Each piece of information is listed below, followed by the argument for the example.

1. Name of the wide data frame object to reshape: data=MPLS.

2. Columns of the data frame constituting the repeated measures: varying=2:5.

3. Quoted subject identification number variable: idvar="subid".

3.4 Reshaping Data

4. Quoted name of the response variable to be created in long format: `v.names="read"`.

5. Quoted name of the time variable to be created in long format: `timevar="grade"`.

6. Values of the time variable to be created: `times=5:8`.

7. Quoted format of the new data set: `direction="long"`.

Suppose the long-format data frame is named `MPLS.L`, with "L" denoting long format. Consider the reshaping syntax below.

```
> MPLS.L <- reshape(data = MPLS, varying = 2:5, v.names = "read", timevar = "grade",
+                   times = 5:8, idvar = "subid", direction = "long")
```

The `varying=` argument identifies the repeated measures columns, and the `times=` argument sets the values of the time variable, `grade` in this case. If the `times=` argument is omitted, `reshape()` will code the time variable as waves, that is, with the counting numbers denoting order of observation. Lists of consecutive integers for `varying=` and `times=` are created using the colon (`:`) notation.

The `reshape()` function is very flexible and will accommodate wide formats other than the one in the example. The `varying=` argument can read noncontiguous columns by use of the concatenation function, for example, `varying=c(2,4,6,8)`. A similar strategy is used with the `times=` argument when the repeated observations are not mapped to contiguous integers, such as when the grades are 1, 3, and 5. The `varying=` argument accepts variable names for the columns, such as `varying=c("read.5", "read.6", "read.7", "read.8")`. Additional options and examples are found by typing `?reshape`; also see the optional Section 3.9.

Running the above syntax resulted in no errors, an indication the reshaping was successful. The first 10 rows of the data frame are printed to the computer screen using the `n=` option with `head()`.

```
> head(MPLS.L, n = 10)
```

	subid	risk	gen	eth	ell	sped	att	ell2	riskC	risk2	grade	read
1.5	1	HHM	F	Afr	0	N	0.94	No	DADV	DADV	5	172
2.5	2	HHM	F	Afr	0	N	0.91	No	DADV	DADV	5	200
3.5	3	HHM	M	Afr	0	N	0.97	No	DADV	DADV	5	191
4.5	4	HHM	F	Afr	0	N	0.88	No	DADV	DADV	5	200
5.5	5	HHM	F	Afr	0	N	0.85	No	DADV	DADV	5	207
6.5	6	HHM	M	Afr	0	N	0.90	No	DADV	DADV	5	191
7.5	7	POV	M	Afr	1	N	0.97	Yes	DADV	DADV	5	199
8.5	8	POV	F	His	1	Y	0.97	Yes	DADV	DADV	5	191
9.5	9	POV	F	Afr	0	Y	0.97	No	DADV	DADV	5	149
10.5	10	POV	F	Afr	0	N	0.96	No	DADV	DADV	5	200

The data frame is currently sorted by grade. This is not a particularly helpful ordering because the repeated measures for an individual are not seen. It is convenient to sort the data frame by the subject identification numbers (subid) and then by the repeated measures (grade). This results in the repeated measures being sorted within subject, or to put it differently, the repeated measures index changes faster than the subject index.

Sorting applies to the rows of the data frame and is accomplished by using the order() function in the row index of the object. The column index is blank, indicating sorting for all the variables. The sorted data frame is saved as HHM.LS with "S" standing for sorted.

```
> MPLS.LS <- MPLS.L[order(MPLS.L$subid, MPLS.L$grade), ]
> head(MPLS.LS, n = 10)
```

	subid	risk	gen	eth	ell	sped	att	ell2	riskC	risk2	grade	read
1.5	1	HHM	F	Afr	0	N	0.94	No	DADV	DADV	5	172
1.6	1	HHM	F	Afr	0	N	0.94	No	DADV	DADV	6	185
1.7	1	HHM	F	Afr	0	N	0.94	No	DADV	DADV	7	179
1.8	1	HHM	F	Afr	0	N	0.94	No	DADV	DADV	8	194
2.5	2	HHM	F	Afr	0	N	0.91	No	DADV	DADV	5	200
2.6	2	HHM	F	Afr	0	N	0.91	No	DADV	DADV	6	210
2.7	2	HHM	F	Afr	0	N	0.91	No	DADV	DADV	7	209
2.8	2	HHM	F	Afr	0	N	0.91	No	DADV	DADV	8	NA
3.5	3	HHM	M	Afr	0	N	0.97	No	DADV	DADV	5	191
3.6	3	HHM	M	Afr	0	N	0.97	No	DADV	DADV	6	199

As seen in the output, the data frame is now sorted such that grade elapses within each block defined by subid. The data set has the same structure as Table 3.2, albeit the variables are in a different order and some additional ones have been created.

The nature of the sorting is also reflected in the first column of rownames, which are labels for the rows. This column is not a variable in the data frame, as reflected by the fact there is no column label. The row labels are a concatenation of subid and grade. The row names are accessed and changed using rownames().

In certain circumstances, it is desirable to set the row names to the counting numbers in the sorted data frame. The row names are set to the counting numbers with the following syntax.

```
> rownames(MPLS.LS) <- NULL
```

For future use, the MPLS.LS data frame can be saved as a Rdata file. Recall that the Rdata file is only used with R and is not portable to other programs. It is convenient to save an Rdata file for the long-format data frame because the text file does not need to be read in again and reshaped. Once an Rdata file is saved, it is loaded with the load() function.

The syntax below is applicable for a Windows machine. The argument select=-riskC is used to delete riskC prior to saving the data frame. The subset() function syntax overwrites the MPLS.LS object.

3.4 Reshaping Data

```
> MPLS.LS <- subset(MPLS.LS, select = -riskC)
> save(MPLS.LS, file = "C:/Mine/MPLS.LS.Rdata")
> load(file = "C:/Mine/MPLS.LS.Rdata")
```

3.4.2 LONG TO WIDE FORMAT

The `reshape()` function is also used to reshape from long to wide format. The reshaping in this case is a bit easier. The time variable already exists in the long-format data frame and can be used to determine the number and ordering of the repeated measures columns for the wide format.

Consider the reshaping of `MPLS.LS` from long to wide format. The syntax below is used to do this, with the resulting wide data frame object being `MPLS.W`. The variables `riskC` and `ell2` are dropped in the reshaping to make things more tidy.

```
> MPLS.W <- reshape(data = MPLS.LS, v.names = "read", idvar = "subid",
+        drop = c("riskC", "ell2"), timevar = "grade", direction = "wide")
> MPLS.W
```

	subid	risk	gen	eth	ell	sped	att	risk2	read.5	read.6	read.7	read.8
1.5	1	HHM	F	Afr	0	N	0.94	DADV	172	185	179	194
2.5	2	HHM	F	Afr	0	N	0.91	DADV	200	210	209	NA
3.5	3	HHM	M	Afr	0	N	0.97	DADV	191	199	203	215
4.5	4	HHM	F	Afr	0	N	0.88	DADV	200	195	194	NA
5.5	5	HHM	F	Afr	0	N	0.85	DADV	207	213	212	213
6.5	6	HHM	M	Afr	0	N	0.90	DADV	191	189	206	195
7.5	7	POV	M	Afr	1	N	0.97	DADV	199	208	213	218
8.5	8	POV	F	His	1	Y	0.97	DADV	191	194	194	NA
9.5	9	POV	F	Afr	0	Y	0.97	DADV	149	154	174	177
10.5	10	POV	F	Afr	0	N	0.96	DADV	200	212	213	NA
11.5	11	POV	F	Whi	0	N	0.98	DADV	218	231	233	239
12.5	12	POV	F	Whi	0	Y	0.96	DADV	228	232	248	246
13.5	13	ADV	F	Whi	0	N	0.99	ADV	228	236	228	239
14.5	14	ADV	M	Afr	1	N	0.99	ADV	199	210	225	235
15.5	15	ADV	F	Whi	0	N	1.00	ADV	218	223	236	NA
16.5	16	ADV	M	Whi	0	N	0.97	ADV	228	226	234	227
17.5	17	ADV	M	Whi	0	N	0.98	ADV	201	210	208	219
18.5	18	ADV	M	Whi	0	N	1.00	ADV	218	220	217	221
19.5	19	ADV	F	Whi	0	N	0.96	ADV	215	216	221	NA
20.5	20	ADV	F	Afr	0	N	0.95	ADV	204	215	219	214
21.5	21	ADV	M	Whi	0	N	0.98	ADV	237	241	243	NA
22.5	22	ADV	F	Afr	0	N	0.96	ADV	219	233	236	NA

The row names can be set to the counting numbers with the syntax previously mentioned. The labels of the repeated measures columns are a concatenation of `subid` and `grade`. Notice the `grade` variable is not retained in the wide format, but it does provide the label indexing for the repeated measures.

Some caution is warranted when reshaping from long to wide format. Irregular timing of observations among the subjects can result in a wide format that is unwieldy and contains many NA values. This topic is discussed in Section 3.6.

3.5 Basic Statistics for Long-Format Data

Basic statistics can be computed with the long-format data frame. This is convenient if the data are entered directly in long format, or if one does not want to switch between formats.

3.5.1 MEANS, VARIANCES, AND CORRELATIONS

The `ddply()` function of `plyr` is used to compute means and SDs conditional on the time predictor. The function requires the response variable (`.data=`), the time predictor (`.variables=.()`), the statistic to be computed (`.fun=`), and optional arguments for handling missing data (`na.rm=TRUE`). Below is the syntax for computing the mean for each grade removing the missing data. The `each()` option is used to provide the column name for the mean in the output. When a single variable is analyzed, it must be enclosed in the `data.frame()` function as shown below.

```
> ddply(.data = data.frame(MPLS.LS$read), .variables = .(grade = MPLS.LS$grade),
+       each(read.mean = mean), na.rm = TRUE)
```

	grade	read.mean
1	5	205.1364
2	6	211.4545
3	7	215.6818
4	8	218.0000

The output shows grade in the first column and the reading means in the second column. If one chooses, the output can be saved to a data frame object, and the column names can be changed with `colnames()`.

SDs and other univariate descriptive statistics are computed by making the proper replacements in the `each()` argument. When switching statistics, the naming should also be replaced for proper output labeling, for example, `sd.read=sd`. Multiple statistics can be computed simultaneously by listing them like the following: `each(mean.read=mean,sd.read=sd)`.

Correlations and covariances are much easier to compute with the wide-format data set, as this is required for the `cor()` and `cov()` functions. Working from the long data frame, the repeated measures must be formatted using the `split()` and `do.call()` functions from the `base` package. The `split()` function splits the long-format data frame into separate column pieces according to the time predictor. The `do.call()` function binds the columns together and returns a data frame. The `cbind()` function name is supplied to accomplish this, along with the object that has the column pieces.

```
> mylist <- split(MPLS.LS$read, MPLS.LS$grade)
> myread <- do.call(cbind, mylist)
> colnames(myread) <- paste("grade.", as.character(5:8), sep = "")
> myread
```

3.5 Basic Statistics for Long-Format Data

```
       grade.5 grade.6 grade.7 grade.8
 [1,]     172     185     179     194
 [2,]     200     210     209      NA
 [3,]     191     199     203     215
 [4,]     200     195     194      NA
 [5,]     207     213     212     213
 [6,]     191     189     206     195
 [7,]     199     208     213     218
 [8,]     191     194     194      NA
 [9,]     149     154     174     177
[10,]     200     212     213      NA
[11,]     218     231     233     239
[12,]     228     232     248     246
[13,]     228     236     228     239
[14,]     199     210     225     235
[15,]     218     223     236      NA
[16,]     228     226     234     227
[17,]     201     210     208     219
[18,]     218     220     217     221
[19,]     215     216     221      NA
[20,]     204     215     219     214
[21,]     237     241     243      NA
[22,]     219     233     236      NA
```

The above syntax is a substitute for `reshape()`. Having created a wide-format data frame with the reading scores, the covariance and correlation matrices are computed. The option `use="pairwise.complete.obs"` is used, so that missing values are omitted on a pair-by-pair basis—that is, pairwise deletion is used.

```
> cov(myread, use = "pairwise.complete.obs")
```

```
         grade.5   grade.6   grade.7   grade.8
grade.5 399.7424  386.8874  355.3788  383.5385
grade.6 386.8874  402.4502  361.1039  396.4615
grade.7 355.3788  361.1039  378.1320  361.6923
grade.8 383.5385  396.4615  361.6923  375.5385
```

```
> cor(myread, use = "pairwise.complete.obs")
```

```
          grade.5    grade.6    grade.7    grade.8
grade.5 1.0000000  0.9645804  0.9140704  0.8825860
grade.6 0.9645804  1.0000000  0.9256661  0.9287729
grade.7 0.9140704  0.9256661  1.0000000  0.9227732
grade.8 0.8825860  0.9287729  0.9227732  1.0000000
```

The correlations and covariances are identical to those computed directly with the wide-format data (see Section 3.3.1). The only difference is in the column and row labels.

3.5.2 MISSING DATA STATISTICS

Missing data statistics are computed with the long format using `ddply()`. To compute the proportion of missing data at each time point, the `is.na()` function is used on `read`, and then the mean is calculated conditional on `grade`. The proportion of missing data is labeled `prop.miss`.

```
> ddply(.data = data.frame(is.na(MPLS.LS$read)),.variables = .(grade = MPLS.LS$grade),
+       each(prop.miss = mean))
```

	grade	prop.miss
1	5	0.0000000
2	6	0.0000000
3	7	0.0000000
4	8	0.3636364

The output is identical to that produced with the wide format (see Section 3.3.2). The output can be saved as an object and graphed, which is shown in the next chapter.

3.5.3 CONDITIONING ON STATIC PREDICTORS

The output column listing of `ddply()` is particularly handy when conditioning is based on static predictors. Conditioning on multiple variables is accomplished by supplying a list in the `.variables=.()` argument.

The syntax below computes the reading mean by grade and gender. To illustrate that output can be saved, the output is assigned to the data frame object `mgrge` (mean, grade, gender).

```
> mgrge <- ddply(data.frame(MPLS.LS$read),.(grade = MPLS.LS$grade,gender= MPLS.LS$gen),
+            each(mean.read = mean), na.rm = TRUE)
> mgrge
```

	grade	gender	mean.read
1	5	F	203.5000
2	5	M	208.0000
3	6	F	210.6429
4	6	M	212.8750
5	7	F	214.0000
6	7	M	218.6250
7	8	F	217.4286
8	8	M	218.5714

The output has a nested structure, with gender groups nested within grade. This means the levels of gender change faster than the levels of grade when going down the rows of the output. The means for Grade 5 are in rows labeled 1–2, with the mean for females in the first row and the mean for males in the second row. The same pattern of female, then male mean is repeated for the remainder of the output.

As a second example of conditioning on static predictors, consider the mean reading score at each grade for a median split of attendance proportion.

3.5 Basic Statistics for Long-Format Data

Previously, the `ifelse()` function was used to create a dummy code for the median split. A more convenient approach is to use the `cut_number()` function from the `ggplot2` package. The function attempts to create groups with the same number of scores. Creation of equal-numbered groups may not be possible, as when a median split is requested and there is an odd number of scores. In such cases, `cut_number()` will create only approximately equally numbered groups. Additional details are provided in the next chapter.

The `cut_number()` function requires the name of the quantitative variable to be grouped (`att`) and the number of groups to be formed (`n=`). In the case of a median split, there are two groups, hence `n=2`. In the syntax below, `cut_number()` is used within `ddply()` to compute means based on the median split. The `factor()` function is used to create value labels.

```
> mgrat <- ddply(data.frame(MPLS.LS$read), .(grade = MPLS.LS$grade,
+                           att.range = cut_number(MPLS.LS$att, n = 2)),
+                           each(read.mean = mean), na.rm = TRUE)
> mgrat
  grade   att.range  read.mean
1     5 [0.85,0.97]   199.6000
2     5   (0.97,1]    217.0000
3     6 [0.85,0.97]   205.4000
4     6   (0.97,1]    224.4286
5     7 [0.85,0.97]   210.3333
6     7   (0.97,1]    227.1429
7     8 [0.85,0.97]   211.0000
8     8   (0.97,1]    230.6000
```

```
> mgrat$att.range <- factor(mgrat$att.range, labels = c("Low","High"))
> mgrat
  grade att.range read.mean
1     5       Low  199.6000
2     5      High  217.0000
3     6       Low  205.4000
4     6      High  224.4286
5     7       Low  210.3333
6     7      High  227.1429
7     8       Low  211.0000
8     8      High  230.6000
```

The output shows that attendance group (`att.range`) is nested within grade. The `Low` attendance group is the group at or below the median of 0.97, and the `High` group is above the median. This is indicated in the first output as [0.85,0.97] and (0.97,1], respectively, with a bracket indicating the interval including the median and a parenthesis indicating the interval excluding the median.

Using `n=2` in `cut_number()` creates groups based on a median split. A quartile split is created using `n=4`. Additional types of splits are possible using various values for `n=`.

Missing data proportions can be computed conditional on the time predictor and static predictors. Suppose conditioning is on gender as well as grade, and the goal is to compute the proportion of missing values.

```
> ddply(data.frame(is.na(MPLS.LS$read)), .(grade = MPLS.LS$grade, gender = MPLS.LS$gen),
+                  each(prop.miss = mean))
```

```
  grade gender prop.miss
1     5      F     0.000
2     5      M     0.000
3     6      F     0.000
4     6      M     0.000
5     7      F     0.000
6     7      M     0.000
7     8      F     0.500
8     8      M     0.125
```

The output has gender nested within grade. The last two lines of output show the missing data proportion for the gender groups at Grade 8. The female group has a higher proportion of missing values (0.5) than the male group (0.125).

3.6 Data Structures and Balance on Time

Wide format is especially convenient for entering and displaying data when the response variable is *balanced on time* (Ware, 1985). This means the time points are common among subjects, or the researcher is willing to treat the data as such.

An example of balance on time is the MPLS data of Table 1.6. For each wave of measurement, the subjects are observed at the same grade, and a single column is used for the response scores at each time point. A missing value code is used when an observation is intended, but not collected, as with the second subject at Grade 8.

Table 3.4 Data unbalanced on time.

				Grade				
Subject	5	6	7	8	9	10	11	12
1	172	NA	185	NA	179	NA	194	NA
2	NA	200	NA	210	NA	209	NA	NA

When the response scores are not balanced on time, known as *unbalanced*, time points are not common among participants, or not common enough to be considered balanced. An example is shown in Table 3.4. The data in the table come from the first two subjects of the balanced data set, only here it is induced to be unbalanced. The subjects in Table 3.4 each have four waves of data, but the waves are staggered. The second subject is always measured a year later than the first subject. In this case, missing value codes are used to "pad" the data, in addition to denoting intended but unrealized values.

The unbalanced data in Table 3.4 can be balanced by wave rather than grade. This will produce an array identical to Table 1.6 with the column headings of the repeated measures being 1, 2, 3, and 4 to represent the waves. Balancing by wave has the advantage of minimizing the missing values. However, it has the disadvantage of misrepresenting the time scale, as observations measured at different times are not treated as such. If the goal is to make inferences about change over the duration of the study (e.g., Grades 8–12), then the wave-balanced data should not be used.

The NAs of the unbalanced data are a concern. The extent to which valid inferences can be made depends on the reasons for the imbalance, or equivalently, the reasons for the missing values. Reasons for missing values and implications for LMER analysis are discussed later in this chapter.

Unbalanced data require a more complex wide-format data frame. As shown in Table 3.4, several columns are required to accommodate the variety of time points among the subjects. When there are many unique time points, the wide format can be rather unwieldy and sparse, with a large number of missing data values required to pad the data frame. In such cases, alternative forms of wide format might be considered, which are discussed in the optional Section 3.9.

In the case of unbalanced data, it is suggested that the data be entered directly into long format. Care must be taken when entering the data, as keying mistakes are perhaps more likely due to the unfamiliarity of the format. Furthermore, when unbalanced data are saved in long format, caution should be used when reshaping to wide format. The resulting data frame might have many columns containing many NAs.

Similar caution is required when computing statistics based on the long-format data frame. If there is imbalance on time, the descriptive statistics for some or all the time points might be based on only a few cases, or even a single case. Missing data information is crucial in this situation, so that the researcher knows the number of available scores on which a statistic is computed. Interpretation of statistics should be tempered by the sample size used to compute them.

3.7 Missing Data in LMER Analysis

As previously seen, statistical functions in R have particular defaults for dealing with missing data. These defaults are changed by using optional arguments, such as na.rm=TRUE in the mean() function.

Apart from the arguments of the statistical functions, the treatment of missing data is controlled through the data structure. If, for example, all the NAs are deleted prior to using mean(), the result will be equivalent to using the na.rm=TRUE argument.

In the LMER analysis discussed in future chapters, missing data will be ignored. This means any row of the long-format data frame that has a NA will be omitted. The pattern of the NAs determines if the omission constitutes part or all of a subject's repeated measures. When NAs occur only for the response variable, a subject is included in the LMER analysis as long as he or she has at least one nonmissing time point. When NAs occur for a static predictor, then the entire record of the subject is ignored, meaning the subject is omitted from the analysis.

To examine the effects of different missing value patterns, the na.omit() function is used with a subset of the MPLS.LS data frame. The na.omit() function will omit any rows of a data frame that have at least one NA. This is the default behavior of the function used for LMER analysis to be introduced in Chapter 5.

To illustrate na.omit(), consider the first three subjects of the long-format MPLS.LS data frame. This example will use the variables subid, read, grade, and gen. The subset() function is used for the selection of the variables. The function requires the name of the data frame from which to select, a condition for selection (subid < 4), and the variable names to be included.

```
> MPLS.LS3 <- subset(MPLS.LS, subid < 4, select = c(subid, read, grade, gen))
> MPLS.LS3
```

	subid	read	grade	gen
1	1.5	1	172	5	F
2	1.6	1	185	6	F
3	1.7	1	179	7	F
4	1.8	1	194	8	F
5	2.5	2	200	5	F
6	2.6	2	210	6	F
7	2.7	2	209	7	F
8	2.8	2	NA	8	F
9	3.5	3	191	5	M
10	3.6	3	199	6	M
11	3.7	3	203	7	M
12	3.8	3	215	8	M

The subject number is used to verify that the records for the first three subjects are in the data frame MPLS.LS3. Line 9 of the output shows that the second subject has a missing value for Grade 8.

Suppose the na.omit() function is applied to the MPLS.LS3 data frame. The result is saved as omit1.

```
> MPLS.LS3 <- subset(MPLS.LS, subid < 4, select = c(subid, read, grade, gen))
> omit1 <- na.omit(MPLS.LS3)
> omit1
```

3.7 Missing Data in LMER Analysis

```
    subid  read  grade  gen
1   1.5    1     172    5    F
2   1.6    1     185    6    F
3   1.7    1     179    7    F
4   1.8    1     194    8    F
5   2.5    2     200    5    F
6   2.6    2     210    6    F
7   2.7    2     209    7    F
8   3.5    3     191    5    M
9   3.6    3     199    6    M
10  3.7    3     203    7    M
11  3.8    3     215    8    M
```

The line numbers show the data frame has lost a row, and inspection of the output will show the omitted row had the NA. The second subject's available observations will be used in the analysis, and only the Grade 8 observation will be ignored. Note that no information is lost in omitting the second subject's NA row because the response score is not available at Grade 8. The static predictor information is still available based on the other grades.

As another example, suppose missing values are induced for a static predictor. Consider the assignment of NA to gen for the first subject. Prior to inducing the missing values, a copy of the original data frame is created and named MPLS.LS3a.

```
> MPLS.LS3a <- MPLS.LS3
> MPLS.LS3a[1:4,4] <- NA
> MPLS.LS3a
```

```
    subid  read  grade  gen
1   1.5    1     172    5    <NA>
2   1.6    1     185    6    <NA>
3   1.7    1     179    7    <NA>
4   1.8    1     194    8    <NA>
5   2.5    2     200    5    F
6   2.6    2     210    6    F
7   2.7    2     209    7    F
8   2.8    2     NA     8    F
9   3.5    3     191    5    M
10  3.6    3     199    6    M
11  3.7    3     203    7    M
12  3.8    3     215    8    M
```

Lines 2 to 5 show that the first subject has missing values for gender. Since static predictors have their constant values repeated over time for each subject, there is an NA for each grade.

Now na.omit() is applied to the MPLS.LS3a data frame, and the result is saved as omit2.

```
> omit2 <- na.omit(MPLS.LS3a)
> omit2
```

```
   subid  read  grade  gen
2.5    2   200     5    F
2.6    2   210     6    F
2.7    2   209     7    F
3.5    3   191     5    M
3.6    3   199     6    M
3.7    3   203     7    M
3.8    3   215     8    M
```

The line numbers indicate that five rows of data have been omitted. One row is omitted for Subject 2 and four rows for Subject 1. All the repeated measures for Subject 1 are gone, meaning the person is not included in the analysis.

To summarize, *a subject will be included in a LMER analysis when he or she has missing data on the response variable, but no missing data on the static predictors.* There needs to be at least one nonmissing response score for the subject to be included in the analysis. If there are missing data on at least one static predictor, the subject will be eliminated from the analysis regardless of the amount of missingness on the response. The caveat here is that if the missing static predictor is not to be used in the analysis, then the subject can be included provided there is at least one nonmissing response score.

Due to spotty missing values, it may be the case that the number of subjects changes for different analyses. Suppose one subject has missing data only on a static predictor, but not on the response. The subject will be included if the static predictor is not used, and the subject will be excluded if the static predictor is used. This can lead to a shifting sample size based on which predictors are in the model. *It is strongly recommended that the sample size be held constant for all analyses, especially if comparisons among various fitted LMER models are to be made.*

3.7.1 RETAIN OR OMIT MISSING DATA ROWS?

For LMER analysis, there are two options considered for the long-format data frame. The NA values can be left in the data frame, or `na.omit()` can be used to eliminate the rows containing NA. The statistical results will be identical either way because missing data only occur for the response in the MPLS data set. For other data sets having missing data on multiple variables, the results may not be identical.

If NA values occur only for the response variable, and the response is balanced on time, then it is probably best to leave the NA values in the data frame. Each subject will have an equal number of rows, and the padding can facilitate inspection when displaying the data frame. On the other hand, if the analysis is exploratory, or a number of descriptive statistics are to be computed, it might be more convenient to omit the missing value rows. Then optional arguments for treating missing values are not needed.

Missing data for static predictors present a potential dilemma. In the event that subjects have missing values on the static predictors and not the response, the number of subjects for the analysis will change depending on whether the static predictors are included. In the example above, the first subject will be retained in the analysis if gender is not used, but excluded in the analysis if gender is used. The same idea applies when different subjects have missing data on different static predictors.

It is not valid to allow the number of subjects to change in an analysis. The inferential methods to be introduced in later chapters are based on the comparisons of models with a constant sample size. Therefore, it is assumed throughout this book that there are no missing values for static predictors in the data frame used for the analysis. In many empirical studies, having no missing values for the static predictors is not a problem. The static predictors are often measured very early in the study, prior to or at the first measurement period.

In the event the researcher does have missing values on the static predictors, every attempt should be made to obtain the realized values. In lieu of that, it is recommended that na.omit() be applied to the data frame so that the number of subjects will be set for all analyses. This should certainly be mentioned in the write-up of the results and listed as a limitation of the analysis.

Another instance in which missing values might be retained is when the data frame contains more than one response variable, and the pattern of missingness differs. If the response variables are to be analyzed separately, it might be tolerable to have the number of subjects vary based on the response variable analyzed. This is arguably a better scenario than having the number of subjects vary based on the static predictors.

3.8 Missing Data Concepts

The missing data approach used throughout this book is to omit a row of data from the long-format data frame if there is at least one NA in the row. The validity of this approach for statistical analysis rests on assumptions about how the missing data came to be. It is important, then, to discuss some missing data concepts to aid the researcher in assessing the degree of validity in a LMER analysis. Throughout the discussion, it is assumed that missing data occur only for the response variable.

The justification for ignoring missing data in LMER analysis is based on assumptions about the *missing data mechanism*. The missing data mechanism is the process responsible for the missing data. Three missing data mechanisms suggested by Rubin (1976) will be considered.

- *Missing completely at random* (MCAR)
- *Missing at random* (MAR)
- *Not missing at random* (NMAR)

For those just learning the concepts, it is helpful to focus on special cases of the missing data mechanisms, which are considered below. General treatments can be found in Allison (2009), Fitzmaurice et al. (2004, chap. 14), and Molenberghs and Kenward (2007, chap. 1).

The missing data mechanisms are explained by imagining a *complete* sample data set, in which every intended response is realized. In reference to the discussion earlier in this chapter, the complete sample data set results when every instance of NA is replaced with the value that would occur if the researcher were able to actually collect the intended observation. It is emphasized that the complete sample data set is like a mythical creature and never observed. One does "see" the observed sample data set, which is the data frame with the NA values. The observed sample data set is *incomplete*, in the sense that hypothetically realized values in the complete data set are missing in the observed data set.

The missing data mechanism can be thought of as the process that acts on the unobserved complete sample data set to produce the incomplete observed data set. The nature of the process defines the missing data mechanism. To illustrate the mechanisms, consider the reading achievement scores at seventh grade from the MPLS data set. The data are complete for this grade, so this grade will act as the hypothetical complete data set. This offers an opportunity to illustrate how the different missing data mechanisms, in effect, set some values to NA for the incomplete observed data.

Illustrations of the missing data mechanisms are shown in Table 3.5. To make the identification of NA easier, each missing value is boxed. The dichotomous risk coding is included in the table as a key variable. To make the presentation easier, the number of subjects in the risk groups is balanced by arbitrarily omitting Subjects 5 and 7. The data are sorted first by risk2 in decreasing alphabetic order and then by read.7 in ascending order. This sorting is helpful to contrast the mechanisms represented in the table.

The variable unif is a random number from 0 to 100 that is used to assign NA for MCAR and MAR. The runif() random number generator was used to generate the values for unif. Each type of mechanism assigns five NA values, which constitutes 25% missing data. The read.7 column constitutes the complete unobserved data, and the remaining columns are the incomplete observed data with NA values assigned by the missing data mechanism.

It is stressed that the researcher never knows the missing data mechanism. Informed guesses as to the mechanism are made based on knowledge of the content under study, the data collection process, and the subjects. Reasons for nonresponse and other forms of missingness might emerge as data collection starts, with subjects sometimes volunteering reasons why they dropped out.

3.8.1 MISSING COMPLETELY AT RANDOM

MCAR means the incomplete observed sample is a random sample of the complete unobserved data. Another way of saying this is that the NA values are randomly assigned. In the MCAR column of Table 3.5, the NA values are assigned based on the five smallest values of unif. Because the assignment values are randomly generated, setting the five smallest values to NA constitutes a completely random missing data scenario.

3.8 Missing Data Concepts

Table 3.5 Missing data examples.

subid	risk2	unif	read.7	MCAR	MAR	NMAR
9	DADV	94.47	174	174	174	NA
1	DADV	26.55	179	NA	NA	NA
8	DADV	89.84	194	194	194	NA
4	DADV	90.82	194	194	194	NA
3	DADV	57.29	203	203	NA	NA
6	DADV	20.17	206	NA	NA	206
2	DADV	37.21	209	209	NA	209
10	DADV	66.08	213	213	213	213
11	DADV	62.91	233	233	233	233
12	DADV	6.18	248	NA	NA	248
17	ADV	76.98	208	208	208	208
18	ADV	49.77	217	217	217	217
20	ADV	99.19	219	219	219	219
19	ADV	71.76	221	221	221	221
14	ADV	17.66	225	NA	225	225
13	ADV	20.60	228	NA	228	228
16	ADV	38.41	234	234	234	234
15	ADV	68.70	236	236	236	236
22	ADV	77.74	236	236	236	236
21	ADV	38.00	243	243	243	243

In contrast to the other missing data mechanisms, `risk2` is not related to the assignment of the NA values. As compared to the ADV students, there is one additional DADV student who was assigned an NA, however, this occurred by chance. With MCAR, the assignment is unrelated to any observed data and unrelated to the unobserved (complete) data.

In the real world, one might think about situations consistent with the MCAR mechanism. In the case of the MPLS study, if students miss the testing day because of illness, and getting sick is completely random, this qualifies as an MCAR process. In such a situation, missingness is not related to risk or any other variable, observed or unobserved.

3.8.2 MISSING AT RANDOM

The MAR mechanism considered here is conditionally random. *The NA values are randomly assigned conditional on risk.* The MAR column of Table 3.5 provides an illustration. The NA values are assigned based on the five smallest values of `unif`, but only for the disadvantaged group. The advantaged group does not have any missing data.

The result is that missing data are related to the observed `risk2` variable, yet not to the complete unobserved reading variable (`read.7`). Disadvantaged students have a higher proportion of missing data. However, within this group, the missing data are random. Because the MAR mechanism allows additional reasons for missingness beyond random sampling of the complete data set, it is thought to be a more plausible assumption than MCAR for many empirical situations (Molenberghs & Fitzmaurice, 2009, chap. 4).

What real-world scenarios are consistent with the MAR mechanism? In the MPLS study, suppose the disadvantaged students are more prone to being out sick due to poorer nutrition. In this sense, risk is a predictor of missingness. In addition, if illness among the disadvantage students occurs randomly, this qualifies as an MAR mechanism. There is random missingness due to illness conditional on risk.

It should be mentioned that MAR is more general than the case presented here. MAR covers additional situations in which missingness is predictable from observed data and not from unobserved data. This more general notion is especially convenient for longitudinal studies. In longitudinal studies, it is common for some subjects to provide initial data, and then to drop out over time. When this occurs, the observed data from earlier time points are often predictive of missing data at latter time points. This lends plausibility to the MAR assumption for longitudinal studies that may not be enjoyed by cross-sectional studies.

3.8.3 NOT MISSING AT RANDOM

NMAR indicates that missing data are not random in any way. The NMAR process assigns NA in a systematic fashion based on the complete unobserved data values. An example is shown in the NMAR column of Table 3.5. The four smallest values of read.7 are assigned NA. The assignment is entirely dictated by the unobserved complete data values, and it is systematic because the smallest values determine the assignment.

NMAR is the process not covered by MCAR or MAR, so there is no random assignment of NA values. In the example, the NA values assigned by the NMAR process all occur in the disadvantaged group. However, unlike MAR, the assignment is not random within the group. Rather, the five smallest values in the disadvantaged group are missing. NMAR also covers the case in which the largest values are set to NA, or any other scenario in which the assignment is nonrandom.

What is a reason the NMAR mechanism might operate? For the MPLS study, one possibility is that the lowest scoring students have an inkling they will do poorly on the reading test and do not show up for the testing day. These students, in effect, have low unobserved scores and self-select out of the study, possibly due to embarrassment. The poor reading scores are a part of the complete unobserved data set. Self-selection out of the measurement results in an observed incomplete data set, with the smallest unobserved scores missing. In this example, the missing data are predicted by the complete unobserved data. Those with unobserved lower reading scores will have a greater probability of missingness.

3.8.4 MISSING DATA MECHANISMS AND STATISTICAL ANALYSIS

Having introduced the missing data mechanisms, the issue now is what implication the mechanisms have for statistical analysis. An attempt is made to answer this question for the examples illustrated in Table 3.5. Recall that the missing data mechanism is never known, so what follows is meant as an illustration rather than a recommendation regarding practice. Recommendations are discussed later.

Suppose the goal of the analysis for the Table 3.5 incomplete observed data is to estimate the population seventh-grade mean reading achievement. Risk may or may not be relevant to this goal, depending on the type of missing data mechanism with which one is dealing.

If the missing data mechanism is MCAR, then risk is irrelevant, and the traditional formula for estimating the population mean is used. This is the sum of the observed reading scores divided by the number of students who contribute observed scores. Students with missing data are not involved in the calculation. In terms of the observed data, the mean() function is used for the calculation with na.rm=TRUE to deal with the missing values.

In the case of MAR, risk is relevant and should be considered in the estimation of the population mean. For the MAR scenario of Table 3.5, missing values only occur for the disadvantaged students. This indicates there is imbalance on risk, and this imbalance may be accounted for in different ways.

When the risk groups are unbalanced, the traditional sample mean formula is a weighted (wt) sample mean. Suppose N_D stands for the number of disadvantaged students with observed scores, and N_A stands for the number of advantaged students with observed scores. In the MAR column of Table 3.5, $N_D = 5$ and $N_A = 10$. Then the weighted mean is

$$\hat{\mu}_{wt} = \frac{1}{N} \cdot \sum_{i=1}^{N} y_i = \frac{N_D \cdot \bar{y}_D + N_A \cdot \bar{y}_A}{N_D + N_A}, \quad (3.8.1)$$

where $\bar{y}_D$ is the mean of the disadvantaged group, and $\bar{y}_A$ is the mean of the advantaged group. As Equation 3.8.1 shows, the disadvantaged and advantaged group means are weighted by $N_D/(N_D+N_A)$ and $N_A/(N_D+N_A)$, respectively.

An alternative to the weighted mean is the unweighted (unwt) mean, which gives equal weighting to the group means. The unweighted sample mean has the following formula:

$$\hat{\mu}_{unwt} = \left(\frac{1}{2}\right) \left(\frac{\sum_{i=1}^{N_D} y_i}{N_D}\right) + \left(\frac{1}{2}\right) \left(\frac{\sum_{i=1}^{N_A} y_i}{N_A}\right) = \frac{\bar{y}_D + \bar{y}_A}{2}. \quad (3.8.2)$$

The formula shows that the unweighted mean is the average of the group means. One way to look at it is the unequal sample size is taken into account "prior" to the group averaging, not "during" the group averaging, as with the weighted mean.

When the groups are balanced, as with the complete data of Table 3.5 (read.7), then Equations 3.8.1 and 3.8.2 are equivalent. In theory, MCAR will produce balanced groups, as NAs are randomly assigned. In this case, both the weighted and unweighted mean will estimate the sample population mean. The sample mean is unbiased regardless of whether the weighted or unweighted type is used. As will be shown in a moment, the same cannot be said when the mechanism is MAR or NMAR. In the case of MAR, only the unweighted mean is unbiased, and with NMAR, both types are biased.

3.8.5 MISSING DATA SIMULATION

To make things more concrete, it is useful to provide an illustration of how the sample mean is affected by the different missing data mechanisms. A tidy illustration is difficult to carry out using the small number of cases in Table 3.5. Therefore, the illustration will rely on data simulated in R to yield a much larger sample size. The simulation will involve complete unobserved data with $N_D = N_A = 500$, yielding an overall complete sample size of $N_D + N_A = 1000$. Incomplete observed data will be induced by assigning NA according to one of the missing data mechanisms. In all cases, there will be 25% missingness, meaning 250 cases will be set to NA in the incomplete observed data sets.

In the following syntax, the mydat data frame is created with simulated values of risk2, read.7, and unif. The reading scores are generated from a normal distribution with $\mu = 200, \sigma = 40$. The unif random numbers are from a uniform distribution ranging from 0 to 100. The set.seed() function allows the reader to replicate the example.

```
> set.seed(222)
> mydat <- data.frame(risk2 = c(rep("DADV", 500), rep("ADV", 500)),
+              read.7 = sort(rnorm(1000, mean = 200, sd = 40)))
> set.seed(333)
> mydat$unif <- runif(1000, min = 0, max = 100)
> head(mydat)
```

	risk2	read.7	unif
1	DADV	89.02132	46.700066
2	DADV	95.87990	8.459815
3	DADV	96.00647	97.348527
4	DADV	98.83332	57.130558
5	DADV	102.27519	2.011937
6	DADV	102.35023	72.355739

Having generated the complete data and random numbers for assigning NA, missing data are now induced based on the MCAR mechanism. To accomplish

3.8 Missing Data Concepts

this, values of `read.7` associated with the 250 smallest values of `unif` are set to NA. It should be noted that `risk2` is completely ignored in this process. The resulting reading variable with missing data is `read.7m`.

```
> MCAR <- mydat                          # Copy data frame.
> MCAR$read.7m <- MCAR$read.7            # Copy complete variable.
> MCAR <- MCAR[order(MCAR$unif), ]       # Sort by random numbers.
> MCAR$read.7m[1:250] <- NA              # Assign NAs.
```

The weighted and unweighted means are computed for the reading variable with missing data. As mentioned, the weighted mean is computed with the `mean()` function using the `na.rm=TRUE` argument. The result is saved as the object `wt`. For the example, the mean of the complete data is also computed with the `mean()` function, but `na.rm=TRUE` is omitted, as there are no missing data.

Computation of the unweighted mean is more involved. The risk group means must be computed first and then averaged. The `ddply()` function is used for the first step, and the `mean()` function is used for the second step. The results are saved in the data frame `myresults1` and printed with rounding to one decimal place.

```
> wt <- mean(MCAR$read.7m, na.rm = TRUE)
> unwt <- ddply(data.frame(MCAR$read.7m),.(MCAR$risk2),each(Mean = mean),na.rm = TRUE)
> unwt <- mean(unwt$Mean)
> myresults1 <- data.frame(complete = mean(MCAR$read.7),wt.mean = wt,unwt.mean = unwt)
> rownames(myresults1) <- "MCAR"
> round(myresults1, 1)
     complete wt.mean unwt.mean
MCAR    199.4   199.1     199.1
```

Recall that $\mu = 200$, so the mean based on the complete data slightly underestimates the population mean. This underestimation is a result of vagaries in the generating process, which can be taken to represent sampling variation. The output shows that the weighted and unweighted means are equal to each other and approximately equal to the complete data mean. Nothing is lost in estimating the population mean from the incomplete data induced by the MCAR mechanism. The mean estimate based on the incomplete data is an unbiased estimate of the population mean, regardless of whether risk is accounted for or not.

Now consider the MAR mechanism as conceptualized in Table 3.5. As opposed to MCAR, this time NA is assigned for the smallest 250 values of `unif`, *but only for the disadvantaged subjects*. The missing data are random conditional on risk.

```
> MAR <- mydat
> MAR$read.7m <- MAR$read.7
> ## Sort by risk2 (decreasing) and unif (increasing).
> MAR <- MAR[order(MAR$risk2,-MAR$unif, decreasing = TRUE),]
> MAR$read.7m[1:250] <- NA
> head(MAR)
```

	risk2	read.7	unif	read.7m
269	DADV	175.2482	0.7072515	NA
439	DADV	192.0899	0.7609383	NA
232	DADV	170.6664	0.7812500	NA
370	DADV	185.5204	1.1813112	NA
388	DADV	187.1371	1.2376774	NA
453	DADV	193.7805	1.3153144	NA

Consider the weighted and unweighted means for the MAR incomplete data.

```
> wt <- mean(MAR$read.7m, na.rm = TRUE)
> unwt <- ddply(data.frame(MAR$read.7m),.(MAR$risk2), each(Mean = mean),na.rm = TRUE)
> unwt <- mean(unwt$Mean)
> myresults2 <- data.frame(complete = mean(MAR$read.7),wt.mean = wt,unwt.mean = unwt)
> rownames(myresults2) <- "MAR"
> round(myresults2, 1)
```

	complete	wt.mean	unwt.mean
MAR	199.4	210.3	199.9

The results are different in comparison to the MCAR mechanism. The weighted mean is much larger than the mean computed on the complete data. The weighted mean shows bias in overestimating the population mean. On the other hand, the unweighted mean is approximately equal to the mean based on the complete data and is very close to the population mean. Based on statistical theory, it can be shown that the unweighted mean is an unbiased estimator of the population mean, and the weighted mean is a biased estimator.

Why is the unweighted mean an unbiased estimator and the weighted mean a biased estimator? The MAR mechanism for the example assigns missing values randomly for the disadvantaged group. This is a MCAR mechanism for the disadvantaged group. Since values are MCAR for disadvantaged students, $\bar{y}_D$ is an unbiased estimator of μ_D; $\bar{y}_A$ is also an unbiased estimator of μ_A, as there are no missing data for advantaged students. The average of two unbiased estimators is itself an unbiased estimator.

The weighted mean is not an unbiased estimator and provides an overestimate. This is due to the disadvantaged group having lower mean scores than the advantaged group. Since only scores from the lower mean group are omitted, the weighted sample mean is larger than it would be if computed on the complete sample data.

For NMAR, the random numbers are not used to assign NA values. In the example, the simulated reading scores are sorted in ascending order, with the smallest values occurring in the disadvantaged group. The NMAR mechanism is simulated by assigning NA to the first 250 subjects, meaning the smallest 250 complete reading values are set to NA in the incomplete observed data set.

```
> NMAR <- mydat
> NMAR$read.7m <- NMAR$read.7
> NMAR$read.7m[1:250] <- NA
> head(NMAR)
```

3.8 Missing Data Concepts

	risk2	read.7	unif	read.7m
1	DADV	89.02132	46.700066	NA
2	DADV	95.87990	8.459815	NA
3	DADV	96.00647	97.348527	NA
4	DADV	98.83332	57.130558	NA
5	DADV	102.27519	2.011937	NA
6	DADV	102.35023	72.355739	NA

Since the bottom 25% of the complete data are omitted, it is expected that the weighted and unweighted means will overestimate the population mean. There is a systematic exclusion of the smallest values in the complete unobserved data set.

```
> wt <- mean(NMAR$read.7m, na.rm = TRUE)
> unwt <- ddply(data.frame(NMAR$read.7m),.(NMAR$risk2),each(Mean = mean),na.rm = TRUE)
> unwt <- mean(unwt$Mean)
> myresults3 <- data.frame(complete = mean(NMAR$read.7), wt.mean = wt, unwt.mean = unwt)
> rownames(myresults3) <- "NMAR"
> round(myresults3, 1)
```

	complete	wt.mean	unwt.mean
NMAR	199.4	216.1	208.6

As anticipated, the weighted mean rather drastically overestimates the population mean. The unweighted mean is a bit better, although it still provides an overestimate. The unweighted mean is biased because $\bar{y}_D$ is biased, due to the nonrandom missingness in the disadvantaged group.

The finding that the unweighted mean is less biased is a result of the data structure. The data were simulated to have a correlation between risk and reading, as the smallest reading values were assigned to the disadvantaged group. The unweighted mean may not necessarily show less bias with real data.

To provide a summary of the simulation results, the data frames of the results are bound together and printed. Rounding is to one decimal place.

```
> round(rbind(myresults1, myresults2, myresults3), 1)
```

	complete	wt.mean	unwt.mean
MCAR	199.4	199.1	199.1
MAR	199.4	210.3	199.9
NMAR	199.4	216.1	208.6

To summarize, the MCAR mechanism does not affect the bias of the sample mean. In terms of the example above, this indicates that risk can be safely ignored. The MAR mechanism does affect the sample mean, and risk must be accounted for by way of computing the unweighted mean. The NMAR mechanism also affects the sample mean, and biased results will occur even when risk is taken into account.

3.8.6 LMER ANALYSIS

The results of the last section illustrate some general principles about the missing data mechanisms.

- When NA values are assigned by the MCAR mechanism, the results of statistical methods are generally valid. No special considerations regarding variables with missing or nonmissing values are necessary. In the example above, conditioning on risk made no difference regarding the sample mean.
- When NA values are assigned by the MAR mechanism, results of statistical methods are valid when predictors of missingness are incorporated into the analysis. In the example, risk was a predictor of missingness, and the unweighted mean provided the necessary conditioning to yield an unbiased sample estimate.
- When NA values are assigned by the NMAR mechanism, the results of statistical methods will be biased to an unknown extent. However, if the systematic missingness is correlated with other variables included in the analysis, the bias might be reduced. This is evident in the example above in which risk was correlated with the nonrandom missingness.

Although it is valuable for applied researchers to be acquainted with the missing data mechanisms, one point needs to be clear: *it is impossible to establish what missing data mechanism is operating based on an analysis of the sample data.* There are some statistical approaches to assessing the plausibility of MCAR (see Diggle, Heagerty, Liang, & Zeger, 2002, chap. 13), but not for MAR or NMAR. Because of the inability to empirically verify the missing data mechanism, *analysis with missing data is always clouded by untestable assumptions* (Ugarte, 2009).

Where does this leave applied researchers who have missing data? Researchers are always going to analyze their data, so two strategies are recommended. The first is to analyze one's data under the assumption of MAR and explicitly state that the results are only valid under this assumption or MCAR. MCAR is a special case of MAR, in which the random missingness is not conditional on an observed variable. Making the assumption explicit will alert the consumer of one's results to the possibility of bias in the reporting of effect sizes and so on. Basic statistics regarding missing data should be presented, as discussed earlier in this chapter.

Second, the researcher should attempt a thought experiment regarding the plausibility of the missing data mechanisms. The thought experiment is based on information about the subjects, the study design, and the data collection. The information and speculation should be reported, so that the consumer can make a judgment regarding the plausibility of the assumed MAR missing data mechanism. It may be based on anecdotes from subjects, or esoteric details of the data collection, such as the physical facilities where measurement occurred.

As an example of a thought experiment, consider the MPLS study. Recall that there are missing data for reading achievement at the eighth grade. District officials reported to the researchers that the missing data were primarily due to students moving out of the school district. There are no exit interviews of the families who move, and one is left with conjectures about the missing data mechanism. If families move out of the district because of a random process, this constitutes an MCAR mechanism. For the MCAR mechanism to be plausible, one has to imagine the families being selected by some sort of a lottery and then willing to move when selected. The lottery notion seems quite far-fetched in this case, and thus, MCAR might be an implausible assumption.

An MAR process seems more plausible. In one MAR scenario, families might move out of the district because of their students' initial observed low reading scores. Perhaps the parents blame low reading scores on the school system and seek a different school system that is perceived to be more effective for their children. In this case, initial reading scores are predictive of dropout, which provides a justification for the MAR mechanism. In such a scenario, it is important to include the students with missing data, so that prediction of missingness is an implicit part of the analysis.

In another MAR scenario, the HHM families might move out of the district at a much higher rate than the other risk groups. Suppose it is plausible that random (or quasi-random) forces are operating among the HHM families to cause them to move from the district. Such forces include changes in availability of space at shelters, or erratic city service budgets. In such a case, there is evidence of random missingness conditional on risk, which perhaps justifies an MAR mechanism. It is important to include the risk variable in the statistical analysis to account for the conditional random missingness.

An even more likely state of affairs is that moving is at least partially dependent on variables that are not collected on the students or their families. For example, unbeknownst to the researchers, suppose the employment status of the parent(s) or guardian(s) changes, precipitating a move out of the district. If moving is caused by extraneous unobserved variables, the dropout mechanism is NMAR. There are no measured variables predictive of dropout, only unmeasured ones.

In the LMER methods to be described in later chapters, missing data can be validly ignored when the missing data mechanism is MCAR or MAR, and some other relatively mild assumptions hold (separation and regularity; see Molenberghs & Kenward, 2007, chap. 7). On a practical level, this means that omitting NA rows from the long-format data frame will probably produce unbiased results regarding mean change over time, assuming MCAR or MAR. As hinted above, it is important to include observed variables that are predictors of missingness. This is to help ensure that unweighted means, or their analogs, are used in the analysis. In most cases, the predictors of missingness are assumed to be earlier, possibly complete, response scores and static predictors.

When the missing data mechanism is NMAR, ignoring the missing data is not valid, and LMER results will be biased to an unknown extent. As mentioned, including observed variables that are correlated with missingness can reduce bias. But in any given situation, the extent of the reduction is unknown and may have only a slight impact. In the NMAR scenario of Table 3.5, missing data are correlated with risk, leading to less bias in the unweighted mean estimate (bias still remains).

Should one worry about assuming MAR in situations for which NMAR is thought to hold? Worries about wrong missing data assumptions probably are only the tip of the iceberg regarding any statistical analysis. From a philosophy of science perspective, although it is wrong to assume MAR under an NMAR mechanism, applied researchers use incorrect models all the time. In fact, it has been argued that "all statistical models are wrong but some are useful" (G. Box, 1979). One never has all the relevant predictors in the regression equation, for example, meaning the true model is never among the candidates considered. A misspecified model for the missing data increases bias, but the amount of increase might be trivial when compared to misspecification of the predictor effects. Leaving out a relevant predictor might have a much greater impact than assuming MAR when, in fact, the mechanism is NMAR. The simplification that comes with assuming MAR might be worth the bias trade-off. Assuming MAR might enable the researcher to expend greater resources on investigation of more important issues, such as determining the relevant predictors for a LMER model.

3.9 Extensions to More Complex Data Structures*

Many longitudinal studies in the behavioral sciences are balanced on time and deal with a single repeatedly measured response variable. In such cases, the reshaping methods previously described will probably suffice.

When there are multiple repeated measures variables and/or the data are not balanced on time, the reshaping procedures must be extended. The `reshape()` function can be used with more complex structures reflected in the wide-format data. This is illustrated for the case of two dynamic variables and an unbalanced response variable. The data sets discussed in this optional section are available from the book website.

3.9.1 MULTIPLE DYNAMIC VARIABLES*

A wide data frame may have multiple dynamic variables. This can occur when the researcher wants to analyze response variables separately, or when at least one of the variables is a dynamic predictor (dynamic covariate). In this case, the syntax of the `reshape()` function is altered to create the proper long-format data frame.

Consider the data in Table 3.6, which depicts two dynamic variables, reading (`read`) and mathematics (`math`) test scores measured over the same four grades. The data frame also contains the risk static predictor.

Suppose the Table 3.6 data are saved as the space-delimited text file `MPLScomp1.txt`. In the syntax below, the wide-format text file is read

3.9 Extensions to More Complex Data Structures*

Table 3.6 Reading and mathematics test scores in wide format.

subid	read.5	read.6	read.7	read.8	math.5	math.6	math.7	math.8	risk
1	172	185	179	194	189	186	183	199	HHM
2	200	210	209	–99	215	206	192	209	HHM
3	191	199	203	215	196	216	206	232	HHM
4	200	195	194	–99	210	175	224	–99	HHM
5	207	213	212	213	206	232	188	–99	HHM
6	191	189	206	195	198	192	223	246	HHM
7	199	208	213	218	205	191	205	200	POV
8	191	194	194	–99	211	218	222	–99	POV
9	149	154	174	177	166	172	199	201	POV
10	200	212	213	–99	195	217	239	–99	POV
11	178	191	193	199	187	213	205	247	POV
12	188	192	208	206	235	215	248	243	POV
13	228	236	228	239	244	266	259	267	ADV
14	199	210	225	235	207	238	215	208	ADV
15	218	223	236	–99	225	237	229	–99	ADV
16	228	226	234	227	218	257	244	260	ADV
17	201	210	208	219	204	215	219	212	ADV
18	218	220	217	221	214	236	243	223	ADV
19	215	216	221	–99	216	210	210	–99	ADV
20	204	215	219	214	212	217	217	217	ADV
21	237	241	243	–99	242	242	242	–99	ADV
22	219	233	236	–99	235	236	238	–99	ADV

in, then the data frame is restructured to long format. Alterations to the `varying=` and `v.names=` arguments are required to properly handle the two dynamic variables. The resulting long data frame is sorted by subject number and grade. Then the data for the first two participants are printed.

```
> MPLSc1 <- read.table("C:\\Mine\\MPLScomp1.txt", header= TRUE, na.strings= c("-99"))
> MPLSc1.L <- reshape(data = MPLSc1, varying = list(2:5, 6:9), idvar = "subid",
+                    v.names = c("read","math"), timevar = "grade", times = 5:8,
+                    direction = "long")
> MPLSc1.L <- MPLSc1.L[order(MPLSc1.L$subid, MPLSc1.L$grade), ]
> head(MPLSc1.L, n = 8)
    subid risk grade read math
1.5     1  HHM     5  172  189
1.6     1  HHM     6  185  186
1.7     1  HHM     7  179  183
1.8     1  HHM     8  194  199
2.5     2  HHM     5  200  215
2.6     2  HHM     6  210  206
2.7     2  HHM     7  209  192
2.8     2  HHM     8   NA  209
```

Notice the use of `list()` with the `varying=` argument and `c()` with the `v.names=` argument. This ensures that the two repeated measures variables are properly identified and named.

The output shows the reading and mathematics scores in separate columns, with the repeated measures correctly depicted, as can be verified from Table 3.6. The risk variable values are repeated for the grades, and the same will be done when additional static predictors are included. The syntax can be extended in a straightforward manner to accommodate any number of dynamic variables.

3.9.2 UNBALANCED DATA*

The previous examples dealt with data balanced on time (grade). *When the data are not balanced on time, it is recommended that the data be entered directly in long format.* An alternative is to alter the wide format to accommodate the imbalance, which is considered here.

Suppose there is a scenario in which the number of waves of measurement is the same for each subject, but the timing of data collection varies. Such a scenario is depicted in Table 3.7.

Table 3.7 has four columns devoted to the repeated measurements of reading, read.1 to read.4, with the column labels reflecting waves rather than grades. There are also four columns for the grades associated with reading, grade.1 to grade.4, and an entry depicts the grade at which a wave is collected. The grades are not common for the waves. For example, the first subject is measured at Grade 4 for the first wave, whereas the second subject is measured at Grade 5.

In this unbalanced scenario, it is assumed the researcher wants to pair the reading scores with the proper time metric, which is grade. Waves are only used here for convenience and will not be part of the analysis. It is difficult to think of a situation in which waves rather than grades are desirable to use, as this constitutes balance on order rather than time.

The decision about anchoring repeated measures to waves rather than time should be carefully considered. Traditional methods, such as RM-ANOVA/MANOVA, require balance on waves in this situation. This is one reason why applied researchers are moving away from the traditional methods.

Reshaping to long format is accomplished using syntax similar to that for two dynamic variables. In this instance, the second dynamic variable (grade) is the time predictor, and the wave of measurement is depicted in the long-format data frame. Consider the syntax and output below.

```
> MPLSc2 <- read.table("C:\\Mine\\MPLScomp2.txt", header = TRUE, na.strings = c("-99"))
> MPLSc2.L <- reshape(data = MPLSc2, varying = list(2:5, 6:9), idvar = "subid",
+                    v.names = c("read", "grade"), timevar = "waves", times = 1:4,
+                    direction = "long")
> MPLSc2.L <- MPLSc2.L[order(MPLSc2.L$subid, MPLSc2.L$grade), ]
> head(MPLSc2.L, n = 8)
```

	subid	risk	waves	read	grade
1.1	1	HHM	1	172	4
1.2	1	HHM	2	185	5
1.3	1	HHM	3	179	6
1.4	1	HHM	4	194	7
2.1	2	HHM	1	149	5
2.2	2	HHM	2	189	6
2.3	2	HHM	3	206	7
2.4	2	HHM	4	195	8

3.9 Extensions to More Complex Data Structures*

Comparing the output to Table 3.7, it can be seen that the grades are appropriately associated with the reading scores. The waves are indexed in the long data frame, and analysis and graphing should be based on `grade`, as this is the appropriate duration variable.

Table 3.7 Reading test scores in wide format but unbalanced on grade.

subid	read.1	read.2	read.3	read.4	grade.1	grade.2	grade.3	grade.4	risk
1	172	185	179	194	4	5	6	7	HHM
2	149	189	206	195	5	6	7	8	HHM
3	201	199	203	215	4	6	7	8	HHM
4	200	210	209	−99	5	6	7	8	HHM
5	200	195	194	−99	4	6	7	8	HHM
6	207	213	212	213	5	6	7	8	HHM
7	199	208	213	218	5	6	7	8	POV
8	191	194	194	−99	4	6	7	8	POV
9	149	154	174	177	5	6	7	8	POV
10	228	212	213	−99	5	6	7	8	POV
11	229	231	233	239	4	5	6	7	POV
12	227	232	248	246	4	6	7	8	POV
13	228	236	228	239	5	6	7	8	ADV
14	225	210	225	235	4	5	6	7	ADV
15	218	223	236	−99	5	6	7	8	ADV
16	218	226	234	227	5	6	7	8	ADV
17	201	210	208	219	4	6	7	8	ADV
18	210	220	217	221	5	6	7	8	ADV
19	215	216	221	−99	4	5	6	7	ADV
20	204	215	219	214	4	6	7	8	ADV
21	237	241	243	−99	5	6	7	8	ADV
22	219	233	236	−99	5	6	7	8	ADV

To understand the scenario a bit more and to illustrate some earlier points, consider reshaping the long data frame back to a wide data frame using `reshape()`. This reshaping does not mimic the original wide format, as the repeated measures are exhaustively listed in columns based on the grade variable.

```
> MPLSc2.W <- reshape(data = MPLSc2.L, v.names = "read", idvar = "subid",
+                    timevar = "grade", direction = "wide", drop = "waves")
> MPLSc2.W
```

	subid	risk	read.4	read.5	read.6	read.7	read.8
1.1	1	HHM	172	185	179	194	NA
2.1	2	HHM	NA	149	189	206	195
3.1	3	HHM	201	NA	199	203	215
4.1	4	HHM	NA	200	210	209	NA
5.1	5	HHM	200	NA	195	194	NA
6.1	6	HHM	NA	207	213	212	213
7.1	7	POV	NA	199	208	213	218
8.1	8	POV	191	NA	194	194	NA
9.1	9	POV	NA	149	154	174	177
10.1	10	POV	NA	228	212	213	NA
11.1	11	POV	229	231	233	239	NA
12.1	12	POV	227	NA	232	248	246

13.1	13	ADV	NA	228	236	228	239
14.1	14	ADV	225	210	225	235	NA
15.1	15	ADV	NA	218	223	236	NA
16.1	16	ADV	NA	218	226	234	227
17.1	17	ADV	201	NA	210	208	219
18.1	18	ADV	NA	210	220	217	221
19.1	19	ADV	215	216	221	NA	NA
20.1	20	ADV	204	NA	215	219	214
21.1	21	ADV	NA	237	241	243	NA
22.1	22	ADV	NA	219	233	236	NA

The output shows that the wide data frame now has five columns rather than four. This is required to represent all the unique values of grade in the long-format data frame. Several missing data values (NA) are required to create the orderly rectangular array. One can imagine that when the long-format data frame has several more unique values than considered here, the wide format resulting from reshape() will have many more columns and many more missing values.

The unbalanced example is tidy because each subject has four waves of data. A characteristic of the unbalanced wide-format data set is that the number of repeated measures columns is equal to the number of columns for the waves. When the number of waves varies among the subjects, the maximum number must be listed, with NAs used to pad the data. For example, if one subject has five waves of data and all other subjects have four, then five columns for the repeated measures must be used for all the subjects. There must also be five columns for the waves, and many missing value codes will fill the fifth column. In such situations, it is probably easier to enter the data directly in long format.

Graphing Longitudinal Data 4

Visual displays of longitudinal data are informative and should be used in every analysis. Graphing can aid in the identification of outliers, provide evidence of consistency with statistical assumptions, reveal unexpected relationships, and help illuminate and explain statistical results.

Graphing can be used prior to, during, or after inferential statistical analysis. This chapter focuses on graphical methods that are likely to be used prior to a LMER analysis. As such, emphasis is on graphs of the raw data, as well as graphs of summaries of the raw data (e.g., means), as opposed to graphs based on fitted LMER models. Chapters 10 and 11 discuss graphing of residuals and fitted values after a LMER model is fit to the data.

4.1 Graphing and Statistical Strategy

Before launching into a discussion of methods, it is important to consider statistical strategy and the role of graphing. Graphing constitutes an examination of the data. Such examinations are viewed differently from confirmatory and exploratory data perspectives. In exploratory analysis, the graphing tends to be extensive, as little is known about the structure of the data and potential effects. Recall that exploratory analysis is chiefly to generate scientific hypotheses for future research (Tukey, 1977).

For longitudinal data, exploratory graphing includes plots of change curves for individual subjects and aggregates of subjects. Graphs of subjects provide information about the extent of individual variability, which is important for suggesting the number of random effects. Graphs of group means and similar summaries are helpful in developing the fixed effects model. Graphs of the response variable conditional on the static predictors are also useful for specifying the fixed effects.

In confirmatory research, the use of graphing is restrained. Graphs are not used to suggest models prior to the analysis, or at least not prominent features like static predictor effects. The focus is on detecting data anomalies that might affect the statistical analysis, such as outliers. Information obtained from the graphing might alter the analysis when, say, outliers are omitted based on preliminary data plots. But the models specified prior to the analysis are not altered based on graphing, or not the important substantive parts of the models.

The multimodel strategy presented in Chapter 1 does not preclude the use of extensive graphing, as long as it occurs *after* the preplanned models are fit to the data. In fact, a thorough analysis involves a second phase of extensive graphing to check the adequacy of the models and a look for unexpected effects that might be important to consider in the future. One should be cautious, however, not to allow graphs of the data to suggest the multiple models to be fit to the very same data. The point of the multimodel strategy is to formulate models as best one can using theoretical information. Anything short of this represents a data-driven strategy to some extent.

The theory-driven and data-driven distinction is sometimes blurred in analysis strategies that use graphing. Graphical methods are an integral part of what might be called *iterative data analysis*. Iterative strategies involve alternating between different analysis steps. Initial graphing is followed by fitting formal statistical models, which is followed by additional graphing, which is followed by additional fitting, and so on. Iterative strategies are very useful for particular purposes, such as fitting an optimal model to the data at hand.

Iterative analysis has been questioned because of its data-driven aspects (Chatfield, 1995; Faraway, 1992). The problem is that graphs are often used to suggest statistical models, or revisions of models, and this activity is typically not taken into account when the final model is presented. SEs for the final parameter estimates, for example, are not adjusted for the graphing and fitting that lead up to the final model.

In this chapter, a variety of graphical methods are presented, with some additional comment on statistical strategy. It is left to the reader to decide which methods are most applicable for a particular situation. Focus is on the analysis of the variables from the MPLS data set, introduced in Chapter 1. All the graphing in this chapter uses data from the long-format data frame, `MPLS.LS` (see the last chapter). This is convenient, in the respect that the same format will be used for statistical analysis with LMER discussed in the coming chapters.

4.2   Graphing With `ggplot2`

The tool to be used for graphing longitudinal data is the `ggplot2` package, written by Hadley Wickham (Wickham, 2009b). The main function for constructing plots in the package is `ggplot()`. The `ggplot2` package must be downloaded, installed, and loaded, as described in Chapter 2.

4.2.1 GRAPH COMPONENTS

A number of important functions are used to construct graphs with `ggplot()`. In the nomenclature of `ggplot2`, these functions are referred to as *components*. The components that will be of primarily concern are grouped into four categories.

- *Aesthetic mappings*
- *Geometric objects*
- *Statistical transformations*
- *Faceting*

Aesthetic mappings, specified with `aes()`, determine how variables are mapped to different graph features. The primary use of `aes()` is to define the *x*-axis in the graphs in terms of the time predictor, and to define the *y*-axis in terms of the response variable. In addition, `aes()` is used to associate subjects with their repeated measures and to group individuals based on static predictors.

Geometric objects consist of features that are drawn on the graph, such as points and lines. A geometric object is drawn by specifying the prefix `geom_` along with the suffix that names the feature to be plotted. For example, `geom_line()` is used for drawing lines, and `geom_point()` is used for drawing points.

Statistical transformations are statistics for graphing. If the goal is to graph means over time, the statistical transformation is the mean of the response for a fixed value of the time predictor. A statistical transformation has the prefix `stat_`, and its suffix is the desired transformation (or set of transformations). Summary statistics, such as means or medians, are plotted using `stat_summary()`.

Statistical transformations also apply to the case in which regression models, or other types of models, are used for summarizing. These types of summaries are computed using `stat_smooth()`.

Faceting creates a separate graph for each subject, or for groups of subjects. A graph of the change curve for each subject is created, for example, using `facet_wrap()`. Facets based on values of static predictors are constructed using `facet_grid()`.

The components discussed in this chapter are listed in Table 4.1. For each component, a brief description is provided, along with a partial list of arguments.

4.2.2 LAYERING

A key feature of `ggplot2` is that graphs are built up in layers. Each layer consists of a sum of components saved as an object. An individual layer can be printed to see the effects of the syntax, or to debug errors. The layers are accumulated as one goes along, and the final object is printed with the `print()`

Table 4.1 Main `ggplot2` components and functions.

Component/Function	Description	Arguments
`ggplot()`	Required first component	`data=, aes()`
`aes()`	Aesthetic mapping	`x=, y=, group=, shape=, linetype=, colour=`
`geom_point()`	Draws points (shapes)	`size=, shape=`
`geom_line()`	Draws lines	`lwd=, linetype=`
`stat_summary()`	Summary statistics	`fun.y=, geom=, aes()`
`stat_smooth()`	Smoothed/regression lines	`method=, se=, aes()`
`facet_wrap()`	Facet by subjects	`~.`
`facet_grid()`	Facet by static predictor(s)	`.~.`
`scale_x_continuous()`	x-axis features	`breaks=, name=`
`scale_y_continuous()`	y-axis features	`breaks=, name=`
`coord_cartesian()`	Zooming	`ylim=, xlim=`
`theme_bw()`	Black-and-white theme	(none)
`theme_gray()`	Gray theme	(none)
`theme_set()`	Sets theme for session	`theme_bw(), theme_gray()`
`scale_linetype()`	Customize lines and legend	`name=`
`scale_shape()`	Customize points and legend	`name=, solid=`
`scale_linetype_manual()`	Customize lines and legend	`name=, values=, breaks=, labels=`
`scale_shape_manual()`	Customize points and legend	`name=, values=, breaks=, labels=`
`scale_colour_brewer()`	Uses RColorBrewer palettes	`palette=`
`opts()`	Various options	`title=, legend.position=`
`print()`	Prints a graph	Graph object (e.g., `print(g1)`)
`cut_number()`	Create equal count groups	`n=`
`cut_interval()`	Create equal length groups	`n=`

command, which constructs the graph. The printed graph is saved from the R graph window, or directly to a graphics file; see ?pdf or ?png.

The ggplot() statement must be the first component in the first layer of the graph. The ggplot() component contains a reference to the data frame and an aesthetic mapping. Since the ggplot() layer contains basic information about the graph, this layer must be executed (or submitted) prior to executing additional layers.

4.3 Graphing Individual-Level Curves

The first type of graph considered is a graph of individual-level curves of observed scores. For each subject, adjacent observed scores are connected by a straight line. If a subject has missing data, then only contiguous scores are connected. The connected lines are superimposed in one graph, or an individual subject can be depicted in his or her own graph. As an option, a subject's individual values can be depicted as points.

Graphs of individual change curves are important for investigating individual variability and outliers. Concerning outliers, a distinction is made between an *individual* being an outlier and an *observation* being an outlier. An individual is an outlier when his or her change curve is very different from the change curve of the other subjects. This can occur when a subject's overall level is extremely high or low relative to the remainder of the sample. A more formal treatment of extreme subjects is provided in Chapter 10 based on realized random effects.

An observation is defined as an outlier in reference to the repeated measures of an individual. That is, an outlier is an extreme score relative to the other observations of a single subject. Outlying observations are easiest to see when subjects are faceted, meaning there is one panel per subject. Outliers arise from mistakes in data entry or sampling vagaries and anomalies. An example of a sampling anomaly is when an individual is mistakenly selected from a different population than the other subjects.

The treatment of outliers is controversial, as not all researchers agree on how they should be handled. Some find it acceptable to omit outliers prior to the statistical analysis, whereas others do not.

Perhaps justification for preanalysis omission is provided from the missing data discussion in the last chapter. When outliers are omitted, this is based on the observed scores, and the deletion is performed by the researcher. As discussed in the last chapter, this omission process is MAR in the taxonomy of missing data mechanisms. If the researcher uses ML estimation, as discussed in the next chapter, it can be shown that the parameter estimates will be unbiased under this scenario.

4.3.1 SUPERIMPOSED INDIVIDUAL CURVES

The first graph to be considered has all the individual change curves superimposed. Sometimes this type of graph is called a *spaghetti plot*, as it can look like wet noodles dropped on a plate. Graphing will be based on the long-format data frame constructed in the last chapter, MPLS.LS. Recall that this data frame has missing values (NA). Rows containing any number of NA values are automatically omitted by ggplot().

Suppose the goal is to plot read by grade. The subject identification number, subid, is used to associate subjects with their repeated measures. The ggplot() statement is used with a data file name and an aesthetic mapping, along with the geom_line() component that draws the lines. When a component has empty parentheses, it inherits the data set and aesthetic mapping defined earlier.

In the syntax below, after loading the Rdata file, a single-layer graph is saved as the object g1 (the object name for a layer is arbitrary). The g1 object is printed, producing a graph in the graphics window.

```
> load("C:/Mine/MPLS.LS.Rdata")
> require(ggplot2)
> g1 <- ggplot(data = MPLS.LS, aes(x = grade, y = read, group = subid)) + geom_line()
> print(g1)
```

In the syntax for g1, the data= argument identifies the data frame. The aesthetic mapping identifies the variables for the axes, and group=subid indicates that the grouping variable is the subject identification number, meaning a line will be drawn for each subject.

The resulting graph is shown in Figure 4.1a. The graph indicates that most subjects increase over time, although the increase does not appear to be straight-line (linear) in many cases. There are some individuals whose reading scores decrease over time. Individual variability is apparent, in terms of scatter about the vertical axis, with one subject having an initial reading score below 160, one subject having an initial score a little below 240, and the other subjects distributed between them. There appears to be no subjects who are outliers; the subject who starts at the smallest value appears not to be extremely different from the other subjects. Likewise, there appear to be no outlying observations (as opposed to individuals), but such outliers are easier to identify with the graphs considered below.

The default graph has a gray background with axes labels that are the variable names. The *x*-axis does not accurately represent the observed grades, as 5.5, for example, is not observed. To change the default behavior, three components are added in two additional layers: theme_bw(), which changes the color theme to black and white; scale_x_continuous(), which controls the scaling and labeling of the *x*-axis; and scale_y_continuous(), which does the same for the *y*-axis. The graph is built in layers, with g1 containing the same elements as previously, as well as the added components and arguments in g2 and g3. Consider the following syntax.

```
> g1 <- ggplot(data = MPLS.LS, aes(x = grade, y = read, group = subid)) + geom_line()
> g2 <- g1 + theme_bw() + scale_x_continuous(breaks = 5:8, name = "Grade")
> g3 <- g2 + scale_y_continuous(name = "Reading Score")
> print(g3)
```

4.3 Graphing Individual-Level Curves

Note that g1 is saved in g2, and g2 is saved in g3. This is an accumulation of the layers that are printed in the final step. The layers can also be printed individually, which is useful for checking for errors, or to see what the syntax produces. The cumulative nature of the layers must be respected, meaning that g2 is not defined and cannot be printed if g1 is not created beforehand, and so forth.

The graph with options is shown in Figure 4.1b. The argument breaks= 5:8 draws four tick marks on the *x*-axis, which accurately represents the observed grades. The background of the new graph is white with gray lines drawn at the tick marks of the axes.

The black-and-white graph theme is consistent with the guidelines for many professional behavioral science journals. Therefore, the remaining graphs in this chapter will be produced with this theme. The black-and-white graph theme is set for a R session using the following syntax.

```
> theme_set(theme_bw())
```

The default gray theme is reinstated using theme_gray().

There are other settings to consider that allow the streamlining of future syntax. The scale_x_continuous() and scale_y_continuous() components are relatively long. They each can be saved with a shorter name and used in subsequent graphs.

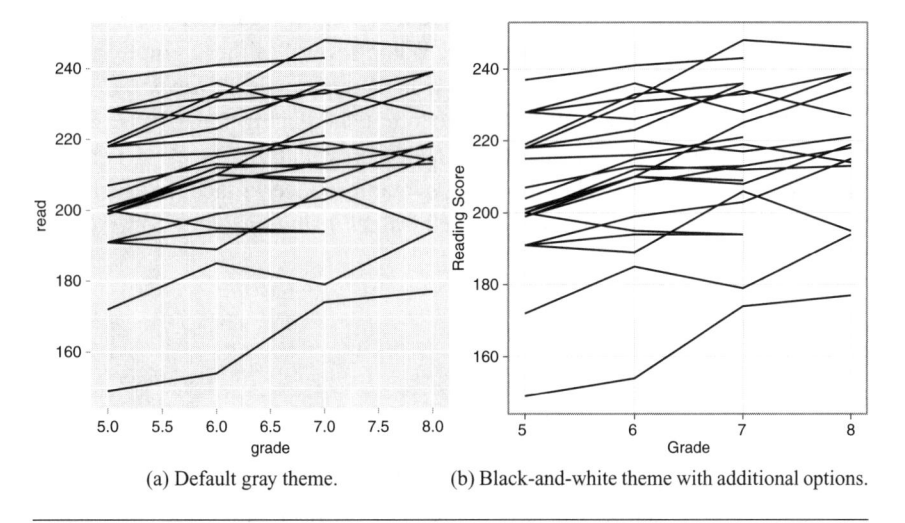

(a) Default gray theme.

(b) Black-and-white theme with additional options.

Figure 4.1 Superimposed individual curves.

```
> myX <- scale_x_continuous(breaks = 5:8, name = "Grade")
> myY <- scale_y_continuous(name = "Reading Score")
```

The objects myX and myY can now be used like any other component. The only caveat is that the ggplot2 package must be loaded prior to running the above syntax. If this is not done, an error message will be produced.

4.3.1.1 SAVING GRAPHS

Once a graph is produced in the R graphics window, it is saved in various graphics formats using the menu options. An alternative is to use the png(), jpeg(), pdf(), or other graphic device functions.

For a Windows-based computer, the following syntax creates a portable network graphics (png) file in the directory specified.

```
> png(filename = "C:/Mine/graph1.png")
> g1 <- ggplot(data = MPLS.LS, aes(x = grade, y = read, group = subid)) + geom_line()
> print(g1)
> graphics.off()
```

The graphics.off() syntax "shuts down" the png() function, causing the graph to be written to the file. It is important to include both print() and graphics.off(), or no graphics file will be constructed. Other devices, such as pdf(), have different shutdown functions such as dev.off(). See the help documentation for the specific device.

4.3.2 FACET PLOTS OF INDIVIDUAL CURVES

The graphs of Figure 4.1 are based on a relatively small sample size ($N = 22$), and still it is a bit difficult to make out the pattern of some of the individual curves. Things can be even more oblique with larger sample sizes.

To better examine the shape of individual trajectories, each subject's change curve can be depicted in its own graph. When several of these graphs appear in the same figure, the graphs are known as panes, panels, or *facets*.

Faceting for individual subjects is accomplished using facet_wrap(). The syntax convention is to list the variable on which the faceting is based, preceded by a tilde (~). The following syntax produces a facet for each subject. Points are drawn for the observed values using geom_point(), in addition to drawing lines.

```
> g1 <- ggplot(data = MPLS.LS, aes(x = grade, y = read, group = subid))
> g2 <- g1 + geom_line() + geom_point() + facet_wrap(~ subid) + myX + myY
> print(g2)
```

The facet graph is shown in Figure 4.2. The subject identification number appears in the banner of each facet. The faceting makes it easier to examine individual curves. Most individuals increase over time, but one subject decreases (Subject 4), and some appear to have little or no change (e.g., Subject 18). A number of subjects have missing data (e.g., Subject 2), and the change curve of some subjects is nonlinear (e.g., Subject 20). Variability among the subjects is evident in terms of overall level, that is, vertical location. In each facet, there does not appear to be any outlying observations, as the reading scores for any one subject are relatively uniform.

Several of the default aspects of the facet plot can be changed. To begin the numbering from the lower left, the argument as.table=FALSE is included

4.3 Graphing Individual-Level Curves

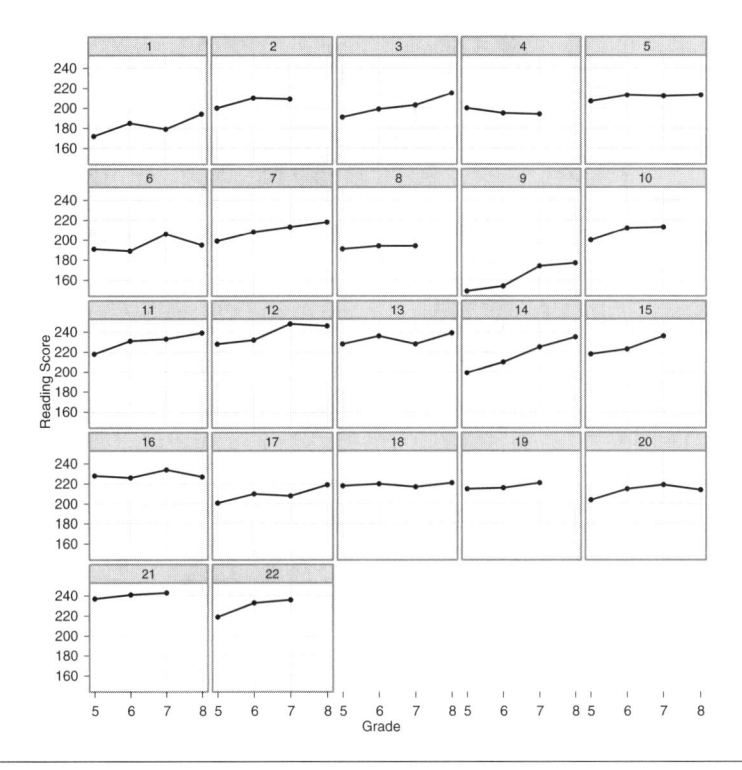

Figure 4.2 Faceted individual change curves.

in `facet_wrap()`. The number of rows or columns is fixed using `ncol=` and `nrow=`, respectively.

In the syntax below, a new facet plot is constructed, numbering from lower left and forcing two rows. Lines and points are drawn as previously.

```
> g1 <- ggplot(data = MPLS.LS, aes(x = grade, y = read, group = subid))
> g2 <- g1 + geom_line() + geom_point() + myX + myY
> g3 <- g2 + facet_wrap(~ subid, nrow = 2, as.table = FALSE)
> print(g3)
```

The graph is shown in Figure 4.3. The panels are elongated to accommodate the fact that there are only two rows, and individuals vary in their initial level. Subject 9 starts particularly low, and Subject 21 starts particularly high, just to name two.

4.3.3 SELECTING SUBSETS

With numerous subjects, a facet plot can have too many panels to be practical, and a superimposed plot can be very busy. For easier comprehension, it is desirable to select a random subset of the sample for graphing.

If the assignment of subject identification numbers is arbitrary, then any range of subject numbers constitutes a random sample. A range of subject numbers is selected by using a conditional statement within the `subset()`

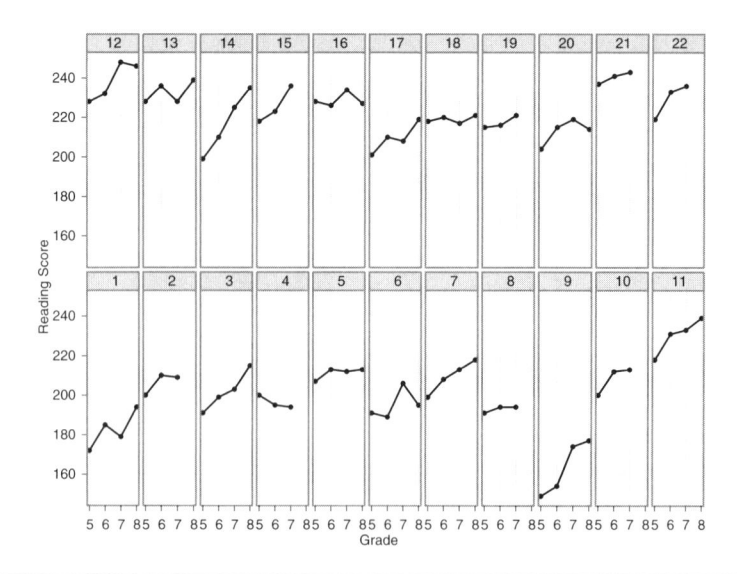

Figure 4.3 Faceted individual lines in two rows.

function. For example, the following syntax selects the first six subjects from the data frame.

```
> mysub6 ← subset(MPLS.LS, subid < 7)
```

Since subjects are identified with the counting numbers (1, 2, 3, ...), selecting those with values less than 7 yields the first six subjects. Again, the selection constitutes a random sample only when the subjects are randomly entered into the data set.

Sometimes the assignment of subject identification numbers is not arbitrary, as when all females are assigned a number in the 10s and all males in the 100s. For this case, selecting a range of subject numbers does not constitute a random sample, and more sophisticated methods must be used.

Within `subset()`, a more complex selection criterion is specified with `unique()`, `sample()`, and `%in%`. The `unique()` function identifies the unique subject identification numbers in the long-format data frame. This is necessary because the subject numbers are repeated for the duration of the measurements in the long data frame; see the discussion in the last chapter. The `sample()` function is used to draw a random sample of the unique subject numbers, and `%in%` is used to select the subjects for the subset.

In the syntax below, a random sample of four subjects is selected, and then a facet graph is constructed. The `set.seed()` function is used with a specific value, so the reader can reproduce the results. As usual, the `set.seed()` function should be omitted in practice, unless the researcher wants to select the same subset in repetitions.

4.3 Graphing Individual-Level Curves

```
> ## Allows reproduction of results (omit in practice).
> set.seed(123)
> ## Select random subset.
> mysub4 <- subset(MPLS.LS, subid %in% sample(unique(MPLS.LS$subid), size = 4))
> ## Graph random subset.
> g1 <- ggplot(data = mysub4, aes(x = grade, y = read, group = subid)) + geom_line()
> g2 <- g1 + geom_point() + facet_wrap(~ subid) + myX + myY
> print(g2)
```

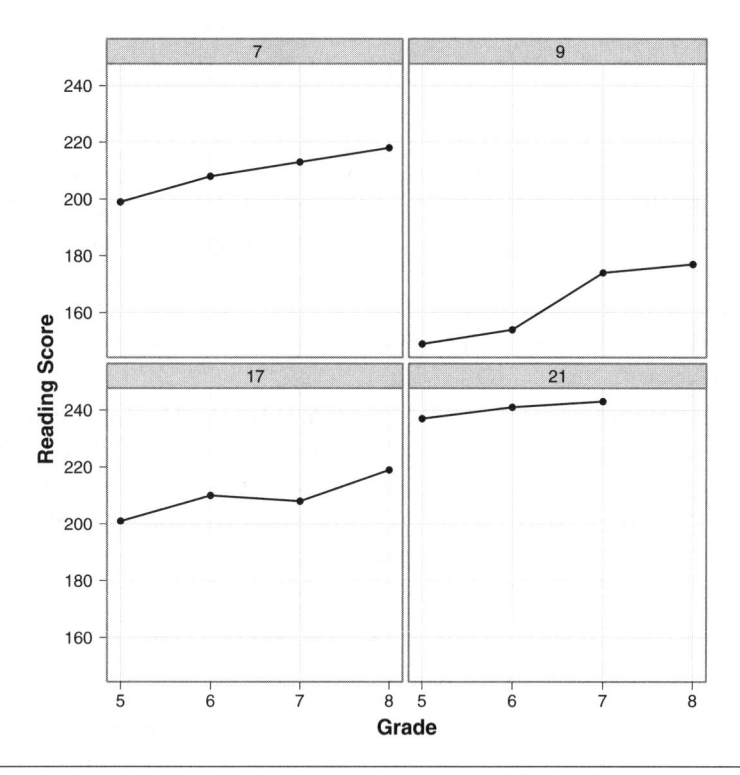

Figure 4.4 Faceted individual lines of a subset of four subjects.

The faceted subsample graph is shown in Figure 4.4. The graph has four panels, one for each of the four subjects randomly selected. The same type of subsample can be used to construct superimposed plots.

4.3.4 GRAPHING FITTED CURVES

Up to now, a change curve has been drawn by connecting a subject's observed values. A curve can also be drawn based on predicted values (or fitted values) from various procedures, such as OLS of traditional regression. Brief examples of OLS were provided in Chapters 1 and 2, and an extended discussion appears in Chapters 5 and 6.

In regard to statistical strategy, drawing curves based on fitted models is generally more consistent with exploratory analysis, as theory is not suggesting the models to be fit. The fitting of individual curves is important in exploratory selection of a change curve shape, as discussed in Chapter 9.

One reason for considering fitted values is that applied researchers usually assume there is measurement error associated with observed values. Measurement error is thought to introduce a degree of random irregularity in the observations. Consequently, the lines connecting the observed values in the graphs previously considered are probably too specific. It is more realistic to consider a type of summary line for each subject, with the observed points scattered about it.

Many types of summary lines can be used with scatterplot data. Two types are considered here: lines based on OLS and lines based on *local smoothing*. Local smoothing works by fitting a regression-type model to subsets of data. The subsets are defined by overlapping segments along the *x*-axis. An overall curve spanning the entire observed time interval is created by connecting each locally fitted curve in a continuous manner. The roughness or bumpiness of the curve is controlled by smoothing parameters that can be set by the analyst.

In contrast to OLS, local smoothers do not fit a model to all the observed points simultaneously. This has the advantage that the overall curve is not unduly influenced by extreme values occurring in a single location. The potential disadvantage is that the local smoothing curve cannot be written in a simple form, such as the regression model of Equation 2.9.1.

4.3.4.1 REGRESSION CURVES

Initial focus is on the fitting of linear curves with OLS. Recall from Chapter 2 that the traditional regression model is an LM, and its parameters can be estimated using the lm() function. The lm() function is used for curve fitting in the stat_smooth() component by including the argument method="lm". This has the default effect of fitting a straight line, in which the time predictor (grade) is the only predictor. After the model is fit, the fitted values of the response for each value of the predictor are computed, and then the fitted values are connected with a line. By default, a confidence interval (CI) about the fitted line is produced, based on the SE of regression. The CI can be turned off by including se=FALSE, which is done below for simplicity.

In the following syntax, points are drawn for the observed values, along with the fitted linear curve. The data of the first six subjects are used, and there is faceting by subjects.

```
> g1 <- ggplot(data = mysub6, aes(x = grade, y = read, group = subid)) + geom_point()
> g2 <- g1 + stat_smooth(method = "lm", se = FALSE) + facet_wrap(~ subid) + myX + myY
> print(g2)
```

4.3 Graphing Individual-Level Curves

The facet graph is shown in Figure 4.5. Each panel has the fitted curve with the observed values scattered about it. In most cases, the graphs appear to be consistent with the idea that the observed points randomly vary about their fitted lines. If the graph is being used to suggest a statistical model, then a linear change curve appears to be a possibility, but see Chapter 9 for a more thorough discussion.

It is often desirable to go beyond linear curves and consider plots of nonlinear curves. A nonlinear curve can be fit by adding power functions of the time variable to a regression equation. The simplest power functions use the counting numbers, which define the polynomials. The linear curve is a polynomial with the time variable having an exponent equal to 1, that is, grade^1 = grade. In the behavioral sciences, the most common nonlinear functions are the quadratic polynomial and the cubic polynomial. The quadratic polynomial has two time-variable transformations, with exponents 1 and 2. The cubic polynomial has three time-variable transformations, with exponents 1, 2, and 3.

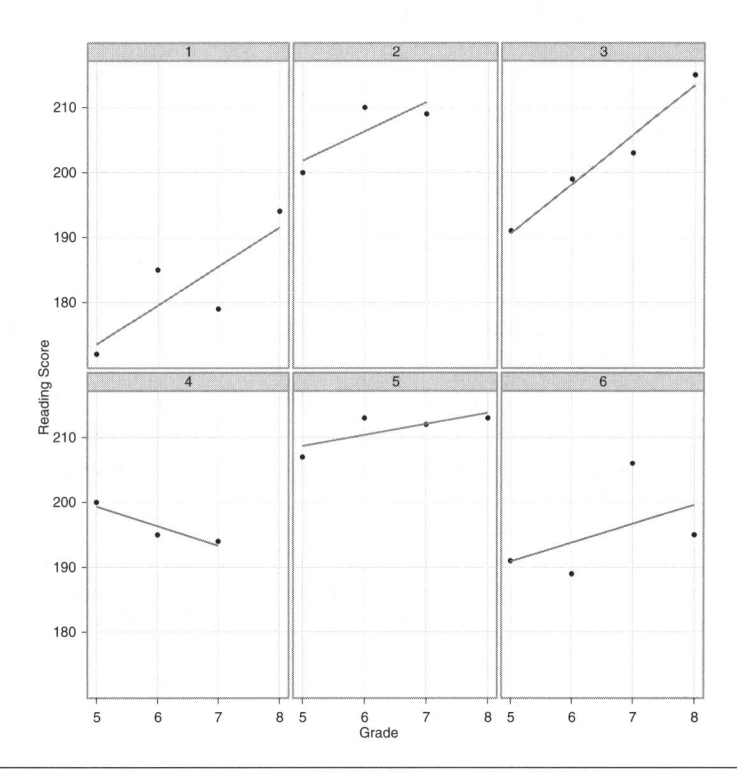

Figure 4.5 Faceted individual regression lines and observed points for a subset of subjects.

Examples of polynomial functions are shown in Figure 4.6. The linear functions are straight-line, whereas the quadratic functions are parabolas, with a single highest point or "peak" or a single lowest point or "valley." The cubic functions have the combination of one peak and one valley, which can be "local," as seen in Figure 4.6.

Consider the LM equations for the linear, quadratic, and cubic polynomials. Below are the fitted value equations.

$$\begin{aligned} \text{Linear:} \quad & \hat{y} = \beta_0 + \beta_1(\text{grade}), \\ \text{Quadratic:} \quad & \hat{y} = \beta_0 + \beta_1(\text{grade}) + \beta_2(\text{grade}^2), \\ \text{Cubic:} \quad & \hat{y} = \beta_0 + \beta_1(\text{grade}) + \beta_2(\text{grade}^2) + \beta_3(\text{grade}^3). \end{aligned} \qquad (4.3.1)$$

The shape of the polynomial is controlled by the sign and magnitude of the β parameters that multiply the time-variable transformations. The polynomials in Equation 4.3.1 are *raw polynomials*, which are correlated. It is possible to construct uncorrelated or *orthogonal* versions of polynomials. The details are discussed in Chapter 12. Here it is simply stated that by using orthogonal polynomials, estimation problems can be avoided that sometimes arise when using correlated polynomials.

Raw and orthogonal polynomials are constructed with the `poly()` function. The function requires the time predictor to be transformed, which in the example is `grade`, and the degree of the highest order term. By default, the function creates orthogonal polynomials, and raw (correlated) polynomials are created by including the argument `raw=TRUE`.

Polynomial functions are fit with `stat_smooth()` by using the `formula=` argument. The argument requires a generic `lm()` formula, similar to what was discussed in Section 2.9. To fit a quadratic polynomial, the syntax `formula=y~poly(x,2)` is used, and a cubic polynomial is fit by replacing 2 with 3. The formula is generic, meaning the symbols *y* and *x* are not replaced by the variable names in the data frame.

The syntax below fits a quadratic polynomial function to each subject's observed values. Points are drawn along with the fitted line, and the subjects are faceted. The `subset6` data frame is used, which contains the data for the first six subjects.

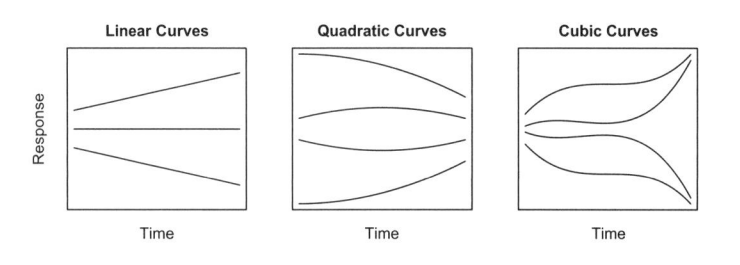

Figure 4.6 Polynomial curves.

```
> g1 <- ggplot(data = mysub6, aes(x = grade, y = read, group = subid)) + geom_point()
> g2 <- g1 + stat_smooth(method = "lm", se = FALSE, formula = y ~ poly(x, 2))
> g3 <- g2 + facet_wrap(~ subid) + myX + myY
> print(g3)
```

4.3 Graphing Individual-Level Curves

The resulting graph is shown in Figure 4.7. The fitted curves are bowed (or parabolic), some to a greater extent than others. For a few subjects (e.g., 1 and 3), the fitted curves deviate only slightly from a straight line, suggesting that nonlinear curves might not be needed. For other subjects (e.g., 2 and 6), the nonlinearity of the curves is more pronounced.

The fitted curves for Subjects 2 and 4 warrant comment. For each subject, the curve passes through all the observed points, indicating perfect fit. The reason for the perfect fit is that the number of β parameters in the LM is equal to the number of observed values (three). In this case, the LM is *saturated* for the subjects.

Saturated models do not summarize, in the respect that the number of estimated parameters is equal to the number of observed values. Because of this, saturated models probably should be avoided when possible. In the example, most subjects have four observations, and the quadratic polynomial is not a saturated model for them. It is tolerable, then, to allow perfect fit for some subjects in assessing the need for nonlinear models of the entire sample.

When the number of repeated measures is less than the order of the polynomial, `poly()` will not fit any curves and will return an error message. For the `subset6` data frame, `poly(x,3)` cannot be used because many subjects have only three data points. To circumvent the problem, subjects can be selected who have a certain number of observations, or equivalently, subjects who have a certain number of missing values.

Missing values. Subjects can be selected based on their number of missing values (or nonmissing values). To select subjects in this way, the NAs for each subject are tallied. Once this is done, the subject identification numbers are selected for those with a particular tally. For example, subjects with no missing data are analyzed by selecting missing value tallies equal to 0.

The number of missing values is tallied using `is.na()` within `ddply()`. See Chapter 3 for a discussion of these functions. Consider the syntax below that selects only those subjects who have no missing data. The `as.numeric (is.na())` functions are used on `read` to assign 0 if a value is not NA and 1 if a value is NA. Then `ddply()` tallies these values for each subject.

```
> mysel <- ddply(.data = data.frame(as.numeric(is.na(MPLS.LS$read))),
+               .variables = .(subid = MPLS.LS$subid), each(missing = sum))
> mysel
```

	subid	missing
1	1	0
2	2	1
3	3	0
4	4	1
5	5	0
6	6	0
7	7	0
8	8	1

```
9     9    0
10    10   1
11    11   0
12    12   0
13    13   0
14    14   0
15    15   1
16    16   0
17    17   0
18    18   0
19    19   1
20    20   0
21    21   1
22    22   1
```

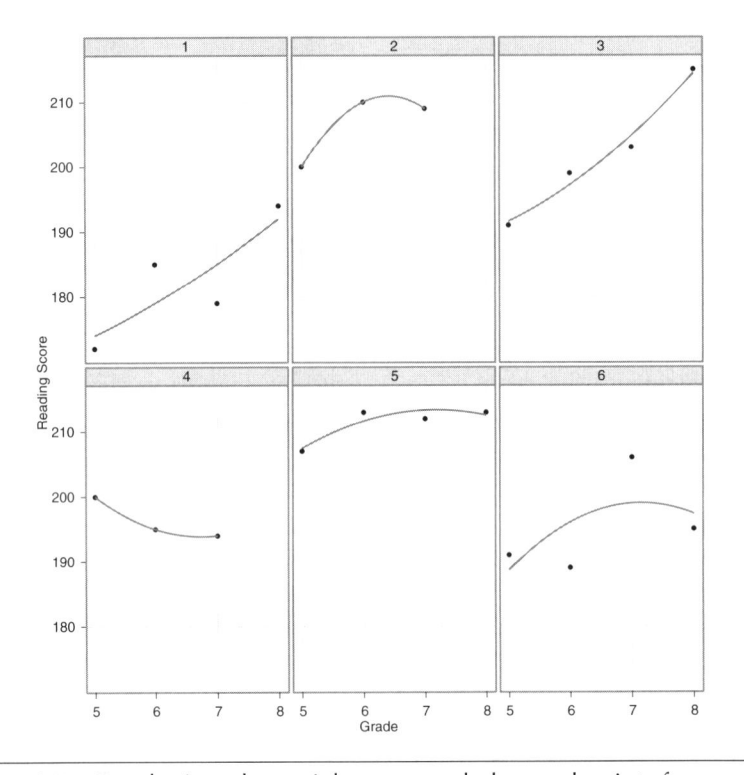

Figure 4.7 Quadratic polynomial curves and observed points for a subset of subjects.

The output shows that the `mysel` data frame contains the subject number in the first column and the missing data tally (`missing`) in the second column. It can be seen that Subject 1, for example, has no missing data, whereas Subject 2 has a missing value at one time point.

With the information in the `mysel` data frame, those subjects who have no missing data are selected. The filtered subject numbers are saved as the

4.3 Graphing Individual-Level Curves

object `myids`. Then the `subset()` function is used to create a data frame of subjects with no missing values.

```
> ## Select subjects with no missing values.
> myids <- with(mysel, subid[missing == 0])
> ## Create subset data frame.
> mysub.comp <- subset(MPLS.LS, subid %in% myids)
> head(mysub.comp)
```

	subid	risk	gen	eth	ell	sped	att	ell2	risk2	grade	read
1.5	1	1	HHM	F	Afr	0	N	0.94	No	DADV	5 172
1.6	1	1	HHM	F	Afr	0	N	0.94	No	DADV	6 185
1.7	1	1	HHM	F	Afr	0	N	0.94	No	DADV	7 179
1.8	1	1	HHM	F	Afr	0	N	0.94	No	DADV	8 194
3.5	3	3	HHM	M	Afr	0	N	0.97	No	DADV	5 191
3.6	3	3	HHM	M	Afr	0	N	0.97	No	DADV	6 199

The `mysub.comp` subset contains subjects who have no missing data. The data frame can now be used with `ggplot()`.

For the methods discussed below, it is convenient to add the missing data information to the existing data frame. The `mysel` data frame has a single missing tally score for each subject identification number. The missing tally score must be repeated for the duration of a subject's repeated measures. This involves a one-to-many mapping that is accomplished with the `merge()` function.

The `merge()` function requires the names of the two data frames to be merged, and the variable common to both data frames by which to match cases (`by=`). In this case, `by=subid` because the merging is by subject number. Consider the following.

```
> MPLS.LS2 <- merge(MPLS.LS, mysel, by = "subid")
> head(MPLS.LS2)
```

	subid	risk	gen	eth	ell	sped	att	ell2	risk2	grade	read	missing
1	1	1	HHM	F	Afr	0	N	0.94	No	DADV	5	172	0
2	1	1	HHM	F	Afr	0	N	0.94	No	DADV	6	185	0
3	1	1	HHM	F	Afr	0	N	0.94	No	DADV	7	179	0
4	1	1	HHM	F	Afr	0	N	0.94	No	DADV	8	194	0
5	2	2	HHM	F	Afr	0	N	0.91	No	DADV	5	200	1
6	2	2	HHM	F	Afr	0	N	0.91	No	DADV	6	210	1

The output shows that the new data frame, `MPLS.LS2`, has the variable `missing` in the last column. The `merge()` function carried out the one-to-many mapping, so that the missing tally score is repeated for the rows of the data frame corresponding to the repeated measures. Now `MPLS.LS2` can be used for further analysis, with selection or splitting by `missing`.

The syntax for faceting by missing data is shown below. For brevity, the graph is not created. A new factor variable, `missing.f`, is constructed with labels that will be used in the title of the facet panels.

```
> MPLS.LS2$missing.f <- factor(MPLS.LS2$missing, labels = c("Not Missing", "Missing"))
> g1 <- ggplot(MPLS.LS2, aes(x = grade, y = read, group = subid)) + geom_point()
> g2 <- g1 + geom_line() + facet_grid(. ~ missing.f) + myX
> print(g2)
```

4.3.4.2 SMOOTHED CURVES

An alternative to polynomials is local smoothing. Local smoothing is perhaps most useful at the group level, as the density of observations is greater than with an individual subject. When local smoothing is used for an individual subject, this results in the observed points being connected with nonlinear segments, rather than the straight-line segments used by geom_line().

Local smoothing is accomplished with stat_smooth() omitting the method= argument. In the syntax below, smoothed curves for the first six subjects are drawn, along with the observed points. Subjects are faceted, and the CIs are turned off for clarity.

```
> g1 <- ggplot(data = mysub6, aes(x = grade, y = read, group = subid)) + geom_point()
> g2 <- g1 + stat_smooth(se = FALSE) + facet_wrap(~ subid) + myX + myY
> print(g2)
```

The facet graphs are shown in Figure 4.8. The points are connected, but the overall curves are more wavy than those produced by geom_line().

Local smoothing is based on the number of available time points. If a subject has few available observations, then it might not be possible to fit a smoothed curve. In such a case, ggplot() produces an error message, and the graph is not constructed. Similar to the case of polynomials, a potential solution is to select a subset of subjects who have a minimum number of nonmissing observations.

4.4 Graphing Group-Level Curves

Group-level curves are useful when interest is in aggregate change. Such curves are produced by changing or omitting the group= argument from aes(). Omitting the argument treats the entire sample as a group, which is illustrated in this section. Group-level curves based on static predictors are considered later in this chapter.

Group-level versions of all the curve types previously considered can be constructed. When focusing on group curves, it is informative to also plot the observed points. There might be, for example, extreme scores influencing the group curve that are important to depict. In all the plots considered below, the geom_point() component is included to draw the observed points.

4.4 Graphing Group-Level Curves

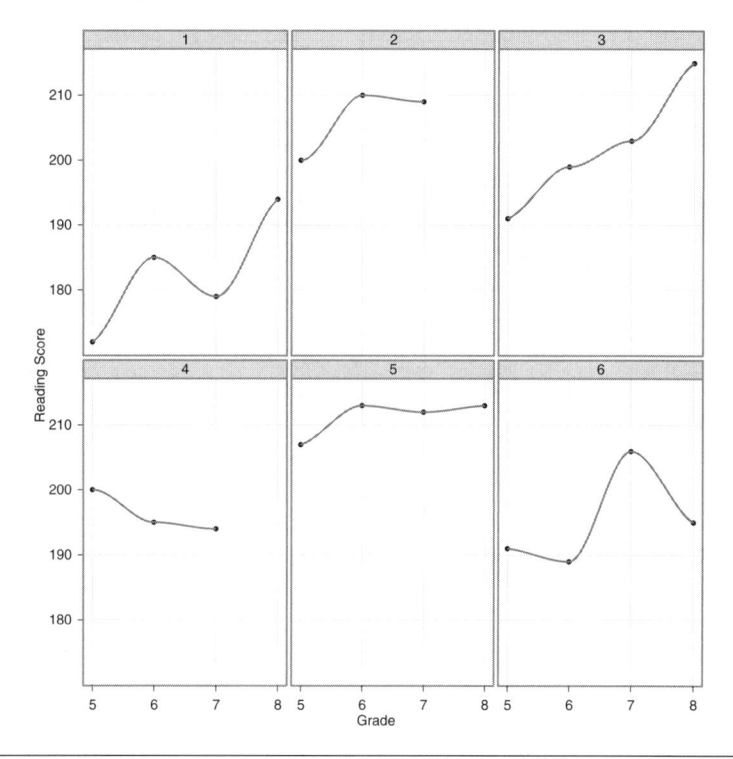

Figure 4.8 Smoothed individual curves and observed points for a subset of subjects.

4.4.1 CURVE OF THE MEANS

The fixed effects portion of LMER concerns mean change over time. Therefore, graphing of the curve of the means is important. This is especially true in exploratory research, where the researcher looks to the data to suggest the type of fixed effects model that might be specified. If the curve of the means is nonlinear, the researcher might consider using polynomials in the fixed effects portion of the model (see Chapter 12).

The curve of the means is drawn with `stat_summary()` using the arguments `fun.y=mean` and `geom="line"`. The `fun.y=mean` argument computes the mean of the response variable for each value of the time predictor, and `geom="line"` draws the line. The means are drawn as points by replacing the latter with `geom="point"`.

The syntax below draws the individual observed points and the curve of the means. The means are also drawn as points. Note that no grouping argument is used in `aes()`.

```
> g1 <- ggplot(data = MPLS.LS, aes(x = grade, y = read)) + geom_point(shape = 1) + myX + myY
> g2 <- g1 + stat_summary(fun.y = mean, geom = "line", lwd = 1.5, linetype = 5)
> g3 <- g2 + stat_summary(fun.y = mean, geom = "point", size=3, shape = 19)
> print(g3)
```

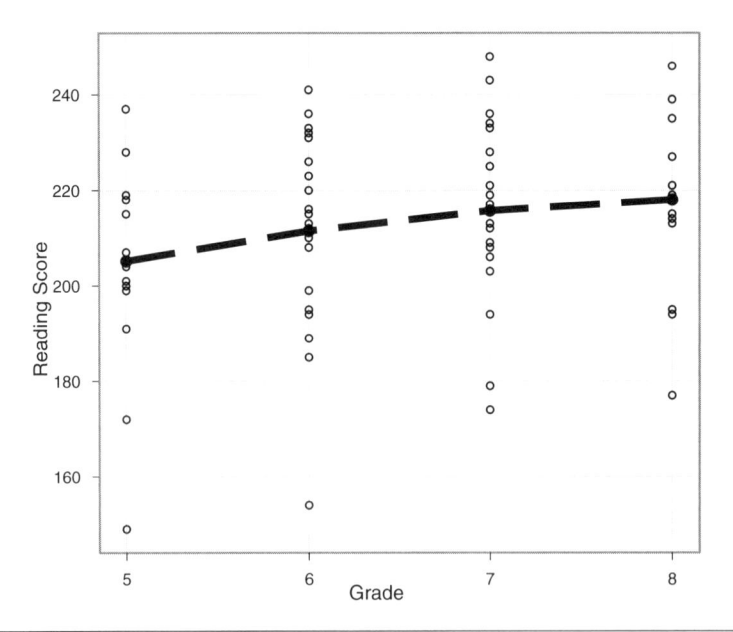

Figure 4.9 Curve of the means with observed points (open circles).

The graph is shown in Figure 4.9. The curve of the means increases over time. The increase is not linear, as there is some deceleration in the curve for the latter grades.

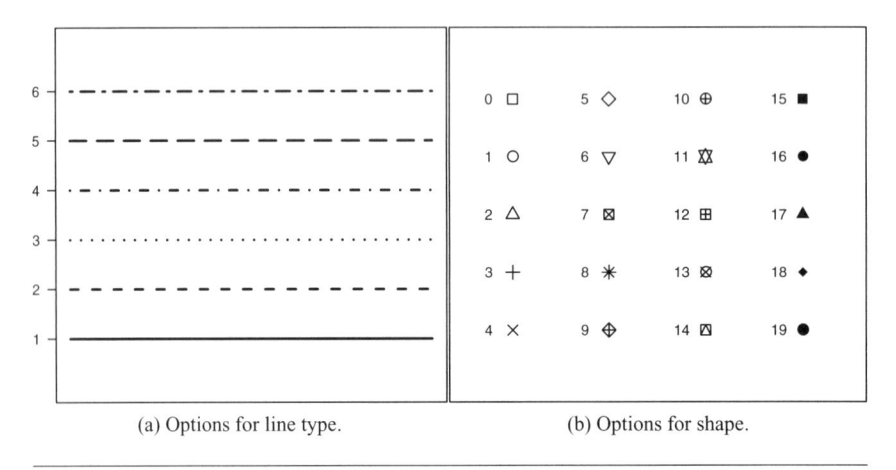

Figure 4.10 Line types, point shapes, and their selection values.

In the syntax above, the argument lwd= controls the line width, and line type= controls the type of line drawn. The arguments size= and shape= control the size and type of the points, respectively. Possible line types are shown in Figure 4.10a, along with the numbers used for their selection. Shape types are shown in Figure 4.10a with their corresponding numbers. The default

4.4 Graphing Group-Level Curves

line width and size is 1, and specifying larger numbers will increase things, whereas smaller numbers will decrease things.

4.4.1.1 MEAN CURVES AND UNBALANCED DATA

A potential complication regarding mean curves is data that are not balanced on time. Recall from the last chapter that unbalanced data refer to repeated measures that are not collected at the same time for all subjects. Such imbalance allows the possibility that the means at any one time point might be based on a very small number of subjects, perhaps only a single subject. Consequently, the mean curve can be very irregular or "bumpy," as there is little or no summarizing among subjects at the time points.

The MPLS.LS data frame is balanced on time, as all subjects are measured at the same grades (when observed). Imbalance is illustrated by adding a small amount of random noise to the grade scores. This is accomplished with the jitter() function.

In the syntax below, a new variable is created in the data frame, jgrade, which is the jittered values of grade. The first eight values of grade and jgrade are printed. The column bind function, cbind(), is used in the head() function to select the desired variables.

```
> ## Jitter grade.
> MPLS.LS$jgrade <- jitter(MPLS.LS$grade)
> ## Print variables.
> with(MPLS.LS, head(cbind(subid, grade, jgrade), n = 8))
```

```
     subid grade    jgrade
[1,]     1     5  5.176187
[2,]     1     6  5.818223
[3,]     1     7  7.011242
[4,]     1     8  8.156968
[5,]     2     5  5.020574
[6,]     2     6  5.982646
[7,]     2     7  7.182733
[8,]     2     8  7.981334
```

The output shows that jitter() adds a small random number to the original grade scores. The output lines [1,] and [5,] show that the first two subjects do not have the same score of jgrade for the first time point. The other output lines can be used to verify that the first two subjects do not have any jgrade scores in common. Thus, the jgrade scores are unbalanced on time.

To see the effect of imbalance on the mean curve, consider a graph of the reading scores plotted as a function of the jittered values of grade. The jgrade variable from the data frame is used, or jitter() can be used within ggplot(). The syntax below considers the former. The scatterplot is printed to illustrate the unbalanced nature of the data, and then the mean curve is drawn.

```
> g1 <- ggplot(data = MPLS.LS, aes(x = jgrade, y = read)) + geom_point()
> print(g1)
> g2 <- g1 + stat_summary(fun.y = mean, geom = "line")
> print(g2)
```

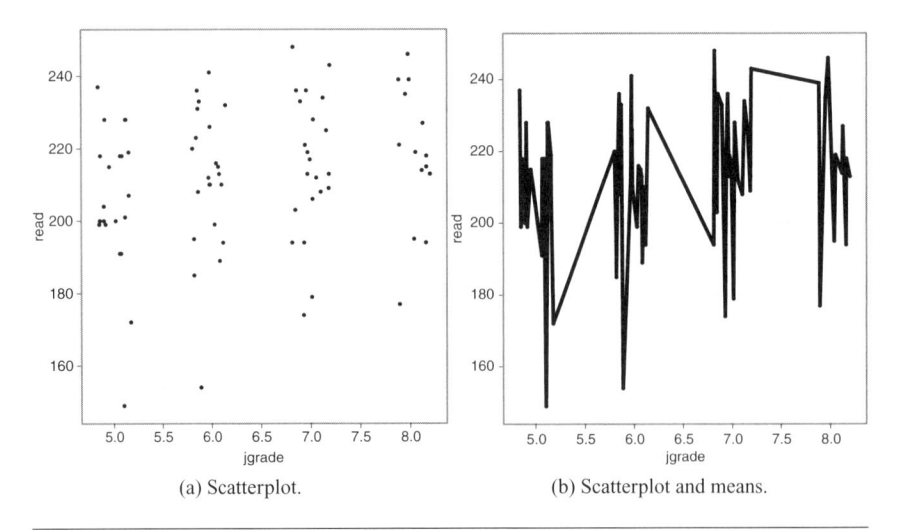

(a) Scatterplot.

(b) Scatterplot and means.

Figure 4.11 Graphs based on jittering grade.

The graphs are shown in Figure 4.11. The scatterplot in Figure 4.11a shows the unbalanced nature of the data. The reading scores are scattered along the grade axis and not arrayed in a series of single vertical columns, as in Figure 4.9. The graph of the means in Figure 4.11b shows many peaks and valleys in an icicle-like pattern.

The mean curve in Figure 4.11b does not provide much summarization, as it mainly connects the observed individual points. A more useful summary curve is based on a regression model, or based on local smoothing. In general, the latter types of curves are recommended for unbalanced data.

4.4.2 GRAPHING FITTED CURVES

Fitted curves based on the LM or local smoothing can be created for group-level data. The same syntax is used as with the individual-level curves, but the `group=` argument is omitted from `aes()`. There is a bit more to discuss with local smoothing compared to regression because the density of points at the group level allows for different degrees of smoothing.

4.4.2.1 REGRESSION CURVES

Fitted curves based on the LM are drawn using `lm()` within `stat_smooth()`. The `poly()` function is used to fit polynomial functions.

The syntax below fits a linear curve for the entire sample. The means are also drawn to get a sense of how well they correspond to the straight line.

4.4 Graphing Group-Level Curves

A new argument is introduced, "aspect.ratio" = 1, that produces a square graph rather than a rectangular graph. Square graphs can sometimes provide a better visual assessment of correspondence between observed points and fitted curves.

```
> g1 <- ggplot(data = MPLS.LS, aes(x = grade, y = read)) + geom_point(shape = 1)
> g2 <- g1 + stat_smooth(method = "lm", se = FALSE, lwd = 2) + myX + myY
> g3 <- g2 + stat_summary(fun.y = "mean", geom = "point", size = 4, shape = 19)
> g4 <- g3 + opts("aspect.ratio" = 1)
> print(g4)
```

The graph is shown in Figure 4.12a. The means closely correspond to the linear curve, showing only a small amount of scatter about the line.

The syntax below fits a quadratic curve at the group level. The means are again drawn as points.

```
> g1 <- ggplot(data = MPLS.LS, aes(x = grade, y = read)) + geom_point(shape = 1) + myX + myY
> g2 <- g1 + stat_smooth(method = "lm", formula = y ~ poly(x,2), se = FALSE, lwd = 2)
> g3 <- g2 + stat_summary(fun.y = "mean", geom = "point", size = 4, shape = 19)
> g4 <- g3 + opts("aspect.ratio" = 1)
> print(g4)
```

The graph is shown in Figure 4.12b. The group curve is bowed, and it passes through all the means.

Unlike the individual curves, it is possible to fit a cubic polynomial to the group data in the example. The reason is that the response variable column in the long-format data frame is treated in its entirety, rather than in subject blocks for the individual-level curves. As long as there are observed points at each grade, a cubic polynomial can be fit. It does not matter that individual subjects have missing data; what matters is that there are observed scores for each grade.

Although a cubic polynomial can be fit for the data in Figure 4.12b, this is undesirable for two reasons. First, the cubic polynomial is a saturated model, as the number of time points is equal to the number of β parameters (four). Second, the quadratic polynomial has near-perfect fit to the means, and there is no point in attempting an improvement.

4.4.2.2 SMOOTHED CURVES

Curves based on local smoothing are drawn with stat_smooth(). It is recommended that multiple curves with different degrees of smoothness be tried. This allows examination of how different curve features are affected by the smoothing. A peak or valley of a curve that is a salient feature under coarse smoothing may still be present when finer smoothing is used. This robustness underscores the importance of the feature. If, on the other hand, a peak or valley disappears under finer smoothing, the feature may not be particularly important.

One way to control the amount of smoothing is through the proportion of data points used in the local fitting, known as the *span*. The default is span = 0.75, and smaller values induce less smoothing, whereas larger values

(a) Linear polynomial.   (b) Quadratic polynomial.

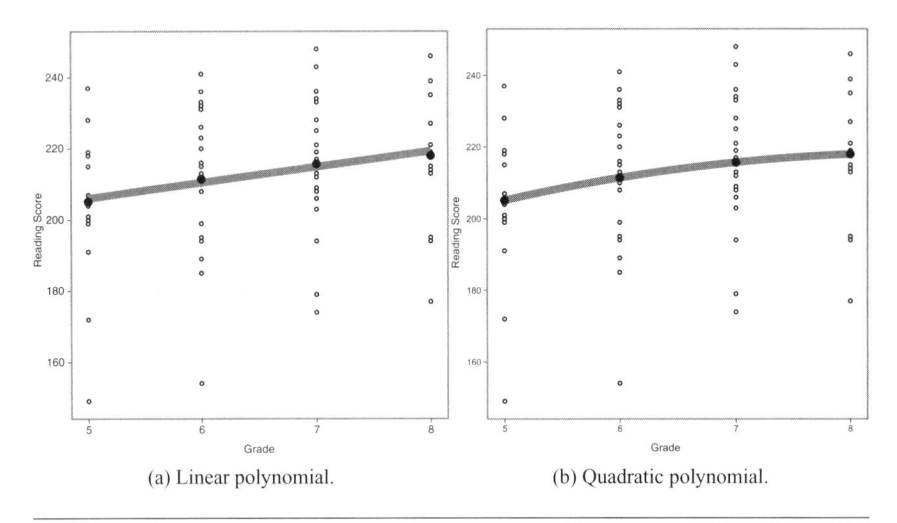

Figure 4.12 Group-level fitted curves based on polynomial regression.

induce greater smoothing. The span is controlled with the `span=` argument in `stat_smooth()`. Below, three graphs are constructed with span = 0.75 (default), 0.50, and 0.90.

```
> g1 <- ggplot(data = MPLS.LS, aes(x = grade, y = read)) + geom_point(shape = 1) + myX + myY
> g2 <- g1 + stat_summary(fun.y = "mean", geom = "point", size = 4, shape = 19)
> g3 <- g2 + stat_smooth(se = FALSE, lwd = 2)
> print(g3)

> g3 <- g2 + stat_smooth(se = FALSE, lwd = 2, span = .5)
> print(g3)
> g3 <- g2 + stat_smooth(se = FALSE, lwd = 2, span = .9)
> print(g3)
```

The graphs are shown in Figure 4.13. The lines based on default smoothing (Figure 4.13a), and span = 0.50 (Figure 4.13b), are more "wiggly" than the line with span = 0.90 (Figure 4.13c). In this example, the different amounts of smoothing do not appear to be particularly important. All three graphs reveal that the means increase, but the rate slows over time.

Local smoothing depends on the number of available observed points. When few observations are available, small span values might not provide enough local points for smoothing. In this case, an error message will be displayed in the console window, and no graphs will be constructed. Using span = 0.20 with the `MPLS` data frame produces such an error. Sometimes the data are so sparse that the default span value is too small to produce a graph. In this case, larger span values might be tried.

4.4.2.3 SMOOTHED CURVES AND UNBALANCED DATA

It was mentioned that smoothed curves and regression curves are more appropriate than mean curves for data unbalanced on time. As an illustration,

4.4 Graphing Group-Level Curves

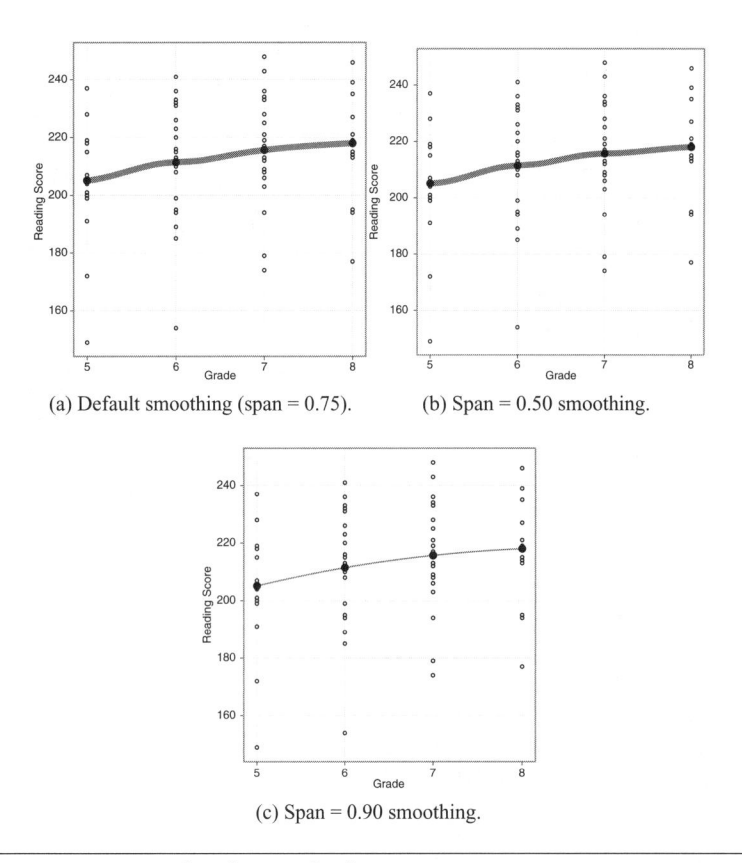

(a) Default smoothing (span = 0.75).

(b) Span = 0.50 smoothing.

(c) Span = 0.90 smoothing.

Figure 4.13 Group-level smoothed curves.

a smoothed curve is fit for the reading scores using the jittered grade variable, `jgrade`. Recall that the mean curve for this graph was very jagged, having an icicle-like pattern (see Figure 4.11b).

```
> g1 <- ggplot(data = MPLS.LS, aes(x = jgrade, y = read)) + geom_point()
> g2 <- g1 + stat_smooth(se = FALSE, lwd = 2) + myX + myY
> print(g2)
```

The graph appears in Figure 4.14. The smoothed curve does not display the peaks and valleys of the mean curve in Figure 4.11. In fact, the smoothed curve of Figure 4.14 is similar to the mean curve of the balanced data. This illustrates that the local smoothing algorithm is relatively resistant to the random noise introduced to the grade variable. For this reason, it is recommended that local smoothing be used routinely with unbalanced data.

4.4.3 GRAPHING INDIVIDUAL-LEVEL AND GROUP-LEVEL CURVES

Individual-level and group-level curves can be superimposed in the same graph. The advantage of such a graph is that the individual variability about

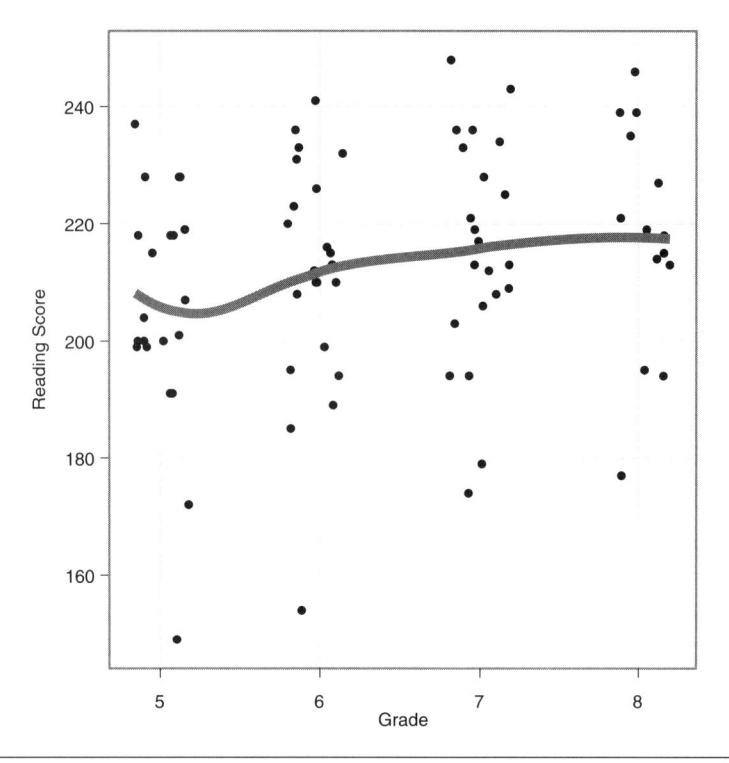

Figure 4.14 Smoothed curve for jittered grade values.

the mean trend can be examined. The key to constructing such graphs is multiple use of the `group=` argument in the aesthetic mapping. Using `group= subid` draws geometric objects for individual subjects, whereas `group=1` draws geometric objects for the entire sample.

In the syntax below, individual lines are drawn for the first six subjects. Then the mean curve and points are constructed based on the entire sample. This is done by using different `data=` and `group=` arguments in `aes()`.

```
> g1 <- ggplot(data = mysub6, aes(x = grade, y = read, group = subid)) + geom_line()
> g2 <- g1 + stat_summary(aes(data = MPLS.LS, group = 1), fun.y = "mean",
+                geom = "line", lwd = 2)
> g3 <- g2 + stat_summary(aes(data = MPLS.LS, group = 1), fun.y = "mean",
+                geom ="point", size = 4) + myX + myY
> print(g3)
```

The graph is shown in Figure 4.15. The individual lines are easy to trace, in contrast to when all the subject lines are drawn. The mean curve reflects the trend of the entire group.

4.5 Conditioning on Static Predictors

The previous sections considered unconditional change, meaning that lines and other geometric objects were not drawn conditional on static predictors.

4.5 Conditioning on Static Predictors

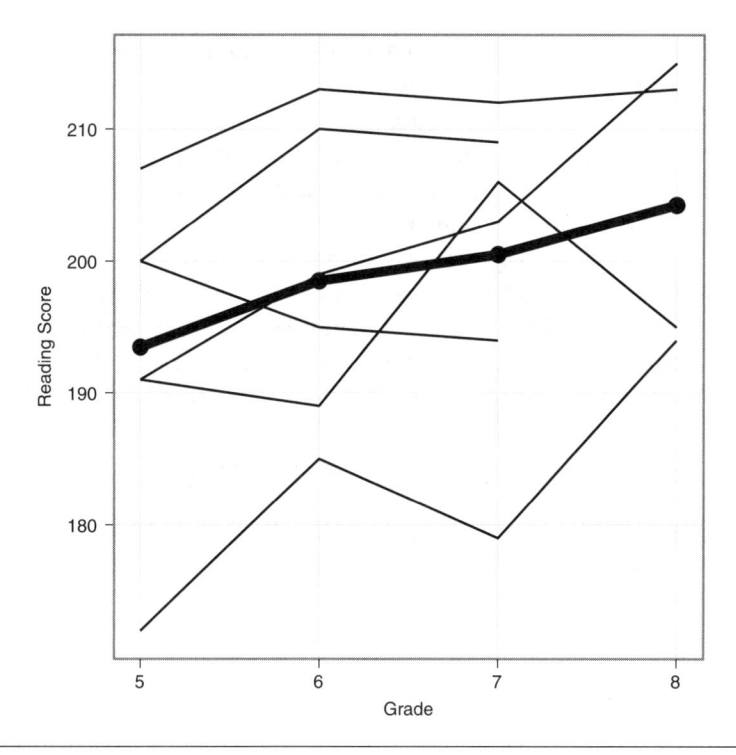

Figure 4.15 Superimposed individual curves (thin lines) and mean curve (thick line).

Another way of saying this is that the static predictors were ignored in the construction of the graphs. When static predictor effects are a priority in the analysis, it is useful to draw graphs based on the static predictor levels. In exploratory analysis, conditional graphs are used to suggest possible static predictor effects. In confirmatory analysis, conditional graphs are used to confirm preconceived notions about the predictor effects, or to investigate potential data anomalies, such as outliers.

Conditional graphs are easiest to construct when the static predictors are categorical. In this situation, a mean curve (or other type of curve) is computed for multiple subjects who are members of the same group. The number of groups is usually not too large, meaning all groups can be depicted in a relatively comprehensible manner.

Constructing conditional graphs with quantitative static predictors is more challenging. Usually there are no natural groups, and multiple individuals might not even share common values for the predictor. An example is provided by the attendance variable (att) in the MPLS.LS data frame. As shown in Table 1.6, each value of the variable is unique for a subject. In this case, it is obviously impossible to compute mean curves based on common values of att.

To make graphing manageable, it is recommended that values of quantitative static predictors be grouped. As mentioned previously, there is debate about the validity of grouping quantitative predictors in statistical analysis

(Gelman & Park, 2008; McClelland & Irwin, 2003). The opinion espoused here is that grouping is fine for constructing graphs, but the number of groups should be varied. This is to help ensure that the grouping does not egregiously misrepresent the nature of the original variable. For the LMER analysis discussed in future chapters, the full range of the quantitative predictor should be used, unless there is a compelling reason not to do so.

Since the creation of groups for quantitative predictors requires special attention, there is a separate discussion of conditional graphs for categorical and quantitative predictors. Similar to graphs already considered, curves for groups can be superimposed on the same graph, or faceted. For faceting based on static predictors, `facet_grid()` is used rather than `facet_wrap()`.

4.5.1 CATEGORICAL STATIC PREDICTORS

Conditional graphs are first considered with categorical static predictors. The focus is on drawing mean curves, but regression curves and smoothed curves can also be drawn.

4.5.1.1 SUPERIMPOSED CURVES

Superimposed mean curves are drawn by providing the static categorical predictor as the conditioning variable in the `group=` argument of the aesthetic component of `stat_summary()`. In contrast to superimposed individual curves, it is helpful to draw different line types and/or point shapes for different groups. A legend is required to identify which group is associated with a particular line/point.

Different line types are drawn by supplying the static predictor name in the `line=` argument of the aesthetic component. Different point shapes are drawn using `shape=` in the aesthetic component. By supplying either or both, a legend is automatically constructed. In addition, if either argument is used, the `group=` argument with the static predictor is not necessary.

Consider the example of mean curves for the dichotomous risk groups based on `risk2`. In the syntax below, the individual observed points are drawn along with the mean curves. The argument `shape=risk2` draws different symbols for the observed points based on the groups. The argument `line=risk2` draws different mean lines for the groups and creates a legend. The component `scale_shape_manual()` is used to specify shapes 1 and 19 from Figure 4.10b for the groups; the line types are chosen automatically.

```
> g1 <- ggplot(data = MPLS.LS, aes(x = grade, y = read, line = risk2)) + geom_point()
> g2 <- g1 + stat_summary(fun.y = mean, aes(line = risk2), geom="line") + myX + myY
> g3 <- g2 + scale_shape_manual(values = c(1, 19))
> print(g3)
```

The graph is shown in Figure 4.16a. The graph indicates that the advantaged group mean is greater than the disadvantaged group mean at Grade 5.

4.5 Conditioning on Static Predictors

The disadvantaged group has a mean increase that is nearly linear. The advantaged group has a mean increase to Grade 7, and then a slight decrease to Grade 8.

By default, the legend is drawn on the right, outside the graph region. The title of the legend is the label of the static predictor (risk2), and the legend key values are the data values (ADV and DADV).

The legend is customized and placed inside the plot area using arguments in opts(). The legend title and values are easiest to change by making a new variable in the data frame. The following syntax performs the customization, along with the drawing of points for the mean values using stat_summary().

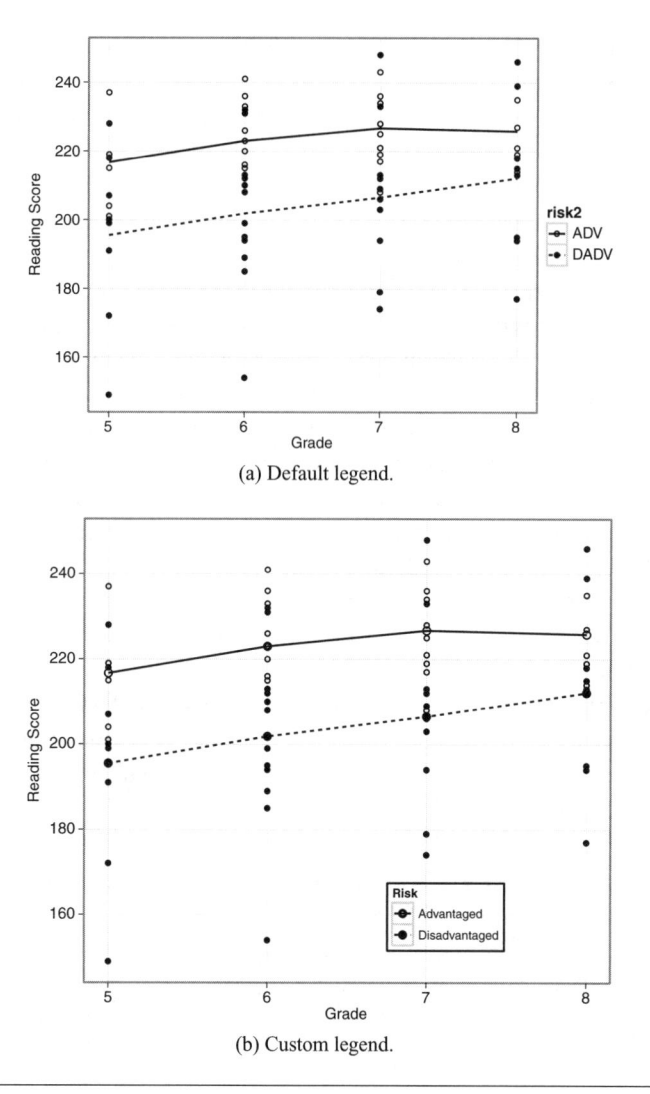

(a) Default legend.

(b) Custom legend.

Figure 4.16 Mean curves by risk group.

```
> ## New variable.
> MPLS.LS$Risk  <- MPLS.LS$risk2
> levels(MPLS.LS$Risk)  <- c("Advantaged", "Disadvantaged")
> ## Custom graph.
> g1  <- ggplot(data = MPLS.LS, aes(x = grade, y = read, shape = Risk)) + geom_point()
> g2  <- g1 + stat_summary(fun.y = mean, aes(line = Risk), geom = "line") + myX + myY
> g3  <- g2 + stat_summary(aes(shape = Risk), fun.y = mean, geom = "point", size = 3)
> g4  <- g3 + opts(legend.position = c(.7, .22), legend.background = theme_rect())
> g5  <- g4 + scale_shape_manual(values = c(1, 19))
> print(g5)
```

The customized graph is shown in Figure 4.16b. The legend position was determined by trial and error. The `theme_rect()` argument draws a rectangle around the legend. In the optional section below, additional customizations are shown.

4.5.1.2 COMBINATIONS OF STATIC PREDICTORS

In certain cases, the researcher may want to examine an interaction among the static predictors. LMER models for such interactions are discussed in Chapter 11. An interaction among the static predictors means that different combinations of static predictors have different effects. For example, reading scores may be different for disadvantaged students who are also receiving special education services. This is in contrast to disadvantaged students who are not receiving such services.

Mean curves are drawn for combinations of static predictors by specifying an interaction among the static predictors in the `line=` argument. Shapes are drawn in a similar fashion with the `shape=` argument. An interaction is specified by using a colon (:) to separate the predictor names.

Suppose the goal is to graph the mean curves of groups defined by the combination of gender and ethnicity. To simplify matters, a dichotomous version of ethnicity is created, `eth2`. The variable has the levels White (W) and non-White (NW). There are four groups defined by the combination of `gen` and `eth2`: F/NW, F/W, M/NW, and M/W.

Prior to graphing the mean curves, it is good to examine a cross-tabulation of the number of subjects who fall in each group. Groups with counts equal to 0 will not be graphed.

In the syntax below, the factor variable `eth2` is created with the `ifelse()` function and saved in the data frame. Then a cross-tabulation with `gen` is produced using the `table()` function. The static predictor scores for Grade 5 are selected using the `with()` function.

```
> ## Dichotomous ethnicity.
> MPLS.LS$eth2  <- factor(ifelse(MPLS.LS$eth == "Whi",yes = "W",no = "NW"))
> ## Save the data frame.
> save(MPLS.LS, file="C:/Mine/MPLS.LS.Rdata")
> ## Cross-tabulation.
> with(MPLS.LS[MPLS.LS$grade == 5, ], table(gen, eth2))
        eth2
    gen NW W
      F  9 5
      M  4 4
```

4.5 Conditioning on Static Predictors

The output shows the following frequencies: `F/NW` = 9, `F/W` = 5, `M/NW` = 4, and `M/W` = 4. There is a sufficient count of subjects in each cross-classification to proceed with graphing of the groups.

In the syntax below, two `stat_summary()` components are used to draw lines and points. In the aesthetic mapping, the interaction between the two static predictors is specified as `gen:eth2`. For simplicity, the individual points are not drawn, and the legend is repositioned inside the graph area.

```
> g1 <- ggplot(data = MPLS.LS, aes(x = grade, y = read)) + myX + myY
> g2 <- g1 + stat_summary(fun.y = mean, aes(line = gen : eth2), geom = "line")
> g3 <- g2 + stat_summary(fun.y = mean, aes(shape = gen : eth2),geom = "point",size= 3)
> g4 <- g3 + opts(legend.position = c(.55, .35), legend.background = theme_rect())
> print(g4)
```

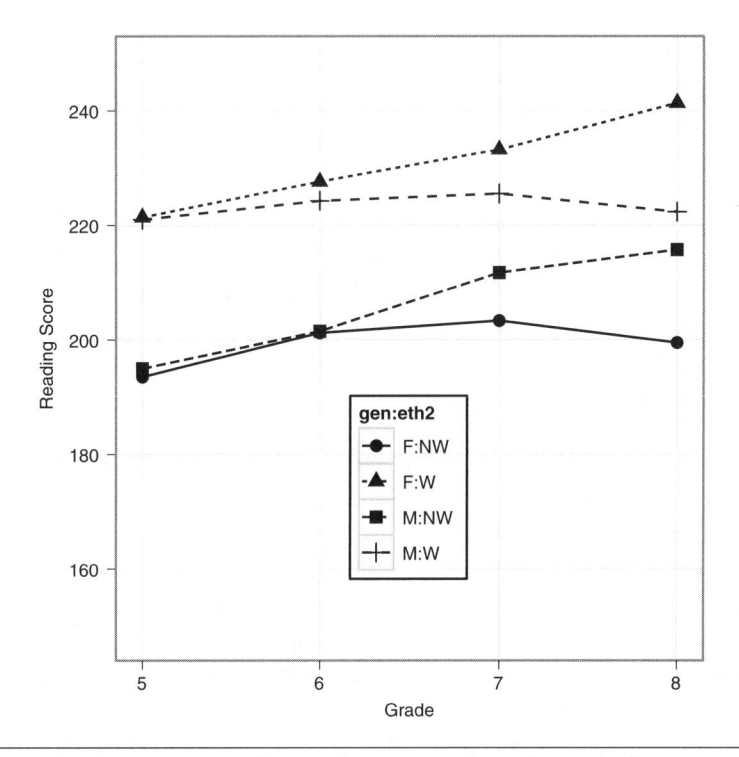

Figure 4.17 Mean curves for combinations of gender and ethnicity.

The graph is shown in Figure 4.17. Overall, the curves for the White students are higher than those for the non-White students. For the White students, females and males have starting values that are nearly equal. White females have increasing means over time, whereas White males have a concave-down pattern with respect to the grade axis. For non-White students, the starting values are also approximately equal. The non-White males have increasing means over time, whereas the non-White females have a concave-down pattern.

4.5.1.3 FACETING

Faceting based on static predictors is performed with `facet_grid()`. Faceting can be by rows or columns with a single static predictor, or both rows and columns with multiple static predictors.

Tilde (~) notation is used with `facet_grid()`, such that row faceting is specified before the tilde and column faceting after the tilde. A period indicates that no faceting occurs for a dimension. For example, `facet_grid(gen~.)` will facet the rows by gender, and `facet_grid(.~gen)` will facet the columns by gender. To facet rows by gen and columns by eth2, the syntax is `facet_grid(gen~eth2)`.

Examples of faceting are first considered with a single static predictor, gender. The syntax below draws individual change curves and mean curves. The faceting is by columns, producing side-by-side graphs.

```
> g1 <- ggplot(data = MPLS.LS, aes(x = grade, y = read, group = subid)) + geom_line()
> g2 <- g1 + stat_summary(fun.y = mean, aes(group = 1), geom = "line", lwd = 3)
> g3 <- g2 + facet_grid(. ~ gen) + myX + myY
> print(g3)
```

The graph is shown in Figure 4.18a. The mean curves are the thick lines, and the subject curves are the thin lines. The graph shows that the initial mean for females is less than that for males. Both mean curves increase over time, and they have approximately the same final value because the male curve plateaus beginning at Grade 7. The individual curves indicate greater variability for females, at least for initial values, as the female curves are more dispersed about the vertical axis.

The title of each facet is based on the value of the static predictor. The title can be changed by creating a new factor variable with the desired value labels in the data frame, as shown previously.

In addition to the facets for the levels of the predictor, a panel for the marginal group is included using `margins=TRUE`. The marginal group is the entire sample, or the unconditional group. The marginal group is useful to include as a point of reference, or to provide information about conditional and unconditional change in the same figure.

In the syntax below, a copy of the gender variable is made, and then the label names are changed from "F" and "M" to the more descriptive "Female" and "Male." The new variable, gen2, is used in `facet_grid()` to create new facet titles. The `margins=TRUE` argument is used to include the graph for the unconditional group.[1]

---

[1] The `margins=TRUE` feature is disabled in `ggplot2` Version 0.8.9, available as of this writing. The feature should be fixed in later versions. An alternative is to copy the data frame, relabel gen2 as (all), stack the original data frame and the altered data frame, and use `ggplot()` on the result. The syntax for relabeling and stacking is the following:

```
MPLS.LSa <- MPLS.LS                      # Copy data frame.
MPLS.LSa$gen2 <- "(all)"                 # Relabel gen2.
plotdata <- rbind(MPLS.LS, MPLS.LSa)     # Stack data frames.
```

4.5 Conditioning on Static Predictors 137

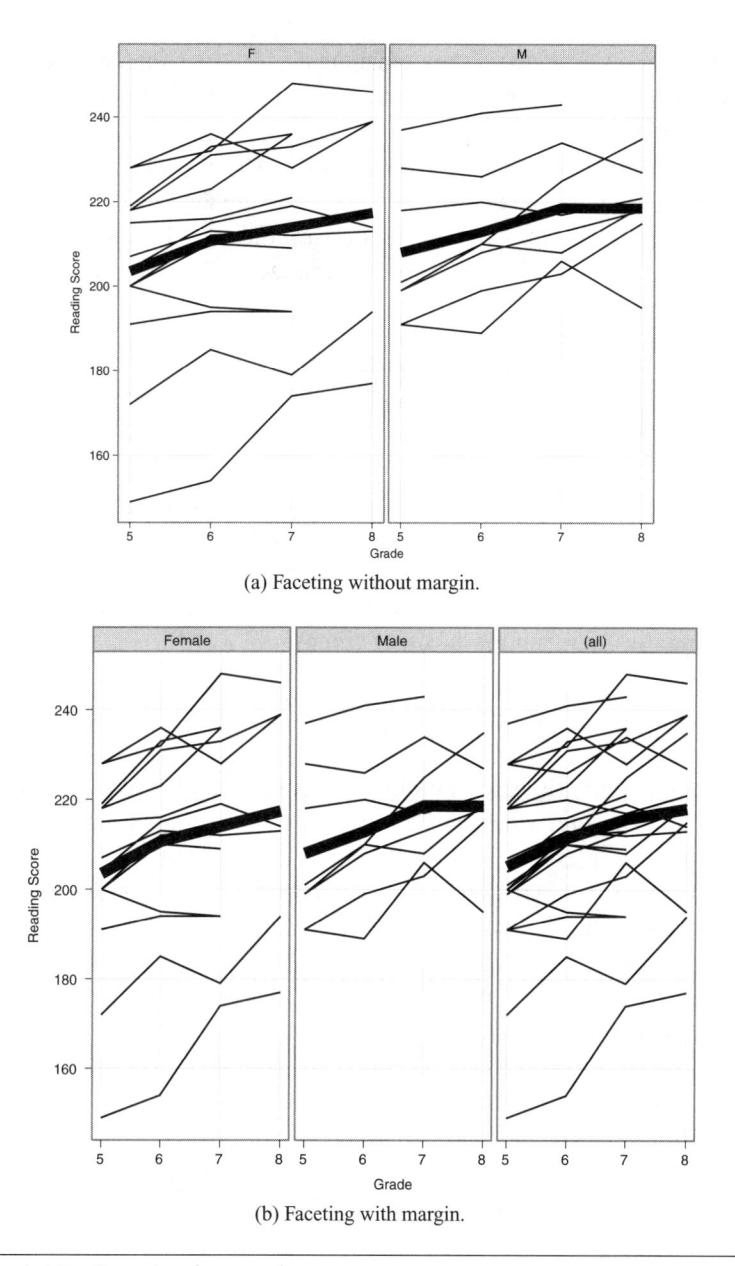

(a) Faceting without margin.

(b) Faceting with margin.

Figure 4.18 Faceting by gender.

```
> ## Make copy of gen2.
> MPLS.LS$gen2 ← MPLS.LS$gen
> levels(MPLS.LS$gen2) ← c("Female", "Male")
> ## New graph.
> g3 ← g2 + facet_grid(. ~ gen2, margins = TRUE)
> print(g3)
```

The resulting graph is shown in Figure 4.18b. The marginal group is labeled as (all). The labels of the new gender variable are used for the titles in the other two panels. The figure shows that the mean curves for the gender groups are similar to the curve of the marginal group. This similarity suggests that the differences between the gender groups might be the result of sampling error, but this cannot be determined in any definitive sense from the graphs.

Faceting can be based on two static predictors. In the syntax below, faceting is by rows for eth2 and by columns for gen. Individual and mean curves are drawn, and the value labels of eth2 are changed to be more descriptive.

```
> levels(MPLS.LS$eth2)  <- c("Non-White", "White")
> g1 <- ggplot(data = MPLS.LS, aes(x = grade, y = read, group = subid)) + geom_line()
> g2 <- g1 + stat_summary(fun.y = mean, geom = "line", lwd = 2, aes(group = 1))
> g3 <- g2 + facet_grid(eth2 ~ gen2) + myX + myY
> print(g3)
```

The graph is shown in Figure 4.19a. Four panels are shown based on the combination of levels of the two static predictors. The mean trends are the same as in the superimposed graph discussed in Section 4.5.1.1. The upper left panel shows there is greater vertical spread of the individual curves for non-White females than for the other groups.

4.5.1.4 SUPERIMPOSING AND FACETING

When conditioning is based on more than one static predictor, presentation is sometimes clearer when curves are superimposed and faceted. The syntax below illustrates this for the gender and ethnicity variables, with faceting by ethnicity and superimposed mean curves for gender. Individual curves are suppressed for clarity of presentation. Two scale_() arguments are used to rename the legend title and specify open shapes, and then the legend is boxed and placed in the graph area with opts(). The components scale_linetype() and scale_shape() are used to name the legend title. The argument solid=FALSE in scale_shape() produces the open shapes (i.e., shapes that are not filled).

```
> g1 <- ggplot(data = MPLS.LS, aes(x = grade, y = read)) + myY + myX
> g2 <- g1 + stat_summary(fun.y = mean, aes(line = gen2), geom = "line")
> g3 <- g2 + stat_summary(fun.y = mean, aes(shape = gen2), geom = "point", size = 3)
> g4 <- g3 + opts(legend.position = c(.78,.3), legend.background = theme_rect())
> g5 <- g4 + scale_linetype(name = "Gender") + scale_shape(name = "Gender", solid = FALSE)
> g6 <- g5 + facet_grid(. ~ eth2)
> print(g6)
```

The graph is shown in Figure 4.19b. The comparison of the female and male mean curves is easier than in the previous two graphs that considered the four groups. It can be seen that for non-White subjects, males increase over time, whereas females have a concave-down pattern. For White subjects, females increase over time, and males have a concave-down pattern. The faceting underscores overall ethnic differences, with the curves for the White subjects shifting higher on the vertical axis than the curves for the non-White subjects.

4.5 Conditioning on Static Predictors

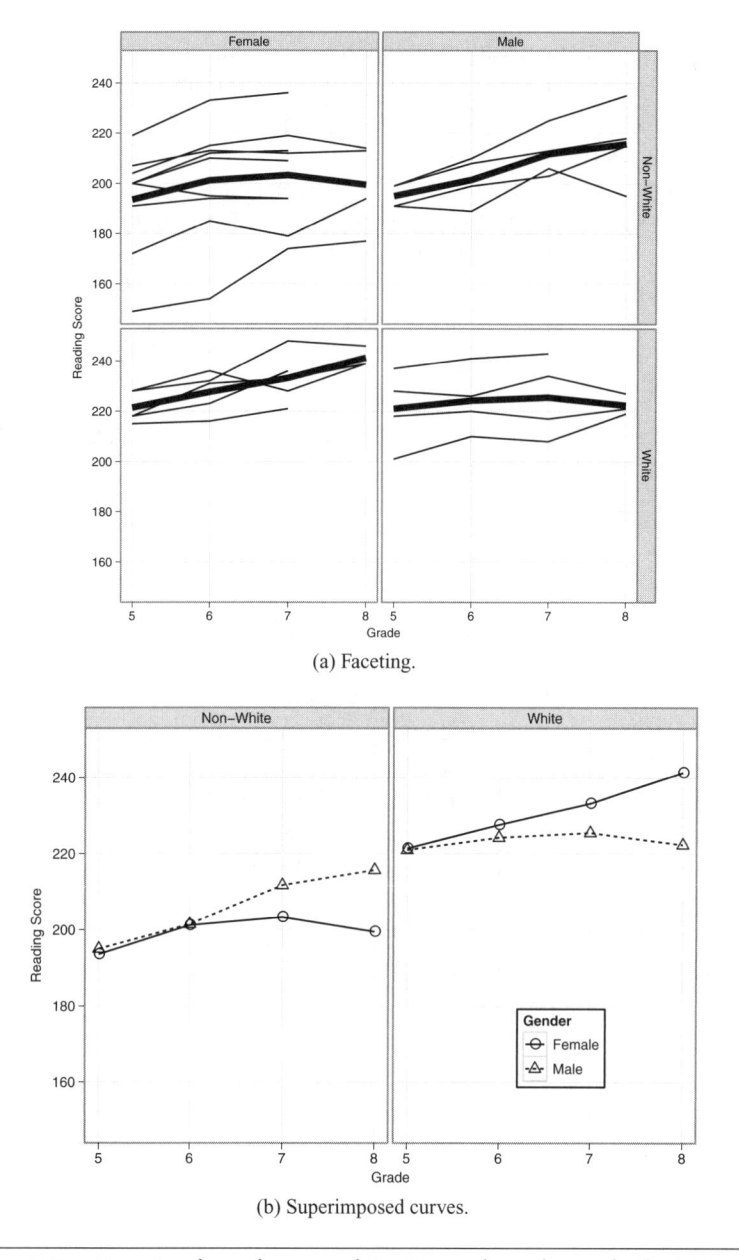

(a) Faceting.

(b) Superimposed curves.

Figure 4.19 Faceting based on combinations of gender and ethnicity.

4.5.2 QUANTITATIVE STATIC PREDICTORS

When the goal is to construct conditional graphs based on a quantitative static predictor, such as attendance proportion, then the values must be grouped. Once the grouping is performed, all the graphs in the preceding sections can be constructed.

Grouping is accomplished with the `cut_interval()` and `cut_number()` functions in the `ggplot2` package. The `cut_interval()`

function divides a quantitative variable into intervals of equal length based on the optional argument n=. The `cut_number()` function divides a quantitative variable into unequal intervals, with equal numbers of observations or counts based on n=; see Chapter 3.

The functions are best illustrated with many more subjects than in the MPLS data set. Therefore, data will be simulated, and the functions will be used with n=4 to create four groups. Data for $N = 100$ subjects are generated from a normal distribution, with $\mu = 100$ and $\sigma = 15$. The `table()` function is used to examine what each function does. First consider `cut_interval()`.

```
> set.seed(123)                              # Enables replication of results.
> x <- rnorm(n = 100, mean = 100, sd = 15)   # 100 scores from normal distribution.
> table(cut_interval(x, n = 4))
```

[65.4,82.2]	(82.2,99.1]	(99.1,116]	(116,133]
7	39	39	15

There are two rows to the output. The top row indicates the limits of the intervals that define the groups. The bottom row is the count or frequency of cases in each group. Notice the counts are not equal for the groups. Four groups were constructed based on the intervals in the top row of the output. A bracket, [or], means the limit is included. A parenthesis, (or), means the limit is not included. The distance of the intervals is determined from the first one, as both limits are included. In this case, $82.2 - 65.4 = 16.8$, so the distribution is cut into four intervals of this length. It is difficult to verify this length from the other limits, as the lower number is not included.

Now consider `cut_number()`, which creates groups of equal frequency. The interval length is allowed to vary. Using n=4 means that four groups of equal frequency are formed.

```
> table(cut_number(x, n = 4))
```

[65.4,92.6]	(92.6,101]	(101,110]	(110,133]
25	25	25	25

The output shows that there are 25 subjects in each group. The intervals narrow or widen to accommodate the equal frequencies.

It is not always the case that `cut_interval()` and `cut_number()` will be able to construct groups of equal interval or equal frequency. The ability to do so is dependent on the sample size and data characteristics, such as tied values (repeated values). For the MPLS.LS example, the sample size is small ($N = 22$), and there are a number of repeated values for the att median, which is 0.97. This can be verified by using the `median()` and `table()` functions. Using the `with()` function, the observations at Grade 5 are selected to avoid repeated values for the same subject.

4.5 Conditioning on Static Predictors

```
> with(MPLS.LS[MPLS.LS$grade == 5,], median(att))
```
```
[1] 0.97
```

```
> with(MPLS.LS[MPLS.LS$grade == 5,], table(att))
```
```
att
0.85 0.88  0.9 0.91 0.94 0.95 0.96 0.97 0.98 0.99    1
   1    1    1    1    1    1    4    5    3    2    2
```

The output shows there are five scores for the median. If cut_number() is used with n=2 to create a median split, the counts will not be equal in the groups. The median values will be binned with the smaller values for the first group, and all the values greater than the median will be binned for the second group. The output shows that the count of the second group will be $3 + 2 + 2 = 7$, so the count of the first group will be $22 - 7 = 15$.

Consider forming the groups using cut_number(att, n=2). The table() function is used in the syntax to see the counts of the groups.

```
> with(MPLS.LS[MPLS.LS$grade == 5,], table(cut_number(att, n = 2)))
```
```
[0.85,0.97]    (0.97,1]
         15          7
```

The output verifies what was said above. The first group has the 15 subjects whose att score is equal to or less than the median. The second group has the 7 subjects whose score is above the median.

Some ggplot2 methods, such as faceting, will only work with variables in a data frame. This means the grouping variable must be created in the data frame, in order to use it for faceting. The cut_number() and cut_interval() functions create factor variables with level labels such as those in the table() output above. The level labels are changed with the levels() function.

In the following syntax, a two-group version of attendance proportion is created, att2. The levels are named, and then a conditional graph is constructed.

```
> MPLS.LS$att2 <- cut_number(MPLS.LS$att, n = 2)               # Create groups.
> levels(MPLS.LS$att2) <- c("Low Attendance", "High Attendance")  # Name levels.
> g1 <- ggplot(data = MPLS.LS, aes(x = grade, y = read, group = subid)) + geom_line()
> g2 <- g1 + stat_summary(fun.y = mean, geom = "line", lwd = 3, aes(group = 1))
> g3 <- g2 + facet_grid(. ~ att2) + myY + myX
> print(g3)
```

The graph is shown in Figure 4.20a. The thin lines are individual change curves, and the thick lines are mean curves. The mean curves show that those in the low group start at a smaller value on average. For both groups, there is an increase over time, though not in a linear fashion. There is more vertical

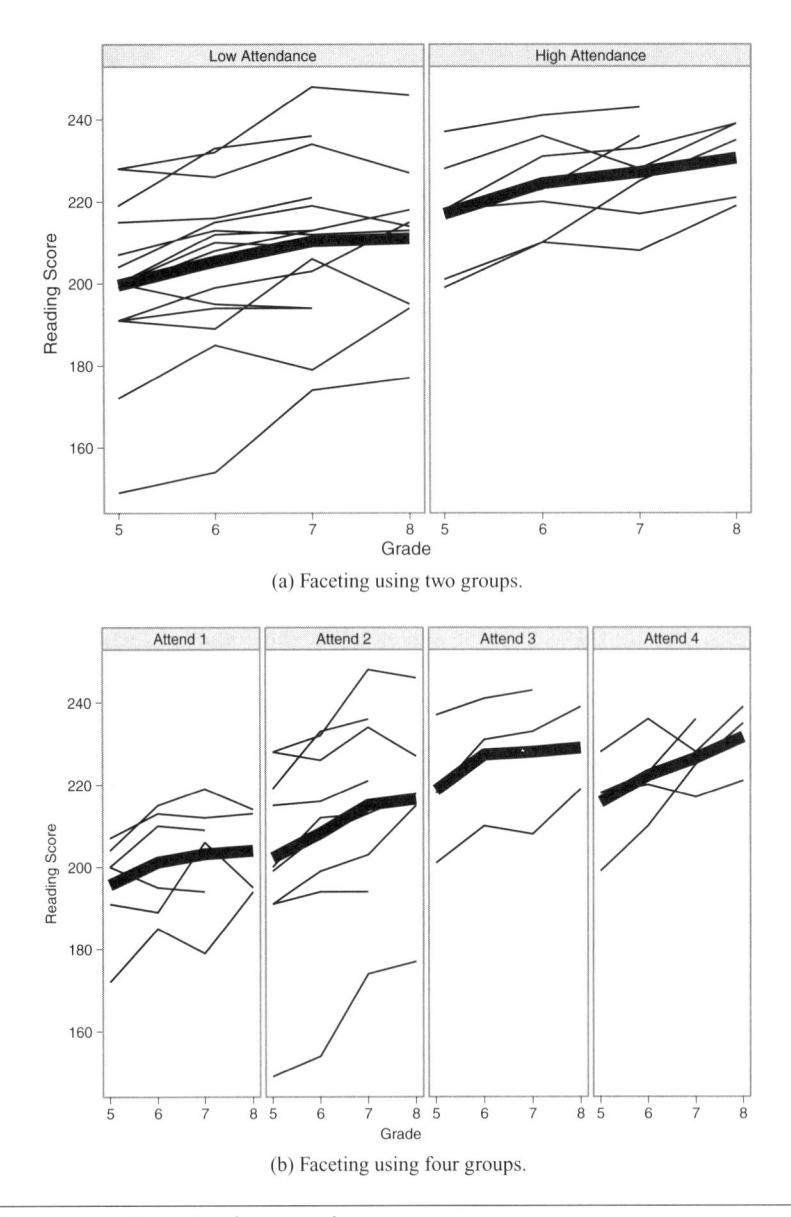

Figure 4.20 Faceting by attendance.

spread among the individual change curves in the low group, but this might be tempered by the fact that this group has more than twice the subjects as the high group.

Using two groups for attendance might be misleading because the variance of the original variable is misrepresented by the grouping. There may be, for example, important differences among subjects with different attendance proportions in the low group, which is currently hidden.

To thoroughly investigate the effects of a static quantitative predictor, it is suggested that multiple groups be formed when possible (e.g., four or more).

In the syntax below, a four-group version of attendance is constructed, `att4`. The levels are numbered, and the new variable is used for faceting.

```
> MPLS.LS$att4 <- cut_number(MPLS.LS$att, n = 4)
> levels(MPLS.LS$att4) <- c("Attend 1", "Attend 2", "Attend 3", "Attend 4")
> g1 <- ggplot(data = MPLS.LS, aes(x = grade, y = read, group = subid)) + geom_line()
> g2 <- g1 + stat_summary(fun.y = mean, geom = "line", lwd = 3, aes(group = 1))
> g3 <- g2 + facet_grid(. ~ att4) + myY + myX
> print(g3)
```

The graph is shown in Figure 4.20b. The four panels reveal information that was not apparent in the two-panel graph, Figure 4.20a. The graph shows that the starting level of the mean curve varies by attendance level, with the two highest levels (Attend 1 and Attend 2) having equal starting points. Thus, there might be important variation among smaller values of attendance.

4.6 Customizing Graphs*

There are several methods available for customizing graphs produced with `ggplot2`. In this optional section, some of the possible customizations for axes, facets, and legends are discussed. Additional customizations are presented in Wickham (2009b) and in the online reference manual at http://had.co.nz/ggplot2/.

4.6.1 CUSTOMIZING AXES*

A common customization for axes is to change the default limits on the range of values. In `ggplot2`, a distinction is made between *zooming* and *limiting*. Zooming changes the range of values that are displayed, and all values are used in any computations. Limiting changes the values that are displayed *and* changes the values used for computations. With limiting, any observations not seen are excluded from any calculations. On the other hand, zooming includes the hidden observations in calculations.

Limiting is performed with the `limits=` argument in `scale_y_continuous()` and `scale_x_continuous()`. The x and y refer to the horizontal and vertical axes, respectively. For example, the following syntax will limit the range of values of the response to (200, 220), and only values in that interval will be used for computing the means.

```
> g1 <- ggplot(data = MPLS.LS, aes(x = grade, y = read, group = subid)) + geom_points()
> g2 <- g1 + stat_summary(fun.y = mean, geom = "line", lwd = 3, aes(group = 1))
> g3 <- g2 + scale_y_continuous(limits = c(200, 220))
```

Zooming is accomplished with `coord_cartesian()` using the arguments `ylim=` or `xlim=`. The following syntax will display response values in the interval (200, 220), but all response values will be used for computing the means.

```
> g1 <- ggplot(data = MPLS.LS, aes(x = grade, y = read, group = subid)) + geom_points()
> g2 <- g1 + stat_summary(fun.y = mean, geom = "line", lwd = 3, aes(group = 1))
> g3 <- g2 + coord_cartesian(ylim = c(200, 220))
```

It is remarked that zooming is probably preferable to limiting. Coordinates are usually changed for aesthetic reasons rather than to exclude values from calculations.

4.6.2 CUSTOMIZING FACETS*

In all the faceting examples considered, the scales of the axes were constant (or fixed) among facets. Sometimes it is preferable to allow the scales of the axes of facets to vary, which is to make them "free." This can be accomplished by using the `scales=` argument in `facet_grid()` or `facet_wrap()`. The following list shows the syntax for particular scalings.

- Allow both axes to vary by facet: `scales = ''free''`
- Allow the *x*-axis to vary by facet: `scales_x = ''free''`
- Allow the *y*-axis to vary by facet: `scales_y = ''free''`

The argument `space=` is used with the same keywords to allow different spacing within facets.

4.6.3 CUSTOMIZING THE LEGEND*

Lines and points can be color-coded based on a static predictor, and the color scheme will be used in the construction of the legend. Color coding is accomplished using the `colour=` argument in the aesthetic mapping; note the British spelling of *colour*. Color palettes are available in ggplot2, and they will be selected automatically if additional syntax is omitted.

Additional color palettes are available in the `RColorBrewer` package, written by Erich Neuwirth (Neuwirth, 2007). To access these palettes, the component `scale_colour_brewer()` is used with the `palette=` argument. The `scale_colour_grey()` component is used to do the same with gray shading; note the variant spelling of *grey*. The following syntax color-codes the gender mean curves and uses an alternative color scheme. For brevity, the graph is not shown.

```
> g1 <- ggplot(data = MPLS.LS, aes(x = grade, y = read))
> g2 <- g1 + stat_summary(fun.y = mean, geom = "line", lwd = 3, aes(colour = gen))
> g3 <- g2 + scale_colour_brewer(palette = 3)
```

The horizontal and vertical orientation of the legend is changed using `hjust=` and `vjust=`. The size and color of the legend title and legend labels are controlled, respectively, using the following arguments:

- `opts(legend.title = theme_text(size = 4, colour = "grey80"))`
- `opts(legend.text = theme_text(size = 3, colour = "red"))`

A list of colors is available on the Internet, for example, http://www.stat.columbia.edu/ tzheng/files/Rcolor.pdf.

The background of the legend is shaded or colored using the following syntax:

- `opts(legend.background = theme_rect(fill = "grey80"))`

As shown previously, the legend label and values are most easily changed by creating a new variable in the data frame. An alternative is to use the appropriate `scale_manual()` arguments. These arguments are also used to change additional features, such as the shape of points and the type of lines. If two types of geometric objects are used in the same graph, it is important to use the same names for the legend titles and values, or separate legends will be drawn for each object.

Consider the graph of `reading` trajectories by `risk2` discussed in Section 4.5.1.1. The following syntax is used to rename the title legend as "Risk Group," rename the value labels as "Advantaged" and "Disadvantaged," and set the line types to 1 and 2 in Figure 4.10a, and point types 1 and 19 in Figure 4.10b. Pound signs (#) demarcate the components that customize the lines and points.

```
> g1 <- ggplot(data = MPLS.LS, aes(x = grade, y = read, shape = risk2)) + geom_point()
> g2 <- g1 + stat_summary(fun.y = mean, aes(line = risk2), geom = "line") + myX + myY
> ################################################################################
> g3 <- g2 + scale_linetype_manual(name = "Risk Group", values = c(1, 2),
+        breaks = c("ADV", "DADV"), labels = c("Advantaged", "Disadvantaged"))
> g4 <- g3 + scale_shape_manual(name = "Risk Group", values = c(1, 19),
+        breaks = c("ADV", "DADV"), labels = c("Advantaged", "Disadvantaged"))
> ################################################################################
> g5 <- g4 + opts(legend.position = c(.7,.22), legend.background = theme_rect())
> print(g5)
```

The numbers for the line types and point types are found in Figure 4.10. Additional customization of points, line types, and legends is possible; see Wickham (2009b).

4.7 Summary of ggplot2 Components

A summary of the main `ggplot2` components discussed in this chapter is shown in Table 4.1. The component or function appears in the first column, followed by a description, and then arguments that were mentioned in the chapter.

Introduction to Linear Mixed Effects Regression 5

Chapter 1 presented a conceptual overview of LMER. In this chapter, details of LMER are presented, along with examples of data analysis using the MPLS data set.

The chapter begins with a review of traditional regression and the LM. The reason for this approach is that LMER can be viewed as an extension of traditional regression to the case of longitudinal data. Specific examples of traditional regression are presented, with an eye toward transitioning to LMER. The lm() function for estimating an LM is discussed, as many of the syntax conventions are also used in estimating a LMER model.

After presentation of the specific LM examples, parallel cases for LMER are discussed. Focus is on models that have only a time predictor and models that add a categorical static predictor. The lmer() function for estimating a LMER model is presented, and details of the output are examined. The output of the LM and LMER solutions is compared.

Following up on the presentation in Chapter 1, additional details of random effects and their role in LMER are discussed. Two conceptualizations of random effects are presented, one focusing on a partitioning of the LMER error term and another focusing on a subject-specific model. To illustrate the latter, a hierarchical, or *multilevel model* depiction of LMER is introduced.

Rather than present general formulas for LMER, the focus in this chapter is on special cases. General formulas can be abstract for the novice, and it is useful to start with models commonly used in longitudinal analysis. Extensions to more complex situations are considered in later chapters. For the interested reader, general formulas for LMER are presented in optional sections at the end of the chapter.

Two sets of fundamental LMER models are discussed. One set focuses on accounting for within-subjects variation using the time predictor. Such models are useful when the focus is on the characteristics of the change curve. The linear change curve is considered in this chapter, and nonlinear change curves are discussed in future chapters, especially Chapter 12.

The other set of models focuses on accounting for between-subjects variation, using one or more static predictors. These models are useful for examining whether the change curve varies as a function of the static predictors. In the case of a two-group categorical predictor considered in this chapter, the question is whether change curves are different for the two groups. Models with additional static predictors are considered in future chapters.

To clearly explicate the ideas, statistical strategy is not directly addressed. This means an analysis is not classified as confirmatory or exploratory. Furthermore, there is no explicit comparison of models, as in the multimodel approach. Focus is on basic concepts, with multimodel analysis being deferred until Chapter 7.

5.1 Traditional Regression and the Linear Model

As a precursor to a discussion of LMER, traditional regression and the LM are presented. This should be a familiar touchstone for most readers. It is useful to sketch the details of some LMs and see how they can be ported over to LMER for the case of longitudinal data.

Since most readers have experience with the LM for multiple regression, the general form of the model is presented, with later discussion of special cases. In anticipation of the transition to LMER, more detailed notation is used than in previous chapters.

The general form of the LM for multiple regression is written as

$$y_i = \beta_0 + \beta_1(x_{1i}) + \beta_2(x_{2i}) + \ldots + \beta_p(x_{pi}) + \varepsilon_i, \tag{5.1.1}$$

where y_i is the response for the ith individual ($i = 1, \ldots, N$), x_{ki} is the kth predictor or correlate ($k = 1, \ldots, p$), β_0 is the intercept, β_k ($k > 0$) is the kth regression coefficient, and ε_i is random error.

The errors are the scatter about the hyperplane defined by the predictor equation, with the hyperplane simplifying to a plane when there are two predictors, and a regression line when there is one predictor. For statistical inference, a normality assumption for the errors is typically made. The errors are assumed to be independent and normally distributed, with mean equal to 0 and constant variance, σ_ε^2.

Several interpretive statements can be made regarding the β_k, for $k > 0$. Perhaps the most detailed is that β_k indicates the change in the response for a unit increase in the kth predictor holding all other predictors at a fixed value (Cohen, Cohen, West, & Aiken, 2003, chap. 3). Sometimes more vague statements are made, such as β_k is the strength of the relationship between the kth predictor and the response controlling for all other predictors.

The LM of Equation 5.1.1 is general, and various types of models are subsumed based on the nature of the predictors. For example, when dummy variables are used as predictors, the one-way and factorial ANOVA models are

5.1 Traditional Regression and the Linear Model

special cases. Recall that a dummy variable takes the value of 0 and 1, and the numbers represent category (or group membership). Predictors can be a mix of dummy variables and quantitative variables, so that ANCOVA is also a special case (Cohen et al., 2003, chap. 5).

An important theme in ANOVA and ANCOVA is the interaction among predictors. As will be seen below, this is also important in LMER. An interaction term consists of the product of two predictors. In the case of factorial ANOVA, the product is among dummy variables. In the case of ANCOVA, the product involves the dummy variable and the quantitative variable.

An interaction term can also be the product of two quantitative predictors. The polynomial functions discussed in the last chapter serve as an example. Suppose x_{1i} is a time predictor. Then $x_{1i} \cdot x_{1i} = x_{1i}^2$ is used to model a nonlinear trend, specifically a quadratic trend.

To set the stage for LMER, it is emphasized that Equation 5.1.1 is a model for a subject, as indicated by the i subscript of the response variable. Although the LM is subject specific, the regression coefficients are group-level parameters, as indicated by the absence of subject subscripts. The regression coefficients index aggregate effects, as they do not vary among the subjects. Because of this, the regression coefficients are referred to as fixed effects, to distinguish them from random variables, such as the random error.

As shown below, the major difference between LM and LMER is that the latter includes subject-specific effects—random effects—in addition to random error. For the moment, the point is that a regression model contains a mix of group-level and subject-level terms. Applied researchers are usually interested in aggregate effects, and so the focus of analysis is on estimation and inference involving the fixed effects.

To emphasize the group-level aspect of the LM, it is common to write the prediction equation,

$$\hat{y}_i = \beta_0 + \beta_1(x_{1i}) + \beta_2(x_{2i}) + \ldots + \beta_p(x_{pi}), \qquad (5.1.2)$$

where $\hat{y}_i$ is referred to as a predicted or *fitted* response value. The presence of the fixed effects in Equation 5.1.2, as well as the absence of the random error, shows that prediction is a group-level enterprise in the LM.

In the traditional conceptualization of the LM, the predictor values are set by the analyst, or treated as such. This translates into the assumption that multiple individuals share common values on the predictor(s), at least in principle. When there is a dummy predictor, multiple subjects share a value of 0, and separate subjects share a value of 1. In such a case, the fitted value for a subject is a *mean value* based on common membership in the levels of the predictor. The concept is perhaps stretched a bit thin when the predictors are quantitative, as few subjects might share a common value, or the values might even be unique to subjects. Nonetheless, the idea of mean prediction still holds with quantitative predictors.

To emphasize the mean prediction aspect of LMs, such as Equation 5.1.2, expected value notation is sometimes used. This is written as $\hat{y}_i = E(y_i)$, where $E(y_i)$ is the long-run average of the response, in the repeated sampling sense discussed in Section 1.6.

5.2 Regression Examples

Examples are presented to illustrate important concepts of the LM and introduce syntax conventions. In anticipation of the transition to LMER, each LM analysis uses the long-format data frame discussed in previous chapters. The LM is appropriate for data collected at a single time point (or cross section). Thus, it is suspect to use the long-format data with LM, especially if the goal is inference regarding the fixed effects. The long-format data frame is used here to provide a comparison with LMER later in the chapter.

The `MPLS.LS` data frame was created in Chapter 3. Having saved the long-format data frame as an object in an Rdata file, the data frame is loaded into R using the `load()` function. This is performed in the syntax below, and the top and bottom portions of the data frame are printed.

```
> load(file="C:\\Mine\\MPLS.LS.Rdata")
> head(MPLS.LS)
> tail(MPLS.LS)
```

	subid	risk	gen	eth	ell	sped	att	ell2	risk2	grade	read
1.5	1	HHM	F	Afr	0	N	0.94	No	DADV	5	172
1.6	1	HHM	F	Afr	0	N	0.94	No	DADV	6	185
1.7	1	HHM	F	Afr	0	N	0.94	No	DADV	7	179
1.8	1	HHM	F	Afr	0	N	0.94	No	DADV	8	194
2.5	2	HHM	F	Afr	0	N	0.91	No	DADV	5	200
2.6	2	HHM	F	Afr	0	N	0.91	No	DADV	6	210

	subid	risk	gen	eth	ell	sped	att	ell2	risk2	grade	read
21.7	21	ADV	M	Whi	0	N	0.98	No	ADV	7	243
21.8	21	ADV	M	Whi	0	N	0.98	No	ADV	8	NA
22.5	22	ADV	F	Afr	0	N	0.96	No	ADV	5	219
22.6	22	ADV	F	Afr	0	N	0.96	No	ADV	6	233
22.7	22	ADV	F	Afr	0	N	0.96	No	ADV	7	236
22.8	22	ADV	F	Afr	0	N	0.96	No	ADV	8	NA

The output of the `tail()` function shows there are missing values for the reading variable (`read`). In the examples below, rows containing missing data are omitted from the analysis automatically by the `lm()` function.

5.2.1 SINGLE QUANTITATIVE PREDICTOR

For the first example, suppose the goal is to use `grade` as the single predictor of `read`. Such an analysis is useful when the aim is to examine linear

5.2 Regression Examples

change in reading scores. Nonlinear change is examined by including transformations of grade, but this consideration is postponed until later chapters.

Using the variable label for the grade predictor from the data frame, the LM is written as

$$y_i = \beta_0 + \beta_1(\text{grade}_i) + \varepsilon_i. \tag{5.2.1}$$

In Equation 5.2.1, y is used rather than the read label to denote the fact that reading scores are assumed to be randomly sampled from the population, and thus, y is a random variable. The grade label is used on the predictor side because it is assumed that the grades are fixed by the researcher, or treated that way.

In Equation 5.2.1, β_1 is the change in mean reading for each additional grade. β_0 is the mean reading score for the 0th grade, or when grade = 0. The 0th grade might not be a meaningful time point, unless kindergarten is coded as 0, for example. Because of this, the intercept is often not imbued with a literal meaning, other than as a vertical location for the regression line. Section 5.4.2 discusses scaling grade to yield an intercept with a more useful interpretation.

The fixed effects interpretations are a consequence of the long-format data frame. That is, a consequence of using a time predictor and a longitudinal response. The interpretations are valid even though the data structure is not appropriate for LM analysis. Traditional regression can certainly be used in a descriptive fashion to get a sense of the relation between grade and read. Of interest here is the fact that a LMER model with the same variables has similar parameters with similar interpretations. This will be seen in a moment.

Equation 5.2.1 is estimated in R using lm(). As discussed in Chapter 2, the major feature of the lm() syntax is that a tilde ($\sim$) is used instead of the equal sign in the regression equation. On the response side, the label of the response variable replaces y. On the predictor side, the sum of the predictor variable labels must be provided, with the intercept term optionally specified with 1. Random error is unobserved, and thus, no specific syntax is devoted to the error term. The lm() syntax for the example is

$$\text{lm}(\text{read} \sim 1 + \text{grade}, \text{data} = \text{MPLS.LS})$$

The data= argument identifies the data frame for the analysis. It is common to assign the above syntax to an object, which is known as the lm() model object, the output object, or the *fitted model object*.

In the syntax below, the single-predictor model is estimated, and the fitted model object is saved as lm.1. The fitted model object is further processed using the summary() function. Additional functions, such as plot(), produce regression diagnostics plots and other useful graphs (Verzani, 2005).

```
> lm.1 <- lm(read ~ 1 + grade, data = MPLS.LS)
> summary(lm.1)
```

```
Call:
lm(formula = read ~ 1 + grade, data = MPLS.LS)

Residuals:
    Min      1Q  Median      3Q     Max
-57.049  -7.512  -0.402  13.704  33.098

Coefficients:
            Estimate Std. Error t value Pr(>|t|)
(Intercept)  183.915     13.238  13.893   <2e-16 ***
grade          4.427      2.056   2.153   0.0344 *
---
Signif. codes:  0 '***' 0.001 '**' 0.01 '*' 0.05 '.' 0.1 ' ' 1

Residual standard error: 19.53 on 78 degrees of freedom
  (8 observations deleted due to missingness)
Multiple R²:  0.05609,    Adjusted R²:  0.04399
F-statistic: 4.635 on 1 and 78 DF,  p-value: 0.03442
```

The lines at the far left are used to reference aspects of the output. Starting at the top, the model syntax is shown in output line 2. Lines 4 to 6 show information about the distribution of the sample residuals. Residuals are taken to be the sample counterparts of population errors, and the residual statistics are useful for assessing assumptions about the population errors. Aspects of the residual output are pointed out for expository purposes. However, it is emphasized that the typical assumption of independence of errors in the LM is not appropriate with longitudinal data. Therefore, the residuals for this example are not to be taken seriously.

The column labels in line 5, Min, 1Q, Median, 3Q, and Max, stand for, respectively, the minimum, the first quartile, the second quantile, the third quartile, and the maximum value. A typical assumption is that the errors are normally distributed with mean 0. Therefore, one might examine the residual statistics for indications of consistency with this assumption. The median is a bit smaller than 0, and the distance from the median to the third quartile is slightly higher than the distance to the first quartile. This provides evidence of slight asymmetry, but overall, there appears to be reasonable consistency with the normality assumption. In an actual cross-sectional analysis, a more thorough inspection of the LM residuals is preferable (Weisberg, 2005).

Lines 8 to 13 contain information about the regression coefficients. In output line 9, the labels Estimate, Std. Error, t value, and Pr(>|t|) stand for, respectively, the parameter estimate ($\hat{\beta}_k$), the estimated SE, the t-ratio, and the p-value. The p-values are labeled with asterisks, with the key shown in the Signif. codes row, line 13. The asterisks are assigned based on the interval in which the p-value falls. To determine this, replace the single quoted symbol in the key by the observed p-value. For example, three asterisks are attached when $0 < p \leq 0.001$, two asterisks when $0.001 < p \leq 0.01$, and so on. Since the LM is not appropriate for inference with longitudinal data, the p-values reported here are suspect.

5.2 Regression Examples

The row labeled (Intercept) in line 10 contains information about the intercept estimate, $\hat{\beta}_0$. The intercept estimate indicates that when grade is 0, the fitted mean reading score is 183.92. The row labeled grade in line 11 contains information about the slope estimate, $\hat{\beta}_1$. The slope estimate indicates there is a mean increase of 4.43 for every additional grade.

At the bottom of the output, lines 15 to 18, information about global fit and missing data appears. Line 15 shows the estimate of the square root of the error variance, $\hat{\sigma}_\varepsilon = 19.53$, which is a "small-is-better" index of model fit. Values closer to 0 indicate better fit, but the metric is not standardized, so that $\hat{\sigma}_\varepsilon$ has meaning only relative to other models. As will be shown in the next three chapters, the relative meaning of $\hat{\sigma}_\varepsilon$ also applies to the fit indexes that are the basis of multimodel inference and the LRT.

Information about missing data is shown on line 16. In this case, eight rows of the data frame were omitted due to missing values.

Line 17 provides the familiar scaled values of global fit, R^2 and *adj.* R^2. Recall that *adj.* R^2 adjusts for the number of predictors and the sample size.

Line 18 shows the omnibus *F*-value, with its associated degrees of freedom (*df*) and *p*-value. *F* is equivalent to the square of the *t*-ratio for the slope in this case, as there is a single predictor. With multiple predictors, *F* is associated with an omnibus null hypothesis and diverges from the individual squared *t*-ratios. Using longitudinal data with the LM points out, among other things, that the *df* are incorrectly calculated for *F*. This casts doubt on the validity of using *F* in this context.

As an aside, notice the *p*-value for the intercept is expressed in scientific notation. The notation 2e-16 indicates that the decimal place for 2 is to be moved 16 places to the left, meaning there are 15 preceding 0s. Scientific notation is suppressed by running the following syntax at any time.

```
> options(scipen = 999)
```

Scientific notation is restored by replacing 999 with 0. A potential problem in turning off scientific notation is that very small (or large) numbers will be displayed with all their digits. This can produce very long output. When portions of the output are printed, as shown below, the round() function is used to display a desired number of digits.

It is helpful to graph the fitted regression line to get a sense of the change curve. This is done by graphing the fitted values that make up the regression line. Conveniently, the fitted values are automatically saved in the fitted lm() output object. They are extracted with the fitted() function.

In the syntax below, the data.frame() function is used to create the plotdata data frame for graphing. Variables from the original data frame are saved, but with the NA rows removed. The new data frame is automatically stored with the lm() output object, and it is accessed in the $model slot. Output slots are learned by using the str() function on the summary()

object, for example, str(summary(lm.1)). Be forewarned that the output can be quite extensive.

In addition to the complete data frame, the fitted values from lm.1 are extracted and saved. The column of fitted values is named fitted, and the complete data frame retains its original column names.

```
> plotdata <- data.frame(lm.1$model, fitted = fitted(lm.1))
> head(plotdata)
```

	read	grade	fitted
1.5	172	5	206.0488
1.6	185	6	210.4756
1.7	179	7	214.9024
1.8	194	8	219.3293
2.5	200	5	206.0488
2.6	210	6	210.4756

The output shows the top portion of the plotdata data frame. By executing summary(plotdata), it can be verified there are no NA rows.

Having created the data frame, the fitted values for the groups are graphed using ggplot2. Observed points are also drawn. Details of the syntax are discussed in Chapter 4.

```
> ## Set some defaults.
> theme_set(theme_bw())
> myX <- scale_x_continuous(breaks = 5:8, name = "Grade")
> myY <- scale_y_continuous(name = "Reading")
> ## Use ggplot().
> g1 <- ggplot(data = plotdata, aes(x = grade, y = read)) + geom_point(shape = 1)
> g2 <- g1 + geom_line(aes(x = grade, y = fitted)) + myX + myY
> print(g2)
```

The graph is shown in Figure 5.1. Consistent with the slope estimate in the output, the regression line is positive. The predicted mean reading achievement increases over grade.

5.2.2 ANALYSIS OF COVARIANCE

As another example of the LM, suppose the goal is to add the dichotomous risk group variable, risk2, as a predictor in the model. By adding the risk group predictor, one can examine if there is a difference in the intercepts of the change curves for the groups. The situation of one quantitative predictor (grade) and one categorical predictor (risk2) is sometimes referred to as *analysis of covariance* (ANCOVA).

When a predictor is categorical, a dummy variable must be used in the LM analysis. Suppose the dummy variable is named risk2DADV and takes the value of 0 when a subject is advantaged (ADV) and takes the values of 1 when a person is disadvantaged (DADV). The LM is written with the dummy variable as follows:

$$y_i = \beta_0 + \beta_1(\text{grade}_i) + \beta_2(\text{risk2DADV}_i) + \varepsilon_i. \quad (5.2.2)$$

5.2 Regression Examples

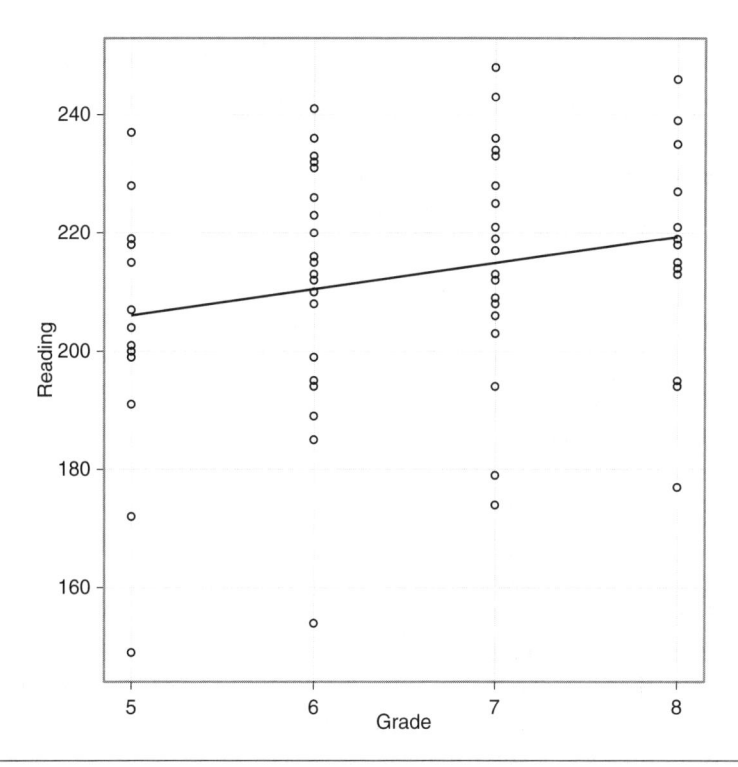

Figure 5.1 Reading scores by grade with regression line and observed points.

In using `lm()` to estimate Equation 5.2.2, one option is to add `risk2DADV` to the data frame and include it as a predictor in the syntax. A more convenient approach is to use `risk2` in the syntax. The `risk2` variable can be used directly because it is saved as a factor variable. If a factor variable is supplied to `lm()`, a dummy variable is automatically created and used in the analysis.

For naming the dummy variable, the convention is to take the original variable name and concatenate it with the value of the level representing the coding of 1. By default, the levels of a dichotomous factor variable are coded in numerical order based on their alphabetical order. In this case, 0 = ADV and 1 = DADV, and the resulting variable name is `risk2DADV`. This coding can be changed, either by creating a new factor variable in the data frame with `factor()`, renaming the levels with `levels()`, or using the contrasts function, `C()`, within the `lm()` syntax; see `?C`. (Be sure to distinguish the contrasts function, `C()`, from the concatenation function, `c()`.)

Consider the following syntax and output for the ANCOVA analysis.

```
> lm.2 <- lm(read ~ 1 + grade + risk2, data = MPLS.LS)
> summary(lm.2)
```

```
Call:
lm(formula = read ~ 1 + grade + risk2, data = MPLS.LS)

Residuals:
    Min      1Q  Median      3Q     Max
-48.035  -9.817   1.548   8.982  41.850

Coefficients:
            Estimate Std. Error t value Pr(>|t|)
(Intercept)  193.886     11.649  16.644  < 2e-16 ***
grade          4.557      1.784   2.554   0.0126 *
risk2DADV    -19.638      3.809  -5.156  1.9e-06 ***
---
Signif. codes: 0 '***' 0.001 '**' 0.01 '*' 0.05 '.' 0.1 ' ' 1

Residual standard error: 16.95 on 77 degrees of freedom
  (8 observations deleted due to missingness)
Multiple R^2:  0.2983,    Adjusted R^2:  0.2801
F-statistic: 16.37 on 2 and 77 DF,  p-value: 1.191e-06
```

Comparing lines 2 and 12, it is seen that supplying the risk2 factor variable causes the risk2DADV dummy variable to be created and used in the analysis. Line 12 shows that the estimated coefficient for risk2DADV is negative, revealing that the disadvantaged group has a lower intercept value than the advantaged group. Additional details are presented below.

In the ANCOVA situation, it is common to consider the relationship between the response and the quantitative predictor, conditioning on the levels of the categorical predictor. In this longitudinal example, the conditioning constitutes an examination of the change curves for the risk groups. That is, reading as a function of grade for advantaged and disadvantaged students. The group change curve equations are obtained by substituting the values of 0 and 1 for risk2DADV into the predicted value version of Equation 5.2.2. Doing so, the following is obtained:

$$\hat{y}_i = \begin{cases} \beta_0 + \beta_1(\text{grade}_i) & \text{if ADV,} \\ (\beta_0 + \beta_2) + \beta_1(\text{grade}_i) & \text{if DADV.} \end{cases} \quad (5.2.3)$$

As the equations show, the groups will have different intercepts when $\beta_2 \neq 0$.

Suppose the parameter estimates from the output ($\hat{\beta}$) are substituted for each β_k. The substitutions yield the following:

$$\hat{y}_i = \begin{cases} 193.89 + 4.56(\text{grade}_i) & \text{if ADV,} \\ 174.25 + 4.56(\text{grade}_i) & \text{if DADV.} \end{cases} \quad (5.2.4)$$

Equations 5.2.3 and 5.2.4 illustrate that risk2DADV in the LM represents an *intercept effect*, as the prediction equations for the groups have the same slope but different intercepts. The group change curves are parallel, and they have different starting points on the vertical (reading) axis. The intercept difference is represented by β_2, and there is no group intercept difference if this parameter is 0.

5.2 Regression Examples

In anticipation of the transition to LMER, *when a static predictor variable appears in the model as a single effect, this represents an intercept effect.* To be clear, this interpretation relies on the first predictor being a time predictor and the second predictor being a static predictor. The idea generalizes to the case of multiple static predictors, although the intercept effects are adjusted for the other predictors in the model. It also generalizes to the case in which the static predictors are quantitative. However, with quantitative static predictors, depictions such as Equation 5.2.3 are more difficult and in some cases may not be possible.

A graphical illustration of the intercept difference is provided by graphing the fitted values based on Equation 5.2.4. As shown previously, the `plotdata` data frame is constructed for use with `ggplot()`.

```
> plotdata <- data.frame(lm.2$model, fitted = fitted(lm.2))
> g1 <- ggplot(data = plotdata, aes(x = grade, y = read, shape = risk2)) + geom_point()
> g2 <- g1 + geom_line(aes(x = grade, y = fitted, linetype = risk2))
> g3 <- g2 + opts(legend.position = c(.8,.3), "aspect.ratio" = 1)
> g4 <- g3 + scale_shape(solid = F) + myX + myY
> print(g4)
```

The graph is shown in Figure 5.2. The regression lines are parallel, and they are shifted apart on the *y*-axis. The predicted increase is the same for the groups over grade, but the advantaged group has a larger intercept than the disadvantaged group.

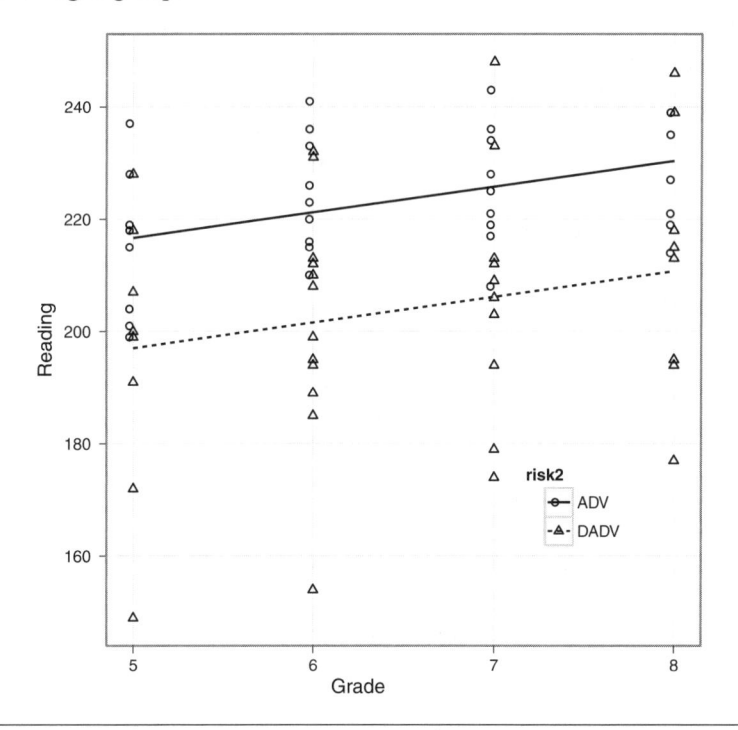

Figure 5.2 Prediction curves illustrating the intercept effect for risk groups.

5.2.3 INTERACTION MODEL

As a final example of the LM, suppose the objective is to add the interaction of grade and risk2 to the model. The interaction term allows the regression lines of the risk groups to have different slopes. This is useful in examining if the rate of change varies by group.

Traditional ANCOVA does not allow regression lines with different slopes, although this possibility is usually investigated (Kleinbaum, Kupper, Muller, & Nizam, 1998, chap. 15). In evaluating the need for different slopes, one compares the ANCOVA model of Equation 5.2.4 to a model that includes an interaction term. As mentioned, an interaction term is a product of two predictors. In this case, the product involves the grade and risk variables, which is really the product of grade and risk2DADV.

The LM with interaction is written as the following:

$$y_i = \beta_0 + \beta_1(\text{grade}_i) + \beta_2(\text{risk2ADV}_i) \\ + \beta_3(\text{grade}_i)(\text{risk2ADV}_i) + \varepsilon_i. \quad (5.2.5)$$

The model has an intercept effect, as represented by β_2, and a *slope effect*, as represented by β_3. In anticipation of the transition to LMER, *when a static predictor by time predictor interaction appears in the model, this represents a slope effect*. Here the time predictor represents linear change. The idea also extends to the nonlinear case, in which interactions are called *trajectory effects*. This more general term is used to denote that groups can have different (non)linear trajectories.

In estimating the model with lm(), one option is to add the product term to the data frame and then include it as a predictor in the syntax. A more convenient option is to specify the product term directly. The product of two variables is denoted by an asterisk (*), or by a colon (:). In lm(), the asterisk is handy as it will automatically include the single effects if they are not separately specified, whereas the colon will not. The following two syntax formulas are equivalent:

read ~ 1 + grade * risk2
read ~ 1 + grade + risk2 + grade : risk2

For simplicity, the first form will often be used, though the second form is more explicit about the effects that are actually estimated. Notice that risk2 is included in the syntax, but the dummy variable, risk2DAVD, is actually used in the calculations.

Consider the syntax and output below.

```
> lm.3 <- lm(read ~ 1 + grade * risk2, data = MPLS.LS)
> summary(lm.3)
```

5.2 Regression Examples

```
Call:
lm(formula = read ~ 1 + grade * risk2, data = MPLS.LS)

Residuals:
    Min      1Q  Median      3Q     Max
-47.264  -8.390   0.391   9.817  41.275

Coefficients:
                 Estimate Std. Error t value Pr(>|t|)
(Intercept)       201.058     17.280  11.636   <2e-16 ***
grade               3.425      2.691   1.273    0.207
risk2DADV         -32.555     23.216  -1.402    0.165
grade:risk2DADV     2.035      3.608   0.564    0.574
---
Signif. codes:  0 '***' 0.001 '**' 0.01 '*' 0.05 '.' 0.1 ' ' 1

Residual standard error: 17.02 on 76 degrees of freedom
  (8 observations deleted due to missingness)
Multiple R²:  0.3013,    Adjusted R²:  0.2737
F-statistic: 10.92 on 3 and 76 DF,  p-value: 4.81e-06
```

Lines 8 to 15 show the table of results for the regression coefficients. Information regarding the single effects are in the rows labeled grade (line 11) and risk2DADV (line 12). Information about the interaction appears in the row labeled grade:risk2DADV (line 13). Although the interaction is specified as grade*risk2 in the syntax, the colon and dummy variable are used for the interaction in the output.

The absolute *t*-ratios are suspect here because a cross-sectional model is used with longitudinal data. It is still possible, however, to compare the *t*-ratios among the predictors to get a sense of relative predictive importance. Lines 12 to 13 show that the absolute *t*-ratio for the interaction term is smaller than that of risk2DADV. This means the standardized slope difference is less than the standardized intercept difference. Furthermore, inspection of the lm.2 output reveals that the risk2DADV *t*-ratio is much higher when the interaction term is not in the model (see the previous output).

Similar to the ANCOVA model, the prediction equations for the risk groups are useful to consider. Substituting values of 0 and 1 for risk2DADV in the predicted value version of Equation 5.2.5, the following is obtained:

$$\hat{y}_i = \begin{cases} \beta_0 + \beta_1(\text{grade}_i) & \text{if ADV,} \\ (\beta_0 + \beta_2) + (\beta_1 + \beta_3)(\text{grade}_i) & \text{if DADV.} \end{cases} \quad (5.2.6)$$

The equations show there is both an intercept effect and a slope effect, with the latter indicating that the slopes vary by risk group. β_2 represents the group intercept difference, and β_3 represents the group slope difference. The groups have the same change curve when the aforementioned parameters are both 0.

Using the parameter estimates from the output, the following is obtained:

$$\hat{y}_i = \begin{cases} 201.06 + 3.43(\text{grade}_i) & \text{if ADV,} \\ 168.50 + 5.46(\text{grade}_i) & \text{if DADV.} \end{cases} \quad (5.2.7)$$

The equations show that the curve for the disadvantaged group starts lower and accelerates at a faster rate than the advantaged group curve. The caveat here is that the intercept difference in the ANCOVA model is relatively large, whereas the slope difference in the interaction model appears to be negligible (according to the t-value). A more thorough determination of the worthiness of the interaction term is warranted and delayed for later.

The regression lines for the groups are graphed using `ggplot()`.

```
> plotdata  <- data.frame(lm.3$model, fitted = fitted(lm.3))
> g1  <- ggplot(data = plotdata, aes(x = grade,y = read,shape = risk2)) + geom_point()
> g2  <- g1 + geom_line(aes(x = grade, y = fitted, linetype = risk2))
> g3  <- g2 + opts(legend.position = c(.8,.3), "aspect.ratio" = 1)
> g4  <- g3 + scale_shape(solid = F) + myX + myY
> print(g4)
```

The graph is shown in Figure 5.3. The lines are not parallel, and they are shifted relative to the y-axis. The disadvantaged group has a lower intercept than the advantaged group, and the vertical gap between the curve narrows a bit at the latter grades. The narrowing gap over time illustrates the slope effect.

5.3 Linear Mixed Effects Regression

Having reviewed the LM and illustrated how parameters are estimated with `lm()`, the time is ripe to transition to LMER. It is helpful to review the LMs considered in the previous sections, as the LMER versions are examples of models commonly used in longitudinal data analysis. In addition to listing the models, the graphs of the fitted curves are included as reference.

1. *Unconditional model:* `grade` as a predictor of `read` (Figure 5.1).

2. *Intercept effect:* `grade` and `risk2` (or `gradeDADV`) as predictors of `read` (Figure 5.2)

3. *Intercept and slope effects:* `grade`, `risk2`, and `grade × risk2` as predictors (Figure 5.3)

The LMER versions of these models are fundamental, in that the models address typical research questions. The first model is used when focus is on unconditional change over time, meaning change that ignores the static predictor. The other models are used when focus is on conditional change, meaning change stratified on the levels of the static predictor. The second model has an intercept effect for the static predictor, and the third model adds

5.3 Linear Mixed Effects Regression

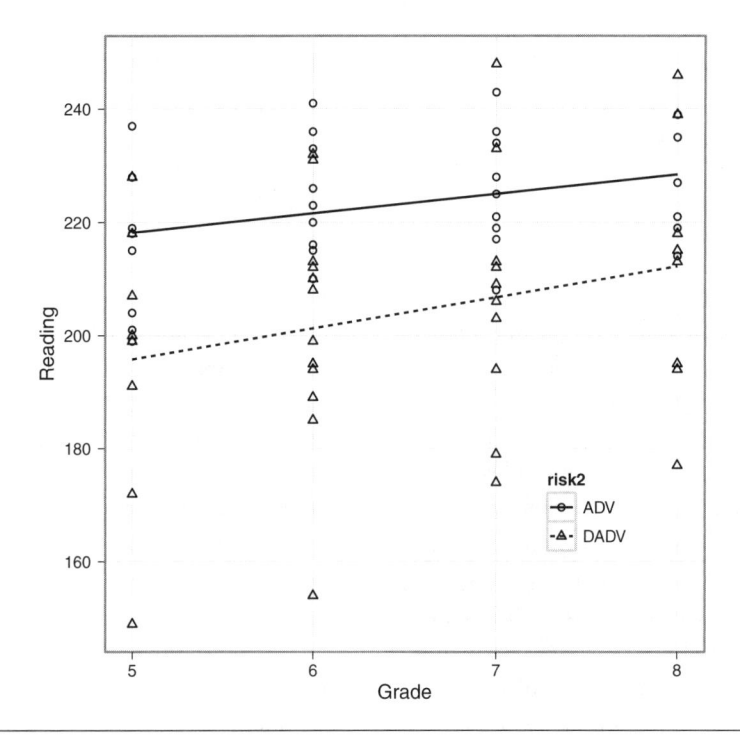

Figure 5.3 Intercept and slope effect.

a slope effect. The details of the LMER version of these models are discussed below.

In the previous sections, all the LMs were fit to longitudinal data structured in long format. The LM is not appropriate for inference with longitudinal data. Consequently, there should be a healthy suspicion regarding the results of such analyses. It is instructive to explore the details of why the LM is wrong for longitudinal data, and how LMER solves the problem.

The main reason that inferences based on LM are incorrect for longitudinal data is the independence assumption of the errors. The independence assumption means that each row of the data frame is treated as a different subject, who is randomly sampled from the population of interest. In the long-format data, this assumption is clearly wrong, as there are repeated observations from the same subjects in the rows. The LM does not properly associate subjects with their repeated observations.

To be more explicit, consider a portion of the long-format MPLS.LS data frame. The first eight rows are printed below.

```
> head(MPLS.LS, n = 8)
```

	subid	risk	gen	eth	ell	sped	att	ell2	risk2	grade	read
1.5	1	HHM	F	Afr	0	N	0.94	No	DADV	5	172
1.6	1	HHM	F	Afr	0	N	0.94	No	DADV	6	185
1.7	1	HHM	F	Afr	0	N	0.94	No	DADV	7	179

1.8	1	HHM	F	Afr	0	N	0.94	No	DADV	8	194
2.5	2	HHM	F	Afr	0	N	0.91	No	DADV	5	200
2.6	2	HHM	F	Afr	0	N	0.91	No	DADV	6	210
2.7	2	HHM	F	Afr	0	N	0.91	No	DADV	7	209
2.8	2	HHM	F	Afr	0	N	0.91	No	DADV	8	NA

As the subject number column (subid) and time column (grade) reveal, blocks of rows contain repeated measurements for single subjects. For this data frame, the LM does not correctly associate an individual with her or his repeated measures (or vector of longitudinal observations). Rather, the LM treats the rows of the data frame as if they are scores from different randomly sampled subjects. Since observations from the same individual are correlated, it certainly is incorrect to treat the rows of data as independent.

How are the subjects properly associated with their repeated measures? One method is to extend the regression model by introducing random effects, as is done in LMER. The random effects embed a subject-specific regression model within the larger model. The subject-specific regression model is defined for a block of repeated observations based on a common subject identification number. For the output immediately above, the first block is defined for the subject with subid = 1, and the second block is defined for subid = 2. Since the blocks of subject observations are taken into account, the random effects allow independence among the subjects, and dependence among the repeated observations within subjects. Thus, LMER is a solid foundation on which to analyze longitudinal data.

LMER is an extension of LM in the respect that the terms appearing in both models have similar interpretations. Common to both models are the fixed effects and random error. The distinction is that LMER adds the random effects. By introducing random effects along with fixed effects, there is a *mix* of effects, which is the essence of LMER. Deeper understanding is facilitated by writing down some special cases of the LMER model.

To write LMER models, the notation is extended to explicitly index subjects, $i = 1, 2, \ldots, N$, and time points, $j = 1, 2, \ldots, n_i$. The subject subscript is used within the time point notation (n_i) to denote missing data. Different subjects can have repeated measures records of different length. In the output immediately above, the first subject has no missing data, and so, $n_1 = 4$. The second subject has a missing value at Grade 8, and so, $n_2 = 3$.

The general form of the LMER model is presented in the optional section at the end of the chapter. To enhance understanding, it is instructive to first consider specific examples that are analogs of the LMs considered above. Paralleling the first LM example in Section 5.2.1, the LMER model having grade as a single predictor is

$$y_{ij} = (\beta_0 + b_{0i}) + (\beta_1 + b_{1i})(\text{grade}_{ij}) + \varepsilon_{ij}, \tag{5.3.1}$$

5.3 Linear Mixed Effects Regression

where b_{0i} and b_{1i} are random effects,[1] β_0 and β_1 are fixed effects similar to the LM, and ε_{ij} is random error, also like the LM.

It is not compulsory to include both random effects, and in some applications to be discussed later, only the random intercept term (b_{0i}) is included. For now, it is important to know that omission of random effects is always from the highest to the lowest, as a higher numbered random effect can never occur without the lower numbered random effect(s) in the model. Graphical and descriptive methods are recommended for selection of the random effects, as presented in Chapter 10. It is recommended the random effects be considered apart from the fixed effects, as discussed in Chapter 7.

An important characteristic of random effects is they have a subject subscript, but not a time subscript. This denotes the fact that the random effects provide a summary over the repeated measures for each subject, as explained below. Assuming random sampling, the random effects allow independence among the subjects, and they account for the dependence among the repeated measures.

The fixed effects in a LMER model, such as Equation 5.3.1, have the same interpretation as in the LM. In the example, β_0 is the group-level intercept, which is the predicted level at the 0th grade. β_1 is the group-level slope, which is the predicted change in mean reading for each additional grade. Similar to the LM, applied researchers are usually interested in estimation and inference for the fixed effects. Other parameters, such as the variance of the errors, might play a role, but it is a tertiary role. As will be seen, the same tertiary role usually characterizes the random effects.

An important practical consideration is that LMER parameters typically are not estimated with OLS. Rather, the more involved ML methods discussed in the next chapter are used. The difference in estimation methods often translates into different fixed effects estimates for the models when there are missing data. However, statistical theory suggests that as the sample size increases, differences among the fixed effects estimates from the two methods will decrease (Jaeger & Kramer, 1998). As illustrated below, the fixed effects estimates can be close, even when the sample size is not large.

Although the LM and LMER fixed effects have a large-sample correspondence, the same is not true of the SEs. LMER takes into account the dependency among the repeated measures, whereas the LM does not. This translates into additional parameters in the LMER model that influence the SEs. The practical implication is that estimated LMER SEs can be very different from those of the LM. These differences are illustrated in an example below.

5.3.1 LMER AS A MULTILEVEL MODEL

In Chapter 1, it was explained that longitudinal response data have two sources of variation: between-subjects and within-subjects. To clarify these

---
[1] In the notation for the random effects, the convention is to list the order of the effect in the first subscript, followed by the subject subscript; that is, b_{ki}, $k = 0, 1, \ldots, q+1$, $i = 1, \ldots, N$.

two sources and how they are modeled, it is helpful to depict the LMER model as a multilevel model. The case of Equation 5.3.5 is first considered.

Throughout this book, it is assumed that the variances of the random effects are never negative values, whether estimated or parameters in a model. Strictly speaking, this assumption is a necessity for the multilevel conception of LMER (Molenberghs & Verbeke, 2004).

The multilevel depiction expresses separate regression models for within-subjects and between-subjects aspects of the longitudinal model. The former is known as the *Level 1 model*, and the latter is known as the *Level 2 model*. The multilevel version of Equation 5.3.5 is

$$\text{Level 1:} \quad y_{ij} = \beta_{0i}^* + \beta_{1i}^*(\texttt{grade}_{ij}) + \varepsilon_{ij}, \quad (5.3.2)$$

$$\text{Level 2:} \quad \begin{cases} \beta_{0i}^* = \beta_0 + b_{0i}, \\ \beta_{1i}^* = \beta_1 + b_{1i}. \end{cases} \quad (5.3.3)$$

Equation 5.3.2 is a subject-specific change curve model. β_{0i}^* is the intercept for the ith subject, and β_{1i}^* is the ith subject's slope. The ε_{ij} are random errors about the subject's regression line.

The Level 1 model pertains to a single subject. As such, the only source of variation is within the subject, pertaining to the repeated measures. Time predictors and any other dynamic variables appear only in the Level 1 model. Whatever is not accounted for by time predictors and other dynamic variables is absorbed by the ε_{ij}; they are like sponges for unaccounted for within-subject variability.

The Level 2 model in 5.3.3 consists of the group-level equations involving the fixed effects. In the Level 2 equations, the response variables are the Level 1 intercepts and slopes. The number of Level 2 equations is determined by the number of Level 1 β^* parameters. Information regarding the repeated measures is summarized in β_{0i}^* and β_{1i}^*, and the focus is only on between-subjects variance. Although not included here, static predictors with their associated fixed effects appear only in the Level 2 model, as they account for between-subjects variation.

Typical of regression models, each Level 2 equation has a single error term, which is a random effect. A random effect is indifferent to the number of fixed effects at Level 2, but there can only be as many random effects as there are Level 2 equations. Not every Level 2 equation need have a random effect, and the omitting of random effects begins with the highest numbered term.

Substitution of the Level 2 equations, 5.3.3, in the Level 1 equation, 5.3.2, yields the LMER model. In developing the LMER model, it is often helpful to begin with the multilevel model, especially when the subject-specific change curve is nonlinear and/or there are numerous static predictors. In such cases, there can be a relatively large number of terms, and it is usually easier to work with separate regression equations than the single LMER equation. Once the multilevel model is constructed, then the LMER equation is obtained by substitution. This last step is helpful, as the syntax for the `lmer()` function maps to the single LMER equation.

5.3 Linear Mixed Effects Regression

The multilevel depiction helps to clarify the nature of the random effects. From the Level 2 model, it can be seen that

$$b_{0i} = \beta_{0i}^* - \beta_0,$$
$$b_{1i} = \beta_{1i}^* - \beta_1.$$

The above formulas show that a random effect is an individual deviation from its associated group-level fixed effect. In the case of b_{0i}, the deviation is the discrepancy between the individual intercept and the fixed intercept. In the case of b_{1i}, it is the discrepancy between the individual slope and the fixed slope. The formulas also point out that a random effect can be a negative value, a positive value, or equal to 0. If an individual's intercept, for example, is less than the fixed intercept, then $\beta_{0i}^* < \beta_0$ and $b_{0i} < 0$. On the other hand, if an individual's intercept is greater than the fixed intercept, then $\beta_{0i}^* > \beta_0$ and $b_{0i} > 0$. Finally, if $\beta_{0i}^* = \beta_0$, then $b_{0i} = 0$.

To help solidify the concepts, consider the graphs in Figure 5.4. A graphical representation of the Level 1 model is shown in Figure 5.4a for Subjects 9 and 11. The dashed lines are the fitted Level 1 curves, and the dancing of the observed points about the regression lines reflects random error. Subject 9 has intercept β_{09}^*, slope β_{19}^*, and errors ε_{9j} ($j = 1, 2, 3, 4$). Subject 11 has intercept β_{011}^*, slope β_{111}^*, and errors ε_{11j} ($j = 1, 2, 3, 4$).

Figure 5.4b shows a graph of the fitted lines for the subjects and the group-level curve. The group-level curve is just the average of the curves for the two individuals in this example. The group-level curve is constant among the subjects, reflecting the fact that its intercept and slope are fixed effects. The random effects are illustrated by the individual dashed curves in relation to the solid fixed effects curve. The individual curves have different intercepts than the fixed effect curve, indicating variability in individual intercepts. The individual curves are not exactly parallel with the fixed effect curve, indicating variability in individual slopes. The lower graphs provide additional details.

Figure 5.4c shows a graph of the subject-level intercepts, β_{0i}^*, and their relation to the fixed intercept, β_0. All intercepts are anchored at Grade 5 in the graphs (see Section 5.4.2). The random intercepts, b_{0i}, are in gray typeface and depict the deviation of the subject-level intercepts from the fixed intercept. This deviation is graphically represented by the vertical gray arrows between the values for which the difference is computed. For example, $b_{09} = \beta_{09}^* - \beta_0 = 147.9 - 182.4 = -36.3$. The sum of the random intercept scores is $36.3 - 36.3 = 0$, reinforcing their role as error terms in summing to 0.

Figure 5.4d shows a graph of the subject-level slopes, β_{1i}^*, and their relation to the fixed slope, β_1. The random slopes, b_{1i}, depict error, as they are the deviation of the subject-level slopes from the fixed slope. The slope of the curve for Subject 9 ($\beta_{19}^* = 10.4$) is greater than that of Subject 11 ($\beta_{111}^* = 6.5$), producing random slopes with different signs. The sum of the random slopes is $1.95 - 1.95 = 0$.

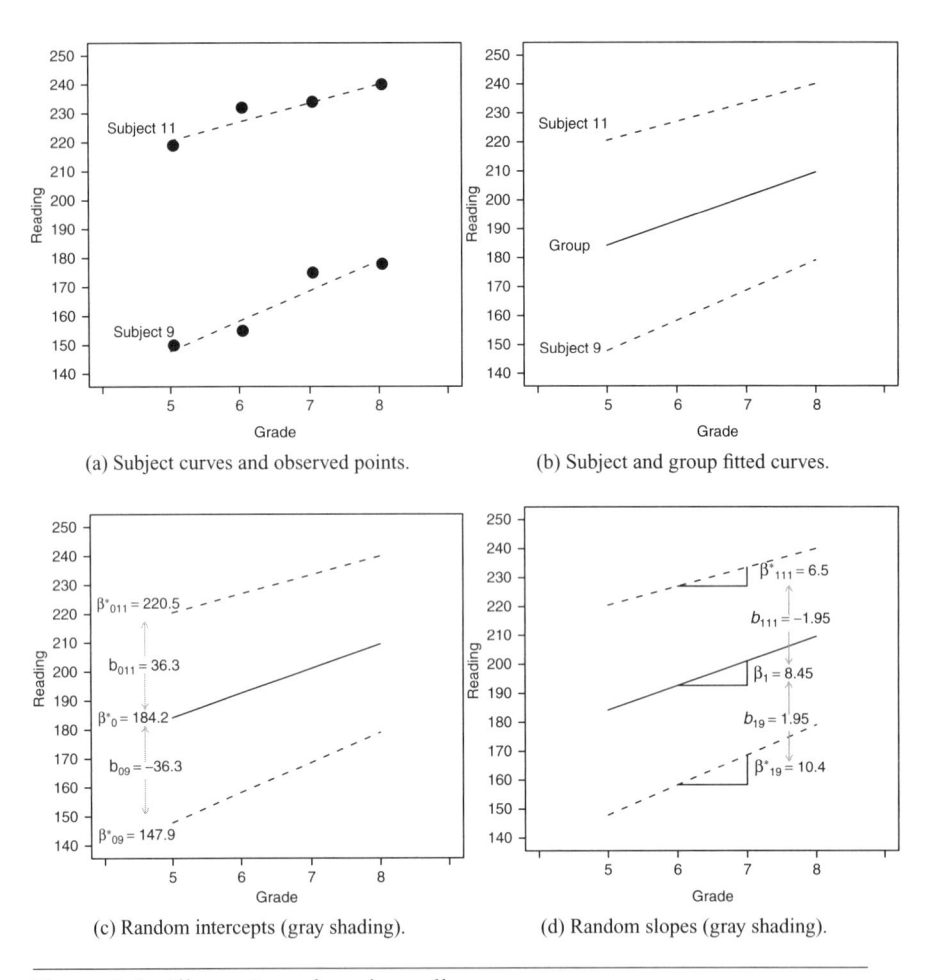

Figure 5.4 Illustration of random effects.

As a slight aside, there is a negative correlation between the subject intercepts and slopes in Figure 5.4. The intercept of Subject 9 is less than that of Subject 11, but Subject 9 increases at a faster rate over the grades.

5.3.1.1 TWO TYPES OF RANDOM EFFECTS?

In LMER, the b_{ki} are referred to as "random effects" because the β_{ki}^* disappear upon substitution. The multilevel depiction introduces a potential confusion, in that, the Level 1 β_{ki}^* coefficients can be interpreted as types of random effects. The Level 2 equations show that the β_{ki}^* are equivalent to the b_{ki} up to a constant, as $\beta_{ki}^* = \beta_k + b_{ki}$. The mean of a β_{ki}^* is a fixed effect, that is, $E(\beta_{ki}^*) = \beta_k$. This is in contrast to the b_{ki}, which have $E(b_{ki}) = E(\beta_{ki}^* - \beta_k) = \beta_k - \beta_k = 0$.

Because of the difference in mean value, the β_{ki}^* are referred to as *mean-uncorrected* random effects, and the b_{ki} are referred to as *mean-corrected*

5.3 Linear Mixed Effects Regression

random effects. Unless stated otherwise, the term random effects refers to the mean-corrected versions, b_{ki}.

The distinction between mean-corrected and mean-uncorrected random effects is not important in the typical LMER analysis. The reason is that the variances and covariances are the focus, rather than the values of the random effects themselves. Recall that adding or subtracting a constant from a variable does not alter its variance. The same can be said for the covariance and correlation between a pair of variables. Therefore, the computations of the variances and covariances are the same regardless of the type of random effects.

The distinction between mean-corrected and mean-uncorrected is important when one wants to estimate the change curve for a subject. In this case, the focus is decidedly on the β_{ki}^* rather than the b_{ki}. Details of the estimation of the mean-corrected random effects are discussed in Chapter 10.

5.3.2 RANDOM EFFECTS AS ERRORS

As shown in the multilevel depiction, the random effects can be conceived of as error terms. This error interpretation can also be emphasized in the LMER model. The alternative LMER expression has a direct parallel to the LM, providing additional insights into both models.

Suppose the random effects are collected together with the random error term and separated from the fixed effects. The model is written in the following way:

$$y_{ij} = \beta_0 + \beta_1(\texttt{grade}_{ij}) + (b_{0i} + b_{1i}(\texttt{grade}_{ij}) + \varepsilon_{ij}). \quad (5.3.4)$$

As explained in the next section, Equation 5.3.4 is a representation of the syntax form that is used in lmer(). That is, lmer() requires that the fixed effects and random effects be separately collected.

Pushing things one step further, define $\varepsilon_{ij}^* = b_{0i} + b_{1i}(\texttt{grade}_{ij}) + \varepsilon_{ij}$. This collects the Level 1 and Level 2 errors into a single term. Then the LMER model is written as

$$y_{ij} = \beta_0 + \beta_1(\texttt{grade}_{ij}) + \varepsilon_{ij}^*. \quad (5.3.5)$$

This equation is very similar in form to the LM. However, the error term of the LM reflects only between-subject deviations. The error term in Equation 5.3.5 is appropriate for longitudinal data, as it reflects both between-subjects and within-subjects deviations.

A final reason for collecting the random effects into ε_{ij}^* is that for the fitted or prediction equation, the random effects drop out along with the random error. This follows from the mean of 0 assumption discussed below. For the example above,

$$\hat{y}_{ij} = E(y_{ij}) = \beta_0 + \beta_1(\texttt{grade}_{ij}). \quad (5.3.6)$$

The expected value notation, $E(y_{ij})$, is commonly used with LMER, although $\hat{y}_{ij}$ is more consistent with the notation often used with the LM. Equation 5.3.6

is the predicted group-level change curve, as it involves only fixed effects parameters. Similar to the LM, the interpretation of the parameters is identical for the observed and fitted LMER models; β_0 is the estimated mean reading score for `grade` $= 0$ (which might not be meaningful), and β_1 indicates the predicted mean response change for each additional grade.

5.3.3 ASSUMPTIONS REGARDING RANDOM EFFECTS AND RANDOM ERROR

Like the LM, statistical inference in LMER is predicated on assumptions about the error term, ε_{ij}^*. Things are a bit more complex in the LMER model of Equation 5.3.5, as there are three components of the error term. Despite this, it is typical to make assumptions that are analogous to those made with the LM.

The following assumptions regarding the random effects and the random error are made throughout this book.

- The random effects have a joint normal distribution.
- The random errors are normally distributed.
- The random errors are independent between time points, and they have constant variance over time.
- The random effects are correlated, but they are independent of the random errors.
- The random effects and the random errors each have a mean equal to 0.

Although not considered here, it is possible for a LMER model to have random effects and errors that have distributions other than the normal distribution (Zhang & Davidian, 2001). It is also possible to include additional terms that allow for autocorrelation among the errors, which can be useful when the spacing of observations is very short (e.g., minutes; Diggle et al., 2002). In addition, the random effects need not be correlated, a possibility that is considered in Chapter 10. Assessing the plausibility of the assumptions listed above based on sample data is also discussed in Chapter 10.

The random error has constant variance σ_ε^2. Because σ_ε^2 is a variance associated with the subject-level change curve (see Equation 5.3.2), its magnitude is influenced by time predictors in the model. When a time predictor is added, σ_ε^2 usually decreases in size, as the time variable will account for some portion of within-subjects variance previously unaccounted for. This concept is illustrated below using sample estimates. Some caveats regarding comparisons of within-subjects variance for different models are discussed in Chapter 9.

The random effects have variances $Var(b_{0i})$ and $Var(b_{1i})$, which index subject variability in intercepts and slopes, respectively. The magnitudes of the variances are influenced by the static predictors in the model. When a static predictor is added, the size of a variance usually decreases, as the static predictor will account for some portion of the between-subjects variance. This is illustrated below using sample estimates. Some caveats regarding comparisons of between-subjects variance are discussed in Chapter 10.

If there is no individual variability in intercepts and slopes, then $Var(b_{0i}) = Var(b_{1i}) = 0$. In this case, there is no need to use LMER, and one can revert to the LM. For the majority of empirical applications, it is expected that both variance components will be greater than 0. Whether a value greater than 0 constitutes a substantial variance depends on the application. Statistical evaluation of variances and covariances is considered in Chapter 10. When random effects are specified by theory, or are at least consistent with theory, they should be included in the model regardless of the size of their variances.

The covariance between the random effects is denoted as $Cov(b_{0i}, b_{1i})$. The covariance is transformed into a correlation by dividing by the product of the square root of the variances. That is,

$$Corr(b_{0i}, b_{1i}) = \frac{Cov(b_{0i}, b_{1i})}{\sqrt{Var(b_{0i})}\sqrt{Var(b_{1i})}}.$$

The correlation indexes the relationship between the subject intercepts and slopes. For example, a positive correlation means that larger intercept values tend to go with larger slope values, and the converse. The correlation between the random effects might be of interest, depending on the research questions.

5.3.4 RANDOM EFFECTS AND CORRELATED OBSERVATIONS

As mentioned, random effects index individual deviations from the group-level fixed effects. What is not obvious from the material presented thus far is that the random effects also provide a model for correlated observations, or the dependency due to repeated measures.

To see this, consider the variance-covariance matrix among the repeated measures of the response variable. For the MPLS data, this matrix consists of the variances and covariances among the reading scores at the four grades. In this case, $\text{grade} = 5, 6, 7, 8$, but $j = 1, 2, 3, 4$. With the subscript values in mind, the variance-covariance matrix among the responses is[2]:

$$\begin{array}{c} \text{grade} \\ 5 \\ 6 \\ 7 \\ 8 \end{array} \begin{array}{cccc} 5 & 6 & 7 & 8 \end{array} \\ \begin{bmatrix} Var(y_{i1}) & Cov(y_{i1}, y_{i2}) & Cov(y_{i1}, y_{i3}) & Cov(y_{i1}, y_{i4}) \\ Cov(y_{i1}, y_{i2}) & Var(y_{i2}) & Cov(y_{i2}, y_{i3}) & Cov(y_{i2}, y_{i4}) \\ Cov(y_{i1}, y_{i3}) & Cov(y_{i2}, y_{i3}) & Var(y_{i3}) & Cov(y_{i3}, y_{i4}) \\ Cov(y_{i1}, y_{i4}) & Cov(y_{i2}, y_{i4}) & Cov(y_{i3}, y_{i4}) & Var(y_{i4}) \end{bmatrix} \quad (5.3.7)$$

---

[2] For clarity, the covariance terms below the diagonal are written in the same way as those above the diagonal. Alternative notation is used in the optional section, Equation 5.6.4.

The above matrix can also be standardized and expressed as a correlation matrix; the details are provided in the optional section.

When the covariances are all equal to 0, there is no dependency among the repeated measures, and there is no correlation between the time points. Such a result would be very strange with longitudinal data. Therefore, in general, the covariances (correlations) are considered to be nonzero.

A statistical model appropriate for longitudinal data should account for the nonzero covariances in Equation 5.3.7. The LMER models do this by way of the random effects and random error. It is shown in the optional section that the variances and covariances in the matrix of Equation 5.3.7 are a function of the grade scores, $Var(b_{0i})$, $Var(b_{1i})$, $Cov(b_{0i}, b_{1i})$, and σ_ε^2. Thus, the random effects provide a model for the correlated observations that characterize longitudinal data.

5.4 Estimating the LMER Model

LMER models are estimated with the lmer() function of the lme4 package written by Douglas Bates (Bates, 2005, 2011). The lmer() function uses syntax similar to lm(), but fixed effects and random effects are collected as in Equation 5.3.4. More specifically, lmer() uses the lm() syntax conventions for the fixed effects portion of the model, with the added requirement that the random effects portion appears in parentheses and explicitly references the subject identification number. This convention reinforces the earlier comment that the random effects properly associate subjects with their vectors of repeated measures. The LMER examples presented below are directly analogous to the LM examples considered earlier in the chapter.

5.4.1 TIME AS A PREDICTOR

Suppose the goal is to estimate the LMER model of Equation 5.3.4 having a single predictor, grade, and two random effects. The model specifies a linear change curve for the longitudinal reading scores. Individual variation is allowed for both intercepts and slopes.

Equation 5.3.4 is rewritten in a slightly different form, in order to closely map to the lmer() syntax.

$$y_{ij} = \beta_0(1) + \beta_1(\text{grade}_{ij}) + (b_{0i}(1) + b_{1i}(\text{grade}_{ij}) + \varepsilon_{ij}). \quad (5.4.1)$$

With the above equation in mind, the lmer() syntax for estimating the model is

$$\text{lmer}(\text{read} \sim 1 + \text{grade} + (1 + \text{grade} | \text{subid}), \text{data}$$
$$= \text{MPLS.LS}, \text{REML} = \text{FALSE}). \quad (5.4.2)$$

5.4 Estimating the LMER Model

Spaces are optional and included for readability. The model formula maps directly to Equation 5.4.1, with the fixed effects portion outside of the inner parentheses and the random effects within the parentheses. For the fixed effects portion, the sum of the multipliers of the βs is listed. For the random effects portion, the sum of the multipliers of the bs is listed, along with a pinning to the subject identification variable, indicated by | subid. The 1s are optional and included here for comprehensibility.

The data= argument identifies the data frame, and REML=FALSE requests that the default restricted maximum likelihood (REML) not be used. REML differs from ML in that it includes a bias adjustment. The bias adjustment can be desirable when the sample size is not large; see the next chapter. However, the bias adjustment is generally undesirable for model comparison (Verbeke & Molenberghs, 2000, chap. 6), which is a major focus of the coming chapters. For the moment, then, only ML is considered.

In the syntax below, the lme4 package is loaded, and then the parameters of the Equation 5.4.1 model are estimated with ML. The standard output is produced with the summary() function; the print() option can also be used.

```
> require(lme4)
> lmer.1 <- lmer(read ~ 1 + grade + (1 + grade | subid), data = MPLS.LS, REML = FALSE)
> summary(lmer.1)
```

```
 1  Linear mixed model fit by maximum likelihood
 2  Formula: read ~ 1 + grade + (1 + grade | subid)
 3     Data: MPLS.LS
 4     AIC  BIC  logLik  deviance  REMLdev
 5    583.7 598  -285.8   571.7    565.8
 6  Random effects:
 7   Groups   Name         Variance  Std.Dev.  Corr
 8   subid    (Intercept)  740.4670  27.2115
 9            grade          6.9662   2.6394   -0.744
10   Residual              18.3152   4.2796
11  Number of obs: 80, groups: subid, 22
12
13  Fixed effects:
14              Estimate  Std. Error  t value
15  (Intercept) 181.3335    6.5614    27.636
16  grade         4.8823    0.7417     6.582
17
18  Correlation of Fixed Effects:
19         (Intr)
20  grade  -0.799
```

The output is organized into four sections. These sections are listed below with the corresponding line numbers in the output.

1. Syntax and data set (1–3)

2. Global fit indexes (4–5)

3. Random effects and random error (6–11)

4. Fixed effects (12–20)

Line 1 indicates that ML rather than REML is used for estimation. The syntax is displayed in line 2 and the data set in line 3.

Lines 4 to 5 show the information about the global fit indexes. In line 4, the labels AIC, BIC, logLik, deviance, and REMLdev stand for, respectively, the Akaike information criterion, the Bayesian information criterion, the log-likelihood value, the deviance value ($= -2 \cdot$ logLik), and the REML deviance. In the next chapter, each of these is discussed in detail. For now, it is important to know that the indexes are used for model comparison, as they each represent global model fit. For every index except logLik, a smaller value indicates better fit of the model to the data. All the measures are unscaled, meaning the values are not interpretable in isolation. The fit indexes are only useful in evaluating *relative fit*, which is helpful for model comparison.

The table titled Random effects appears in lines 6 to 11. The table column labels are Groups, Name, Variance, Std.Dev., and Corr. Groups references whether the table row pertains to a random effect or random error. Random effects are referenced by the subject number label—in this case, subid (line 8). Random error is referenced by the label Residual shown in line 10. Recall that a residual is the sample counterpart of an error. The Name column identifies the specific random effect.

In the example, the random intercepts are denoted as (Intercept) in line 8, and the random slopes are denoted as grade in line 9. The Variance column lists the estimated variances of the random effects and random error (lines 8, 9, 10, respectively). The Std.Dev. column lists the square root of the variance. The Corr column shows the correlation between the random intercepts and random slopes. It is important to keep in mind that the Variance column does not provide estimates of b_{0i}, b_{1i}, and ε_{ij}, but rather estimates of their *variances*. Additional details are provided in Chapter 10.

The estimate of *Var*(b_{0i}) is 740.47, and the estimate of *Var*(b_{1i}) is 6.97. The difference in the magnitude of the estimated variances is expected, as the intercepts and slopes reflect different scales. The scale of the intercepts is the NALT reading scores at the 0th grade. The scale of the slopes is the linear change in the reading scores. Raw scores and change in raw scores are two different things, and it is typical to have different-sized variances for each.

The estimated correlation of the random effects has the value $cor = -0.74$. The negative correlation indicates that those with lower intercepts tend to have higher slopes and the converse. The estimated variance of the random error is listed in the Residual row and has the value $\hat{\sigma}_\varepsilon^2 = 18.32$.

Line 11 at the bottom of the Random effects table shows a listing of the number of rows of data used in the analysis, Number of obs. There are 88 rows in the MPLS.LS data frame, but 8 of these have NA values. Therefore, the total number of rows used in the analysis is 80.

5.4 Estimating the LMER Model

Line 11 also shows the number of subjects `groups: subid`, which is $N = 22$. The proper accounting of subjects and repeated measures is an indication that LMER is an appropriate method for analyzing longitudinal data. Values for the number of rows and number of subjects should be inspected to ensure the data frame is properly constructed, and the model is correctly specified.

Finally, information about the fixed effects appears in output lines 12 to 20. The `Fixed effects` table has the column labels, `Estimate`, `Std.Error`, and `t value`. These stand for, respectively, the β parameter estimates, the estimated SEs, and the *t*-values. A *t*-value is the ratio of the estimated parameter to its estimated SE—the value in the first column divided by the value in the second column. This ratio is also known as the *z*-ratio.

As mentioned, the fixed effects have similar interpretations as the LM regression coefficients. Here, the estimated intercept is $\hat{\beta}_0 = 181.33$, which is the predicted mean reading score when `grade` $= 0$. The estimated slope is $\hat{\beta}_1 = 4.88$, which is the mean increase in reading score for an additional grade.

At the bottom of the output in line 20 is the correlation between the two fixed effects. This value is based on the variance-covariance matrix of the fixed effects discussed in the next chapter. The values are useful for detecting multicollinearity among predictor terms. The printing of the fixed effects correlation is suppressed by using `print(lmer.1, cor = FALSE)`.

Conspicuously absent from the entire output are p*-values*. This underscores the fact that inference with LMER is more involved than with the LM. The random effects table does not even provide SEs, suggesting that inference with variance components may be even more complicated than inference with the fixed effects, which it is. These issues are thoroughly discussed in the upcoming chapters.

At this point, if the reader feels unbearably naked because of the lack of inferential information for at least the fixed effects, then the *t*-ratios in the output can be treated as *z*-ratios. The critical value of 1.96 can be used to evaluate the absolute value *t*-ratios at the $\alpha = 0.05$ level (two-tailed), or 2.58 can be used at the $\alpha = 0.01$ level, and so on. Better yet, one might compute a CI of the form `Estimate` $\pm 1.96 \cdot$ (`Std. Error`). In the next chapter, it is shown how CIs and *p*-values are added to the fixed effects output table. However, these inferential statistics may be inferior to methods based on the AIC (see Chapters 7 and 8).

5.4.1.1 COMPARISON OF LM AND LMER ESTIMATES

To gain insight into the difference between the LM and LMER, the fixed effects estimates for the models are compared. Consider the models with grade as the predictor. This is a comparison of the parameter estimates from the LM of Equation 5.2.1 saved in the object, `lm.1`, and the estimates from the LMER model of Equation 5.3.6 saved in the object, `lmer.1`.

In the syntax below, the fixed effects table of each fitted model object is printed. The LM fixed effects table is in the $coefficients slot of the summary() object, and the LMER fixed effects table is in the @coefs slot of its summary() object. The round() function is used to display four significant digits for the numbers in the tables. The print() function is used to print a table title.

```
> print("-- LM table --", quote = F)
> round(summary(lm.1)$coefficients,4)
> print("-- LMER table -- ", quote = F)
> round(summary(lmer.1)@coefs, 4)
```

[1] -- LM table --

	Estimate	Std. Error	t value	Pr(>|t|)
(Intercept)	183.9146	13.2382	13.8927	0.0000
grade	4.4268	2.0562	2.1529	0.0344

[1] -- LMER table --

	Estimate	Std. Error	t value
(Intercept)	181.3335	6.5614	27.6363
grade	4.8823	0.7417	6.5822

The output shows that the estimates of the fixed effects are similar, with the LMER estimate of the intercept being a bit smaller than the LM estimate, and the LMER estimate of the slope being a bit larger than the LM estimate. Statistical theory suggests even closer agreement as the sample size increases (Jaeger & Kramer, 1998). The large-sample similarity provides some justification for the fitting of regression curves in the graphing procedures presented in the last chapter. Recall that in some instances, OLS fits were used to investigate the nature of the group-level change curves (see Section 4.3.4.1). A similar approach is used in Chapter 9 for selecting time predictors.

Although the fixed effects estimates are similar, the estimated SEs are quite different. The LMER estimates are approximately half as large as the LM estimates. The differences in the parameter estimates result in a *t*-value for the LMER intercept that is approximately two times larger than that of the LM intercept. The *t*-value for the LMER slope is approximately three times larger than the *t*-value of the LM slope.

This example shows that SEs and *t*-values can be radically different for the LM and LMER when applied to longitudinal data. Since LMER accounts for the dependency due to repeated measures, a researcher would certainly want to use the LMER estimates as a basis for inference.

5.4.1.2 COMPARISON OF WITHIN-SUBJECTS VARIANCES

As previously mentioned, the error variance, σ_ε^2, is influenced by time predictors in the model. To illustrate this, look at what happens to the estimated σ_ε^2 when different time predictors are used.

5.4 Estimating the LMER Model

Consider the estimate of σ_ε^2 with grade in the model and with grade omitted from the model. This is a comparison of an intercept-only model and a linear change model. The estimated σ_ε^2 should be larger when grade is omitted from the model, as the unaccounted for within-subjects variance will wind up in the "dustbin" of the estimated errors (i.e., the residuals).

To ensure an even basis for comparison, only random intercepts are included in both models. In the syntax below, the intercept-only and linear change models are estimated, and the fitted output objects are saved.

```
> ## Intercept-only model.
> lmer.0 <- lmer(read ~ 1 + (1 | subid), data = MPLS.LS, REML = FALSE)
> ## Linear model.
> lmer.1 <- lmer(read ~ 1 + grade + (1 | subid), data = MPLS.LS, REML = FALSE)
```

To display the estimated σ_ε^2, the following syntax is used.

```
> se2.0 <- round(summary(lmer.0)@sigma ^ 2, 2)
> se2.1 <- round(summary(lmer.1)@sigma ^ 2, 2)
> ## Printing.
> myse2 <- data.frame(Intercept = se2.0, Linear = se2.1)
> rownames(myse2) <- "Est. Sigma2"
> myse2
```

	Intercept	Linear
Est. Sigma2	66.2	29.17

The output shows the estimated error variance is smaller when grade is in the model. In fact, it is more than two times smaller. This illustrates that grade accounts for a portion of within-subjects variance. When grade is not in the model, the unaccounted for variance is absorbed in the residuals. Reduction in the estimated σ_ε^2 is important in the selection of time predictors. This topic is discussed in Chapter 9.

5.4.2 ANCHORING THE INTERCEPT

To this point, grade has been used as the time predictor. Recall that this produces an interpretation of β_0 as the estimated group reading level for the 0th grade. This interpretation may not have practical value, unless a coding of 0 for grade is meaningful.

To provide a more convenient interpretation for the intercept, a linear transformation of the original time predictor is used. Adding or subtracting a constant value to all the time scores is usually sufficient. Multiplication and division are used when the goal is to transform time into other common scales, such as going from hours to minutes by multiplying by 60.

In many instances, it is convenient to anchor the intercept at the first time point. Then the intercept has the interpretation as the estimated level at the first time point, sometimes referred to as the *estimated initial status*. To anchor the time point in this manner, the minimum value of the time scores must be equal to 0. In the MPLS data example, grade has the minimum value of 5. To produce a minimum score of 0, the value of 5 is subtracted from all the scores. Suppose a new time predictor is computed, `grade5 = grade - 5`, and used in the analysis. The intercept now has the interpretation as the predicted reading level at fifth grade.

There is nothing sacrosanct about the first observed time point. The intercept can be anchored at other time points as well. When interest is in the level at the final outcome or terminal point, anchoring at the last time point may be of interest. Anchoring at eighth grade is accomplished by computing `grade8 = grade - 8`, resulting in the possible values of $-3, -2, -1, 0$. Since 0 occurs at the last time point, this is where the intercept is anchored.

Consider the results for the three different anchorings of the intercept. *It is important to use the same scaling in the fixed effects and the random effects portions.* This is to ensure proper scaling of the random effects. The insulate function, `I()`, is used to help ensure the scaling is properly interpreted (see Section 6.3 for additional details). For the output, the `fixef()` function is used to extract the fixed effects estimates, and `data.frame()` is used for prettier output.

```
> ## Estimation.
> lmer.1a  <- lmer(read ~ I(grade - 5) + (1+ I(grade- 5) | subid),MPLS.LS,REML= FALSE)
> lmer.1b  <- lmer(read ~ I(grade - 8) + (1+ I(grade- 8) | subid),MPLS.LS,REML= FALSE)
> ## Print out coefficients.
> data.frame(grade = fixef(lmer.1), grade5 = fixef(lmer.1a), grade8 = fixef(lmer.1b))
```

	grade	grade5	grade8
(Intercept)	180.754201	205.745124	220.392076
grade	4.984553	4.882314	4.882318

The output shows that the intercept grows larger when there is an increase in the grade at which the anchoring occurs. The slope value changes slightly, which reflects differences in the variances and covariances of the random effects. Although the changes here are slight, they may be more dramatic for some data sets.

As shown in the output above, transformations of the time variable affect parameter estimation and interpretation in the LMER model. If `grade` is used as the time predictor, then $Var(b_{0i})$ will be the variance of the intercepts at 0th grade. If `grade5` is used, the $Var(b_{0i})$ will be the variance of the intercepts at fifth grade. Suppose the individual change curves fan out over time, starting from a common point at `grade = 0`. Then it is possible that $Var(b_{0i}) = 0$ for 0th grade, but $Var(b_{0i}) > 0$ for fifth grade. Since the time transformation is only a rescaling, it is desirable to keep the random intercept term in the model regardless of whether its estimated variance is 0. This recommendation is reiterated in the discussion of inferential methods in Chapter 7.

5.5 LMER With Static Predictors

Static predictor effects are specified in LMER in the same manner as in the LM. Intercept effects are represented by single predictors in the model, and slope effects are represented by interactions with the time predictor. Examples of LMER models are considered that parallel the LMs previously discussed.

5.5.1 INTERCEPT EFFECTS

Suppose the goal is to examine the intercept effect of risk. Similar to the ANCOVA model, the dummy variable risk2DADV is included in the LMER model as a single effect. The LMER model for this case is written as

$$y_{ij} = \beta_0 + \beta_1(\text{grade}_{ij}) + \beta_2(\text{risk2DADV}_i) \\ + (b_{0i} + b_{1i}(\text{grade}_{ij}) + \varepsilon_{ij}). \tag{5.5.1}$$

This is very similar to the LM of Equation 5.2.2, except now there is a time subscript and a more complex error term that includes the random effects.

In the simpler model of Equation 5.3.1 with grade as the predictor, there is a random effect associated with each fixed effect. However, in Equation 5.5.1, no additional random effect is introduced with β_2. *The reason is that in the multilevel model, random effects are specified only in reference to the Level 1 model.* Thus, random effects are only associated with dynamic (time-varying) predictors, in addition to the intercept, as these are the only predictors in the Level 1 model. Since static predictors are included only in the Level 2 model, they never have accompanying random effects.

The reasoning is perhaps clearer if the multilevel version of Equation 5.5.1 is depicted:

$$\begin{aligned} \text{Level 1:} \quad & y_{ij} = \beta_{i0}^* + \beta_{i1}^*(\text{grade}_{ij}) + \varepsilon_{ij}, \\ \text{Level 2:} \quad & \begin{cases} \beta_{0i}^* = \beta_0 + \beta_2(\text{risk2DADV}_i) + b_{0i}, \\ \beta_{1i}^* = \beta_1 + b_{1i}. \end{cases} \end{aligned} \tag{5.5.2}$$

The risk predictor appears in the first Level 2 equation, as it predicts subject intercepts. Since riskDADV is a dummy variable, β_2 is the group difference between the mean intercepts. The Level 1 equation does not change with the inclusion of the risk predictor, so neither does the number of Level 2 equations. The number of random effects is determined by the number of Level 2 equations, so no random effects are added with the inclusion of the risk predictor.

Returning to the LMER model of Equation 5.5.1, consider the estimation of the parameters. The syntax and output appear below. The print() function is used to print out the results with the correlation among the fixed effects suppressed for brevity.

```
> lmer.2 <- lmer(read ~ 1 + grade + risk2 + (1 + grade | subid),
+              data = MPLS.LS, REML = FALSE)
> print(lmer.2, cor = FALSE)

 1  Linear mixed model fit by maximum likelihood
 2  Formula: read ~ 1 + grade + risk2 + (1 + grade | subid)
 3     Data: MPLS.LS
 4     AIC   BIC  logLik deviance REMLdev
 5   577.9 594.6 -282.0   563.9   552.7
 6  Random effects:
 7   Groups   Name        Variance Std.Dev. Corr
 8   subid    (Intercept) 600.3700 24.5024
 9            grade         7.1643  2.6766  -0.782
10   Residual              18.1295  4.2579
11  Number of obs: 80, groups: subid, 22
12
13  Fixed effects:
14              Estimate Std. Error t value
15  (Intercept) 192.4531     7.0479  27.306
16  grade         4.8836     0.7466   6.541
17  risk2DADV   -20.3988     6.6515  -3.067
```

Line 17 shows that the dummy variable, risk2DADV, is included as a single effect. Inspection of the output for lmer.2 and lm.2 shows that the fixed effects estimates are similar. Thus, the graph in Figure 5.2 can be used as an illustration of the intercept differences for the risk group change curves. If this were a serious LMER analysis for a professional publication, the fitted curves would be based on the LMER results, as illustrated in Chapter 11.

Line 8 shows the estimated variance of the random intercepts. Its value is smaller than when risk was not in the model (see the previous output). This indicates that some of the intercept variability among subjects is accounted for by risk.

5.5.2 SLOPE AND INTERCEPT EFFECTS

Similar to the LM with an interaction, Equation 5.2.5, one might want to examine a slope effect for the groups, in addition to an intercept effect. It is instructive to begin with the multilevel form of the model,

$$\text{Level 1:} \quad y_{ij} = \beta_{0i}^* + \beta_{1i}^*(\texttt{grade}_{ij}) + \varepsilon_{ij},$$

$$\text{Level 2:} \quad \begin{cases} \beta_{0i}^* = \beta_0 + \beta_2(\texttt{risk2DADV}_i) + b_{0i}, \\ \beta_{1i}^* = \beta_1 + \beta_3(\texttt{risk2DADV}_i) + b_{1i}. \end{cases} \quad (5.5.3)$$

The Level 2 model has risk2DADV predicting both Level 1 intercepts (β_{0i}^*) and Level 1 slopes (β_{1i}^*). β_3 indexes the relationship between the risk predictor and the subjects' slopes. Since risk2DADV is a dummy variable, β_3 is the mean slope difference between the groups. There are only two random effects, as again, the Level 2 equations are indifferent to the number of static predictors.

5.5 LMER With Static Predictors

Substituting the Level 2 equations in the Level 1 equation yields the LMER model. Collecting the fixed effects and random effects, the model is written as

$$y_{ij} = \beta_0(1) + \beta_1(\text{grade}_{ij}) + \beta_2(\text{risk2DADV}_i) \\ + \beta_3(\text{risk2DADV}_i \cdot \text{grade}_{ij}) + (b_{0i}(1) + b_{1i}(\text{grade}_{ij}) + \varepsilon_{ij}). \tag{5.5.4}$$

The syntax below is used to estimate Equation 5.5.4. The colon (:) syntax is used here rather than the asterisk (*) syntax, so that the model formula maps directly to the equation.

```
> lmer.3 <- lmer(read ~ 1 + grade + risk2 + risk2 : grade + (1 + grade | subid),
+              data = MPLS.LS, REML = FALSE)
> print(lmer.3, cor = FALSE)
```

```
 1  Linear mixed model fit by maximum likelihood
 2  Formula: read ~ 1 + grade + risk2 + risk2:grade+ (1+ grade|subid)
 3     Data: MPLS.LS
 4     AIC    BIC  logLik deviance REMLdev
 5   579.8  598.8  -281.9   563.8   549.9
 6  Random effects:
 7   Groups   Name         Variance  Std.Dev. Corr
 8   subid    (Intercept)  593.6171  24.3643
 9            grade          6.9489   2.6361  -0.779
10   Residual               18.2444   4.2713
11  Number of obs: 80, groups: subid, 22
12
13  Fixed effects:
14                    Estimate Std. Error t value
15  (Intercept)        194.571      8.973  21.685
16  grade                4.570      1.106   4.130
17  risk2DADV          -24.258     12.115  -2.002
18  grade:risk2DADV      0.571      1.489   0.383
```

The fixed effects table appears in lines 13 to 18. The labels in the first column indicate the single predictors of `grade` (line 16) and `risk2DADV` (line 17). The grade-by-risk interaction is indicated by `grade:risk2DADV` (line 18). The *t*-value for the grade-by-risk interaction in line 18 is relatively small, pointing out that the slope difference between the risk groups is negligible in the sample and might be so for the population. More formal evaluation is considered in the next three chapters.

Line 9 contains the estimated variance of the subject slopes. The estimated value is only slightly smaller than in the previous model that omits the risk-by-grade interaction. This is an indication that risk group membership does not account for much variability in subject slopes. In Chapter 10, more formal evaluation of such effects is considered.

5.5.3 INITIAL STATUS AS A STATIC PREDICTOR

In some situations, the researcher wants to control for initial status, especially when the first time point is a baseline measurement. In nonexperimental studies, preexisting differences are not accounted for in the research design, and there may be a desire to use statistical control. One means of doing so is to use the response at the first time point as a static predictor.

In terms of the MPLS data set, this means using reading at the fifth grade as a static predictor. Change is then examined over Grades 6 to 8. Note that the fifth-grade scores are no longer considered in the change over time. Including fifth-grade reading along with risk will provide statistical control for initial differences among the risk groups. It is probably not desirable to provide such control in the case of the MPLS data. Given the research questions regarding risk groups, preexisting differences are something that should be highlighted rather than controlled. In any event, there are other data sets in which such control is warranted.

To create the fifth-grade static predictor, the initial response scores are extracted from the data frame using the `subset()` function. The remaining response scores must also be extracted to a new data frame. The initial response scores are repeated for the duration of the remaining time points. This is accomplished with the `merge()` function. Consider the syntax below, in which fifth-grade reading is treated as the static predictor named `read.int`.

```
> grade5 <- subset(MPLS.LS, grade == 5, select = c(subid, read))
> colnames(grade5)[2] <- "read.int"
> grade6to8 <- subset(MPLS.LS, grade != 5)
> grade6to8a <- merge(grade5, grade6to8, by = "subid")
> head(grade6to8a)
```

	subid	read.int	risk	gen	eth	ell	sped	att	ell2	risk2	grade	read
1	1	172	HHM	F	Afr	0	N	0.94	No	DADV	6	185
2	1	172	HHM	F	Afr	0	N	0.94	No	DADV	7	179
3	1	172	HHM	F	Afr	0	N	0.94	No	DADV	8	194
4	2	200	HHM	F	Afr	0	N	0.91	No	DADV	6	210
5	2	200	HHM	F	Afr	0	N	0.91	No	DADV	7	209
6	2	200	HHM	F	Afr	0	N	0.91	No	DADV	8	NA

As the output shows, the values of `read.int` are repeated over the grades, which indicates this is a static predictor. The repeated measures in the `read` column now span Grades 6 to 8. Reading score at Grade 5 can now be used as a static predictor in a LMER analysis.

5.5.4 EXTENSIONS TO MORE COMPLEX MODELS

The concepts discussed in this chapter have extensions to more complex models. Time transformations, such as `grade`^{2}, can be added to account for nonlinear trends. Additional static predictors can be included, either singly for intercept effects, or as product terms with the time predictor(s) for trajectory effects. The main caveat regarding multiple static predictors is that effects of one predictor are adjusted for the other predictors in the model. This is analogous to the "partialled" or "controlled" effects of traditional multiple regression. For example, if risk and ethnicity are in the model, the risk slope effect is adjusted for ethnicity and vice versa. Such extensions are discussed in Chapter 11.

It is argued in Chapter 7 that care is required when building more complex models. This is especially so if different time predictors and random effects are to be considered along with static predictor effects. For this reason, different chapters are devoted to the evaluation of different effects. Chapters 7 and 8 discuss the evaluation of static predictors, Chapter 9 discusses the selection of time predictors, and Chapter 10 discusses the selection of random effects.

5.5.5 SUMMARY OF lmer() SYNTAX

A summary of the lmer() syntax discussed in this chapter is presented in Table 5.1. The table shows syntax for the case in which read is the response variable, grade is the time predictor, and risk2 is the static predictor. Furthermore, the subject identification variable is subid, the data set is MPLS.LS, and ML rather than REML is used.

5.6 Additional Details of LMER*

The examples of LMER offered in the previous sections are sufficient to continue on with the remaining chapters. For readers who want a deeper understanding, including knowledge of the general form of the LMER model, this optional section is included.

The optional section makes use of matrix algebra, as formulas with other notation (e.g., summation notation) can be quite cumbersome with LMER. A soft introduction to matrix algebra is provided in the Appendix. For the reader completely unfamiliar with matrix algebra, the Appendix should be read before attempting the material below.

Table 5.1 lmer() syntax presented in this chapter.

Static Predictor Effect	RE	Syntax
Unconditional	1	lmer(read ~ grade + (1 | subid), data = MPLS.LS, REML = FALSE)
Unconditional	2	lmer(read ~ grade + (1 + grade | subid), data = MPLS.LS, REML = FALSE)
Intercept	2	lmer(read ~ grade + risk2 + (1 + grade | subid), data = MPLS.LS, REML = FALSE)
Intercept and Slope	2	lmer(read ~ grade + risk2 + grade : risk2 + (1 + grade | subid), data = MPLS.LS, REML = FALSE)
Intercept and Slope	2	lmer(read~grade*risk2 + (1+grade |subid data=MPLS.LS, REML=FALSE)

Note. RE = number of random effects.

The presentation begins with a specific example, and then it is shown how the example is a special case of the general form of the LMER model. Next, there is an illustration of how the variances and covariances among the response variable are modeled based on the random effects and random error. Finally, R matrix operations are used in examples based on the MPLS data set.

5.6.1 GENERAL FORM OF THE LMER MODEL*

To develop ideas, consider the example of Equation 5.5.4 that has `grade` and `risk2DADV` as predictors, with both intercept and slope effects. Consider Equation 5.5.4 for an individual who has four repeated measurements, $n_i = 4$. This is a system of four equations, one for each time point:

$$y_{i1} = \beta_0(1) + \beta_1(\text{grade}_{i1}) + \beta_2(\text{risk2DADV}_i)$$
$$+ \beta_3(\text{risk2DADV}_i \cdot \text{grade}_{i1}) + b_{0i}(1) + b_{1i}(\text{grade}_{i1}) + \varepsilon_{i1},$$
$$y_{i2} = \beta_0(1) + \beta_1(\text{grade}_{i2}) + \beta_2(\text{risk2DADV}_i)$$
$$+ \beta_3(\text{risk2DADV}_i \cdot \text{grade}_{i2}) + b_{0i}(1) + b_{1i}(\text{grade}_{i2}) + \varepsilon_{i2},$$
$$y_{i3} = \beta_0(1) + \beta_1(\text{grade}_{i3}) + \beta_2(\text{risk2DADV}_i)$$
$$+ \beta_3(\text{risk2DADV}_i \cdot \text{grade}_{i3}) + b_{0i}(1) + b_{1i}(\text{grade}_{i3}) + \varepsilon_{i3},$$
$$y_{i4} = \beta_0(1) + \beta_1(\text{grade}_{i4}) + \beta_2(\text{risk2DADV}_i)$$
$$+ \beta_3(\text{risk2DADV}_i \cdot \text{grade}_{i4}) + b_{0i}(1) + b_{1i}(\text{grade}_{i4}) + \varepsilon_{i4}.$$

Collecting terms into matrices, the equations can be expressed with matrix multiplication and addition. The above equations are written as

$$\begin{bmatrix} y_{i1} \\ y_{i2} \\ y_{i3} \\ y_{i4} \end{bmatrix} = \begin{bmatrix} 1 & \text{grade}_{i1} & \text{risk2DADV}_i & \text{risk2DADV}_i \cdot \text{grade}_{i1} \\ 1 & \text{grade}_{i2} & \text{risk2DADV}_i & \text{risk2DADV}_i \cdot \text{grade}_{i2} \\ 1 & \text{grade}_{i3} & \text{risk2DADV}_i & \text{risk2DADV}_i \cdot \text{grade}_{i3} \\ 1 & \text{grade}_{i4} & \text{risk2DADV}_i & \text{risk2DADV}_i \cdot \text{grade}_{i4} \end{bmatrix} \begin{bmatrix} \beta_0 \\ \beta_1 \\ \beta_2 \\ \beta_3 \end{bmatrix}$$
$$+ \begin{bmatrix} 1 & \text{grade}_{i1} \\ 1 & \text{grade}_{i2} \\ 1 & \text{grade}_{i3} \\ 1 & \text{grade}_{i4} \end{bmatrix} \begin{bmatrix} b_{0i} \\ b_{1i} \end{bmatrix} + \begin{bmatrix} \varepsilon_{i1} \\ \varepsilon_{i2} \\ \varepsilon_{i3} \\ \varepsilon_{i4} \end{bmatrix}. \quad (5.6.1)$$

Each of the matrices in Equation 5.6.1 can be denoted with **boldface**. Doing so yields the general form of the LMER model:

$$\boxed{\boldsymbol{y}_i = \boldsymbol{X}_i \boldsymbol{\beta} + \boldsymbol{Z}_i \boldsymbol{b}_i + \boldsymbol{\varepsilon}_i,} \quad (5.6.2)$$

where $\boldsymbol{X}_i$ is the *design matrix* for the fixed effects, $\boldsymbol{Z}_i$ is the design matrix for the random effects, $\boldsymbol{\beta}$ is a vector of fixed effects, $\boldsymbol{b}_i$ is a vector of random effects, and $\boldsymbol{\varepsilon}_i$ is a vector of random errors.

5.6 Additional Details of LMER*

For the special case of Equation 5.6.1, the matrices have the following dimensions: y_i is 4×1, X_i is 4×4, β is 2×1, Z_i is 4×2, b_i is 2×1, and ε_i is 4×1.

Suppose that p is the number of predictors of the fixed effects, and q is the number of predictors for the random effects (both excluding intercepts). Then there are $p+1$ fixed effects and $q+1$ random effects, and the matrices have the following dimensions: y is $n_i \times 1$, X_i is $n_i \times (p+1)$, β is $(p+1) \times 1$, and Z_i is $n_i \times (q+1)$, with $p \geq q$. In addition, b_i is $(q+1) \times 1$, and ε_i is $n_i \times 1$.

The columns of Z_i are typically a subset of the columns of X_i, pertaining to the intercept and time predictor(s). The reason is that random effects are not associated with static predictors. For the special case of Equation 5.6.1, it can be seen that Z_i consists of the first two columns of X_i.

The subject subscript is used to denote the fact that the matrices can be of different lengths based on missing data. All the matrices have an i subscript, except for β. This is because β contains the fixed effects parameters that are shared by all the subjects.

The column dimension of the X_i design matrix is reduced or increased to accommodate various types of models with time predictors, static predictors, dynamic predictors, and functions thereof. Thus, Equation 5.6.2 is the general form of the LMER model in matrix notation.

Equation 5.6.2 has a direct connection to statistical programming, as X_i and Z_i are multipliers of the fixed effects and random effects, respectively. The columns of X_i, as depicted in Equation 5.6.1, are used in the fixed effects portion of the `lmer()` syntax, and the columns of Z_i are used in the random effects portion.

In terms of estimation, the labels in the design matrix of Equation 5.6.1 are replaced by numerical values. For quantitative predictors such as `grade`, the level labels are replaced by the associated values from the data frame. For categorical predictors, such as `risk2DADV`, the level labels are replaced by the associated dummy variable values of 0 and 1.

Conveniently, the X_i design matrix with numerical values is printed using the `model.matrix()` function based on a `lmer()` fitted model object. The `model.matrix()` function actually prints X_i for each participant in long format, with subject matrix stacked upon subject matrix.

Consider the following syntax that prints the head of the design matrix for the case with `grade` as the sole predictor, based on `lmer.1`.

```
> head(model.matrix(lmer.1))
```

	[,1]	[,2]
[1,]	1	5
[2,]	1	6
[3,]	1	7
[4,]	1	8
[5,]	1	5
[6,]	1	6

The first column of the design matrix is a vector of 1s, and the second column is the vector of `grade` values.

As a more complex example, consider the design matrix for the case with the grade predictor, the risk predictor, and their interaction. The output object for this model is `lmer.3`.

```
> head(model.matrix(lmer.3))
     [,1] [,2] [,3] [,4]
[1,]    1    5    1    5
[2,]    1    6    1    6
[3,]    1    7    1    7
[4,]    1    8    1    8
[5,]    1    5    1    5
[6,]    1    6    1    6
```

The first column is the vector of 1s, and the second column is the vector of `grade` values. The third column is the vector of `risk2DADV` values (only scores for disadvantaged students are shown), and the last column is the product of `grade` and `risk2DADV`.

The default `lmer()` output lists the estimated elements of β. The vector of random effects and error are usually implicit, which means they typically are not estimated. Rather, the variances and covariances are estimated, and they appear in the `lmer()` output. Chapters 9 and 10 discuss explicit estimation of random effects and random error, especially for regression diagnostics.

5.6.2 VARIANCE-COVARIANCE MATRIX AMONG REPEATED MEASURES*

Having presented the general form of the LMER model, it is now possible to provide additional details regarding the random effects. The focus is on the role of the random effects in accounting for the dependency inherent in longitudinal data.

To clarify the role of the random effects, the variance-covariance matrix among the repeated measures is first considered. The presentation is much simpler if balance on time is assumed, meaning that the subjects are measured at the same fixed time points. With this assumption, the variance-covariance matrix for a single subject is written as

$$\text{Var-Cov}(y_i) = V_i, \quad (5.6.3)$$

where V_i has dimensions $n_i \times n_i$. Equation 5.6.3 refers to the variances and covariances of y among the time points. For the example of $n_i = 4$ in the MPLS data set, the matrix is Equation 5.3.7, which is reproduced here:

$$V_i = \begin{bmatrix} \text{Var}(y_{i1}) & \text{Cov}(y_{i1}, y_{i2}) & \text{Cov}(y_{i1}, y_{i3}) & \text{Cov}(y_{i1}, y_{i4}) \\ \text{Cov}(y_{i2}, y_{i1}) & \text{Var}(y_{i2}) & \text{Cov}(y_{i2}, y_{i3}) & \text{Cov}(y_{i2}, y_{i4}) \\ \text{Cov}(y_{i3}, y_{i1}) & \text{Cov}(y_{i3}, y_{i2}) & \text{Var}(y_{i3}) & \text{Cov}(y_{i3}, y_{i4}) \\ \text{Cov}(y_{i4}, y_{i1}) & \text{Cov}(y_{i4}, y_{i2}) & \text{Cov}(y_{i4}, y_{i3}) & \text{Var}(y_{i4}) \end{bmatrix}. \quad (5.6.4)$$

5.6 Additional Details of LMER*

The matrix is symmetric, as $Cov(y_{ij}, y_{ij+1}) = Cov(y_{ij+1}, y_{ij})$. $Var(y_{ij})$ indexes the variability at a time point, and $Cov(y_{ij}, y_{ij+1})$ represents the dependency between two time points.

V_i can be decomposed into between-subjects and within-subjects components (Laird & Ware, 1982). The within-subjects component is based on the variance of the random errors, and the between-subjects component is based on the variance-covariance matrix among the random effects. The two components are additive, meaning a sum of two $n_i \times n_i$ matrices.

Let B_i stand for the between-subjects matrix, and let W_i stand for the within-subjects matrix. Then the decomposition is

$$V_i = B_i + W_i. \tag{5.6.5}$$

The within-subjects matrix is based on the random error variance and has the following form:

$$W_i = \sigma_\varepsilon^2 I_i, \tag{5.6.6}$$

where I_i is a $n_i \times n_i$ identity matrix. Consider the example of a subject with $n_i = 4$:

$$W_i = \sigma_\varepsilon^2 I_i = \sigma_\varepsilon^2 \begin{bmatrix} 1 & 0 & 0 & 0 \\ 0 & 1 & 0 & 0 \\ 0 & 0 & 1 & 0 \\ 0 & 0 & 0 & 1 \end{bmatrix} = \begin{bmatrix} \sigma_\varepsilon^2 & 0 & 0 & 0 \\ 0 & \sigma_\varepsilon^2 & 0 & 0 \\ 0 & 0 & \sigma_\varepsilon^2 & 0 \\ 0 & 0 & 0 & \sigma_\varepsilon^2 \end{bmatrix}. \tag{5.6.7}$$

The right-hand matrix in Equation 5.6.7 highlights the assumptions about the random error stated earlier. Namely, the 0 off-diagonal values reflect the independence assumption, and the equal diagonal values indicate constant variance, or *homogeneity of variance* over time.

The between-subjects matrix, B_i, is based on the variance-covariance matrix among the random effects, symbolized as G. Assume there are two random effects, as in most of the models considered in this chapter. Then G is the following:

$$Var\text{-}Cov(b_i) = G = \begin{bmatrix} Var(b_{0i}) & Cov(b_{0i}, b_{1i}) \\ Cov(b_{1i}, b_{0i}) & Var(b_{1i}) \end{bmatrix}. \tag{5.6.8}$$

The matrix is symmetric as $Cov(b_{0i}, b_{1i}) = Cov(b_{1i}, b_{0i})$. In general, G has dimension $(q+1) \times (q+1)$ with the number of unique elements being $\frac{(q+1)(q+2)}{2}$. G does not have a subject subscript, as it is based on all subjects, and thus, constant among subjects.

The between-subjects matrix, B_i, is constructed by pre-multiplying and post-multiplying G by Z_i, the design matrix for the random effects. That is,

$$B_i = Z_i G Z_i^T. \tag{5.6.9}$$

Since Z_i has dimensions $n_i \times (q+1)$, and G has dimensions $(q+1) \times (q+1)$, it follows that B_i has dimensions $n_i \times n_i$.

Putting everything together, the decomposition of the observed variance-covariance matrix is the following:

$$V_i = B_i + W_i = Z_i G Z_i^T + \sigma_\varepsilon^2 I_i. \quad (5.6.10)$$

V_i has the advantage of allowing heterogeneity of variance over time, with the covariances being a function of time spacing. This is advantageous, as much empirical longitudinal data exhibit such characteristics.

The subject subscript of V_i denotes that the dimensions of the matrix can vary based on missing data. For example, a subject with no missing data in the example ($n_i = 4$) will have a 4×4 matrix, whereas a subject with only two time points will have a 2×2 matrix.

5.6.3 IMPORTANCE OF RANDOM EFFECTS*

An important aspect of random effects is that they account for possible heterogeneity over time and dependency among the repeated measures. This implies that the variances and covariances in Equation 5.6.4 are a function of the random effects.

To see the relationship, consider an example of Equation 5.6.10 based on the model of Equation 5.3.5 discussed earlier in the chapter. The model has grade as the only predictor and two random effects. Suppose that $n_i = 4$. Working through Equation 5.6.10, it can be shown that the variance of a response is

$$Var(y_{ij}) = \frac{1}{c}\Big\{(\text{grade}_{ij})^2 \cdot Var(b_{0i}) + Var(b_{1i}) \\
+ \sigma_\varepsilon^2 \cdot Var(b_{0i}) \cdot Var(b_{1i}) - Cov(b_{0i}, b_{1i}) \quad (5.6.11) \\
\big[2 \cdot (\text{grade}_{ij}) - \sigma_\varepsilon^2 \cdot Cov(b_{0i}, b_{1i})\big]\Big\}$$

where

$$c = Var(b_{0i}) \cdot Var(b_{1i}) - \big[Cov(b_{0i}, b_{1i})\big]^2. \quad (5.6.12)$$

This provides greater detail regarding the earlier remark in the chapter: the variance of the response is a function of the time predictor, the variances and covariance among the random effects, and the error variance.

Now consider the covariance between the response at two time points. Again, working through Equation 5.6.10, it can be shown that

$$Cov(y_{ij}, y_{ij+1}) = \frac{1}{c}\Big\{(\text{grade}_{ij}) \cdot (\text{grade}_{ij+1}) \cdot Var(b_{0i}) + Var(b_{1i}) \\
- Cov(b_{0i}, b_{1i})\big[(\text{grade}_{ij}) + (\text{grade}_{ij+1})\big]\Big\} \quad (5.6.13)$$

The covariance is a function of the time predictor, the variances and covariance of the random effects, and the error variance. This illustrates that the random effects form the basis of a model appropriate for longitudinal data.

5.6 Additional Details of LMER*

In contrast to W_i, B_i does not generally have identical diagonal elements, and the off-diagonal elements are not equal to 0. Thus, the variance and covariance pattern in V_i is induced through B_i, meaning the presence of the random effects provides a model of dependency among the repeated measures.

To help examine the dependency structure among the repeated measures, V_i can be standardized, so that the off-diagonal elements are correlations rather than covariances. This also transforms all the variances to be equal to 1. Suppose the standardized matrix is denoted as V_i^*. Then,

$$V_i^* = D_i V_i D, \qquad (5.6.14)$$

where D_i is a diagonal matrix with elements,

$$\frac{1}{\sqrt{Var(y_{ij})}}.$$

5.6.4 WORKING WITH MATRICES IN R*

Equation 5.6.10 or 5.6.14 can be symbolically solved to examine the V_i or V_i^* structure. However, even with a small number of time points (e.g., $n_i = 4$), this involves several terms leading to a relatively complicated matrix.

An alternative approach is to consider a numeric example. Given numerical values for the elements of all the matrices, an example of V_i is computed using the matrix operations available in R. In the syntax below, various matrix functions are used, along with elements extracted from the lmer() output object.

Suppose the goal is to compute the variance-covariance matrix among the repeated measures for the first subject ($i = 1$). The correlation matrix will also be computed. The calculations require the matrices Z_1, $\hat{G}$, and W_1. Consider the LMER model of Equation 5.3.5, which has grade as the predictor, two random effects, and the fitted model object lmer.1.

First, the model.matrix() function is used with indexing to obtain Z_1.

```
> ## Estimate LMER model.
> lmer.1 ← lmer(read ~ grade + (grade|subid),MPLS.LS,REML = FALSE)
> ## Random effects design matrix for first person.
> Z ← model.matrix(lmer.1)[1:4, ]
> Z
```

	[,1]	[,2]
[1,]	1	5
[2,]	1	6
[3,]	1	7
[4,]	1	8

Now the estimated G matrix is extracted using the VarCorr() function. The subject identification variable must be indexed in this operation.

```
> G <- VarCorr(lmer.1)$subid[1:2,1:2]
> G
```

	(Intercept)	grade
(Intercept)	740.46698	-53.403676
grade	-53.40368	6.966213

The output shows the elements of the matrix, with the variances on the diagonal and the covariance on the off-diagonal. The diagonal elements are the same values listed in the Random effects table of the lmer() output.

Now the estimated value of the error variance is extracted. Then the identity matrix, I_1, is created, and the estimate of W_1 is computed. The diag() function is used to create the identity matrix, and * is used for scalar multiplication.

```
> ## Extract and save error variance.
> sigma2 <- summary(lmer.1)@sigma ^ 2
> ## Create 4 x 4 Identity matrix.
> Ident <- diag(4)
> # Compute W.
> W <- sigma2 * Ident
> W
```

	[,1]	[,2]	[,3]	[,4]
[1,]	18.31525	0.00000	0.00000	0.00000
[2,]	0.00000	18.31525	0.00000	0.00000
[3,]	0.00000	0.00000	18.31525	0.00000
[4,]	0.00000	0.00000	0.00000	18.31525

The output shows the matrix is diagonal, with a constant value of 18.32. This agrees with the symbolic illustration in Equation 5.6.7. The diagonal value appears in the Residual row of the lmer() output.

In the syntax below, an estimate of B_1 is computed using the operator for matrix multiplication, %*%, and the transpose, t().

```
> B <- Z %*% G %*% t(Z)
> B
```

	[,1]	[,2]	[,3]	[,4]
[1,]	380.5855	362.0129	343.4403	324.8677
[2,]	362.0129	350.4065	338.8001	327.1937
[3,]	343.4403	338.8001	334.1600	329.5198
[4,]	324.8677	327.1937	329.5198	331.8458

The output shows that the diagonal elements are not constant, and the off-diagonal elements are nonzero. Contrasting the above matrix with the estimate of W_1, it can be seen that the dependency pattern in the off-diagonal is accounted for by the between-subjects matrix. That is, the variance-covariance pattern among the repeated measures is induced by the variance-covariance among the random effects.

5.6 Additional Details of LMER*

The final step is to compute V_1. The plus symbol (+) is for matrix addition.

```
> V ← B + W
> V
```

```
           [,1]      [,2]      [,3]      [,4]
[1,]   398.9008  362.0129  343.4403  324.8677
[2,]   362.0129  368.7218  338.8001  327.1937
[3,]   343.4403  338.8001  352.4752  329.5198
[4,]   324.8677  327.1937  329.5198  350.1611
```

The output shows the estimate of V_1. The diagonal elements are model-based estimates of the variances of the reading scores over grade. The off-diagonal elements are estimates of the covariance between reading scores at pairs of grades. The diagonal elements indicate heterogeneity of variance, with the variance decreasing over time.

Inspection of the off-diagonal elements reveals that the magnitude of the covariance is a function of the time interval. Observations more closely spaced have a higher covariance than observations more distantly spaced. This is the decay pattern that characterizes much empirical longitudinal data.

It is also desirable to examine the correlations among the repeated measures. To compute the estimated V_1^* matrix, the following syntax is used.

```
> ## Create diagonal matrix, D.
> D ← diag(1 / sqrt(diag(V)))
> ## Compute Vstar.
> Vstar ← D %*% V %*% D
> Vstar
```

```
            [,1]       [,2]       [,3]       [,4]
[1,]   1.0000000  0.9439353  0.9159137  0.8692410
[2,]   0.9439353  1.0000000  0.9397880  0.9105875
[3,]   0.9159137  0.9397880  1.0000000  0.9379577
[4,]   0.8692410  0.9105875  0.9379577  1.0000000
```

The correlations show a decay pattern similar to the covariances.

The features of heterogeneity of variance and decay are common for longitudinal data. In this respect, the V_i matrix of LMER provides a realistic model for longitudinal data. On the other hand, LMER provides only one of a number of possible methods of accounting for correlated data. Alternative models are beyond our scope, and the interested reader is referred to the relevant chapters of Diggle et al. (2002), Fitzmaurice et al. (2004), or Pinheiro and Bates (2000).

Overview of Maximum Likelihood Estimation 6

In the last chapter, LMER models commonly used in longitudinal analysis were introduced. The emphasis was on conceptual understanding and practical aspects of estimating the models. This chapter goes a step deeper. Details of estimation are discussed, along with the foundations for the inferential methods considered in the remaining chapters.

There are three primary objectives of estimation and inference with LMER models:

- Computing point estimates of parameters,
- Computing indexes of uncertainty for the point estimates in the form of SEs, and
- Comparing different models based on global fit.

To accomplish these objectives, a general approach is considered, known as the method of *maximum likelihood* (ML) due to Ronald A. Fisher (Fisher, 1922). More recent treatments include Edwards (1992), Royall (1996), and Sprott (2000).

The intent of this chapter is to provide an overview of ML to aid in the successful specification and estimation of LMER models and the interpretation of output. The material is also helpful for troubleshooting problems in estimation. This chapter stresses conceptual issues important for applied research; for a more rigorous treatment, see texts such as Azzalini (1996). There is a discussion of some mathematical details related to ML, but this is provided to enhance overall understanding. Focus is on the normal distribution and its foundational role in ML estimation with LMER.

ML provides a foundation for the two main methods of inference discussed in this book. The first method is the relatively new approach of multimodel inference using the AIC. As discussed in Chapter 1, multimodel inference involves examining the AIC of many hypothesized models. The AIC is presented in this chapter, but its justification and use in multimodel inference are discussed in Chapter 7.

The second method is the LRT. The LRT is used to examine two nested models, with nesting meaning a smaller model is inside a bigger model. The LRT falls under the umbrella of traditional NHST. Although the LRT is introduced in this chapter, its use is more thoroughly discussed in Chapter 8. Additional inference methods, such as the Wald test and CIs, are also mentioned in this chapter.

To keep things manageable, ML is first discussed in the context of the LM before moving on to LMER. This mirrors the approach taken in Chapter 5, and it shows that many concepts applicable with the LM also apply to LMER.

6.1 Conceptual Overview

ML begins with the following question: for which parameter value are the data most likely? Or, more specifically, given the data and the model, what are the most likely values of the parameters? ML provides a framework for answering these questions. ML is a system in which the level of uncertainty in estimating the parameters is the smallest possible, considering the randomness of the data and the statistical model under consideration. Uncertainty is the bane of statistical analysis, but it is unavoidable when working with sample data. In principle, ML provides a means of minimizing the curse of uncertainty.

Generally speaking, ML provides a method of linking the crucial ingredients necessary for sound inference: the sample data, the unknown model parameters, and the statistical assumptions (e.g., normality). The ML framework enables the "wringing" of all the statistical information from the sample data and bringing it to bear on problems of inference. All the knowledge about the population parameters contained in the sample data can be extracted. The extraction provides results that have attractive properties, which are favorable for rigorous statistical inference.

On a facile level, ML is similar to OLS, as there is an optimization criterion that is the basis for computing estimates of parameters. As shown below, OLS is considered a special case of ML. With OLS, the optimization criterion is the sum of squared errors (SSE). SSE is "optimal" at its minimum or least value, hence the name ordinary *least* squares. When estimating the LM with sample data, the fixed effects estimates are chosen such that SSE is as small as possible.

In the case of ML, the optimization criterion is the *likelihood function*, or a transformation of it known as the *deviance function*, but the idea is the same as in OLS. The fixed effects estimates and other estimates are chosen so that the deviance is as small as possible. A complication with ML is that the deviance function is a probability model for the longitudinal responses, which includes all the parameters of the LMER model. Thus, the ML setup is more complex than the one for OLS. In the following sections, some of the complexities are discussed, and necessary concepts for overall understanding are introduced.

6.1 Conceptual Overview

One of the major points is that ML estimation yields not only values for the parameter estimates in the models, but also a global fit index. This index is the minimum of the deviance function obtained in the actual data analysis. The minimum deviance, or a transformation thereof, is used to compare the fit of different models to the same data. As will be seen in the next two chapters, many common research questions are addressed by model comparison based on the deviance.

An advantage of ML is that it produces statistics or, in ML terminology, *estimators*,[1] which have desirable large-sample (asymptotic) properties. For example, under certain regularity conditions that are assumed to hold throughout this book (see Azzalini, 1996), the ML estimators are consistent and asymptotically normally distributed. Consistency roughly means that as the sample size increases, the estimator converges to its goal. If the sample size is large but finite, these properties are expected to approximately hold.

"Large sample" means the sample size increases without bound. This is a convenient assumption in deriving certain results, such as the normality of the estimators. The large-sample assumption is often necessary due to the difficulty in deriving exact results for finite samples. With this in mind, it is important to remember that statistics derived under large-sample assumptions may not work well for situations in which the sample size is small. In such cases, applied researchers often "hope for the best" and assume without confirmation that the large-sample properties are valid when carrying out the analysis.

This brings up an important point about ML as applied in this text. Since the samples are finite and there are missing data, the ML results of this book are always approximate. The approximations can be quite good, so this should not be too startling a revelation. Furthermore, applied researchers should not shy away from approximate methods, as they are the stuff of science. As Betrand Russell said, "Although this may seem a paradox, all exact science is dominated by the idea of approximation" (Russell, 1931, p. 42).

On the other hand, approximate results suggest that one should not get too hung up on rigid rules of practice. For instance, it does not much matter whether a CI for a fixed effect is computed as Estimate± 2·(Std. Error) or as Estimate ± 1.96·(Std. Error). It is also the case that inflexible cutoffs, such as $\alpha = 0.05$, for declaring "statistical significance" are not warranted. In the next two chapters, an argument for an effect size approach to statistical inference is made that largely avoids the use of rigid cutoff values.

This chapter considers what are called *regular problems*, which means that ML solutions are possible. For all the inferential methods to be discussed, there is an assumption of a repeated sampling scenario. This is a concept from traditional statistics in which sample data are assumed to come from a hypothetical and infinite population. The data are assumed to be generated

---

[1] Estimators are statistics and can loosely be thought of as the formulas used to obtain numerical *estimates* with sample data.

by repetitions of the same underlying phenomenon (Sprott, 2000, chap. 1). In this scenario, no matter how many random samples have been drawn, it is supposed that another random sample can always be selected. This repeatability idea is a fundamental theme in the development of the properties of the ML estimators and the AIC.

6.2 Maximum Likelihood and LM

In the development of ML, a familiar starting point is the traditional regression model. In contrast to the last chapter, a cross section of the MPLS data set is selected for analysis, rather than the entire long-format data frame. The data at only one grade will be selected for each subject. Thus, longitudinal data will not be considered initially. For ease of explication, the cross-sectional data to be considered have no missing values.

Suppose a cross-section of data for the first, third, fifth, and seventh subjects are selected from the MPLS.LS data frame. For each subject, a unique grade is selected, along with the associated reading score. There are no repeated measures, random sampling is assumed, and the data are appropriate for traditional regression analysis. However, it should be emphasized that the sample size is much too small to draw any serious conclusions.

In the syntax below, the subset is selected, and the new data frame is printed. Then a graph of the observed points with the line of best fit is constructed.

```
> ## Select subset.
> mysubset <- subset(MPLS.LS, subid == 1 & grade == 5 | subid == 3 & grade == 6 |
+ subid == 5 & grade == 7 | subid == 7 & grade == 8,
+ select = c(subid, read, grade))
> mysubset
```

	subid	read	grade
1.5	1	172	5
3.6	3	199	6
5.7	5	212	7
7.8	7	218	8

```
> ## Graph with regression line.
> theme_set(theme_bw())
> myx <- scale_x_continuous(breaks = 5:8)
> g1 <- ggplot(mysubset, aes(grade, read)) + geom_point()
> g2 <- g1 + stat_smooth(method = "lm", se = FALSE) + myx
> print(g2)
```

The graph is shown in Figure 6.1. The points indicate an increasing trend over grade that is evident in the regression line. It is emphasized that each point in Figure 6.1 comes from a different subject.

Suppose that using the data in Figure 6.1, the goal is to estimate the value of the slope of the line. There is a traditional formula for computing this value,

6.2 Maximum Likelihood and LM

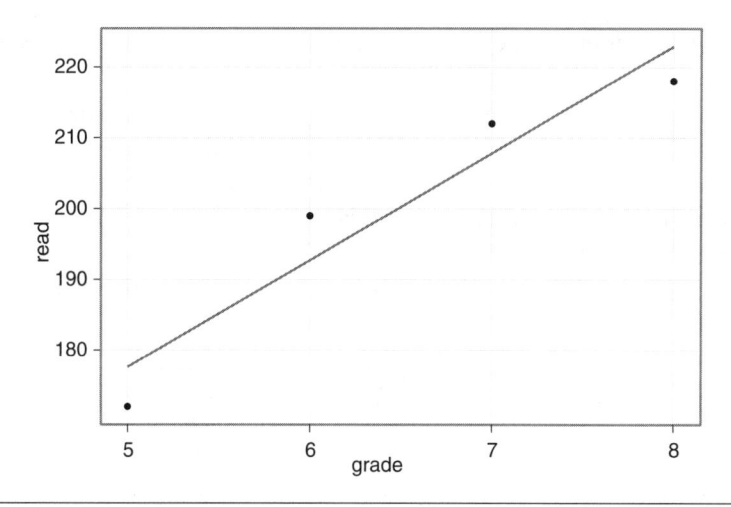

Figure 6.1 Scatterplot and regression line based on four subjects.

but for the moment, assume the formula is unknown. The reason for feigning ignorance is so that the concepts underlying ML can be illustrated.

In this example, ML estimation attempts to answer the following question: *Given the data and the model, what is the most likely value of the unknown slope parameter?* The first concern is the "given" in the last sentence. Obviously, the data are "given" as they reside in the mysubset data frame. What needs to be fleshed out is what is meant by a "given model."

For this example, the model consists of the traditional regression equation, with the enhancement of an explicit probability model. Based on Figure 6.1, the regression equation will have grade as the single predictor. As for the explicit probability model, a normal probability distribution is assumed, but other distributions are possible. The enhancement means the traditional regression equation is embedded in a normal probability model. The details of the embedding are provided below.

The probability model is specified before the analysis and gives the probability of all the possible samples for the parameters in the model. Inferences about the slope are made according to the model after the sample data are selected. Although the probability model is used for the ML setup, inferences are based on something called the *likelihood*, not probability. Philosophically speaking, the likelihood supplies an order of preference (or plausibility) among possible parameter values, given the observed data and the model (Sprott, 2000, chap. 2). The likelihood is denoted as *Lik*.

It is helpful to be more specific regarding the probability model for the regression example. In contrast to OLS, ML begins with a probability model for each and every observed score. In the context of traditional regression, this means an LM with a distributional assumption regarding the errors. For the example, the model of Section 5.3 is relevant and is written here again for convenience:

$$y_i = \beta_0 + \beta_1(\text{grade}_i) + \varepsilon_i. \quad (6.2.1)$$

As usual, it is assumed the ε_i are normally distributed with mean $\mu_\varepsilon = 0$ and variance $\sigma_\varepsilon^2 > 0$.

So far, nothing new is stated in comparison with the discussion in Chapter 5. However, the setup is not complete. To finish the ML setup, Equation 6.2.1 is expressed in terms of the normal probability model. It is instructive, then, to show the details of how this is accomplished.[2]

The ML setup for the example relies on the normality assumption for the errors. The normal distribution for the errors can be written in the following way:

$$\varepsilon_i \sim \mathcal{N}(\mu_\varepsilon, \sigma_\varepsilon^2) = f(\varepsilon_i) = \frac{\exp\left[-\frac{(\varepsilon_i - \mu_\varepsilon)^2}{2\sigma_\varepsilon^2}\right]}{\sqrt{2\pi\sigma_\varepsilon^2}},$$

where $\pi = 3.14159\ldots$ and $\exp(a) = e^a$. As per the error assumptions, $\mu_\varepsilon = 0$, and there is an additional simplification,

$$f(\varepsilon_i) = \frac{\exp\left[-\frac{\varepsilon_i^2}{2\sigma_\varepsilon^2}\right]}{\sqrt{2\pi\sigma_\varepsilon^2}}. \tag{6.2.2}$$

Equation 6.2.2 is a probability model, as there are different probabilities associated with different individual errors. Error values closer to the mean have a higher probability of being selected in a random draw, which is in contrast to error values farther from the mean. For every ε_i that is plugged into the equation, a corresponding probability value of $f(\varepsilon_i)$ is computed, representing the height of the normal curve at the value of ε_i.

As a slight aside, it is assumed that the ε_i are discrete values, so a probability is associated with each. There is an empirical argument for assuming discrete values: observations in the real world are always measured to a finite precision (Lindsey, 1999). This does lead to a contradiction of sorts, as the normal distribution is a continuous distribution. No attempt is made to reconcile these ideas.

To illustrate the concepts, it is shown how the probability, $f(\varepsilon_i)$, is computed for a specific value of ε_i. In R, this is accomplished using dnorm(). The dnorm() function has three main arguments: the value of the random variable (ε_i in this case), the value of the population mean ($\mu_\varepsilon = 0$), and the value of the population SD ($\sqrt{\sigma_\varepsilon^2}$).

Suppose for the example, $\sigma_\varepsilon^2 = 1$ and $\varepsilon_1 = -1$. Then the height of the curve, $f(\varepsilon_i)$, over $\varepsilon_1 = -1$ is the following.

```
> dnorm(-1, mean = 0, sd = sqrt(1))

[1] 0.2419707
```

---

[2] Some properties that might be useful for this section are $e^a \cdot e^b = e^{a+b}$, $\log(a \cdot b) = \log(a) + \log(b)$, $\log(a^b) = b \cdot \log(a)$, $\log(\frac{a}{b}) = \log(a) - \log(b)$, and $\log(e^a) = a$.

6.2 Maximum Likelihood and LM

The output shows the probability associated with $\varepsilon_1 = -1$ is $f(\varepsilon_i) = 0.24$.

It is helpful to use dnorm() to obtain $f(\varepsilon_i)$ for many values of ε_i. Then one can examine how the height of the curve—that is, the probability—changes as the ε_i change.

In the following syntax, a data frame of the ε_i is created, called norm.ex. The errors are incremented by 0.1 for values in the range of $(-4, 4)$. That is, $\varepsilon_i = -4.0, -3.9, -3.8, \ldots, 3.8, 3.9, 4.0$. The value of $f(\varepsilon_i)$ is computed for each ε_i, and then a graph is constructed.

```
> norm.ex <- data.frame(eps = seq(from = -4, to = 4, by = 0.1) )
> norm.ex$f.of.eps <- dnorm(norm.ex$eps, mean = 0, sd = 1)
> head(norm.ex)
    eps     f.of.eps
1  -4.0   0.0001338302
2  -3.9   0.0001986555
3  -3.8   0.0002919469
4  -3.7   0.0004247803
5  -3.6   0.0006119019
6  -3.5   0.0008726827
```

```
> g1 <- ggplot(data = norm.ex, aes(x = eps, y = f.of.eps)) + geom_line()
> g2 <- g1 + geom_abline(intercept = 0, slope = 0, linetype = 2)
> g3 <- g2 + ylab(expression(italic(f)(epsilon)))
> g4 <- g3 + xlab(expression(paste("Epsilon ", (epsilon))))
> print(g4)
```

The graph is shown in Figure 6.2. The curve shows the typical bell shape of the normal distribution. As an aside, the expression() function is used with ggplot2 to provide special typesetting in this chapter.

Having introduced the details of the normal distribution, attention is now turned to its role in ML estimation. The central feature of ML is the *Lik* function, which is the basis for all inferential methods in ML. The *Lik* function consists of a probability model for each and every potential observation. For the LM, this means that under the assumption of independence, the normal distribution of Equation 6.2.2 is defined for each ε_i, and then the individual models are multiplied.[3] Using the left-hand notation of Equation 6.2.2, the *Lik* function is

$$Lik = \left[f(\varepsilon_1)\right] \cdot \left[f(\varepsilon_2)\right] \cdot \cdots \cdot \left[f(\varepsilon_{N-1})\right] \cdot \left[f(\varepsilon_N)\right]$$
$$= \left(\frac{1}{\sqrt{2\pi\sigma_\varepsilon^2}}\right)^N \cdot \exp\left(-\frac{\sum_i^N \varepsilon_i^2}{2\sigma_\varepsilon^2}\right). \quad (6.2.3)$$

The product of normal distributions is relatively difficult to work with, and it is more convenient to take the natural log of the *Lik* function, which is the

---
[3] Recall that the joint probability of two or more events is the product of their individual probabilities. For example, the probability of getting two "heads" for the tosses of two fair coins is $0.5 \cdot 0.5 = 0.25$.

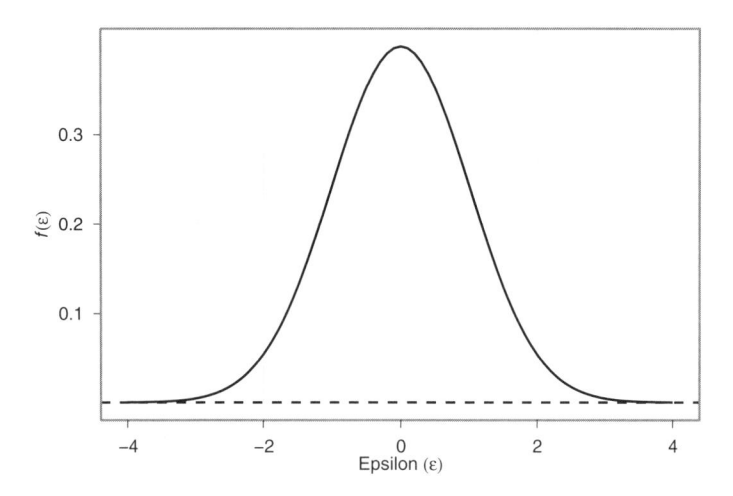

Figure 6.2 Graph of $f(\varepsilon)$ by ε.

log-likelihood (*logLik*) function.[4] Using the right-hand side of Equation 6.2.2 and keeping in mind there are N equations, the *logLik* function is

$$logLik = log(Lik) = -\frac{N}{2} \cdot log(2\pi\sigma_\varepsilon^2) - \frac{1}{2\sigma_\varepsilon^2} \cdot \sum_i^N \varepsilon_i^2. \qquad (6.2.4)$$

An additional simplification is to multiply the *logLik* function by -2, yielding the *deviance function*. The deviance function is written as

$$\begin{aligned} deviance &= -2 \cdot logLik \\ &= N \cdot log(2\pi\sigma_\varepsilon^2) + \frac{1}{\sigma_\varepsilon^2} \cdot \sum_i^N \varepsilon_i^2 \qquad (6.2.5) \\ &= N \cdot log(2\pi\sigma_\varepsilon^2) + \frac{1}{\sigma_\varepsilon^2} \cdot \sum_i^N (y_i - \beta_0 - \beta_1 \cdot \texttt{grade}_i)^2. \end{aligned}$$

It may not be clear to every reader how Equation 6.2.5 is obtained from Equation 6.2.2 and Equation 6.2.3; see footnote 2. However, it is hoped that every reader will have at least an intuitive sense that the terms, such as π, come from the equation for the normal distribution, and N and $\sum_i^N$ are a result of having a normal distribution for each of the N potential observations (i.e., the ε_i).

The logic underlying ML estimation is illustrated with the deviance function. The deviance function is chosen because it makes the math easier and produces some similarities with OLS. The main idea behind ML is that once observations are collected and a model is adopted, values for the unknown parameter(s)—for example, β_1—are chosen so that the deviance function is at its smallest possible value (or smallest value in a practical sense).

---

[4]Throughout this book, *log* refers to the natural logarithm.

6.2 Maximum Likelihood and LM

To get an intuitive sense of this minimization process, consider the observed data of the four subjects in the `mysubset` data frame previously shown. From the printing of `mysubset`, it can be verified that

$$(read_1, grade_1) = (172, 5),$$
$$(read_2, grade_2) = (199, 6),$$
$$(read_3, grade_3) = (212, 7),$$
$$(read_4, grade_4) = (218, 8).$$

For purposes of illustration, a relatively implausible case is considered, one in which the researcher knows the values of the population intercept and error variance. Later in the chapter, a more plausible situation is discussed, one in which none of the parameters are known. Assume the LM of Equation 6.2.1, with $\beta_0 = 102$ and $\sigma_\varepsilon^2 = 49$. Given the model with the known parameter values and the observed data, the object is to select the best value for the slope, β_1. The "best value" means the number that when substituted into Equation 6.2.5, will produce the smallest deviance. In terms of ML theory, this is the estimate of β_1 that is maximally likely, given the model and the observed data—hence the term *maximum likelihood*.

Under the above scenario, everything is a known value in Equation 6.2.5, except for β_1. The idea is to express the deviance as a function of the unknown parameter. Using the known parameter values, the data values, and $N = 4$, the deviance is the following.

$$\begin{aligned} deviance = {} & 4 \cdot log(2 \cdot \pi \cdot 49) + \frac{1}{49} \cdot (172 - 102 - \beta_1 \cdot 5)^2 \\ & + (199 - 102 - \beta_1 \cdot 6)^2 + (212 - 102 - \beta_1 \cdot 7)^2 \\ & + (218 - 102 - \beta_1 \cdot 8)^2. \end{aligned} \quad (6.2.6)$$

Given the data and the model, what are likely and unlikely values of the population slope, β_1? Based on Figure 6.1, it appears relatively unlikely that $\beta_1 < 0$. It is unlikely to obtain the data in Figure 6.1 sampling from a population with a negative slope, although it should be pointed out that seemingly odd things can happen with a very small sample size. It appears more likely that the data arose from a population with a positive slope. It is desirable to be more precise, and ML provides a systematic way of searching for the most likely slope parameter candidate.

Using calculus, the analytic formula for the best candidate of β_1 can be derived. The result is the familiar formula of the covariance of reading and grade, divided by the variance of grade; see Equation 1.3.1. For purposes of illustration, suppose the analytic formula for obtaining the best candidate is not known.

Without the formula for the sample slope, one approach to finding the best value for β_1 is to substitute in several candidate values, compute the deviance of Equation 6.2.6 for each, and then pick the β_1 candidate that produces the smallest deviance. In R, this is accomplished by writing a function for Equation 6.2.6, creating a range of candidate values for β_1, solving the function for each candidate value, and saving the results. Once the computations are finished, the results are inspected for the candidate value associated with the smallest deviance.

In the syntax below, the dev.func() function is created, and mdply() is used to compute the deviance based on candidate values of β_1. The β_1 values are incremented by 0.1 in the range (13, 17) using the seq() function. This range of search values is chosen to facilitate the illustration and will not necessarily produce the optimal result. The results are stored in the data frame, dev.store. Note the value of π is specified as pi in R.

```
> ## Create the function.
> dev.func <- function(B1) {4 * log(2 * pi * 49) + (1 / 49) *
+ sum((mysubset$read - 102 - B1 * mysubset$grade) ^ 2)}
> ## Generate the values of the deviance and the store results.
> dev.store <- mdply(data.frame(B1 = seq(from = 13, to = 17, by = 0.1)),
+ dev.func)
> colnames(dev.store)[2] <- "deviance"
> head(dev.store)
```

	B1	deviance
1	13.0	41.10246
2	13.1	39.63593
3	13.2	38.24042
4	13.3	36.91593
5	13.4	35.66246
6	13.5	34.48001

What candidate value of β_1 should be picked from among the list in dev.store? As was said, the best candidate is the one for which the deviance is the smallest. The row of dev.store having the smallest value of deviance can be selected with subset().

```
> subset(dev.store, deviance == min(deviance))
```

	B1	deviance
22	15.1	25.21961

The output reveals that the 22nd row of dev.store contains the smallest value of deviance, which is 25.22. Thus, the best candidate for β_1 is $\hat{\beta}_1 = 15.1$. This last value is the *maximum likelihood estimate*, which is the estimate of the population slope, symbolized as $\hat{\beta}_1$.

The deviance value has no meaning in isolation, as it is not on a standard scale like other quantities, such as R^2. The deviance does have relative meaning and is useful for model comparison. This topic is explored below.

Additional insight is gained by graphing the deviance as a function of the β_1 candidate values, which can be done using ggplot2. In addition to constructing the graph, the geom_abline() component is used to draw a horizontal line based on the smallest deviance value in the data frame.

6.2 Maximum Likelihood and LM

```
> g1 <- ggplot(data = dev.store, aes(x = B1, y = deviance)) + geom_line()
> g2 <- g1 + geom_abline(intercept = min(dev.store$deviance), slope = 0, linetype = 2)
> g3 <- g2 + ylab(expression(italic(deviance))) + xlab(expression(beta[1]))
> print(g3)
```

The graph is shown in Figure 6.3. The curve is convex with respect to the horizontal axis (or concave-up), with its minimum occurring at deviance = 25.22, B1 = 15.1. The dashed horizontal line is the tangent at the aforementioned point. The intercept of the tangent line is the value of the deviance associated with the ML estimate of the slope parameter. Typically, it is this minimum deviance and only this value that is reported in statistical output, as will be seen below. When the context is clear, the minimum deviance based on sample data will be referred to as the *deviance*.

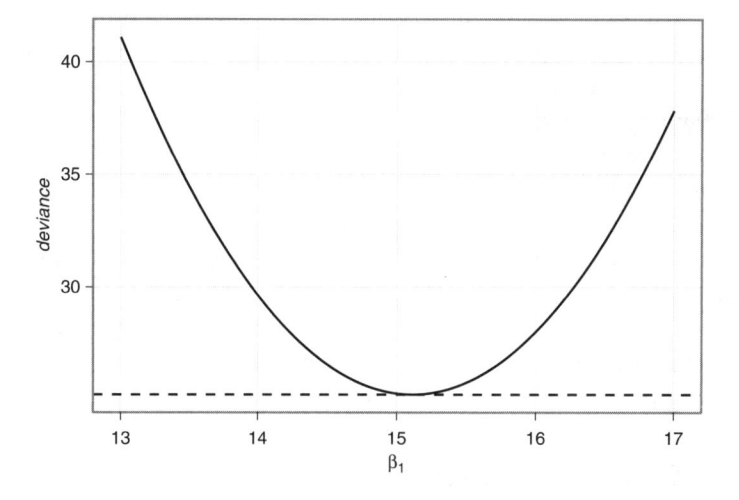

Figure 6.3 Graph of deviance by candidate values of β_1.

At this point, the reader may have some questions regarding the need for the search process for $\hat{\beta}_1$ just described. After all, there is a formula for computing $\hat{\beta}_1$ directly from observed data. Although the details are not presented, it can be shown that the traditional formula for $\hat{\beta}_1$ "cuts to the chase," in the respect that the best $\hat{\beta}_1$ is directly computed without having to perform the type of search just described. The traditional formula computes $\hat{\beta}_1$ for which the deviance is the smallest possible. The obvious advantage of the traditional formula is that an exhaustive search can be avoided.

In the case of multiple regression, equations for the ML estimators can be derived directly from the deviance function. This is accomplished by taking the partial derivative of Equation 6.2.5 with respect to each parameter, setting it to 0, and then solving for the unknown parameter. Once the formulas are derived, it is obviously easier to use them than to perform an exhaustive search. If the traditional formula for $\hat{\beta}_1$ finds the optimal value directly, then why introduce the exhaustive search concepts of this section? There are several reasons.

First, for more complex models including LMER models, estimation is not so straightforward as plugging in observed values to a set formula. In general, formulas are not available for ML estimators. Thus, one must use exhaustive search methods, or closely related iterative procedures known as *numerical methods* (Bolker, 2008, chap. 7).

With LMER, a deviance function (or *logLik* function) more complex than that of Equation 6.2.5 is defined. Then a tangent line such as the horizontal line in Figure 6.3—or something analogous to it in multidimensional space—must be searched for and hopefully discovered. Computer algorithms for this search constitute a good portion of the "guts" of functions such as lmer(). Although the specifics of these algorithms are not considered, it is good to have a general idea of what they do—hence the purpose of the illustration.

Second, it is important to discuss the deviance function. From an ML perspective, the deviance function contains all the inferential information of the sample for a particular model (Berger & Wolpert, 1988; Edwards, 1992; Lindsey, 1999; Royall, 1996). By this, it is meant that any type of inference based on the sample data is accomplished most effectively through the deviance function. This includes parameter estimation, quantification of uncertainty, and model comparison. Details are provided in a moment.

Third, by considering the details of the ML setup for LM and LMER, insight is gained into how the two models differ. More specifically, the ML setup for LMER provides an indication of how the random effects account for the dependency due to the repeated observations. It also provides clues about what can go wrong in the estimation process and how to fix such problems.

6.2.1 SEVERAL UNKNOWN PARAMETERS

In the last section, the case of only one unknown parameter was considered, β_1. This is an implausible situation, as the researcher usually does not know the value of the intercept or the slope. The value of σ_ε^2 is also unknown, but let us take one step at a time. Eventually, the case in which none of the parameters are known will be discussed.

Consider the simple LM from above, only this time assume that the value of the population intercept and slope are unknown. Using the observed data, and again assuming $\sigma_\varepsilon^2 = 49$, the deviance function with the sample data is

$$deviance = 4 \cdot log(2 \cdot \pi \cdot 49) + \frac{1}{49} \cdot (172 - \beta_0 - \beta_1 \cdot 5)^2$$
$$+ (199 - \beta_0 - \beta_1 \cdot 6)^2 + (212 - \beta_0 - \beta_1 \cdot 7)^2 \quad (6.2.7)$$
$$+ (218 - \beta_0 - \beta_1 \cdot 8)^2 .$$

β_0 and β_1 both appear in Equation 6.2.7, meaning they are the two unknowns. In this case, the deviance function is a plane in three-dimensional space, with each point having the coordinates $x = \beta_0, y = \beta_1, z = deviance$. Although formulas for the intercept and slope are available (see Equation 1.3.1), here

6.2 Maximum Likelihood and LM

a search is used to find the best values. Candidate values for both β_0 and β_1 must be considered simultaneously.

In the syntax below, the `dev.func()` function is written to carry out the search. For the candidate values, `expand.grid()` is used to create a data set that combines every value of β_0 with every value of β_1. For ease of exposition, the search increments are by 0.1 for each value in the range of $(89, 106)$ for β_0 and $(12, 18)$ for β_1. The ranges are chosen to facilitate illustration and to avoid the creation of a very large data frame.

```
> ## Create the function.
> dev.func <- function(B0, B1) {4 * log(2 * pi * 49) + (1 / 49) *
+ sum((mysubset$read - B0 - B1 * mysubset$grade) ^ 2)}
> ## Generate the values of the deviance and store the results.
> dev.store <- mdply(expand.grid(B0 = seq(98,106,by = 0.1), B1 = seq(12,18,by = 0.1)),
+ dev.func)
> colnames(dev.store)[3] <- "deviance"
> head(dev.store)
```

	B0	B1	deviance
1	98.0	12	74.20450
2	98.1	12	73.80940
3	98.2	12	73.41593
4	98.3	12	73.02410
5	98.4	12	72.63389
6	98.5	12	72.24532

The `expand.grid()` function creates a data frame with many rows (4941). Therefore, only the beginning of the data frame is printed.

The row of `dev.store` associated with the minimum deviance is again selected using `subset()`.

```
> subset(dev.store, deviance == min(deviance))
```

	B0	B1	deviance
2553	102.1	15.1	25.21879

The output shows that row 2553 contains the minimum deviance. The ML estimates in this situation are $\hat{\beta}_0 = 102.1$ and $\hat{\beta}_1 = 15.1$.

In the case of two unknown parameters, the graph of the deviance function requires three dimensions (3-D). It is not possible to produce 3-D graphs with `ggplot2`, and an alternative is considered. The alternative is `wireframe()`, which is part of the `lattice` package that is automatically installed with the `lme4` package. The author of `lattice` is Deepayan Sarkar (Sarkar, 2007). The syntax for `wireframe()` should be evident to the reader at this point, and it is presented below without comment.

```
> wireframe(deviance ~ B0 * B1, dev.store)
```

The graph is shown in Figure 6.4. The arrows indicate increasing values for the axes. The plane has its minimum at the 3-D point $B0 = 102.1, B1 = 15.1, \text{deviance} = 25.22$. It is this low point that is associated with the ML estimates.

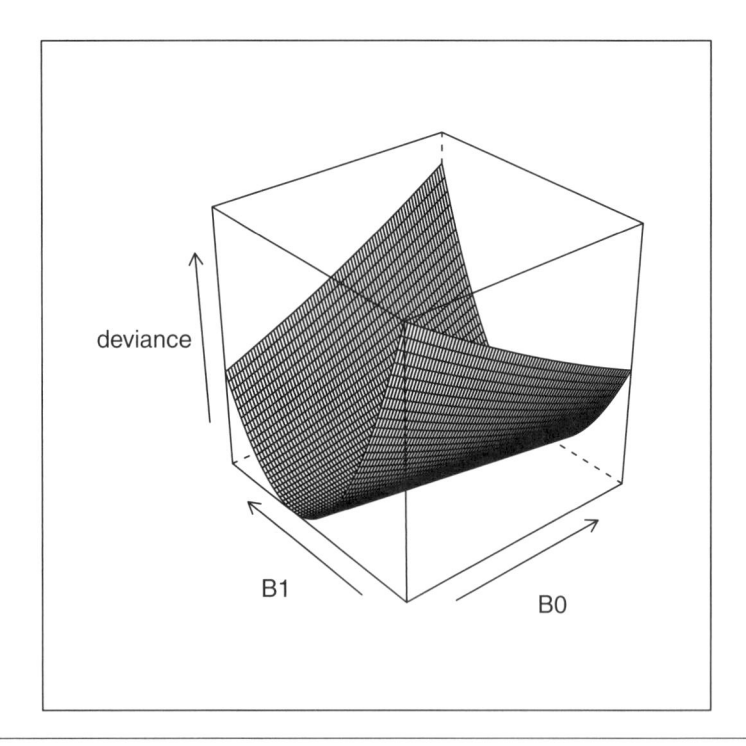

Figure 6.4 Graph of *deviance* by candidate values of β_0 and β_1.

The floor of the graph in Figure 6.4 is the horizontal plane on which the function "rests." The function has its minimum deviance at the floor. It is this floor that needs to be found in an actual analysis. It yields the minimum deviance and also the best candidate values for the parameters. In more complex situations, such as with LMER, the floor may not be so easy to identify. In such cases, numerical methods are typically used rather than an exhaustive search.

To this point, knowledge of σ_ε^2 has been assumed. In the most realistic case, none of the three parameters are known (β_0, β_1, σ_ε^2). With three unknowns, the level of complexity increases. The deviance function is now a hyperplane in 4-D space, which is rather difficult to depict graphically.

One can imagine with more predictors or different models such as LMER, the number of parameters can proliferate, leading to a relatively complex function. Regardless of the complexity, the goal is always to find the minimum point at which the deviance is the smallest. The candidate values at the minimum point are the ML estimates. Again, the internal workings of functions such as `lmer()` contain algorithms for performing such searches (thank goodness for computers!).

6.2.2 EXHAUSTIVE SEARCH AND NUMERICAL METHODS

Each example above using `dev.func()` is an instance of an exhaustive search to find the minimum deviance and the ML estimates. The examples

6.2 Maximum Likelihood and LM

are artificial, in that convenient ranges are set that are known to contain the ML estimates. In practice, such ranges are rarely known, and a much more expansive search grid must be used.

In addition to expanding the ranges of the search, the grid over which the search is performed is usually finer than considered in the examples. In the case of the unknown intercept and slope just considered, the search was incremented by 0.1 for the candidate values of β_0 and β_1. In practice, a more thorough search is preferable to allow for a finer resolution. A search increment of 0.001 might be used, for example. Given the relatively gross searches performed above, the "ML estimates" might not be particularly accurate. Serious estimation involves more precise methods and greater accuracy.

One problem with a finer and expanded search grid is computing time and memory. Incrementing by 0.001 over a greater range of values will result in a very large `dev.store` object that can take a long time to compute. For many problems, it is not clear over what range to search. Searching over too narrow a range can lead to incorrect solutions, and searching over a very broad range with a fine resolution can result in a very time-consuming and memory-consuming process. LMER models with many parameters compound the problems, and exhaustive searches may not be feasible.

As an alternative to an exhaustive search, numerical methods based on calculus are used. One of the best known is the *Newton-Raphson method* (Bolker, 2008, chap. 7). Such methods constitute much of the internal workings of functions such as `lmer()`. Numerical methods are saddled with the so-called regularity assumption, meaning that the deviance function is smooth, is continuous, and has a single minimum value. In most applications, this is true, or it is safe to assume it is true. However, in theory, deviance (and likelihood) functions can be wiggly and have gaps.

Given the regularity assumptions about the deviance function, numerical methods use first and second derivatives to move very quickly to the minimum deviance. This results in a much faster and less resource-intensive process than an exhaustive search. Once the algorithm is in the neighborhood of the minimum deviance, there is a much more limited type of "search" than with the exhaustive search method. This limited search consists of iterations involving derivatives and roots of derivatives, and it stops when the solution is close enough to the minimum to call it a day. For additional details and illustrations using R, see Bolker (2008, chap. 7).

For an illustration of the iterative process just described, consider a foray into LMER analysis with the MPLS data set. The object is to show that `lmer()` uses iterative numerical methods, and information regarding these procedures can be extracted if desired.

Output related to the iterative process is printed by using the optional argument `verbose=TRUE`. Consider the estimation of the model having `grade` as the predictor with one random effect term (random intercepts).

```
> print(lmer.0 <- lmer(read ~ grade + (1 | subid), MPLS.LS,
+ REML = FALSE, verbose = TRUE), cor = FALSE)
```

```
 1  0:   630.28212:  0.856349
 2  1:   588.35548:  1.85635
 3  2:   582.39837:  2.24625
 4  3:   578.88930:  2.72023
 5  4:   578.00143:  3.02706
 6  5:   577.82774:  3.20530
 7  6:   577.81509:  3.26311
 8  7:   577.81487:  3.27154
 9  8:   577.81487:  3.27187
10  9:   577.81487:  3.27187
11 Linear mixed model fit by maximum likelihood
12 Formula: read ~ grade + (1 | subid)
13 Data: MPLS.LS
14   AIC     BIC      logLik     deviance    REMLdev
15  585.8   595.3     -288.9      577.8       572.5
16 Random effects:
17  Groups   Name          Variance   Std.Dev.
18  subid    (Intercept)   312.315    17.6724
19  Residual               29.174      5.4013
20 Number of obs: 80, groups: subid, 22
21
22 Fixed effects:
23             Estimate    Std. Error    t value
24 (Intercept)  177.211      5.301        33.43
25 grade          4.968      0.582         8.54
```

Output lines 1 to 10 show the iterations. The regular `lmer()` output begins on line 11. The first column in the top part of the output indicates the iteration number. The initial starting point is represented by 0. The output indicates that nine iterations were required to find the "close enough" minimum deviance.

The first numerical column shows the deviance for each iteration. The deviance *decreases* as `lmer()` iterates, showing that it is closing in on the minimum value. The deviance in the last iteration was chosen as the minimum (line 10). The deviance in line 10 is the same value as in line 15 of the default output (`deviance` column) rounded to one decimal place.

The last column in the iteration output is the ratio of the estimated SD of the intercept to the estimated SD of the random error—that is, an estimate of $\sqrt{Var(b_{0i})}/\sqrt{\sigma_\varepsilon^2}$. As the iterations progress, the ratio increases in this example, but the result is not to be taken as typical. The reader should confirm that the ratio of the SDs in lines 18 and 19 is equal to the value in the last column of line 10, $3.2719/5.4013 = 3.2719$.

The verbose output need not be routinely produced. In fact, the default is `verbose=FALSE`. In certain troubleshooting situations, when `lmer()` produces an error message or does not provide proper estimates, the verbose output is helpful for diagnosing the problem.

6.2.3 RESTRICTED MAXIMUM LIKELIHOOD

As mentioned, calculus can be used with the deviance function to obtain equations for the ML estimators. This includes the ML estimator of σ_ε^2 in the LM. Although the details of the derivation are skipped, it can be shown that the estimator of the ML error variance, $\hat{\sigma}_{\varepsilon,\mathrm{ML}}^2$, is

$$\hat{\sigma}_{\varepsilon,\mathrm{ML}}^2 = \frac{\sum_i^N \hat{\varepsilon}_i^2}{N}, \qquad (6.2.8)$$

where the subscript contains "ML" for reasons to be explained in a moment.

It can be shown that Equation 6.2.8 is a biased estimator of the population error variance. This means that under repeated sampling, the average or expected value of $\hat{\sigma}_{\varepsilon,\mathrm{ML}}^2$ is not equal to the population value. Specifically, the expected value *underestimates* the population value, meaning the sample estimate tends to be too small.

To correct the bias, an alternate denominator is used. The result is called the *restricted maximum likelihood* (REML) estimator of σ_ε^2. The REML estimator is

$$\hat{\sigma}_{\varepsilon,\mathrm{REML}}^2 = \frac{\sum_i^N \hat{\varepsilon}_i^2}{N - p - 1}, \qquad (6.2.9)$$

where $p =$ the number of predictors in the LM. The square root of Equation 6.2.9 is known as the *residual standard error* (RSE), which is printed by default in the summary() listing of the fitted lm() object.

ML without the bias correction is known as *full ML*, or simply ML. REML is standard with both lm() and lmer(), but its use is not emphasized for the following reasons.

First, when the sample size is large, ML and REML results will be very close. In fact, as the sample size increases without bound, the ML and REML results converge. This means that the ML estimators are nearly unbiased for large sample sizes. Most of the ML results used for inference are based on large-sample theory. Using a large-sample variance is consistent with this general approach.

Second, and more important, REML is a correction for variances, but the nature of the correction depends on the fixed effects structure of the model. The problem for LMER is that there is a term in the REML correction that is affected by the fixed effects structure. This means that two nested models, for example, will differ not only in their number of fixed effects, but also in their correction terms. This does not provide a common basis for comparing the models, and it follows that REML should not be used for such comparisons (Pinheiro & Bates, 2000, chap. 2). ML does not suffer from this problem, and thus, provides a sound basis for model comparison. Because model comparisons are a major part of the remaining chapters, ML rather than REML is emphasized throughout this book. Additional details are provided in the optional section at the end of the chapter.

6.2.4 EXTRACTING THE LOG-LIKELIHOOD AND THE DEVIANCE

For purposes of model comparison, it is useful to extract the deviance from fitted model objects. As seen below, the `deviance()` function is used for this purpose with a `lmer()` output object. For an `lm()` object, the *logLik* value must be extracted and multiplied by −2 to compute the deviance.[5]

First consider the previous LM example with the output object `lm.1`. The `logLik()` function is used to extract the *logLik*, and then the deviance is computed.

```
> ## Estimate the model.
> lm.1 <- lm(read ~ grade, data = mysubset)
> ## Extract the log-likelihood.
> ll.1 <- logLik(lm.1)
> ## Compute the deviance.
> dev.1 <- -2 * as.numeric(ll.1)
> dev.1
```

```
[1] 24.70525
```

The output indicates that *deviance* = 24.71. The `as.numeric()` function is necessary because `logLik()` saves some additional pieces of information, such as the sample size and the number of estimated parameters.

6.2.5 COMPARING MODELS

The deviance is a solid foundation for comparing models. Deviance is the basis for the AIC and the LRT, which are the two major methods of inference discussed in the next two chapters.

As an illustration of model comparison based on deviance, consider the fit of the simple regression model of Equation 6.2.1, with an even simpler intercept-only model. The intercept-only model is the equation for a horizontal line,

$$y_i = \beta_0 + \varepsilon_i. \quad (6.2.10)$$

The horizontal line has the vertical location (intercept) of β_0.

The linear model was previously fit to the `mysubset` data. Suppose the intercept-only model is fit as well. Scatterplots with the regression lines for the models are shown in Figures 6.5a and 6.5b. The vertical dotted lines are the estimated errors or residuals.

The graphs show the unsurprising result that the residuals are larger for the intercept-only model (Figure 6.5a), except for sixth grade. Therefore, the fit of the linear model should be better than that of the intercept-only model. This will be reflected in the deviance of the models.

---
[5] When the `deviance()` function is used with a `lm()` object, the sum of squared residuals is computed rather than −2·(*logLik*).

6.2 Maximum Likelihood and LM

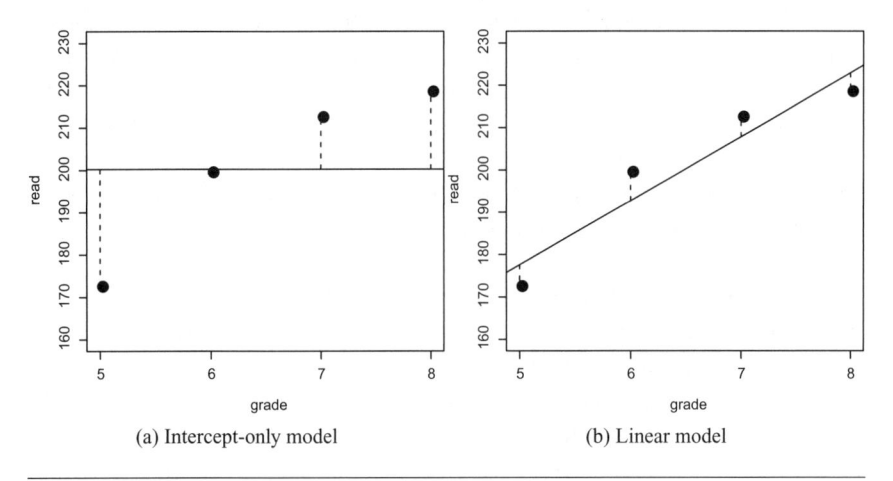

Figure 6.5 Regression lines for two models with the same data.

(a) Intercept-only model

(b) Linear model

If the ML estimator of Equation 6.2.8 is used, then the deviance function simplifies to

$$\begin{aligned} deviance &= N \cdot log(2 \cdot \pi \cdot \hat{\sigma}^2_{\varepsilon,\text{ML}}) + N \\ &= N\left[log\left(2 \cdot \pi \cdot N^{-1} \cdot \sum_i^N \hat{\varepsilon}_i^2\right) + 1 \right]. \end{aligned} \qquad (6.2.11)$$

The term $\sum \hat{\varepsilon}_i^2$ is the sum of squared residuals (SSR), which is the only quantity in Equation 6.2.11 that is not a constant. For a fixed sample size, the SSR is the sole influence on the size of the deviance. Therefore, minimizing Equation 6.2.11 is equivalent to minimizing the SSR. Since OLS is based on minimizing the same thing, it can be considered a special case of ML. An important qualification is that this special case is only for the LM and not LMER.

Based on Figures 6.5a and 6.5b, it is expected that the SSR will be smaller for the linear model compared to the intercept-only model. It follows that the deviance for the linear model should also be smaller.

The linear model was estimated above and saved as `lm.1`. Now the intercept-only model is estimated and saved as `lm.0`. The deviance is computed for both models.

```
> lm.0 <- lm(read ~ 1, mysubset)
> comp <- data.frame(deviance = c(-2 * logLik(lm.1), -2 * logLik(lm.0)))
> rownames(comp) <- c("Linear", "Intercept-only")
> comp
```

```
                deviance
Linear          24.70525
Intercept-only  34.33872
```

As the output shows, the deviance for the linear model (*deviance* = 24.71) is less than that for the intercept-only model (*deviance* = 34.34). It can be shown that any model with additional parameters will fit the sample data better than any model with fewer parameters. The SSR will always decrease when predictors are added to the model. Therefore, the deviance will always be *smaller* for the more complex model. This is analogous to R^2, which always improves when predictors are added to the model (the same is *not* true of *adj.* R^2).

It may be the case that the added predictors are worthless, in the sense of having population regression weights equal to 0. In such a case, the SSR will still decrease relative to a model omitting the worthless predictors. Except in some contrived or anomalous situations, additional predictors will make the more complex model conform more closely to the sample data, even if this conformity is to random error. Much more will be said about this topic in the next chapter.

To help guard against adding potentially worthless predictors, the deviance can be "penalized" by adding a term that is a function of the number of parameters in the model. The penalized indexes considered here are known generally as *information criteria* (IC), and have the form

$$IC = deviance + penalty.$$

Similar to the deviance, *smaller IC values indicate better fit*. The penalty term is always nonnegative and increases as parameters are added to the model. IC are based on a trade-off between fit to the data—as represented by the deviance—and complexity of the model—as represented by the penalty term. IC have the advantage that they will not necessarily decrease when worthless predictors are added to the model. In fact, the IC values can *increase* in this situation. The added predictors have to come with a sufficient improvement in fit in order for the IC value to decrease. This provides a sound basis for comparing models of different complexity.

There are several IC, two of the most popular being the AIC (Akaike, 1973, 1974, 1981) and Schwartz's Bayesian information criterion (BIC; Schwarz, 1978). The AIC has the penalty of $2 \cdot K$, where K is the total number of estimated parameters. The BIC has the penalty $K \cdot log(N^*)$, where $N^* = N$ for the LM, and $N^* = \sum_i^N n_i$ for LMER. The IC are summarized in Table 6.1.

Table 6.1 Information criteria.

Information Criterion	LM	LMER
AIC	$deviance + 2 \cdot K$	$deviance + 2 \cdot K$
BIC	$deviance + K \cdot log(N)$	$deviance + K \cdot log\left(\sum_i^N n_i\right)$

Note. K = number of model parameters.

There is debate over which IC should be used in practice, as they each have advantages depending on the goals of the analysis (Burnham & Anderson, 2004; Kuha, 2004). The use of the AIC is emphasized in this book for reasons given in the next chapter.

The deviance is also the basis for a statistical test of two nested models. Two models are nested when parameters of the more complex model, known as the *full model*, can be set to 0 to yield the simpler model, known as the *reduced model*. For example, the reduced intercept-only model of Equation 6.2.10 is nested in the full linear model of Equation 6.2.1. The models are nested because $\beta_1 = 0$ can be set in the full model to obtain the reduced model.

Assuming the sample size increases without bound, it can be shown that the difference between the deviances of the full and reduced model has a chi-squared distribution (χ^2), with *df* equal to the difference in the number of parameters (Sprott, 2000, chap. 6). Suppose that *deviance_R* stands for the deviance of the reduced model, and *deviance_F* stands for the deviance of the full model. It is assumed that the reduced and full models are nested, so it will always be the case that *deviance_F* ≤ *deviance_R*.

The likelihood ratio statistic is a comparison of the two deviance values. It forms the basis for the LRT, which is the main test statistic discussed in Chapter 8. The likelihood ratio statistic, X^2, is defined as

$$X^2 = deviance_R - deviance_F. \qquad (6.2.12)$$

Because X^2 is defined as a difference, it may be unclear why the word *ratio* is used in LRT. The genesis is the fact that Equation 6.2.12 can also be written as the ratio of two likelihoods (see, e.g., Verbeke & Molenberghs, 2000, chap. 5).

In theory, X^2 ranges from 0 to ∞, with larger values indicating superior fit of the full model over the reduced model. If the full model has equal fit to the reduced model, then *deviance_R* − *deviance_F* = 0. If the full model has better fit than the reduced model, *deviance_R* − *deviance_F* > 0.

How large does the difference have to be to prefer the full model to the reduced model? This is usually determined by the LRT *p*-value (LRT-*p*) associated with the test statistic. The LRT-*p* is determined by comparing X^2 to the χ^2 distribution. As with other test statistics, the LRT-*p* has a reciprocal relationship with X^2. Holding the *df* constant, the LRT-*p* decreases as the test statistic increases, and vice versa.

In a sense, the LRT penalizes the deviance difference in a fashion similar to the IC. For a constant deviance difference, as the *df* increase, the *p*-value increases. Therefore, in principle, the LRT-*p* cannot be made to be smaller by adding worthless predictors that do not sufficiently change the deviance difference. Additional parallels between the AIC and the LRT are discussed in Chapter 8.

As expounded upon later, the LRT-*p* can be used as a measure of evidence, with relatively small values favoring the full model over the reduced model.

However, the LRT is usually used to make a decision about the reduced model, using a rule such as "reject" when LRT-$p \leq 0.05$. Details regarding such uses are discussed in Chapter 8.

6.3 Maximum Likelihood and LMER

To this point, ML has been discussed in the context of traditional regression. ML also provides the basis for inference with LMER. The deviance function (or *logLik* function) is defined for LMER models in a similar fashion as discussed in the last sections. For a given LMER model, ML estimators are derived from the deviance function to obtain estimates based on observed data. Models can be compared using the deviance, AIC (or BIC), or the LRT as previously described.

The LMER equations are more complex than in traditional regression, as there are additional parameters related to the random effects. But the concepts are similar, and there is now a switch over to LMER to discuss issues pertinent to the analysis of longitudinal data.

In contrast to lm(), the default output of lmer() lists the values of the *logLik*, the deviance, and the IC. Examples can be seen in the last chapter, but as a reminder, the relevant portion of the output for lmer.1 is shown below. The slot in the summary() output object containing the crucial information is @AICtab. Consider the longitudinal model with grade as a predictor of read, with two random effects (random intercepts and random slopes).

```
> ## Estimate linear model.
> lmer.1 <- lmer(read ~ grade + (grade | subid), MPLS.LS, REML = FALSE)
> ## Print ML information.
> summary(lmer.1)@AICtab
```

	AIC	BIC	logLik	deviance	REMLdev
	580.9591	595.2513	-284.4796	568.9591	563.2774

In light of the discussion in the last section, perhaps the only unfamiliar column label is REMLdev. This is the value of the deviance using the REML variances, as opposed to the ML variances (see Section 6.2.3). It is reiterated that the REML deviance cannot be used for comparison of models with different fixed effects. Such comparisons are very important in applied analysis, and thus, focus is almost exclusively on ML estimation in this book.

Additional functions can be used to compute the AIC, as well as transformations of the AIC based on a lmer() model object. These functions are discussed in the next chapter.

To perform the LRT, the anova() function is used by supplying the fitted output objects of the reduced and full models. As an example, consider lmer.1 as the reduced model and an estimated full model that adds the

6.3 Maximum Likelihood and LMER

square of grade, grade². It is common to include the square of a time predictor to account for a nonlinear change curve trend; see Chapter 12 for more details.

The squaring of grade is performed within the insulate function, I(), to ensure that lmer() interprets the transformation for the predictor and not for the parameter (i.e., grade² and not β_1^2). The new output object is saved as lmer.2, and the models are compared with anova(), listing the reduced model first.

```
> ## Estimate the full model.
> lmer.2 <- lmer(read ~ grade + I(grade ^ 2) + (grade | subid), MPLS.LS, REML = FALSE)
> ## LRT.
> anova(lmer.1, lmer.2)
```

```
Data: MPLS.LS
Models:
lmer.1: read ~ grade + (grade | subid)
lmer.2: read ~ grade + I(grade^2) + (grade | subid)
       Df    AIC    BIC  logLik   Chisq Chi Df Pr(>Chisq)
lmer.1  6 580.96 595.25 -284.48
lmer.2  7 581.12 597.79 -283.56  1.8408      1     0.1749
```

The first four lines of output provide information about the data and show the lmer() syntax for the models. The first four numeric columns of lines 6 to 7 show the output for the individual fitted models. The last three columns of line 7 contain the output related to the LRT.

The first numeric column, labeled Df, lists the number of estimated parameters of the models. Line 6 shows that the reduced model has six parameters, and line 7 shows the full model has seven parameters. The tally of the parameters is the following. For the reduced model, there are estimates for the two fixed effects, the three unique variance components of the random effects, and the error variance. The full model adds the third fixed effect for the squared term.

The second numeric column lists the AIC for each model, followed by the BIC in the next column, and then the *logLik*. According to both IC, the reduced model has better fit than the full model. The deviance is not listed but can easily be computed if desired ($-2 \cdot$ logLik).

The last three columns in line 7 list X^2 (Chisq), the *df* (Chi Df), and the LRT-*p* (Pr(>Chisq)). In this case, $X^2 = 1.84$, $df = 1$, and LRT-*p* = 0.17. The LRT-*p* is relatively large by conventional standards, which argues for the reduced model; there is a detailed discussion in Chapter 8.

A word regarding notation is appropriate at this juncture. There is a potential for confusion when interpreting the anova() output, as Df is used for indexing the number of estimated parameters of a single model. The number of estimated parameters is denoted as *K* in the formulas of this chapter. In addition, Chi Df is used for the degrees of freedom in the LRT, which is denoted as *df* in the formulas of this chapter.

6.3.1 LMER DEVIANCE FUNCTION

Thus far, practical information regarding `lmer()` output has been presented, relying on the generalization of concepts developed for the LM. Insight into LMER and how it differs from traditional regression can be gained by examining some of the details of the ML setup.

Similar to what was already discussed, ML estimation with LMER is based on the deviance function. Because of the addition of random effects, the ML setup in LMER is more complex than with the LM. For this reason, a full explication is perhaps best accomplished with matrix algebra. Since knowledge of matrix algebra is not assumed, the approach here is to present a special case. The special case is that of only two time points. The two-time point case illustrates important concepts that can be generalized to additional time points. Thus, the example below will help provide insight into generic concepts regarding ML estimation of LMER models. For readers familiar with matrix algebra, the optional section at the end of the chapter provides a general overview.

Similar to what was discussed previously, the ML setup begins with a probability model for an individual observation. This is the LMER model, with the associated normality assumptions for the random effects and random error. To keep things simple, consider the LMER model for linear change with no static predictors:

$$y_{ij} = (\beta_0 + b_{0i}) + (\beta_1 + b_{1i})(\texttt{grade}_{ij}) + \varepsilon_{ij}. \quad (6.3.1)$$

It is assumed the subjects are randomly sampled, and thus, there is independence among the subjects. As usual, the repeated observations within subjects are assumed to be correlated. The same assumptions as discussed in the last chapter are made regarding the random effects and error, the most pertinent being normality (see Section 5.3.3).

An important aspect of the ML setup is that the normality assumption of the random effects and error implies that the response is normally distributed conditional on grade. To see this, consider the fact that besides the random effects and error, everything else on the right-hand side of Equation 6.3.1 is fixed or constant. This means the random response variable is a linear combination of the random effects and error. It follows that the response variable has the distributional properties implied by the linear combination of the random variables. Thus, the response variable is assumed to have a multivariate normal distribution, and the variance-covariance matrix among the y_{ij} is a function of the variance components of the random effects and random error. As the y_{ij} are assumed correlated among the time points, it is necessary to include the variances and covariances among the y_{ij} in the deviance function.

Consider the case of Equation 6.3.1 with two time points, Grade 5 ($j = 1$) and Grade 6 ($j = 2$). It is stressed that two time points are insufficient to estimate the model, and the example is only for illustration purposes. After establishing some results with the two time points, it is easy to see how things are extended to additional time points and models that can be estimated.

6.3 Maximum Likelihood and LMER

With two time points, there is a single covariance between y_{i1} and y_{i2}, denoted as $Cov(y_{i1}, y_{i2})$. This is the covariance between the response scores at Grades 5 and 6. In addition, there is a variance for each time point, $Var(y_{i1})$ and $Var(y_{i2})$.

As shown in the optional sections of the last chapter, the variances and covariances of the responses are a function of the variance components of the random effects and random error. Specifically,

$$Var(y_{i1}) = Var(b_{0i}) + Var(b_{1i}) + 2 \cdot Cov(b_{0i}, b_{1i}) + \sigma_\varepsilon^2,$$
$$Var(y_{i2}) = 5^2 \cdot Var(b_{0i}) + 6^2 \cdot Var(b_{1i}) + (2 \cdot 5 \cdot 6) \cdot Cov(b_{0i}, b_{1i}) + \sigma_\varepsilon^2,$$
$$Cov(y_{i1}, y_{i2}) = 5 \cdot Var(b_{0i}) + 6 \cdot Var(b_{1i}) + (5+6) \cdot Cov(b_{0i}, b_{1i}),$$
(6.3.2)

where values of 5 and 6 are the grades. The last equation is a mathematical representation of how the random effects account for the dependency due to the repeated measures. The covariance between the response scores is defined by the linear combination of the variance components of the random effects weighted by the `grade` values. Without the random effects variance components, there would be no accounting for the correlation of the longitudinal observations. The variances are defined by a different linear combination at each time point, which indicates the variances can change over time, either increasing or decreasing depending on the value of the covariance.

Given the information above, it can be shown that the LMER deviance function is

$$deviance = (2 \cdot N) \cdot log(2 \cdot \pi) + N \cdot log \Big[Var(y_{i1}) \cdot Var(y_{i2}) - 2 \cdot Cov(y_{i1}, y_{i2}) \Big]$$
$$+ \frac{\sum_i^N \Big[Var(y_{i1}) \cdot \varepsilon_{i2}^2 + Var(y_{i2}) \cdot \varepsilon_{i1}^2 - 2 \cdot Cov(y_{i1}, y_{i2}) \cdot \varepsilon_{i1} \cdot \varepsilon_{i2} \Big]}{Var(y_{i1}) \cdot Var(y_{i2}) - Cov(y_{i1}, y_{i2})^2}, \quad (6.3.3)$$

where $\varepsilon_{ij} = y_{ij} - (\beta_0 + \beta_1 \cdot \text{grade}_{ij})$. The numerator of the last term illustrates a stark contrast with the corresponding term in the LM setup of Equation 6.2.5. In the LM case, the numerator is the SSE. In the LMER case of Equation 6.3.3, the numerator is a *weighted* SSE, the weights being the variances and covariance among the responses. The weighted SSE is known as *generalized least squares* (GLS), and the formulas for the fixed effects obtained from Equation 6.3.3 are known as GLS estimators.

The deviance provides insight regarding some practical issues of estimation with LMER. The denominator of the last term must be nonzero, or the deviance is not defined. Such a denominator will occur when one or both of the variances equal 0, as either of these conditions imply a covariance of 0. Unfortunately, a variance estimate need not be exactly 0 to create problems in estimation.

In practice, when the estimate of a variance is 0, or nearly so, `lmer()` will issue an error message but attempt to provide a result anyway. Alternatively, an error message will not be issued, but the correlation between the random effects may be unusually high or perfect (±1). In either case, the integrity of the result is in question, and the analyst may want to alter the underlying model. This usually implies that the random effects structure be simplified, perhaps setting the covariance equal to 0 or dropping the random slope term. These topics are discussed in Chapter 10.

Equation 6.3.3 can be generalized to accommodate additional time points and additional fixed effects. Regardless of the added complexity, the concepts illustrated in the deviance function of Equation 6.3.3 are the same. The squared errors and products are weighted by the variances and covariances among the observed responses. The latter are in turn defined by the variances and covariances among the random effects. Thus, all the components of the LMER models are incorporated in the deviance function: the fixed effects structure, the random effects structure, and the random errors.

Another pertinent issue for applied analysis is *identifiability*. Loosely, a model is identified in an analysis when the number of observed quantities is equal to or greater than the number of parameters. This is a necessary condition for proper estimation of the model. In LMER, the fixed effects structure is a model for mean change, and there must be at least as many observed means as there are fixed effects, including the intercept. It is strongly recommended that there be many more observed means than fixed effects. This is to help avoid estimation problems and possible conceptual problems, such as perfectly fitting change curves. In the example with two time points, there are two means and two fixed effects parameters, meaning the linear change curve fits perfectly.

When estimating the variance components of the random effects and random error, there must be at least as many observed variances and covariances as there are parameters. With two time points, there are two observed variances and one covariance. However, Equation 6.3.2 shows four unique variance component parameters. Therefore, the model of Equation 6.3.1 is not identified and cannot be properly estimated.

The lmer() function might produce results in the case of nonidentified models, but there will be indications of problems in the output. The correlation between the random effects might be at the extreme value, or some estimates might not appear at all. Such results suggest that a simplification of the model is warranted.

There is an unfortunate truth that applied researchers sometimes do not want to face: *small data sets simply will not support the use of complex models*. Complex inferences require a large amount of information that is not contained in small data sets. *Small* in this case can refer to the number of subjects and/or the number of time points.

6.3.2 ML STANDARD ERRORS

To this point, the focus has been on obtaining the minimum deviance and ML *point estimates*. A point estimate is a number based on the sample data taken as the best candidate for the parameter in question. Because

6.3 Maximum Likelihood and LMER

of sampling fluctuations, uncertainty is an inevitable part of any analysis. For every ML point estimate, then, an indication of uncertainty should be reported. A method of quantifying the uncertainty associated with a point estimate is its SE. The term *precision* is used to refer to the extent of uncertainty indexed by the SE.

Precision is numerically indexed in a number of ways. One of the most common is to compute the ratio of the estimate to its estimated SE, which is referred to as the *t*-ratio or *z*-ratio. Suppose the notation $\widehat{SE}(\hat{\beta}_k)$ is used for the estimated SE of the *k*th fixed effect. With this notation in place, the *t*-ratio is defined as

$$t = \frac{\hat{\beta}_k}{\widehat{SE}(\hat{\beta}_k)}. \quad (6.3.4)$$

To the extent that the estimated SE is large relative to the estimated fixed effect, there is uncertainty in estimation. Absolute value *t*-ratios close to 0 indicate relatively low precision, and larger absolute values reflect relatively high precision. High precision seems desirable, as this is an indication the value of the ML estimate may change little under repeated sampling.

The *t*-ratio is a type of standardized effect size, and its use as a relative measure is emphasized without regard to statistical tests or cutoff values. The *t*-ratio can be used, for example, to make judgments about the predictive ability of different static predictors in the same model.

Consider a LMER model with risk and ethnicity intercept effects. To keep things simple, the dichotomous versions of the static predictors are used, `risk2` and `eth2`. As usual, `read` is the response and `grade` is the time predictor. The model is estimated, and the fixed effects table is printed. The fixed effects table resides in the `@coefs` slot of the `lmer()` output object.

```
> lmer.2 <- lmer(read ~ grade + risk2 + eth2 + (grade | subid), MPLS.LS, REML = FALSE)
> summary(lmer.2)@coefs
                Estimate Std.      Error     t value
(Intercept)  193.0265794    7.629504  25.30001570
grade          4.7791299    0.733152   6.51860660
risk2DADV    -26.7628227    5.696248  -4.69832490
eth2W         -0.3587849    5.763682  -0.06224926
```

The `Estimate` column contains $\hat{\beta}_k$, the `Std. Error` column contains the estimated SEs, and the `t value` column lists the *t*-values. The `risk2 DADV` row lists the intercept effect for risk, controlling for ethnicity. The `eth2W` row lists the intercept effect for ethnicity, controlling for risk. Recall that the row labels are a concatenation of the original variable names (`risk2`, `eth2`) and the category coded as one in the data frame, `DADV` and `W`, respectively.

The *t*-value for risk is much higher in absolute value ($t = -4.7$) than that of ethnicity ($t = -0.06$). The intercept effect for risk is much stronger than that of ethnicity, when both static predictors are in the model. In fact, the ethnicity *t*-value is close to 0, indicating it has a negligible sample effect with risk in the model.

An alternative method of quantifying precision is to compute a CI. A CI for a fixed effect is computed as

$$\hat{\beta}_k \pm 2 \cdot \widehat{SE}(\hat{\beta}_k), \tag{6.3.5}$$

although 2 can be replaced by other values, such as 1.96.

The CI is an interval providing a rough estimate of the plausible values of the population parameter. This definition is meant to be helpful for applied researchers who want to judge evidence provided by their sample data. The reader should be aware there are other interpretations of the CI. Alternatives include the traditional long-run interpretation regarding the behavior of the CI under infinite repeated samplings. The long-run interpretation is considered to be unhelpful because it focuses on the behavior of the CI, rather than on the evidence offered by the sample data in a particular analysis (Berger, 2003; Christensen, 2005; Hubbard & Bayarri, 2003). Related discussions on evidential interpretations of traditional hypothesis testing are provided in Chapters 7 and 8.

CIs can be added to the fixed effects coefficients table. The table must be saved as a data frame, and then the calculations are performed and stored as additional columns. The new columns, `LCI` and `UCI`, stand for lower CI limit and upper CI limit, respectively.

```
> mytable  <- as.data.frame(summary(lmer.2)@coefs)
> mytable$LCI <- mytable$Estimate - 2 * mytable$"Std.Error"
> mytable$UCI <- mytable$Estimate + 2 * mytable$"Std.Error"
> mytable
```

	Estimate	Std. Error	t value	LCI	UCI
(Intercept)	193.0265794	7.629504	25.30001570	177.767571	208.285588
grade	4.7791299	0.733152	6.51860660	3.312826	6.245434
risk2DADV	-26.7628227	5.696248	-4.69832490	-38.155318	-15.370327
eth2W	-0.3587849	5.763682	-0.06224926	-11.886148	11.168578

Consider the risk and ethnicity intercept effects. The CI for risk is $(-38.16, -15.37)$, indicating that the population risk group intercept difference might be somewhere in this range. The CI for ethnicity is $(-11.89, 11.17)$. There is considerable uncertainty for ethnicity, as the CI is nearly symmetric about the value of 0. This means the fixed effect parameter could have a positive sign, a negative sign, or be equal to 0. In contrast, the CI for risk is a range of negative numbers.

Given a large sample size, it is probably safe to treat the *t*-ratio as a *z*-ratio. The standard normal distribution probably can be used as a relatively accurate basis for inference regarding a fixed effect. The *t*-ratio as test statistic is used to test the null hypothesis $H_0: \beta_k = 0$.

It is emphasized that the *z*-test (*t*-test) is really a comparison of a model that includes β_k and a model that excludes β_k. One potential problem is that

6.3 Maximum Likelihood and LMER

lmer() output usually contains many *t*-ratios, as shown in the above output. Therefore, many model comparisons are being performed simultaneously. Some of these comparisons may be irrelevant to the research questions at hand. Irrelevant *t*-ratios can be distracting and/or confusing, especially when they are large relative to the relevant *t*-ratios. For this reason, it is advocated that the LRT be used in place of such tests. The LRT requires the researcher to specify the β_k to be tested, thus lowering the chance of distracting irrelevant tests.

The *t*-ratio is a special case of a more general form of statistic known as the *Wald statistic*. With the Wald statistic, one "rejects" H_0 if $p \leq \alpha$ and does not reject otherwise. It is almost universal that $\alpha = 0.05$, but it need not be. General issues regarding the use and interpretation of such tests are considered in the next two chapters.

The *p*-values can be attached to the table of fixed effects. Below, the pnorm() function is used to compute two-tailed *p*-values. Only two-tailed hypotheses are considered in this book; see Chapter 8 for details. The pnorm() function requires the absolute value *t* (q=abs()) be supplied, and the upper tail area must be requested (lower.tail=FALSE). The result is multiplied by 2 in order to return the two-tailed *p*-value.

```
> mytable$p.value <- pnorm(q = abs(mytable$"t value"), lower.tail = FALSE) * 2
> round(mytable, 4)
```

	Estimate	Std. Error	t value	LCI	UCI	p.value
(Intercept)	193.0266	7.6295	25.3000	177.7676	208.2856	0.0000
grade	4.7791	0.7332	6.5186	3.3128	6.2454	0.0000
risk2DADV	-26.7628	5.6962	-4.6983	-38.1553	-15.3703	0.0000
eth2W	-0.3588	5.7637	-0.0622	-11.8861	11.1686	0.9504

The *p*-values agree with the CIs, in the respect that a CI covering the value of 0 will have a relatively large associated *p*-value. Conversely, a CI that does not cover 0 will have a relatively small *p*-value. This suggests another interpretation of a CI as an interval containing candidate values for the null hypothesis that will not be rejected (Christensen, 2005).

The general form of the Wald statistic can be used to test a multiparameter null hypothesis, such as $H_0: \beta_k = \beta_{k'} = 0$. The test is based on the estimated fixed effects and their associated estimated variances and covariances. Multiparameter Wald tests are not considered, as they have some disadvantages compared to the LRT.

The Wald test and the LRT tend to agree for very large sample sizes, though they may not for smaller sample sizes. Therefore, it is recommended that either the Wald test or the LRT be used, but not both. Although the Wald statistic is convenient for evaluating a single-parameter null hypothesis, the LRT is recommended as a replacement. A disadvantage of the Wald test is there is no explicit alternative hypothesis. The LRT has an explicit H_0, the reduced model, and an explicit H_A, the full model. This characteristic is favorable for calibrating *p*-values, as discussed in Chapter 8. Another problem is the Wald test can give different results when equivalent varied forms of the

H_0 are tested (see Greene, 2008, chap. 16). The LRT does not suffer from this problem.

6.3.3 ADDITIONAL SE DETAILS

All ML point estimates are obtained from the deviance function, including the SEs. An interesting relation is that the size of an SE is determined by the curvature of the deviance function. Curvature is loosely defined as the extent of deviation from a flat line.

If the deviance function is relatively flat, there is greater uncertainty regarding the candidate values for any one parameter, and its SE will be large. The flatness means that the deviance values for the candidates differ relatively little about the minimum. Upon repeated sampling, the optimal candidate value might jump around, and there is relatively high imprecision associated with any one sample result. The imprecision is reflected in a larger SE.

In contrast, when the function has greater curvature, the deviance values about the minimum are relatively dissimilar. This means greater consistency upon repeated sampling, in that the optimal value is expected to vary less than in the previous scenario. For any one sample, there is greater precision in guessing the best candidate value, which is reflected in a smaller SE.

To help fix the curvature concepts, consider the made-up deviance functions in Figure 6.6. The graphs represent a deviance function in which the linear slope is unknown, analogous to Equation 6.2.6. The right-hand graph is flatter, and thus, has less curvature than the left-hand graph. Both deviance functions have minimum value of *deviance* = 8, which is associated with $\beta_1 = 1.5$.

Suppose the interval of $\beta_1 = (1, 2)$ is arbitrarily picked in both graphs. For the right-hand graph, the β_1 values in the interval have associated deviance values that are very similar. For example, $\beta_1 = 1$ is associated with *deviance* = 8.25, which is very close to the optimal value of 8 with $\beta_1 = 1.5$.

For the left-hand graph, the β_1 values in the same interval have associated deviance values that are much less similar. For example, $\beta_1 = 1$ has *deviance* = 9.5, which is a greater distance from the optimal value than in the right-hand graph. Therefore, the precision is greater in the left-hand graph, meaning the SE for β_1 is smaller.

As mentioned, the estimated SE for a parameter can be obtained from the deviance function. To be more specific, the estimated variance-covariance matrix *of the fixed effects* can be obtained from the deviance function. It is the square root of the estimated variances that are the estimated SEs.

Several variances and covariances have already been discussed: those among the random effects (b_{ki}), and those among the observed responses (y_{ij}). The SEs are based on the diagonal of the variance-covariance matrix among the fixed effects (β_k). Table 6.2 is provided to help clarify the different types of variances and covariances. The general formula for the variance-covariance matrix among the fixed effects is provided in the optional section at the end of this chapter.

6.3 Maximum Likelihood and LMER

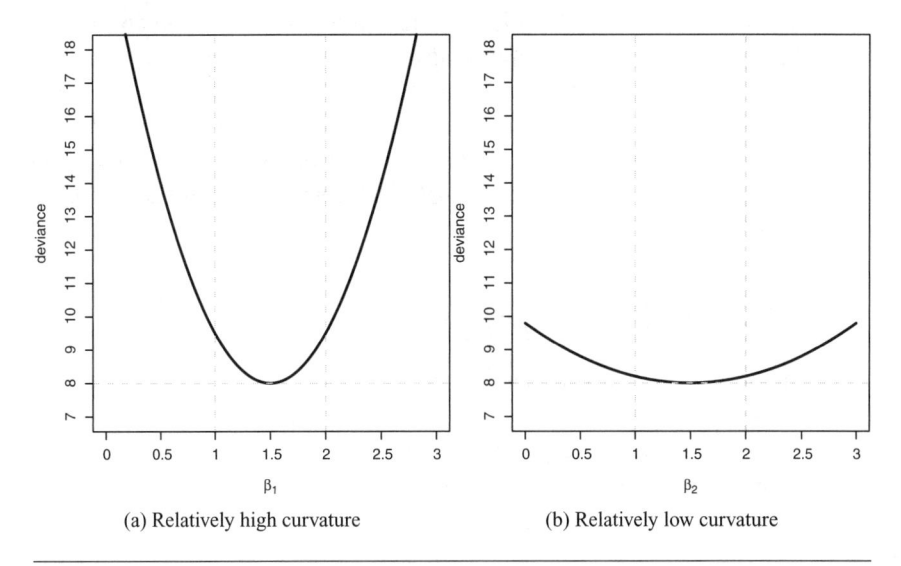

Figure 6.6 Graphs of deviance by β_1.

(a) Relatively high curvature

(b) Relatively low curvature

It is useful to examine the SE formulas for the special case of two time points previously mentioned. Given no missing data and the LMER model of Equation 6.3.1, it can be shown that the SEs of the fixed effects are

$$SE(\hat{\beta}_0) = \sqrt{\frac{6^2 \cdot Var(y_{i1}) + 5^2 \cdot Var(y_{i1}) - 2 \cdot 5 \cdot 6 \cdot Var(y_{i1})}{N}},$$

$$SE(\hat{\beta}_1) = \sqrt{\frac{Var(y_{i1}) + Var(y_{i1}) - 2 \cdot Var(y_{i1})}{N}}.$$

Table 6.2 Varieties of variances and covariances in LMER.

Object	Notation	Importance
Random effects	$Var(b_{0i})$, $Var(b_{0i})$, $Cov(b_{0i}, b_{1i})$	Indexes individual variation and covariation of change curve components
Response	$Var(y_{i1})$, $Var(y_{i2})$, $Cov(y_{i1}, y_{i2})$	Indexes variability and dependency of the observed responses
Fixed effects	$Var(\beta_0)$, $Var(\beta_1)$, $Cov(\beta_0, \beta_1)$	Square root of variance is the SE; basis for inference with fixed effects

The formulas are important, as they illustrate an inferential principle that should be kept in mind. The scores for the grades (5, 6) appear in the SE for the intercept, but not for the slope. A linear transformation of grade will change the grade values, affecting the SE for the intercept, and not the SE for the slope.

Thus, the *t*-ratio of the slope is not affected by the linear transformation, only the *t*-ratio for the intercept is affected. This concept generalizes to models with additional terms, such as `grade`^{2}. The point is that only the *t*-ratio for the highest order term is insensitive to linear transformations of the time predictor. It follows that all lower order *t*-ratios are only tentative, in that they are sensitive to such transformations. More will be said about this in future chapters.

6.3.4 DEFAULT `lmer()` OUTPUT

As mentioned in the last chapter, the default `lmer()` output does not include *p*-values, CIs, or SEs for variance components. Reasons for these omissions are provided in this section.

Estimated SEs for fixed effects are expected to be relatively accurate when the sample size is large, with "large" pointedly being undefined. Accuracy is reduced when the sample size is not large. With small sample sizes, the CIs and *p*-values previously considered may be overly optimistic. This means the CIs are too narrow, and the *p*-values are lower than they should be.

Rather than use the standard normal distribution as a basis for inference, a traditional cure for the small-sample problem is to use quantiles from a *t*-distribution, with *df* estimated from the data. For basic problems, such as the one-sample mean test, the method for computing the *df* is relatively straightforward. Unfortunately, it is unclear what method, if any, is appropriate for computing *df* in LMER (Baayen, Davidson, & Bates, 2008). Among other problems, when there are missing data or imbalance on time, it is unclear what constitutes the "effective sample size" from which the number of estimated parameters is subtracted.

Recall in the one-sample mean problem, the *t*-test of $H_0: \mu = \mu_0$ is based on $df = N - 1$, with N being the (effective) sample size. For the case of LMER, it is not clear what value replaces N in the analogous equation. It is known that the effective sample size is somewhere between the number of subjects (N) and the number of observations ($\sum n_i$), but it is difficult to establish something more specific.

Several methods of estimating *df* based on the data have been proposed (see, e.g., Littell, Milliken, Stroup, Wolfinger, & Schabenberger, 2006, chap. 5). However, there is no agreed upon best approach, and the different *df* methods can lead to CIs of different lengths and differing *p*-values. Because there is no standard method for computing *df*, CIs and *p*-values are not computed by `lmer()` and do not appear in its output.

Rather than discuss various *df* methods, the use of the *t*-ratio as an effect size measure is emphasized. If one is truly forced to test H_0, the *t*-value can be treated as a Wald statistic, which should be sufficient for many empirical situations. A caveat is that the LRT is a better method to use than the Wald test. Furthermore, for the researcher who is concerned about the accuracy of *p*-values, the parametric bootstrap of the LRT should be used, which is discussed in Chapter 8.

Besides CIs and p-values, another omission in the `lmer()` output is estimated SEs for the random effects variance components. The reason for this omission is they are prone to two types of misuse. First, SEs are necessary for computing CIs, and the usefulness of conventional two-sided CIs for variances has been questioned (Bates, 2009, 2011). Since variances are bounded below by 0 and unbounded above, their sampling distribution is not symmetric. The asymmetric sampling distribution can result in CIs having implausible negative values at the lower end (variances are squared things and can only be ≥ 0). It is possible to truncate the lower CI bound at 0, but this only hides the underlying conceptual problem.

Second, an SE is necessary to construct a Wald test for the variance of a random effect. This is a test of $H_0 : Var(b_{ki}) = 0$. The Wald test avoids the CI problem of implausible values. However, it can been shown (Self & Liang, 1987) that the reference distribution for evaluating $H_0 : Var(b_{ki}) = 0$ is not the χ^2 distribution, regardless of the sample size. The reason is that the null value of 0 is exactly the lower bound of the value that the parameter estimate might take. This means that accurate p-values for testing H_0 require nonstandard distributions, known as mixture distributions.

The use of mixture distributions is not straightforward (see, e.g., Verbeke & Molenberghs, 2000, chap. 6). Therefore, the SEs are omitted so as to remove the temptation to construct potentially inaccurate Wald tests. As a possible remedy to these problems, bootstrap methods for testing random effect variances and covariances are suggested and discussed in Chapter 10.

6.3.5 ASSUMPTIONS REGARDING MISSING DATA

As discussed in Chapter 3, the strategy adopted for handling missing data is to ignore it. This means any row of the data frame that contains an NA will be omitted from the analysis. Omission is performed by default with the `lmer()` function. When ML is the basis of inference, it can be shown (e.g., Verbeke & Molenberghs, 2000, chap. 15) that ignoring the missing data will provide unbiased estimates, under the assumption that the missing data mechanism is MCAR or MAR; see Chapter 3.

As previously discussed, MAR is perhaps a more plausible assumption than MCAR for applied analysis, although MAR is impossible to verify based on the sample data. It follows that all the results in this book are conditional on unverifiable missing data assumptions. This appears to be an inevitable state of affairs for applied research (Ugarte, 2009).

When MAR or MCAR does not hold, LMER results will be biased to an unknown extent. Information about the robustness of results assuming different missing data mechanisms can be obtained from a sensitivity analysis. However, this topic is beyond our scope, and the interested reader is referred to sources such as Molenberghs and Kenward (2007).

Missing data can arise from the researcher omitting observations. This is usually done when preliminary graphs or descriptive statistics reveal outliers. When outliers are omitted, this is based on the observed scores, and the deletion is performed by the researcher. As discussed in Chapter 3, this omission process is MAR in the taxonomy of missing data mechanisms. Thus, in theory, a statistical analysis using ML will yield unbiased estimates when outliers are omitted.

6.4 Additional Details of ML for LMER*

This optional section is for the reader interested in additional details of the ML setup for LMER. Formulas in this section make use of matrix algebra. A soft introduction to matrix algebra is provide in the Appendix. If the reader is new to matrix algebra, the Appendix material should be read prior to this section.

General formulas are provided for the deviance function, the GLS estimator of β, the variance-covariance matrix among $\hat{\beta}$, and the REML deviance. The goal of the presentation is to facilitate conceptual understanding. Readers wishing a presentation closely tied to the programming algorithms of lmer() are referred to Bates (2011) and Pinheiro and Bates (2000).

As discussed in the optional Section 5.6, the formula for the variance-covariance matrix among the responses is

$$V_i = Z_i G Z_i^T + \sigma_\varepsilon^2 I_i, \tag{6.4.1}$$

where Z_i is a $n_i \times (q+1)$ design matrix for the random effects (there are $q+1$ random effects), G is a $(q+1) \times (q+1)$ matrix, Z_i^T is the transpose of Z_i, and I_i is a $n_i \times n_i$ identity matrix.

Under the assumptions of random sampling of subjects and normality, the formula for the LMER deviance function is

$$\begin{aligned} deviance &= \sum_i^N n_i \cdot log(2\pi) + \sum_i^N log|V_i| \\ &+ \sum_i^N (y_i - X_i\beta)^T V_i^{-1} (y_i - X_i\beta), \end{aligned} \tag{6.4.2}$$

where X_i is a $n_i \times (p+1)$ design matrix for the fixed effects (there are $p+1$ fixed effects), β is a $(p+1) \times 1$ vector of fixed effects, $|V_i|$ is the determinant, and V_i^{-1} is the inverse (see the Appendix).

The GLS estimator of β is obtained from the deviance function. It can be shown (e.g., Fitzmaurice et al., 2004, chap. 6) that the GLS estimator is

$$\hat{\beta} = \left\{ \sum_i^N (X_i^T V_i^{-1} X_i) \right\}^{-1} \sum_i^N (X_i^T V_i^{-1} y_i), \tag{6.4.3}$$

where y_i is the $n_i \times 1$ vector of response scores for the ith subject. When estimating a model in practice, V_i is replaced by its ML or REML estimate, with the former being emphasized in this book. Since V_i is a function of

6.4 Additional Details of ML for LMER*

the variances and covariances of the random effects, the estimator takes into account both the individual variability among subjects, and the correlation due to repeated measures (see the optional sections of Chapter 5).

The variance-covariance matrix among the fixed effects is important for inference, especially for computing CIs. It can be shown that the variance-covariance among the fixed effects is

$$Cov\left(\hat{\beta}\right) = \left\{\sum_{i}^{N} (X_i^T V_i^{-1} X_i)\right\}^{-1}. \qquad (6.4.4)$$

The square root of the diagonal elements are the SEs for the associated fixed effects.

Finally, the REML deviance function subtracts a correction term from the ML deviance function. The REML deviance is expressed as

$$deviance_{REML} = deviance_{ML} - \log\left|Cov\left(\hat{\beta}\right)\right|^{\frac{1}{2}}, \qquad (6.4.5)$$

where $deviance_{ML}$ is the ML deviance of Equation 6.4.2. The equation illustrates that the correction term changes based on the fixed effects in the model. If there is only an intercept and a time predictor, then $Cov\left(\hat{\beta}\right)$ is a 2 × 2 matrix. However, if a second time predictor is added (e.g., grade²), then the matrix is 3 × 3. The determinant in each case will be different, yielding a correction term that is particular to the model in question. This provides an unsound basis for comparing models. The changing dimension means that ML rather than REML should be used to evaluate models with different fixed effects, as ML does not suffer from this problem.

Multimodel Inference and Akaike's Information Criterion

7

One of the common goals in longitudinal analysis is to examine static predictor effects. Chapter 5 introduced two static predictor models: one with intercept effects and the other with intercept and slope effects. A single static predictor was considered in Chapter 5, which was the binary risk variable, with categories of DADV and ADV. The risk variable is categorical in nature, so the intercept effect is the mean difference between the intercepts of the change curves of the groups. The slope effect is the mean difference in slopes of the groups.

In Chapter 5, the static predictor models were presented without regard to whether all the effects were needed in the model. In this chapter, emphasis is on evaluating models with different static predictor effects and making judgments regarding these models (and effects). The multimodel approach is presented, in which the models to be evaluated are formulated based on theoretical considerations, prior to the data analysis. The approach relies on the AIC, as well as transformations of the AIC, for assessing the plausibility of the models in the set.

Discussion of model evaluation is limited to static predictors, with selection of time predictors and random effects left for future chapters. There are several reasons for this initial emphasis. LMER is more complex than traditional regression, due to the mix of fixed and random effects. Since the types of effects are correlated, it can be quite a daunting task to select both the fixed effects and the random effects at the same time. As a consequence, usually one structure is held constant while the other structure is selected. Static predictor effects are often the most important in terms of addressing primary research questions. Random effects are important for a proper model of longitudinal data, but they are not the primary objects of inference. Therefore, the first concern will be the selection of fixed effects holding the random effects structure constant.

Another complication is that the fixed effects structure involves time predictors and static predictors. The shape of the change curve influences the fixed effects structure, as different time predictors are required for linear and nonlinear curves. Similar to the issue with fixed and random effects, it is difficult to simultaneously select the shape of the change curve and the static predictor effects. As a consequence, the change curve and the random effects are considered to be "preselected" and held constant when examining static predictor effects. Ideally, the preselection is based on theory, but exploratory methods using graphs and descriptive statistics can also be used. Exploratory methods for selecting time predictors are discussed in Chapter 9, and methods for selecting random effects are discussed in Chapter 10.

In this chapter and throughout the remainder of the book, statistical inference is treated as a model evaluation problem, or equivalently, a model comparison problem. This approach subsumes traditional hypothesis testing because a hypothesis test can be translated into a nested model comparison problem. For instance, to examine the statistical reliability of a slope difference among risk groups, a model including the slope difference can be compared to a model excluding the slope difference (the latter model is nested within the former).

As previously mentioned, the dominant paradigm for comparing models in the behavioral sciences is NHST. Because of this dominance, the entire next chapter is devoted to the LRT that can be used for NHST with LMER. The current chapter focuses on alternative approaches to model evaluation, based on the work of Hirotugu Akaike (Akaike, 1973, 1974, 1981) using his information criterion (AIC).

Statistical inference based on the AIC has many advantages over NHST. Models can be rank-ordered in terms of fit, and the global effect size of each model can be calculated. This provides a direct evaluation of models, with a focus on effect size not afforded by NHST. A considerable amount of space in this chapter is devoted to the theoretical underpinnings of the AIC and its associated effect size measures.

The nature of the AIC is amenable to the statistical strategy of multimodel inference, introduced in Chapter 1. Multimodel inference using the AIC is relatively new to the behavioral sciences. For this reason, several details of the method are presented, including an extensive example using `lmer()` and functions from the `AICcmodavg` package. Contrasts with NHST are discussed, and a case is made for the use of the AIC rather than NHST.

7.1 Objects of Inference

Statistical inference is a reasoned judgment about population unknowns based on sample data. The unknowns are broadly defined and include parameters in the LMER model, as well as global characteristics of population models. As

7.1 Objects of Inference

discussed in Chapter 6, all statistical inference with LMER will be based on ML methods.

This chapter is limited to statistical inference for static predictor effects. An example is evaluating if there is statistical evidence to suggest that risk groups have different population intercepts and/or different slopes. Another example is examining if population risk group effects endure when another variable, such as ethnicity, is added to the model.

Because of the complexity of LMER, there are different possible objects of inference. By this, it is meant that various types of parameters are of potential interest in model evaluation. All LMER models considered in this book have the following three additive components.

1. Fixed effects structure

2. Random effects structure

3. Random error structure

Of the three, the fixed effects structure is the focus of most applied research, although the other two structures are important for properly modeling longitudinal data.

The random effects and random error are random variables, and thus, are typically not estimated. Rather, it is the variances and covariances (correlations) of the random effects, as well as the variance of the random error, that are estimated. The term *variance component* is used to refer to any of these. The variance components of the random effects contain potentially useful information regarding individual differences. However, questions regarding individual differences are usually secondary to questions of aggregate effects that pertain to the fixed effects.

It might not be too extreme to say that in many instances, the variance components of the random effects and random error are treated as nuisance parameters. This means that the fixed effects are the focus, and the other two structures are primarily included to account for the dependency due to the repeated measures. There is a tilt toward this view, which is based on published results of LMER analysis. The fixed effects estimates are almost always the primary focus of discussion when LMER results are reported and interpreted.

Another complication is presented by the situation in which the shape of the change curve is unknown. As shown in the multilevel model presentation in Chapter 5, the number of possible random effects is determined by the number of subject-specific parameters, β_{ki}^*. If the subject-specific change curve is a horizontal line, then $y_{ij} = \beta_{0i}^* + \varepsilon_{ij}$, and only one random effect is possible. With a linear model, $y_{ij} = \beta_{0i}^* + \beta_{1i}^*(\text{grade}_{ij}) + \varepsilon_{ij}$, and two random effects are possible, and so on.

It follows that selection of the shape of the change curve has implications for the selection of the random effects. There often is an "automatic" inclusion of a random effect for every Level 1 parameter. For a subject-specific linear model, this means the automatic inclusion of a random intercepts term (b_{0i}) and a random slopes term (b_{1i}). The danger of automatic inclusion is that some variance components might not be needed. Including unneeded variance components can lower statistical efficiency. However, the loss in efficiency can be slight, and the trade-off for simplicity in model specification is probably worthwhile in many circumstances.

The point of all this is that the complexity of the statistical inference depends on what needs to be selected for inclusion in the model. Suppose, for example, the goal is to evaluate whether there are intercept and slope effects for the risk group static predictor. If it is known that a linear change curve and two random effects are adequate, then the only objects of statistical inference are the fixed effects of the static predictor. In this scenario, the change curve fixed effects and the variance components are automatically included in the model, similar to the way that the intercept term and error variance are automatically included in traditional regression. The change curve fixed effects and the variance components are not objects of inference, so model evaluation focuses only on the fixed effects associated with the risk groups. The change curve fixed effects and the variance components are estimated, but the inferential focus is on the risk group intercept difference and the risk group slope difference.

Contrast the above with the situation in which the shape of the change curve is unknown. This also implies that the number of random effects is unknown. In such a case, statistical inference might involve several models with many different terms. One might consider a subject-specific cubic change curve to be the most complex possible. The predictors would be grade, grade^2, and grade^3, and each might have its associated random effect. Several simpler models might be considered by dropping some of the grade transformations, along with their random effects. Given the possible combinations of terms, the number of potential models is quite large.

To compound problems, the addition of a single random effect causes several variance components to be added to the model. For instance, suppose there is a random intercept term in the model, and a random slope term is added. As usual, the variance-covariance matrix among the random effects is not constrained, meaning every unique element is estimated. Adding the random effect results in the addition of two variance components, the variance of the slopes, and the covariance between the intercepts and slopes. The number of variance components grows even more with the addition of a third random effect, and so on.

It is hoped that the picture is becoming clear that formal inference involving both fixed effects and random effects is not a standard problem. To help make LMER analysis more manageable, preselection of the time predictor(s) and associated random effects is recommended, so that static predictor effects are the objects of inference in model evaluation. Preselection means effects are constant across all models considered, and thus, are not considered in model comparisons. The result is that formal inference will concern only fixed effects of the static predictors.

7.1 Objects of Inference

The recommendation is perhaps most justifiable when the shape of the change curve is dictated by theory. The random effects might also be suggested by theory, or their inclusion can be automatic by providing a random effect for each time predictor and time transformation in the subject-specific model, including the intercept. In the case when the shape of the change curve is not known, it is recommended that graphing be used to suggest the shape. Graphs of the data can also be used to suggest the number of random effects (see Chapters 9 and 10).

When the shape of the change curve is suggested by graphing, the analysis will have a data-driven element prior to the use of formal inferential methods. The data-driven portion will inevitably introduce uncertainty not accounted for by the formal inferential methods (Chatfield, 1995; Faraway, 1992). It is believed that the introduction of additional uncertainty is worth the gain in simplicity of the inferential analysis in many situations. For the reader who does not agree, formal inferential methods for random effects and the time predictors are discussed in the chapters indicated above.

The preselection recommendation is consistent with regression textbooks that implicitly or explicitly suggest the use of iterative analysis. Iterative analysis alternates between analysis steps using graphical methods and inferential methods (Faraway, 2005). The reader must be cautioned, however, that graphical and descriptive analysis used to preselect the change curve and random effects will be completely ignored by the inferential methods discussed in this chapter. Preselection means the model uncertainty will be underestimated, leading to the introduction of bias. The extent of such bias is unknown, and it is not clear if it can ever be known (Chatfield, 1995; Faraway, 1992). This may be one reason why the issue of model uncertainty is rarely raised when iterative analysis steps are used.

Much of the discussion in this section is summarized in Table 7.1, which depicts three scenarios for model evaluation. For each scenario, there is an indication of whether the parameters associated with the particular effects are treated as preselected, or (to be) selected. The second to last column lists the types of parameters that are the objects of inference. The last column lists the chapter in which the indicated selection is discussed.

Table 7.1 Scenarios for analysis.

Scenario	Change Curve	Random Effects	Static Predictors	Objects of Inference	Chapter
1	Preselected	Preselected	Selected	FE	7
2	Preselected	Selected	Selected	FE, VC	10
3	Selected	Selected	Selected	FE, VC	9, 12

Note. FE = fixed effects; VC = variance components.

Scenario 1 is the simplest, as inferential methods are limited to the fixed effects of the static predictors. *It is recommended that inferential analysis assuming Scenario 1 be used when possible.*

Scenarios 2 and 3 are substantially more complex, as fixed effects and variance components are the focus of inferential procedures. Scenario 2 is turned into Scenario 1 by automatically including a random effect for every Level 1 parameter. An alternative is to use graphs and other exploratory methods to suggest the number of random effects.

Scenario 3 is the most difficult. Scenario 3 is turned into Scenario 1 by first using graphs and other exploratory methods to suggest the time predictors and transformations, as discussed in Chapters 9 and 11. This is followed by automatically including a random effect for each subject-level parameter, or using descriptive/inferential methods to select the random effects.

In the remainder of this chapter, Scenario 1 is assumed. Thus, the various models considered all have the same change curve and random effects, but they differ in the number of static predictors, or differ in the number of static predictor effects.

7.2 Statistical Strategy

Philosophy is important, as it facilitates the examination and sharpening of the premises under which applied researchers labor. It is probably fair to say that the philosophy guiding statistical practice for many behavioral scientists is mostly implicit, with activities arising largely by tradition, or the researcher's sense of what constitutes correct scientific practice. Making one's statistical philosophy explicit is valuable, as the scientist and the scientist's audience will better understand the guiding principles motivating particular activities. With this in mind, some space is taken to sketch a philosophy of statistical analysis.

Applied research begins with a substantive problem or a research question. The research question usually taps theoretical notions as to how the system under study "works," including the proposed influences that may be responsible for patterns in the sample data. In the context of the MPLS data set, examples of research questions include "What is the nature of risk group differences in reading achievement over time?" and "What type of longitudinal risk group differences exist when ethnicity is considered?"

The research questions give rise to *working hypotheses*, which are specific assertions about the phenomenon under study. For example, "The advantaged group has a different mean intercept than the disadvantaged group," or "The growth rate of the advantaged group is different than that of the disadvantaged group controlling for ethnicity." Although the distinction is often blurred between research questions and working hypotheses, the latter are thought to be more closely related to the *statistical models* used in the analysis.

There are various definitions of a statistical model (Cox, 1990). In this book, a statistical model is considered to be a statistical hypothesis (Forster, 2000; Kieseppä, 2001). Statistical models are the translation of the verbal working hypotheses into mathematical equations, such as those listed in Chapter 5. The translation of a working hypothesis into a statistical model is often

7.2 Statistical Strategy

inexact. The statistical model can have additional aspects and assumptions not explicitly stated in the working hypothesis, such as the normality assumption. The converse is also a possibility.

One of the hallmarks of the statistical philosophy advocated here is that the parameters of the models are assumed to vary, but they never include the value of 0. The models, then, are akin to alternative models in traditional NHST, as opposed to null models that have parameter values of 0. One characteristic of the multimodel inference described later is the absence of null models, as such models do not represent statistical hypotheses of interest.

As an example, consider the risk group model from Chapter 5:

$$y_{ij} = (\beta_0 + b_{0i}) + (\beta_1 + b_{1i})(\text{grade}_{ij}) + \beta_2(\text{riskDADV}_i)$$
$$+ \beta_3(\text{grade}_{ij} \cdot \text{riskDADV}_i) + \varepsilon_{ij}. \qquad (7.2.1)$$

The model contains a risk intercept effect indexed by β_2, and a risk slope effect indexed by β_3. These fixed effects parameters are always assumed to be values other than 0. If one of the effects could possibly be 0, then an additional hypothesis must be represented by another model that excludes the zero-valued parameter(s).

It is typical for there to be multiple statistical models, as there are usually multiple working hypotheses. In fact, the formulation of several working hypotheses prior to data analysis is encouraged, and this practice has a long history in science (Chamberlain, 1890; Peirce, 1903). Platt (1964) lists multiple working hypotheses as a necessary component for "strong inference" in scientific research, and Feyerabend (1968) considers this essential for a researcher to be a "good empiricist."

As an example, suppose the research question is "What is the nature of risk group intercept differences in reading achievement when ethnicity is considered?" One tact for addressing this question is to consider three working hypotheses and three corresponding statistical models. These are shown in Table 7.2. To address the questions regarding intercept differences, it is preferable to anchor the intercept at the fifth grade. Thus, in Table 7.2, grade5 = grade−5 is used for all the models. The same variable is used for estimation (see below).

The hypotheses and models in Table 7.2 represent conjectures that have bearing on the research question. The primary means of addressing the research question is to evaluate the models using sample data. Inferences regarding the research question are made based on the results of the model evaluation.

Consider Model 1 and Model 3. Model 1 implies $\beta_2 \neq 0$ and $\beta_3 = 0$, whereas Model 3 implies $\beta_2 \neq 0$ and $\beta_3 \neq 0$. If Model 1 is equally plausible as Model 3, then ethnicity does not account for risk group differences.

Now consider Model 2 and Model 3. If Model 2 is just as plausible as Model 3, then ethnicity does account for risk group differences. Or, stated another way, ethnicity effects do not become negligible when risk is in the model.

Table 7.2 Working hypotheses and statistical models for a research question about risk group differences.

Number	Working Hypothesis	LMER Model
1	Change is linear; intercept difference among the advantaged and disadvantaged risk groups	$y_{ij} = (\beta_0 + b_{0i})$ $+ (\beta_1 + b_{1i})(\texttt{grade5}_{ij})$ $+ \beta_2(\texttt{risk2DADV}_i) + \varepsilon_{ij}$
2	Change is linear; intercept difference among the White and non-White ethnic groups	$y_{ij} = (\beta_0 + b_{0i})$ $+ (\beta_1 + b_{1i})(\texttt{grade5}_{ij})$ $+ \beta_2(\texttt{eth2NW}_i) + \varepsilon_{ij}$
3	Change is linear; intercept difference among the risk groups controlling for ethnicity	$y_{ij} = (\beta_0 + b_{0i})$ $+ (\beta_1 + b_{1i})(\texttt{grade5}_{ij})$ $+ \beta_2(\texttt{risk2DADV}_i)$ $+ \beta_3(\texttt{eth2NW}_i) + \varepsilon_{ij}$

What does it mean for one model to be more "plausible" than another? This means there is greater statistical evidence based on the sample data for one model over another. Statistical evidence is quantified in different ways, and the ML methods of the last chapter provide a solid foundation.

As discussed in the last chapter, the deviance function (or the *logLik* function) is the mathematical representation of the statistical evidence in the data (Berger & Wolpert, 1988; Blume, 2002). This means that all inferences one might want to make can be gleaned from the deviance function. The deviance "wrings" from the data all the information about the population parameters of interest. The minimum deviance value shown in the `lmer()` output is a type of global measure of relative statistical evidence for a fitted model. It follows that the deviance is the preferred basis for assessing the relative plausibility of models.

One drawback of the deviance is that it will always decrease when the number of estimated parameters increases. The deviance will indicate better fit, even when the predictors being added are worthless. "Worthless" means that the predictors have no relation with the response variable in the population. To account for the possibility of adding worthless predictors, it is preferable to penalize the deviance based on the number of parameters in the model. The penalty provides a trade-off between fit, on the one hand, and model complexity, on the other hand.

Two penalization approaches will be emphasized in this chapter and the next. The first approach uses the AIC, which adjusts the deviance upward to account for the number of estimated parameters. The second is the LRT, whose penalty is realized through the *df* of the χ^2 sampling distribution. The LRT-*p* takes into account the difference in the number of estimated parameters of two nested models, whereas the AIC can be used for nested or nonnested models.

The LRT-*p* falls under the umbrella of the dominant statistical paradigm in the behavioral sciences, NHST. NHST is a hybrid of methods due to Ronald

Fisher (Fisher, 1922, 1925), and Jerzy Neyman and Eagon Pearson (Neyman & Pearson, 1928a, 1928b). In Fisher's conception, the method involves a null hypothesis that is assumed to be true before any data are analyzed. Based on the sample data, a *p*-value is computed that is the probability of obtaining the observed result or one more extreme, given the truth assumption about the null hypothesis. The magnitude of the *p*-value is taken as evidence against the null hypothesis, with smaller values indicating greater evidence (Berger, 2003; Christensen, 2005).

It has been argued that when used cautiously and in appropriate circumstances, NHST can be of benefit to applied researchers (Abelson, 1997; Krantz, 1999). However, there is much disagreement on this point (Cohen, 1994; Gigerenzer, Krauss, & Vitouch, 2004; Hubbard & Lindsay, 2008). Rather than sift through all the relevant arguments, focus is on reasons why model comparison based on the AIC may be superior to using LRT-*p* and NHST. These issues are treated below. But first, specifics of the AIC are presented to facilitate better understanding when discussing the contrasts with the LRT-*p*.

7.3 AIC and Predictive Accuracy

The AIC may be new to some readers, due to its relatively recent development (1970s) and its scant use in the behavioral sciences. For this reason, a heuristic overview is provided. The AIC has an intimate connection with the framework known as Kullback-Leibler information theory (Kullback & Leibler, 1951). This is the basis for the term, Akaike's *information criterion*. In addition to this connection, the AIC is an estimate of *predictive accuracy*, which is the ability of a model to predict new data (or out-of-sample data). The discussion of the AIC provided here focuses on predictive accuracy, as this touches on many themes familiar to applied researchers.

Recall that the AIC has the formula

$$\text{AIC} = \textit{deviance} + 2 \cdot K, \qquad (7.3.1)$$

where K is the total number of estimated parameters, which is the number of the fixed effects and variance components in LMER. A smaller deviance indicates better fit, and the same goes for the AIC. The AIC penalizes the deviance by 2 times the number of estimated parameters. This penalty helps to guard against improving fit simply by adding worthless predictors. The AIC will not decrease (i.e., improve) with the addition of predictors, unless there is an accompanying improvement of fit as indexed by a decrease in the deviance. In this way, the AIC balances fit and complexity.

In the sense just described, the AIC is similar to *adj*. R^2 of traditional regression. However, the theoretical justification of the two measures is very different. Although the AIC has a simple form, it is based on sophisticated statistical theory, as laid down by Akaike (1973, 1974, 1981) and illustrated by Burnham and Anderson (2002, 2004) and Forster and Sober (Forster, 2002;

Forster & Sober, 1994, 2011; Sober, 2002). As explicated by Forster and Sober, the AIC can be expressed as a measure of predictive accuracy. Predictive accuracy involves important concepts for applied analysis, such as the reproducibility of results and parsimony in model selection.

Similar to the last two chapters, the concepts underlying the AIC are initially illustrated with traditional regression models assuming independent (nonlongitudinal) data. Then the extension to LMER is discussed, and examples for longitudinal data analysis are provided using the MPLS data set.

Predictive accuracy illustration. For the sake of illustration, suppose a researcher has knowledge of the model that generates the sample data. By this, it is meant there is a population model with known form and known parameter values. This model is known as the generating model or the *true model*. It is stressed that the true model is never known. If the true model were known, there would be no reason for the analysis of sample data.

Let the true model be a cross-sectional regression model (LM), relevant for the MPLS data set. Suppose the response variable is reading achievement (read), and the predictor is attendance proportion (att) at Grade 5. To be clear, there is only one time point considered (Grade 5), so the data are cross-sectional and not longitudinal. Suppose the true model is the LM:

$$\begin{aligned} y_i &= \beta_0 + \beta_1(\text{att}_i) + \varepsilon_i \\ &= \beta_0 + 0 \cdot (\text{att}_i) + \varepsilon_i \\ &= \beta_0 + \varepsilon_i. \end{aligned} \quad (7.3.2)$$

The ε_i are normally distributed with mean of 0 and constant variance σ_ε^2. There is no relationship between reading and attendance in the true model, meaning $\beta_1 = 0$. Because of this, the slope parameter and predictor drop out of Equation 7.3.2. Despite the 0 slope, there are still att_i values for all the subjects in the population.

Equation 7.3.2 indicates the true regression line is a horizontal line with intercept β_0. Because of the random error term, the population observed values are scattered about the true regression line. If the form of the true regression line is unknown, which is usually the case, then the goal of the analysis is to make a best guess as to its form. This best guess is based on the evaluation of different models with the sample data.

To make things concrete, suppose the `simulate()` function from the `lme4` package is used to generate a sample of response scores from the true model of Equation 7.3.2. The data set will be called Sample A, with associated data frame `sample.a`. The `simulate()` function is supplied a fitted model whose estimates ($\hat{\beta}_k$) are treated as the population parameters, or true model parameters. New response data are generated based on the normality assumption for the errors. The predictor scores are treated as fixed, meaning they are the values from the original sample. This treatment of the predictor is consistent with the assumptions of traditional regression and LMER.

7.3 AIC and Predictive Accuracy

In the syntax below, the intercepts-only model of Equation 7.3.2 is fit to the original sample data in the `MPLS.LS` data frame. Then the `simulate()` function is used to generate a new response variable. The new response is put in a data frame, along with the original predictor variable to form Sample A. The `set.seed()` function is used to allow a reproduction of the results.

```
> ## Select grade 5 data.
> mysample <- subset(MPLS.LS, grade == 5)
> ## Fit true Model 0.
> model.0 <- lm(read ~ 1, mysample)
> ## Simulate Sample A.
> set.seed(1)                              # Reader can reproduce the results.
> sim.dv <- unlist(simulate(model.0))      # Generate response.
> sample.a <- data.frame(read = sim.dv, att = mysample$att)
> head(sample.a)
```

```
          read      att
sim_11  188.9370  0.94
sim_12  205.1828  0.91
sim_13  184.7422  0.97
sim_14  233.4919  0.88
sim_15  208.1080  0.85
sim_16  185.0463  0.90
```

The row names in the output are a result of using `simulate()`, and they can be omitted or altered if desired. A scatterplot of the sample data, along with the true regression line, is shown in Figure 7.1.

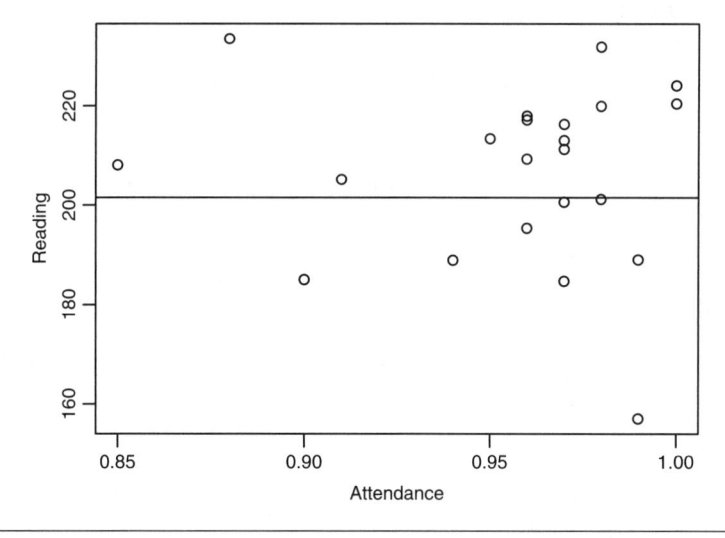

Figure 7.1 Scatterplot of Sample A with the true regression line.

With the data frame in hand, suppose the researcher asks a colleague to investigate the relationship between reading achievement and attendance by fitting regression models. (Graphical methods can also be used but are not considered here.) The colleague does not know the true model, and based on the supplied variables, the colleague decides to fit two models. The first is a linear model, with attendance as a predictor. The second is a nonlinear quadratic model, with attendance and attendance squared as the predictors. These two models are known as *candidate models*. One of the candidate models is usually "elected" as the best guess of the true model, based on the statistical analysis. A summary of the models for the example is provided in Table 7.3.

Table 7.3 Models used in the AIC illustration.

Model	Equation
True Model 0	$y_i = \beta_0 + \varepsilon_i$
Candidate Model 1	$y_i = \beta_0 + \beta_1(\text{att}_i) + \varepsilon_i$
Candidate Model 2	$y_i = \beta_0 + \beta_1(\text{att}_i) + \beta_2(\text{att}_i^2) + \varepsilon_i$

It is emphasized that both candidate models are *false*, as they both have extraneous predictors and parameters. Model 1 is "less false" than Model 2, in the sense that Model 1 has one less extraneous parameter. Of the two candidate models, Model 1 is a better *approximating model* than Model 2, as Model 1 is closer to the truth. The true model is never known in applied analysis, and thus, the best approximating model is also never known. An informed guess as to the best approximating model can be made based on the following theoretical scenario.

Back to the example. The colleague will fit Model 1 and Model 2 for Sample A of Figure 7.1. Suppose the colleague measures fit using the deviance. Before Sample A is analyzed, is it known which model will have superior fit? The answer is yes, as the model with the larger number of predictors (and parameters) will have superior fit. This is Model 2, with attendance and attendance squared as the predictors. As an illustration, consider the deviance for the fitted Model 1 and Model 2.

```
> model.1a  <-  lm(sample.a$read  ~  sample.a$att)
> model.2a  <-  lm(sample.a$read  ~  sample.a$att + I(sample.a$att ^ 2))
> dev.a  <-  data.frame(deviance = c(deviance(model.1a), deviance(model.2a)))
> rownames(dev.a)  <-  c("Model.1a", "Model.2a")
> dev.a
```

```
         deviance
Model.1a 6672.761
Model.2a 6615.108
```

The output shows that Model 2 (`Model.2a`) has the smaller deviance, and thus, the better fit. Since the true regression line is horizontal, the predictors att and att^2 are fitting random error, as there is nothing "real" to be fit beyond the intercept term. This spurious superiority is really *over-fit* of the data. A more complex model always has the ability to conform itself to the

7.3 AIC and Predictive Accuracy

observed data more closely than a model with fewer parameters. Because of the susceptibility to over-fitting, one does not always want to favor models with additional predictors and parameters. Additional complexity is desired only if this constitutes a genuine effect.

If increasingly complex models always have superior fit to the data at hand, how is one to know if a particular fitted model is genuine or a case of over-fitting? A way forward is to examine how well the fitted models of Sample A predict new data generated by the true model. If Model 1 is closer to the truth than Model 2, it is expected that Model 1 will have better average fit to new data than Model 2.

Model 2 is able to conform itself better than Model 1 to the same data set. In a new data set generated by the true model, the pattern of random error is different, and the conformity of Model 2 to the old data set should work against it in predicting the new data. The over-fitting of random error for the old data set should "penalize" Model 2 in fitting new data. The same should happen for Model 1, as it too is a false model. However, Model 1 is closer to the true model. Less over-fitting is expected with Model 1, leading to better prediction for new data. Let us see if these expectations are borne out.

Here is what is meant by prediction of new data. The fitted model objects for Sample A are model.1a and model.2a. These objects contain, among other things, the fitted values produced by the estimated regression equations. For example, consider the display of the estimated regression parameters and the first few fitted values for model.1a.

```
> model.1a$coefficients
(Intercept)   sample.a$att
   232.09883      -26.74164

> head(model.1a$fitted.values)
       1         2         3         4         5         6
206.9617  207.7639  206.1594  208.5662  209.3684  208.0313
```

Suppose a second sample is generated, Sample B, based on the true model of Equation 7.3.2. The data are generated in the same manner as Sample A. After generating the data, the researcher again asks the colleague to compute the deviance using the *fitted values from Sample A and the observed values from Sample B*. The deviance in this case is not computed solely on the data at hand, but is a type of cross-sample *predictive deviance*. Since Model 1 is closer to the truth than Model 2, Model 1 is expected to have a smaller predictive deviance than Model 2, in contrast to the regular deviance previously computed.

Suppose the researcher generates Sample B and hands it over to the colleague to fit the same models as fit with Sample A. This scenario is represented in the syntax below.

```
> ## Generate Sample B.
> set.seed(13)
> sim.dv <- unlist(simulate(model.0))
> sample.b <- data.frame(read = sim.dv, att = mysample$att)
> ## Fit candidate models.
> model.1b <- lm(sample.b$read ~ sample.b$att)
> model.2b <- lm(sample.b$read ~ sample.b$att + I(sample.b$att ^ 2))
> dev.b <- data.frame(deviance = c(deviance(model.1b), deviance(model.2b)))
> rownames(dev.b) <- c("Model.1b", "Model.2b")
> dev.b
```

	deviance
Model.1b	7154.775
Model.2b	6689.174

Once again, the deviance of Model 2 is smaller. This indicates a better fit to the data at hand. The question is how the models fare in terms of predictive deviance.

The goal here is to compare the predictive deviance of both models. The deviance for a model is computed using the equations from the last chapter. The SSR is computed using the response from Sample B, `sample.b$read`, and the fitted values based on Sample A, `model.1a$fitted.values` and `model.2a$fitted.values`. The residual formula is the following,

$$\tilde{\varepsilon}_i = y_{Bi} - \hat{y}_{Ai}, \quad (7.3.3)$$

where y_{Bi} is the response from Sample B, and $\hat{y}_{Ai}$ is the fitted values from Sample A, with $\hat{\beta}_0$ and $\hat{\beta}_1$ estimated based on the Sample A data. Using the formulas from the last chapter, it can be shown that the predictive deviance is

$$deviance_p = N\left[log\left(2 \cdot \pi \cdot N^{-1} \cdot \sum_i^N \tilde{\varepsilon}_i\right)\right]. \quad (7.3.4)$$

Consider the following computation of predictive deviance for each model.

```
> N <- nrow(sample.b)
> prdev.1b <- N * (log(2 * pi * sum((sample.b$read - model.1a$fitted.values)^ 2)) + 1)
> prdev.2b <- N * (log(2 * pi * sum((sample.b$read - model.2a$fitted.values)^ 2)) + 1)
> prdev.b <- data.frame(preddev = c(prdev.1b, prdev.2b))
> rownames(prdev.b) <- c("Model 1", "Model 2")
> prdev.b
```

	preddev
Model 1	258.9184
Model 2	260.0115

The predictive deviance is smaller for Model 1, which indicates better prediction of the new data of Sample B. Another way to say this is that the fitted values of Model 1 for Sample A have a closer association with the observed data of Sample B. This is comforting, as the linear model is closer to the true model that generated the data.

The above result suggests a method for dealing with the over-fitting phenomenon: *attempt to determine how accurate a model is in predicting new*

7.3 AIC and Predictive Accuracy

data. Unfortunately, applied researchers rarely have access to repeated samples to assess predictive accuracy. However, the scenario depicted here is the theoretical underpinning of the AIC, which can be used as an approximation.

To continue the example, suppose yet another sample is generated from the true model. This new sample will be labeled as Sample C. The researcher again hands over the data to the colleague for analysis, using the same linear and quadratic models.

```
> set.seed(21)
> sample.c <- data.frame(read = unlist(simulate(model.0)), att = mysample$att)
> model.1c <- lm(sample.c$read ~ sample.c$att)
> model.2c <- lm(sample.c$read ~ sample.c$att + I(sample.c$att ^ 2))
> dev.c <- data.frame(deviance = c(deviance(model.1c), deviance(model.2c)))
> rownames(dev.c) <- c("Model.1c", "Model.2c")
> dev.c
```

	deviance
Model.1c	9681.264
Model.2c	8989.102

Once again, Model 2 fits the data at hand better than Model 1. Consider the predictive deviance using the fitted values from Sample B and the response from Sample C.

```
> prdev.1c <- N * (log(2 * pi * sum((sample.c$read - model.1b$fitted.values)^ 2))+ 1)
> prdev.2c <- N * (log(2 * pi * sum((sample.c$read - model.2b$fitted.values)^ 2))+ 1)
> prdev.c <- data.frame(preddev = c(prdev.1c, prdev.2c))
> rownames(prdev.c) <- c("Model 1", "Model 2")
> prdev.c
```

	preddev
Model 1	264.7495
Model 2	268.0598

The output shows that the fitted Model 1 is superior for predicting new data. The above process can be repeated many times, but the reader is spared the tedium. Figure 7.2 shows the general predictive accuracy scenario. The figure uses letters for the samples, but it is assumed the lettering can be infinite, with doubles (AA), triples (AAA), and so on. The regular deviance is represented as a vertical arrow, as this deviance is computed based on a single sample. The predictive deviance ($deviance_p$) is represented by a diagonal arrow, as this deviance is computed based on two samples, the fitted values of the first sample, and the observed values of the second sample.

For the simulation scenario just described, the regular deviance along with the predictive deviance is shown in Table 7.4. The last line of the table shows the average. As seen in the table, Model 2 has superior fit to the data at hand, but it is known this is due to over-fitting (Model 0 is the true model). Model 1 has superior average fit for predicting new data. The average predictive deviance accounts for the fact that Model 2 is uselessly more complex than Model 1, in relation to the true model.

The average predictive deviance is an important concept in regard to the AIC. Suppose infinite samples from the true model are generated. For each sample, the predictive deviance is computed as represented in Figure 7.2. *Given a large sample size, the normality assumption, and the endless repeated sampling scenario, the AIC is an unbiased estimator of the average of the predictive deviance* (Forster & Sober, 1994). The penalty term of the AIC, $2 \cdot K$, acts as an adjustment for over-fitting that is an estimate of the adjustment that is "naturally" accomplished by the average predictive deviance. To put it another way, predictive accuracy is based on the long-run idea of predicting new data.

In practice, there is usually only one sample data set, and the true model is not known. To be thorough, then, an additional condition is that the AIC is an estimate of predictive accuracy, *given the true model is never known*. In addition to not knowing the true model, it is not known which of the candidate models is closest to the truth. In this case, the AIC can be computed for each candidate model. Since the AIC is an unbiased estimate of the average long-run predictive deviance, the model with the smallest AIC is the best guess as to the model closest to the truth. The model closest to the truth is referred to as the *best approximating model*. In the examples of Table 7.4, the best approximating model is known to be Model 1, and the AIC values in all cases (Samples A, B, and C) confirm this. In the example, the AIC is not needed, as the true model is known. In real applications, the AIC is needed.

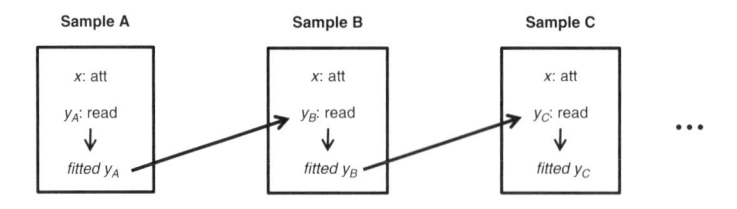

Figure 7.2 Illustration of predictive accuracy. A vertical arrow represents deviance and a diagonal arrow represents predictive deviance.

The AIC is extracted from a `lmer()` object by accessing the slot, `@AICtab$AIC`, of the `summary()` output object. The last two columns of Table 7.4 show the AIC for each model computed on each sample. As shown in the table, the AIC indicates Model 1 is preferable to Model 2, which is consistent with the average predictive deviance, as it should be. In most applied research, there is only one sample, and a single AIC value for each model is computed one time.

A caveat about Table 7.4 is that it is "textbook perfect," meaning that all the information is consistent with the predictive accuracy underlying the AIC. It should be mentioned that for any pair of samples, the predictive deviance can be *smaller* for Model 2. The theory only specifies that on average, the predictive deviance will be smaller for Model 1. In addition, the AIC can be

7.3 AIC and Predictive Accuracy

Table 7.4 Deviance, predictive deviance, and AIC for sample data generated by the same underlying true model.

Data	dev. 1	dev. 2	pred. dev. 1	pred. dev. 2	AIC 1	AIC 2
Sample A	6672.76	6615.11	—	—	194.16	195.97
Sample B	7154.78	6689.17	258.92	260.01	195.69	196.21
Sample C	9681.26	8989.1	264.75	268.06	202.35	202.71
Average	6672.76	6615.11	258.92	260.01	194.16	195.97

Note. 1 = linear model; 2 = quadratic model; dev. = deviance.

in error, meaning it incorrectly identifies a model as the best approximating model when, in fact, it is not. The extent of uncertainty in identifying the best approximating model can be quantified, and this quantification is the basis of effect size measures considered below.

AIC details. Some details of the AIC are important to keep in mind. AIC values are not standardized and can be negative, positive, very large, or very small. The AIC does not offer a method of statistical testing. The term *statistically significant* should never be used with the AIC. Furthermore, long-run error probabilities of traditional NHST are irrelevant. This points out, among other things, that there is no "multiple testing" problem when many models are evaluated.

Rather than statistical testing, the AIC offers a method of rank-ordering models in a set and determining the models' relative effect sizes in terms of distance from the truth. Models need not be nested, so all models in a set can be directly evaluated.

The AIC is affected by sample size, underlining that comparisons across studies are not possible. In addition, the AIC cannot be used when the response variable changes among models. Therefore, the AIC cannot be used to investigate different transformations of the response variable, although different transformations of variables on the predictor side are valid.

The example above involved a true model that was simpler than the two candidate models. Predictive accuracy and the AIC also works in a similar manner when the true model is more complex than the candidate models. In this scenario, the more complex model has better predictive accuracy, indicating the additional predictors are warranted because they reflect "real" effects.

7.3.1 EXTENSION TO LMER

The heuristic overview of the AIC focused on multiple regression, but the AIC is valid for other methods, including LMER (Anderson, 2008, chap. 3). What is required for valid application is an appropriate deviance function having a probability distribution with relevant parameters that account for the dependency due to repeated measures. As seen in the last chapter, the deviance function for LMER qualifies as appropriate in this regard. Consequently, the AIC can be used for identifying the best approximating model.

There are some caveats, however, regarding the use of the AIC with LMER. The first is that the AIC is most appropriate for the selection of fixed effects. The AIC is an unbiased guide to selecting the best approximating model only when the models under consideration differ in the number of fixed effects (Liang, Wu, & Zou, 2008; Vaida & Blanchard, 2005). Bias can result when the AIC is used to select models with a different number of random effects, or associated variance components (see Chapter 10).

A related second issue is that the predictive accuracy in LMER refers only to the fitted values based on the fixed effects. Over-fitting in LMER is more complex than with the LM. Worthless predictors may conform themselves not only to random error, but also to individual variability represented by the random effects. This implies that the random effects model should be "adequate," so as to decrease (or eliminate) a source of spurious over-fitting. For a linear change curve, two random effects are considered adequate.

When there are many models, it is convenient to use a function for extracting the AIC of each model. In anticipation of things to come, the aictab() function of the AICcmodavg package is introduced, written by Marc Mazerolle (Mazerolle, 2010).

The aictab() function requires the fitted model objects be supplied in a list, using cand.set=list(). In addition, names for the models must be supplied in a character vector (modnames=). The names vector is created below with the paste() function. To compute the AIC rather than its variant to be discussed below, the optional argument second.ord=FALSE is used. Since aictab() computes several additional measures, as.data.frame() is used to limit the output to the names of the models, the number of estimated parameters, and the AIC.

For this example, the LMER models of Table 7.2 are considered. The time predictor, grade5, is constructed providing anchoring of the intercept at fifth grade.

```
> ## Create grade5.
> MPLS.LS$grade5 ← MPLS.LS$grade - 5
> ## Estimate models.
> model.1 ← lmer(read ~ grade5 + risk2 + (grade5 | subid), MPLS.LS, REML = FALSE)
> model.2 ← lmer(read ~ grade5 + eth2 + (grade5 | subid), MPLS.LS, REML = FALSE)
> model.3 ← lmer(read ~ grade5 + risk2 + eth2 + (grade5|subid), MPLS.LS, REML = FALSE)
> ## Compute AIC.
> mynames ← paste("M", as.character(1:3), sep = "")
> myaic ← aictab(cand.set = list(model.1, model.2, model.3),
+                modnames = mynames, sort = FALSE, second.ord = FALSE)
> as.data.frame(myaic)[ ,1:3]
```

	Modnames	K	AIC
1	M1	7	563.8856
2	M2	7	579.2080
3	M3	8	565.8819

The Modnames column contains the model names created with paste(). The K column lists the number of estimated parameters. Model 1 and Model

7.3 AIC and Predictive Accuracy

2 have seven estimated parameters, so these models are not nested. The last column lists the AIC.

As seen in the output, the AIC shows that Model 1 has the best fit, followed by Model 3 and then Model 2. Model 1 is considered the best approximating model in this analysis. How much superior is the fit of Model 1 to the other models? Or, put another way, how sound is it to assume that Model 1 is the best approximating model? These questions will be answered in the following sections. But first, a variant of the AIC is introduced that provides a small-sample correction.

7.3.2 AIC CORRECTED

The correction term of $2 \cdot K$ in Equation 7.3.1 has a large-sample justification. When the sample size is not large, a bias-adjusted form of the AIC should be used, the AIC-corrected or AICc (Hurvich & Tsai, 1989). A justification for the use of the AICc with LMER is provided by Azari, Li, and Tsai (2006).

For longitudinal data, the AICc is computed as

$$\text{AICc} = \text{AIC} + \frac{2 \cdot K \cdot (K+1)}{\left(\sum_{i}^{N} n_i\right) - K - 1}, \qquad (7.3.5)$$

where the summation is the total number of observed time points (for the LM, the summation is replaced with N). As the sum in the denominator increases, the second term approaches 0, meaning the AICc approaches the AIC. Because of this, the AICc should be regularly used rather than the AIC, to cover both small- and large-sample situations.

The AICc is not a panacea for a small sample size. A small sample size means there is limited information in the sample. A researcher may not be able to address all the pertinent research questions with a small sample size. In such cases, one might have to pare back the models by reducing the number of static predictors.

The AICc is computed with `aictab()`. Consider computation of the AICc for the models of Table 7.2. The argument `second.ord=` is omitted, meaning the AICc is computed by default. As in the last illustration, `as.data.frame()` is used to print only the relevant columns of output.

```
> myaicc <- aictab(cand.set = list(model.1, model.2, model.3),
+                  modnames = mynames, sort = FALSE)
> as.data.frame(myaicc)[ ,1:3]

  Modnames K     AICc
1       M1 7 565.4412
2       M2 7 580.7635
3       M3 8 567.9101
```

The first column lists the model names, the second column shows the number of estimated parameters, and the third column lists the AICc. The ordering of the models is the same as with the AIC, but the separation between the models is slightly greater.

7.4 AICc and Effect Size

A desirable aspect of the AICc (and AIC) is that it can be used as a basis for effect size. The predictive accuracy underlying the AICc is a relative concept. It is relative because one never knows the true model, and therefore, cannot estimate its distance from a candidate model. What can be done is to estimate the relative proximity to the true model for two or more candidate models. This is taken as an indication of the plausibility that a candidate model is the best approximating model, or the plausibility the best-fitting model is the closest to the truth.

Given two or more candidate models, the model with the smallest AICc is the most plausible candidate for being the best approximating model. Candidate models with larger values are not as plausible. Not only does the order of the models matter, but also the similarity or dissimilarity of the AICc. If the values of the models are very similar, there is uncertainty regarding the best approximating model. Since the AICc is a sample statistic, it is influenced by sampling fluctuations and is not a completely reliable indicator of the best approximating model. Two models with similar values are almost equally plausible in regard to the best approximating model. On the other hand, when two models have very dissimilar values, then there is much more confidence that the one with the smaller AICc is the best approximating model.

Effect size is a quantification of the (dis)similarity among the candidate models in terms of being the best approximating model. There are a number of ways to express effect size, and three of these are considered below. The first subtracts out from each AICc the minimum value in the set. The second transforms the AICc values to be on a probability scale ranging from 0 to 1. The third is a ratio of probabilities yielding an odds of plausibility. Each type of effect size measure is considered for the LMER models in Table 7.2.

7.4.1 DELTA

The first measure of effect size is *delta*, symbolized as Δ. Delta is the difference between each AICc and the smallest AICc of the candidate models. More formally, for the hth model,

$$\Delta_h = \text{AICc}_h - \text{AICc}_{min}, \tag{7.4.1}$$

where $h = 1, \ldots, H$, with H being the number of models, and AICc_{min} is the smallest AICc value in the set of H models.

7.4 AICc and Effect Size

Δ_h is a calibration of model fit, using the best fitting as the standard. The best-fitting model is the touchstone, as it is the most plausible to be the best approximating model. The best-fitting model has $\Delta_h = 0$, and all other models have $\Delta_h > 0$. Δ_h is interpreted as an estimate of the difference in the plausibility of model h and the best-fitting model, in terms of being the best approximating model. Echoing what was said above, this definition is conditional on the data, the set of models, and the inability to know the true model.

Since the best-fitting model is the most likely candidate for the best approximating model, it also is a prime candidate to be judged as plausible. Models with a short distance from the best fitting have a relatively small Δ_h and are relatively plausible candidates. On the other hand, models more distant from the best fitting have a relatively large Δ_h and are relatively implausible candidates.

It is not always the case that a Δ_h value will be extreme for the most distant, worst-fitting model. In this case, it might not be possible to distinguish among the models in the set as candidates for the best approximating model. Such indistinguishable cases should not necessarily be viewed as negative, but as an indication of the relatively high uncertainty of the analysis. On the other hand, it seems desirable to have lower uncertainty in any analysis, so one might hope for relatively large Δ_h for all models except the best fitting (the best fitting always has $\Delta_h = 0$).

There are some guidelines for what constitutes an "appreciable" Δ_h (Anderson, 2008, chap. 4). A value of $\Delta_h = 4$ constitutes what is considered a "strong" difference between model h and the best-fitting model, and $\Delta_h > 8$ is considered a "very strong" difference. The reader is cautioned to not use these values as cutoffs, as when 0.05 is used with the *p*-value in NHST.

There is no testing performed with the Δ_h. The intention is to present values for all the models in order to paint a complete picture regarding the candidate set. As Anderson (2008) puts it, "Science is about estimation and understanding; it is not about cutoffs or dichotomies" (p. 85). Furthermore, the guidelines are established assuming independence of observations, so they are expected to be only approximate for longitudinal models. As an alternative to such guidelines, two other types of measures are favored, as presented below.

The Δ_h are computed by default with `aictab()`. Consider printing the `myaicc` output object previously saved, but this time showing the first four columns.

```
> as.data.frame(myaicc)[ ,1:4]
  Modnames K     AICc Delta_AICc
1       M1 7 565.4412   0.000000
2       M2 7 580.7635  15.322307
3       M3 8 567.9101   2.468887
```

The `Delta_AICc` column lists Δ_h. The output shows that $\Delta_1 = 0$, $\Delta_2 = 15.3$, and $\Delta_3 = 2.5$. In words, the difference in the AICc of Model 2 and the best-fitting Model 1 is 15.3. The difference in AICc for Model 3 and the best-fitting Model 1 is 2.5. Model 1 is the most plausible, followed not too far behind by Model 3. Model 2 is fairly distant and relatively implausible.

7.4.2 WEIGHT OF EVIDENCE

The delta measure is a convenient means of quickly seeing the distance from the best approximating model. However, the delta scale is not bounded above, and its metric might be unfamiliar to researchers new to the AICc.

An alternative scaling that will be familiar to most applied researchers is the *weight of evidence*. The weight of evidence for the *h*th model, W_h, is a probability scaling of Δ_h. This scaling is convenient, as the W_h have a range of 0 to 1, and the W_h sum to 1.

The weight of evidence of the *h*th model is computed as

$$W_h = \frac{exp(-0.5 \cdot \Delta_h)}{\sum_{h}^{H} exp(-0.5 \cdot \Delta_h)}, \qquad (7.4.2)$$

where the sum is over all the models in the set. *Given the data, the set of models, and the unknowable true model, W_h indicates the probability that model h is the best approximating model.* The model with the largest weight of evidence is the best-fitting model of the set. The larger the Δ_h, the smaller the W_h, and the less probable that model *h* is the best approximating model. Conversely, the smaller the Δ_h, the larger the W_h, and the more probable the model in question is the best approximating model.

The weight of evidence can be used as a representation of the extent of *model evaluation uncertainty*. This refers to the uncertainty that a model in question is, in fact, the best approximating model. The uncertainty arises from the reality that models are evaluated based on a single sample. There are no guarantees the models will be judged similarly in a replication, using another sample of the same size from the same population.

How large does the weight of evidence need to be in order for a researcher to have high certainty about a model or set of models? This requires judgment on the part of the researcher, but it has been suggested that $W_h = 0.90$ and $W_h = 0.95$ are reasonable benchmarks (Anderson, 2008, chap. 4). A researcher can probably be fairly confident the best-fitting model is, in fact, the true best approximating model—*not* the true model—if its probability of being so is at least 0.90.

It is not always the case that a single model will have such a large probability. In such cases, it is convenient to form a *confidence set* of the models whose probabilities sum to 0.90 or 0.95. Confidence statements about the set are similar to those of individual models. There is uncertainty regarding the models within the confidence set. However, if the confidence for the set is high (e.g., 0.95), there is considerable confidence that one of the models in the set is the best approximating model.

7.4 AICc and Effect Size

To provide a sense of how the weight of evidence is used in an analysis, consider the graphs in Figure 7.3 that illustrate two separate made-up scenarios involving five candidate models. The bar graph on the left of Figure 7.3 shows the case in which the best-fitting model has a weight of evidence that is large, with the remaining models having much smaller weights. The weight of evidence of an individual model is indicated at the top of its bar.

In this example, Model 3 is the best fitting ($W_3 = 0.95$), followed by Model 5 ($W_5 = 0.027$), then Model 1 ($W_1 = 0.01$), and so on. There is relatively high confidence that if a new sample is drawn from the population, Model 3 will again be judged as the best fitting. Model 3 comprises its own confidence set, as its weight is $W_3 = 0.95$. This bolsters the status of Model 3 in terms of its candidacy as the best approximating model. The scenario represents a relatively high level of certainty for identifying a single candidate for the best approximating model. It is important to keep in mind that although Model 3 is clearly the best approximating model in this example, it may still be very distant from the true model. The large probability speaks only to the relative fit of the model, not the absolute fit. The issue of relative versus absolute fit is revisited below and in Chapter 11.

Now consider the bar graph on the right of Figure 7.3. In this case, the best-fitting model has a weight of evidence that is relatively similar to the other models. Model 3 is again the best fitting ($W_3 = 0.21$), but the second best-fitting model, Model 5, has a weight that is similar ($W_5 = 0.19$), as does the third best model ($W_1 = 0.17$), and so on. There is relatively low confidence that Model 3 will be selected as the best in a replication. In fact, any of the models in the set have the potential to be judged as best under replication. This constitutes a relatively low level of certainty, in that any of the models in the set might, in fact, be the best approximating model.

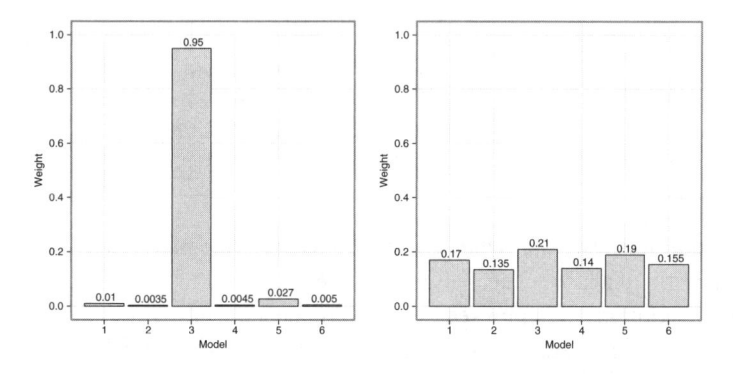

Figure 7.3 Two examples of weight of evidence: low model evaluation uncertainty (left) and high model evaluation uncertainty (right). Individual weights are shown at the top of the bars.

In terms of a confidence set for the right-hand graph, the sum of the probabilities for the five best-fitting models is only 0.865. This constitutes a 87%

confidence set, which is indeed a very uncertain situation! All the models in the confidence set have similar probabilities, and the confidence in any one being the best approximating model is low. It is stressed that the low certainty in this situation does not speak to the absolute worth of the models. The entire set could be very close to the true model, or very far. If very close, then it probably matters little which model is selected for interpretation, as all the models have a similar distance from the truth.

Subsets of models are judged as plausible or implausible based on the weight of evidence. The best-fitting model is always a plausible candidate relative to the other models in the set. This does not mean the best-fitting model is good or correct in any way. The approach does not ensure that any of the models are good in the sense of explaining a substantial portion of within-subjects or between-subjects response variance. The approach only attempts to identify the model that is the most plausible given the data, the set of models considered, and the unknowable true model. After the most plausible model is identified, the researcher might want to go on to examine some type of R^2 measure to assess the model's goodness in an absolute sense. This is discussed in Chapter 11.

The W_k are computed by default with aictab(). Up to this point, default sorting of the results has been suppressed by using sort=FALSE. If this is set to TRUE or omitted, then the output is sorted by the weight of evidence, and the cumulative weight of evidence is also computed. The cumulative weight of evidence can be used to form confidence sets. In what follows, aictab() is rerun, this time sorting by the weight of evidence. For brevity, the printing of the *logLik* for the models is suppressed in the print() statement.

```
> myaicc <- aictab(list(model.1, model.2, model.3), modnames = mynames)
> print(myaicc, LL = FALSE)
```

```
Model selection based on AICc :

    K   AICc  Delta_AICc  AICcWt  Cum.Wt
M1  7  565.44       0.00    0.77    0.77
M3  8  567.91       2.47    0.23    1.00
M2  7  580.76      15.32    0.00    1.00
```

The output shows that when print() is used, the model name column is printed without a label. The weight of evidence is in the AICcWt column, and from this column, it can be seen that the models are sorted by fit. The model name column indicates the order of fit, with the best-fitting Model 1 in the first row.

The output shows that, given the data, the models in the set, and the unknowable true model, Model 1 has a 0.77 probability of being the best approximating model, Model 2 has a probability of almost 0, and Model 3 has a probability of 0.23. The output is rounded to two decimal places, suggesting that Model 2 has a weight of 0. It is always the case that $W_h > 0$, but the weight for Model 2 is very close to 0 in this example.

7.4 AICc and Effect Size

The cumulative weight of evidence is shown in the Cum.Wt column. Model 1 by itself constitutes a 77% confidence set. Model 1 and Model 3 constitute a > 99% confidence set. The rounding makes it appear this is a 100% confidence set, but it is always the case that $\Sigma_h^H W_h = 1$. For the set of Model 1 and Model 3, a researcher might have very high confidence that the best approximating model is in this set. Model 2 is certainly considered to be implausible in this example, in terms of candidacy for the best approximating model.

With only three models, the confidence set is easy to determine by inspecting the output. However, with additional models, it is convenient to use the confset() function in AICcmodavg. The function requires the list of fitted model objects and the model names.

```
> confset(cand.set = list(model.1, model.2, model.3), modnames = mynames)
```

```
Confidence set for the best model

Method:  raw sum of model probabilities

95% confidence set:
     K    AICc  Delta_AICc  AICcWt
M1   7  565.44        0.00    0.77
M3   8  567.91        2.47    0.23

Model probabilities sum to 1
```

The default confidence is 95%, but this can be changed with the level= argument. Consider the following 75% confidence set.

```
> confset(cand.set = list(model.1,model.2,model.3), modnames = mynames,level = 0.75)
```

```
Confidence set for the best model

Method:  raw sum of model probabilities

75% confidence set:
     K    AICc  Delta_AICc  AICcWt
M1   7  565.44           0    0.77

Model probabilities sum to 0.77
```

The confidence set contains only Model 1, as $W_h = 0.77$, which exceeds the 0.75 cutoff for the set. There are methods for defining confidence sets other than the sum of the weight of evidence; see ?confset.

Returning to the 95% confidence set, a judgment might be made as to how strong a difference is represented by the probabilities for Model 1 and Model 3. A 77% to 23% comparison might be compelling for some researchers, but to further aid in this judgment, an additional effect size measure is introduced.

7.4.3 EVIDENCE RATIO

A third measure of effect size is the *evidence ratio*. This measure expresses the difference between the best-fitting model and a worse-fitting model in terms of odds. The evidence ratio for the hth model is

$$E_h = \frac{W_{max}}{W_h}, \qquad (7.4.3)$$

where W_{max} is the maximum weight of evidence in the set, which is the value for the best-fitting model. The best-fitting model has $E_h = 1$, and all other models have $E_h > 1$. E_h indicates how many times greater the best-fitting model is than the hth model. Since E_h is a ratio of probabilities, it also can be interpreted as the odds that model h is *not* the best approximating model. The higher the odds, the more confidence that the hth model is not the best approximating model.

The reference for interpretation of the evidence ratio is the value of 1, as this is the odds of the best-fitting model, $\frac{W_{max}}{W_{max}} = 1$. As an example of interpretation for other models, consider again the left-hand graph of Figure 7.3. The second best-fitting model is Model 5, and its evidence ratio is $E_5 = \frac{0.95}{0.027} = 35.19$. This indicates that the best-fitting Model 3 has a weight of evidence more than 35 times greater than the second best-fitting Model 5. There is an estimated odds of approximately 35 to 1 that Model 5 is not the best approximating model. This appears to be "strong" evidence against Model 5. The odds are even greater for the other models, providing rather convincing sample evidence in support of Model 3 and against the other models.

For another example, consider the right-hand graph of Figure 7.3. Model 5 is again the second best-fitting model, but its evidence ratio is $E_5 = \frac{0.21}{0.19} = 1.11$. This means that Model 3 is only 1.11 times better than Model 5, or the odds are only 1.11 to 1 against Model 5. This does not constitute convincing sample evidence in support of Model 3 relative to Model 5. Furthermore, the graph shows that even the worst-fitting Model 2 has $E_2 = \frac{0.21}{0.135} = 1.56$. This shows that Model 2 is only about one and a half times worse than the best-fitting model. There is little support for dismissing even the worst-fitting model, and the researcher might consider all the models in the set as plausible candidates for the best approximating model.

It is stressed that the graphs in Figure 7.3 are invented scenarios, showing two extremes of model evaluation uncertainty. In practice, the researcher might find a situation that is at neither extreme. In the next section, such a situation is illustrated with the MPLS data set.

A single E_h is computed using the `evidence()` function in AIC cmodavg. The name of the `aictab()` output object is supplied.

```
> evidence(myaicc)
```

```
Evidence ratio between models ' M1 ' and ' M3 ':
3.44
```

7.4 AICc and Effect Size

The default of the function is to return the evidence ratio for the best-fitting model and the second best-fitting model. Values for other models are computed using the optional `model.low=` argument, which contains the quoted model name as originally used in `aictab()`. For example, `model.low=''M2''` computes the evidence ratio for Model 2.

To compute the E_h for the entire set of models, it is convenient to work with the `aictab()` output object. After the `aictab()` object is saved as a data frame, the AICcWt values can be used for the computation. The `max()` function is used to compute the maximum value of the weight of evidence.

```
> ## Save data frame, exclude logLik.
> myaicc2 <- as.data.frame(myaicc)[ ,-7]
> myaicc2$Eratio <- max(myaicc2$AICcWt) / myaicc2$AICcWt
> ## Print with rounding to two decimal places.
> data.frame(Model = myaicc2$Modnames, round(myaicc2[ ,-1], 2))
  Model K   AICc Delta_AICc ModelLik AICcWt Cum.Wt  Eratio
1    M1 7 565.44       0.00     1.00   0.77   0.77    1.00
3    M3 8 567.91       2.47     0.29   0.23   1.00    3.44
2    M2 7 580.76      15.32     0.00   0.00   1.00 2124.21
```

The output shows that $E_2 = 2124.2$, $E_3 = 3.4$, and $E_1 = 1$ (the best-fitting model always has $E_h = 1$). Regarding the interpretation, Model 2 is more than 2000 times less likely to be the best approximating model than Model 1. Model 3 is 3.4 times less likely to be the best approximating model than Model 1.

Judgment must be used to interpret the evidence ratio of the models. For some researchers, an odds of 3.4 constitutes a large enough value to consider Model 3 as implausible. In such a case, only Model 1 is treated as plausible, and additional details of the estimated model are presented. These details include all the parameter estimates, estimated SEs, and t-ratios, where applicable (e.g., for fixed effects but not for variance components).

For other researchers, an odds of 3.4 does not constitute a large enough value to dismiss Model 3. One strategy is to show the details of both Model 1 and Model 3. Alternatively, the details of only Model 1 are presented, but the model uncertainty is acknowledged. In a write-up of the results, these issues are mentioned initially in the results section, and then amplified in the discussion.

As a potential aid to making judgments, repeated sampling from the same population can be simulated with the parametric bootstrap. The parametric bootstrap treats the sample estimates as population parameters. Replications of data are generated based on the normal distribution assumptions for the random effects and random error. Details are provided in the optional Section 7.8.

7.5 AICc and Multimodel Inference

As shown in the last section, the effect size measures based on the AICc are used to assign a value to each model in a set. This assignment makes it possible to present information regarding all the models considered in the analysis. Such an approach is known as *multimodel inference* (Anderson, 2008; Burnham & Anderson, 2002, 2004).

Multimodel inference is a natural way to deal with the multiple working hypotheses that typically characterize applied research. The multimodel approach involves the translation of the working hypotheses into mathematical models that are directly evaluated based on sample data. For longitudinal data, the mathematical models are LMER models, and the direct evaluation is via the effect size measures of the last sections.

As Cox (1995) has pointed out, problems of formulation are more important than problems of solution. As such, it is important that sufficient resources are spent in formulating the set of LMER models to be analyzed. The multimodel approach is well suited to evaluating models that are formulated prior to examining the data. A thorough review of all theoretical issues related to the problem at hand should be undertaken, to help ensure the scientific soundness of the preanalysis models.

Once a set of LMER models is formed, the models are evaluated to determine the following:

1. Rank order of the models in terms of plausibility

2. Relative effect size

On the basis of the effect size measures, the researcher makes judgments regarding the relative plausibility of the models. Some models might have relatively poor fit and constitute implausible candidates. Other models might have relatively good fit and be plausible candidates. After the analysis is completed, it is expected the plausible set of models will be revised. Several iterations of such analyses with new data will lead to an evolution of the model set; some old models will exit, and some new models will be introduced. In this sense, the multimodel approach is amenable to a program of research, rather than a one-shot analysis.

The intention of multimodel inference is to assemble a portfolio of plausible models, which are subject to continual change. Tukey (1995) eloquently refers to the portfolio concept as a "bouquet of models." He summarizes the multimodel approach as the following.

> The most acceptable pattern, as far as I am concerned, for the development of a bouquet of models begins with a predata choice of a collection of models likely to be relevant in the field in question, followed by an examination of the reasonability of the data in light of each model.

Tukey's quote is taken as a sketch of how to carry out multimodel research.

7.5.1 CONTRAST WITH NHST

Multimodel inference is used routinely in some disciplines, such as ecology and wildlife biology (Anderson & Burnham, 2002; Richards, 2005). However, its use in the behavioral sciences is relatively rare (for an example, see Klimes-Dougan et al., 2010). Perhaps the reason for the limited use is the relatively recent development of multimodel inference (early 21st century) and the AIC (1970s), as compared to NHST (1920s).

As mentioned, NHST is the dominant method of analysis in the behavioral sciences. NHST is fundamentally sound when used in the proper context. For experimental research where randomization is possible, NHST is extremely useful for making inferences (Krantz, 1999). However, in nonexperimental research, it is argued that multimodel inference has advantages. This is especially the case when nonexperimental research is coupled with regression analysis, such as LMER.

Although NHST has its place, it should not be regarded as the default method for statistical analysis. For the analysis of nonexperimental data, multimodel analysis using the AICc provides a simpler and clearer evaluation of statistical models and working hypotheses. As the American Psychological Association (APA) Task Force on Statistical Inference phrased it, "If the assumptions and strength of a simpler method are reasonable for your data and research problem, use it" (Wilkinson & APA Task Force on Statistical Inference, 1999, p. 10).

For readers new to multimodel inference, it is useful to provide a detailed contrast with NHST. This will aid in determining which approach is most appropriate for a proposed analysis. The major issues are the following.

1. AICc can handle the simultaneous comparison of many models, whereas NHST only considers two models at a time.

2. AICc can be used to compare models that are nested or not nested, whereas NHST only handles the former.[1]

3. AICc does not use arbitrary cutoffs for judging models, whereas NHST does.

4. AICc provides a basis for a clear measure of effect size, whereas NHST does not.

5. AICc does not require the assumption that at least one of the candidate models is true, whereas NHST does.

6. AICc allows one to determine evidence for a model, whereas NHST does not.

---

[1] It is assumed the likelihood ratio test will be used for NHST. There are alternative statistical methods for evaluating nonnested models (see, e.g., Golden, 2000).

These points are expanded upon below.

To illustrate the difference among the approaches, consider evaluation of the three LMER models in Table 7.2. The AICc and associated measures allow for the assigning of effect size values directly to each model. The models can be rank-ordered in terms of their candidacy as the best approximating model and also in terms of their probability (given the data, the particular set of models, and the unknowable true model). Based on the results from the last section, clear statements can be made that Model 1 is the prime candidate for the best approximating model with probability $W_1 = 0.77$, followed by Model 3 ($W_3 = 0.23$) and then Model 2 ($W_2 < 0.001$). Model 3 is 3.4 times worse fitting than Model 1, and Model 2 is 2124.2 times worse fitting.

The multimodel approach treats two models or 200 models in the same manner—each is assigned a measure of relative predictive accuracy or a transformation thereof. The presentation of the effect size information of multiple models poses no theoretical problem, although the presentation of long tables may pose a practical problem. Long-run error probability, such as the Type I error rate, is irrelevant, so there is no multiple testing problem with multimodel inference.

In contrast to the above, direct evaluation of all the models using NHST is not possible. Since models must be nested, it is only possible to compare Model 1 to Model 3 and Model 2 to Model 3. Model 1 and Model 2 cannot be directly compared.

For the models that can be compared, it is not clear if NHST will provide an indication of their relative plausibility. It is dubious whether the LRT-p can be used to rank-order the models. In Fisher's framework of NHST, the LRT-p is interpreted as a measure of evidence against the null hypothesis (Christensen, 2005). The smaller the LRT-p, the stronger the evidence against the null hypothesis provided by the sample data. However, in the comparison of multiple models, it is unclear how the LRT-p reflects effect size, if at all (Goodman, 1999).

For those steeped in the NHST tradition, it is perhaps disconcerting to think of retaining or discarding models based on AICc effect size measures, rather than the dichotomous decisions of NHST. The AICc approach is consistent with the APA Task Force recommendation that researchers move away from a routine reliance on NHST and move toward effect size measures (Finch, Thomason, & Cumming, 2002; Wilkinson & APA Task Force on Statistical Inference, 1999). More compelling is the fact that the AICc measures constitute statistical evidence under ML theory, and such evidence is more fundamental than the decision-based declarations of NHST. The AICc evidence may be used in decision making if the researcher wishes, but more generally, it can be used to adjust prior beliefs about working hypotheses, or simply used to reduce uncertainty.

One criticism of NHST is that it is often used with a rigid, arbitrary cutoff that seems to run afoul of scientific intuition (Anderson et al., 2000; Gelman & Stern, 2006). The p-value is regularly evaluated against a cutoff of 0.05.

7.5 AICc and Multimodel Inference

Results are declared as "statistically significant" or "not statistically significant," depending on which side of the cutoff the *p*-value happens to fall. The cutoff of 0.05 is near universal, despite the fact that neither Fisher nor Neyman and Pearson were wedded to a particular value. In fact, both parties advocated flexibility, with an appropriate cutoff being determined by the demands of the research situation (Hubbard & Bayarri, 2003).

The problem with a rigid cutoff is illustrated by way of some examples shown in Table 7.5. Each scenario concerns the same two nested model comparisons, Model 1 versus Model 3, and Model 2 versus Model 3. Suppose the 0.05 cutoff is used, and the traditional (or standard) interpretation of the outcome is made. In Scenario 1, LRT-p = 0.01 for the comparison of Model 1 versus Model 3, and LRT-p = 0.03 for the comparison of Model 2 versus Model 3. The simpler model is the null model in each comparison, and under Fisher's system, the *p*-value is the extent of evidence against the null. Both *p*s are less than 0.05, meaning Model 3 is selected over the other models. There is slightly more evidence that Model 2 and Model 3 are more similar than Model 1 and Model 3, although "slightly more" is not rigorously quantified here.

Scenario 2 has LRT-p = 0.04 for 1 versus 3 and LRT-p = 0.06 for 2 versus 3. The traditional interpretation takes the 0.05 cutoff value seriously, and the conclusion is there is evidence against Model 1, but *not* against Model 2. Strictly speaking, LRT-p_2 = 0.06 is treated as *no* evidence against Model 2, as the model is "not rejected," roughly meaning it is equally plausible as Model 3. This interpretation is odd, by virtue of the fact that the difference in *p*-values (i.e., 0.02) is equal to the first scenario, in which the evidence is slightly greater against Model 1.

Table 7.5 Fictional *p*-value scenarios using the LRT to compare models.

Scenario	Null	Alternative	LRT–p	Traditional Conclusion
1	Model 1 Model 2	Model 3 Model 3	0.01 0.03	Model 3 is preferred over 1 and 2 but moreso over 1.
2	Model 1 Model 2	Model 3 Model 3	0.04 0.06	Model 3 is preferred over 1 but not 2.
3	Model 1 Model 2	Model 3 Model 3	0.10 0.50	Model 3 is not preferred over 1 or 2.

It has been noted that two effects with *p*-values close to but on either side of 0.05 usually do not have a difference that is statistically significant (Gelman & Stern, 2006). Yet, drawing the arbitrary 0.05 line in the sand somehow imbues the *p*-value just south of the line with a scientific status not afforded the *p*-value just north of the line. Behavioral scientists appear to recognize the arbitrariness and try to patch things up by labeling *p*-values slightly above

0.05 as "suggesting of" or "trending toward" statistical significance. However, the meaning of these verbal declarations is unclear, and they seem to be statements of belief rather than of evidence (Goodman & Royall, 1988).

Consider Scenario 3, in which LRT-p = 0.10 for 1 versus 3, and LRT-p = 0.50 for 2 versus 3. In a Fisherian evidential sense, the difference between Models 1 and 3 is much greater than between Models 2 and 3. However, taking the cutoff seriously, these p-values are treated equally. In the traditional interpretation, there is no variance in the category of "not statistically significant." Yet, if p-values are evidential, the pair of "not statistically significant" p-values in Scenario 3 represent the greatest difference between the models of all three examples. There is a difference of 0.40 as compared to a difference of 0.02 in the other two scenarios. How many instances of strong relative effects have been ignored in the behavioral sciences because of the arbitrary designation of "not statistically significant?"

These examples are not to be regarded as unrealistic or flippant. As evidence for this point, many readers have no doubt felt a palpable annoyance upon finding that p = 0.06 rather than, say, p = 0.04. This testifies to the fact that the arbitrary 0.05 line is a fixture in some disciplines. The status of a result is treated differently, at least in the minds of some, depending on which side of the line the p-value happens to land. This is unfortunate, as the cutoff is arbitrary, and arbitrariness seems to be an enemy of science.

As discussed in Section 7.3, the predictive accuracy underlying the AICc is based on the concept of distance from a true model. No candidate model is ever considered as true, only an approximation to the truth. This is in contrast to NHST, which is saddled with the assumption that at least one model is true (recall that a model is defined as a statistical hypothesis). For instance, in the comparison of Model 1 and Model 3, the null model is Model 1. LRT-p is the probability of obtaining the observed X^2 or one greater, *under the assumption that Model 1 is true*.

The requirement that a candidate model be true is troubling, as no model—statistical or otherwise—is true (G. Box, 1979; Cohen, 1994; DeLeeuw, 1988; Forster, 2000; Lindsey, 1999; Taper, 2004). In fact, the history of science is a history of false models, with models of planetary motion being just one example (Forster, 1999). Since all candidate models are false, the p-value never has its textbook definition as a probability under a true null hypothesis. It is unclear if this renders the p-value as a useless device. But there is concern as to whether a method that assumes truth can aid in selecting models of approximate truth (Weakliem, 2004).

The necessity of a null hypothesis also contributes to a related problem, the examination of uninteresting working hypotheses. Consider again the nested comparisons of the models in Table 7.2. What if both nested comparisons, 1 versus 3 and 2 versus 3, are not statistically significant? Is Model 3 implausible in this scenario? It can be argued that such a judgment is difficult to make, as Model 3 is not adequately evaluated. There is no direct investigation of the need for *both* the static predictors in the model because the null model in Table 7.2 always contains one static predictor. To address the shortcoming, NHST seems to beg the introduction of another model, one without any static predictors. Assume this model is labeled Model 0. The comparison of Model 0 and Model 3 allows a test for the need of the two static predictors, or more specifically, the need for *any* of the static predictor effects.

The introduction of Model 0 brings up serious scientific issues, as the model is ad hoc and does not represent any working hypothesis. Assuming even a pedestrian knowledge of educational achievement issues, would one ever assume absolutely no effect of either risk or ethnicity? The answer is an emphatic no, which is reflected by the omission of Model 0 from the set of models in Table 7.2. If Model 0 is a plausible model, it should be added to the set of models prior to the analysis.

If Model 0 is a priori implausible, there seems to be no scientific reason to compare Model 0 and Model 3. Remember that the *p*-value provides evidence against the null hypothesis. Prior to the data, there is already sufficient evidence against Model 0 to omit it from the set of working hypotheses. In this sense, Model 0 is a nothing or *nil hypothesis*, set up as a straw man to be almost surely burned down (Cohen, 1994). The rejection of a straw man hypothesis does not seem to work to the advancement of science.

The reader may protest that evidence against the null is really evidence for the alternative. This means there is evidence for Model 3, in Scenarios 1 and 2 of Table 7.2. Curiously, such interpretations are not consistent with the NHST of Fisher's framework. The *p*-value never provides information for a hypothesis, only against it.

At the heart of the issue is the fact that a *p*-value indexes the rarity of an event under a hypothesis. If the *p*-value is very small, then "either the hypothesis is not true, or an exceptionally rare outcome has occurred" (Fisher, 1960, p. 8). The trouble is an exceptionally rare outcome occurs when the *p*-value is very small, but also when the *p*-value is very large (Schervish, 1996). For example, LRT-$p = 0.01$ represents a rare event under a hypothesis, but so does LRT-$p = 0.99$. The former *p*-value cuts off the upper 1% (lower 99%) of the chi-squared distribution, but the latter cuts off the lower 1% (upper 99%). Thus, exceptionally small values of LRT-p and exceptionally large values both provide evidence against a hypothesis, in terms of rarity of an event (Christensen, 2003; Schervish, 1996).

In NHST, then, it is unclear what constitutes evidence *for* a hypothesis. It certainly cannot be stated that a "small" LRT-p is evidence in favor of an alternative hypothesis, as a "large" value indicates the same thing. It seems that all that can be said is that an *extreme* LRT-p is evidence against a null hypothesis. As Sprott (2000, p. 88) states plainly, "The logic of *p*-values is incapable of providing evidence in favor of H [a hypothesis]."

It seems self-evident that when data agree with a preplanned model predicted from theory, this constitutes evidence *for* the theory (Thompson, 2007, chap. 11). Researchers want to build the case for accepting models, not just rejecting them. As an early critic of NHST poetically phrased it (Berkson,

1942), when confronted with a dead body at a crime scene, one does not say, "Here is evidence against the hypothesis that no one is dead." What one does say is, "Evidently someone has been murdered."

The AICc effect size measures provide evidence *for* a model, in terms of its candidacy for the best approximating model. This allows a straightforward evaluation of the models in question, avoiding the potential convolutions when NHST is used to evaluate multiple models.

7.6 Example of Multimodel Analysis

To illustrate the multimodel approach using the AICc and associated measures, the evaluation of additional models to those in Table 7.2 is considered. The models are estimated with `lmer()` using the `MPLS.LS` data frame, and the `aictab()` function is used to compute the effect size measures.

Since some readers might be new to multimodel evaluation and the effect size measures, the discussion below is rather exhaustive. An applied researcher might choose to present less material in a professional publication or other write-up. A condensed example of a write-up for the results is offered in Section 7.7.

7.6.1 GUIDELINES FOR MODEL FORMULATION

Predata LMER models should be formulated to reflect a researcher's working hypothesis about the problem at hand. To reiterate one of John Tukey's points above (Tukey, 1995), all the predata models should be *relevant*. This means the typical null models used in NHST are not included unless they represent plausible working hypotheses. The working hypotheses might represent theories regarding the underlying mechanism of the phenomenon of study. On the other hand, they might be more speculative in nature and only identify variables that have been found to be, or believed to be, important in prediction.

In translating working hypotheses to LMER models, there are some guidelines to consider to help ensure interpretable results. These guidelines are general and also apply to the case of NHST considered later. It is suggested that LMER models be constructed with the following three constraints.

1. For all the predictors in the LMER model (time and static predictors), all higher order terms should have the associated lower order terms included.

2. No higher numbered random effect should appear without also including all lower numbered random effects.

3. No random effect should appear in the model without its associated fixed effect, but not necessarily the converse.

7.6 Example of Multimodel Analysis

The first two constraints are to help ensure that the LMER parameters are interpretable under linear transformations, especially transformations of the original time predictor. The third constraint is to ensure that a random effect is properly scaled with a mean of 0.

The first constraint in the list is relevant when either polynomial transformations of the time variable are used, or interactions among two or more static predictors are included. As an example of the first, if grade_{ij}^2 is used as a predictor, then grade_{ij} should also be included in the model (a somewhat different view is presented in Chapter 12). As an example of the second, if ($\text{risk2DAVD}_i \cdot \text{att}_i$) is used as a predictor, then risk2DAVD_i should be included as a single predictor, and att_i should also be included as a single predictor. To summarize: *If an interaction term is a predictor in the LMER model, then the main effects should also be included.* These topics will be revisited in future chapters, especially Chapter 11.

7.6.2 EXAMPLE SET OF MODELS

To illustrate the multimodel approach, we revisit and extend the research questions involving the MPLS data set discussed in Chapter 1. An additional static predictor, ethnicity, is considered along with the risk predictor previously introduced. Risk and ethnicity are selected because of their relevance to the study of reading achievement gaps. It is emphasized that the model formulation and evaluation are for illustrative purposes. To seriously address issues regarding achievement gaps, a much larger sample size is required, along with additional relevant variables.

Several longitudinal studies have reported initial and ongoing differences in reading achievement among ethnic groups, as well as socioeconomic groups (e.g., Chatterji, 2006; Xue & Miesels, 2004). Advantaged students tend to have higher achievement scores than disadvantaged students, and majority students tend to have higher scores than minority students. A complication is that socioeconomic status and ethnic status are correlated, with ethnic minority students having a higher rate of poverty than majority students (Obradović et al., 2009; Zill & West, 2001).

A research question important to achievement gaps is *to what extent risk status acts as a proxy for ethnic effects, or vice versa* (Lee, 2002). Recall that for the risk2 variable, the DADV students are classified as such if they meet eligibility for free or reduced-price meals based on federal standards. The ADV students have high enough family incomes to disqualify them from disadvantaged status.

One way to address the proxy question is to consider LMER models that represent different plausible proxy scenarios. A model including both ethnicity and risk group as static predictors indicates that both have a nonnegligible effect when considered as a set. A model with only ethnicity represents the scenario in which there is no appreciable effect of risk group when ethnicity is considered, and the former variable can be omitted. A model with only risk group represents the case when there is no appreciable effect of ethnicity when risk is considered.

In addition to the proxy question involving the static predictors, an important issue is *the duration of the achievement gap*. Based on at least one body of achievement literature (Lee, 2002), there is conflicting evidence regarding the persistence of achievement gaps. Depending on the epoch considered (e.g., the 1990s), early differences tend to endure over time or, alternatively, show a tendency for initial gaps to either narrow or widen (Applebee & Langer, 2006; Campbell, Hombo, & Mazzeo, 2000; Caro et al., 2009; Dearing et al., 2006; Hedges & Nowell, 1999). The enduring-gap scenario represents intercept-only differences, whereas the changing-gap scenario represents intercept and slope differences (assuming linear change; see below).

Consistent with the discussion in the last section, the change curve and random effects for the analysis are considered to be preselected. A linear change curve is adopted at both the subject and group levels, and a random intercept term and a random slope term are included in every model. Change curves of achievement tend to be nonlinear when the observed period of time is relatively extensive, say from Grade 1 to Grade 12 (Shin et al., 2009). However, the observed time period is relatively short for the data set (Grades 5–8), so a linear model should be adequate. Furthermore, the exploratory methods presented in Chapters 9 and 12 also suggest the reasonableness of a linear change curve.

Given a linear change curve, two random effects are automatically included: random intercepts and random slopes. The exploratory methods presented in Chapter 10 suggest that two random effects are reasonable.

Considering all possible combinations of static predictors (risk, ethnicity, both) and gap (constant, changing), six models are proposed for evaluation. The models are shown in Table 7.6.

Recall that the static predictor, risk2DADV, is a dummy variable with ADV = 0 and DADV = 1. The static predictor, eth2W, is a dummy variable created in Chapter 4 with NW = 0 (non-White) and W = 1 (White).

The models in Table 7.6 are consistent with the constraints mentioned in Section 7.6.1. The models differ only in the number of fixed effects (static predictors effects). All the models have the same response variable, y_{ij}; the same change curve (linear); and two random effects, b_{0i} and b_{1i}.

There are pairs of models in Table 7.6 that are nested and pairs that are not nested. Recall that a simpler model is nested within a more complex model when parameters of the latter can be set to 0 to obtain the former. In Table 7.6, Model 2 is nested within Model 3 because $\beta_3 = 0$ can be set in Model 3 to obtain Model 2. This is equivalent to omitting ethnicity. On the other hand, Model 1 and Model 2 are not nested, as there is no parameter in one model that can be set to 0 to yield the other model.

The analysis begins by estimating each model in Table 7.6. The lmer() syntax shown below is written in its most compact form, so the 1 used to represent an intercept term is omitted, and an asterisk (*) is used for an

7.6 Example of Multimodel Analysis

Table 7.6 Set of hypothesized models.

Model	Static Predictors	Gap	Fixed Effects Structure
1	Risk	Constant	$\beta_0 + \beta_1(\texttt{grade5}_{ij})$ $+\beta_2(\texttt{risk2DADV}_i)$
2	Ethnicity	Constant	$\beta_0 + \beta_1(\texttt{grade5}_{ij})$ $+\beta_2(\texttt{eth2W}_i)$
3	Risk, ethnicity	Constant	$\beta_0 + \beta_1(\texttt{grade5}_{ij})$ $+\beta_2(\texttt{risk2DADV}_i)$ $+\beta_3(\texttt{eth2W}_i)$
4	Risk	Changing	$\beta_0 + \beta_1(\texttt{grade5}_{ij})$ $+\beta_2(\texttt{risk2DADV}_i)$ $+\beta_3(\texttt{grade5}_{ij} \cdot \texttt{risk2DADV}_i)$
5	Ethnicity	Changing	$\beta_0 + \beta_1(\texttt{grade5}_{ij})+$ $+\beta_2(\texttt{eth2W}_i)$ $+\beta_3(\texttt{grade5}_{ij} \cdot \texttt{eth2W}_i)$
6	Risk, ethnicity	Changing	$\beta_0 + \beta_1(\texttt{grade5}_{ij})$ $+\beta_2(\texttt{riskDADV}_i)$ $+\beta_3(\texttt{eth2W}_i)$ $+\beta_4(\texttt{grade5}_{ij} \cdot \texttt{risk2DADV}_i)$ $+\beta_5(\texttt{grade5}_{ij} \cdot \texttt{eth2W}_i)$

Note. For all models, $\varepsilon_{ij}^* = b_{0i} + b_{1i}(\texttt{grade5}_{ij}) + \varepsilon_{ij}$.

interaction, rather than a colon (:). ML rather than REML, is requested using REML=FALSE. Recall that the dummy variables in Table 7.6 are not listed in the `lmer()` syntax; rather, the original variable labels are used, `risk2` and `eth2`.

```
> model.1 <- lmer(read ~ grade5 + risk2 + (grade5 | subid), MPLS.LS, REML = FALSE)
> model.2 <- lmer(read ~ grade5 + eth2 + (grade5 | subid), MPLS.LS, REML = FALSE)
> model.3 <- lmer(read ~ grade5 + risk2 + eth2 + (grade5 | subid), MPLS.LS, REML= FALSE)
> model.4 <- lmer(read ~ grade5 * risk2 + (grade5 | subid), MPLS.LS, REML = FALSE)
> model.5 <- lmer(read ~ grade5 * eth2 + (grade5 | subid), MPLS.LS, REML = FALSE)
> model.6 <- lmer(read ~ grade5 * risk2 + grade5 * eth2 + (grade5 | subid),
+             MPLS.LS, REML = FALSE)
```

After submitting the above syntax, no statistical output is displayed in the R console window. The reason is that the output for each analysis is saved as a fitted model object.

Having saved the output objects, the AICc and related quantities are computed with `aictab()`. Recall that `aictab()` requires a list of the model objects enclosed by `list()` and a character vector of the model names. Sorting of the results is suppressed by using `sort=FALSE`, which also automatically suppresses the computation of the cumulative weight of evidence. Results are saved and then printed as a data frame to facilitate additional manipulation.

```
> mynames    <- paste("M", as.character(1:6), sep = "")
> mymodels   <- list(model.1, model.2, model.3, model.4, model.5, model.6)
> myaicc     <- as.data.frame(aictab(cand.set = mymodels, modnames = mynames,
+                              sort = FALSE)[,-c(5,7)])
> myaicc$Eratio <- max(myaicc$AICcWt) / myaicc$AICcWt
> data.frame(Modnames = myaicc$Modnames, round(myaicc[,-1], 2))
```

```
  Modnames  K    AICc Delta_AICc AICcWt   Eratio
1       M1  7  565.44       0.00   0.61     1.00
2       M2  7  580.76      15.32   0.00  2124.21
3       M3  8  567.91       2.47   0.18     3.44
4       M4  8  567.73       2.29   0.19     3.14
5       M5  8  582.09      16.65   0.00  4133.44
6       M6 10  572.01       6.57   0.02    26.71
```

The first labeled column of the output contains the model number. The second column lists the number of estimated parameters, followed by the AICc, Δ_h, W_h, and E_h.

The output shows that Model 1 is the best-fitting model of the set, as it has $\Delta_1 = 0$ and $W_1 = 0.61$. Model 4 is the next best fitting, with $\Delta_4 = 2.29$ and $W_4 = 0.19$. Model 3 is the next best fitting, with $\Delta_3 = 2.47$ and $W_3 = 0.18$, and so on. Further interpretation is provided below.

7.6.3 BAR GRAPHS OF RESULTS

To aid in the interpretation of the results, bar graphs of the weights of evidence and evidence ratios are constructed. This is accomplished using ggplot2 with the geom_bar() component.

```
> ## Define components for later use.
> myx    <- scale_x_continuous(breaks = 5:8)
> theme_set(theme_bw())
> ## Create bar graphs.
> g1 <- ggplot(myaicc, aes(x = Modnames, y = AICcWt)) + ylab("Weight")
> g2 <- g1 + geom_bar(fill = "grey80", colour = "black") + xlab("Model")
> g3 <- g2 + scale_y_continuous(limits = c(0,1))
> print(g3)
```

The optional argument, scale_y_continuous(limits=c(0,1)), sets the range of the y-axis. It is recommended that the entire probability range of 0 to 1 be displayed, so as to facilitate interpretation of the size of the weights. The resulting bar graph is shown in the upper left corner of Figure 7.4.

To get a sense of the relative size of the weights, a bar graph of the evidence ratios is constructed. In addition to using geom_bar(), a reference line is drawn for $E = 1$ with the geom_hline() component.

7.6 Example of Multimodel Analysis

```
> g1 <- ggplot(myaicc, aes(x = Modnames, y = Eratio)) + ylab("Ratio")
> g2 <- g1 + geom_bar(fill = "grey80", colour = "black") + xlab("Model")
> g3 <- g2 + geom_hline(aes(yintercept = 1), linetype = 2)
> print(g3)
```

The resulting graph is shown in the upper right corner of Figure 7.4. The values tend to fall at two extremes, making the resolving power of the graph low for smaller values.

Another approach to the construction of the bar graphs is to sort by the weight of evidence, which also sorts the evidence ratio. In the syntax below, the `myaicc` data frame is sorted by AICc in ascending order. This results in the weight of evidence being sorted in descending order, and the evidence ratio being sorted in ascending order. Bar graphs are constructed for each sorted variable. By default, `ggplot()` sorts based on the *x* variable. To suppress the sorting, `I(as.character())` is used.

```
> ## Sort data frame.
> myaicc2 <- myaicc[order(myaicc$AICc), ]
> ## Bar graph of weight of evidence.
> r1 <- ggplot(myaicc2,aes(x = I(as.character(Modnames)),y = AICcWt)) + ylab("Weight")
> r2 <- r1 + geom_bar(fill = "grey80", colour = "black") + xlab("Model")
> r3 <- r2 + scale_y_continuous(limits = c(0,1))
> print(r3)
> ## Bar graph of evidence ratio.
> s1 <- ggplot(myaicc2,aes(x = I(as.character(Modnames)),y = Eratio)) + ylab("Weight")
> s2 <- s1 + geom_bar(fill = "grey80", colour = "black") + xlab("Model")
> s3 <- s2 + geom_hline(aes(yintercept = 1), linetype = 2)
> print(s3)
```

The graphs are shown in the bottom row of Figure 7.4. The weight of evidence graph is in the lower left corner, and the evidence ratio graph is in the lower right corner. The horizontal axis of the graphs lists the model number in the order of model fit.

The resolving power of the graph in the bottom right is low because of the great difference in evidence ratios. One might want to construct an alternative graph, omitting the two values that are extremely large (M2 and M5).

7.6.4 INTERPRETATION OF GLOBAL RESULTS

The discussion of the results begins with the weight of evidence and the evidence ratio. As seen in the left-hand graphs of Figure 7.4, Model 1 has the largest weight of evidence, indicating it is the prime candidate for the best approximating model. Moreover, $W_1 = 0.61$, showing that Model 1 accounts for the majority of probability.

However, the lower left-hand graph of Figure 7.4 implies that Model 1 may not be the only viable candidate for the best approximating model. Two other models have relatively high weights of evidence, Model 4, followed by Model 3.

It is helpful to compute the cumulative weight of evidence when the models are sorted on fit, from best to worst. This is done automatically by `aictab()`, omitting `sort=` or setting it to `TRUE`. As mentioned, the `confset()` function can also be used to form confidence sets.

```
> myaicc <- as.data.frame(aictab(cand.set = mymodels, modnames = mynames)[ ,-c(5,7)])
> myaicc$Eratio <- max(myaicc$AICcWt) / myaicc$AICcWt
> data.frame(Modnames = myaicc$Modnames, round(myaicc[ ,-1], 2))
```

	Modnames	K	AICc	Delta_AICc	AICcWt	Cum.Wt	Eratio
1	M1	7	565.44	0.00	0.61	0.61	1.00
4	M4	8	567.73	2.29	0.19	0.80	3.14
3	M3	8	567.91	2.47	0.18	0.98	3.44
6	M6	10	572.01	6.57	0.02	1.00	26.71
2	M2	7	580.76	15.32	0.00	1.00	2124.21
5	M5	8	582.09	16.65	0.00	1.00	4133.44

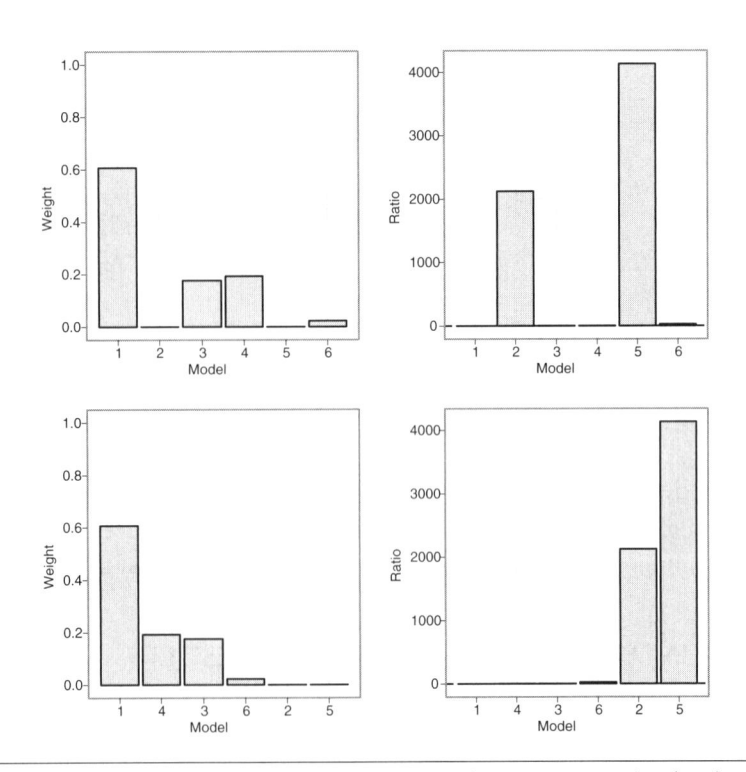

Figure 7.4 Weight of evidence (left) and evidence ratio (right) for the estimated models. Graphs in the bottom row have models sorted by weight (left) and ratio (right).

As the output shows, Models 1, 3, and 4 account for 0.98 of the total probability. This is an indication of the high plausibility of this set of models. It is highly plausible given the data, all the models, and the unknowable true model, that the best approximating model is among 1, 3, or 4. Common to these models is the risk intercept effect. In terms of the research question,

7.6 Example of Multimodel Analysis

there is strong evidence of real risk group differences, at least intercept differences. More is said about this point in a moment.

Things can also be worded negatively. It is highly implausible that the best approximating model is among 2, 5, or 6, as collectively, these models account for only $1 - 0.98 = 0.02$ of the total probability. Common to all of these models is the ethnicity slope effect, which casts doubt on the importance of this effect. Model 6 is certainly more plausible than Model 2 and Model 5, but the evidence ratio of Model 6 is approximately 27. This is considered to be a high enough value to also judge Model 6 as relatively implausible.

The two models that include only ethnicity, Models 2 and 5, have extremely high evidence ratios. As shown in the graph in the lower right corner of Figure 7.4, the odds that Model 5 is not the best approximating model is more than 4000 to 1, and the odds against Model 2 is more than 2000 to 1. In terms of the research question, there is strong statistical evidence that ethnicity is not a proxy for risk.

The above results are accentuated by computing a 99% confidence set. This is a very high level of confidence, and any models outside the set would certainly be considered implausible.

```
> confset(cand.set = mymodels, modnames = mynames, level = 0.99)
```

```
Confidence set for the best model

Method:   raw sum of model probabilities

99% confidence set:
    K    AICc  Delta_AICc  AICcWt
M1  7  565.44       0.00    0.61
M4  8  567.73       2.29    0.19
M3  8  567.91       2.47    0.18
M6 10  572.01       6.57    0.02

Model probabilities sum to 1
```

The output verifies the previous results. Model 2 and Model 5 are not in the 99% confidence set, and they are considered implausible.

Returning to the plausible set of models, Models 3 and 4 have evidence ratios that are not particularly large. Model 4 has an evidence ratio close to 3 ($E_4 = 3.14$). This means the odds that Model 1 is the best approximating model is about 3 to 1 over Model 4. Model 3 is just slightly behind Model 4. There is a tendency in this case to consider Model 1 as the most plausible, but not to immediately rule out Model 3 or Model 4.

The interpretations above are admittedly subjective, as the only point of reference for evaluating the odds of the models is the value of 1. The extreme cases are probably not controversial to most readers. Reasonable researchers will probably be convinced that an odds of 4000 to 1 against are much too large to seriously entertain the plausibility of a model. It is the less extreme cases, say of Model 3 and Model 4, that are more difficult to interpret.

One approach to providing a point of reference is a parametric bootstrap procedure. The parametric bootstrap is a simulation procedure that treats the best-fitting Model 1 as the true model and then generates random samples from this true model. The bootstrap evidence ratio for the known best approximating model (Model 1) is computed for each replication. The resulting bootstrap distribution of evidence ratios is used to evaluate the evidence ratios computed on the original sample. Details are presented in the optional Section 7.8.

Another approach to evaluating evidence ratios is to appeal to scientific principles that have historically been important to applied researchers. The primary one is the *principle of parsimony*, which roughly means to pursue the simplest adequate hypothesis (Sober, 2006). From a parsimony perspective, Model 1 is certainly attractive. Not only is it the most plausible model, but it is the simplest of all the models that one might be willing to judge as plausible (see Table 7.6).

Another consideration is consistency of effects among the most plausible models. In the example, the risk group intercept effect is in the three most plausible models, providing evidence for its importance. One probably cannot completely rule out the possibility of an additional ethnicity intercept effect (Model 3) or a risk slope effect (Model 4), but there is evidence that the risk intercept effect is an important consideration.

In summary, Model 1 is favorable. Model 1 includes the risk intercept effect that is common to all the plausible models, but it pares additional effects that appear to be questionable. In reporting results, it is common to provide detailed information regarding the best approximating model, which is done below. Although details of only one model are presented, the point of multimodel analysis is that fit information about the other models in the set is provided. This allows plausibility comments to be made about all the models (sometimes in batches).

Presenting at least limited information about the set of models seems scientifically advantageous. No single observational study is expected to hit the bull's-eye and discover the true model because the true model is never known. The best a researcher can hope for is that results of individual studies cluster about the bull's-eye, some closer to the center than others. When information about multiple models is presented, it is easier to see common themes among different study results. This approach may widen the definition of what constitutes "successful replication" or "consistent findings," but such a widening seems desirable, especially for nonexperimental research.

7.6.5 DETAILS OF MODELS

The last section focused on global model features, with judgments focusing on the relative plausibility of the models. Details of the models, such

7.6 Example of Multimodel Analysis

as parameter estimates and *t*-ratios, are also important to consider when interpreting the results. Usually such details are reported for the best approximating model, but specifics for additional models can also be useful.

At this point, an interpretation is offered for what the multimodel analysis has to say regarding the overarching research question. Models including ethnicity, but not risk, appear to be relatively implausible, suggesting that ethnicity may not be a proxy for risk. On the other hand, the most plausible models have a risk intercept effect, suggesting an initial reading difference in the risk groups that endures over the observed grade span. The possibility of an ethnicity intercept effect, along with a risk intercept effect, cannot be definitively ruled out. Finally, the possibility of a change in the reading gap for the risk groups also cannot be definitively ruled out.

Several lingering questions about the analysis have not been addressed thus far. Consider the following list.

1. Based on the best approximating model (Model 1), what is the estimated direction and size of the risk group intercept difference?

2. Based on the best approximating model, what is the estimated rate of change for the risk groups?

3. For the model with risk and ethnicity intercept effects (Model 3), what is the estimated relative size of these effects?

4. For the model with the risk group slope effect (Model 4), what is the estimated direction and size of this effect?

These types of questions are addressed by considering additional details of the fitted model objects. What is required is an inspection of the fixed effects parameter estimates, their estimated SEs, the *t*-ratios, and the CIs.

To address the first two questions, consider a printing of the fixed effects coefficients table of `model.1`. This table resides in the `@coefs` slot of the `summary()` output object.

```
> mytab ← as.data.frame(summary(model.1)@coefs)
> mytab
```

	Estimate	Std. Error	t value
(Intercept)	216.677017	3.9911887	54.288843
grade5	4.779081	0.7332994	6.517231
risk2DADV	-26.582297	4.8271322	-5.506851

Suppose the lower CI bound (LCI) and the upper CI bound (UCI) for the fixed effects are added to the table. The table is printed, omitting the *t*-values column.

```
> mytab$LCI  <- mytab$Estimate - 2 * mytab$"Std. Error"
> mytab$UCI  <- mytab$Estimate + 2 * mytab$"Std. Error"
> round(mytab[ ,-3], 2)
```

	Estimate	Std. Error	LCI	UCI
(Intercept)	216.68	3.99	208.69	224.66
grade5	4.78	0.73	3.31	6.25
risk2DADV	-26.58	4.83	-36.24	-16.93

The output can be used to address the questions regarding the magnitude of the group differences. To do so, it is advantageous to consider the expected value equation,

$$E(y_{ij}) = \beta_0 + \beta_1(\text{grade5}_{ij}) + \beta_2(\text{risk2DADV}).$$

Substituting the numeric values for risk2DADV (i.e., 0 and 1) yields the following:

$$E(y_{ij}) = \begin{cases} \beta_0 + \beta_1(\text{grade5}_{ij}) & \text{if ADV,} \\ (\beta_0 + \beta_2) + \beta_1(\text{grade5}_{ij}) & \text{if DADV.} \end{cases}$$

The output indicates that $\hat{\beta}_2 = -26.58$. This means the sample disadvantaged group intercept is less than the advantaged group by the stated amount. The point estimate should be tempered by the CI, which gives some indication of the statistical reliability of the difference.

As for the estimated change in reading achievement, the model proposes there is a yearly increase of β_1 for both groups. The estimate of this increase is $\hat{\beta}_1 = 4.78$, which again should be tempered by the CI.

To get an overall sense of the effects, the observed means and the fitted curves for the risk groups are graphed. The fitted values are based on the estimated fixed effects, as this is the focus of the analysis. The fitted values are computed by post-multiplying the design matrix or model matrix by the fixed effects vector. The model matrix is a data frame based on the original data set. It omits missing values and uses the risk dummy variable rather than the original factor variable. The details of computing fitted values based on the fixed effects estimates are presented in Chapter 11. Here it is simply said that matrix multiplication is needed, which is performed using %*%. The model matrix is extracted using model.matrix() (see the optional section of Chapter 5 and the Appendix). In the syntax below, a data frame for plotting is constructed, and then ggplot2 is used to construct the graph.

```
> ## Create data frame for graphing.
> plotdata  <- model.1@frame
> plotdata$pred  <- model.matrix(model.1) %*% fixef(model.1)
> plotdata$grade  <- plotdata$grade + 5
> ## ggplot2.
> g1  <- ggplot(plotdata, aes(x = grade, y = read, linetype = risk2))
> g2  <- g1 + stat_summary(fun.y = "mean", geom = "point", cex = 2)
> g3  <- g2 + stat_summary(aes(y = pred), fun.y = "mean", geom = "line")
> g4  <- g3 + myx + opts(legend.position = c(0.54, 0.3), legend.title = theme_blank())
> print(g4)
```

7.6 Example of Multimodel Analysis

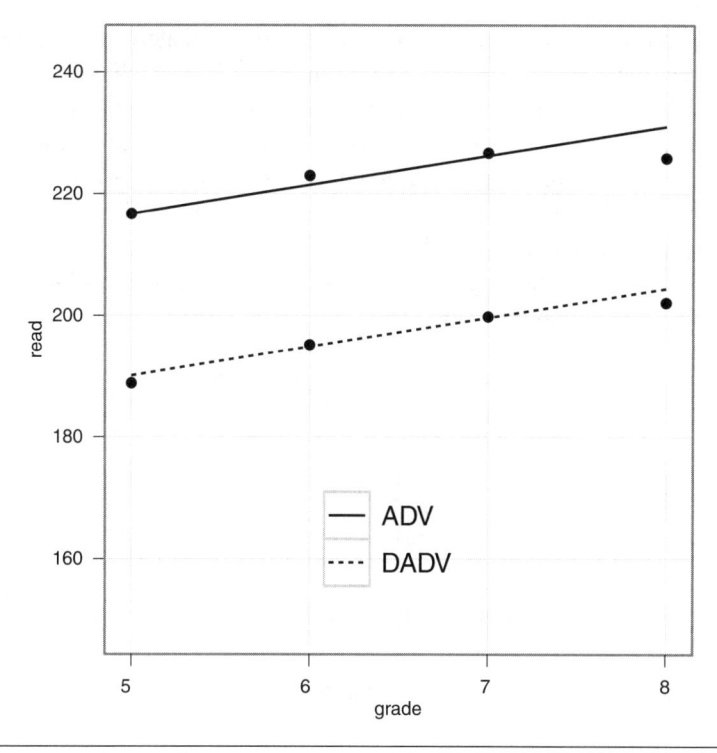

Figure 7.5 Observed means (points) and fitted curves (lines) for risk groups.

The graph is shown in Figure 7.5. The intercept difference is evident, and the change curves are parallel. This shows the persistence of the reading gap, which is characteristic of Model 1.

Now consider the question regarding the relative effects of Model 3. The coefficients table of model.3 is printed, and the output is interpreted.

```
> summary(model.3)@coefs
```

	Estimate	Std. Error	t value
(Intercept)	216.922336	5.6542928	38.36418552
grade5	4.779125	0.7331515	6.51860475
risk2DADV	-26.762825	5.6963106	-4.69827353
eth2W	-0.359036	5.7637445	-0.06229214

The output label, eth2W, is a reminder that the dummy coding is NW = 0, W = 1. The estimated fixed effect for ethnicity is $\hat{\beta}_3 = -0.36$, indicating the White group has a slightly smaller intercept than the non-White group, controlling for risk. The risk variable and the ethnicity variable are on the same scale, as they are both dichotomous dummy variables. Therefore, a direct comparison of the intercept effects is possible based on the estimated fixed effects. As the output shows, the partialled ethnicity difference is very small, as compared to that of risk. A difference of approximately 27 is substantial for the reading measure, whereas a difference of 0.36 is negligible.

The difference is also reflected in the *t*-values of the two fixed effects estimates. The *t*-value for the risk difference is relatively large in absolute value, $t = -4.7$, whereas the value for ethnicity is close to 0, $t = -0.06$. Although the global model analysis indicates that Model 3 has some plausibility, the ethnicity effect is relatively small.

For the final question regarding the risk slope effect in Model 4, the fixed effects table is printed for model.4.

```
> mytab2 <- as.data.frame(summary(model.4)@coefs)
> mytab2$LCI <- mytab2$Estimate - 2 * mytab2$"Std. Error"
> mytab2$UCI <- mytab2$Estimate + 2 * mytab2$"Std. Error"
> mytab2
```

	Estimate	Std. Error	t value	LCI	UCI
(Intercept)	217.5139399	4.447690	48.9049258	208.618560	226.409320
grade5	4.4290901	1.085066	4.0818608	2.258957	6.599223
risk2DADV	-28.1116330	6.021277	-4.6687161	-40.154187	-16.069079
grade5:risk2DADV	0.6341161	1.460646	0.4341339	-2.287176	3.555409

The relevant expected value formulas are the following:

$$E(y_{ij}) = \begin{cases} \beta_0 + \beta_1(\text{grade5}_{ij}) & \text{if ADV,} \\ (\beta_0 + \beta_2) + (\beta_1 + \beta_3)(\text{grade5}_{ij}) & \text{if DADV.} \end{cases}$$

Since the sign of the estimate of β_3 is positive, the disadvantaged group increases at a faster rate than the advantaged group over the observed grade period. However, there is a greater intercept effect than in Model 1 (see above). In addition, the *t*-value of the slope effect is relatively close to 0 ($t = 0.43$), indicating the estimated effect is not large. The CI contains negative and positive values, so the reading gap may increase or decrease over time. Such ambiguity perhaps lessens the enthusiasm for considering Model 4 as a plausible model.

Summary. To summarize the last two sections, the following pieces of evidence are important in the evaluation of multiple models.

1. Weight of evidence
2. Evidence ratio
3. Estimates of fixed effects
4. Estimated SEs of fixed effects (precision estimates)
5. *t*-ratios associated with fixed effects
6. CIs of fixed effects

One usually begins with the first two, as they are global indexes. Then the other pieces of information are discussed as the occasion arises. An example write-up of the results is offered in Section 7.7.

7.6.6 COMMENTS REGARDING THE MULTIMODEL APPROACH

The multimodel approach has much to its credit. There is no statistical testing, so there is no concern for types of errors that give rise to the use of cutoff values and multiple testing problems. Models are formulated beforehand, so the examination of evidence constitutes confirmatory analysis. The ability to rank-order and assess relative effect sizes goes a long way in making judgments about the set of models. Much can be gained by simply examining the graphs in Figure 7.4.

There are some caveats, however, that a researcher should keep in mind when interpreting the multimodel results. First, the weight of evidence and the evidence ratio are *relative*, meaning they apply only to the set of models considered. There might be other good candidates for the best approximating model apart from the six considered in the example above. If any of the excluded models are included in the set, all the weights of evidence and evidence ratio values will change. The change might be slight or substantial, depending on the (dis)similarity to the models in the set. This is one reason why it is important to think carefully about the construction of the predata hypotheses and their representative models.

Second, the researcher is required to make judgments regarding what models are plausible and implausible. These judgments do not seem out of the ordinary for the interpretation of statistical results, but there can be disagreement over this point. Some might feel that an evidence ratio of 3 or greater constitutes substantial evidence of the implausibility of a model. This seems reasonable for the present example, as the evidence ratio is accompanied by parameter estimates that have relatively weak (small) effect sizes. Others might want a more objective criterion for judging the worth of a model. Those seeking a more objective reference point for evaluating evidence ratios may want to consider the parametric bootstrap, as described in the optional Section 7.8. The drawback of the parametric bootstrap is the additional programming and time required.

Finally, the weight of evidence and the evidence ratio do not indicate if a model—including the best fitting—is "good" in any absolute sense. To help assess the goodness of the models, the researcher should compute an absolute fit index rather than a relative fit index, at least for the best-fitting model. One such index is R^2 for LMER, which is similar to the statistic computed in traditional regression analysis. Details are discussed in Chapter 11.

7.6.7 POST HOC MODELS

In applied analysis, it is not always possible to write down every relevant hypothesis and every relevant model beforehand. Sometimes additional research questions arise during or after the analysis. These questions might provoke the formulation of additional models that the researcher would like to examine.

There are at least two ways to treat models that are not formulated before the analysis. One approach is to treat such models as if they occurred prior to the analysis and include them in the predata set. Another approach is to treat them as post hoc models. In either case, the additional models can be added to the set, and the AICc and other measures recomputed. In the post hoc treatment, a table of initial results is presented, excluding the post hoc models. Then a second table of results is presented, with the post hoc models along with the initial models.

If the additional models are treated as predata models, then the interpretations follow along the lines outlined above. If the models are treated as post hoc, then the recalculated weights of evidence and evidence ratios should be interpreted in this light. One should have additional suspicion about post hoc models, especially if an initial result was used to suggest the formulation of one or more of these models.

As an example of a post hoc model, suppose that after producing the results of the six models, it is decided that it is important to include a model with gender. Suppose this idea motivates two additional models, one with intercept effects for risk, ethnicity, and gender (Model 7), and a second with intercept and slope effects for the same three predictors (Model 8). It should be reinforced that the data set is much too small to support serious inference based on such models. Thus, this exercise is for illustration purposes.

In the syntax below, the additional models, Model 7 and Model 8, are estimated. `aictab()` is used to compute the AICc and related measures for all eight models.

```
> model.7 <- lmer(read ~ grade5 + risk2 + eth2 + gen + (grade5 | subid),
+                MPLS.LS, REML = FALSE)
> model.8 <- lmer(read ~ grade5 * risk2 + grade5 * eth2 + grade5 * gen + (grade5 | subid),
+                MPLS.LS, REML = FALSE)
> mymodels <- list(model.1, model.2, model.3, model.4, model.5, model.6, model.7, model.8)
> mynames <- paste("M", as.character(1:8), sep="")
> myaicc <- as.data.frame(aictab(mymodels, mynames))[ ,-c(5,7)]
> myaicc$Eratio <- max(myaicc$AICcWt) / myaicc$AICcWt
> data.frame(Modnames = myaicc$Modnames, round(myaicc[ ,-1], 2))
```

	Modnames	K	AICc	Delta_AICc	AICcWt	Cum.Wt	Eratio
1	M1	7	565.44	0.00	0.57	0.57	1.00
4	M4	8	567.73	2.29	0.18	0.76	3.14
3	M3	8	567.91	2.47	0.17	0.92	3.44
7	M7	9	570.21	4.77	0.05	0.98	10.88
6	M6	10	572.01	6.57	0.02	1.00	26.71
8	M8	12	577.24	11.80	0.00	1.00	365.59
2	M2	7	580.76	15.32	0.00	1.00	2124.21
5	M5	8	582.09	16.65	0.00	1.00	4133.44

Model 7 and Model 8 are post hoc models, and their weights of evidence and evidence ratios should be taken less seriously than those of the predata models. "Less seriously" means that the values of the post hoc models might be somehow informally downgraded. An alternative is to present the results on the initial six models separately from the results on the eight models.

The output shows that adding the additional models changes the values of all the measures. Model 1 is still the best fitting, but its weight of evidence is a bit lower compared to omitting the additional models. The reason is that the total probability must now be spread out over the additional models.

Model 8 is relatively easy to judge, as its weight of evidence is very low, and its evidence ratio is very high. It appears that gender does not have important intercept or slope effects when risk and ethnicity are in the model.

The judgment of Model 7 is more difficult, as it is the fourth best-fitting model. It is now necessary to include the model to form a 95% confidence set, or a 98% confidence set as the case may be. On the other hand, the weight of evidence for the model is relatively low, $W_7 = 0.05$, and its evidence ratio is appreciably higher than the next best-fitting model, $E_7 = 10.88$. Since Model 7 is a post hoc model and its evidence ratio is relatively large, it appears to be a relatively implausible candidate for the best approximating model. The introduction of the two post hoc models does not change the interpretation of the overall result in this example.

7.7 Example Write-up

To encourage the use of multimodel inference using the AICc measures, an example write-up of the results of the six-model analysis is presented. For researchers familiar with the publication manual of the American Psychological Association (2010), this is an example of what would be written for the results section of a journal article. It is assumed the working hypotheses and statistical models have been introduced and discussed prior to the material below.

Results

Fit information for the six hypothesized models is shown in Table 7.7. The models are sorted in terms of goodness of fit, with the best-fitting model in the first row. As the table shows, Model 1 had the best fit and Model 5 had the worst fit. The weight of evidence for Model 1 was $W_1 = 0.61$, indicating that it accounted for the majority of probability. The sum of the probability for the first three models was 0.98, indicating very high plausibility for the set of Models 1, 3, and 4.

On the other hand, Models 2, 5, and 6 had a combined probability of only 0.02. Each model in this second set had an ethnicity slope effect, which casts doubt on the need for such an effect. Furthermore, the models that included only ethnicity (2 and 5) had especially low weights of evidence and very high evidence ratios (see Table 7.7).

Table 7.7 Fit information for hypothesized models.

Model	AICc	K	Δ	W	E
1	565.44	7	0.00	0.61	1.00
4	567.73	8	2.29	0.19	3.14
3	567.91	8	2.47	0.18	3.44
6	572.01	10	6.57	0.02	26.71
2	580.76	7	15.32	0.00	2124.21
5	582.09	8	16.65	0.00	4133.44

Given the results in Table 7.7, focus is on the most plausible set of Models 1, 3, and 4. Emphasis is on Model 1, as it had a probability that was more than three times greater than the next best-fitting Model 4. The common effects among the best three models were a linear change curve and a risk group intercept effect. For all models, the parameter estimates (not reported) indicated a linear increase in reading over time, with the disadvantaged group having a lower intercept than the advantaged group. Model 4 included a risk group slope effect, with the disadvantaged group having a slightly higher rate of increase over time. However, the t-value for this effect was close to 0, $t = 0.43$, and the confidence interval contained 0, $(-2.29, 3.56)$. Model 3 included an ethnicity intercept effect, and the parameter estimates indicted this was a weak effect, $t = -0.06$.

Models 3 and 4 had evidence ratios greater than 3, and as mentioned, the additional effects not included in Model 1 were relatively weak. Furthermore, Model 1 was the most parsimonious of the top three models. Given these findings, additional details of Model 1 are presented.

Table 7.8 shows the parameter estimates for Model 1. Because of the dummy coding (0 = advantaged, 1 = disadvantaged), $\hat{\beta}_0 = 216.68$ is the sample intercept value for the advantaged group. The estimate of β_2 indicates the disadvantaged group had a sample intercept value of $216.68 - 26.58 = 190.09$. For both groups, the estimated slope indicated an increase of $\hat{\beta}_1 = 4.78$ per grade. The lower portion of the table shows the estimated variance components. The estimated correlation, -0.64, indicated that individuals with smaller intercepts tended to have larger slopes and vice versa.

In addition to the material above, comments would be made in the discussion section regarding the model uncertainty of the analysis. The substantive discussion might center on Model 1, but it would also be reiterated that other models might be plausible, such as Models 3 and 4.

Table 7.8 Estimates for Model 1.

Effect	Estimate	Std. Error	95% LCI	95% UCI
Intercept	216.68	3.99	208.69	224.66
Slope	4.78	0.73	3.31	6.25
Risk	−26.58	4.83	−36.24	−16.93
Var(Inter)	184.79			
Var(Slope)	6.75			
Corr.	−0.64			

7.8 Parametric Bootstrap of the Evidence Ratio*

To aid in the interpretation of the evidence ratio, a simulation method can be used known as the *parametric bootstrap* (Efron & Tibshirani, 1993). The parametric bootstrap provides a benchmark of the values that might result when the evidence ratio of the known best approximating model is computed on repeated samples. This provides a basis for judging how typical or atypical the evidence ratios for the original sample happen to be.

To prevent things from becoming too abstract, focus is on the previous analysis, using the set of six models in Table 7.6. Recall that Model 1 was the best fitting in the sample, and thus, the prime candidate for the best approximating model. All the other models had an evidence ratio greater than 3, but it is unclear if such a ratio constitutes substantial evidence against these models. The parametric bootstrap can aid in making such judgments.

Suppose Model 1 is treated as the true model, meaning all the estimates of the fixed effects and variance components are imagined to be the population parameters. Data are repeatedly generated from this true model, simulating a replication scenario like that for predictive accuracy. For each replication, all the candidate models are fit in the set, Model 1 to Model 6, and the AICc and weight of evidence are computed. In this scenario, it is expected that Model 1 will be selected as the best approximately most of the time, that is, in the majority of replications. It will not be selected every time because of simulation variation, which is taken to be indicative of idiosyncrasies of sampling due to chance events.

Using the simulated data of the bth bootstrap replication ($b = 1, \ldots, B$), the following evidence ratio is computed:

$$E_b^* = \frac{W_{max(b)}^*}{W_{1b}^*}, \qquad (7.8.1)$$

where the star (*) in the superscript denotes the fact that the quantities are computed on each replication sample. $W_{max(b)}^*$ is the maximum weight of evidence for the bth bootstrap replication, and W_{1b}^* is the weight of evidence for Model 1 for the bth bootstrap replication.

Model 1 is in the denominator of Equation 7.8.1, as this model is known to be the best approximating model for each replication. To be clear, the value of W_{1b}^* will vary from replication to replication. Regardless of this fact, the weight of Model 1 is always in the denominator because it is the best approximating model of the simulation.

The numerator can be the weight of any of the models, Model 1 through Model 6. Since Model 1 is the known best approximating model for the simulation, the expectation is that $W_{max(b)}^* = W_{1b}^*$ most of the time, yielding $E_b^* = 1$. However, sampling vagaries will result in other models (2–5) being the best fitting for some replications. When this occurs, $W_{max(b)}^* > W_{1b}^*$ and $E_b^* > 1$.

The case of $E_b^* > 1$ constitutes an erroneous deviation from the correct value of $E_b^* = 1$. It occurs because of chance fluctuations under a repeated sampling scenario. The distribution of the E_b^* over B bootstrap replications is an estimate of the sampling distribution of the evidence ratio for the known best approximating model. This provides an indication of how much the evidence ratio can vary for the model that is known to be the actual best approximating model.

The distribution of the E_b^* provides a reference for evaluating the evidence ratios of the original sample. Say, for example, that based on a large number of replications (see below), 99% of the E_b^* happen to be less than 3. Then it is very improbable to get an evidence ratio for the known best approximating model (Model 1) larger than 3 in repeated sampling. Or, it is reasonable (probable) to get an evidence ratio less then 3, when the best approximating model is known. This benchmark is used for all the evidence ratios of the initial sample. Any evidence ratio greater than 3 is considered exceedingly rare and not simply a result of sampling fluctuations. The rare values are taken as evidence the model in question is not the best approximating model.

7.8.1 PERFORMING THE PARAMETRIC BOOTSTRAP*

Data generation based on a fitted model object is performed with `simulate()`. When a fitted model object, such as `model.1`, is supplied to `simulate()`, data are generated treating the parameter estimates as the population parameters, or the parameters of the true model. The random effects and random error are drawn from normal distributions, with means of 0, and variance and covariance parameters fixed to the estimated values. The same number of subjects and repeated measures is generated as in the original sample, and the missing data pattern is also the same. Only response variable data are generated, as the original time and static predictor(s) are considered fixed (constant) among samples.

For each replication, the models are fit to the generated data using the `refit()` function of the `lme4` package. Then `aictab()` is used to compute the AICc and the weight of evidence. The evidence ratio of Equation 7.8.1 is computed and stored.

It is convenient to write a function to perform the above operations and then use `rdply()` of the `plyr` package to perform the function a large number

7.8 Parametric Bootstrap of the Evidence Ratio*

of times (e.g., $B = 9999$). The function requires the number of bootstrap replications and the name of the function to be executed. An advantage of `rdply()` is that a progress bar can be requested to track the progression of the computing process, although a progress bar can be made without using `rdply()` (see Section 8.9).

As a first step, consider the estimation of the six models of Table 7.6 and the computation of the AICc effect size measures. The results are sorted by AICc values for ease of interpretation.

```
> model.1 <- lmer(read ~ grade5 + risk2 + (grade5 | subid), MPLS.LS, REML = FALSE)
> model.2 <- lmer(read ~ grade5 + eth2 + (grade5 | subid), MPLS.LS, REML = FALSE)
> model.3 <- lmer(read ~ grade5 + risk2 + eth2 + (grade5 | subid), MPLS.LS, REML = FALSE)
> model.4 <- lmer(read ~ grade5 * risk2 + (grade5 | subid), MPLS.LS, REML = FALSE)
> model.5 <- lmer(read ~ grade5 * eth2 + (grade5 | subid), MPLS.LS, REML = FALSE)
> model.6 <- lmer(read ~ grade5 * risk2 + grade5 * eth2 + (grade5 | subid),
+                MPLS.LS, REML = FALSE)
> mynames <- paste("M", as.character(1:6), sep = "")
> mymodels <- list(model.1, model.2, model.3, model.4, model.5, model.6)
> myaicc <- as.data.frame(aictab(mymodels, mynames))[ ,-c(5,7)]
> myaicc$Eratio <- max(myaicc$AICcWt) / myaicc$AICcWt
> myaicc
```

	Modnames	K	AICc	Delta_AICc	AICcWt	Cum.Wt	Eratio
1	M1	7	565.4412	0.000000	0.6070287135	0.6070287	1.000000
4	M4	8	567.7313	2.290062	0.1931650774	0.8001938	3.142539
3	M3	8	567.9101	2.468887	0.1766432949	0.9768371	3.436466
6	M6	10	572.0110	6.569755	0.0227302888	0.9995674	26.705719
2	M2	7	580.7635	15.322307	0.0002857673	0.9998531	2124.206666
5	M5	8	582.0949	16.653730	0.0001468581	1.0000000	4133.438401

The next step is to write a function for the operations that will be carried out for each bootstrap replication. Four operations must be performed.

1. Simulate the response data using `simulate()`.

2. Fit each model with the simulated data using `refit()`.

3. Compute the weight of evidence using `aictab()`.

4. Compute the replication evidence ratio of Equation 7.8.1.

For each bootstrap replication, the response data are stored in the object `simdv`. This object name, as well as that of the fitted model object, is supplied to `refit()`.

In the syntax below, a function named `boot.func()` is written to carry out the four operations. Nothing explicit will be passed to the function, so the parentheses of `function()` will be empty. The bootstrap evidence ratio is computed in the last line of code.

```
> boot.func <- function(){
+ ## Simulate response vector based on best fitting Model 1.
+ simdv <- simulate(model.1)
+ ## Fit models using refit() and save aictab() output.
+ mynames <- paste("M", as.character(1:6), sep = "")
+ mymodels <- list(refit(model.1, simdv[ ,1]), refit(model.2, simdv[ ,1]),
+                  refit(model.3, simdv[ ,1]), refit(model.4, simdv[ ,1]),
+                  refit(model.5, simdv[ ,1]), refit(model.6, simdv[ ,1]))
+ myaicc <- aictab(mymodels, mynames, sort = F)
+ ## Compute bootstrap evidence ratio. Denominator is initial best model (Model 1).
+ b.eratio <- max(myaicc$AICcWt) / myaicc$AICcWt[1]
+ }
```

After running the above syntax, nothing is printed to the R console window, as the function is merely defined. It should be noted that the function is specific to the example. If the reader has a different number of models, or if the best-fitting initial one is not Model 1, the above code must be altered in a straightforward manner.

To execute `boot.func()` numerous times, the `rdply()` function is used. The number of bootstrap replications must be supplied (`.n=`), as well as the name of the function (`.expr=`) and an indication that the optional progress bar is desired (`.progress="text"`). The number of bootstrap replications should be large, such as $B = 9999$. To save time for the reader replicating the results, $B = 999$ is used in the illustration. The `set.seed()` function is set to a specific value to allow the reader to replicate the results shown below.

```
> set.seed(1)
> B <- 999
> mystorage0 <- rdply(.n = B, .expr = boot.func, .progress = "text")
```

After submitting the above syntax, a progress bar will appear in the R console window. The percentage to the extreme right indicates the progress, and an equal sign (=) is added to the progress bar as the replications proceed. A fancier progress bar can be created on Windows machines using `.progress="win"`.

Having executed the replications, the quantiles based on the bootstrap replications can now be computed. The selection of quantiles is arbitrary, but researchers usually feel comfortable with values in the 0.90s. Here the 0.90, 0.95, and 0.99 quantiles are considered. It is noted that the number of bootstrap replications needs to be large, say $B = 9999$, to provide an accurate 0.99 quantile.

The `mystorage0` object has two columns, the first containing the replication number and the second containing the replication evidence ratio. In the syntax below, the evidence ratio is extracted and sorted, and then the results are stored as `mystorage`. The row number of the sorted vector is selected pertaining to the desired quantile. The row number is determined by the formula $(B+1)(1-a)$, where $a = (0.90, 0.95, 0.99)$ contains the quantiles of interest, and B is the total number of replications. A comment on this formula appears below.

```
> ## Extract and sort bootstrap ratios.
> mystorage.s <- sort(mystorage0[ ,2])
> ## Compute empirical quantiles.
> a <- c(.1, .05, .01)                              # a values.
> b <- (B + 1) * (1 - a)                            # b values.
> myquant <- as.data.frame(mystorage.s[b])  # Save and display quantiles.
> colnames(myquant) <- "quantile"
> rownames(myquant) <- c("90%", "95%", "99%")
> myquant
```

7.8 Parametric Bootstrap of the Evidence Ratio*

```
        quantile
90%     3.017103
95%     6.005801
99%    35.523984
```

The quantiles are shown in the output. These values are used to inform judgments regarding the evidence ratios based on the original sample analysis. However, it is cautioned that the quantiles should not be used as hard-and-fast cutoff values to decide the plausibility or worth of the models. Recall the admonition of Anderson (2008, p. 85) that science is not about holding to rigid cutoffs rules.

The 0.99 quantile is 35.52, and one might judge any model with an evidence ratio greater than this value to be "very implausible." If $E_h > 35.52$, then either an exceedingly rare event has occurred, or the h candidate model is not the best approximating model. For the example, this pertains to Model 2 ($E_2 = 2124$) and Model 5 ($E_5 = 4133$).

Model 6 has an evidence ratio of $E_6 = 27$ that falls between the 0.95 and 0.99 quantiles. This is not quite as extreme as the models above. At the risk of being haunted by the "0.05 specter," one might judge this outcome to be relatively extreme, as it is among the top 5%. This might be enough to consider Model 6 "implausible."

Model 3 has $E_3 = 3.4$ that falls between the 0.90 and 0.95 quantiles. This model appears to be on the cusp of implausibility. A cautious researcher might regard Model 3 as plausible, but perhaps "with suspicion." The same can probably be said of Model 4, although its evidence ratio is close to the 0.90 quantile.

A summary of the bootstrap analysis is provided in Table 7.9. The last column of the table lists possible judgment statements a researcher might make, based on the value of the evidence ratio and the bootstrap quantiles. The best-fitting model is always the most plausible, and the information in the table is most relevant for the models other than Model 1. In addition, the researcher must think about how the judgments in Table 7.9 relate to the research questions at hand. There is reason to favor Model 1, but perhaps a researcher would not be especially willing to discount Model 3 and Model 4.

Table 7.9 Bootstrap evaluation of evidence ratios.

Model	Inequality	Judgment
1	$E_1 < Q_{.90}$	Plausible
2	$Q_{.99} < E_2$	Very implausible
3	$Q_{.90} < E_3 < Q_{.95}$	Plausible with suspicion
4	$Q_{.90} < E_4 < Q_{.95}$	Plausible with suspicion
5	$Q_{.99} < E_5$	Very implausible
6	$Q_{.95} < E_6 < Q_{.99}$	Implausible

Note. $Q =$ bootstrap quantile; $E =$ evidence ratio.

7.8.2 CAVEATS REGARDING THE PARAMETRIC BOOTSTRAP*

The main caveat regarding the bootstrap procedure is that it can take a long time to run. The $B = 999$ bootstrap replications above take approximately 11 minutes on a modern laptop computer. To avoid bias introduced by the bootstrap procedure, the number of replications should be larger, say in the thousands (Davison, Hinkley, & Young, 2003). If the sample size is large and/or the LMER models are complex, it can take a long time to carry out thousands of bootstrap replications.

The `rdply()` function is timed by enclosing it in `system.time()`. One can start with a smallish number of bootstrap replications and time how long the process takes. Then a rough estimate of the total time for the full number of replications can be calculated. In the example, a very rough estimate for the total time using $B = 9999$ is $(10)(11) = 111$ minutes.

An alternative to a single run is to perform the replications in batches of, say, 1000 replications at a time. This requires different storage objects for the replications, which are concatenated to produce the single final vector of total replications.

Finally, the bootstrap replication distribution has a finite number of values. A quantile is determined by the integer row number that cuts off a certain proportion of the vector, say the bottom 0.95. Since the row number is determined by $(B + 1)(1 - a)$, integer values will occur if B ends in 99. This is known as the "99" rule (Boos, 2003) and explains the nature of the quantile formula.

7.9 Bayesian Information Criterion*

Alternative types of an information criterion can be used in the multimodel approach. For a review, see Kadane and Lazar (2004). One of the most popular is the Bayesian information criterion (BIC; Schwarz, 1978). The BIC for LMER is defined as

$$\text{BIC} = deviance + log\left(\sum_i^N n_i\right) \cdot K,$$

where the sum is the total number of observations, and K is the number of parameters (fixed effects and variance components).

The effect size measures previously considered for the AIC (and AICc) can be computed based on the BIC. For example, delta is computed by substituting the BIC for the AICc in Equation 7.4.1. The empirical BIC value is in the `@AICtab$BIC` slot of the `summary()` output object (e.g., `summary(model.1)@AICtab$BIC`).

Similar to the AIC (and AICc), a smaller value of BIC indicates more favorable evidence for a model. However, there are fundamental differences in philosophy and interpretation of the AIC and the BIC. The most relevant difference is that the BIC is not an unbiased estimator of predictive accuracy (it is biased). This is no drawback for advocates of the BIC, as it is not intended as an estimator of predictive accuracy. Rather, the BIC is an estimator of the *Bayes factor*. The Bayes factor is a type of evidence ratio of models in the Bayesian paradigm (Wasserman, 2000). One apparently need not be a Bayesian to use the BIC, but one must be willing to switch from an estimator of predictive accuracy to an estimator of the Bayes factor.

If one feels particularly rigid about theoretical frameworks, then the AIC and the BIC should not be used together, as they estimate two different things. Evidently, writers of much statistical software do not feel particularly passionate about this, as the AIC and BIC are routinely printed in output, as with lmer(). For practical analysis, the BIC tends to favor simpler models than the AIC. Sometimes the BIC has been suggested when parsimony is a priority (Kadane & Lazar, 2004). The BIC can lead to similar judgments about models as the AICc, when the sample size is not large (Ward, 2008).

On a theoretical level, the BIC is less desirable for model evaluation than the AIC (and AICc). The main drawback is that the researcher must assume that the true model is among the candidate models in the set (Berger & Pericchi, 1996). Recalling the discussion above, a true model can never be known. This fact seems to render a dubious theoretic status on the BIC as a model evaluation criterion in applied research.

There have been solutions offered for this philosophical problem, one being that the researcher need not believe that one of the candidate models is true, only that the researcher "operates as if truth were in the model set" (Link & Barker, 2006). It is unclear what the difference is between assuming one candidate model is true and assuming there is "truth in the model set." For this reason, the philosophical underpinnings of the AICc are favored, as the researcher can make the more realistic assumption that none of the candidate models are true. In fact, the researcher can make the reasonable assumption that the true model is unknowable.

Likelihood Ratio Test 8

The last chapter dealt with the selection of static predictor effects using multimodel inference and the AIC. In this chapter, the focus is on selection using the LRT.

As previously mentioned, the prime concern in evaluating models is that a more complex model will always have superior fit to the data at hand than a less complex model. But this superiority can be spurious. An added effect, say a static predictor, can improve fit by conforming to random error and/or random individual variability. Such conforming is not representative of the genuine fixed effects of the underlying true model.

It is of prime importance to account for potentially spurious improvement in model fit when extraneous predictors are added to the model. In Chapter 7, this was dealt with using the concept of predictive accuracy, for which the AIC is an unbiased estimator under widely applicable assumptions. Predictive accuracy is the ability of a model fit on initial data to predict the data of another sample drawn from the same population, or generated from the same true model (Forster & Sober, 1994). Predictive accuracy is one means of accounting for the possibility of overfitting data.

In this chapter, the LRT will be discussed as an alternative method of accounting for overfit. Like the AIC, the LRT balances fit and parsimony, but the LRT does not use a penalty term to adjust the deviance. Rather, the LRT relies on the χ^2 distribution, with its associated df.

The AIC and LRT have many similarities, and these are discussed in the first part of the chapter. What is different about the two methods is the way they are typically used. The AIC is closely associated with multimodel inference, with evidence values assigned directly to models that may or may not be nested. This makes it possible to order models in terms of approximations to the truth and determine meaningful distances between models. Issues of traditional analysis, such as statistical significance and Type I error rate, are irrelevant in multimodel analysis.

In contrast to the AIC, the LRT is typically used for NHST. The LRT is a method for comparing two nested models, a more complex full model, and a less complex reduced model. Under the assumption that the reduced model is true, the LRT-p is computed, and some type of evaluation is made by the researcher. The evaluation often boils down to a decision of whether to "accept" or "reject" the null model, which, by complement, entails a decision about the alternative model. In many analyses, the decision is made multiple times, constituting the overall model evaluation. Multiple decisions are required when there are more than two models to be evaluated. Since the LRT handles only two models at a time, one of the two models is left behind in some respect—usually being labeled as a "reject"—so that additional models can be evaluated.

The philosophy adopted here is that a dichotomous accept/reject use of the LRT is not compulsory. To this end, evidential interpretations of the LRT-p are discussed, focusing on the evidence for the full model in a given comparison. Discussion centers on parallels of the AIC and the LRT, and it is shown how LRT-ps can be calibrated based on predictive accuracy.

For the evaluation of multiple nested models with the LRT, two methods are discussed. The first is the *step-up* approach, in which the models to be tested increase in complexity. The second is the *top-down* approach, in which the models decrease in complexity. Both approaches can be used in confirmatory and exploratory analysis, and illustrations of each type are presented.

There are two additional topics: the parametric bootstrap for the LRT and a simulation method for estimating required sample size. The LRT bootstrap is desirable when the sample size is not large and/or the number of parameters tested is large. In such situations, the bootstrap p-value can be more accurate than the analytic LRT-p.

The simulation method for estimating required sample size is important when a researcher is planning a study. In research planning, there is often a need to estimate the number of subjects to measure. The estimated sample size can be computed based on a parametric bootstrap, provided that a pilot data set is available to the researcher.

Similar to the last chapter, the focus is again on evaluating fixed effects of static predictors. The time predictors and random effects are assumed to be preselected. Thus, the LRT is used only to compare models that differ in their number of fixed effects. The use of the LRT for selecting time predictors is discussed in Chapter 9, and selection of random effects is discussed in Chapter 10.

8.1 Why Use the Likelihood Ratio Test?

In the last chapter, the virtues of the AIC and multimodel inference were extolled. Although the methods of the last chapter are preferred, there are reasons why an applied researcher might want to use the LRT for selecting static predictor effects. These reasons include the following.

8.1 Why Use the Likelihood Ratio Test?

1. The researcher must adhere to standards of the "*p*-value culture" (Nelder, 1999), and analyze their data and interpret their results consistent with this culture.

2. The researcher is satisfied with comparing only nested models, and comparing them two at a time.

3. The researcher wants to use a criterion for balancing fit and parsimony other than the AIC (or AICc).

4. The researcher is planning a study and needs to estimate the number of subjects required to reject a null hypothesis at a specified probability level (power level).

The first reason acknowledges that there are sociological constraints in certain areas of the behavioral sciences. These constraints act to discourage the use of multimodel inference, perhaps because of an unfamiliarity with the AIC. Another reason is an unfavorableness in working without a dichotomous framework that does not declare statistical significance or nonsignificance for results of an analysis. A researcher may feel his or her results will not be taken seriously by journal editors or academic committees unless *p*-values are computed and asterisks assigned to especially small values, such as "***p < .001." This practice is codified by authoritative journals and publication guidelines such as the *Publication Manual of the American Psychological Association* (American Psychological Association, 2010, chap. 8). Nelder (1999) summarizes the attitude in the following way:

> Many experimenters who have taken a statistics course are left with the belief that the purpose of an analysis is to calculate a *p*-value. If this value is sufficiently small then an editor might look kindly on their paper.

Although most researchers know better, results that pass under the arbitrary $\alpha = 0.05$ bar are often imbued with an air of scientific definitiveness not afforded to effect size measures (Krantz, 1999). It has long been argued that the use of arbitrary cutoffs for declaring dubious states of reality like "statistical significance" may slow the advancement of science (Anderson et al., 2000; Berkson, 1942; Cohen, 1994; Hubbard & Lindsay, 2008; Johnstone, 1986; Smedslund, 2006). The opinion here is that the LRT can be used without necessarily making dichotomous decisions. Rather, the LRT-*p* can be used as an index of effect size. The basis for this interpretation is presented below.

The second reason above addresses the fact that in regression analysis, researchers often formulate nested models to answer their research questions. However, in some studies, it is unclear if this formulation is a logical implication of the research questions, or a consequence of using statistical methods that only accommodate nested models. Two-at-a-time evaluation can be problematic, as it is not always consistent with the natural strategy that a researcher might adopt for evaluating multiple models. When the evaluation of pairs of nested models does fit one's analysis strategy, then the LRT can provide clear answers.

The third reason listed above arises from the fact that the AIC tends to favor more complex models than the LRT when the latter is used with traditional cutoffs, such as $\alpha = 0.05$. As shown below, the AIC can favor the full model in situations where the LRT-p does not lead to the rejection of the reduced model. Thus, even though the LRT provides a trade-off between fit and parsimony, decisions regarding the plausibility of the models can be different with the LRT-p and the AIC. This will be somewhat of a nonissue after considering the calibration of LRT-p based on predictive accuracy.

The fourth reason may be particularly compelling for researchers who need to estimate how many subjects to measure in the future. Granting agencies, dissertation committees, and the like often want to know if certain resources are sufficient to ensure with a high likelihood that the results will be statistically reliable. This usually translates into an estimation of the number of subjects required to favor a full model at a high probability. An optional section is provided that discusses a simulation method based on the bootstrap for estimating such a sample size.

Finally, the strategy throughout this chapter is to present LRT-p as a useful statistic, which can be reported in the evaluation of two nested models. The LRT-p is emphasized as an effect size measure, both in a traditional sense and also in a modern sense. The former is based on the ideas of Ronald Fisher, and the latter is based on calibration of the LRT-p using the AIC. Focus is on the AIC rather than the AICc because the former is most comparable to the LRT. Like the AIC, the LRT is based on large-sample properties. For researchers concerned about small-sample accuracy, an optional section is provided that discusses a parametric bootstrap procedure for the LRT.

8.2 Fisher and Neyman-Pearson

The LRT is often used for dichotomous reject/accept decisions about statistical hypotheses. As mentioned, such decisions use arbitrary cutoffs that may be of dubious scientific value. It has long been argued that effect size measures are a better way to express scientific evidence (Berkson, 1942; Goodman & Royall, 1988; Hacking, 1972; Royall, 1996, 2000).

There has been a recent renewed interest in effect size, as it is now recommended by several authorities in the behavioral sciences as an integral part of reporting statistical results (American Educational Research Association, 2006; American Psychological Association, 2010; Fidler, 2002; Thompson, 2002; Wilkinson & APA Task Force on Statistical Inference, 1999). Consistent with these sentiments, focus is on the interpretation of the LRT and LRT-p in terms of effect size.

To clarify and perhaps justify the use of LRT-p as a measure of evidence, there is brief mention of an important distinction often glossed over in

8.2 Fisher and Neyman-Pearson

presentations of statistical inference. The distinction is between the ideas of Fisher (Fisher, 1922, 1925) and Neyman and Pearson (Neyman & Pearson, 1928a, 1928b). Statistical inference, as taught in the behavioral sciences and many other fields, is a hybrid of the ideas from both frameworks. This hybrid has been described as a "marriage of convenience that neither party would have condoned" (Hubbard & Bayarri, 2003). Although both frameworks involve common elements, such as the computation of a p-value, the goals and interpretation of statistical analysis are quite different. Highlighting these distinctions is important for clarifying the philosophical approach taken in the remainder of the chapter.

The Neyman-Pearson system is concerned with the long-run error probabilities associated with *decisions*. The focus of the decisions are the null hypothesis (H_0) and the alternative hypothesis (H_A). One implication of the decision focus is that an exact p-value is unimportant, other than to indicate whether a sample result falls in the rejection or acceptance region (Berger, 2003). The regions are dictated by two types of error probabilities, Type I (α) being the probability of rejecting H_0 when it should not be rejected, and Type II being the probability of failing to reject H_0 when it should be rejected. If $p \leq \alpha$, then H_0 is rejected, and H_A is accepted, with the word *accepted* being an appropriate term in the Neyman-Pearson system (Goodman, 1993). If $p > \alpha$, H_A is rejected, and H_0 is accepted. It is almost universal that $\alpha = 0.05$, although Neyman and Pearson advocated flexibility based on the context of the analysis (Mayo, 1992).

Fisher's system is concerned with the *statistical evidence* offered by a single sample. The focus is on the extent of evidence against a single hypothesis, H_0. There is no explicit H_A in Fisher's framework. The exact p-value is of prime importance, as it provides the measure of evidence against H_0, with smaller values indicating greater evidence (Berger, 2003; Christensen, 2005; Hubbard & Bayarri, 2003). Although Fisher stressed the evidential nature of p-values, he allowed for a decision to be made regarding H_0, which was to reject it if the p-value was below a cutoff, or fail to reject if the p-value was above. Fisher's philosophy was strictly falsificationist, meaning a researcher never accepts H_0 if it is not rejected. This follows from the view of Popper (1959) that evidence can only be garnered against a hypothesis, never for it (Greenland, 1998).

Because both approaches use p-values, cutoff values, and decisions about hypotheses, there is little mystery as to why they have become conflated. For applied researchers, it is important to contrast the fact that Fisher interpreted the p-value as a measure of evidence for a single analysis, whereas Neyman and Pearson did not. The Neyman-Pearson approach is only about the long-run implications of decisions, as in their system, "no test based upon a theory of probability can by itself provide any valuable evidence of the truth or falsehood of a hypothesis" (Neyman & Pearson, 1933, pp. 290–291).

To amplify, the Neyman-Pearson approach is not evidential, meaning that under their framework, the researcher cannot obtain evidence for or against statistical models based on a single analysis (Hubbard & Bayarri, 2003). As a consequence, it has been remarked that the Neyman-Pearson framework is most appropriate for applications such as industrial quality control (Mayo, 1992). In such applications, the focus is not on whether a particular batch of light bulbs, for example, should be rejected because they are defective. Rather, the focus is on whether the decision process leading to rejection is good business practice over the long run.

It seems almost scientifically necessary that researchers in the behavioral sciences adopt a Fisherian view to make sense of the results of a single statistical analysis. It has been remarked that the Neyman-Pearson approach requires a decision-like attitude that Neyman himself did not use when analyzing actual data (Cox, 1999).

The long-run decision rates associated with statistical methods can be an important justification for their use, but long-run behavior should not be the goal in using statistical methods. Rather, the purpose of using statistical methods is they allow the researcher to make inferences about hypotheses from an individual analysis. *Scientists want evidence, not abstractions.*

The Fisherian attitude is at least tacitly acknowledged in many quarters of the behavioral and social sciences. For example, the *Publication Manual of the American Psychological Association* suggests an evidential interpretation of p-values by recommending their exact value be reported rather than an inequality such as $p < 0.05$, or a lonely declaration of (non)statistical significance (American Psychological Association, 2010, chap. 5). Furthermore, the majority of professional journals implicitly or explicitly require the use of asterisks for expressing different p-value levels in tables of results (Fidler, 2002). The Neyman-Pearson approach would require only one asterisk, `*p <.05`.

The stance of this chapter is to treat the LRT as a pragmatic and evidential device. This means the LRT-p will be regarded as providing evidence for and against hypotheses in a single analysis. The view goes beyond what Fisher would consider appropriate, as the LRT-p will be considered an index of evidence *for* a hypothesis. Furthermore, α will not be interpreted as a long-run error rate, as in the Neyman-Pearson system. Instead, α will be treated as a cutoff with no long-run characteristics, as in Fisher's system (Hubbard & Bayarri, 2003).

A consequence of the adopted approach is that there will be no concern with the number of model comparisons in the analysis. In the case of multiple testing, some researchers feel they should adjust the model evaluation criterion to guard against false-positive results. This approach only seems useful if there is a chance that all the null hypotheses might be true (Lindquist & Gelman, 2009; Nelder, 1999). A null hypothesis is never true in observational research. Thus, any long-run error rate contingent on such truth assumptions is not applicable for the analysis at hand (Forster, 2000). Because of the unrealistic underlying assumptions, Nelder (1971) has starkly said that "multiple comparison methods have no place at all in the interpretation of data."

Finally, deviance is a random variable having changing values for different samples. This means the AIC and the LRT-p are also random variables (Murdoch, Tsai, & Adcock, 2008). It seems appropriate to use them as measures of evidence for a single analysis. However, replication is the key to making definitive scientific statements. Fisher believed that H_0 is only convincingly discredited when there are repeated tests that result in sufficiently small p-values (Johstone, 1987). Such repetition may not be possible in observational research. But Fisher's general idea of the value in repeated similar findings should be appreciated.

8.3 Evaluation of Two Nested Models

In this chapter, focus is on the evaluation of two nested models, as this is a requirement of the LRT. The two major components of the LRT are the X^2 test statistic, and the χ^2 distribution from which the LRT-p is derived. As discussed in Chapter 6, X^2 is the empirical deviance of the reduced model minus the empirical deviance of the full model:

$$X^2 = deviance_R - deviance_F. \qquad (8.3.1)$$

The reduced model is nested within the full model, meaning the former can be obtained from the latter by setting at least one fixed effect to 0.

The larger the value of X^2, the greater the separation between the deviances, and the better the fit of the full model relative to the reduced model. In practical applications, it is always the case that $X^2 > 0$ because the fit is always better for the full model to the data at hand (see Chapter 7).

The LRT, in effect, penalizes the X^2 statistic by obtaining LRT-p from a χ^2 distribution based on the df, the difference in the number of parameters of the full and reduced models. The df determine the shape of the χ^2 distribution, for which the LRT-p is the upper tail area.

As an example of the LRT, consider the comparison of the following two LMER models. The reduced model has `grade5`, and the full model adds an `eth2` intercept effect.

Reduced: $y_{ij} = (\beta_0 + b_{0i}) + (\beta_1 + b_{1i})(\text{grade5}_{ij}) + \varepsilon_{ij},$
Full: $y_{ij} = (\beta_0 + b_{0i}) + (\beta_1 + b_{1i})(\text{grade5}_{ij}) + \beta_2(\text{eth2}_i) + \varepsilon_{ij}.$

The reduced model can be obtained from the full model by setting $\beta_2 = 0$. It follows that the comparison of the above two models is an evaluation of $H_0 : \beta_2 = 0$ versus $H_A : \beta_2 \neq 0$. The hypothesis setup is always two-tailed, as one-tailed tests do not allow the elimination of the parameter in question from the full model (Weakliem, 2004).

Fitted LMER models are compared using the `anova()` function. The reduced and full models must be fit with the same sample data. If there are missing values for the static predictor(s), the sample size will differ for the reduced and full models, and the `anova()` function will produce an error message. In such cases, the `na.omit()` function can be used on the data set when estimating the models (see the discussion in Chapter 3).

The names of the fitted model objects are supplied with the reduced model listed first. Suppose the reduced model object is `model.0`, and the full model object is `model.1`.

```
> model.0 <- lmer(read ~ grade5 + (grade5 | subid), MPLS.LS, REML = FALSE)
> model.1 <- lmer(read ~ grade5 + eth2 + (grade5 | subid), MPLS.LS, REML = FALSE)
> anova(model.0, model.1)
```

```
Data: MPLS.LS
Models:
model.0: read ~ grade5 + (grade5 | subid)
model.1: read ~ grade5 + eth2 + (grade5 | subid)
         Df    AIC    BIC   logLik  Chisq Chi Df Pr(>Chisq)
model.0   6 580.96 595.25 -284.48
model.1   7 579.21 595.88 -282.60 3.7512      1    0.05277 .
---
Signif. codes:  0 '***' 0.001 '**' 0.01 '*' 0.05 '.' 0.1 ' ' 1
```

The output shows that $X^2 = 3.75$, and LRT-p = 0.0528. For the researcher trained to use a rigid cutoff of $\alpha = 0.05$, the LRT-p might be troublesome, as it just misses the mark. Probably to the chagrin of many applied researchers, H_0 is not rejected here. This "almost but not quite" result is sometimes dealt with by labeling the LRT-p as "trending" toward statistical significance or "marginally" significant. The meanings of these verbal descriptions are unclear at best, and later it is shown that they can be replaced by statements of evidence. Below it is argued that p-values in the neighborhood of $\alpha = 0.05$ (e.g., LRT-p = 0.04, 0.05, 0.06) all can be interpreted as providing "moderate evidence" for the full model.

The difference in empirical deviance—that is, X^2—is a natural means of assessing the relation between hypotheses and sample evidence (Hacking, 1972; Lindsey, 1999; Royall, 1996, 2000). Despite this, the deviance difference should not be taken at face value because of the overfitting problem (Forster & Sober, 2004; Rao, 1992). The deviance difference somehow needs to be adjusted or penalized for the difference in the complexity of the reduced and full models. The AIC and the LRT both penalize the test statistic, but in different ways. Insight can be gained by examining the details. Much of what follows is based on material presented by Sakamoto, Ishiguro, and Kitagawa (1986).

As discussed in Chapter 7, one basis for a penalty is the predictive accuracy underlying the AIC. Chapter 7 dealt with the general case of evaluating many models, nested or not. Here, focus is on using the AIC to evaluate two nested models. The AIC rather than the AICc is considered, as it has a close parallel to the LRT in that both are large-sample methods.

Consider the comparison of two nested models with the AIC. The difference in AIC of two nested models is denoted as ΔAIC, with the full-model

8.3 Evaluation of Two Nested Models

AIC (AIC_F) always being subtracted from the reduced-model AIC (AIC_R). The difference can be written in the following way:

$$\begin{aligned}
\Delta AIC &= AIC_R - AIC_F \\
&= (deviance_R + 2 \cdot K_R) - (deviance_F + 2 \cdot K_F) \\
&= (deviance_R - deviance_F) - 2 \cdot (K_F - K_R) \qquad (8.3.2) \\
&= X^2 - 2 \cdot (K_F - K_R) \\
&= X^2 - 2 \cdot \Delta K.
\end{aligned}$$

K_R is the number of parameters of the reduced model, K_F is the number of parameters of the full model, and ΔK is the difference. $\Delta K > 0$ because the full model always has at least one additional parameter.

The last line of Equation 8.3.2 shows that ΔAIC penalizes the X^2 statistic based on the difference in complexity of the models. In order for ΔAIC to increase in value, the added parameters of the full model must increase in fit, as indexed by X^2.

Unlike X^2, ΔAIC can be negative or positive. $\Delta AIC < 0$ if the reduced model has superior fit, as AIC_R is less than that of the full model. On the other hand, $0 < \Delta AIC$ results when the full model has superior fit.

Based on ΔAIC, the weight of evidence for the models can be computed. When nested models are considered, the weight of evidence for the reduced model, W_R, is computed as

$$W_R = \frac{exp(-0.5 \cdot \Delta AIC)}{1 + exp(-0.5 \cdot \Delta AIC)}. \qquad (8.3.3)$$

The denominator results because one of the models is always the best fitting, producing $\Delta = 0$ and $exp(0) = 1$. A convenient relation is $W_F = 1 - W_R$ because the weights must sum to 1.

Suppose the following are computed for the two nested models considered above: ΔAIC, W_R, and W_F. The results are concatenated to the standard anova() output and printed.

```
> myout <- anova(model.0, model.1)
> ## Compute delta.aic.
> myout$delta.aic <- myout$Chisq - 2 * myout$"Chi Df"
> ## Weight of evidence.
> myout$w.r <- exp(-.5 * myout$delta.aic) / (1 + exp(-.5 * myout$delta.aic))
> myout$w.f <- 1 - myout$w.r
> ## Print excluding columns 3 and 4.
> myout[ ,-(3:4)]
          Df     AIC  Chisq Chi Df Pr(>Chisq) delta.aic    w.r    w.f
model.0    6  580.96
model.1    7  579.21 3.7512      1    0.05277    1.7512 0.29409 0.70591
```

The output shows that $\Delta AIC = 1.75$, $W_R = 0.29$, and $W_F = 0.71$. The evidence ratio for the full model is $0.7/0.3 = 2\frac{1}{3}$. Given the data, the two models, and that neither model is true, there is approximately a 0.7 probability the full model is the best approximating model, or the model closest to the truth. From this perspective, there certainly is evidence for the full model. Based on what will be shown below, since $0.6 < W_F < 0.9$, the result might be characterized as "moderate" evidence for the full model. Although judgment is required in classifying the size of the effect, there is no need to refer to vague concepts such as "trending toward significance."

Both the AIC and LRT approaches provide a trade-off between fit, as represented by X^2, and model complexity, as represented by ΔK. The LRT is saddled with a truth assumption regarding the reduced model, as the reduced model is always H_0. Under the assumption the reduced model is true, LRT-p is the probability of getting a X^2 at least as weird as the observed one (Christensen, 2005).

An obvious question with the LRT is, what constitutes a weird result? It is arbitrary but conventional to define this in terms of the cutoff, $\alpha = 0.05$. Fisher advocated flexibility regarding α (Hubbard & Bayarri, 2003), but this is often a hard sell in the *p*-value culture.

In traditional NHST, when LRT-$p \le 0.05$, one rejects H_0, and when LRT-$p > 0.05$, one does not reject. Although not supported by the theory of Fisher or Neyman-Pearson, applied researchers appear to take the rejection of the reduced model as evidence *for* the full model. The Neyman-Pearson framework supports a *decision* to accept the full model, but this is very different from *evidence* for the full model (Mayo, 1992).

This treatment is especially common when more than two nested models are compared. When many models are evaluated in multiple steps, statistical significance means that a previous full model (H_A) is treated as a true reduced model (H_0) in a subsequent test. From a Fisherian perspective, one model is assumed to be a priori true in one step, but perhaps not in another step. This seems to tread on thin philosophical ice, which may be why some assume "truth all around" and state the hypotheses in nested comparisons as H_0 : the reduced model holds true, and H_A : the full model holds true (e.g., Rao & Wu, 2001).

When ΔAIC is used, the strength of evidence for a hypothesis can be expressed in terms of the probability of being the best approximating model (see Chapter 7). Alternatively, the evidence ratio can be computed, which expresses strength of evidence in terms of odds.

In contrast, strength of evidence is a relatively vague concept with the LRT-p (Goodman, 1993). When effect size statements about *p*-values are made, they are usually gleaned from Fisher's writings (e.g., Fisher, 1954, chap. 20). To provide touchstones for interpreting *p*-values as effect sizes, Efron and Gous (2001) provide common α cutoff values and their associated verbal descriptions. These are listed in Table 8.1.

Referencing Table 8.1, LRT-$p = 0.02$ constitutes "substantial" evidence against the reduced model and for the full model. On the other hand, LRT-$p = 0.06$ provides only "borderline" evidence against the reduced model and for the full model. Are these statements reasonable? There is an attempt to answer this question from a predictive accuracy perspective.

8.3 Evaluation of Two Nested Models

Table 8.1 Cutoff value (α) and strength of evidence descriptions.

α	Strength of Evidence
0.100	Borderline
0.050	Moderate
0.025	Substantial
0.010	Strong
0.005	Very strong
0.001	Overwhelming

8.3.1 CALIBRATING *P*-VALUES BASED ON PREDICTIVE ACCURACY

To assess the strength of evidence represented in Table 8.1, a predictive accuracy approach is adopted. This means the X^2 common to both the LRT and ΔAIC is used as a basis to compare the weight of evidence and *p*-values. If a mapping of LRT-*p* to W_F is obtained, this can be used to determine what strength of evidence is represented by the former. Values of LRT-*p* can be interpreted in terms of the plausibility that the full model (and, by complement, the reduced model) is the best approximating model. This provides a type of calibration of LRT-*p* based on predictive accuracy.

As a point of departure, first consider the case in which the full model and the reduced model differ by one parameter, so that $df = \Delta K = 1$. Recall that $\Delta AIC < 0$ when the reduced model has superior fit, and $\Delta AIC > 0$ when the full model has superior fit. Based on Equation 8.3.2, $\Delta AIC > 0$ when $X^2 > 2 \cdot \Delta K = 2$. The full model will have superior fit, as indexed by the difference in AIC, when the test statistic is greater than 2. The value of $X^2 = 2$, then, will be considered a benchmark value.

From Equation 8.3.2, it can be determined that $X^2 = 2$ results in $\Delta AIC = 2 - 2 = 0$. Using Equation 8.3.3, it can be shown that $W_R = \frac{1}{1+2} = 0.5$, and $W_F = 1 - W_R = 0.5$. In this case, the reduced model and the full model are equally plausible, in terms of being the best approximating model. This is the most uncertain situation as far as the weight of evidence is concerned, as there is a 50–50 chance that either model is closest to the truth. Because of the principle of parsimony, the reduced model may be favored in this case, but this is based on reasoning apart from the weight of evidence.

Since the LRT and ΔAIC share X^2, it is interesting to see what α is associated with $X^2 = 2$, based on $df = \Delta K = 1$. The areas under the curve can be computed with the function `pchisq()`. The values of X^2 (q=) and ΔK (df=) are supplied, and `lower.tail=FALSE` is used to obtain the upper tail probability.

```
> pchisq(q = 2, df = 1, lower.tail = FALSE)
```
```
[1] 0.1572992
```

The output shows that $\alpha = 0.1573$ when $W_R = W_F = 0.5$. This means LRT-$p = 0.1573$ is judged as less than "borderline," perhaps "negligible." It is heartening for advocates of NHST to know that when there is equal weight of evidence for and against the full model, the LRT-p is not even "borderline." Something would be amiss if the LRT-p indicated, say, "strong" evidence for the full model in the most uncertain case according to the weight of evidence.

Now consider the case of $X^2 = 8$, still assuming $\Delta K = 1$. It can be shown that $\Delta AIC = 6$, $W_R = 0.0474$, and $W_F = 0.9526$. There is a 0.9526 probability the full model is the best approximating model, given the data, the two models, and the unknown true model. In this case, there is strong or very strong evidence that the full model is the best approximating model. What is the LRT-p cutoff?

```
> pchisq(q = 8, df = 1, lower.tail = FALSE)
[1] 0.004677735
```

The output indicates $\alpha = 0.0047$, and an LRT-p of this size would be considered "very strong" evidence for the full model according to Table 8.1. Again, this may be encouraging to researchers interested in using NHST, as there appears to be some correspondence between the magnitude of evidence as measured by the LRT-p, and the weight of evidence.

To learn more about the relationship between the LRT-p cutoff and W_F, consider the value of both quantities for several values of X^2, say every 0.05 value of $X^2 \in (0, 12)$.

```
> mychi  <- data.frame(chisq = seq(from = 0, to = 12, by = 0.05))
> mychi$alpha  <- pchisq(q = mychi$chisq, df = 1, lower.tail = FALSE)
> mychi$delta.aic  <- mychi$chisq - 2
> mychi$w.r  <-  exp(-.5 * mychi$delta.aic) / (1 + exp(-.5 * mychi$delta.aic))
> mychi$w.f  <- 1 - mychi$w.r
> head(mychi)
  chisq     alpha delta.aic       w.r       w.f
1  0.00 1.0000000     -2.00 0.7310586 0.2689414
2  0.05 0.8230633     -1.95 0.7261150 0.2738850
3  0.10 0.7518296     -1.90 0.7211152 0.2788848
4  0.15 0.6985354     -1.85 0.7160598 0.2839402
5  0.20 0.6547208     -1.80 0.7109495 0.2890505
6  0.25 0.6170751     -1.75 0.7057850 0.2942150

> tail(mychi)
    chisq     alpha delta.aic         w.r       w.f
236 11.75 0.0006084324      9.75 0.007577241 0.9924228
237 11.80 0.0005923072      9.80 0.007391541 0.9926085
238 11.85 0.0005766135      9.85 0.007210359 0.9927896
239 11.90 0.0005613394      9.90 0.007033587 0.9929664
240 11.95 0.0005464738      9.95 0.006861119 0.9931389
241 12.00 0.0005320055     10.00 0.006692851 0.9933071
```

8.3 Evaluation of Two Nested Models

Having computed α and W_F, the values are graphed using `ggplot2`. Dotted lines are drawn at landmark values of both variables using `geom_hline()` and `geom_vline()`.

```
> g1 <- ggplot(mychi, aes(x = w.f, y = alpha)) + geom_line(lwd = 1.5) + theme_bw()
> g2 <- g1 + geom_hline(yintercept = c(0.01, 0.05), linetype = 2)
> g3 <- g2 + geom_vline(xintercept = c(0.50, 0.90, 0.95), linetype = 2)
> g4 <- g3 + scale_x_continuous(breaks = seq(0.20, 1, 0.05))
> g5 <- g4 + scale_y_continuous(breaks = seq(0, 1, 0.05))
> g6 <- g5 + xlab("Full model weight of evidence")
> g7 <- g6 + ylab(expression(paste("Alpha (", alpha, ")")))
> print(g7)
```

The graph is shown in Figure 8.1. The graph indicates that α is a nonlinear function of W_F. Larger values of α are associated with smaller values of W_F, and smaller values of α are associated with larger values of W_F. The monotonic relationship supports the general evidential interpretation of the LRT-p: smaller values indicate stronger evidence against the reduced model and for the full model.

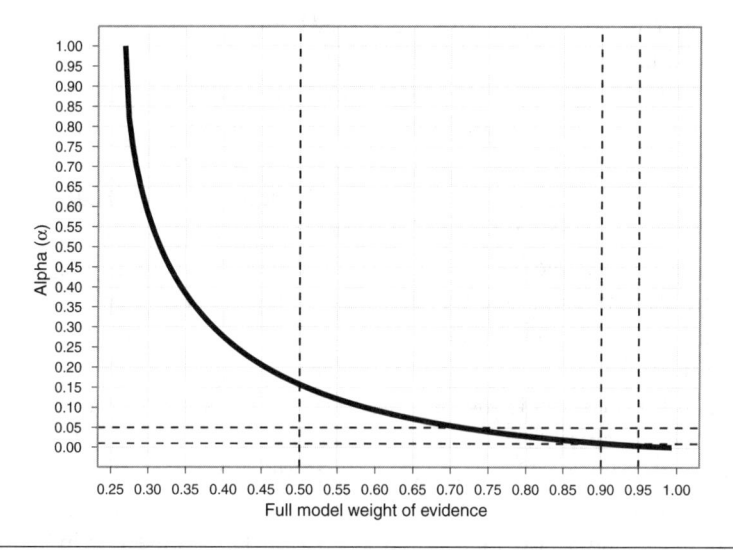

Figure 8.1 Alpha as a function of the full-model weight of evidence, $df = \Delta K = 1$.

Several things can be learned from Figure 8.1. First, depending on the values of the researcher, the traditional interpretation of the LRT-p cutoff in Table 8.1 may underrepresent the evidence for the full model. A vertical dotted line is drawn at $W_F = 0.5$, as this is the borderline for values that reflect superior fit of the reduced model ($W_F < 0.5$), and superior fit of the full model ($W_F > 0.5$). If the researcher wants to consider *any evidence* for the full model, then the cutoff of approximately LRT-$p < 0.15$ is used. This cutoff reflects less than "borderline" evidence in the traditional interpretation (see Table 8.1). However, when LRT-$p < 0.15$, the borderline is crossed into the territory where the weight of evidence is for the full model. In this respect, the traditional interpretation underrepresents the evidence for the full model.

Regarding the other descriptions in Table 8.1, there appears to be fairly good support based on Figure 8.1. From a predictive accuracy perspective, having $0.9 < W_F$ probably constitutes "strong" evidence for the full model, as there is at least a 0.9 probability that the full model is closer to the truth than the reduced model. The lowest horizontal dotted line is drawn at $\alpha = 0.01$, which approximately coincides with $W_F = 0.9$. It can also be seen that when α is slightly lower than 0.01, this coincides with $W_F \approx 0.95$. There appears to be grounds for dubbing $\alpha = 0.01$ as the threshold for "strong" evidence regarding the full model.

There also appears to be support for using $\alpha = 0.05$ as a "moderate" evidence threshold. The higher dotted horizontal line in Figure 8.1 marks $\alpha = 0.05$. It can be seen that the dotted line coincides with the solid line at $W_F \approx 0.7$. This means that $E_F = \frac{0.7}{0.3} = 2\frac{1}{3}$. It seems reasonable to label such values as "moderate", as there is evidence for the full model but certainly not substantial evidence.

Although threshold values are mentioned above, Figure 8.1 shows the absurdity of using a rigid cutoff for decisions regarding the reduced model and the full model. Consider the weight of evidence in the neighborhood where $\alpha = 0.05$ intersects with the curve. It can be shown by the methods used above that $W_F = 0.71$ is associated with LRT-$p = 0.051$, and $W_F = 0.72$ is associated with LRT-$p = 0.049$. Surely the weights constitute nearly the same amount of evidence for the full model. The first weight has an evidence ratio of 2.45, and the second has a ratio of 2.55. Yet the first result is judged as "not statistically significant," and the second is judged as "statistically significant," when using $\alpha = 0.05$ in a traditional manner. One could argue that the values in the range of, say, $W_F = (0.65, 0.75)$ each constitute "moderate" evidence for the full model, rendering dichotomous decisions within this range to be highly questionable.

Although the use of a dichotomous decision is discouraged, classifications of effect sizes can be helpful for judging results of statistical analysis. For this reason, the strength of evidence for LRT-p and W_F is presented in Table 8.2. The values in the table are based on a one-parameter difference between the reduced and full models, so that $df = \Delta K = 1$. Flexibility is advocated with the values in Table 8.2, and the reader is cautioned against using the endpoints of these categories as rigid rules for decisions. It is strongly urged that the term *statistically significant* not be used, as it seems inextricably linked to rigid cutoff values. Rather, the LRT-p can be described in terms of the strength of evidence shown in Table 8.2.

If any rigid cutoffs are to be used, it seems that $\alpha = 0.15$ is one good candidate, as this is the threshold for evidence against the full model ($W_F < 0.5$) and evidence for the full model ($W_F > 0.5$). Another good candidate is $\alpha = 0.01$, as this is the threshold for $W_F = 0.9$, representing "strong" evidence in terms of predictive accuracy. Which one to use depends on the values of the researcher. If the researcher values a "weak" test, then $\alpha = 0.15$ is used. If the researcher values a "strong" test, then $\alpha = 0.01$ is used.

8.3 Evaluation of Two Nested Models

Table 8.2 Ranges of LRT-p and strength of evidence based on $df = \Delta K = 1$.

LRT-p Range	W_F Range	Full Model Evidence
0.15 < LRT-p	W_F < 0.50	None[a]
0.10 < LRT–p ≤ 0.15	0.50 < W_F < 0.70	Weak
0.01 < LRT–p ≤ 0.10	0.70 ≤ W_F < 0.90	Moderate
0.001 < LRT–p ≤ 0.01	0.90 ≤ W_F < 0.99	Strong
LRT–p ≤ 0.001	0.99 < W_F	Very strong

a. There is evidence against the full model.

Again, the use of rigid cutoffs is discouraged, but it is acknowledged that their use is virtually ingrained in the minds of some researchers. Even when $W_F < 0.5$ and LRT-$p > 0.15$, the researcher is encouraged to report the results. It has been argued that the presentation of only "statistically significant" results has caused a strong publication bias in many fields, including the social and behavioral sciences (Hedges & Olkin, 1985, chap. 1). Treating LRT-p as an effect size measure can help alleviate the bias of publishing only results deemed arbitrarily significant. This can potentially go a long way in helping to provide crucial information relevant for meta-analysis (Anderson et al., 2000).

Table 8.2 is for the case when the full model has one more parameter than the reduced model. Table 8.2 is approximately valid when the df are a little larger, say, up to $df = 4$. However, when the df increase above this, LRT-p can no longer be judged with the strength of evidence descriptions listed in the table. The reason is that the sampling distribution of X^2 is no longer accurately represented by a χ^2 distribution (Pinheiro & Bates, 2000, chap. 2). The LRT-p tends to be too small in this situation, overestimating the strength of evidence.

As an illustration, consider the case in which the full and reduced models differ by eight parameters, so that $df = \Delta K = 8$. In the following syntax, X^2 values are generated in the interval $(0, 30)$, by an increment of 0.05. Then α and W_F are computed.

```
> mychi      <- data.frame(chisq = seq(from = 0, to = 30, by = 0.05))
> mychi$alpha <- pchisq(q = mychi$chisq, df = 8, lower.tail = FALSE)
> mychi$delta.aic <- mychi$chisq - 2 * 8
> mychi$w.r  <- exp(-0.5 * mychi$delta.aic) / (1 + exp(-0.5 * mychi$delta.aic))
> mychi$w.f  <- 1 - mychi$w.r
> head(mychi)
  chisq     alpha    delta.aic         w.r              w.f
1  0.00  1.0000000     -16.00    0.9996646       0.0003353501
2  0.05  1.0000000     -15.95    0.9996562       0.0003438366
3  0.10  0.9999997     -15.90    0.9996475       0.0003525378
4  0.15  0.9999988     -15.85    0.9996385       0.0003614591
5  0.20  0.9999962     -15.80    0.9996294       0.0003706061
6  0.25  0.9999908     -15.75    0.9996200       0.0003799845

> tail(mychi)
```

	chisq	alpha	delta.aic	w.r	w.f
596	29.75	0.0002339987	13.75	0.0010322310	0.9989678
597	29.80	0.0002292921	13.80	0.0010067708	0.9989932
598	29.85	0.0002246786	13.85	0.0009819380	0.9990181
599	29.90	0.0002201563	13.90	0.0009577171	0.9990423
600	29.95	0.0002157236	13.95	0.0009340930	0.9990659
601	30.00	0.0002113785	14.00	0.0009110512	0.9990889

Having generated the above data frame, `ggplot2` is used to create a graph of α as a function of the weight of evidence for the full model.

```
> g1 <- ggplot(mychi, aes(x = w.f, y = alpha)) + geom_line(lwd = 1.5) + theme_bw()
> g2 <- g1 + geom_hline(yintercept = c(0.01, 0.05), linetype = 2)
> g3 <- g2 + geom_vline(xintercept = c(0.5, 0.90, 0.95), linetype = 2)
> g4 <- g3 + scale_x_continuous(breaks = seq(0, 1, 0.1))
> g5 <- g4 + scale_y_continuous(breaks = seq(0, 1, 0.05))
> g6 <- g5 + xlab("Full model weight of evidence")
> g7 <- g6 + ylab(expression(paste("Alpha (", alpha, ")")))
> print(g7)
```

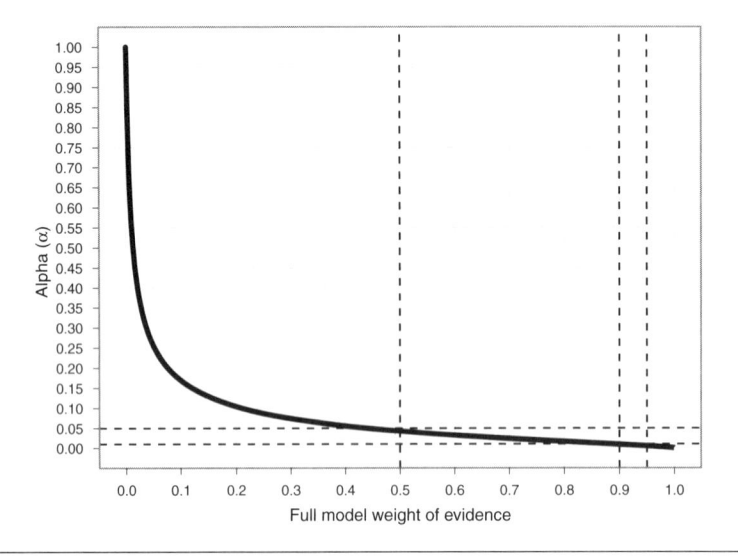

Figure 8.2 Alpha as a function of the full-model weight of evidence, $df = \Delta K = 8$.

The graph is shown in Figure 8.2. The values of α are associated with very different weights of evidence, as compared to the case of $df = 1$. Smaller values of α are required to maintain the same strength of evidence. The graph shows that the traditional $\alpha = 0.05$ cutoff is associated with $W_F < 0.5$, indicating there is more evidence *against* the full model than the reduced model. The phenomenon illustrated in Figure 8.2 has an interpretation in terms of traditional NHST: the Type I error rate of the LRT is inflated as the df increase (Pinheiro & Bates, 2000, chap. 2).

Because of the distortion in LRT-p caused by large df, the LRT is not recommended for testing a large number of fixed effects (i.e., more than four).

This should be kept in mind when formulating models to address the research questions of interest. One can always replace a large *df* comparison with a series of smaller ones. For example, suppose the goal is to investigate intercept and slope effects for ethnicity. One can perform a single $df = 2$ comparison of a reduced model with none of the effects, to a full model with both of the effects. An alternative is to perform two $df = 1$ comparisons, adding the ethnicity intercept effect, and then the slope effect. Recall that from a predictive accuracy perspective, multiple testing is not an issue (see above).

8.4 Approaches to Testing Multiple Models

Up to this point, the focus has been on the comparison of two models. Certain research questions imply that many models will be tested in the analysis. Such a case was encountered in the last chapter, where research questions concerned the effect of risk and ethnicity on reading achievement. Here the research questions are revisited, but this time the analysis is performed using the LRT.

In multimodel inference, there is an emphasis on formulating models prior to the analysis. The same emphasis applies to the LRT. Planning is an important guard against spurious results that arise from the use of data-driven methods. Similar to variable selection in traditional multiple regression, data-driven analysis with LMER can yield misleading results. If enough time is invested and a sufficient number of LRTs are performed, some type of pattern can always be found, even if the predictors are worthless (Miller, 2002, chap. 1). Because of this, data-driven approaches are sometimes pejoratively labeled as "data grubbing," "fishing for results," or "torturing the data until it confesses" (Chatfield, 1995; Lovell, 1983).

One of the best defenses against spurious results is to bring one's scientific knowledge to bear on the analysis. In terms of the LRT, this knowledge is used to suggest which models to evaluate and the order of the evaluation. The conforming of the results with expectations is valuable information for validating the theory in question. Contrariwise, if the results do not conform to expectations, this is valuable for invalidating, or at least questioning, the theory.

If the results do not comport with expectations, then further exploratory analysis may be used in the same analysis. There is nothing wrong with having both confirmatory and exploratory aspects of an analysis, as long as these are clearly demarcated in the reporting of the results. What seems to especially muddy the scientific waters is an exploratory analysis dressed up as a confirmatory analysis.

There are many ways of evaluating more than two models with the LRT. Two approaches are considered:

- Step-up
- Top-down

The step-up method begins with a simple model, and the LRT is used to see if the model can be made more complex by adding predictors or predictor effects. When the steps are data-driven, the method is known as *forward selection*.

The top-down method begins with the most complex model, and the LRT is used to see if the model can be simplified by omitting predictors or predictor effects. When the simplification process is data-driven, this is known as *backward elimination*.

In the examples below, a planned, theory-driven, step-up procedure is shown. Then a data-driven, backward elimination approach is illustrated.

Regardless of the approach, the guidelines of Section 7.6.1 should be followed when the LRT is used. In the step-up approach, this means that intercept effects are always examined prior to slope effects. Any slope effect should be examined with its associated intercept effect in the model, regardless of the statistical significance of the latter. This is to ensure the model provides proper predictions and is valid under arbitrary linear transformations, such as when a constant is added to the time predictor to anchor the intercept (Morrell, Pearson, & Brant, 1997).

It is emphasized that only tests of the highest order terms are invariant under linear transformations. The *p*-values of the lower order terms will change under arbitrary linear transformations, and one can induce almost any values by judicious choice of the transformations. This property means that lower order terms and their *p*-values only have a tentative status, and caution needs to be exercised if they are to be interpreted when higher order terms are in the model (Griepentrog, Ryan, & Smith, 1982; Magee, 1998).

In the analysis below, the same principle is followed as in the AIC multimodel analysis of the last chapter. All the models considered vary only in their static predictors (or static predictor effects). It is crucial when using the LRT that the models differ only in the number of fixed effects. Particular problems of interpretation and statistical theory arise when fixed effects and random effects are simultaneously tested with the LRT (see Chapters 7 and 10).

In the general regression context, the LRT is frequently used to select a single model, with specific inferences being based on the best-fitting model. Detailed results, such as parameter estimates, are often presented only for the best model. As in multimodel analysis, it is advantageous to present limited information on all the model evaluation steps, so that some sense of model evaluation uncertainty can be conveyed.

8.5 Step-Up Approach

The step-up approach has an intuitive appeal, as it is common in regression analysis to estimate a model, and then test to see if additional predictors are needed. In the example presented here, the models are formulated prior to the analysis. The order of testing is such that simpler models are tested before more complex models. In addition, focus is on models that differ by a single parameter, so that $df = \Delta K = 1$.

8.5 Step-Up Approach

The strategy in the step-up approach is to accept the full model if there is sufficient evidence for it, based on either LRT-p or W_F, according to Table 8.2. By "accept," it is meant that the full model is considered the best approximating model of the two considered. No statistical model is ever assumed to be true. If there is not sufficient evidence for the full model, then the reduced model is accepted. Since the models and order of testing are planned, there is no adherence to the common data-driven practice of stopping upon the first acceptance of a reduced model.

The criterion for acceptance should be determined prior to the procedure. That is, the researcher should have a sense of what strength of evidence will be sufficient to accept the full model. At the very least, this will be an LRT-p less than 0.15, with an associated weight of evidence greater than 0.5. At the other extreme, one might accept a full model only if there is "strong" or "very strong" evidence for it. In this case, an LRT-p less than 0.01 is used. The strategy for the example will be the less stringent approach, accepting the full model when LRT-$p < 0.15$. For each analysis, the size of the effect will be noted, based on the ranges listed in Table 8.2.

When a full model is accepted, it then turns into the reduced model for the next comparison. The most complex model that is accepted is usually the model for which additional details are reported. The details include a table of the fixed effects estimates, with SEs, t-values, and estimates of the variance components.

Recall the analysis from Chapter 7 involving risk, ethnicity, and reading achievement. Suppose an analysis is planned to address the two research questions previously discussed. Recall the first question is: to what extent does risk status act as a proxy for ethnicity? The second question is the following: do achievement gaps based on risk and/or ethnicity persist over time?

To address the above questions in a step-up fashion, a graded series of models is formulated. Rather than list the details of the models, the predictors are shown below. Each model includes two random effects. A commentary on each model follows the list.

0. grade5,
1. grade5, eth2;
2. grade5, eth2, risk2;
3. grade5, eth2, risk2, (grade5 · eth2);
4. grade5, eth2, risk2, (grade5 · eth2), (grade5 · risk2).

Model 0 is not of substantive interest in this case, but it is included to test Model 1. An alternative is to omit Model 0 and begin with the comparison of Models 1 and 2.

Model 1 includes the ethnicity intercept effect, and Model 2 adds the risk intercept effect. The comparison of Model 1 and Model 2 can be used to investigate the proxy question for intercept effects. If the intercept effect of risk is redundant with ethnicity, then the difference between 1 and 2 is expected to not be great. On the other hand, if the predictors are not completely redundant, then there might be sufficient separation between the models to justify the inclusion of risk.

Model 3 adds the ethnic slope effect, and Model 4 adds the risk slope effect. The comparison of Model 3 and Model 2 addresses the question of the persistence of an ethnic reading achievement gap over time. The comparison of Model 3 and Model 4 addresses whether risk is needed in addition to (or in place of) ethnicity, to account for the achievement gap.

Consistent with the guidelines in Section 7.6.1, Model 4 and Model 5 will be evaluated regardless of whether the lower order full models are accepted. This is to meet the requirement that intercept effects be in the model when slope effects are evaluated. There is some debate as to whether Model 2 or Model 3 should be the reduced model for evaluating Model 4. If the ethnicity-by-grade interaction has a very small effect size, then perhaps Model 2 should be considered the reduced model. We do not want to change our order of testing, lest the analysis deteriorate into a data-driven exercise. Therefore, the models will be evaluated in the order shown above. Consider the following.

```
> ## Estimate models.
> model.0 <- lmer(read ~ grade5 + (grade5 | subid), MPLS.LS, REML = FALSE)
> model.1 <- lmer(read ~ grade5 + eth2 + (grade5 | subid), MPLS.LS, REML = FALSE)
> model.2 <- lmer(read ~ grade5 + eth2 + risk2 + (grade5 | subid),MPLS.LS,REML= FALSE)
> model.3 <- lmer(read ~ grade5 + eth2 + risk2 + grade5 * eth2 +
+                  (grade5 | subid), MPLS.LS, REML = FALSE)
> model.4 <- lmer(read ~ grade5 + eth2 + risk2 + grade5 * eth2 + grade5 * risk2 +
+                  (grade5 | subid), MPLS.LS, REML = FALSE)
> ## LRT.
> myout <- anova(model.0, model.1, model.2, model.3, model.4)
> ## Effect size.
> myout$delta.aic <- c(myout$Chisq - 2 * myout$"Chi Df")
> myout$weight.f <- (1 - exp(-0.5 * myout$delta.aic)/(1 + exp(-0.5*myout$delta.aic)))
> myout$eratio.f <- myout$weight.f / (1 - myout$weight.f)
> ## Print.
> myout[ ,-c(3:4)]
```

	Df	AIC	Chisq	Chi Df	Pr(>Chisq)	delta.aic	weight.f	eratio.f
model.0	6	580.96						
model.1	7	579.21	3.7512	1	0.05277	1.7512	0.70591	2.40
model.2	8	565.88	15.3260	1	0.00009	13.3260	0.99872	782.91
model.3	9	566.83	1.0522	1	0.30500	-0.9478	0.38369	0.62
model.4	10	568.82	0.0072	1	0.93251	-1.9928	0.26965	0.37

In the output, the Df column shows the number of estimated parameters for each model. It can be seen that each more complex model adds an additional fixed effect. The LRT-p is in the Pr(>Chisq) column, and the last three columns contain ΔAIC, W_F, and the full-model evidence ratio (how many times better the full model fits over the reduced model). It is important to keep in mind that the values in the output are only relevant for evaluating a particular pair of nested models. The weight of evidence, for example, cannot be used to rank-order all the models, as was performed in Chapter 7. The weight of evidence only can be used to rank-order the two models in the pair.

8.5 Step-Up Approach

Based on Table 8.2, the evidence for Model 1 is "moderate" because LRT-$p = 0.0528$ and $W_F = 0.71$. Model 1 is accepted rather than Model 0, and the next comparison is considered. Model 1 is now the reduced model, and Model 2 is the full model.

For the comparison of Model 1 and Model 2, LRT-$p < 0.001$ and $W_F < 0.99$. This is a "very strong" effect, and the full Model 2 is accepted. Model 2 is now the reduced model for the next comparison.

For the comparison of Model 2 and Model 3, LRT-$p = 0.305$ and $W_F = 0.38$. Since the weight of evidence is less than 0.5, there is more evidence for Model 2 (the reduced model) than for Model 3 (the full model). Model 2 is accepted.

The last comparison sets Model 3 as the reduced model, which may seem in conflict with the previous result. As mentioned, there may be debate as to whether Model 3 or Model 2 is the proper reduced model for comparison with Model 4. We do not want to alter the testing strategy, so the last line of the results is interpreted, and there is relatively strong evidence *against* the full model (against Model 4).

Based on the step-up procedure, Model 2 is selected, as it is the most complex full model accepted. It is recommended that the output for all the model comparisons be presented, so that a consumer of the results can get a sense of the model evaluation uncertainty. In this case, the ethnic intercept effect is not nearly as strong as the risk intercept effect. There is very strong evidence that the risk intercept effect needs to be added when ethnicity is already in the model. There is only moderate evidence that ethnicity needs to be added when no static predictors are in the model.

It is useful to print additional details of Model 2. Printing includes the parameter estimates, the estimated SEs, and the t-values for the fixed effects. These are all accessible from the fitted model object.

```
> print(model.2, cor = FALSE)
Linear mixed model fit by maximum likelihood
Formula: read ~ grade5 + eth2 + risk2 + (grade5 | subid)
   Data: MPLS.LS
   AIC   BIC  logLik deviance REMLdev
  565.9 584.9 -274.9   549.9   534.6
Random effects:
 Groups   Name        Variance Std.Dev. Corr
 subid    (Intercept) 185.254  13.6108
          grade5        6.749   2.5979  -0.641
 Residual              18.460   4.2965
Number of obs: 80, groups: subid, 22

Fixed effects:
            Estimate Std. Error t value
(Intercept) 216.9224     5.6542   38.36
grade5        4.7791     0.7332    6.52
eth2W        -0.3591     5.7637   -0.06
risk2DADV   -26.7628     5.6962   -4.70
```

From the output it can be seen that the t-value for the ethnic intercept effect is quite small in absolute value, $t = -0.06$. In contrast, the absolute value for risk is relatively large, $t = -4.7$. The risk intercept effect is much stronger than the ethnicity effect when both predictors are in the model. In fact, the ethnicity effect appears negligible when risk is in the model.

8.5.1 ORDER OF TESTING

The order of testing is crucial, as different results can be obtained. Consider what happens when risk is entered before ethnicity.

```
> ## Estimate models.
> model.0 <- lmer(read ~ grade5 + (grade5 | subid), MPLS.LS, REML = FALSE)
> model.1 <- lmer(read ~ grade5 + risk2 + (grade5 | subid), MPLS.LS, REML = FALSE)
> model.2 <- lmer(read ~ grade5 + risk2 + eth2 + (grade5 | subid), MPLS.LS, REML = FALSE)
> model.3 <- lmer(read ~ grade5 + risk2 + eth2 + grade5 * eth2 +
+    (grade5 | subid), MPLS.LS, REML = FALSE)
> model.4 <- lmer(read ~ grade5 + risk2 + eth2 + grade5 * risk2 + grade5 * eth2 +
+    (grade5 | subid), MPLS.LS, REML = FALSE)
> ## LRT.
> myout <- anova(model.0, model.1, model.2, model.3, model.4)
> ## Effect size.
> myout$delta.aic <- c(myout$Chisq - 2 * myout$"Chi Df")
> myout$weight.f <- (1 - exp(-0.5 * myout$delta.aic) / (1 + exp(-0.5 * myout$delta.aic)))
> myout$eratio.f <- myout$weight.f / (1 - myout$weight.f)
> myout[ ,-c(3:4)]
```

	Df	AIC	Chisq	Chi Df	Pr(>Chisq)	delta.aic	weight.f	eratio.f
model.0	6	580.96						
model.1	7	563.89	19.0735	1	0.00001	17.0735	0.99980	5098.7
model.2	8	565.88	0.0037	1	0.95133	-1.9963	0.26931	0.4
model.3	9	566.83	1.0522	1	0.30500	-0.9478	0.38369	0.6
model.4	10	568.82	0.0072	1	0.93251	-1.9928	0.26965	0.4

As seen in the output, Model 1 with the risk variable has a very strong effect. Model 2 with ethnicity has evidence *against it*, as do the remaining models. Model 1 is accepted in this analysis, which is contrary to Model 2 selected in the last section. The reason for the disagreement is the order of testing. In the previous analysis, ethnicity was added prior to risk, and there was no a priori plan to *remove* ethnicity for later models. The fitted model with both ethnicity and risk in the first analysis (Model 2) reveals a negligible effect, but this effect is carried along in the additional model comparisons. In the second analysis, when risk is considered first, ethnicity is not added.

The ability to reconcile results of different testing order can vary. The researcher needs to consider what order of testing will be most useful for addressing the research question at hand. There is a danger in trying different orders of testing, as a preplanned analysis can quickly deteriorate into a data-grubbing exercise.

One of the strengths of multimodel inference is that testing order is irrelevant. Models can be compared directly, and their evidence is not obscured by a compulsory two-at-a-time evaluation.

8.5.2 COMMENTS ON THE STEP-UP APPROACH

Some qualifications should be mentioned regarding the step-up approach. First, in the conception presented here, the initial analysis step involves Model 0, which is not a model motivated by the research questions. Model 0 is invented so that the LRT can be used to evaluate the ethnicity intercept effect. It is desirable to only consider models that are scientifically interesting and justifiable. To address this, the evaluation should probably begin with Model 1 versus Model 2. On the other hand, if the evaluation of Model 1 is crucial, Model 0 must be included.

Second, in the step-up approach, the intercept effects are evaluated prior to the slope effects. Another way of saying this is that the main effects are evaluated prior to adding the interactions. Caution must be exercised when interpreting the results, as the main effects will change when the interactions are in the model. A previously important main effect can be rendered as negligible when an interaction is added to the model.

Recall that when slope effects are not in the model, the intercept effects need not be qualified, as the change curves of the groups are parallel. When slope effects are added, the intercept effects must be qualified, as the change curves of the groups are not parallel. By "qualified," it is meant that the magnitude of the group intercept difference varies based on the time (or grade) at which the intercept is anchored. In the step-up approach, the intercept effects are first tested as unqualified and then as qualified. In the case where the slope effects do belong in the model, this order of testing is misleading. When there are genuine slope effects, the intercept effects are qualified, and they should not be tested as unqualified.

Third, a planned analysis was presented, but the step-up approach can be used in a data-driven fashion. In forward selection, the first step is to estimate the effect of each static predictor in isolation. A model with no predictors is the reduced model, and the model with the single static predictor with the largest effect is the full model. If the reduced model is accepted, the evaluation stops. If the full model is selected, it becomes the reduced model for the next step. The next step compares the reduced model with a full model that adds the predictor with the next largest effect. The process proceeds until a reduced model is accepted. Forward selection is labor intensive, as an individual main effect model must be fit for each static predictor.

8.6 Top-Down Approach

In contrast to step-up, top-down begins with the most complex model. The LRT is used to potentially remove predictors, or predictor effects, from the model. At the first step, the most complex model is the full model, and the reduced model is the one omitting the fixed effect(s). If the LRT favors the reduced model, it is accepted, and it becomes the full model in a subsequent comparison. The process ends when no additional predictors can be removed. At that point, the last acceptable full model is selected.

The term top-down is used when the removal of predictors is theory-driven and planned. In this case, the most complex model is specified by the researcher, and it represents the highest level of complexity the researcher is willing to entertain. The term backward elimination is used when the removal is data-driven. The most complex model for backward elimination is selected by the researcher, or it is the model with all the possible effects. In the context of the example, the model with all the possible effects is the one with all the intercept and slopes effects of all the static predictors. With backward elimination, the number of steps is not planned. Rather, the results of the LRT at any one step are used to determine if one goes on to an additional step.

An advantage of the top-down approach is that interactions are always tested before main effects. This is consistent with traditional analysis, such as ANOVA, where the interaction is tested first and only omitted if it has a negligible effect (Harrell, 2001, chap. 2). In terms of LMER models, using the top-down procedure means that a slope effect is tested prior to an intercept effect. Like the illustration in the last section, the order of exclusion of the predictors is important, and it can result in different models being selected.

To provide another perspective on LMER analysis, backward elimination is illustrated in this section. However, data-driven approaches to LMER analysis are not generally recommended.

In the first step of backward elimination, the most complex model is fit. The t-values of the predictors are inspected to identify a fixed effect candidate, or multiple candidates, for removal from the model. *Consistent with the guidelines of Section 7.6.1, the candidates for removal must be only from among the highest order terms.* This means only the slope effects are considered for initial exclusion. The fixed effect with the smallest slope effect t-value is the prime candidate for exclusion, but fixed effects with t-values that are just a bit larger might also be considered for elimination.

As an illustration of backward elimination, suppose the most complex model the researcher is willing to consider is the model with intercept and slope effects for ethnicity and risk. Consider estimation of the model and inspection of the fixed effects table.

```
> model.1 <- lmer(read ~ grade5 * risk2 + grade5 * eth2 + (grade5 | subid),
+          MPLS.LS, REML = FALSE)
> round(summary(model.1)@coefs, 2)
```

	Estimate	Std. Error	t value
(Intercept)	214.99	6.70	32.09
grade5	5.52	1.57	3.52
risk2DADV	-26.22	7.11	-3.69
eth2W	3.63	7.20	0.50
grade5:risk2DADV	-0.14	1.66	-0.09
grade5:eth2W	-1.59	1.67	-0.95

8.6 Top-Down Approach

In the output, it can be seen that the smallest absolute t-value is that of the risk-by-grade interaction, `grade:risk2DADV`. This is the prime candidate for elimination. The first LRT comparison, then, has Model 1 as the full model. The reduced model, which is called Model 2, excludes the risk-by-grade interaction.

```
> model.2 <- lmer(read ~ grade5 + risk2 + grade5 * eth2 + (grade5 | subid),
+                 MPLS.LS, REML = FALSE)
> myout <- anova(model.2, model.1)
> myout$delta.aic <- c(myout$Chisq - 2 * myout$"Chi Df")
> myout$weight.f <- (1 - exp(-0.5 * myout$delta.aic)/(1 + exp(-0.5*myout$delta.aic)))
> myout$eratio.f <- myout$weight.f / (1 - myout$weight.f)
> myout[ ,-c(3:4)]
```

```
        Df    AIC    Chisq Chi Df Pr(>Chisq)  delta.aic  weight.f  eratio.f
model.2  9  566.83
model.1 10  568.82  0.0072      1    0.93251    -1.9928   0.26965    0.3692
```

The output shows there is relatively strong evidence *against the full model and for the reduced model*. To consider just one measure, $W_F = 0.27$, which is relatively small. Therefore, the reduced model is accepted and becomes the *full model* for the next comparison. The `grade:risk2DADV` interaction is removed from further consideration.

Since there is only one remaining interaction (ethnicity by grade), this is automatically the candidate for exclusion. The full model is Model 2. The reduced model, which is called Model 3, excludes `grade:ethW`.

```
> model.3 <- lmer(read ~ grade5 + risk2 + eth2 + (grade5 | subid), MPLS.LS, REML = FALSE)
> myout <- anova(model.3, model.2)
> myout$delta.aic <- c(myout$Chisq - 2 * myout$"Chi Df")
> myout$weight.f <- (1 - exp(-0.5 * myout$delta.aic) / (1 + exp(-0.5 * myout$delta.aic)))
> myout$eratio.f <- myout$weight.f / (1 - myout$weight.f)
> myout[ ,-c(3:4)]
```

```
        Df    AIC    Chisq Chi Df Pr(>Chisq)  delta.aic  weight.f  eratio.f
model.3  8  565.88
model.2  9  566.83  1.0522      1      0.305    -0.9478   0.38369   0.62257
```

As seen in the output, there is evidence against the full model and for the reduced model. Model 3 is accepted, and both the slope effects are excluded (the `grade:ethW` interaction is no longer considered).

To determine the next reduced model, t-values of the main effects of Model 3 are examined.

```
> round(summary(model.3)@coefs, 2)
```

	Estimate	Std. Error	t value
(Intercept)	216.92	5.65	38.36
grade5	4.78	0.73	6.52
risk2DADV	-26.76	5.70	-4.70
eth2W	-0.36	5.76	-0.06

The output shows that ethnicity has the smallest t-value and thus is the prime candidate for exclusion. It follows that the full model includes ethnicity (Model 3). The reduced model, which is called Model 4, excludes ethnicity.

```
> model.4 <- lmer(read ~ grade5 + risk2 + (grade5 | subid), MPLS.LS, REML = FALSE)
> myout <- anova(model.4, model.3)
> myout$delta.aic <- c(myout$Chisq - 2 * myout$"Chi Df")
> myout$weight.f <- (1 - exp(-0.5 * myout$delta.aic)/(1 + exp(-0.5*myout$delta.aic)))
> myout$eratio.f <- myout$weight.f / (1 - myout$weight.f)
> myout[ ,-c(3:4)]
```

	Df	AIC	Chisq	Chi Df	Pr(>Chisq)	delta.aic	weight.f	eratio.f
model.4	7	563.89						
model.3	8	565.88	0.0037	1	0.95133	-1.9963	0.26931	0.36857

The results indicate there is evidence against the full model (Model 3) and for the reduced model (Model 4). The reduced model omitting ethnicity is accepted.

As a final step, one can investigate the evidence for removing risk from the model. The full model includes risk (Model 4), and the reduced model excludes it. The reduced model, which is called Model 5, has no static predictors and is equivalent to Model 0 of the last section.

```
> model.5 <- lmer(read ~ grade5 + (grade5 | subid), MPLS.LS, REML = FALSE)
> myout <- anova(model.5, model.4)
> myout$delta.aic <- c(myout$Chisq - 2 * myout$"Chi Df")
> myout$weight.f <- (1 - exp(-0.5 * myout$delta.aic)/(1 + exp(-0.5*myout$delta.aic)))
> myout$eratio.f <- myout$weight.f / (1 - myout$weight.f)
> myout[ ,-c(3:4)]
```

	Df	AIC	Chisq	Chi Df	Pr(>Chisq)	delta.aic	weight.f	eratio.f
model.5	6	580.96						
model.4	7	563.89	19.073	1	1.2578e-05	17.073	0.9998	5098.7

As can be seen above, there is very strong evidence for the full model containing risk (Model 4). Therefore, Model 4 is selected as the final step of the analysis.

8.7 Comparison of Approaches

Which approach is better, step-up or top-down? Conceptually, there appears to be merit in the step-up procedure because it is common to "build" models in regression analysis, going from the simpler to the more complex. However, the top-down procedure is recommended because it provides the correct order of testing—interactions are evaluated before the main effects.

A drawback of the top-down procedure is that it is not always evident what constitutes the most complex model. Furthermore, if there are many static

8.7 Comparison of Approaches

predictors, the most complex model can be very complex and difficult to estimate. In such cases, a step-up approach might be appropriate.

What about the approaches of this chapter and the multimodel approach? Consulting Chapter 7, it can be seen that the AIC and the LRT backward selection procedure both identified the best-fitting model as the one with the risk intercept effect. The LRT step-up procedure identified the model that also included the ethnicity intercept effect. The discrepancy highlights that the AIC and the LRT might not always agree regarding the best-fitting model, depending on the criteria used to accept or reject models. As seen earlier in the chapter, comparing two models based on the AIC is approximately the same as using the LRT with a relatively high α-level (Greven & Kneib, 2010). The same result approximately holds for the AICc, especially if the sample size is large. Using two different methods that, in essence, have two different magnitudes of statistical power can lead to divergence in model selection.

The multimodel approach and the LRT are distinctive in how research questions are addressed. The AIC provides a logical framework for interpreting model fit with sample data, in terms of candidates for the best approximating model. This concept is not a part of the formal theory of NHST, although applied researchers might act as if this were the case (Cox, 1995). The strategy of selecting the best approximating model was adopted in this chapter, as LRT-p values were calibrated using the AIC. The limitation is that only nested models were considered, one pair at a time. Following Burnham and Anderson (Anderson, 2008; Burnham & Anderson, 2002, 2004), a main point is that the multimodel approach using information criteria is a more comprehensive means of evaluating research problems than NHST. Model comparisons are not limited to nested models, and several models can be evaluated simultaneously. It is mainly for this reason that the multimodel approach is recommended.

The multimodel approach stresses a careful preanalysis consideration of theory, extent literature, researcher expertise, and common sense. This information is distilled down to a set of several LMER models that are directly evaluated. The same preanalysis considerations can certainly be made with NHST using the LRT, but it seems less likely that predata models can be evaluated directly. The AIC (or AICc) provides a means of attaching a number to a fitted model, indicating its relative fit. This one-to-one mapping means that the models can be rank-ordered, and the distances between them meaningfully expressed in terms of probabilities or odds.

With LRT/NHST strategies, there is a lower chance of a direct one-to-one mapping of predata models and effect size, making evaluation of a set more vague. The requirement of nesting makes it difficult to evaluate nonnested models, for example, Model 1 and Model 2 in Table 7.6. One could use the LRT to compare Model 1 to a model without any static predictors, do the same for Model 2, and then compare the p-values. This focuses on the p-value as statistical evidence rather than as a decision device, similar to the multimodel approach. However, it seems that one would be better off using the AIC in a direct manner.

For the MPLS data, the top-down method selected the same best-fitting model as the AIC, but the status of the other models is unclear. Were any of the rejected models approximately as good fitting as the selected model? This question appears difficult to answer using LRT alone. Such information is important in forming a complete scientific picture. Empirical research will inevitably involve some situations in which the evidence is equivocal (Royall, 1996). NHST strategies seem to hide this fact, as it is difficult to provide an overall indication of effect size for all the models in a set. Models declared as "not statistically significant" are often relegated to the dustbin of the analysis history, and those models are often treated as if they have little or no scientific information to offer. This is probably fine to do in the case where a single model is clearly outstanding to the rest. However, with data arising from observational studies, there is a proneness to having a relatively subtle gradation of models. Ignoring the gradation prevents a complete picture from being painted. To reiterate an earlier point, it seems to be a good scientific strategy to rank-order the models under consideration, and provide some indication as to the distance between the best-fitting model and the rest.

For researchers ensconced in the world of NHST, the multimodel approach using the AIC might suggest a paradigm shift, requiring a different way of thinking. The AIC does not lend itself to automatic decision-making mechanisms about models. It is true that the best-fitting model of a set can be unequivocally identified with the AIC. However, the determination of what constitutes additional plausible models requires judgment on the part of the researcher and is open to interpretation. It is argued that such judgments and interpretations are no different than similar ones made in LRT/NHST strategies, and they are part and parcel of sound data analysis.

8.8 Parametric Bootstrap*

The LRT-p can be inaccurate when the sample size is small and/or when the number of parameters to be estimated is large (Pinheiro & Bates, 2000, chap. 2). For large df, Figure 8.2 shows that the inaccuracy is such that the LRT-p tends to overestimate the strength of evidence. For instance, given a sufficiently large df, LRT-$p = 0.04$ can actually represent evidence *against* the full model. Yet, using a traditional $\alpha = 0.05$ cutoff, the full model would be accepted (the null model would be rejected).

The LRT is based on large-sample properties that can only be expected to approximately hold, at best, for small samples (Cox, 1995). In such cases, the sampling distribution of X^2 is not χ^2, or not well approximated by it. To improve the accuracy of the LRT-p, the parametric bootstrap can be used. The parametric bootstrap provides an approximate sampling distribution of X^2, based on models that are fit to simulated data. The observed value of X^2 from the LRT is located in the bootstrap distribution, and the proportion in the upper tail is taken as the bootstrap LRT-p value.

8.8 Parametric Bootstrap*

The basics of the parametric bootstrap are presented in Section 7.8. To provide a concrete example for the LRT, consider the case of the parametric bootstrap in the first step of the step-up problem in Section 8.5. For the LRT, the reduced model has no static predictor effects (Model 0), and the full model includes an ethnicity intercept effect (Model 1). The goal is to estimate the sampling distribution of X^2 under the reduced model (Model 0), and use it to evaluate the X^2 statistic that is computed on the data with the reduced and full models.

Suppose a bootstrap sample is generated using simulate(), as described in Section 7.8. The bootstrap sample is generated under the reduced model (Model 0). For the bootstrap sample, both the reduced and the full models (Model 1) are fit. Then X_b^{*2} is computed, which is the bth bootstrap chi-squared test statistic under the reduced model ($b = 1, \ldots, B$). The value of X_b^{*2} is recorded, and the process is repeated a large number of times (e.g., $B = 9999$). When the simulation is terminated, the observed statistic, X^2, is located in the X_b^{*2} distribution, and the upper tail proportion is the bootstrapped p-value.

Before examining the function used to carry out the parametric bootstrap, consider a single bootstrap sample. In the syntax below, simulate() is used to generate a sample based on the fitted reduced model object. Then refit() is used to fit the full and reduced models based on the simulated data. The X_b^{*2} is computed with deviance().

```
> ## Estimate models.
> model.0 <- lmer(read ~ grade5 + (grade5 | subid), MPLS.LS, REML = FALSE)
> model.1 <- lmer(read ~ grade5 + eth2 + (grade5|subid), MPLS.LS, REML = FALSE)
> ## Simulate bootstrap sample data.
> simDV <- simulate(model.0)
> ## Fit full and reduced models.
> b.full <- refit(model.1, simDV[ ,1])
> b.reduced <- refit(model.0, simDV[ ,1])
> ## Compute bootstrap chi-squared statistic.
> chisq.star <- deviance(b.reduced) - deviance(b.full)
> chisq.star
```

```
[1] 3.411622
```

chisq.star is the bootstrapped chi-squared statistic obtained under the reduced model or, equivalently, under the null hypothesis. In this case, $X_1^{*2} = 3.41$.

In the syntax above, a single bootstrap chi-squared statistic was computed, but many replications are required to generate an accurate bootstrap distribution. The strategy for producing many replications is to create a function based on the above syntax, and use rdply() to execute the syntax a large number of times. To make the function general, the variables r and f are taken to stand for the reduced model and full model objects actually fit to the observed data. In the example above, r = model.0, and f = model.1.

The simulation function is named boot.fun(), and its syntax is similar to what appears above, only the fitted model objects are replaced with the variables, r and f. The return() function is used so that rdply() knows what to store in the output data frame. Consider the syntax below.

```
> boot.func  <-  function(r, f){              # r (reduced), f (full).
+    simDV     <-  simulate(r)
+    b.full    <-  refit(f, simDV[ ,1])
+    b.reduced <-  refit(r, simDV[ ,1])
+    chisq.star <- deviance(b.reduced) - deviance(b.full)
+    return(chisq.star)}
```

When the syntax is executed, no output appears in the R console window, as the function has only been defined for future use. Now rdply() can be used to execute boot.func() a large number of times.

The rdply() function requires the number of replications be supplied (.n=), the name of the function, and the arguments for r and f (.expr=). An optional progress bar can be set with .progress="text". In this illustration, $B = 999$ replications are performed, and the process is timed with system.time(). The set.seed() function is used so that the reader can replicate the results. The variables, r and f, are set to the appropriate fitted model objects.

```
> set.seed(101)                          # Allows reader to replicate results.
> system.time(store.chisq.star  <-  rdply(.n = 999,
+                                 .expr = boot.func(r = model.0, f = model.1),
+                                 .progress = "text"))
```

The progress is monitored in the console window. When the process is finished, the elapsed time is shown in seconds. In replicating this result, the reader might find there are warnings regarding convergence failure printed to the console window. This is due to the small sample size. Because this is a toy example, the warnings are ignored. If one is using a large sample size and encounters such warnings, simplification of the models under consideration might be warranted.

The X_b^{*2} are stored in store.chisq.star, and the top few rows are printed using the head() function.

```
> head(store.chisq.star)
```

	.n	V1
1	1	0.07636475
2	2	1.34104400
3	3	1.07151693
4	4	1.83267776
5	5	0.52259862
6	6	0.25292024

8.8 Parametric Bootstrap*

Having simulated many X_b^{*2} values, the empirical distribution can be used as a reference for the observed X^2 value. In the syntax below, the observed X^2 is computed based on the original fitted model objects, `model.0` and `model.1`. Then there is a determination of how many X_b^{*2} values are greater than the observed X^2, the proportion of which yields a bootstrap LRT-*p*. Consider the following.

```
> ## Compute observed chi-squared.
> chisq.obs ← deviance(model.0) - deviance(model.1)
> round(as.numeric(chisq.obs), 2)
```

```
[1] 3.75
```

```
> ## Compute bootstrap LRT-p.
> mean(store.chisq.star[ ,2] > chisq.obs)
```

```
[1] 0.08108108
```

The `mean()` function provides a pithy way of computing the proportion of cases above the observed X^2 value. The estimated LRT-*p* value is relatively large, which is in line with the LRT-*p* obtained with `anova()` in Section 8.5. For this example, it does not much matter if the analytic or bootstrap *p*-value is used.

In general, when a large analytic *p*-value is observed, the parametric bootstrap *p*-value will also tend to be large. For such occasions, the extra computing time might not be worth the trouble.

8.8.1 COMMENTS ON THE PARAMETRIC BOOTSTRAP*

Although the bootstrap is by no means a panacea for distortions caused by small sample size and/or high *df*, there is evidence it can yield greater accuracy than the traditional test statistics in the broad context of regression analysis (see, e.g., Godfrey, 1998). Nevertheless, there are some important issues to be considered in the use of the bootstrap.

Perhaps the most important issue is that the parametric bootstrap demands more time and devotion on the part of the researcher than the LRT. As mentioned at the end of Section 7.8, the parametric bootstrap can take a considerable time to run. The $B = 999$ replications of the example above took approximately 10 minutes on a modern PC. To avoid bias, a larger number of replications should be used, such as $B = 9999$.

The time issue is compounded by the fact that the parametric bootstrap must be used for each comparison in the data analysis. This means that `rdply()` might need to be used multiple times in a step-up or top-down approach. This is in contrast to the bootstrap used in multimodel analysis, which need only be run one time.

8.9 Planning a Study*

This second optional section is concerned with planning a study. One of the crucial aspects of planning a study is determining the number of subjects, or the *required sample size*. The required sample size is sometimes decided upon by what is convenient, or by what resources are available to the researcher. In other cases, the required sample size is identified based on the future statistical analysis—the analysis to be performed when all the measurements are collected. Funding agencies, for example, want to know if the requested amount of resources is sufficient to yield statistically reliable results.

Simulation with the parametric bootstrap can be used to estimate the required sample size based on statistical criteria. The key concept is *statistical power*, which is the ability to correctly reject H_0 for a fixed level of α. In the context of the LRT, this is the ability to correctly accept the full model for a fixed level of α.

The method discussed here applies only to the case in which the researcher has pilot data. The pilot data are assumed to be a random sample from the same population as the future subjects. It is further assumed the future data will have roughly the same number of time points, roughly the same pattern of missing data, and roughly the same static predictor scores. The final requirement is the specification of at least one set of reduced and full models that will be compared with the future data. If one plans to compare a reduced model with an ethnicity intercept effect to a full model with ethnicity intercept and slope effects, then these two models constitute the set for the parametric bootstrap. There can be multiple model comparisons, and each should address the major research questions of the proposed study.

The idea behind the parametric bootstrap for estimating required sample size is to simulate data *according to the full model*. This is contrary to the last section, in which the object was to simulate data under the reduced model. For each simulated data set under the full model, the reduced and full models are fit, and $X_b^{\star 2}$ is computed. For each $X_b^{\star 2}$, its associated bootstrap LRT-p is computed, denoted as $p_b^{\star}$. Based on the criteria of Table 8.2, each $p_b^{\star}$ is evaluated to see if the full model is favored or accepted. The proportion of times the full model is accepted is taken as the estimated power.

The above process is first performed using the sample size of the pilot data. Then it is repeated for larger sample sizes.[1] As the sample size increases, the proportion of full-model acceptance will increase. When an arbitrary threshold of power is reached, the associated sample size is taken as the estimated required sample size for fixed α. The arbitrary but traditional threshold for acceptable power in the behavioral sciences is 0.80 (Cohen, 1988, chap. 1).

To keep things manageable, the sample size will be increased by the size of the original sample. As an example, the MPLS data set is treated as pilot

---

[1] Implicit here is the belief the pilot sample size will yield low power. If it does not, there may be no reason to collect additional data.

8.9 Planning a Study*

data, since $N = 22$. The bootstrap sample size will be increased by 22 for each power calculation. Thus, there will be bootstrap sample sizes of $N_c^* = 22, 44, 66, 88, \ldots N_C^*$. The maximum bootstrap sample size, N_C^*, should be large enough to allow the power curve discussed below to surpass the 0.80 threshold. This can take some trial and error to determine. In the example below, $N_C^* = 22 \cdot 10 = 220$. The c and C subscripts are used rather than b and B, as the sample sizes are distinct from the bootstrap replications.

The sample size is increased by generating multiple samples with `simulate()` and then concatenating the result. The time and static predictor scores are treated as fixed. Thus, the original sample values are concatenated to fill out the bootstrap data frame.

For each sample size, the bootstrap power procedure should be carried out a large number of times, say $B = 9999$. This is to help ensure the accuracy of the estimated power at the cth sample size value.

The *power curve* consists of the estimated power values as a function of the sample size for fixed α. Several values of α can be considered if desired. The concatenation approach to increasing the sample size may be rather coarse, as it omits potentially important intervening sample sizes. To help account for this, a smoother will be applied to the estimated values, so that the power curve will be smooth (see Chapter 4). The approach should suffice for the majority of applications. If one desires more accuracy, a different strategy of concatenation can be used for increasing the sample size. For example, one might increase the bootstrap sample size by half the original sample size.

In the syntax below, the `power.func()` function is illustrated, which can be used to estimate power for various sample sizes, with the fixed α values of $0.01, 0.05, 0.15$. The syntax of the function is relatively involved, and a detailed explanation is not provided. Annotation is contained in the body of the function for the interested reader. To enable use of the function, the following syntax is executed.

```
> ###########################################################
> ## power.func()
> ###########################################################
> power.func <- function(r, f, sample.rep, power.rep){
+ power.results <- data.frame(matrix(ncol = 4, nrow = sample.rep))
+ ## Sample size loop.
+ for(k in 1:sample.rep){
+ ## Print to console.
+ cat("", "\n")
+ cat(paste("Sample Size =", k*length(unique(r@frame[,ncol(r@frame)]))),"\n")
+ ## Storage vector.
+ pvalue <- numeric(power.rep)
+ ## Progress bar.
+ pb <- txtProgressBar(max = power.rep, style=3)
+ ## Power replications.
+ for(j in 1:power.rep){
+ Sys.sleep(0.001); setTxtProgressBar(pb, j) # Update progress bar.
+ ## Simulate response data, put in vector.
+ simdv <- matrix(unlist(simulate(f, nsim = k)), ncol = 1)
```

```
+ ## Simulate predictor data, renumbering subject ID.
+ mm <- NULL; mm1 <- NULL; c <- 0
+ ## Concatenate sample size.
+ for(i in 1:k) {
+ mm1 <- f@frame
+ mm1[ ,ncol(mm1)] <- as.integer(mm1[ ,ncol(mm1)] + c)
+ c <- max(mm1[ ,ncol(mm1)])
+ mm <- rbind(mm, mm1)
+ }
+ ## Run anova().
+ mm[ ,1] <- simdv
+ s.full <- lmer(formula(f), mm, REML = F)
+ s.reduced <- lmer(formula(r), mm, REML = F)
+ pvalue[j] <- anova(s.reduced, s.full)[2,7]
+ ## Progress bar cleanup.
+ Sys.sleep(.002)
+ close(pb)
+ }
+ ## Bootstrap sample size.
+ power.results[k,1] <- max(mm[ ,ncol(mm)])
+ ## Power calculations for different alpha.
+ power.results[k,2] <- mean(pvalue <= .01)
+ power.results[k,3] <- mean(pvalue <= .05)
+ power.results[k,4] <- mean(pvalue <= .15)
+ ## Clean up for console screen.
+ cat("", "\n")
+ }
+ cat("", "\n")
+ cat("Finished", "\n")
+ cat("", "\n")
+ ## Return power results.
+ colnames(power.results) <- c("N","alpha.01","alpha.05","alpha.15")
+ return(power.results)
+ }
```

When the syntax above is executed, nothing is returned in the console window, as the function is only defined for future use. Once the above syntax is executed, power.fun() can be used with its required arguments.

Four arguments must be supplied to power.fun(). In order, these are (1) the name of the fitted reduced model object, (2) the name of the fitted full-model object, (3) the number of sample sizes (e.g., $C = 10$), and (4) the number of bootstrap power replications (e.g., $B = 9999$). The number of sample sizes determines how many concatenations of the original sample will be used. Each increase in the sample size increases the bootstrap sample size by the original value (e.g., 22, 44, 66, ...). As usual, the bootstrap power replications should be large (e.g., $B = 9999$) and end in 99.

In what follows, the reduced and full models are estimated based on the MPLS sample data, which are treated as pilot data. Then power.func() is used with $C = 10$ sample sizes and $B = 999$ bootstrap power replications. The process is timed using system.time(), and the results are saved to

8.9 Planning a Study*

the data frame `power.results`. For readers running the example on their own computer, be forewarned that the function can take a very long time to finish.

```
> ## Estimate models.
> model.0 <- lmer(read ~ grade5 + eth2 + (grade5 | subid), MPLS.LS, REML = FALSE)
> model.1 <- lmer(read ~ grade5 * eth2 + (grade5 | subid), MPLS.LS, REML = FALSE)
> ####################################################
> ## power.func(r, f, sample.rep, power.rep):
> ## r = reduced model object
> ## f = full model object
> ## sub.rep = subject size replication (e.g., 10)
> ## pow.rep = power replication (e.g., 999).
> ####################################################
> system.time(power.results <- power.func(model.0, model.1, 10, 999))
```

As the function is running, the progress for each sample size is printed to the console window. The assignment within `system.time()` saves the results to the data frame `power.results`. This data frame can be used for graphing the power curve.

It is useful to plot the power curves for each level of α. Since there are sizable gaps between the sample sizes, a smoother is used to produce smooth curves. The syntax below graphs the estimated power as points and fits a smoother for each curve.

```
> g1 <- ggplot(power.results, aes(x = N, y = alpha.15)) + geom_point() + theme_bw()
> g2 <- g1 + stat_smooth(se = FALSE) + ylab("Power")
> g3 <- g2 + geom_point(aes(y = alpha.05)) + stat_smooth(aes(y = alpha.05), se = FALSE)
> g4 <- g3 + geom_point(aes(y = alpha.01)) + stat_smooth(aes(y = alpha.01), se = FALSE)
> g5 <- g4 + annotate("text", x = 45,  y = .7, label = "alpha == .15", parse = TRUE)
> g6 <- g5 + annotate("text", x = 115, y = .6, label = "alpha == .05", parse = TRUE)
> g7 <- g6 + annotate("text", x = 145, y = .5, label = "alpha == .01", parse = TRUE)
> g8 <- g7 + scale_x_continuous(breaks = seq(25, 225, 25))
> print(g8)
```

The graph is shown on the left-hand side of Figure 8.3. Often the smoothed curves are presented without the points. This can be accomplished by removing the `geom_point()` components. The smoothed curves alone are shown in the right-hand graph of Figure 8.3.

As the graphs shows, a bit fewer than 100 subjects are required for 80% power with $\alpha = 0.15$. Fewer than 150 subjects are required for $\alpha = 0.05$, and approximately 225 subjects are required for $\alpha = 0.01$. Since $df = \Delta K = 1$, $\alpha = 0.15$ corresponds to "weak" evidence for the full model, $\alpha = 0.05$ corresponds to "moderate" evidence for the full model, and $\alpha = 0.01$ corresponds to "strong" evidence for the full model (see Table 8.2).

The above information can be used to make a decision regarding the number of subjects to measure. If the researcher wants a 0.8 probability of demonstrating "strong" evidence for the full model, then approximately 225 subjects should be selected. If the researcher wants a 0.8 probability of demonstrating "moderate" evidence for the full model, then approximately 150 subjects should be selected. Finally, if the researcher wants a 0.8 probability of demonstrating "weak" evidence for the full model, then approximately 100 subjects should be selected.

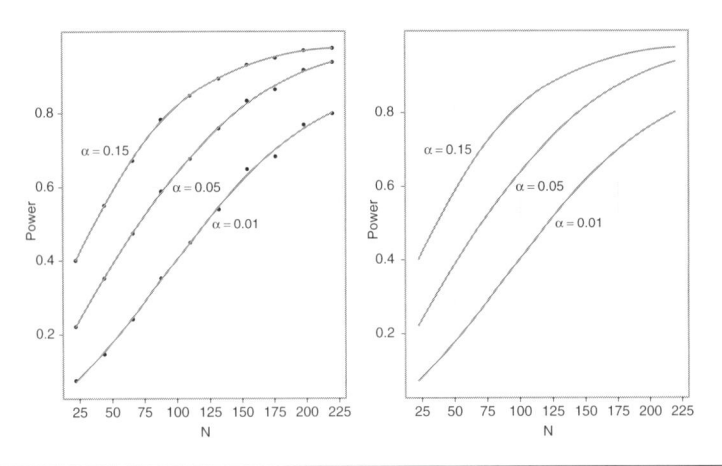

Figure 8.3 Power curves for three α levels, with (left) and without (right) individual estimates.

8.9.1 COMMENT ON THE PROCEDURE*

A potentially important issue with `power.fun()` is that is can take an extensive time to run. The above procedure took 64 minutes on a modern PC. The required time can be much greater if the pilot data are larger than in this example, if the sample size replications are increased, if power replications are increased, or if the models involved are more complex.

Analytic approaches to estimating required sample size in LMER are also available (Diggle et al., 2002, chap. 2). However, these approaches usually involve overly simple models, such as models with only random intercepts. Such simplifications may or may not be valid for a particular empirical problem.

Finally, it is possible to use a bootstrap procedure when no pilot data are available. If estimated values of all the parameters of the full model are known, then syntax can be written to simulate data from the full model using the estimates as parameters. This requires that quantities, such as the estimated variance components, be reported in the results of published studies. Although such reporting is increasing in frequency, it may be difficult to obtain estimates for all parameters. In such cases, best guesses must be used, or the values can be varied in the simulations. The details of programming such procedures are beyond our scope.

Selecting Time Predictors 9

The last two chapters dealt with the evaluation of static predictor effects assuming the time predictors and the random effects were preselected. Preselection means the time predictors and the random effects are set beforehand and appear in all the models being compared. This chapter and the next present methods for aiding in the preselection. The selection of time predictors is discussed in this chapter, and the selection of random effects is covered in the next chapter.

Recall that the simultaneous selection of the time predictors, random effects, and static predictor effects is a daunting task. To make LMER analysis manageable, it is desirable to hold the time predictors and random effects constant and have the models of the evaluation differ only in the static predictor effects. This strategy assumes the static predictor effects are the most important types of effects, which is probably the case for much applied analysis.

To hold the time predictors constant in an analysis, they must be decided upon prior to examining the static predictor effects. The best basis for preselection is theory, previous research, or the like. For example, a linear change curve was adopted in the previous two chapters because of the relatively short time span (4 years) and the particular grade epoch (fifth–eighth grades). If the time span was longer, or covered a different epoch, then a nonlinear curve might be appropriate.

Another means of preselection is to graph the data, which was discussed in Chapter 4. The current chapter discusses statistical methods that can be used along with graphing.

Choosing time predictors based on graphs is not always straightforward. Individual and group-level curves can be perturbed by random error, which might be difficult to detect visually. Scaling, aspect ratio, and other graph features can distort particular characteristics of change curves. Nonlinear aspects of curves, for example, can be either exaggerated or understated, depending on the choice of limits of the graph axes (Cleveland, 1993, chap. 1).

When there is little or no theory to guide interpretation of graphs, the researcher might want to include the use of statistical analysis. This can involve both descriptive and inferential statistics, and similar to graphing, it can be targeted at the group or subject level. Group-level analysis uses aggregates of subjects who might or might not be stratified based on static predictors.

Subject-level analysis focuses on fitting change curves to individuals, and then using the information to make judgments about collections of subjects. For example, the statistical fit of regression lines for individual subjects might be determined and then the information used to suggest a group-level curve.

The main distinction between subject-level and group-level selection in this chapter is that the former uses only descriptive statistics, whereas the latter uses inferential statistics. The group-level analysis will focus on inference using the AIC and the LRT. The subject-level analysis will focus on description using statistics such as R^2, computed for each subject.

Group-level analysis has some potential limitations, especially when the role of static predictors is unclear. Aggregating over subgroups with different shapes of change curves can result in a potentially misleading depiction of change. Subject-level analysis addresses some of the potential problems. Assuming a multilevel model, focus is on the Level 1 model for an individual, which is indifferent to static predictors. Subject-level change curves can be clustered to suggest potential static predictor effects, or to suggest the level of complexity needed for the group-level model. This last topic is discussed in an optional section at the end of the chapter.

9.1 Selection of Time Transformations

There are two main uses of time transformations. The first is to anchor the intercept at a particular time point, and the second is to model nonlinear trends. Anchoring by adding a constant was discussed in Chapter 5, and in this chapter, the focus is on time transformations to account for nonlinear change.

The most common method of modeling nonlinear trends in the behavioral sciences is to use polynomials. Polynomials are power transformations of the original time predictor. The time predictor is the base, and the exponents are the nonnegative integers. For the MPLS data, the time predictor is grade, and the polynomial terms are

$$\text{grade}^0, \text{grade}^1, \text{grade}^2, \text{grade}^3, \ldots,$$

with $\text{grade}^0 = 1$, and grade^1 commonly being written as grade.

The *order* (or degree) of the polynomial is the value of its largest exponent. The 0th-order polynomial is used to define an intercept-only model discussed below. The first-, second-, and third-order polynomials are often referred to as *linear*, *quadratic*, and *cubic* polynomials, respectively. Additional details of

9.1 Selection of Time Transformations

polynomials and alternative types of nonlinear transformations are considered in Chapter 12.

Polynomials are used in LMER models to account for nonlinear change. To keep things simple, assume for the moment the LMER models do not have static predictors. The expected value form of the LMER model with the polynomials is written as

$$E(y_{ij}) = \beta_0(\text{grade}_{ij}^0) + \beta_1(\text{grade}_{ij}^1) + \beta_2(\text{grade}_{ij}^2)$$
$$+ \beta_3(\text{grade}_{ij}^3) + \cdots + \beta_p(\text{grade}_{ij}^p).$$

The number of polynomial terms is $p + 1$, which is also the number of fixed effects. The number of predictors is p, as $\text{grade}_{ij}^0 = 1$ is a constant, and it is not a predictor in the traditional sense.

The convention is followed that when a higher order polynomial term is included in the model, all lower order terms are automatically included (however, see the discussion of fractional polynomials in Chapter 12). For example, if grade^2 is in the model, then grade is also included. The inclusion of the lower ordered terms is without regard to statistical results for the terms, such as t-ratios. Recall that linear transformations of the time variable, such as $\text{grade5} = \text{grade} - 5$, will change the t-ratios for all the lower ordered terms, but not for the highest order polynomial term. Therefore, statistical results should not be used to determine the inclusion or exclusion of lower order terms.

It is also desirable to avoid saturated models, as they do not summarize the data. Saturated models have as many fixed effects as the total number of possible time points. The fixed intercept is counted along with the fixed effects for the polynomial terms. Saturated models are avoided by considering polynomials whose order is at least *two* less than the total number of possible time points. In the MPLS data set, $max(n_i) = 4$, so at the most, a quadratic polynomial with a total of three fixed effects would be considered.

The selection of time transformations is fundamental, in that the order of the polynomial determines the potential number of random effects and the potential number of static predictor interaction terms. Consider the case of the linear and quadratic polynomials. Suppose grade5 is the time predictor, and there is the single static predictor, ethW, the dummy predictor for ethnicity. The first two polynomial models are the following:

Linear: $y_{ij} = (\beta_0 + b_{0i}) + (\beta_1 + b_{1i})(\text{grade5}_{ij}) + \beta_1(\text{ethW}_i)$
$\qquad\qquad + \beta_2(\text{grade5}_{ij} \cdot \text{ethW}_i) + \varepsilon_{ij},$

Quadratic: $y_{ij} = (\beta_0 + b_{0i}) + (\beta_1 + b_{1i})(\text{grade5}_{ij})$
$\qquad\qquad + (\beta_2 + b_{2i})(\text{grade5}_{ij}^2) + \beta_3(\text{ethW}_i)$
$\qquad\qquad + \beta_4(\text{grade5}_{ij} \cdot \text{ethW}_i) + \beta_5(\text{grade5}_{ij}^2 \cdot \text{ethW}_i) + \varepsilon_{ij}.$

The above equations show that the shape of the change curve affects the random effects and the static predictors. The linear model has two random effects and a single interaction term involving the static predictor, (grade5_{ij}·

ethW$_i$). The quadratic model adds an additional random effect, and there is an additional interaction term involving the static predictor, (grade5$_{ij}^2$·ethW$_i$). The linear model has three variance components associated with the random effects, whereas the quadratic model has six. Adding the single random effect, b_{2i}, adds three unique elements to the variance-covariance matrix among the random effects, $Var(b_{2i})$, $Cov(b_{0i}, b_{2i})$, and $Cov(b_{1i}, b_{2i})$. This point is taken up again in the next chapter.

Because of the fundamental nature of the time transformations, they are usually selected in the initial step of the analysis, the preselection step. When theory dictates the shape of the change curve, this step might be skipped, or there might be a limited confirmatory analysis. For example, if theory dictates a linear curve, a quadratic curve might also be examined to confirm that a nonlinear trend is not needed. In exploratory research, the selection of time transformations is more involved, perhaps dealing with the evaluation of several polynomial models.

For the selection of time transformations, it is important to consider the role of static predictors and random effects. Consistent with the previous two chapters, *when considering the selection of time transformations, the number of static predictors and random effects is held constant among the models.* Comparisons are made among models that differ only in the number of polynomial terms. The reason is that interpretations are clearer if there is one influence on model fit. If the number of polynomial terms and random effects is allowed to vary, it is not clear if an improvement in fit is due to an additional time transformation, an additional variance component, or both.

The number of random effects is held constant by including one greater than the lowest order polynomial in every model. For example, if there is a comparison of the linear ($p_1 = 1$), quadratic ($p_2 = 2$), and cubic models ($p_3 = 3$), all three would we have two random effects: a random intercept term, and a random slope term. The strategy is to allow for additional random effects to be added later, possibly after the static predictors have been selected. The number of random effects might also be reduced, or perhaps specific variance components omitted, such as the covariance between two random effects. This strategy places a higher priority on the fixed effects than the random effects, which is consistent with the value system of many applied researchers. The details are discussed in the next chapter.

Another consideration is whether static predictors should be involved in the selection of time transformations. Subgroups defined by the strata of static predictors can have different change curves. For example, advantaged students might have a steeper linear slope than disadvantaged students. Selection methods that ignore such differences can lead to misleading results. Graphs go a long way in this regard and are recommended for guiding the statistical analysis. Extensive discussion of graphing is found in Chapter 4.

The selection of time transformations is simplified when static predictors are not going to be examined. Researchers might not consider static predictors when the analysis is exploratory. In some nascent areas of research, static predictors are not yet identified, and the focus of the analysis is developing models of change for the response variable.

9.2 Group-Level Selection of Time Transformations

The first consideration is the group-level selection of polynomials. The focus is on the selection of the appropriate polynomial in the fixed effects structure of the LMER model. The potential strength of the group-level approach is that formal inferential methods (the AIC and the LRT) can be used.

The exploratory/confirmatory analysis continuum is important in group-level analysis. Polynomial selection might be part of a confirmatory analysis, when the goal is to formally verify that an aggregate change curve is a hypothesized pattern rather than another pattern. An example would be the case in which a linear curve is hypothesized. In such a circumstance, a first-order polynomial would be estimated, but a second-order polynomial would also be estimated. The second-order polynomial is estimated to confirm that the required curve is indeed linear rather than quadratic.

In exploratory research, the selection of polynomials might constitute a preliminary step of the analysis. Alternatively, the selection of polynomials might be the focus of the analysis. As mentioned in the last section, the terms of the change curve determine the maximum number of possible random effects and the maximum number of possible static predictor terms. In this respect, selection of time transformations is fundamental to LMER for longitudinal data analysis.

Another important issue is whether static predictors should be involved in the polynomial selection. If the change curve is expected to be similar for levels of the static predictors, then the static predictors can probably be ignored in the selection. Aggregating among the subgroups of the static predictors will not distort the shape of the curve for any given subgroup.

This is illustrated by the hypothetical scenario in the left-hand graph of Figure 9.1. The solid lines are the subgroup change curves, and the dotted line is the mean curve that results by aggregating the subgroups. In the left-hand scenario, polynomial selection can be based on the aggregate, as the dotted curve is parallel to the subgroups curves. A quadratic polynomial selected for the dotted line, for example, also accurately characterizes change for the subgroups.

A contrasting scenario is shown in the right-hand graph of Figure 9.1. In this case, the subgroups do not have the same shape. The subgroup curves are both nonlinear, but the upper one is concave with respect to the time axis, whereas the lower one is convex. This results in an aggregate curve that is linear. Selection based on the aggregate curve is misleading regarding the curves for the subgroups. In this case, the differences among static predictor levels should be accounted for, so that the conditional curves will be properly specified as nonlinear curves.

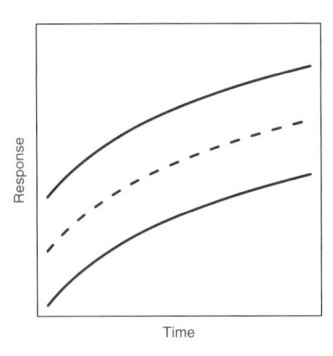

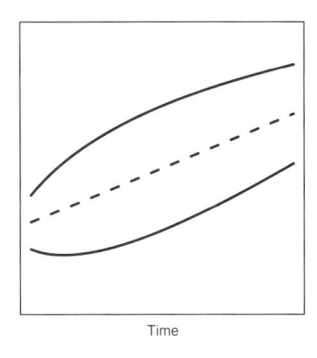

Figure 9.1 Hypothetical subgroup curves (solid) and aggregate curve (dashed). Left: subgroups have same change curves. Right: subgroups have different change curves.

Graphs are useful for evaluating if static predictors should be included in the polynomial selection. However, in some situations, static predictors might not be available, or an inadequate list might be available. In such cases, clustering of individual curves can be used, as discussed later.

To summarize points made in this section and the previous one, guidelines for group-level selection are listed in Table 9.1. These guidelines are suggested regardless of whether the AIC or the LRT is used to compare models.

Table 9.1 Guidelines for the selection of time transformations.

1. Graphs should be used in concert with statistical methods.
2. Include all lower order terms in polynomial models.
3. Avoid saturated models.
4. Compare models that differ only in their polynomial terms.
5. Static predictor interactions should be included if such interactions are a possibility.

9.3 Multimodel Inference

When static predictors are not considered in the analysis, the models in the set can be evaluated using multimodel inference and the AIC (or AICc). In this situation, the set of models varies only in the number of polynomial terms. For example, the linear model might have grade5 as the only predictor, and the quadratic model might have grade5 and grade5^2.

When static predictors are considered along with time transformations, the multimodel approach is not recommended. Since the models differ in both the static predictor effects and the number of polynomial terms, it can be difficult to assess the source of (mis)fit. For this reason, it is suggested that the AICc (or

9.3 Multimodel Inference

AIC) be used for preselection of the polynomial models. Then a subsequent analysis might be multimodel, focusing on models that vary in terms of their static predictor effects.

9.3.1 ANALYSIS WITHOUT STATIC PREDICTORS

Consider the example of polynomial models without static predictors. Recall that such models are referred to as unconditional. It is assumed there will be no subsequent analysis involving static predictors. As usual, the number of random effects is forced to be the same among the models. After identification of the best-fitting model, a post hoc analysis can be performed to determine if additional random effects are needed (see the next chapter).

Consider the selection of polynomial models with the MPLS data set. Assuming a completely exploratory analysis, three models are in the set.

1. Model I: Intercept-only model, which is a horizontal or flat-line model having only a fixed intercept term, β_0.

2. Model L: Linear model with the single predictor, grade5.

3. Model Q: Quadratic model with predictors grade5 and grade5^2.

The cubic model is not considered because there is a maximum of four time points. As indicated above, the models have the intercept anchored at fifth grade for the analysis.

Consistent with the earlier discussion, each of the models will have only a random intercept term. The reason is that Model I can accommodate only a random effects term, and this dictates the number of random effects included in all the models.

In the syntax below, the three models are estimated with lmer(). After estimating the models, aictab() is used to compute AICc, Δ, and the weight of evidence (W). The evidence ratio (E) is also computed.

```
> ## Estimate models.
> model.i  <- lmer(read ~ 1 + (1 | subid), MPLS.LS, REML = FALSE)
> model.l  <- lmer(read ~ grade5 + (1 | subid), MPLS.LS, REML = FALSE)
> model.q  <- lmer(read ~ grade5 + I(grade5 ^ 2) + (1 | subid), MPLS.LS, REML = FALSE)
> mynames  <- c("I", "L", "Q")
> ## AICc, etc.
> myaicc  <- as.data.frame(aictab(cand.set = list(model.i, model.l, model.q),
+                                 modnames = mynames))[ ,-c(5,7)]
> ## Evidence ratio:
> myaicc$eratio  <- max(myaicc$AICcWt) / myaicc$AICcWt
> ## Print.
> data.frame(Model = myaicc[ ,1], round(myaicc[ ,2:7], 4))

  Model K      AICc Delta_AICc AICcWt Cum.Wt       eratio
2     L 4  586.3482     0.0000 0.6922 0.6922 1.000000e+00
3     Q 5  587.9693     1.6211 0.3078 1.0000 2.249100e+00
1     I 3  630.8464    44.4982 0.0000 1.0000 4.598991e+09
```

The output shows that Model L has the best fit and is the most plausible model. Model I has a weight of evidence that is extremely small and an evidence ratio that is extremely large (e+09 means move the decimal place nine to the right). Model I is judged as implausible and not considered further.

The quadratic model has a weight of evidence that is less than half that of the linear model. The quadratic model has an evidence ratio that is not especially large, indicating it is plausible to some extent. How plausible is the quadratic model? To address this question, it is helpful to examine the fixed effects table for the estimated Model Q. Recall this table resides in the @coefs slot of the summary() object.

```
> summary(model.q)@coefs
```

	Estimate	Std. Error	t value
(Intercept)	201.6079191	3.9236125	51.3832393
grade5	6.3923647	1.8467767	3.4613631
I(grade5^2)	-0.5058592	0.6229319	-0.8120618

The estimates for the quadratic term are in the row labeled I(grade5^2). The output indicates the estimated quadratic coefficient has a negative sign ($\hat{\beta}_2 = -0.51$). This means that the aggregate sample change curve has some concavity with respect to the grade axis. More specifically, there is a slowing down or deceleration for the later grades. The *t*-ratio for the quadratic term fixed effect is relatively close to 0, confirming the results of the model comparison.

As a slight aside, the *t*-ratios for grade5 and (Intercept) are not evaluated. The linear and intercept terms are of lower order than the quadratic term and are included in the model regardless of the statistical results. As will be seen in a moment, the *t*-ratios of lower order terms can change dramatically when the highest order term is omitted from the model. It follows that the *t*-ratios of lower order terms cannot be used to judge the importance of effects.

The fixed effects table of the estimated Model L provides additional information.

```
> summary(model.l)@coefs
```

	Estimate	Std. Error	t value
(Intercept)	202.05155	3.8932107	51.898437
grade5	4.96813	0.5820497	8.535577

The output shows that the *t*-ratio for the linear effect is relatively large ($t = 8.54$). The *t*-ratio for grade5 is much larger than when grade5² is in the model. It is reiterated that *t*-ratios should not be used to assess the importance of lower order effects when higher order effects are in the model. The importance of grade5 can certainly be evaluated in the output above, but not when grade5² is in the model.

The multimodel analysis suggests that the best approximating change curve model is linear. The results should be tempered by the fact that the sample size is relatively small ($N = 22$), and there is a limited grade range (5–8). Increasing the sample size and/or the grade range might result in the quadratic polynomial having the best fit.

9.3.2 ANALYSIS WITH STATIC PREDICTORS

When static predictors are considered along with time transformations, the approach to take in the analysis is not clear-cut. It is possible to use the multimodel approach to evaluate models that differ in both static predictors and time transformations. However, the results of such an analysis are vulnerable to misinterpretation, as shown in an example below. For this reason, it is recommended that the multimodel approach be used only for a set of models that differ in either static predictor effects, or polynomials, but not both.

To illustrate the potential interpretation problems with the multimodel approach, consider Model 1 and Model 3 from the analysis presented in Section 7.6.2. For convenience, the LMER equations for the models are written here:

$$\text{Model 1:} \quad y_{ij} = (\beta_0 + b_{0i}) + (\beta_1 + b_{1i})(\text{grade5}_{ij}) + \beta_2(\text{risk2DADV}_i) + \varepsilon_{ij},$$

$$\text{Model 3:} \quad y_{ij} = (\beta_0 + b_{0i}) + (\beta_1 + b_{1i})(\text{grade5}_{ij}) + \beta_2(\text{risk2DADV}_i) + \beta_3(\text{eth2W}_i) + \varepsilon_{ij}.$$

Model 1 is a linear change curve model with a risk intercept effect. Model 3 is also a linear change curve model with risk and ethnicity intercept effects.

Suppose in addition to selecting the static predictor effects, the goal is to select time transformations in the same analysis. From the graphs presented in Chapter 4, there is a suspicion that a quadratic change curve might be needed. Therefore, quadratic change curve versions of Model 1 and Model 3 are constructed, labeled as Model 1q and Model 3q, respectively. The LMER models are the following:

$$\text{Model 1q:} \quad y_{ij} = (\beta_0 + b_{0i}) + (\beta_1 + b_{1i})(\text{grade5}_{ij}) + \beta_2(\text{grade5}_{ij}^2) + \beta_3(\text{risk2DADV}_i) + \varepsilon_{ij},$$

$$\text{Model 3q:} \quad y_{ij} = (\beta_0 + b_{0i}) + (\beta_1 + b_{1i})(\text{grade5}_{ij}) + \beta_2(\text{grade5}_{ij}^2) + \beta_3(\text{risk2DADV}_i) + \beta_4(\text{eth2W}_i) + \varepsilon_{ij}.$$

Comparing Model 1 and Model 1q, it can be seen that the latter has one additional fixed effect for the quadratic term. The same can be said about Model 3 and Model 3q.

The set for the multimodel approach consists of the four models, 1, 1q, 3, and 3q. In the syntax below, the models are estimated, and the AICc and related measures are computed.

```
> ## Estimate Models.
> model.1   <- lmer(read ~ grade5 + risk2 + (grade5 | subid), MPLS.LS, REML = FALSE)
> model.1q  <- lmer(read ~ grade5 + risk2 + I(grade5 ^ 2) + (grade | subid),
+                   MPLS.LS, REML = FALSE)
> model.3   <- lmer(read ~ grade5 + risk2 + eth2 + (grade5 | subid),MPLS.LS,REML= FALSE)
> model.3q  <- lmer(read ~ grade5 + risk2 + eth2 + I(grade5 ^ 2) + (grade | subid),
+                   MPLS.LS, REML = FALSE)
> ## AICc.
> mynames <- c("1", "1q", "3", "3q")
> myaicc  <- as.data.frame(aictab(cand.set = list(model.1,model.1q,model.3,model.3q),
+                   modnames = mynames))[ ,-c(5,7)]
> myaicc$eratio <- max(myaicc$AICcWt) / myaicc$AICcWt
> myaicc
```

	Modnames	K	AICc	Delta_AICc	AICcWt	Cum.Wt	eratio
1	1	7	565.4412	0.0000000	0.4193874	0.4193874	1.000000
2	1q	8	565.7574	0.3161956	0.3580588	0.7774462	1.171281
3	3	8	567.9101	2.4688874	0.1220403	0.8994865	3.436466
4	3q	9	568.2982	2.8570065	0.1005135	1.0000000	4.172449

The output shows that Model 1 is the best fitting, followed by Model 1q, Model 3, and Model 3q. The evidence ratio is small for Model 1q and moderate for Models 3 and 3q. In terms of the static predictor effects, the models that have only risk effects (1 and 1q) have much better fit than the models that add ethnicity effects (3 and 3q). In terms of candidates for the best approximating model, Model 1 is favored, with Model 1q perhaps not far behind.

Judgments regarding the shape of the change curve for the best approximating model are more difficult. Because Model 1q is the second best-fitting model, it is tempting to conclude that the best approximating model might have a quadratic change curve. However, this conclusion is suspect. Model 1q is the second best fitting because it shares the same static predictor with Model 1, not because it includes the quadratic term. A comparison of Models 1 and 1q shows that the quadratic term is actually a liability, causing *worse* fit. The same can be seen in the comparison of Models 3 and 3q. If the quadratic term worsens fit, then the best approximating model is probably a linear model. With respect to the change curve, then, Model 3 is more plausible than Model 1q, which is in contradiction to the AICc and the other measures.

Perhaps more troubling is the fact that the quadratic term in Model 1q can be completely worthless, yet Model 1q can still be as good fitting as

9.3 Multimodel Inference

Model 3 and better fitting than Model 3q. "Completely worthless" means that grade5^2 accounts for no additional within-subject variance, with the result being that the deviance of Model 1q is identical to that of Model 3. This cannot happen in practice, but for illustration, let us assume this is the case.

Using the formulas for the AICc in Chapter 7, it can be shown that if the quadratic term does not decrease (improve) the deviance of Model 1 at all, then the AICc for Model 1q will be equal to 567.9. Likewise, if ethnicity is completely worthless, then the AICc value of Model 3 will also be 567.9, and that of Model 3q will be 570.5. This shows that a model with a completely spurious quadratic term can still have the second best fit, as long as the risk intercept effect is in the model. It is not clear, then, how the rank-order fit based on the AICc can be used to make judgments about the appropriate order of polynomials in this case.

The illustrations above indicate there can be ambiguity when the multimodel approach is used with models that differ in both static predictor effects and time transformations. For this reason, it is suggested that the multimodel approach be used for models differing in only one aspect. When static predictors are to be included, it is recommended the time transformations be preselected.

The AICc can be used along with graphing for the preselection of polynomial terms. If it appears from graphs of the data that the predictor effects will be only intercept effects, then the static predictors need not be included in the polynomial selection. The change curve for the subgroups defined by the static predictors will be parallel, and thus, the same curve shape will apply for the subgroups and when the groups are aggregated.

For the MPLS data, the graphs in Chapter 4 show the change curves of the ethnicity and risk groups to be approximately parallel. This suggests an analysis ignoring static predictors is appropriate for preselection of the polynomial. Preselection does involve a decision regarding what order of polynomial to use in the multimodel analysis. For this reason, one should always select the polynomial model that has the smallest AICc value. Information about the fit of all the polynomial models is considered, but the AICc is used to make a decision, as opposed to judgments of plausibility.

When change curves of static predictor subgroups are not parallel, or it is unclear, then the order of the polynomial should be selected with static predictor interactions in the model. In this case, subgroups have different curve shapes, and ignoring the static predictors can lead to selection of an aggregate curve that is not appropriate. This is the scenario shown in the right-hand graph of Figure 9.1.

As an example, suppose the intention is to evaluate models that differ in ethnicity and risk effects. Three polynomial models are examined that have the two static predictors as single effects and all the possible interactions. Similar to the last section, the polynomials consist of an intercept-only model (Model I), a linear model (Model L), and a quadratic model (Model Q). The LMER equations are the following:

Model I: $y_{ij} = (\beta_0 + b_{0i}) + \beta_1(\texttt{risk2DADV}_i) + \beta_2(\texttt{eth2W}_i) + \varepsilon_{ij}$,

Model L: $y_{ij} = (\beta_0 + b_{0i}) + \beta_1(\texttt{grade5}_{ij}) + \beta_2(\texttt{risk2DADV}_i)$
$\qquad + \beta_3(\texttt{eth2W}_i) + \beta_4(\texttt{grade5}_{ij} \cdot \texttt{risk2DADV}_i)$
$\qquad + \beta_5(\texttt{grade5}_{ij} \cdot \texttt{eth2W}_i) + \varepsilon_{ij}$,

Model Q: $y_{ij} = (\beta_0 + b_{0i}) + \beta_1(\texttt{grade5}_{ij}) + \beta_2(\texttt{grade5}_{ij}^2)$
$\qquad + \beta_3(\texttt{risk2DADV}_i) + \beta_4(\texttt{eth2W}_i)$
$\qquad + \beta_5(\texttt{grade5}_{ij} \cdot \texttt{risk2DADV}_i)$
$\qquad + \beta_6(\texttt{grade5}_{ij} \cdot \texttt{eth2W}_i)$
$\qquad + \beta_7(\texttt{grade5}_{ij}^2 \cdot \texttt{risk2DADV}_i)$
$\qquad + \beta_8(\texttt{grade5}_{ij}^2 \cdot \texttt{eth2W}_i) + \varepsilon_{ij}$.

Model Q has all the possible interaction effects. Another possibility is to include only linear interaction effects, but that is not pursued here.

In the syntax below, the three models are estimated, and the AICc and weight of evidence are computed.

```
> model.i  <- lmer(read ~ risk2 + eth2 + (1 | subid), MPLS.LS, REML = FALSE)
> model.l  <- lmer(read ~ grade5 * risk2 + grade5 * eth2 + (1 | subid),
+              MPLS.LS, REML = FALSE)
> model.q  <- lmer(read ~ grade5 * risk2 + grade5 * eth2 + I(grade5 ^ 2) * risk2 +
+              I(grade5 ^ 2) * eth2 + (1 | subid), MPLS.LS, REML = FALSE)
> mynames  <- c("I", "L", "Q")
> myaicc   <- as.data.frame(aictab(cand.set = list(model.i, model.l, model.q),
+                            modnames = mynames))[ ,-c(5,7)]
> data.frame(Modnames = myaicc[ ,1], round(myaicc[ ,-1], 4))
```

	Modnames	K	AICc	Delta_AICc	AICcWt	Cum.Wt
2	L	8	575.0007	0.0000	0.9663	0.9663
3	Q	11	581.7098	6.7091	0.0337	1.0000
1	I	5	616.1857	41.1850	0.0000	1.0000

The results show that the linear model has a very large weight of evidence, and the other models have very small weights. The linear model is selected for the subsequent multimodel analysis.

As a final comment for this section, it is possible to use the AICc in a post hoc manner with a multimodel analysis. Rather than preselecting the polynomial, one can compare the best-fitting model in the set to alternatives with different polynomial terms. As an illustration, consider again the multimodel analysis of Section 7.6.2. All the models in the set had linear change curves based on graphs of the data. The best-fitting model was found to be Model 1, considered in this section.

A post hoc check on the adequacy of the linear model can be conducted by comparing Model 1 to a model that includes a quadratic term, which is Model 1q. Consider the following syntax and output.

```
> print(aictab(cand.set = list(model.1, model.1q),
+                modnames = c("1","1q")),LL = FALSE)

Model selection based on AICc :

    K    AICc  Delta_AICc  AICcWt  Cum.Wt
1   7  565.44        0.00    0.54    0.54
1q  8  565.76        0.32    0.46    1.00
```

Similar to the previous analysis, the output shows the weight of evidence for the linear models is slightly higher than for the quadratic model. There is evidence that the linear polynomial is sufficient. Even though the weight of evidence is nearly equal for the linear and quadratic models, the linear model is definitely selected, as it is more parsimonious. The theme of parsimony is also relevant when using the LRT, which is discussed in the next section.

9.4 Likelihood Ratio Test

One advantage of using the AICc is that the fit of several alternative models can be examined. A more traditional approach is to use NHST to select polynomials. As discussed in Chapter 8, the LRT is the primary means of obtaining p-values for testing nested models.

Recall that the guidelines listed in Table 9.1 are pertinent for evaluation based on the AICc and the LRT. Therefore, a distinction is again made between analysis with and without static predictors. Model comparisons should be considered only for models that differ in the time transformations.

9.4.1 ANALYSIS WITHOUT STATIC PREDICTORS

Analysis considering only polynomial terms can be performed with the LRT using a step-up or top-down approach. Recall that both approaches compare two nested models at a time, with the reduced model having fewer parameters than the full model. For any comparison, if the LRT-p is not sufficiently small, this argues against the need for the additional parameters of the full model. Thus, the more parsimonious reduced model is adopted. The more complex full model is retained when the LRT-p is sufficiently small. For simplicity, $p \leq 0.05$ constitutes "sufficiently small" throughout this chapter, consistent with the traditional definition of statistical significance. Emphasis below will be on a dichotomous decision regarding the reduced and full models, whether to accept or reject. This is a subtly different use of the LRT-p than as an effect size measure (see Chapter 8).

In the step-up approach, the starting point is a simplistic polynomial model, and this is compared to a polynomial model of the next highest order. For example, the process might commence with an intercept-only model as the reduced model and the linear model as the full model. If the LRT is not statistically significant, the reduced model is accepted and the testing terminates. If the LRT is statistically significant, the full model is accepted, and then it is compared to the next highest order polynomial model. Testing usually terminates upon the first nonsignificant result, but sometimes a rule of two successive nonsignificant results is used (Ryan, 1997, chap. 8).

In the top-down approach, the first step involves a complex polynomial model, and this is compared to the polynomial model of the next lowest order. As an example, testing might commence with the cubic model as the full model and the quadratic model as the reduced model. If the result is statistically significant, the full model is accepted and the testing terminates. If the LRT is not statistically significant, the reduced model is accepted and then compared to the next lowest order polynomial model. Testing usually terminates upon the first statistically significant result.

As an illustration of the step-up and top-down approaches, consider the three polynomial models analyzed in Section 9.3.1: the intercept-only model (Model I), the linear model (Model L), and the quadratic model (Model Q). In the syntax below, the models are estimated, and the fitted output objects are saved. The `anova()` function is used to perform the LRT for each nested pair.

```
> model.i <- lmer(read ~ 1 + (1 | subid), MPLS.LS, REML = FALSE)
> model.l <- lmer(read ~ grade5 + (1 | subid), MPLS.LS, REML = FALSE)
> model.q <- lmer(read ~ grade5 + I(grade5 ^ 2) + (1 | subid), MPLS.LS, REML = FALSE)
> anova(model.i, model.l, model.q)
```

```
Data: MPLS.LS
Models:
model.i: read ~ 1 + (1 | subid)
model.l: read ~ grade5 + (1 | subid)
model.q: read ~ grade5 + I(grade5^2) + (1 | subid)
        Df    AIC    BIC   logLik   Chisq Chi Df Pr(>Chisq)
model.i  3 630.53 637.68 -312.26
model.l  4 585.81 595.34 -288.91 46.7157      1  8.207e-12 ***
model.q  5 587.16 599.07 -288.58  0.6564      1     0.4178
---
Signif. codes:  0 '***' 0.001 '**' 0.01 '*' 0.05 '.' 0.1 ' ' 1
```

Output lines 3 to 5 show the syntax for each model. Lines 6 to 9 show the table of fit information. The `Df` column indicates Model I has three estimated parameters, and an additional parameter is added as the order of the polynomial increases. Information for the first LRT, comparing Models I and L, is shown on line 8. The likelihood ratio statistic is large, $X^2 = 46.72$, producing a very small LRT-p, which is statistically significant. The second LRT, comparing Models L and Q, is shown on line 9. The likelihood ratio statistic is small, $X^2 = 0.66$, producing a relatively large LRT-p, which is not statistically significant.

Using the `anova()` output for a step-up analysis, comparison begins with Models I and L. The LRT is statistically significant, so the linear model is accepted, and this model is compared to the quadratic model. The LRT for Model L versus Q is not statistically significant. The linear model is accepted, and the testing terminates.

The same `anova()` output is used for the top-down analysis. This time, testing begins with the LRT for Model Q versus L. It is not statistically significant, so the more parsimonious linear model is accepted, and this is compared to the intercept-only model. The LRT for Model L versus I is statistically significant, leading to the acceptance of the more complex linear model, and the testing terminates.

In the example, the linear model is selected with both approaches. However, there is no guarantee that the approaches will always select the same model.

9.4.2 ANALYSIS WITH STATIC PREDICTORS

Testing is relatively straightforward when static predictors are not a concern. When static predictors are to be analyzed, things become more cloudy. A way forward is to follow the same themes as in the discussion of the AICc. If the static predictor effects are thought to be only intercept effects, the approaches of the last section can be used as an initial step in the analysis. This is similar to the preselection analysis discussed with the AICc. When there is evidence of static predictor interactions or the possibility of such, then polynomials should be selected with the interaction terms in the model.

9.5 Cautions Concerning Group-Level Selection

Group-level selection of polynomials has the advantage that inferential statistics can be used. This helps to account for sampling vagaries to distinguish "real" data patterns from spurious ones.

There are some cautions concerning the group-level selection of polynomials. As shown in the right-hand graph of Figure 9.1, aggregating over subgroups defined by static predictors is sometimes misleading. If aggregate curves have a different shape than subgroup curves, then an inappropriate polynomial model might be adopted.

In confirmatory analysis, the researcher has an adequate list of relevant static predictors, and graphs can be used to guide or check polynomial selection with inferential statistics. In situations of exploratory analysis, the relevant static predictors might be unknown, or only partially known. There seems to be more danger in basing selection on aggregate curves, as it is not known if relevant subgroups are being collapsed, providing a distorted picture of the change pattern. For this reason, the subject-level selection of the next section may be preferable.

9.6 Subject-Level Selection of Time Transformations

The goal of the subject-level approach is to use individual change curves to suggest what type of polynomial should be used in the fixed effects structure of the LMER model. The subject-level approach uses only descriptive statistics. A goodness-of-fit index, such as R^2, is computed for each subject to quantify the adequacy of a particular polynomial model. The individual information is summarized in graphs, or pooled to compute a single descriptive statistic. Then judgments regarding the appropriate polynomial model are made for the group as a whole, or for subgroups possibly stratified by the static predictors.

When subgroups differ in curve shape, the highest order polynomial should be fit to all the subjects. For the subgroup with the simpler shape, the parameter estimate for the higher order term(s) will tend to be close to 0. This will, in effect, allow for the fitting of different curve shapes for the subgroups. A primary goal, then, is to determine the highest order polynomial that is required. When the relevant static predictors are unknown or partially known, clustering of subject-level change curves is useful.

The subject-level approach starts at the most fundamental level, that of the individual change curve. Since there is no aggregation among subjects, static predictors do not need to be taken into account. The subject-level curves only concern within-subject variation, as opposed to between-subject variation.

The disadvantage of the subject-level approach is that the procedures are descriptive, so that statistical theory cannot be used to judge sample effects. This means that the subject-level information is relatively ambiguous, since inferential theory is not used to assess over- or underfitting for the individual models. Furthermore, missing data complicate the analysis, and it might not be possible to fit the same polynomial model for all the subjects.

9.6.1 LEVEL 1 POLYNOMIAL MODEL

Change curves are either connected observed values or connected fitted values. Observed change curves are not model based, whereas fitted change curves are model based. The model for the fitted curves is the subject-specific Level 1 from the multilevel model depiction (see Chapter 5).

Consider the Level 1 model with polynomial terms. Using grade5 as the time variable, the Level 1 polynomial model is

$$y_{ij} = \beta^*_{0i} + \beta^*_{1i}(\text{grade5}_{ij}) + \beta^*_{2i}(\text{grade5}^2_{ij}) \\ + \cdots + \beta^*_{pi}(\text{grade}^p_{ij}) + \varepsilon_{ij}, \qquad (9.6.1)$$

where grade5^p_{ij} is the pth order polynomial with $p + 1 < n_i$, and β^*_{ki} ($k > 0$) is a subject-specific regression weight. Since $i = 1, \ldots, N$, there are N Level 1 equations of the form of Equation 9.6.1. Equation 9.6.1 does not

9.6 Subject-Level Selection of Time Transformations

involve static predictors—it is a model that concerns only within-subjects variance.

For subject-level analysis, the correlation among the repeated measures is ignored in Equation 9.6.1, and OLS is used for estimation. This is justified because the concern is only with description. As discussed in Chapter 5, OLS can provide valid estimates of fixed effects for the Level 1 model, even when the data are longitudinal. (SEs and any inferential statistics are *not* valid, however.)

In subject-level analysis, the goal is to select the appropriate order of the polynomial in Equation 9.6.1. This is considered on a subject-by-subject basis. The idea is to find the highest order polynomial required, even if some subjects require a simpler model. For the subjects who have a simpler model, the estimated regression coefficients for the higher order terms will be 0, or approximately so. This has the effect of potentially reducing the model on a case-by-case basis. For example, the process might yield a quadratic model for some subjects and a linear model for others.

As an example, suppose that some subjects require a quadratic polynomial, up to $grade5^2$, and other subjects require a linear polynomial, up to $grade5$. The more complex model is used for all subjects, as those requiring only a linear polynomial will have $\beta^*_{2i} = 0$. Thus, the quadratic model will, in effect, be simplified to a linear model for those with straight-line change.

9.6.2 MISSING DATA

Missing data are an important issue with the subject-level approach. The requirement $n_i > p + 1$ sets a limit on the order of the polynomial that can be fit for a subject with missing data. It is desirable to create a variable that indexes the number of missing (or nonmissing) data points. With such a variable, individuals can be excluded based on some criterion, such as those who have data at only a single time point.

The same method is used as in Section 4.3.4.1 for indexing missing data. Below is the syntax, which makes use of ddply() from the plyr package. The reader is referred to Chapter 4 for a detailed explanation.

```
> MPLS.LS$miss  <-  as.numeric(is.na(MPLS.LS$read))
> mysel  <-  ddply(.data = data.frame(MPLS.LS$miss),
+                  .variables = .(MPLS.LS$subid), .fun = sum)
> colnames(mysel)  <-  c("subid", "totmiss")
> MPLS.LS2  <-  merge(MPLS.LS, mysel, by = "subid")
> head(subset(MPLS.LS2, select = -c(riskC, ethC)))
```

	subid	risk	gen	eth	ell	sped	att	grade	read	risk2	eth2	grade5	miss	totmiss
1	1	HHM	F	Afr	0	N	0.94	5	172	DADV	NW	0	0	0
2	1	HHM	F	Afr	0	N	0.94	6	185	DADV	NW	1	0	0
3	1	HHM	F	Afr	0	N	0.94	7	179	DADV	NW	2	0	0
4	1	HHM	F	Afr	0	N	0.94	8	194	DADV	NW	3	0	0
5	2	HHM	F	Afr	0	N	0.91	5	200	DADV	NW	0	0	1
6	2	HHM	F	Afr	0	N	0.91	6	210	DADV	NW	1	0	1

The output shows that the new data frame, `MPLS.LS2`, has the variable `totmiss` in the last column, which indexes the total number of missing time points. This variable is treated as a static predictor, as its values are repeated for each grade. Now `MPLS.LS2` can be used for further analysis, with selection or splitting based on `totmiss`.

9.6.3 SUBJECT-LEVEL FITS

One aid in determining the appropriate order of the polynomial is to inspect subject-level curves as discussed in Section 4.3. Graphs are usually relatively clear when the sample size and the number of time points are not very large. This is the case with the MPLS data consisting of $N = 22$ subjects and a maximum of four time points, $max(n_i) = 4$.

When there is a larger number of subjects and/or a greater number of time points, graphs of individual change curves can be cumbersome. In such cases, it is helpful to use a summary of curve fit, such as R^2, to investigate the plausibility of polynomials. If the researcher is willing to consider models that are not saturated, a penalized fit index, such as $adj.\ R^2$, can also be computed and graphed (see below).

Comparisons based on R^2. Consider computing R^2 for each subject to assess the fit of a polynomial model. R^2 is one of the statistics computed by default with `lm()`, and it is accessed in the `$r.squared` slot of the `summary()` output object. The notation, R_i^2, denotes the value for the ith subject.

To estimate a polynomial model for each subject, a user-defined function is included in `dlply()`. The user-defined function makes use of `lm()`, which produces a fitted model object for each subject. An initial list object is produced, with each element consisting of the `lm()` fitted model object for one subject.

The user-defined function consists of a `lm()` statement with the appropriate variable names from the data frame, `read` and `grade5`. With the `lm()` syntax, `data=x` is set, meaning the argument is a variable. When used in conjunction with the `.data=MPLS.LS` and `.variables=MPLS.LS$subid` arguments in `dlply()`, the `data=x` argument results in the data being supplied to `lm()` in blocks defined by `subid`. The syntax below fits a linear polynomial for each subject. The results are saved as the list object, `mylm.1`.

```
> mylm.1 <- dlply(.data = MPLS.LS, .variables = .(MPLS.LS$subid),
+                 .fun = function(x) {lm(read ~ grade5, data = x)})
```

If the reader wishes to use the above syntax with his or her own data frame, the names of the response and predictor need to be changed in the `lm()` syntax.

9.6 Subject-Level Selection of Time Transformations

The `mylm.1` object is not convenient for viewing, as each element is a fitted model object. It is more useful to extract elements of the output and display them for the subjects. The `ldply()` function in `plyr` is used to display the estimated regression coefficients for each individual. The `.data=` argument takes the `mylm.1` list object, and `.fun=` takes a new user-defined function. Consider the following.

```
> ldply(.data = mylm.1, .fun = function(x) {x$coefficients})
```

	MPLS.LS$subid	(Intercept)	grade5
1	1	173.5000	6.0
2	2	201.8333	4.5
3	3	190.6000	7.6
4	4	199.3333	-3.0
5	5	208.7000	1.7
6	6	190.9000	2.9
7	7	200.2000	6.2
8	8	191.5000	1.5
9	9	147.9000	10.4
10	10	201.8333	6.5
11	11	180.5000	6.5
12	12	188.0000	7.0
13	13	229.0000	2.5
14	14	198.8000	12.3
15	15	216.6667	9.0
16	16	228.0000	0.5
17	17	201.7000	5.2
18	18	218.1000	0.6
19	19	214.3333	3.0
20	20	207.9000	3.4
21	21	237.3333	3.0
22	22	220.8333	8.5

The function passes each element of `mylm.1` to the function. This means that each output object replaces the variable x, resulting in the regression coefficients being extracted. The `ldply()` function returns a data frame.

Turning to the output, the `(Intercept)` column lists the estimated intercept, $\hat{\beta}_{0i}^*$, and the `grade5` column lists the estimated slope, $\hat{\beta}_{1i}^*$. Each row pertains to a particular subject, as shown by the subject identification numbers listed in the first column (`MPLS.LS$subid`). Subject 4 has a negative linear slope, but all the other subjects have positive linear slopes.

As an aside, the scores in the `mylm.1` are mean-uncorrected random effects scores (see Chapter 5). When the focus is on such scores, OLS is arguably not the best method of computation. An alternative method for computing random effects scores based on a fitted `lmer()` object is discussed in the next chapter.

To estimate a quadratic model for each subject, `grade5` and `grade5`^{2} are included as predictors. In the syntax below, the output for each subject is saved in the list object, `mylm.2`. The `ldply()` function displays the subject-specific estimates.

```
> mylm.2 <- dlply(.data = MPLS.LS, .variables = .(MPLS.LS$subid),
+                 .fun = function(x) {lm(read ~ grade5 + I(grade5 ^ 2), data = x)})
> ldply(mylm.2, function(x) {x$coefficients})
```

	MPLS.LS$subid	(Intercept)	grade5	I(grade5^2)
1	1	174.00	4.50	0.50
2	2	200.00	15.50	-5.50
3	3	191.60	4.60	1.00
4	4	200.00	-7.00	2.00
5	5	207.45	5.45	-1.25
6	6	188.65	9.65	-2.25
7	7	199.20	9.20	-1.00
8	8	191.00	4.50	-1.50
9	9	147.40	11.90	-0.50
10	10	200.00	17.50	-5.50
11	11	178.75	11.75	-1.75
12	12	186.50	11.50	-1.50
13	13	229.75	0.25	0.75
14	14	198.55	13.05	-0.25
15	15	218.00	1.00	4.00
16	16	226.75	4.25	-1.25
17	17	202.20	3.70	0.50
18	18	218.60	-0.90	0.50
19	19	215.00	-1.00	2.00
20	20	203.90	15.40	-4.00
21	21	237.00	5.00	-1.00
22	22	219.00	19.50	-5.50

Along with the intercept and slope, the estimated quadratic coefficient, $\hat{\beta}_{2i}^*$, is listed in the `I(grade5^2)` column. Most subjects have a negative sign for the quadratic coefficient, but some have a positive sign. The signs represent shape differences, with negative values indicating a quadratic component that is concave to the grade axis, ∩, and the positive values indicating a quadratic component that is convex to the grade axis, ∪.

Inclusion of the quadratic component does not mean that it will necessarily dominate the overall curve. As shown in Equation 9.6.1, the quadratic component is added to the linear component (and intercept), with the values of the coefficients determining the overall curve shape. For subjects with a quadratic coefficient close to 0, their change curve will be close to linear. Subject 1 is an example of a person with a near-linear curve.

With the MPLS data set, there is little point in going on to fit the cubic polynomial. Because $max(n_i) = p + 1 = 4$, the cubic polynomial model will be saturated, yielding $R^2 = 1$ for each subject. Missing values in the data set mean there are some subjects for whom the quadratic model is saturated. For this reason, it is important to graph values of R_i^2 conditional on the missing value tally.

9.6 Subject-Level Selection of Time Transformations

Having estimated the linear and quadratic polynomial models for each subject, the R_i^2 values can now be extracted. This is performed with the `ldply()` function. In this case, the `summary()` function is applied to each list element of `mylm.1`, and then the `$r.squared` slot of the `summary()` object is accessed to extract R_i^2.

```
> temp1 <- ldply(.data = mylm.1, .fun = function(x) summary(x)$r.squared)
> colnames(temp1) <- c("subid", "Rsq")
> head(temp1)
```

	subid	Rsq
1	1	0.6896552
2	2	0.6675824
3	3	0.9626667
4	4	0.8709677
5	5	0.5838384
6	6	0.2434153

It is convenient to store the missing value tallies along with R_i^2 in the data frame. The syntax below accomplishes this and saves the result as `Rsq1`.

```
> Rsq1 <- merge(mysel, temp1, by = "subid")
> Rsq1
```

	subid	totmiss	Rsq
1	1	0	0.68965517
2	2	1	0.66758242
3	3	0	0.96266667
4	4	1	0.87096774
5	5	0	0.58383838
6	6	0	0.24341534
7	7	0	0.97563452
8	8	1	0.75000000
9	9	0	0.91197302
10	10	1	0.80732484
11	11	0	0.89989350
12	12	0	0.81939799
13	13	0	0.32981530
14	14	0	0.99434768
15	15	1	0.93822394
16	16	0	0.03225806
17	17	0	0.81939394
18	18	0	0.18000000
19	19	1	0.87096774
20	20	0	0.47377049
21	21	1	0.96428571
22	22	1	0.87753036

The output shows that `Rsq1` has three columns listing the subject number (`subid`), the missing value tally (`totmiss`), and the R_i^2 value (`Rsq`). The same is done for the quadratic model using the syntax below. The data frame is saved as Rsq2.

```
> temp2   <- ldply(.data = mylm.2, .fun = function(x) summary(x)$r.squared)
> colnames(temp2) <- c("subid", "Rsq")
> Rsq2    <- merge(mysel, temp2, by = "subid")
> Rsq2
```

	subid	totmiss	Rsq
1	1	0	0.6934866
2	2	1	1.0000000
3	3	0	0.9760000
4	4	1	1.0000000
5	5	0	0.8363636
6	6	0	0.3606368
7	7	0	0.9959391
8	8	1	1.0000000
9	9	0	0.9136594
10	10	1	1.0000000
11	11	0	0.9520767
12	12	0	0.8494983
13	13	0	0.3535620
14	14	0	0.9946763
15	15	1	1.0000000
16	16	0	0.1935484
17	17	0	0.8254545
18	18	0	0.2800000
19	19	1	1.0000000
20	20	0	0.9983607
21	21	1	1.0000000
22	22	1	1.0000000

The totmiss and Rsq columns reveal that the quadratic polynomial fits perfectly for the subjects with missing data. The reason is that the number of Level 1 parameters is equal to the number of time points (three).

Having saved the two data frames, the R_i^2 for the linear and quadratic models can be graphed. The graphs are informative regarding the relative fit of the polynomial models for the subjects. Boxplots of the R_i^2 are constructed, as they provide a handy means of summarizing the distributions. Boxplots are created in ggplot2 using geom_boxplot().

To graph the R_i^2 for each polynomial, a data frame is created by stacking the objects Rsq1 and Rsq2 in a single vector. It is also convenient to create a stacked vector of 1s and 2s indicating the order of the polynomial, and a stacked vector of the missing data tally. For graphing purposes, it is desirable to save the missing data tally and the order of the polynomial as factor variables. Consider the following.

```
> N <- nrow(Rsq1)                  # Number of subjects.
> plotdata <- data.frame(rbind(Rsq1, Rsq2), c(rep(1, N), rep(2, N)))
> colnames(plotdata)[4] <- "poly"
> plotdata$poly.f <- factor(plotdata$poly, labels = c("Linear", "Quadratic"))
> plotdata$missing.f <- factor(plotdata$totmiss, labels = c("Complete", "Missing"))
> head(plotdata)
```

9.6 Subject-Level Selection of Time Transformations

```
  subid totmiss       Rsq poly poly.f missing.f
1     1       0 0.6896552    1 Linear  Complete
2     2       1 0.6675824    1 Linear   Missing
3     3       0 0.9626667    1 Linear  Complete
4     4       1 0.8709677    1 Linear   Missing
5     5       0 0.5838384    1 Linear  Complete
6     6       0 0.2434153    1 Linear  Complete
```

In the example, subjects either have complete data ($n_i = 4$) or have missing data at Grade 8 ($n_i = 3$). Thus, the factor variable, missing.f, has the levels Complete and Missing.

The boxplots of the R_i^2 are constructed conditional on the order of the polynomial and the missing value categories. In the syntax below, geom_boxplot() is used along with the fill= option that colors the boxplots. To produce a scatter of points about the boxplots, jittering is used with geom_point(position="jitter") (see Chapter 4). Jittering is used so that equal R_i^2 values will not be superimposed. Finally, the expression() function is used within ylab() to create a typeset label for the y-axis.

```
> g1 <- ggplot(plotdata, aes(x = poly.f, y = Rsq)) + geom_boxplot(fill = "grey80")
> g2 <- g1 + geom_point(position = "jitter") + facet_grid(. ~ missing.f)
> g3 <- g2 + theme_bw() + xlab("Polynomial") + ylab(expression(R ^ 2))
> print(g3)
```

The graph is shown in Figure 9.2. The left-hand panel shows the boxplots for the subjects with complete data, and the right-hand panel shows those for subjects with missing data (i.e., those missing Grade 8). The left-hand panel indicates the median R_i^2 value is just below 0.8 for the linear model and just above 0.8 for the quadratic model. The right-hand panel reveals the median value is above 0.8 for the linear model, and all values are equal to 1 for the quadratic model, resulting in the boxplot being a single horizontal line.

The exact values of the medians are obtained with the ddply() function. In this case, the goal is to compute the median of Rsq, conditioning on poly.f and missing.f. The optional argument na.rm=TRUE must be used with median() in the syntax.

```
> ddply(.data = data.frame(plotdata$Rsq),
+       .variables=.(plotdata$missing.f, plotdata$poly.f),
+       .fun = each(Md = median), na.rm = TRUE)
```

```
  plotdata$missing.f plotdata$poly.f        Md
1           Complete          Linear 0.7545246
2           Complete       Quadratic 0.8429310
3            Missing          Linear 0.8709677
4            Missing       Quadratic 1.0000000
```

There are several features one might consider in the evaluation of Figure 9.2 and the ddply() output. These include the spread of the R_i^2 for each polynomial, and the median values for both polynomials. In the present evaluation, more weight is given to the subjects with complete data as they provide the most information regarding change.

The ddply() output indicates that the median value for the linear model with no missing data is $Md = 0.75$. This value is relatively high, indicating that for at least the top half of the cases, the linear polynomial accounts for three fourths or more of the within-subjects variation.

The increase in the median value for the quadratic model with no missing data is $0.84 - 0.75 = 0.09$. The increase is approximately 11%, which is not particularly dramatic in light of the fact that R_i^2 will increase with the addition of a worthless predictor. Thus, the increase might not be large enough to justify the quadratic model.

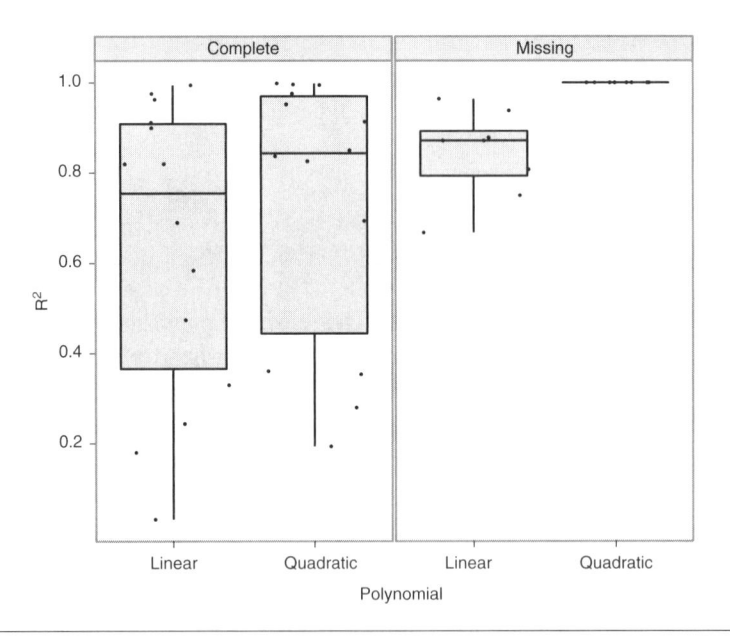

Figure 9.2 Boxplots of R_i^2 by polynomial order and missing value status.

Comparisons based on adjusted R^2. A drawback of using R_i^2 is that it will always increase when a polynomial term is added to the model. The measure does not penalize for the inclusion of worthless predictors. A subjective judgment must be made about what constitutes a large enough difference to support the adoption of a higher order polynomial.

An alternative is to use a penalized measure, such as *adj.* R_i^2, which is symbolized as $\bar{R}_i^2$. The measure is defined as

$$\bar{R}_i^2 = 1 - (1 - R_i^2)\left(\frac{n_i - 1}{n_i - p - 1}\right), \tag{9.6.2}$$

where p is the number of predictors or, equivalently, the number of polynomial terms greater than the 0th.

9.6 Subject-Level Selection of Time Transformations

Care must be taken when computing $\bar{R}_i^2$. It is not defined for saturated models in which $n_i = p + 1$, as the denominator in Equation 9.6.2 is 0. Saturation can easily occur when there are missing data. It should also be noted that $\bar{R}_i^2$ can be negative, even when $n_i > p + 1$. Using Equation 9.6.2, it can be shown that for the quadratic polynomial and $n_i = 4$, $\bar{R}_i^2 < 0$ when $R_i^2 < .75$.

The $\bar{R}_i^2$ are extracted from a list object in a similar manner as the R_i^2. The appropriate slot of the summary() object is $adj.r.squared. Suppose the goal is to compare linear and quadratic models. Since $max(n_i) = 4$, those who have missing data must be excluded, as there is a requirement of $n_i \geq p + 1$, and $p + 1 = 3$ with the quadratic model. The subset() function is used to select the subjects with no missing data. This is performed below, and the resulting data frame is saved as mysub.

```
> mysub <- subset(MPLS.LS2, totmiss == 0)
```

The next step is to include mysub in the dlply() function, in order to fit the linear and polynomial model for each subject.

```
> mylm.1 <- dlply(.data = mysub, .variables = .(mysub$subid),
+                 .fun = function(x) {lm(read ~ grade, data = x)})
> mylm.2 <- dlply(.data = mysub, .variables = .(mysub$subid),
+                 .fun = function(x) {lm(read ~ grade + I(grade ^ 2), data = x)})
```

The ldply() function extracts the $\bar{R}_i^2$ and saves them in a data frame. This is performed for the linear and quadratic fits. The user-defined function is created outside of ldply(), illustrating another approach to the syntax.

```
> myfunc <- function(x) summary(x)$adj.r.squared   # Define the function.
> ## Linear.
> adjRsq1 <- ldply(.data = mylm.1, .fun = myfunc)
> colnames(adjRsq1) <- c("subid", "adjRsq")
> ## Quadratic.
> adjRsq2 <- ldply(.data = mylm.2, .fun = myfunc)
> colnames(adjRsq2) <- c("subid", "adjRsq")
```

Having constructed the two data frames, aRsq1 and aRsq2, they are stacked to create the data frame for graphing. Then the boxplots of the $\bar{R}_i^2$ are constructed. Consider the following syntax.

```
> N <- nrow(adjRsq1)
> ## Create plot data.
> plotdata <- data.frame(rbind(adjRsq1, adjRsq2), c(rep(1, N), rep(2, N)))
> colnames(plotdata)[3] <- "poly"
> plotdata$poly.f <- factor(plotdata$poly, labels = c("Linear", "Quadratic"))
> ## ggplot().
> g1 <- ggplot(plotdata, aes(x = poly.f, y = adjRsq)) + geom_boxplot(fill = "grey80")
> g2 <- g1 + geom_point(position = "jitter")
> g3 <- g2 + theme_bw() + xlab("") + ylab(expression(bar(R)^2))
> print(g3)
```

The boxplots are shown in Figure 9.3. The dispersion is much wider for the quadratic model, indicating some $\bar{R}_i^2$ decrease a large amount in going from

[Boxplot figure showing R² on y-axis (ranging from about -1.0 to 0.5+) for Linear and Quadratic polynomials]

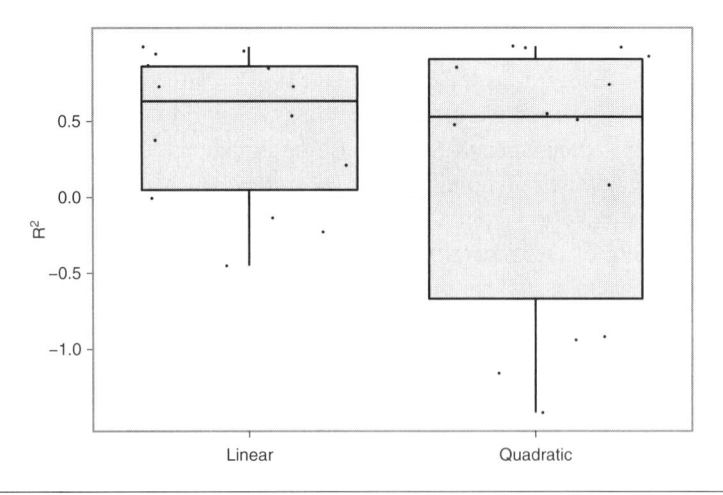

Figure 9.3 Boxplots of $\bar{R}_i^2$ by polynomial.

the linear to the quadratic polynomial. The median of the $\bar{R}_i^2$ for the linear model is higher than for the quadratic model. This suggests the linear model is appropriate.

9.6.4 POOLED MEASURES OF FIT

An alternative to working with the distribution of R_i^2 or $\bar{R}_i^2$ is to pool information from all subjects into a single summary statistic. The information to be combined is based on the subject-level sums of squares, which are the building blocks of R_i^2 and $\bar{R}_i^2$. The main advantage is that subjects who have missing data can be included in the calculations.

Recall that R^2 can be expressed in terms of sums of squares. In this context, R_i^2 is written as

$$R_i^2 = 1 - \left[\frac{SSR_i}{SST_i}\right] = 1 - \left[\frac{\sum_{j}^{n_i}(y_{ij} - \hat{y}_{ij})^2}{\sum_{j}^{n_i}(y_{ij} - \bar{y}_{ij})^2}\right], \quad (9.6.3)$$

where $\hat{y}_{ij}$ is a predicted value from the OLS solution, and $\bar{y}_{ij}$ is the mean among the repeated measures for the ith subject. SSR_i is the *sum of squares residuals*, and SST_i is the *sum of squares total*.

9.6 Subject-Level Selection of Time Transformations

Following Verbeke and Molenberghs (2000), a pooled version of R_i^2 is defined by replacing each individual sum of squares in Equation 9.6.3 by the sum among all the subjects. The pooled measure is

$$R_{meta}^2 = 1 - \left[\frac{\sum_i^N SSR_i}{\sum_i^N SST_i} \right]. \qquad (9.6.4)$$

As indicated in Equation 9.6.4, the individual sum of squares terms are combined. This allows information from all the subjects to be used for the summary measure. The word *meta* appears in the subscript. This is to denote that the pooling is similar to the idea of combining information as in a meta-analysis. The summations in Equation 9.6.4 are over all the subjects, so that any subject with at least one nonmissing time point is included. The syntax for computing R_{meta}^2 is considered in a moment.

R_{meta}^2 shares the property of R_i^2, in that it will increase when a predictor is added to the model. Therefore, R_{meta}^2 will always be larger for a higher order polynomial, even if the additional term is worthless. For this reason, it is preferable to use a penalized fit index that adjusts for the number of predictors. Two penalized measures are considered. The first is a pooled version of the *residual standard error* (RSE), known as RSE_{meta}. The second is a pooled version of $\bar{R}_i^2$, known as $\bar{R}_{meta}^2$.

RSE_{meta} is the pooled analog of the subject-level measure, RSE_i. The subject-level measure is defined as

$$RSE_i = \sqrt{\frac{SSR_i}{n_i - p_i - 1}}, \qquad (9.6.5)$$

where $n_i - p_i - 1$ is the residual degrees of freedom.

With RSE_{meta}, the subject-level sum of squares in Equation 9.6.5 is replaced with the sum among the subjects. The residual degrees of freedom are also replaced with a pooled version. The formula for RSE_{meta} is

$$RSE_{meta} = \sqrt{\frac{\sum_{i=1}^N SSR_i}{\sum_{i=1}^N (n_i - p_i - 1)}}, \qquad (9.6.6)$$

where $\sum_{i=1}^N (n_i - p_i - 1)$ is the meta residual degrees of freedom.

RSE_{meta} is computed with the following syntax. For clarity, the individual coefficients are again estimated for the subjects. The `resid()`

function is used to compute the residuals, and the residual *df* reside in the `$df.residual` slot of the output object.

```
> ## Estimate coefficients.
> my1 <- dlply(MPLS.LS, .(MPLS.LS$subid), function(x) lm(read ~ grade, data = x))
> my2 <- dlply(MPLS.LS, .(MPLS.LS$subid), function(x) lm(read ~ grade + I(grade ^ 2),
+                                                         data = x))
> ## SSE.
> sse1 <- sum(ldply(my1, function(x) sum(resid(x) ^ 2))[, 2])
> sse2 <- sum(ldply(my2, function(x) sum(resid(x) ^ 2))[, 2])
> ## Residual df.
> df1 <- sum(ldply(my1, function(x) x$df.residual)[, 2])
> df2 <- sum(ldply(my2, function(x) x$df.residual)[, 2])
> ## Compute RSE meta.
> RSEmeta.1 <- sqrt(sse1/df1)
> RSEmeta.2 <- sqrt(sse2/df2)
> RSEmeta.1
```

```
[1] 4.261803
```

```
> RSEmeta.2
```

```
[1] 5.623293
```

The output shows that $RSE_{meta} = 4.26$ for the linear model, and $RSE_{meta} = 5.62$ for the quadratic model. Since the value for the linear model is smaller, there is evidence that the linear model is sufficient.

The other penalized measure is $\bar{R}^2_{meta}$. $\bar{R}^2_{meta}$ is computed by dividing the numerator and denominator terms of R^2_{meta} by their respective meta degrees of freedom. The formula is

$$\bar{R}^2_{meta} = 1 - \frac{\left[\dfrac{\sum_{i=1}^{N} SSR_i}{\sum_{i=1}^{N}(n_i - p_i - 1)}\right]}{\left[\dfrac{\sum_{i=1}^{N} SST_i}{\sum_{i=1}^{N} n_i - N}\right]}, \qquad (9.6.7)$$

where $\sum_{i=1}^{N} n_i - N$ is the meta total degrees of freedom.

RSE_{meta} and $\bar{R}^2_{meta}$ are constructed based on OLS formulas, which assume independence among the repeated measures observations, not just among the subjects. Since this assumption is not tenable with longitudinal data, *the penalized measures cannot be used as a basis for inference*. It is emphasized that these measures are used only as descriptive devices to provide evidence concerning the appropriate order of the polynomial.

9.6 Subject-Level Selection of Time Transformations

The syntax below is used to compute R^2_{meta} and $\bar{R}^2_{meta}$ based on a list of `dlply()` objects. In the example, the objects `mylm.1` and `mylm.2` are for the linear and quadratic models, respectively. With more than four time points, there might be additional objects for a cubic polynomial, and so on, and each can be included in the list of objects to be analyzed.

Rather than explain each line of syntax, focus is on the first three lines, as these are the only lines that need to be altered by the reader. In the first two lines below, the `dlply()` objects are created. In the third line, the object names are provide as a quoted list within `c()`. The remainder of the syntax does not need to be altered by the user. Consider the following.

```
> ################################################################
> mylm.1    <- dlply(MPLS.LS, .(MPLS.LS$subid), function(x) lm(read ~ grade, data = x))
> mylm.2    <- dlply(MPLS.LS, .(MPLS.LS$subid), function(x) lm(read ~ grade+ I(grade^ 2),
+                                                              data = x))
> lm.objects <- c("mylm.1", "mylm.2")
> ################################################################
> Rsqmeta    <- numeric(length(lm.objects))
> adjRsqmeta <- numeric(length(lm.objects))
> for(i in 1:length(lm.objects)){
+     ## Define functions.
+     myfunc1 <- function(x) sum((x$model[ ,1] - mean(x$model[ ,1])) ^ 2)   # SST.
+     myfunc2 <- function(x) sum(resid(x) ^ 2)                              # SSR.
+     myfunc3 <- function(x) length(x$model[ ,1]) - 1                       # df Total.
+     myfunc4 <- function(x) x$df.residual                                  # df Resid.
+     ## SST.
+     SSTotal <- ldply(eval(parse(text = lm.objects[i])), myfunc1)
+     ## SSE.
+     SSResid <- ldply(eval(parse(text = lm.objects[i])), myfunc2)
+     ## Rsq-meta.
+     Rsqmeta[i] <- 1 - (sum(SSResid[ ,2]) / sum(SSTotal[ ,2]))
+     ## Degrees of freedom.
+     dfTotal <- sum(ldply(eval(parse(text = lm.objects[i])), myfunc3)[ ,2])
+     dfResid <- sum(ldply(eval(parse(text = lm.objects[i])), myfunc4)[ ,2])
+     ## Adjusted Rsq-meta.
+     adjRsqmeta[i] <- 1 - ((sum(SSResid) / dfResid) / (sum(SSTotal) / dfTotal))
+ }
> Rsq.meta    <- data.frame(lm.objects, Rsqmeta)
> adjRsq.meta <- data.frame(lm.objects, adjRsqmeta)
```

The last two lines of syntax above create the data frames containing the values of R^2_{meta} and $\bar{R}^2_{meta}$, respectively. Their contents are printed below.

```
> Rsq.meta
```

	lm.objects	Rsqmeta
1	mylm.1	0.8298182
2	mylm.2	0.8847786

```
> adjRsq.meta
```

	lm.objects	adjRsqmeta
1	mylm.1	0.6432226
2	mylm.2	0.2961982

The output shows that $R^2_{meta} = 0.83$ for the linear model, and $R^2_{meta} = 0.88$ for the quadratic model. The values for the models are closer than the median values considered in the last section. R^2_{meta} for the linear model is rather large, and the increase for the quadratic model is not impressive. There is evidence that the linear model is sufficient.

The output also shows that $\bar{R}^2_{meta} = 0.64$ for the linear model, and $\bar{R}^2_{meta} = 0.30$ for the quadratic model. The value for the linear model is more than twice that of the quadratic model. It seems to be the case that one can be confident that the linear model is sufficient.

Syntax details*. For the reader curious about the above syntax, some space is devoted here to an explanation of the details. The argument, `numeric (length(lm.objects))`, is used twice to define a numeric vector of length 2 that is used to store the R^2_{meta} and $\bar{R}^2_{meta}$ values. The `for()` loop is used to compute R^2_{meta} and $\bar{R}^2_{meta}$ for each object listed in `lm.objects`. The generic function, `myfunc1`, computes SST_i, with the response scores being accessed at the `$model[,1]` slot. The second generic function, `myfunc2`, uses the `resid()` function to compute the SSR_i.

The last two generic functions, `myfunc3` and `myfunc4`, are used to extract the degrees of freedom for each subject. Within `ldply()`, the syntax `eval(parse(text = lm.objects[i]))` takes one of the quoted strings in `lm.objects` and evaluates it as an object rather than as a name. Finally, the `sum()` function is used to sum a numeric vector.

9.6.5 CLUSTERING OF SUBJECT CURVES*

This optional section considers selection of a change curve for exploratory analysis. In exploratory analysis, not only is the shape of the change curve unknown, but relevant static predictors are also unknown. There can be additional complicating conditions, such as a wide variety of observed change curves and/or a large sample size.

For such situations, it is useful to cluster subject trajectories. Clustering helps the researcher identify the variety of curve shapes and potential subgroups of currently unidentified static predictors. The clustering might constitute a preliminary or preselection step of the analysis, or it might be the primary analysis.

There are two major families of clustering methods, *model based* and *partitioning based*. Model-based procedures involve statistical assumptions such as normality, and often involve formal tests to check the validity of the clustering. Many of these methods are related to mixture modeling or latent class analysis (see, e.g., Nagin, 1999).

Partitioning methods are algorithm-based and do not require any parametric assumptions. In exploratory analysis, it is perhaps best to make as few assumptions as possible. Thus, the focus in this section is on a partitioning method known as *K-means clustering*. The idea behind K-means clustering is to automatically partition the data into a number of groups. This is performed in such a way that the data within the same cluster are similar, and the

9.6 Subject-Level Selection of Time Transformations

data belonging to different clusters are dissimilar. The algorithm considered chooses the number of clusters by attempting to simultaneously maximize the variability between clusters and minimize the variability within clusters.

The K-means algorithm focuses on the distance between the centers of clusters, called the *centroids*. There is one centroid per cluster, and initially, a predetermined number of k centroids ($k > 1$) are randomly determined. Data values in the neighborhood of a centroid are grouped into a cluster. The positions of the centroids are then reestimated and located in the center of the cluster to which they correspond. This procedure, data clustering and centroid reestimation, is repeated until the k centroids are fixed. The final clusters produced by K-means are sensitive to the initial placement of the centroids, so the procedure is repeated several times to identify stable centroid positions and provide more robust results. The repetitions are referred to as *reruns*.

As with all clustering methods, it is unclear if the K-means method is capable of finding the "correct" number of clusters (Hardy, 1996). To complicate matters, the clustering of individual change curves involves intercepts and trajectories, and the clusters can be defined for each, or by a combination. The goal, then, is not to attempt to identify the correct number of clusters. Rather, the object is to examine a number of cluster solutions for clues regarding the variety of curve shapes and intercept values.

K-means clustering for longitudinal data is performed with the kml() function of the KmL package written by Christophe Genolini (Genolini & Falissard, 2010). *The data to be clustered must be in wide format* (see Chapter 3). Missing values are permissible, which indicates that the data need not be complete or balanced, although things go easier if there is balance on time. The wide-format data frame must have the subject number as the first column, with the remaining columns consisting of the repeated measures of the response variable and nothing else. Recall that with the wide-format data frame, the time metric is implied by the number of columns of the repeated measures.

In the syntax below, the repeated measures are reshaped into wide format. The subset() function is used to select only the subject identification number (subid), the reading variable (read), and the grade variable (grade).[1] Then reshape() is used to create the wide-format data frame, which is named read.wide.

```
> temp <- subset(MPLS.LS, select = c(subid, read, grade))
> read.wide <- reshape(temp, v.names = "read", timevar = "grade",
+                     idvar = "subid", direction = "wide")
> read.wide
```

---

[1] For the K-means procedure, it does not matter if the original time metric or a transformation is used.

	subid	read.5	read.6	read.7	read.8
1.5	1	172	185	179	194
2.5	2	200	210	209	NA
3.5	3	191	199	203	215
4.5	4	200	195	194	NA
5.5	5	207	213	212	213
6.5	6	191	189	206	195
7.5	7	199	208	213	218
8.5	8	191	194	194	NA
9.5	9	149	154	174	177
10.5	10	200	212	213	NA
11.5	11	178	191	193	199
12.5	12	188	192	208	206
13.5	13	228	236	228	239
14.5	14	199	210	225	235
15.5	15	218	223	236	NA
16.5	16	228	226	234	227
17.5	17	201	210	208	219
18.5	18	218	220	217	221
19.5	19	215	216	221	NA
20.5	20	204	215	219	214
21.5	21	237	241	243	NA
22.5	22	219	233	236	NA

The output shows that the read.wide data frame has one row per subject, with the first column being the subject number, and the remaining columns being the repeated measures. There are missing data at the last time point, and NA values are used to fill in the missing observations.

After creating the wide-format data frame, an additional preparation step must be performed. The kml() function only works with a class of objects known as ClusterizLongData. To create an object of this class, the data frame must be saved with the as.cld() function. The function also allows a specification of the time metric, which is Grades 5 to 8. Consider the following.

```
> require(kml)
> mycld ← as.cld(read.wide, timeReal = 5:8)
```

The new object is named mycld. Having created this object, clustering can now proceed with the kml() function.

At a minimum, the kml() function requires the name of the Clusteriz LongData object (mycld). By default, the number of clusters fit is two to six, but this can be altered by using the nbClusters= argument. Because of the sensitivity to initial centroid assignment, the K-means algorithm is rerun a number of times. The default number of reruns is 20, but this can be changed with the nbRedrawing= argument.

For each rerun and each number of clusters ($k = 2, \ldots, 6$), an index of fit is computed, known as the *Calinski and Harabasz criterion* (CHC; Calinski

9.6 Subject-Level Selection of Time Transformations

& Harabasz, 1974). The CHC is a weighted ratio of the between-cluster variance over the within-cluster variance, *and larger values indicate more optimal clustering*. There is an inclination to select the number of clusters based on the largest CHC value. However, the reader is cautioned that discovering the correct number of clusters by any criterion is known to be a difficult task (Hardy, 1996).

The results of `kml()` are best depicted graphically, with the cluster curves superimposed with individual curves, and the letter having a color coding to reflect cluster membership. The rerun process can be viewed in real time by including the optional arguments `print.cal=TRUE` and `print.traj=TRUE`, which display graphs of the CHC and the cluster trajectories, respectively. With these options, `kml()` will open a R graphics window, and the CHC and trajectory graphs will appear side by side. The graphs will continually change until all 20 reruns for all cluster sizes have been completed. Rather than depict the rerun process, focus is on interpreting graphs at the termination of the reruns.

In the syntax below, the `kml()` function is used with optional arguments to show the real-time graphs of the reruns.

```
> kml(Object = mycld, print.cal = TRUE, print.traj = TRUE)
```

Information about the reruns is automatically added to the `mycld` object. Thus, this object is referenced when presenting the results.

After the reruns have terminated, a graph of the CHC by the number of clusters is examined to see potential candidates for the optimal cluster size. This is accomplished with the `plotCriterion()` function. To construct a graph with a nice appearance, two parameters are set prior to graphing using `par()`. The argument, `mfrow=c(1,1)`, sets a single frame for plotting, and `pty="s"` produces a square graph (as opposed to a rectangular one). Following `plotCriterion()`, `mtext()` is used to label the axes in the graph. Consider the following.

```
> par(mfrow = c(1, 1), pty = "s")
> plotCriterion(mycld)
> mtext("Cluster Number (k)", side = 1, line = 3)    # Set label in bottom margin.
> mtext("CHC", side = 2, line = 3)                    # Set label in left margin.
```

The graph is shown in Figure 9.4. The CHC is largest for $k = 4$, followed by $k = 5$ and then $k = 6$. For now, judgment regarding the optimal number of clusters is deferred, as the graphs of the trajectories provide additional relevant information.

More important than the CHC graph is the graph of the cluster trajectories. These are the curves of the means for the clusters. The cluster trajectories are graphed using `plot()`. The optional argument `y=` determines what cluster

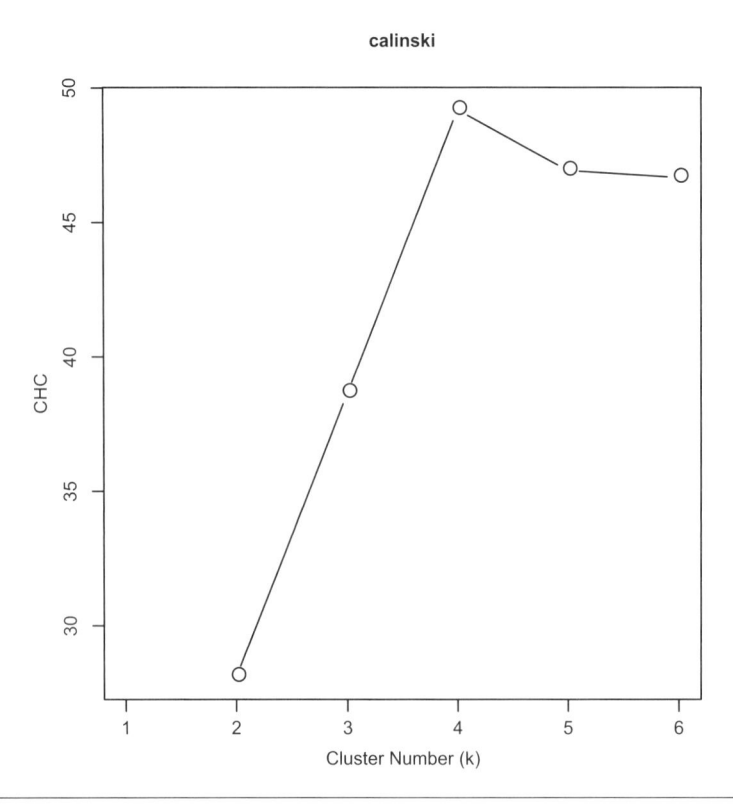

Figure 9.4 Graph of the Calinski and Harabasz criterion (CHC) by number of clusters.

size is graphed. In the syntax below, a 2 × 2 matrix is defined for plotting, and a graph is drawn at each cell location for cluster size $k = 2, \ldots, 5$.

```
> par(mfrow = c(2,2), pty = "s")                              # 2 x 2 matrix, square graphs.
> plot(mycld, y = 2, ylab = "Response", main = "k = 2")       # Optional labeling included.
> plot(mycld, y = 3, ylab = "Response", main = "k = 3")
> plot(mycld, y = 4, ylab = "Response", main = "k = 4")
> plot(mycld, y = 5, ylab = "Response", main = "k = 5")
> par(mfrow = c(1,1), pty = "m")                              # Default settings.
```

The graphs are shown in Figure 9.5. In each graph, the individual change curves are draw with thin lines, and the cluster-level curves are draw with thick lines. A letter denotes the cluster and is drawn at the centroid. There is a legend for each graph showing the percentage of cases in each cluster. The clusters are labeled with capital letters (A, B, etc.).

The goal of the clustering is to get a sense of (1) the variety of curve shapes, (2) potential intercept effects, and (3) potential trajectory effects. The first of these can aid in the selection of a change curve for the analysis. The second two can suggest effects that might be conditional on static predictors.

Regarding the shape of the curves, most of the curves based on the larger percentages of cases are close to linear. This suggests that a linear change

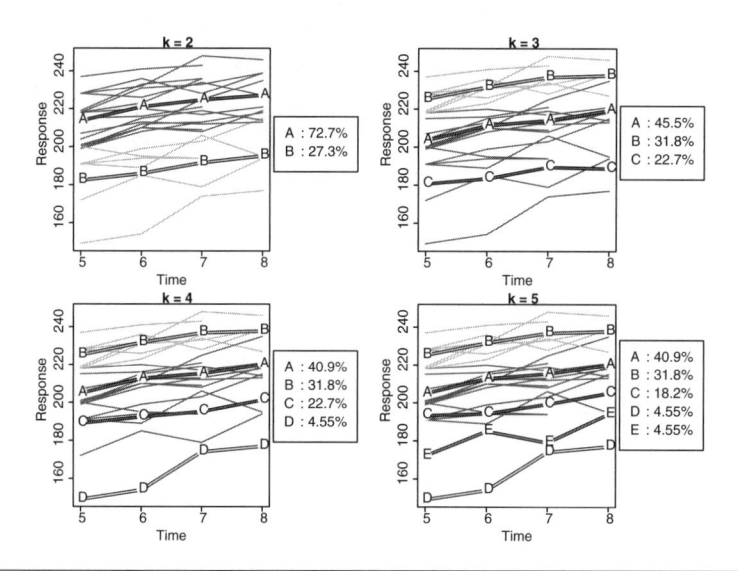

9.6 Subject-Level Selection of Time Transformations

Figure 9.5 Graph of cluster trajectories over time; k is the number of clusters.

curve is sufficient for further analysis. The curves at the bottom of the $k = 4$ and $k = 5$ graphs have a greater degree of nonlinearity. However, these curves are based on clusters consisting of less than 5% of the data. Since the sample size is small ($N = 22$), a cluster of less than 5% consists of a single subject. A single-subject cluster cannot be valid, as the trajectory is almost surely an overfit. Therefore, the D and E trajectories do not represent patterns of interest. Furthermore, one might consider the optimal clustering to be $k < 4$. The single-subject D cluster in the $k = 4$ graph appears to be a result of the subject being an outlier.

Regarding intercept effects, all the graphs indicate there might be such effects. For example, the $k = 2$ graph shows two nearly parallel curves with different starting points. Although no static predictors are considered here, it is known from earlier chapters that the cluster intercept effects can be accounted for by the risk static predictor. Perhaps the other graphs ($k > 2$) suggest intercept effects for additional risk categories.

As for trajectory effects, most of the curves are close to parallel, especially those based on the higher percentages of cases. This indicates a lack of trajectory effects based on unknown static predictors. This is consistent with analyses of the previous chapters that show no appreciable trajectory effects based on risk and ethnicity.

This section ends by mentioning that model-based clustering using mixture models can be performed with the mmlcr package written by Steve Buyske (Buyske, 2006). The package is based on the predecessor to the lme4 package, which is the lme package. The syntax for lme is not discussed in this book, but it is required for use of mmlcr. Details of lme can be found in several Web sources, or in the book by Pinheiro and Bates (2000).

Selecting Random Effects 10

As discussed in the previous chapters, it is a daunting task to select static predictor effects, time predictors, and random effects simultaneously. A simplifying strategy is to preselect the time predictors and random effects and use multimodel analysis with the AIC or stepwise analysis with the LRT to evaluate static predictor effects. Selection of time predictors was discussed in Chapter 9, and the selection of random effects is discussed in this chapter.

Random effects are an essential part of the LMER model for longitudinal data. It is by way of the random effects that individual differences are accounted for, as well as the dependency due to repeated measures.

Strategies for selection of random effects have been delayed to this point because their inclusion is influenced by the time predictors. As discussed in Chapter 9, the number of possible random effects is determined by the order of the polynomial of the change curve. The selection of the random effects can be automatic, provided the researcher decides to include a random effect for each polynomial term, starting with the 0th (intercept).

There are situations in which automatic inclusion is not optimal. When the order of the polynomial is greater than 1, the addition of a single random effect can add several variance components to the LMER model. Some of these parameters might be superfluous, which affects statistical efficiency. Inclusion of unneeded variance components can cause estimation problems and inaccuracy of the parameter estimates. For this reason, the researcher might want to evaluate the random effects in terms of worthiness for inclusion in the model.

Similar to the preceding chapter, descriptive and inferential approaches to the selection of random effects are considered. Two types of descriptive methods are introduced. The first focuses on OLS estimates of the subject-level change curves. The second focuses on the residuals from different model fits. Two types of inferential methods are also discussed, NHST based on the LRT and model comparison based on the AICc.

The selection of random effects is dissimilar to that of fixed effects in important ways. First, random effects are rarely, if ever, the primary focus of analysis. For this reason, there is an emphasis on the selection of random effects either prior or subsequent to a fixed effects analysis. Second, the inferential methods discussed below have variances as their main object of inference. Inferences with variances are more complicated than with fixed effects. For example, the sampling distribution under the null hypothesis for the LRT is not well approximated by the χ^2 distribution. This leads to bias in favor of simpler models with too few random effects.

The above issues, especially the bias problem, require careful consideration and special remedies. Regarding inference, one solution is the bootstrap. Different types of bootstrap methods are applicable for various situations, and a "fast" version and a "slow" version are discussed, each named for their required computing time. Unlike previous chapters, the bootstrap methods are not relegated to optional sections. The reason is that bootstrap methods are compelling compared to other methods for selecting random effects or their variance components.

In addition to methods for selecting random effects, certain ancillary topics are also presented. Among these topics is computing predicted random effects scores based on a fitted LMER model. Such predicted scores are useful for evaluating statistical assumptions and for providing information about change for a specific individual.

10.1 Automatic Selection of Random Effects

In the longitudinal LMER models considered in this book, the maximum number of random effects is determined by the number of time transformations in the model. If p is the number of time transformations, then there are $p + 1$ fixed effects for the change curve and the same number of potential random effects. For example, when the only time predictor is grade5, then at a maximum there can be two random effects. When grade5 and grade5² are the predictors, there can be a maximum of three random effects, and so on.

One approach to the selection of random effects mentioned in past chapters is to include a random effect for the intercept and every time predictor. This automatic approach seems appropriate when the number of time predictors is small, as in the case of the linear change curve. Although the linear model might include potentially needless variance components, such as the variance of the slopes, these are kept to a minimum.

For the LMER models considered in this book, the only means of accounting for the correlation due to repeated measures is through the random effects. In this sense, there is some justification in automatically including at least a small number of random effects in the model at the outset. As will be demonstrated in the following sections, two random effects provide a covariance (correlation) structure among the repeated measures that appears to be appropriate for much empirical data. *Therefore, a rule of thumb is to include at least two random effects in the model unless there is compelling evidence to the contrary.*

The automatic approach is less appealing when the change curve is nonlinear, as the addition of a single time transformation can result in the addition of several variance components. For instance, the automatic inclusion of random effects when increasing from the linear to quadratic change curve model will result in three additional parameters. Increasing from the quadratic model to the cubic model will result in four additional parameters, and so on.

The inclusion of additional random effects presents the possibility of adding unneeded variance components to the model. The variance of the quadratic random effect might be 0, for example. In this case, not only is the variance term superfluous, but the covariances involving the quadratic random effect are also unnecessary. (A covariance will be 0 when at least one variance is 0.)

There are at least two potential problems when unnecessary variance components are included in the model. First, the relative statistical efficiency is decreased. This means, for example, that SEs are larger than they should be compared to when the unnecessary variance components are omitted. Second, superfluous variance components can lead to estimation problems. Estimated variances that are near 0 present problems for estimation algorithms. The result can be inaccurate parameter estimates. In extreme cases, the estimation algorithm can fail altogether. The lmer() function will issue an error message regarding *convergence failure* for such cases.

To avoid these problems, the researcher may want to use descriptive or inferential methods to evaluate the need for particular random effects and variance components. Another potential use for the methods is to evaluate research hypotheses regarding the variance components themselves. A fundamental research question might be whether there is individual variation in the rate of change over time. The methods discussed in the following sections can be used to address this type of question.

10.2 Random Effects and Variance Components

In a discussion of random effects, it is important to distinguish between the random effects themselves and the variance components of the random effects. The random effects are random variables, whereas the variance components are the variances and covariances of those random variables. In LMER analysis, it is typical to estimate the variances and covariances and not deal directly with the random effects. The reason is that applied researchers are usually interested in aggregate effects, which are indexed by the variance components.

As a touchstone for the discussion, consider the LMER model with grade5 as the sole predictor and two random effects in the model:

$$y_{ij} = (\beta_0 + b_{0i}) + (\beta_1 + b_{1i})(\texttt{grade5}_{ij}) + \varepsilon_{ij}. \quad (10.2.1)$$

Recall that random effects are individual deviations from the fixed effects, with b_{0i} being the ith individual's deviation from the group intercept, and b_{1i} being the deviation from the group slope. The variance of a random effect indexes individual variability, with $Var(b_{0i})$ indexing variability of intercepts, and $Var(b_{1i})$ indexing variability of slopes. For inferences with LMER, the common assumption is made that the random effects and random errors are normally distributed, with means equal to 0. The random effects may be correlated, but each is independent of the random errors.

The variance-covariance matrix[1] among the random effects is symbolized as G. G is a symmetric matrix, meaning the upper triangle is a mirror image of the lower triangle with equivalent corresponding elements. Suppose that q is the number of predictors of the random effects, and $q^* = q + 1$ is the total number of random effects (including the intercepts). The maximum possible number of unique elements in G is $\frac{q^*(q^*+1)}{2}$. If there are two random effects, then G has the structure

$$G = \begin{bmatrix} Var(b_{0i}) & Cov(b_{0i}, b_{1i}) \\ Cov(b_{0i}, b_{1i}) & Var(b_{1i}) \end{bmatrix}. \quad (10.2.2)$$

The variances are on the diagonal, and the off-diagonal contains the covariance.

It is not always the case that each element of G is required. In some instances, a single random effect will suffice, meaning G consists of the single element, $Var(b_{0i})$. In other cases, the random effects are uncorrelated, and then $Cov(b_{0i}, b_{1i}) = 0$, and only the variances in G are nonzero.

The three scenarios are depicted in Table 10.1. The models in the table illustrate that the selection of random effects and the selection of variance components are distinct. For example, Model 2 and Model 3 have the same number of random effects, but a different number of nonzero variance components.

All the models in Table 10.1 have the same fixed effects structure, so why might one want to select a model with a particular structure of G? The answer is twofold. First, based on theory or the nature of the data, the researcher may have expectations that are consistent with one structure or another. For instance, if there is an expectation that subjects will vary in their intercepts but not their rate of change over time, Model 1 is desirable.

Second, based on preliminary graphical or statistical analysis, there may be indications that one structure is more appropriate than another. Suppose in the initial estimation, the estimated $Var(b_{1i})$ in Model 3 is near to 0, and the estimated $Cov(b_{0i}, b_{1i}) = -1$. The perfect negative correlation and small estimated variance are an indication that G has too many parameters (Bates, 2011; Pinheiro & Bates, 2000). Model 2 or even Model 1 would be desirable candidates in this case.

In the sections to follow, some details of estimating the variance components using `lmer()` are discussed. Specifics are presented regarding how

---

[1]This section discusses some fundamentals of matrices. A soft introduction is provided in the Appendix. The reader new to matrix representations should peruse at least the first section of the Appendix prior to reading this section.

10.2 Random Effects and Variance Components

various structures of G give rise to models of dependency among the repeated measures. This information can help in a preliminary selection of a structure for G.

Table 10.1 Models differing in variance components.

Model	LMER Equation	G
1	$y_{ij} = (\beta_0 + b_{0i})$ $+\beta_1(\text{grade5}_{ij}) + \varepsilon_{ij}$	$\left[Var(b_{0i}) \right]$
2	$y_{ij} = (\beta_0 + b_{0i})$ $+(\beta_1 + b_{1i})(\text{grade5}_{ij}) + \varepsilon_{ij}$	$\begin{bmatrix} Var(b_{0i}) & 0 \\ 0 & Var(b_{1i}) \end{bmatrix}$
3	$y_{ij} = (\beta_0 + b_{0i})$ $+(\beta_1 + b_{1i})(\text{grade5}_{ij}) + \varepsilon_{ij}$	$\begin{bmatrix} Var(b_{0i}) & Cov(b_{0i}, b_{1i}) \\ Cov(b_{0i}, b_{1i}) & Var(b_{1i}) \end{bmatrix}$

10.2.1 RESTRICTED MAXIMUM LIKELIHOOD

Decisions about the inclusion of random effects, or their variance components, should be based on models estimated with REML rather than ML. ML yields variance components that are biased downward, meaning they are smaller than they should be. REML corrects for this downward bias.

To illustrate the difference in REML and ML, consider the linear change curve model of Equation 10.2.1. In previous chapters, ML was used for estimation by including the argument REML=FALSE in the lmer() syntax. REML estimation is the default with lmer(), and it can be used by either setting REML=TRUE or omitting the argument altogether. In the syntax below, the same model is estimated using ML and REML.

```
> reml.out  <-  lmer(read ~ grade5 + (grade5 | subid), MPLS.LS)
> ml.out    <-  lmer(read ~ grade5 + (grade5 | subid), MPLS.LS, REML = FALSE)
```

The random effects table in the output is printed by accessing the @REmat slot in the summary() output object. Consider the following for the REML solution.

```
> print(summary(reml.out)@REmat, quote = FALSE)

 Groups   Name          Variance   Std.Dev.   Corr
 subid    (Intercept)   398.6429   19.9660
          grade5          7.1406    2.6722    -0.528
 Residual                18.6601    4.3197
```

The output is a matrix object, but this is not apparent. If quote=FALSE was not used, then all the values would be quoted, as a matrix object has only one type of data (see Chapter 3). The values are character strings, and it is more convenient to obtain numerical output for the purposes below.

Numeric output is obtained by using the VarCorr() function in the lme4 package. The fitted output object name is supplied to the function as illustrated below.

```
> VarCorr(reml.out)
```

```
$subid
            (Intercept)      grade5
(Intercept)  398.64294   -28.162414
grade5       -28.16241     7.140641
attr(,"stddev")
(Intercept)      grade5
 19.966045      2.672198
attr(,"correlation")
            (Intercept)      grade5
(Intercept)   1.0000000   -0.5278484
grade5       -0.5278484    1.0000000

attr(,"sc")
[1]  4.319734
```

There are four sections of the output. Lines 1 to 4 show the estimated G matrix. This matrix is referenced by the subject identification variable prefaced by a dollar sign, which is listed in line 1. Lines 5 to 7 show the square root of the diagonal of the estimated G matrix, which contains the SDs of the random effects (*not* the SEs). The SDs are extracted with the attr() function as shown in a moment. Lines 8 to 11 show the correlation matrix of the random effects. This is the standardized version of the estimated G matrix. Lines 13 to 14 show the table of the square root of the estimated error variance, $\hat{\sigma}_\varepsilon$.

The attr() function is used to print the SDs, the correlation matrix, and $\hat{\sigma}_\varepsilon$. The VarCorr() statement must appear referencing the subject variable. This is followed by the appropriate keyword shown in the output above, "stddev", "correlation", or "sc". Below the correlation matrix is printed.

```
> attr(VarCorr(reml.out)$subid, "correlation")
```

	(Intercept)	grade5
(Intercept)	1.0000000	-0.5278484
grade5	-0.5278484	1.0000000

To extract the estimated G matrix alone, the as.data.frame() function is used, and reference is made to the subject identification variable. The

10.2 Random Effects and Variance Components

syntax is shown below. The matrix for the REML solution and the ML solution is printed for purposes of comparison.

```
> print("--- REML ---", quote = FALSE); as.data.frame(VarCorr(reml.out)$subid)
```

```
[1] --- REML ---
```

	(Intercept)	grade5
(Intercept)	398.64294	-28.162414
grade5	-28.16241	7.140641

```
> print("---  ML  ---", quote = FALSE); as.data.frame(VarCorr(ml.out)$subid)
```

```
[1] ---  ML  ---
```

	(Intercept)	grade5
(Intercept)	380.20163	-26.817849
grade5	-26.81785	6.558018

As the output shows, the variance components for the model estimated with ML are all *smaller* than their counterparts estimated with REML. This illustrates the downward bias of the ML estimators.

The extent of similarity of the REML and ML solutions depends on the sample size. As the sample size increases, the REML and ML solutions converge. Thus, for large-sample problems, the parameter estimates for the solutions will be very similar. Conversely, the solutions will have greater divergence for small sample sizes.

10.2.2 RANDOM EFFECTS AND CORRELATED DATA

The dependency among the repeated measures of the response variable is accounted for by the random effects in the LMER model. Specifically, the variance-covariance matrix among the repeated measures, V_i, is a function of G, the multipliers of the random effects arrayed in the Z_i matrix, and the within-subjects error variance, σ_ε^2. For details, see the optional Section 5.6.

A discussion of the matrix algebra underlying V_i is not presented. Rather, focus is on examples using the MPLS data set. In addition to examining V_i, it is helpful to examine its standardized version, V_i^*, which is the correlation matrix among the repeated measures.

For the MPLS data, there are four time points consisting of Grades 5, 6, 7, and 8. Recall the response variable is reading scores repeatedly measured at the grades. The data are balanced on time, although there are some missing values. For a subject with no missing data, V_i is a 4 × 4 matrix with the diagonal elements consisting of the reading variances of the grades, and the off-diagonal elements consisting of the reading covariances among the grades. V_i^* is also a 4 × 4 matrix, with diagonal elements of 1, and off-diagonal elements consisting of the correlations among the grades.

In what follows, the pattern of the estimated V_i and V_i^* is considered when the number of random effects and variance components is varied. For simplicity, the case of a subject with no missing data is presented. To compute the estimated V_i and V_i^*, the syntax of two functions is introduced, V.func() and Vstar.func().

No random effects. When there are no random effects, the within-subjects variance and between-subjects variance are collected into the error variance. V_i is a diagonal matrix with the error variance on the diagonal.

Models with no random effects cannot be estimated with lmer(), so lm() is considered in the examples. In the syntax below, the square root of the error variance is extracted from the sigma slot of the summary() output object. A diagonal 4 × 4 matrix is constructed using the diag() function.

```
> s0  <- summary(lm(read ~ grade5, data = MPLS.LS))$sigma  # Estimated error SD.
> V0  <- diag(s0 ^ 2, nrow = 4, ncol = 4)                   # 4 by 4 diagonal matrix.
> round(V0, 2)                                              # Round results.
```

	[,1]	[,2]	[,3]	[,4]
[1,]	350.79	0.00	0.00	0.00
[2,]	0.00	350.79	0.00	0.00
[3,]	0.00	0.00	350.79	0.00
[4,]	0.00	0.00	0.00	350.79

The output shows that the estimated reading variance at every grade is $\widehat{Var}(y_{ij}) = 350.79$. This illustrates the typical homogeneity of variance assumption of the linear model: the variance of the response is assumed constant for the values of the predictor(s). Each off-diagonal element is 0, indicating there is no dependency between any two time points. That is, reading scores are not correlated among the grades.

To transform any estimated V_i matrix into an estimated V_i^* matrix, the following user-defined function is used.

```
> Vstar.func  <- function(x) diag(1 / sqrt(diag(x))) %*% x %*% diag(1 / sqrt(diag(x)))
```

The function requires the name of the estimated V_i matrix, which is V0 in the example above.

For a diagonal covariance matrix, as in this example, the correlation matrix will also be diagonal (with the value of 1 on the diagonal).

```
> Vstar0  <- Vstar.func(V0)
> round(Vstar0, 2)
```

	[,1]	[,2]	[,3]	[,4]
[1,]	1	0	0	0
[2,]	0	1	0	0
[3,]	0	0	1	0
[4,]	0	0	0	1

10.2 Random Effects and Variance Components

The output shows the reading correlation between any two time points is 0.

The model with no random effects is unrealistic for longitudinal data. In the case of the MPLS data set, it is expected that the reading scores are correlated. For this reason, *there should always be at least one random effect term in the model when dealing with longitudinal data.* This is reinforced by the fact that `lmer()` will not estimate a model unless this condition is met. An error message is printed if no random effects are included in the `lmer()` syntax.

Random intercepts. The inclusion of a single random effect is a substantial change compared to the model with no random effects. Including random intercepts means the off-diagonal elements of V_i are no longer 0. To see this, consider the estimation of Model 1 from Table 10.1. The fitted model object is saved as `linear.1`. After fitting the model, the estimated G matrix is printed along with the estimate of σ_ε.

```
> linear.1  <-  lmer(read ~ grade5 + (1 | subid), data = MPLS.LS)
> G1  <-  matrix(as.numeric(VarCorr(linear.1)$subid), ncol = 1)
> s1  <-  attr(VarCorr(linear.1), "sc")
> G1; s1
```

```
           [,1]
[1,]  327.4523
```

```
[1] 5.448451
```

The first number in the output is an estimate of $Var(b_{0i})$, and the second number is an estimate of σ_ε.

To compute an estimate of V_i, the `V.func()` function is defined below. Four things must be supplied to the function.

1. w = number of times points assuming balance on time and no missing data.

2. x = estimated G.

3. y = estimated σ_ε.

4. z = fitted model object, from which x and y are extracted.[2]

The syntax below must be submitted to R in order to use the function.

```
> V.func  <-  function(w, x, y, z){
+     nRE  <-  nrow(summary(z)@REmat) - 1           # Count random effects.
+     Z  <-  matrix(model.matrix(z)[1:4,1:nRE], ncol = nRE)  # Create Z matrix.
+     R  <-  diag(w) * y ^ 2                          # Create R matrix.
+     V  <-  Z %*% x %*% t(Z) + R                     # Compute V.
+ }
```

---
[2] The variables w, x, y, and z are arbitrary and should not be confused with any other notation used in this chapter or other chapters.

The function is for use only with a `lmer()` fitted model object. The resulting estimated V_i matrix is for a subject with no missing data.

After executing the above syntax, the estimated V_i matrix is computed for the example by supplying the number of time points (4), `G1`, `s1`, and `linear.1`, in that order. Consider the following.

```
> V1 <- V.func(4, G1, s1, linear.1)
> round(V1, 2)
      [,1]   [,2]   [,3]   [,4]
[1,] 357.14 327.45 327.45 327.45
[2,] 327.45 357.14 327.45 327.45
[3,] 327.45 327.45 357.14 327.45
[4,] 327.45 327.45 327.45 357.14
```

The resulting matrix shows the characteristics that result from having only random intercepts in the model. The diagonal contains the variances of the reading measure by grade. Similar to the case with no random effects, the variance is constant among grades, meaning the inclusion of the random intercept term induces homogeneity of variance. The covariances are not 0, but they are constant, indicating the same strength of relationship between reading scores regardless of the spacing of the observations. The covariance between reading scores at Grades 5 and 6 (indexes `[,1]` and `[2,]`) is the same as the covariance between Grades 5 and 8 (indexes `[,1]` and `[4,]`).

The syntax below is used to compute and print the estimated V_i^* matrix.

```
> Vstar1 <- Vstar.func(V1)
> round(Vstar1, 2)
     [,1] [,2] [,3] [,4]
[1,] 1.00 0.92 0.92 0.92
[2,] 0.92 1.00 0.92 0.92
[3,] 0.92 0.92 1.00 0.92
[4,] 0.92 0.92 0.92 1.00
```

Like the covariances, the correlations are constant. The correlation between reading scores at two different grades is 0.92, regardless of the spacing of the grades. The correlation is relatively large in this example and should not be taken as typical.

The constant variance and constant covariance (correlation) pattern is referred to as *compound symmetry*. This is the same type of structure that is used in the traditional RM-ANOVA (Verbeke & Molenberghs, 2000). Although having random intercepts is an improvement over no random effects, the compound symmetry pattern is thought to have limited applicability. The pattern is appropriate when subjects vary in their intercepts, but not in their rate of change over time. In many empirical instances, subjects are expected to vary in their rate of change. Thus, the compound symmetry pattern is considered to be overly restrictive.

10.2 Random Effects and Variance Components

Compound symmetry is applicable to the case when repeated measures are collected over conditions of an experiment rather than time. In experiments, the order of presentation of the conditions can be randomized among subjects. In principle, this means there is a chance jumbling of the within-subjects effects among the conditions, resulting in a constant variance for conditions, and constant covariance (correlation) between conditions.

Two uncorrelated random effects. Individual variability in rate of change and variability in intercepts are accounted for by including two random effects in the LMER model. The focus is first on the case in which the two random effects are uncorrelated, meaning their covariance (correlation) is 0.

Consider the estimation of Model 2 in Table 10.1. To include two random effects and set their covariance to 0, two arguments must be used for the random effects portion in the lmer() syntax. The first argument is (1|subid), which specifies a random intercept term. The second argument is (0+grade5 |subid), which includes a random slope term. The use of 0 has the effect of setting the covariance to that value. Consider the syntax below.

```
> linear.2 <- lmer(read ~ grade5 + (1 | subid) + (0 + grade5 | subid), MPLS.LS)
```

To view the estimated G matrix, the VarCorr() function is used within the as.data.frame() function.

```
> as.data.frame(VarCorr(linear.2))
```

	X.Intercept.	grade5
(Intercept)	368.0262	6.937469

The output shows the *diagonal* of the G matrix, here printed as a row vector. The diagonal consists of the estimates of $Var(b_{0i})$ and $Var(b_{1i})$, in that order.

The estimates are put into a matrix with the diag() function. But to do so, the as.numeric() function must be used. In addition to constructing the estimated G matrix, the estimate of σ_ε is also extracted.

```
> G2 <- diag(as.numeric(VarCorr(linear.2)))
> s2 <- attr(VarCorr(linear.2), "sc")
> G2; s2
```

```
         [,1]      [,2]
[1,] 368.0262  0.000000
[2,]   0.0000  6.937469
```

```
[1] 4.331744
```

The output shows the estimated G matrix followed by the estimate of σ_ε. The estimated V_i matrix is the following.

```
> V2 <- V.func(4, G2, s2, linear.2)
> round(V2, 2)
```

	[,1]	[,2]	[,3]	[,4]
[1,]	386.79	368.03	368.03	368.03
[2,]	368.03	393.73	381.90	388.84
[3,]	368.03	381.90	414.54	409.65
[4,]	368.03	388.84	409.65	449.23

There are two new features of this matrix. First, the variances are not constant on the diagonal, indicating two random effects allow for heterogeneity of variance over time. In this case, the reading variance increases over time, suggesting that individual change curves tend to fan out.

Second, the reading covariances are not constant. The constant values in the first row and column are a consequence of anchoring the intercept at Grade 5, that is, a consequence of using grade5 as a predictor rather than, say, grade. This can be shown using the matrix equations in the optional Section 5.6.

To gain further insight, the correlations among the repeated measures are computed.

```
> Vstar2 <- Vstar.func(V2)
> round(Vstar2, 2)
```

	[,1]	[,2]	[,3]	[,4]
[1,]	1.00	0.94	0.92	0.88
[2,]	0.94	1.00	0.95	0.92
[3,]	0.92	0.95	1.00	0.95
[4,]	0.88	0.92	0.95	1.00

The correlation matrix has a pattern different from the case of the single random intercept. The correlation changes as a function of the spacing of the time points. Specifically, the correlation decreases as the spacing between the grades increases. The correlation between reading scores at Grades 5 and 6 is estimated to be 0.94, whereas the correlation between Grades 5 and 8 is estimated to be 0.88.

As mentioned in past chapters, when the correlation decreases as the spacing of the time points increases, this is referred to as a decay pattern. The decay pattern is observed in much empirical data, which makes the inclusion of at least two random effects attractive for general use.

Two correlated random effects. How are things different when the random effects are allowed to correlate? To investigate this question, Model 3 in Table 10.1 is estimated. In the syntax below, the estimated G matrix is computed, and the estimate of σ_ε is extracted. To use the estimated G matrix in V.func(), it must be saved as a matrix. This is done by using the matrix() function.

10.2 Random Effects and Variance Components

```
> linear.3 ← lmer(read ~ grade5 + (grade5 | subid),data = MPLS.LS)
> G3 ← matrix(as.numeric(VarCorr(linear.3)$subid), ncol = 2)
> s3 ← attr(VarCorr(linear.3), "sc")
> G3; s3
```

	[,1]	[,2]
[1,]	398.64294	-28.162414
[2,]	-28.16241	7.140641

| [1] 4.319734 |

The output shows a negative covariance (correlation) between the two random effects.

The estimated V_i matrix is the following.

```
> V3 ← V.func(4, G3, s3, linear.3)
> round(V3, 2)
```

	[,1]	[,2]	[,3]	[,4]
[1,]	417.30	370.48	342.32	314.16
[2,]	370.48	368.12	328.44	307.42
[3,]	342.32	328.44	333.22	300.67
[4,]	314.16	307.42	300.67	312.59

There are two differences between this matrix and the corresponding matrix for the uncorrelated random effects. First, the reading variances now *decrease* over time rather than increase. This indicates that individual change curves tend to converge rather than fan out over time. Second, the covariances show a decay pattern not shown with the uncorrelated random effects.

To further understand any differences, consider the correlations among the grades.

```
> Vstar3 ← Vstar.func(V3)
> round(Vstar3, 2)
```

	[,1]	[,2]	[,3]	[,4]
[1,]	1.00	0.95	0.92	0.87
[2,]	0.95	1.00	0.94	0.91
[3,]	0.92	0.94	1.00	0.93
[4,]	0.87	0.91	0.93	1.00

The correlations show a decay pattern, but the rate of decay is greater than in the case of the uncorrelated random effects. For example, the decrease between Grades 5 and 6, as well as Grades 5 and 8, is $0.95 - 0.87 = 0.08$. This is larger than the corresponding difference for the uncorrelated random effects, which is 0.06.

It should be emphasized that the decreasing variances for the correlated random effects model is due to their negative correlation. If the random effects are positively correlated, then the variances will increase over time. The ability to accommodate both increasing and decreasing variances over time makes the correlated random effects model quite flexible and attractive for general use.

Three correlated random effects. To round out the illustrations, consider a quadratic model with three random effects. The LMER model is

$$y_{ij} = (\beta_0 + b_{0i}) + (\beta_1 + b_{1i})(\text{grade5}_{ij})$$
$$+ (\beta_2 + b_{2i})(\text{grade5}_{ij}^2) + \varepsilon_{ij}. \qquad (10.2.3)$$

Equation 10.2.3 includes a random effect for the quadratic term, b_{2i}, which is the individual deviation from the quadratic fixed effect.

As will be seen below, there is relatively little evidence that the model of Equation 10.2.3 is needed for the MPLS data. Furthermore, the estimation of many variance components is always tenuous with a small sample size. Therefore, the model of Equation 10.2.3 is only estimated for purposes of illustration. The syntax for estimating the model is the following.

```
> quad.4 <- lmer(read ~ grade5 + I(grade5 ^ 2) + (grade5 + I(grade5 ^ 2) | subid),
+               data = MPLS.LS)
```

The estimates of G and σ_ε are extracted and saved as objects.

```
> G4 <- matrix(as.numeric(VarCorr(quad.4)$subid), ncol = 3)
> s4 <- attr(VarCorr(quad.4), "sc")
> G4; s4
```

	[,1]	[,2]	[,3]
[1,]	392.168131	-15.0345006	-5.30040843
[2,]	-15.034501	5.9188591	0.17212664
[3,]	-5.300408	0.1721266	0.07181923

[1] 4.264052

The variance of the third (quadratic) random effect is relatively small, and its covariance with the second (linear) random effect is close to 0.

For further insight, consider the correlations among the random effects.

```
> attr(VarCorr(quad.4)$subid, "correlation")
```

	(Intercept)	grade5	I(grade5^2)
(Intercept)	1.0000000	-0.3120569	-0.9987409
grade5	-0.3120569	1.0000000	0.2640029
I(grade5^2)	-0.9987409	0.2640029	1.0000000

The correlation between the random intercepts and the random quadratic terms is almost perfect, yet it can be seen that the estimated variance of the

10.3 Descriptive Methods

quadratic random effect is close to 0. This is an indication there are too many parameters in the G matrix. The quadratic random effect is probably not needed, but the example is continued for the sake of illustration.

Below, estimates of V_i and V_i^* are computed.

```
> V4 <- V.func(4, G4, s4, quad.4)
> round(V4, 2)
```

```
        [,1]   [,2]   [,3]   [,4]
[1,]  410.35 371.83 340.90 299.36
[2,]  371.83 376.02 333.72 299.49
[3,]  340.90 333.72 335.39 291.35
[4,]  299.36 299.49 291.35 293.12
```

```
> Vstar4 <- Vstar.func(V4)
> round(Vstar4, 2)
```

```
      [,1] [,2] [,3] [,4]
[1,]  1.00 0.95 0.92 0.86
[2,]  0.95 1.00 0.94 0.90
[3,]  0.92 0.94 1.00 0.93
[4,]  0.86 0.90 0.93 1.00
```

The pattern of the covariance and the correlation matrices is very similar to the corresponding matrices for two correlated random effects.

The demonstration here that two correlated random effects can give similar results as three random effects suggests it may be desirable to simplify the structure of G when possible. As mentioned, the inclusion of needless variance components can adversely affect statistical efficiency by increasing the size of SEs and causing problems with estimation. The following sections provide descriptive and inferential methods for selecting random effects and their variance components.

10.3 Descriptive Methods

One means of selecting random effects is to examine graphs and descriptive statistics. The graphs presented in Chapter 4 can be used to assess the extent of evidence for variability in individual intercepts, slopes, and other change curve components. In this section, additional descriptive methods are presented to aid in judgments regarding the need for random effects and their variance components.

Two approaches are discussed. The first is based on OLS estimates of the change curve parameters for each subject. In Chapter 9, the OLS estimates were used to help determine the need for time transformations. In this chapter, the variability and covariability of the estimates are examined to provide clues about the random effects and variance components.

The second approach is the examination of residuals from fitted models that vary in the number of random effects. Relative change in the residual variability is used as an indication of the need for additional random effects. For instance, a substantial reduction in residual variability going from a less complex to a more complex model is an indication that the additional random effect is needed.

10.3.1 OLS ESTIMATES

OLS estimates can be used to assess the extent of individual variability and covariability. Such information is useful for suggesting what random effects might be included in the model.

As shown in Chapter 9, OLS estimates of each subject's change curve parameters are computed using `lm()` in `dlply()`. Once the estimates are extracted with the `ldply()` function, graphs can be constructed with `ggplot2`, or descriptive statistics can be computed with other functions.

In the syntax below, a linear model is estimated for each subject. Nonlinear models can be estimated using the `I()` function as described in Chapter 9. In what follows, the `my.ols` list object is created, and OLS estimates of the intercept and slope are extracted using `coef()`. The results are saved as the data frame object `my.coefs`.

```
> my.ols <- dlply(.data = MPLS.LS, .variables = .(MPLS.LS$subid),
+           .fun = function(x) {lm(read ~ grade5, data = x)})
> my.coefs <- ldply(my.ols, function(x) coef(x))
> my.coefs
```

	MPLS.LS$subid	(Intercept)	grade5
1	1	173.5000	6.0
2	2	201.8333	4.5
3	3	190.6000	7.6
4	4	199.3333	-3.0
5	5	208.7000	1.7
6	6	190.9000	2.9
7	7	200.2000	6.2
8	8	191.5000	1.5
9	9	147.9000	10.4
10	10	201.8333	6.5
11	11	180.5000	6.5
12	12	188.0000	7.0
13	13	229.0000	2.5
14	14	198.8000	12.3
15	15	216.6667	9.0
16	16	228.0000	0.5
17	17	201.7000	5.2
18	18	218.1000	0.6
19	19	214.3333	3.0
20	20	207.9000	3.4
21	21	237.3333	3.0
22	22	220.8333	8.5

10.3 Descriptive Methods

The output indicates that the `my.coefs` data frame contains the estimated intercepts (`(Intercept)`) and slopes (`grade5`).

It is informative to compute the variance-covariance matrix among the OLS estimates. This is analogous to the G matrix. The matrix is computed using the `cov()` function. The first column of subject number is excluded using -1 in the columns index of the `my.coefs` object.

```
> cov(my.coefs[ ,-1])
```

	(Intercept)	grade5
(Intercept)	404.53293	-29.13626
grade5	-29.13626	13.13610

The output shows that the variance of the OLS intercepts is 404.53, and the variance of the OLS slopes is 13.14. The variance of the intercepts is much larger than that of the slopes. This is reasonable, as the scale of the reading measure at the first time point is expected to be larger than the scale of the change over time.

The variability of the OLS estimates can be visualized by constructing boxplots. In the syntax below, a data frame friendly for graphing is created, which includes a phantom character variable, `ph`. The phantom is used as the x-axis variable to make the resulting graph look nicer. The data frame contains the stacked intercept and slope estimates, and the `label` variable is constructed for identification. Consider the following.

```
> plotdata <- data.frame(coef = c(my.coefs[,2], my.coefs[,3]),
+                       label = c(rep("Intercept", nrow(my.coefs)),
+                                 rep("Slope", nrow(my.coefs))),
+                       ph = rep(" ", nrow(my.coefs)))
> head(plotdata)
```

```
       coef     label    ph
1  173.5000  Intercept
2  201.8333  Intercept
3  190.6000  Intercept
4  199.3333  Intercept
5  208.7000  Intercept
6  190.9000  Intercept
```

Notice the `ph` variable has blank labels.

Having constructed the `plotdata` data frame, boxplots for the estimates will be produced. The function `geom_boxplot()` is used, along with `facet_grid()`, which includes the optional argument `scales="free"`, to allow for the different scales of the graphs.

```
> g1 <- ggplot(plotdata, aes(x = ph, y = coef)) + geom_boxplot() +
+       theme_bw()
> g2 <- g1 + facet_grid(label ~ ., scales = "free") + xlab("") +
+       ylab("Scale")
> print(g2)
```

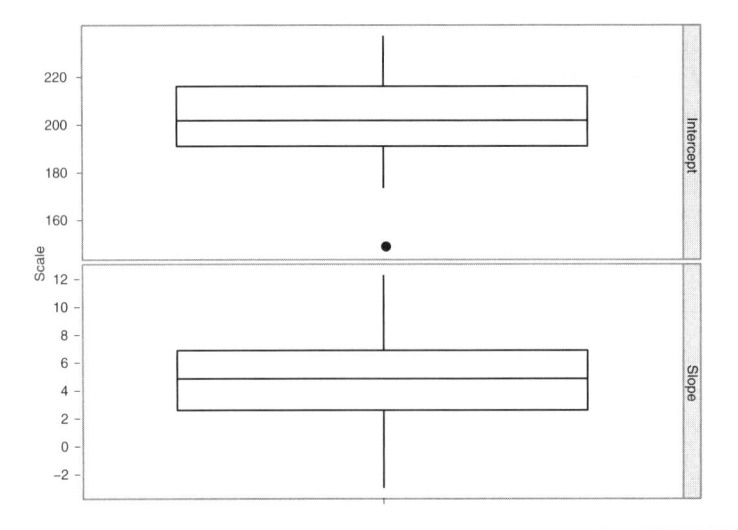

Figure 10.1 Boxplot of OLS estimates for intercepts and slopes.

The boxplots are shown in Figure 10.1. The upper panel is the boxplot for the intercepts, and the lower is for the slopes. Notice the vertical axis is scaled differently for each random effect. The intercepts are slightly negatively skewed, and there is a potential outlier denoted by the filled circle. The distribution of the slopes appears to be symmetric, or nearly so.

In addition to examining the variability of each random effect, it is useful to consider their joint distribution. The joint distribution can be important for evaluating whether the random effects should be allowed to correlate in the LMER analysis.

The covariance computed above is one means of assessing dependence among the OLS estimates, but its value is not on a standard scale. To address this, the correlation among the estimates is computed using cor().

```
> cor(my.coefs[ ,-1])
```

	(Intercept)	grade5
(Intercept)	1.0000000	-0.3996903
grade5	-0.3996903	1.0000000

From the output, it is seen that the correlation is $cor = -0.4$, which is modest. The LMER model-based estimate of the correlation from the previous output is somewhat larger, $cor = -0.53$.

The bivariate distribution can be depicted with a scatterplot and a superimposed linear regression line. The following syntax accomplishes these tasks.

```
> g1 <- ggplot(my.coefs, aes(x = my.coefs[ ,2], y = my.coefs[ ,3])) + geom_point()
> g2 <- g1 + stat_smooth(method = "lm", se = FALSE)
> g3 <- g2 + theme_bw() + xlab("Intercept") + ylab("Slope")
> print(g3)
```

10.3 Descriptive Methods

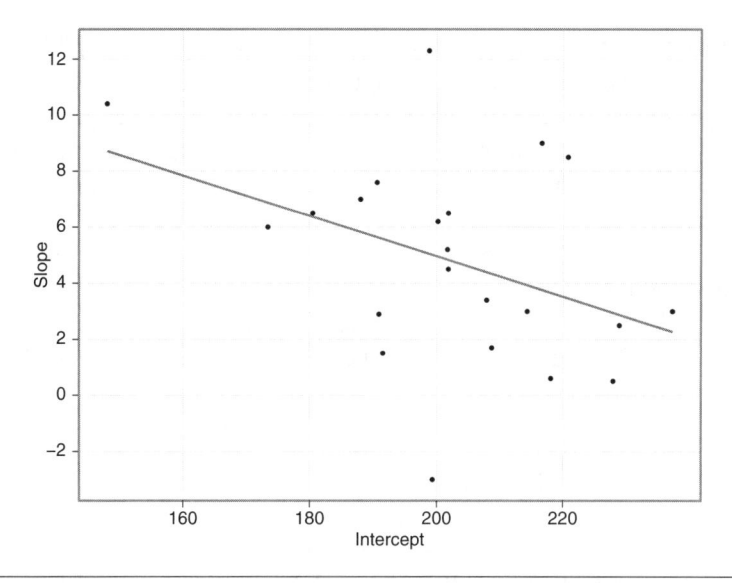

Figure 10.2 Scatterplot of OLS estimates of intercepts and slopes.

The graph is shown in Figure 10.2. There are some candidates for outliers, such as the person who has a negative value for his or her slope estimate at the bottom of the graph.

Correlations with static predictors. In the event that static predictor are to be examined, the correlations with the OLS estimates can be computed. This is informative about whether static predictor effects might be included in the model. The caveat here is that the approach is data-driven, which should be kept in mind when interpreting the results.

Consider the squared correlation coefficient, R^2, between the OLS estimates and the two-group risk variable, `risk2`. The risk values from only the first time point are selected, and `lm()` is used for the calculation.

```
> inter.r2 <- summary(lm(my.coefs[,2] ~ MPLS.LS$risk2[MPLS.LS$grade == 5]))$r.squared
> slope.r2 <- summary(lm(my.coefs[,3] ~ MPLS.LS$risk2[MPLS.LS$grade == 5]))$r.squared
> round(inter.r2, 2); round(slope.r2, 2)
```

```
[1] 0.49
```

```
[1] 0
```

The first output value is the R^2 between the OLS intercepts and risk, and the second is the R^2 between the OLS slopes and risk. The values indicate that risk might be a predictor of intercepts, but not of slopes. This is consistent with the findings of the previous chapters. Additional static predictors can be examined in a similar manner.

Conclusion. The descriptive methods of this section are helpful for suggesting how many random effects might be included in a LMER model, and what type of covariance (correlation) structure might suffice. A potential issue is that the descriptive methods do not account for chance fluctuations that arise in repeated sampling. Thus, there might be a hesitation to make judgments regarding the need for random effects based on the methods of this section. Although the graphs and statistics of this section are informative, they may be considered supplementary information for more formal methods. The formal methods are inferential, based on the LRT and AICc. Inferential methods are discussed in the sections below, but first, the topic of residuals is broached.

10.3.2 EXAMINING RESIDUALS

A weakness of examining the OLS estimates is a lack of clearly defined criteria for making decisions regarding the extent of variation of the random effects. For example, Figure 10.1 indicates there is variability in the OLS intercepts and slopes. It is not clear if the variability represented in the boxplots is substantial enough to justify the inclusion of random effects. It is helpful to have a point of reference other than 0 (no variance).

A point of reference is provided by considering individual variability for models that differ in the number of random effects. This model comparison idea is similar to what was used in the last few chapters to evaluate the need for fixed effects.

The presentation begins with descriptive methods for examining the residuals of various models. Inferential methods for model comparisons are considered later.

Evidence for the need of random effects is provided by changes in the residual variability when random effects are added to or omitted from the model. Since random effects account for between-subject variability, there should be a reduction in residual variability if a needed random effect is added to the model, and an increase when it is omitted. The change in residuals is indexed by the residual variance.

To set ideas, assume the goal is to evaluate the need for random intercepts. For simplicity, static predictors are not considered, and it is assumed that a linear change curve is adequate. The need for random intercepts is assessed based on the comparison of the following two models.

$$y_i = \beta_0 + \beta_1(\text{grade5}_i) + \varepsilon_i, \quad (10.3.1a)$$
$$y_{ij} = (\beta_0 + b_{0i}) + \beta_1(\text{grade5}_{ij}) + \varepsilon_{ij}. \quad (10.3.1b)$$

Equation 10.3.1a is a LM treating the repeated measures as independent, with the only source of variance on the predictor side being ε_i. Equation 10.3.1b is a LMER model with two sources of variance on the predictor side, b_{0i} and ε_{ij}.

10.3 Descriptive Methods

Consider the errors of the models, which are obtained by solving for ε_i and ε_{ij}, respectively.

$$\varepsilon_i = y_i - \beta_0 - \beta_1(\texttt{grade5}_i), \qquad (10.3.2a)$$

$$\varepsilon_{ij} = y_{ij} - \beta_0 - b_{0i} - \beta_1(\texttt{grade5}_{ij}). \qquad (10.3.2b)$$

The concern is with the variance of the errors in each equation. Given the independence of the random effects and error, it can be shown that the variance of the errors is a function of the variance of the random variables on the right side of each equation. Time predictors, such as `grade5`, are not random variables, as they are considered fixed by the researcher (or treated as such). This means there is one random variable on the right side of Equation 10.3.2a, y_i, and two random variables on the right side of Equation 10.3.2a, y_{ij} and b_{0i}.

It can be shown that the variance of the errors for each model is the following.

$$Var(\varepsilon_i) = Var(y_i), \qquad (10.3.3a)$$

$$Var(\varepsilon_{ij}) = Var(y_{ij}) - Var(b_{0i}), \qquad (10.3.3b)$$

where Equation 10.3.3a is the error variance of the LM, and Equation 10.3.3b is that of the LMER model. The above equations indicate that if $Var(b_{0i}) > 0$, the error variance of the LMER model will be *smaller* than that of the LM.

With sample data, the residuals rather than the errors are relevant. The extent of reduction in the LMER residual variance is an index for the need of the random intercepts, with greater reduction indicating greater need.

To assess the difference of the models, it is convenient to compute a *proportion reduction in error* (PRE) measure. The formula for the models in Equation 10.3.1 is

$$\text{PRE} = \frac{Var(\varepsilon_i) - Var(\varepsilon_{ij})}{Var(\varepsilon_i)}. \qquad (10.3.4)$$

The range of values is $0 \leq \text{PRE} \leq 1$, with larger values indicting a greater proportion reduction in residual variance. For analysis with sample data, the error variances in Equation 10.3.4 are replaced by the residual variances.

To compute the PRE measure, first the models of Equations 10.3.1a and 10.3.1b are fit, and the residual variances of the fitted model objects are extracted. Then the ratio of Equation 10.3.4 is computed. The syntax and output are shown below.

```
> ## Estimate the models.
> lm.1     <- lm(read ~ grade5, MPLS.LS)
> lmer.1   <- lmer(read ~ grade5 + (1 | subid), MPLS.LS)
> ## Residual variances.
> lm.s2    <- summary(lm.1)$sigma ^ 2
> lmer.s2  <- attr(VarCorr(lmer.1), "sc")
> names(lmer.s2) <- ""
> data.frame(lm.s2, lmer.s2, row.names = "")
```

```
       lm.s2    lmer.s2
    350.7917   5.448451
```

```
> ## PRE measure.
> PRE <- (lm.s2 - lmer.s2) / lm.s2
> PRE
```

```
0.9844681
```

The last line of the output indicates there is a 98.45% reduction in the residual variance when the random intercept term is added to the model. This is a strong sample effect, which will also be seen in the results of the bootstrap method of Section 10.4.1 below.

As a graphical indication of the residual variance reduction, a boxplot of the residuals for each subject is constructed. Since the mean of the residuals is 0 in both models, variation of the boxplots about 0 is a graphical index of the extent of the residual variance.

Residuals for both models are computed using the resid() function. To be clear, the function computes the sample counterparts on the left side of Equation 10.3.2, based on the estimated parameters and observed values of grade5. For LMER, the predicted random effects discussed in Section 10.6 are also used in the calculations.

In anticipation of plotting the residuals, the following data frame is constructed. The first column contains the subject numbers extracted from the lmer() fitted model object. The next two columns contain the residuals from the LM and LMER, respectively, and the last two columns are labels for the models.

```
> my.resid <- data.frame(subid = lmer.1@frame$subid,
+                        lm.resid = resid(lm.1),
+                        lmer.resid = resid(lmer.1),
+                        lm.1 = I("LM"), lmer.1 = I("LMER"))
> head(my.resid)
```

```
      subid    lm.resid  lmer.resid  lm.1  lmer.1
1.5       1  -30.767184   -3.644907    LM    LMER
1.6       1  -21.661863    4.386049    LM    LMER
1.7       1  -31.556541   -6.582995    LM    LMER
1.8       1  -20.451220    3.447961    LM    LMER
2.5       2   -2.767184   -1.384431    LM    LMER
2.6       2    3.338137    3.646525    LM    LMER
```

Having constructed the above data frame, another data frame is constructed that is convenient for plotting with ggplot2. The c() function is used to stack variables, resulting in a new data frame consisting of three columns.

```
> plotdata <- with(my.resid, data.frame(subid = c(subid, subid),
+                                       resid = c(lm.resid, lmer.resid),
+                                       model = c(lm.1, lmer.1)))
> head(plotdata)
```

10.3 Descriptive Methods

```
  subid        resid  model
1     1   -30.767184     LM
2     1   -21.661863     LM
3     1   -31.556541     LM
4     1   -20.451220     LM
5     2    -2.767184     LM
6     2     3.338137     LM
```

Using the `plotdata` data frame, boxplots of residuals for each subject are constructed. There is also faceting by the type of model.

```
> g1 <- ggplot(data = plotdata, aes(x = subid, y = resid, groups = subid)) + theme_bw()
> g2 <- g1 + geom_boxplot(fill = "grey80") + coord_flip() + geom_hline(yintercept = 0)
> g3 <- g2 + facet_grid(. ~ model) + ylab("Residual") + xlab("Subject") + ylim(-50, 50)
> print(g3)
```

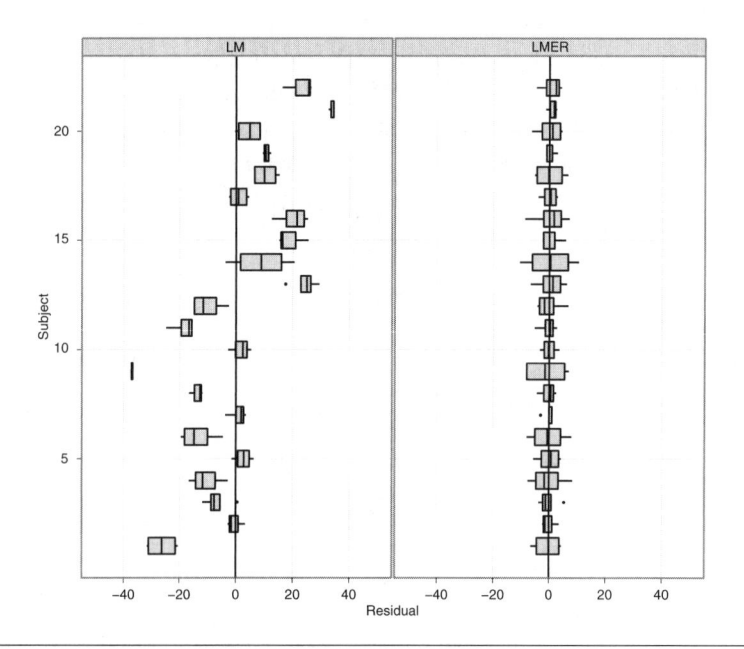

Figure 10.3 Subject intercept residual boxplots by model type.

The boxplots are shown in Figure 10.3. The left panel is for the LM, and the right panel is for LMER. Comparison of the panels provides dramatic visual evidence of the need for random intercepts. The LM boxplots display much greater variation about 0 than the LMER boxplots. The tighter band of variation about 0 in the LMER panel illustrates the extreme reduction in residual variation when random intercepts are included.

In addition to considering random intercepts, the need for higher order random effects can also be evaluated. This is illustrated for random slopes, and the ideas can be extended to more complex situations of nonlinear change.

Assessing the need for random slopes involves a comparison of two LMER models. The first is the random intercepts model of Equation 10.3.1b. The second model adds random slopes,

$$y_{ij} = (\beta_0 + b_{0i}) + (\beta_1 + b_{1i})(\texttt{grade5}_{ij}) + \varepsilon_{ij}. \quad (10.3.5)$$

Consider the related equation for the errors:

$$\varepsilon_{ij} = y_{ij} - b_{0i} - b_{1i}(\texttt{grade5}_{ij}) - \beta_0 - \beta_1(\texttt{grade5}_{ij}). \quad (10.3.6)$$

Based on Equation 10.3.6, it can be shown that the error variance is a function of the variances of the random effects and their covariance. For details, see Section 5.6.

A comparison of Equation 10.3.6 with Equation 10.3.2b reveals that, if the random slopes are needed in the model, the error variance will be reduced when the random slopes are added to the model. This idea generalizes to models with additional random effects (e.g., a random quadratic term).

Suppose the error variance of a simpler reduced model with fewer random effects is denoted as $Var(\varepsilon_{ij})_R$. The error variance of a more complex full model with additional random effects is denoted as $Var(\varepsilon_{ij})_F$. For example, $Var(\varepsilon_{ij})_R$ might be the error variance for Equation 10.3.2b, and $Var(\varepsilon_{ij})_F$ might be that for Equation 10.3.6. Then the PRE measure is

$$\text{PRE} = \frac{Var(\varepsilon_{ij})_R - Var(\varepsilon_{ij})_F}{Var(\varepsilon_{ij})_R}.$$

With sample data, the error variances are replaced with the residuals variances.

In the syntax below, the Equation 10.3.5 model is fitted, and the sample PRE measure is computed.

```
> lmer.2    <- lmer(read ~ grade5 + (1 + grade5 | subid), MPLS.LS)
> lmer.1.s2 <- lmer.s2
> lmer.2.s2 <- attr(VarCorr(lmer.2), "sc")
> names(lmer.2.s2) <- ""
> PRE <- (lmer.1.s2 - lmer.2.s2) / lmer.1.s2
> PRE
```

```
0.207163
```

The output shows the reduction in the residual variance is 20.72%. The evidence for including random slopes is less compelling than the case of random intercepts. However, the reduction in residual variance appears large enough to justify the inclusion of random slopes.

Subject boxplots of the residuals are constructed as previously discussed. Below is the syntax to directly construct the stacked data frame for plotting. This avoids the need to construct an initial residual data frame as was done above. The `rep()` and `factor()` functions are used to make plotting more convenient. The coding scenario below will force the reduced model to be displayed before the full model when the facet panels are created.

10.3 Descriptive Methods

```
> plotdata <- data.frame(subid = c(lmer.2@frame$subid, lmer.2@frame$subid),
+                        resid = c(resid(lmer.1), resid(lmer.2)),
+                        model = c(rep(1,nrow(lmer.2@frame)),rep(2,nrow(lmer.2@frame))))
> plotdata$model <- factor(plotdata$model, labels = c("Reduced", "Full"))
> head(plotdata)
```

	subid	resid	model
1	1	-3.644907	Reduced
2	1	4.386049	Reduced
3	1	-6.582995	Reduced
4	1	3.447961	Reduced
5	2	-1.384431	Reduced
6	2	3.646525	Reduced

Having constructed the `plotdata` data frame, the subject residual boxplots are now produced.

```
> g1 <- ggplot(data = plotdata,aes(x = subid, y = resid,groups = subid)) + theme_bw()
> g2 <- g1 + geom_boxplot(fill = "grey80") + coord_flip() + geom_hline(yintercept = 0)
> g3 <- g2 + facet_grid(. ~ model) + ylab("Residual") + xlab("Subject")
> print(g3)
```

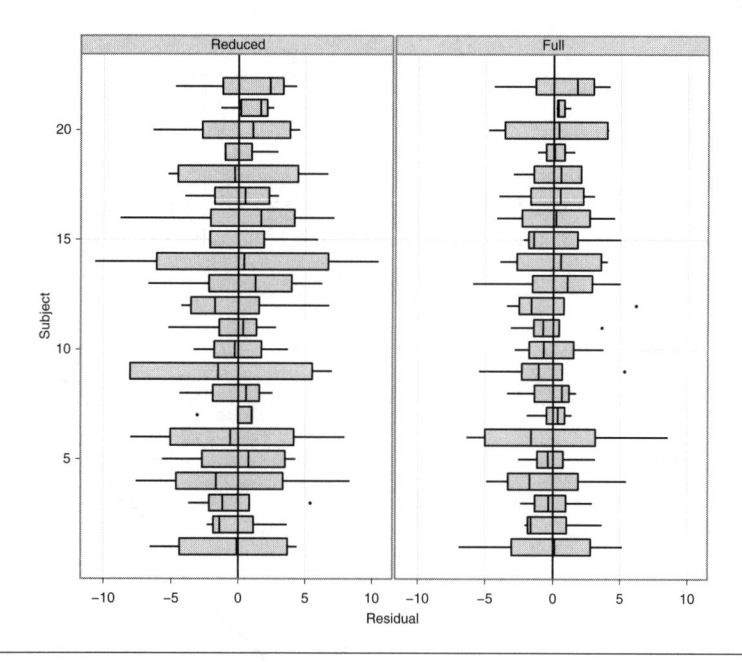

Figure 10.4 Subject slope residual boxplots by model type.

The boxplots are shown in Figure 10.4. The boxplots for the reduced model are on the left, and those for the full model are on the right. For the most part, the boxplots for the full model are shorter than for the reduced model. In addition, the full model medians appear to be a bit closer to 0 on the whole, indicating less variation.

10.3.3 RESIDUALS AND NORMALITY

As an aside, recall that normality is a key assumption in LMER regarding the distribution of the random effects and random error. In the midst of discussing random error and residuals, this seems like an appropriate time to mention that the residuals can be used to assess the normality assumption of the errors. One means of doing so is the Q-Q plot (Wilk & Gnanadesikan, 1968). If the quantiles of the sample residuals are similar to those of a normal distribution, the points should approximately lie on a diagonal line.

As a reference for evaluating the sample residuals, data are generated from a normal distribution. This provides a benchmark for determining the extent of deviation from the Q-Q line when sampling from a known normal distribution.

In the syntax below, a data frame is constructed with the sample residuals and generated data. For the latter, the `rnorm()` function is used, supplying the sample size and SD of the sample residuals (the mean is 0). The `stat="qq"` option is used in the `geom_point()` component to construct the Q-Q plots.

```
> lmer.2 <- lmer(read ~ grade5 + (1 + grade5 | subid), MPLS.LS)
> myresid <- data.frame(resid = resid(lmer.2))
> myrand <- data.frame(resid = rnorm(n = nrow(myresid), mean = 0, sd = sd(myresid)))
> plotdata <- data.frame(resid = rbind(myresid, myrand),
+                        type = c(rep("Sample", nrow(myresid)),
+                                 rep("Generated", nrow(myresid))))
> g1 <- ggplot(plotdata, aes(sample = resid)) + geom_point(stat = "qq")
> g2 <- g1 + facet_grid(. ~ type) + theme_bw()
> print(g2)
```

The Q-Q plots are shown in Figure 10.5. The Q-Q plot for the generated residuals is similar to the plot for the sample residuals. There is evidence of consistency with the normality assumption.

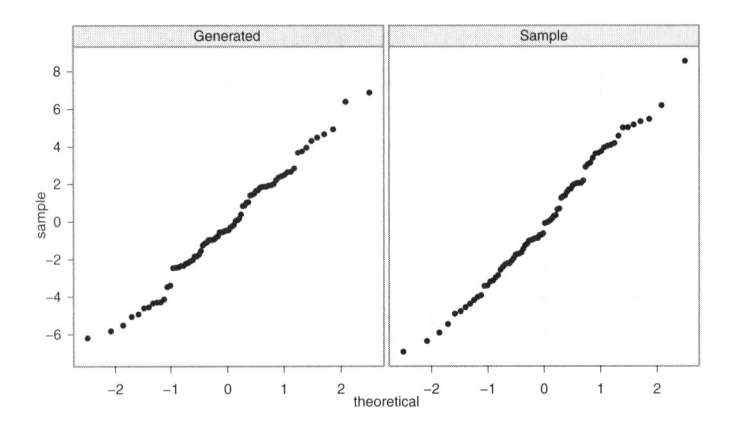

Figure 10.5 Q-Q plot of generated residuals (left) and sample residuals (right).

10.4 Inferential Methods

In certain analysis situations, the researcher wants to go beyond description and use inferential methods for the selection of random effects. The primary motivation is that sample data are subject to sampling fluctuations. The PRE measure and boxplots of residuals will always be misleading to some extent. For instance, it is unknown if the last PRE value from the previous section could arise when sampling from a population in which random slopes are not needed. For situations in which the sample size is not enormous, inferential methods are important for indicating if the interpretation of the sample effects should be tempered.

For inferences with fixed effects, SEs can be used to construct CIs, or t-ratios (z-ratios) can be used. SEs for variance components, especially variances, are perhaps less useful. The reason is that the sampling distribution of the variance is bounded below at 0 and skewed. SEs used to compute confidence intervals and z-ratios are problematic for bounded and skewed distributions. CIs for variances can contain impossible negative values, and z-tests can have inaccurate p-values. For this reason, the output of lmer() does not contain SEs for variance components (Bates, 2009).

Rather than rely on CIs or z-ratios, focus is on the LRT and the AICc for selecting random effects and variance components. The selection of random effects is usually ancillary to the selection of static predictors and time predictors. For this reason, the multimodel approach is not considered for selection of random effects. The AICc is used to evaluate multiple models, but the emphasis is on selecting the number of random effects or variance components, rather than entertaining a bouquet of models.

The discussion begins with the LRT. Bootstrap methods are featured for reasons described below.

10.4.1 LIKELIHOOD RATIO TEST

The discussion begins with the test of the variance of a random effect. Tests of covariances are treated in a moment.

The LRT was used in the previous two chapters for comparing nested models with different fixed effects. The LRT, being a general method, is also applicable for the comparison of models with different random effects (or variance components). There is a complication, however, for testing null hypotheses with variances of random effects. The complication is that the sampling distribution of X^2 is not χ^2.

Recall that the likelihood ratio statistic is the difference of the deviances of the full and reduced models, $X^2 = deviance_R - deviance_F$. When testing fixed effects, if the sample size is large, the number of fixed effects to be tested is not excessive, and the normality assumptions hold, the null sampling distribution of X^2 is reasonably approximated by a χ^2 distribution, with df

equal to the number of fixed effects omitted from the full model. In such cases, the `anova()` function should provide a reasonably accurate *p*-value for evaluating the null hypothesis that the reduced model is sufficient (see Chapter 8 for additional details).

For the LRT variance test, the full model includes the variance in question, and the reduced model omits it. For example, in Table 10.1, Model 1 is the reduced model and Model 2 is the full model. Model 2 includes $Var(b_{1i})$, whereas Model 1 does not.

Since the full and reduced models differ by a single variance, the null hypothesis is that the variance is equal to 0, and the alternative hypothesis is that the variance is greater than 0. In symbols,

$$H_0: Var(b_{ki}) = 0, \qquad H_A: Var(b_{ki}) > 0. \qquad (10.4.1)$$

When $k = 0$, the hypotheses pertain to the variance of the random intercepts. When $k = 1$, they pertain to hypotheses of the variance of the slopes, and so on.

The value of 0 in the null hypothesis of Equation 10.4.1 is the minimum possible for the parameter. Because this null hypothesized value is on the "edge" of the possible values, it can be shown that the sampling distribution of the likelihood ratio statistic is not well approximated by a χ^2 distribution (Self & Liang, 1987; Stram & Lee, 1994). This is the case regardless of the sample size, meaning the LRT has a general bias for testing the variance of a random effect. The nature of the bias is such that the LRT is "conservative," with its *p*-value tending to be *too large*. Using the LRT, then, can lead to the selection of an overly simple model, with too few random effects and/or too few variance components.

A practical but ad hoc method of adjusting for the conservative nature of the LRT is to change the rejection rule. For instance, one might reject H_0 when $p \leq 0.10$ rather than $p \leq 0.05$ (Fitzmaurice et al., 2004, chap. 8). This suggestion seems reasonable for the researcher who is willing to use the LRT as a rough indicator of the need for random effects and variance components. However, in some worst-case scenarios, the *p*-value of the LRT can be twice what it should be (Pinheiro & Bates, 2000), and it is unknown how well the adjusted rejection rule will work.

For those requiring greater accuracy, the bootstrap can be used with the LRT to approximate the sampling distribution under the null hypothesis. There are two types of bootstrap methods presented, a *fast bootstrap* and a *slow bootstrap*. The names reflect differences in required computing time. As will be seen below, the two methods can provide similar results, which argues for general use of the fast bootstrap.

The fast bootstrap is due to Crainiceanu and Ruppert (2004) and requires very little computing time. The reason is that the method does not require the calculation of the deviance of the reduced and full models. Rather, the method relies on a transformation (decomposition) of the design matrix of the predictors, which is the same for the reduced and full models. In this context,

10.4 Inferential Methods

the full and reduced models have the same number of fixed effects, and thus, the same design matrices (see the optional Section 5.6). The fast bootstrap is performed with the `exactRLRT()` function of the `RLRsim` package, written by Fabian Scheipl (Scheipl, Greven, & Küchenhoff, 2008).

The slow bootstrap is the parametric bootstrap discussed in Chapter 8. The parametric bootstrap involves simulating data under the fitted reduced model, and then fitting the reduced and full models for each simulation. The difference in deviance of the two models under simulation is computed. The distribution of the difference is an approximation of the actual sampling distribution of X^2. A bootstrap p-value is computed by comparing the deviance difference computed on the sample data to the set of bootstrap deviance differences. The bootstrap p-value is the proportion of simulated differences that is greater than the sample-based difference.

The slow bootstrap is more flexible than the fast bootstrap in regard to assumptions and the type of null hypotheses that can be tested. For example, with the slow bootstrap, one can test the need for an additional variance and covariance. On the other hand, the slow bootstrap can take a relatively long time to run on a common laptop or desktop computer. It also requires a user-defined function, as discussed below.

It is important to note that not all the methods presented below are based on model comparisons of REML solutions. The `anova()` function uses the ML deviance even if REML is used for estimation. The author of `lme4`, Doug Bates, appears to think that the benefits of the REML unbiasedness are perhaps overstated, due to the skewed nature of the distribution of variance estimators (Bates, 2009). This is taken as an indication that the author thinks that ML model comparison is a good general approach, regardless of the types of effects being evaluated.

Testing the variance of the intercepts. The first case considered is the testing of the variance of the random intercepts. The full model in this situation has only random intercepts, and the reduced model does not have any random effects. The null and alternative hypotheses are

$$H_0: Var(b_{0i}) = 0, \quad H_A: Var(b_{0i}) > 0.$$

Care must be taken in interpreting H_0, as it does not necessarily imply that no random effects are needed. H_0 only implies there is no variance for a particular anchoring of the intercept. Additional comment is made on this issue in a moment.

The fast bootstrap is used for testing H_0. The fast bootstrap provides a very close approximation of the null sampling distribution of the LRT statistic, and it does not require fitting of multiple models, as with the slow bootstrap.

The fast bootstrap is performed with the `exactRLRT()` function of the `RLRsim` package. The syntax is relatively simple, requiring only the name of the fitted output object of the random intercepts reduced model. Recall from the previous section this object is `linear.1`.

```
> require(RLRsim)
> exactRLRT(linear.1)

    simulated finite sample distribution of RLRT. (p-value based on 10000
    simulated values)

data:
RLRT = 114.8226, p-value < 2.2e-16
```

In the output, RLRT stands for restricted LRT, which is the LRT based on REML. The test statistic in this case is relatively large, $X^2 = 114.82$, and the p-value is extremely small, indicating rejection of $H_0 : Var(b_{0i}) = 0$. There is strong evidence that random intercepts should be in the model.

It should be noted that the fast bootstrap relies on a random number generator. This means the results obtained here will probably not be exactly replicated by the reader. This applies for the results below as well.

In principle, the analytic (non-bootstrap) LRT and the slow bootstrap can be used to test $H_0 : Var(b_{0i}) = 0$, but there are practical reasons why these methods cannot be used. The anova() function cannot be used with a mix of lm() and lmer() objects. Furthermore, although the deviance can be calculated based on a lm() object, it is not clear if this deviance is comparable to one computed on a lmer() object. For this reason, the fast bootstrap is considered the only viable method for testing $H_0: Var(b_{0i}) = 0$.

Having demonstrated how $H_0 : Var(b_{0i}) = 0$ is tested, it should be mentioned that a failure to reject this null hypothesis is only one consideration in the decision to retain $Var(b_{0i})$ and b_{0i} in the LMER model. There are several reasons why b_{0i} might be retained despite the failure to reject H_0.

First, the failure to reject might be due to the anchoring of the intercept. Suppose that individual variability is very small initially, but it increases over time. If the intercept is anchored at the first time point, or a previous time point, then this can produce an estimate of $Var(b_{0i})$ that is close to 0. However, anchoring at some other time, such as the terminal time point, might produce a substantially large estimate of $Var(b_{0i})$, leading to the rejection of H_0. In the latter case, $Var(b_{0i})$ is important to retain, so that the results will be valid under linear transformations of the time metric.

Second, even if the estimate of $Var(b_{0i})$ is near to 0, b_{0i} should be retained in the model if any higher order random effects are in the model, such as b_{1i}. Recall that similar to polynomials, all lower order random effects are always included in the model. Again, this is to ensure the LMER model is valid under various linear transformations of the time variable. Under rescaling of the time variable, a researcher probably would not want the random intercept effects to wind up in the random error term.

Finally, omitting all variance components including $Var(b_{0i})$ seems extreme, as there will be no random effects in the model. In this case, there is no LMER model, and the longitudinal data will be treated as independent within subjects. The assumption of independence may be reasonable for special cases of

10.4 Inferential Methods

distantly collected measures. If observations occur every 10 years, for example, the correlation between time points might be very weak. But even in this extreme case, it seems desirable to account for whatever correlation does exist among the repeated measures. In the event the correlations are very close to 0, at least one is using a model that is appropriate for longitudinal data. For this reason, even small variance components can be meaningful and important to include in the model (Carroll, 2003).

Testing with uncorrelated random effects. The second case to consider is a test of the variance of the random slopes. It is assumed that the random intercept term is also in the model, and the covariance (correlation) between the random effects is 0. The case of correlated random effects is considered later.

For the case of the variance of the slopes, the null and alternative hypotheses are

$$H_0: Var(b_{1i}) = 0, \qquad H_A: Var(b_{1i}) > 0.$$

The null hypothesis is equivalent to saying that b_{1i} is not needed in the model, with the caveat that b_{0i} and b_{1i} are uncorrelated.

First consider the fast bootstrap for testing the null hypothesis. To use `exactRLRT()`, three models must be fit.

1. The full model including b_{0i} and b_{1i} with their covariance set to 0.

2. A first reduced model that includes only b_{0i}.

3. A second reduced model that includes only b_{1i}.

The third model is estimated only as a means of testing H_0, and it is not considered a viable model of interest. Recall from the discussions in Chapters 7 and 8 that sometimes an uninteresting null model must be used to test other models of interest.

The three models are fit to the data in the order listed above. The syntax is similar to that in Section 10.2.2.

```
> full          <- lmer(read ~ grade5 + (1 | subid) + (0 + grade5 | subid), MPLS.LS)
> reduced.int   <- lmer(read ~ grade5 + (1 | subid), MPLS.LS)
> reduced.slope <- lmer(read ~ grade5 + (0 + grade5 | subid), MPLS.LS)
```

The three fitted model objects are supplied to `exactRLRT()` in a specific order. Of the three fitted model objects, `reduced.slope` contains the estimated variance to be tested. This model is listed first. Then the `full` model is listed with both the estimated variances. Finally, the `reduced.int` model is listed with only the variance of the intercepts estimated. Consider the following syntax and output.

```
> exactRLRT(reduced.slope, full, reduced.int)
```

```
            simulated finite sample distribution of RLRT.   (p-value based on 10000
            simulated values)
data:
RLRT = 5.4989, p-value = 0.0079
```

The output indicates the value of the LRT statistic is $X^2 = 5.5$ and $p = 0.0079$. Therefore, H_0 is rejected, which suggests the need for the random slopes in the model.

Two alternative methods for testing H_0 are the slow bootstrap and the analytic LRT using the χ^2 reference distribution. The results of these methods are considered for comparison. The LRT can be easily performed with `anova()` by supplying the full-model object with both estimated variances, and the reduced model object that omits the variance of the slopes. The full and reduced models correspond to the `full` and `reduced.int` fitted model objects above. To make things more understandable, the reduced model is saved as `reduced`.

```
> reduced  <-  reduced.int
> anova(reduced,  full)
```

```
Data: MPLS.LS
Models:
reduced: read ~ grade5 + (1 | subid)
full: read ~ grade5 + (1 | subid) + (0 + grade5 | subid)
        Df     AIC     BIC  logLik   Chisq Chi Df Pr(>Chisq)
reduced  4  585.82  595.35 -288.91
full     5  582.92  594.83 -286.46  4.9026      1    0.02682 *
---
Signif. codes:  0 '***' 0.001 '**' 0.01 '*' 0.05 '.' 0.1 ' ' 1
```

It is useful to compare the results of the LRT to the results of the fast bootstrap. However, it should be mentioned that the fast bootstrap is based on the REML solution, whereas `anova()` is based on the ML solution. The `anova()` output shows a smaller value for the LRT statistic, $X^2 = 4.9$, and a larger p-value, LRT-$p = 0.0268$. The difference illustrates the conservative nature of the LRT for testing variances of random effects.

The slow bootstrap is similar in form to the bootstrap of the LRT considered in Chapter 8. In the syntax below, the function `slow.b()` is defined to carry out the slow bootstrap. The reader is referred to the optional sections of Chapters 7 and 8 for a detailed discussion of the code.

```
> slow.b  <-  function(x, y, z) {
+     chisq.star  <-  numeric(x)                                     # Storage vector.
+ for(i in 1:x){                                                     # Loop for bootstrap.
+     simDV  <-  simulate(y)                                         # Simulate on reduced model.
+     full.s  <-  refit(z, simDV[ ,1])                               # Refit full model.
+     reduced.s  <-  refit(reduced, simDV[ ,1])                      # Refit reduced model.
+     chisq.star[i]  <-  -2*(logLik(reduced.s) - logLik(full.s))     # Store the LR statistic.
+ }
+ mean(anova(y, z)[2,5] < chisq.star)                                # p-value.
+ }
```

10.4 Inferential Methods

When `REML=TRUE` or the `REML` statement is omitted in the initial model fits, the slow bootstrap will use the REML deviance. The ML deviance can be used by setting `REML=FALSE`.

After the above syntax is submitted to R, `slow.b()` is used by supplying the number of bootstrap replications, the reduced fitted model object, and the full fitted model object, in that order. The number of replications is limited to $B = 999$ in the example below, but a larger number should be used in practice, such as $B = 9999$. The reduced and full models from the last example are considered here.

```
> slow.b(999, reduced, full)
```
```
[1] 0.01201201
```

The *p*-value for the slow bootstrap is between that of the LRT and that of the fast bootstrap. Additional replications are needed for the slow bootstrap to approach the *p*-value of the fast bootstrap. The slow bootstrap relies on a random number generator, and the results obtained here will probably not be exactly replicated by the reader.

Testing with correlated random effects. To this point, it has been assumed that the random effects are uncorrelated, with their covariance (correlation) being equal to 0. This assumption is unrealistic for general situations, and it is probably preferable to test $H_0: Var(b_{1i}) = 0$, assuming b_{0i} and b_{1i} are correlated.

Correlated random effects present a complication, as the test of $Var(b_{1i})$ must necessarily involve $Cov(b_{0i}, b_{1i})$. The covariance cannot be different from 0 when at least one variance is equal to 0. Therefore, the null hypothesis when the random effects are correlated is

$$H_0: Var(b_{1i}) = Cov(b_{0i}, b_{1i}) = 0. \qquad (10.4.2)$$

The alternative hypothesis is that at least $Var(b_{1i}) > 0$. H_0 is equivalent to saying the random slope term is not needed in the model.

The H_0 of Equation 10.4.2 involves both a variance and a covariance, and the relevant sampling distribution is a joint distribution. The nature of this distribution is not well known. For this reason, the accuracy of the fast bootstrap can vary as a function of the correlation between the random effects.

Based on simulation studies, there is evidence the fast bootstrap will be reasonably accurate if the correlation between the random effects is not extremely large (Scheipl et al., 2008). However, the meaning of "extremely large" is unclear. If the simulation results are to be believed, then the fast bootstrap is probably safe for general use—that is, safe to use for both the correlated and uncorrelated random effects situations.

Similar to the case of testing a single variance, the analytic LRT is expected to not be accurate in testing the H_0 of Equation 10.4.2. The inaccuracy is such that the likelihood ratio statistic will be smaller than it should be and the *p*-value too large.

The slow bootstrap is perhaps the best option for testing Equation 10.4.2. The slow bootstrap approximates the actual joint distribution, although an accurate approximation requires a large number of replications. The computing time can be substantial for an acceptable degree of accuracy.

In considering the three methods, it is important to examine the estimate of the correlation between the random effects. If this value is not very high, then the fast bootstrap is probably the best strategy. The value of the correlation among the random effects can be printed using `attr()`. The full-model output object for this situation is `linear.3`.

```
> attr(VarCorr(linear.3)$subid, "correlation")
             (Intercept)      grade5
(Intercept)   1.0000000   -0.5278484
grade5       -0.5278484    1.0000000
```

The absolute value of the correlation is rather large ($cor = -0.53$), indicating the fast bootstrap p-value may have limited accuracy. A better strategy may be the slow bootstrap, which can be performed using the `slow.b()` function.

As will be seen below and in Table 10.2, the fast bootstrap provides a result that is similar to the slow bootstrap for the MPLS data. The correlation between the random effects is considered to be relatively high, perhaps providing evidence for the validity of the fast bootstrap.

The fast bootstrap was performed in the last section. Here the output is shown again.

```
    simulated finite sample distribution of RLRT.  (p-value based on 10000
    simulated values)
data:
RLRT = 5.4989, p-value = 0.0079
```

The output shows that $p = 0.0079$. This is used for a reference value in comparing results with the slow bootstrap and analytic LRT.

The slow bootstrap is performed below. The reduced model is the same as that used in the last slow bootstrap, namely, the output object `reduced`. The full-model object is `linear.3`, which is renamed as `full` for clarity.

```
> full   <- linear.3
> cor.re <- slow.b(999, reduced, full)
> cor.re
[1] 0.008008008
```

The output shows that the p-value for the slow bootstrap is $p = 0.008$. This is similar to the p-value for the fast bootstrap. Based on either method, there is evidence the random slopes are needed in the model.

To carry out the analytic LRT, `anova()` is used with the two nested models.

10.4 Inferential Methods

```
> anova(reduced, full)
```

```
Data: MPLS.LS
Models:
reduced: read ~ grade5 + (1 | subid)
full: read ~ grade5 + (grade5 | subid)
        Df    AIC    BIC  logLik  Chisq Chi Df Pr(>Chisq)
reduced  4 585.82 595.35 -288.91
full     6 580.98 595.28 -284.49 8.8375      2    0.01205 *
---
Signif. codes:  0 '***' 0.001 '**' 0.01 '*' 0.05 '.' 0.1 ' ' 1
```

The output shows this is now a 2 df test, indicating that $Var(b_{1i})$ and $Cov(b_{0i}, b_{1i})$ are omitted from the full model to obtain the reduced model. The output shows that the likelihood ratio statistic is a bit larger, and the *p*-value a little smaller, than in the case of uncorrelated random effects. In addition, LRT-*p* is larger than the one in the fast and slow bootstrap.

Testing the covariance. In addition to testing a null hypothesis for a variance, the null hypothesis that a covariance is equal to 0 can also be tested. Focus is first on the case of the covariance between the random intercepts and the random slopes. In this situation,

$$H_0: Cov(b_{0i}, b_{1i}) = 0, \qquad H_A: Cov(b_{0i}, b_{1i}) \neq 0.$$

It is assumed the two corresponding random effects are in both the reduced and full models, which distinguishes the H_0 here from the one in Equation 10.4.2.

The fast bootstrap cannot be used to test H_0, so focus is on the slow bootstrap and the analytic LRT. First consider the analytic LRT. Since the parameter value in the null hypothesis is no longer on the edge of the parameter space, the LRT using `anova()` is expected to provide a more accurate *p*-value than the previous cases.

The syntax below estimates the reduced and full models. The fitted model objects are then used in `anova()`.

```
> reduced <- lmer(read ~ grade5 + (1 | subid) + (0 + grade5 | subid), data = MPLS.LS)
> full <- lmer(read ~ grade5 + (grade5 | subid), data = MPLS.LS)
> anova(reduced, full)
```

```
Data: MPLS.LS
Models:
reduced: read ~ grade5 + (1 | subid) + (0 + grade5 | subid)
full: read ~ grade5 + (grade5 | subid)
        Df    AIC    BIC  logLik  Chisq Chi Df Pr(>Chisq)
reduced  5 582.92 594.83 -286.46
full     6 580.98 595.28 -284.49 3.9349      1    0.04729 *
---
Signif. codes:  0 '***' 0.001 '**' 0.01 '*' 0.05 '.' 0.1 ' ' 1
```

The output shows that LRT-$p = 0.0473$. H_0 is rejected, but the LRT-p is perhaps uncomfortably close to the traditional cutoff value.

The slow bootstrap is performed below.

```
> cov.test <- slow.b(999, reduced, full)
> cov.test
```

```
[1] 0.04004004
```

The output shows that the p-value is very similar to LRT-p. Again, H_0 is rejected. The similarity of the p-values of the two methods underscores that the testing of the covariance is not saddled with the "edge of the parameter space" problem encountered in testing variances.

Summary. A summary of the results in the sections above is provided in Table 10.2. A blank in the table indicates the method cannot be used to test the variance component in question.

Table 10.2 shows that a test for the need of random intercepts can be conducted only with the fast bootstrap. For a test of the slopes assuming uncorrelated random effects, the fast bootstrap had the smallest p-value, followed by the slow bootstrap and the LRT. For a test of the slopes assuming correlated random effects, the fast and slow bootstrap had very similar p-values, which were much smaller than the LRT-p. For testing the covariance, the fast bootstrap cannot be used; the slow bootstrap and the LRT had very similar p-values.

Table 10.2 Summary of results for testing variance components.

Component	Fast Boot	Slow Boot	LRT
Intercepts	0.0000		
Slopes, Uncorr.	0.0079	0.0120	0.0268
Slopes, Corr.	0.0079	0.0080	0.0120
Covariance		0.0400	0.0473

Additional summary and commentary on the methods are provided in Table 10.3. Each method can be used to test additional types of hypotheses that are not depicted in the table. For example, the slow bootstrap can be used to test if the variance of a random quadratic effect and its covariance with the other terms are required in the model.

10.4 Inferential Methods

Table 10.3 Summary of methods for testing variance components.

Method	Function	Example H$_0$	Comment
Fast bootstrap	`exact RLRT()`	H$_0$: Var(b_{0i}) = 0, H$_0$: Var(b_{1i}) = 0	Assumes uncorrelated random effects
Slow bootstrap	`slow.b()`	H$_0$: Var(b_{1i}) = 0, H$_0$: Var(b_{1i}) = Cov(b_{0i}, b_{1i}) = 0	Computing time can be substantial; not applicable for H$_0$: Var(b_{0i}) = 0
Analytic LRT	`anova()`	H$_0$: Var(b_{1i}) = 0, H$_0$: Var(b_{1i}) = Cov(b_{0i} b_{1i}) = 0	Results are conservative; not applicable for H$_0$: Var(b_{0i}) = 0

10.4.2 AICc

Another method of selecting random effects and variance components is to use the AICc. The AICc can be used to compare a set of fitted models differing in the number of variance components. It is recommended that the AICc be used to decide on the number of variance components rather than to evaluate a set of candidate models, as in a multimodel analysis. The variance components are rarely the primary focus of the analysis, and emphasis is on preselection for subsequent fixed effects evaluation.

A problem in using the AICc is that it essentially has the same bias properties as the LRT (Greven & Kneib, 2010). This means the AICc values for fitted models with different variance components will be more similar than they should. Thus, there is a tendency to select models that are too simple. This should be kept in mind when using the AICc for the selection of random effects.

In the syntax below, the three different models of Table 10.1 are estimated. All have the same fixed effects structure, but different variance components. Recall the nature of the three models.

1. Intercepts-only model

2. Model with uncorrelated random intercepts and slopes

3. Model with correlated random intercepts and slopes

The AICc is computed for the set using `aictab()`.

```
> model.1 <- lmer(read ~ grade5 + (1 | subid), data = MPLS.LS)
> model.2 <- lmer(read ~ grade5 + (1 | subid) + (0 + grade5 | subid), data = MPLS.LS)
> model.3 <- lmer(read ~ grade5 + (grade5 | subid), data = MPLS.LS)
> print(aictab(cand.set = list(model.1, model.2, model.3),
+       modnames = c("M1", "M2", "M3")), LL = FALSE)
```

```
Model selection based on AICc :

     K   AICc  Delta_AICc  AICcWt  Cum.Wt
M3   6  576.40    0.00      0.63    0.63
M2   5  577.82    1.42      0.31    0.94
M1   4  581.04    4.64      0.06    1.00
```

The output shows that the model with the correlated random effects is the best-fitting (Model 3). This result is consistent with that of the previous section. That is, the AICc suggests the same number of variance components (three) as the LRT and bootstrap methods. Although the methods show agreement for this example, there is no assurance of agreement in general.

10.5 Variance Components and Static Predictors

The examples of the previous sections did not involve static predictors. This may be justified when the researcher wants to preselect the random effects, and then move on to fixed effects model comparison.

It is also possible to examine the need for random effects after the fixed effects models have been selected. For example, say that the best-fitting models have the predictors grade5, risk2, and eth2. Suppose the fixed effects models are compared using two random effects, and the researcher desires to test for the need of the second random effect (random slopes). The fast bootstrap syntax for this comparison is shown below.

```
> full          <- lmer(read ~ grade5 + risk2 + eth2 + (1 | subid) + (0 + grade5 | subid), MPLS.LS)
> reduced.int   <- lmer(read ~ grade5 + risk2 + eth2 + (1 | subid), MPLS.LS)
> reduced.slope <- lmer(read ~ grade5 + risk2 + eth2 + (0 + grade5 | subid), MPLS.LS)
> exactRLRT(reduced.slope, full, reduced.int)
```

```
        simulated finite sample distribution of RLRT.  (p-value based on 10000
        simulated values)

data:
RLRT = 4.3256, p-value = 0.0202
```

The output indicates the *p*-value is small. The result suggests that the random slope term is needed in the final model.

10.6 Predicted Random Effects

In applied analysis, the focus is usually on the variance components of random effects, and not the random effects themselves. There are, however, special

10.6 Predicted Random Effects

cases in which a researcher is interested in computing and examining predicted random effects scores. Two uses of the predicted random effects scores are considered in this section.

- The first use is to judge consistency with statistical assumptions. Graphs of the predicted random effects can be inspected for evidence of consistency with normality, which is a key assumption for inference with LMER.
- The second use is to obtain information on change for an individual. The predicted random effects can be used to compute predicted scores for a subject. The scores are often used to assess the subject's standing relative to the group change curve.

Each of these uses is explored in turn. But prior to doing so, some issues related to the random effects scores are discussed.

The fitted lmer() model can be used to compute random effects values for each subject. There is some question regarding whether these realized values should be referred to as *predicted random effects* or *estimated random effects*. The terminology depends on whether one adopts a LMER perspective or a multilevel model perspective.

In the LMER model, random effects are random variables. The only parameters are those of the (joint) distribution of the random effects, the means (assumed to be 0), variances, and covariances (correlations). Since realizations of random variables are not parameter estimates, the term predicted random effects is appropriate from a LMER perspective.

From a multilevel model perspective, the regression coefficients in the Level 1 model, β_{ki}^*, are subject-specific parameters. These have been referred to as uncorrected random effects, as the β_{ki}^* are sums of Level 2 means (fixed effects) and random Level 2 errors (corrected random effects). Considering only one subject in isolation, it is reasonable to treat the β_{ki}^* as parameters because the subject is fixed, and the only random variation in the Level 1 model is the error. In this sense, the $\hat{\beta}_{ki}^*$ might be referred to as estimated random effects.

There is yet another interpretation of the predicted random effects. Under the normality assumption, the predicted random effects are interpreted as conditional means, given the response vector and the estimated fixed effects. These means are known as the *best linear unbiased predictors* (BLUPs). When the predicted random effects are computed based on the fitted lmer() model, they are known as *empirical best linear unbiased predictors* (EBLUPs).

To make the concepts clearer, consider the equation for the predicted value of the response based on the estimated fixed effects and predicted random effects.

$$\tilde{y}_{ij} = (\hat{\beta}_0 + \hat{b}_{0i}) + (\hat{\beta}_1 + \hat{b}_{1i})(\text{grade5}_{ij}). \quad (10.6.1)$$

The $\hat{b}_{ki}$ are the BLUPs, and the $\hat{\beta}_k$ are the REML estimators. When realized values are obtained using lmer(), there are EBLUPs and REML estimates.

Equation 10.6.1 can be expressed as

$$\tilde{y}_{ij} = \hat{\beta}_{0i}^* + \hat{\beta}_{1i}^*(\text{grade5}_{ij}), \qquad (10.6.2)$$

where

$$\hat{\beta}_{0i}^* = \hat{\beta}_0 + \hat{b}_{0i},$$
$$\hat{\beta}_{1i}^* = \hat{\beta}_1 + \hat{b}_{1i}.$$

Equation 10.6.2 is used to obtain the predicted values of the response variable over time for a particular subject.

Similar to the distinction made in Section 5.3.1.1, the realized values of $\hat{b}_{ki}$ are referred to as *corrected EBLUPs* and the $\hat{\beta}_{ki}^*$ as *uncorrected EBLUPs*. The reason is that the $\hat{b}_{ki}$ have a mean of 0, and thus, are mean corrected. The $\hat{\beta}_{ki}^*$ have a mean of $\hat{\beta}_k$ and are not mean corrected.

The corrected EBLUPs are extracted from a lmer() fitted model using the ranef() function. In the syntax below, a LMER model is estimated, and ranef() is used within ldply() to save a data frame with the EBLUPs.

```
> my.lmer    ← lmer(read ~ grade5 + (grade5|subid), MPLS.LS)
> my.c.re    ← ldply(ranef(my.lmer))[-1]
> colnames(my.c.re) ← c("b0i", "b1i")
> my.c.re
```

	b0i	b1i
1	-28.3935529	1.2569094
2	-0.5156510	-0.1043502
3	-10.1590239	1.8770524
4	-7.6026541	-2.6471705
5	4.9002556	-1.9934296
6	-12.4801137	-0.9306980
7	-1.2058438	0.8551081
8	-12.8452671	-0.7835362
9	-51.8963150	4.3795263
10	0.6960155	0.5978739
11	-21.0156890	1.4183836
12	-13.1307841	1.5701007
13	25.9329855	-1.9126508
14	0.7817642	4.5189316
15	17.3005722	0.9385674
16	23.8017482	-3.0854327
17	-0.2432981	0.2296886
18	13.8181926	-2.8326267
19	11.2918691	-1.0836195
20	5.0385717	-0.9643664
21	34.6898058	-1.9164057
22	21.2364122	0.6121443

10.6 Predicted Random Effects

The corrected EBLUPs of the random intercepts are in the first column, and those of the random slopes are in the second column. To be clear, these are the values of $\hat{b}_{0i}$ and $\hat{b}_{1i}$ in Equation 10.6.1.

To illustrate that `my.c.re` contains the mean-corrected EBLUPs, the mean is computed for each column.

```
> round(mean(my.c.re), 8)

b0i b1i
  0   0
```

As the output shows, the mean of each column is equal to 0, to at least eight decimal places.

10.6.1 EVALUATING THE NORMALITY ASSUMPTION

Having extracted the EBLUPs into a data frame, one use for them is to assess the consistency of each distribution with a normal distribution. Recall that inferential methods in LMER are predicated on this assumption. Various types of graphs of the EBLUPs are constructed: density plots, boxplots, and Q-Q plots.

In the syntax below, six graphs are constructed, three for the EBLUPs of the random intercepts and three for those of the random slopes. The `opts("aspect.ratio" = 1)` component is used to construct square graphs. It is shown in a moment how the graphs are printed on a single page.

```
> ## Density plot b0i.
> d1 <- ggplot(my.c.re, aes(x = b0i)) + geom_density(fill="grey80")
> d2 <- d1 + theme_bw() + opts("aspect.ratio" = 1)
> ## Boxplot b0i.
> b1 <- ggplot(my.c.re, aes(x = "b0", y = b0i)) + geom_boxplot()
> b2 <- b1 + theme_bw() + opts("aspect.ratio" = 1)
> ## Q-Q plot b0.
> q1 <- ggplot(my.c.re, aes(sample = b0i)) + geom_point(stat = "qq")
> q2 <- q1 + theme_bw() + opts("aspect.ratio" = 1)
> ## Density plot b1.
> dd1 <- ggplot(my.c.re, aes(x = b1i)) + geom_density(fill="grey80")
> dd2 <- dd1 + theme_bw() + opts("aspect.ratio" = 1)
> ## Boxplot b1.
> bb1 <- ggplot(my.c.re, aes(x = "b1", y = b1i)) + geom_boxplot()
> bb2 <- bb1 + theme_bw() + opts("aspect.ratio" = 1)
> ## Q-Q plot b1.
> qq1 <- ggplot(my.c.re, aes(sample = b1i)) + geom_point(stat= "qq")
> qq2 <- qq1 + theme_bw() + opts("aspect.ratio" = 1)
```

After submitting the above syntax, the saved graphs are printed on a single page. This printing facilitates comparison of the graphs. The following syntax prints the graphs in two rows with three columns each. The graphs for the intercepts are in the top row, and those for the slopes are in the bottom row.

```
> vplayout <- function(x,y) viewport(layout.pos.row = x,layout.pos.col = y)
> grid.newpage()
> pushViewport(viewport(layout = grid.layout(2, 3)))
> print(d2,   vp = vplayout(1, 1))
> print(b2,   vp = vplayout(1, 2))
> print(q2,   vp = vplayout(1, 3))
> print(dd2,  vp = vplayout(2, 1))
> print(bb2,  vp = vplayout(2, 2))
> print(qq2,  vp = vplayout(2, 3))
```

To save the page to a graphics file, the menu options are accessed within the graph window. An alternative is to enclose the above syntax between, say, a pdf() statement and the dev.off() statement. Alternative formats are also possible; see ?png.

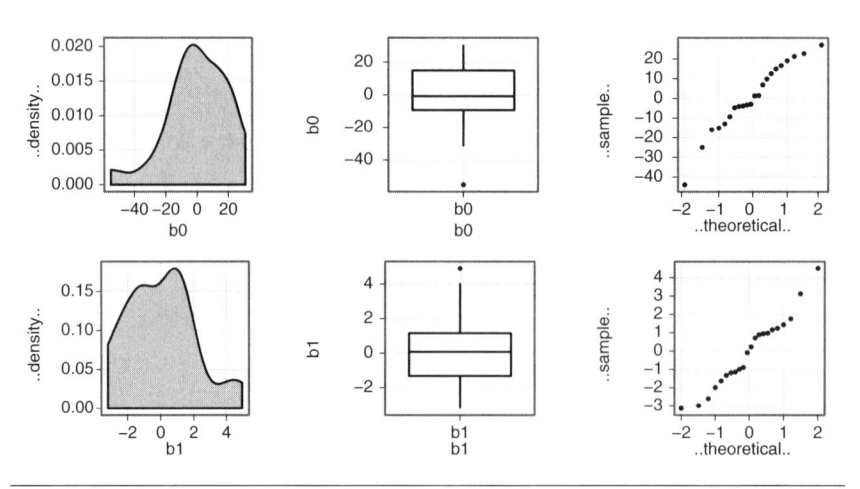

Figure 10.6 Graphs for assessing normality of predicted random intercepts (top row) and predicted random slopes (bottom row). First column: density plots. Second column: boxplots. Third column: Q-Q plots.

The graphs are shown in Figure 10.6. The graphs for the intercepts indicate the distribution is negatively skewed, with a potential outlier. The Q-Q plot in the upper right indicates slight discontinuity. The graphs for the slopes also show slight asymmetry of the distribution, but in the positive direction. Given the small sample size, the asymmetry evident in the graphs is not extreme enough to cause serious doubt regarding the plausibility of the normality assumption for either set of EBLUPs.

10.6 Predicted Random Effects

Although not pursued here, an additional step can be performed for the evaluation of the normality assumption. One can randomly generate scores from a normal distribution and create the same plots as in Figure 10.6. This helps provide a reference for how the plots might look for sample data that are known to come from a normal distribution. The rnorm() function is used for the generation, with means equal to 0 and SDs being those of the EBLUPs. The syntax below generates the random data for intercepts and slopes, which is used with ggplot2.

```
> sim.data <- data.frame(sim.b0i = rnorm(n = 22, mean = 0, sd = sd(my.c.re[ , 1])),
+                        sim.b1i = rnorm(n = 22, mean = 0, sd = sd(my.c.re[ , 2])))
```

10.6.2 PREDICTED VALUES FOR AN INDIVIDUAL

Another use of the EBLUPs is to provide information about change for an individual. In particular situations, it is desirable to compute the predicted values over time based on the EBLUPs for a subject. Or, at least provide the predicted intercept and slope. A parent, for example, might want to know if her daughter's reading scores are increasing at a rate consistent with the average rate for her school. Such questions are addressed with the *uncorrected* EBLUPs of $\hat{\beta}_{0i}^*$ and $\hat{\beta}_{1i}^*$ in Equation 10.6.2.

Based on Equation 10.6.2, the scores are computed by summing the corrected EBLUPs of the random effects with their associated fixed effects. Recall the EBLUPs of the random effects are saved in the data frame my.c.re. In the syntax below, the my.beta data frame is created with the same number of rows and columns as my.c.re, but with the fixed effects estimates repeated.

```
> my.beta <- data.frame(matrix(fixef(my.lmer), nrow = nrow(my.c.re),
+                              ncol = ncol(my.c.re), byrow = TRUE))
> colnames(my.beta) <- c("B0", "B1")
> head(my.beta)
        B0       B1
1 202.1441  4.82925
2 202.1441  4.82925
3 202.1441  4.82925
4 202.1441  4.82925
5 202.1441  4.82925
6 202.1441  4.82925
```

The output shows the estimated fixed intercept in the first column and the estimated fixed slope in the second column.

The next step is to sum my.c.re and my.beta on an element-by-element basis using the summation operator (+). The result is saved as my.un.re.

```
> my.un.re <- my.beta + my.c.re
```

```
> colnames(my.un.re) <- c("B0i", "B1i")
> my.un.re
        B0i       B1i
1  173.7506  6.086160
2  201.6285  4.724900
3  191.9851  6.706303
4  194.5415  2.182080
5  207.0444  2.835821
6  189.6640  3.898553
7  200.9383  5.684359
8  189.2989  4.045714
9  150.2478  9.208777
10 202.8402  5.427124
11 181.1284  6.247634
12 189.0134  6.399351
13 228.0771  2.916600
14 202.9259  9.348182
15 219.4447  5.767818
16 225.9459  1.743818
17 201.9008  5.058939
18 215.9623  1.996624
19 213.4360  3.745631
20 207.1827  3.864884
21 236.8339  2.912845
22 223.3805  5.441395
```

The first column contains the uncorrected EBLUPs for the intercepts, and the second column contains those for the slopes.

It is important to distinguish the uncorrected EBLUPs in my.un.re from the OLS estimates obtained with lm(). Of the two, EBLUPs are "best" in that they have a smaller variance. In addition, the EBLUPs "borrow" strength from the fixed effects, meaning that information from the entire group of subjects is used, rather than the information from only a single subject. For these reasons, the EBLUPs rather than OLS estimates should be used for evaluating change information for an individual.

There are many uses for the uncorrected EBLUPs. Here it is illustrated how change information for a single subject is evaluated vis-à-vis the group change curve. Rather than work with the EBLUPs directly, it is convenient to compute the predicted or fitted values for each subject, $\tilde{y}_{ij}$. These are the fitted values based on the fixed and random effects in Equation 10.6.1, as opposed to those based solely on the fixed effects.

The fitted values are computed using the fitted() function, by supplying the name of the lmer() output object. In the syntax below, a data frame is constructed with the original variables used in the analysis (in the @frame slot) and the fitted values (fitted.re). The fixed effects are saved in a separate data frame and used to draw the same group curve for each subject. A subject facet plot is created with the EBLUP prediction line. The group curve is drawn in each panel, in addition to the observed values.

10.6 Predicted Random Effects

```
> ## Fit LMER model using REML.
> lmer.1 <- lmer(read ~ grade5 + (grade5 | subid), MPLS.LS)
> ## Create data frame 1.
> plotdata <- data.frame(lmer.1@frame, fitted.re = fitted(lmer.1))
> head(plotdata)
```

	read	grade5	subid	fitted.re
1.5	172	0	1	173.7506
1.6	185	1	1	179.8367
1.7	179	2	1	185.9229
1.8	194	3	1	192.0091
2.5	200	0	2	201.6285
2.6	210	1	2	206.3534

```
> ## Create data frame 2.
> fixed <- data.frame(fixef(lmer.1))
> fixed
```

	fixef.lmer.1.
(Intercept)	202.14414
grade5	4.82925

```
> ## ggplot().
> g1 <- ggplot(plotdata, aes(x = grade5, y = read)) + geom_point()
> ## Facet.
> g2 <- g1 + facet_wrap(~ subid, nrow = 2)
> ## Individual fitted curve.
> g3 <- g2 + geom_line(aes(y= fitted.re),linetype= 2)+ scale_x_continuous(breaks= 0:3)
> ## Group fitted curve.
> g4 <- g3 + geom_abline(intercept = fixed[1,1], slope = fixed[2,1]) + theme_bw()
> print(g4)
```

The facet plots are shown in Figure 10.7. The solid line is the same for each panel, as it is the group fitted curve. The group curve is drawn using `geom_abline()`. The dotted line in each panel is the fitted curve based on the EBLUPs. Each panel reveals the change of an individual in relation to group change. For example, Subject 14 begins at the same predicted value as the group, but increases at a rate faster than the group. Subject 22 starts higher than the group, but has a rate of change that is nearly identical to the group.

As mentioned, the OLS estimates and the EBLUPs have different properties and result in different prediction curves for the subjects. To see the difference between the OLS estimates and the EBLUPs, consider a plot of both types of predicted curves.

```
> g1 <- ggplot(plotdata, aes(x = grade5, y = read)) + geom_point()
> g2 <- g1 + facet_wrap(~ subid, nrow = 2)
> ## EBLUP lines.
> g3 <- g2 + geom_line(aes(y = fitted.re), linetype = 2) + scale_x_continuous(breaks = 0:3)
> ## OLS lines.
> g4 <- g3 + stat_smooth(method = "lm", se = F) + theme_bw()
> print(g4)
```

The facet plots are shown in Figure 10.8. The fitted curves based on OLS are solid, and the fitted curves based on the EBLUPs are dotted. The OLS

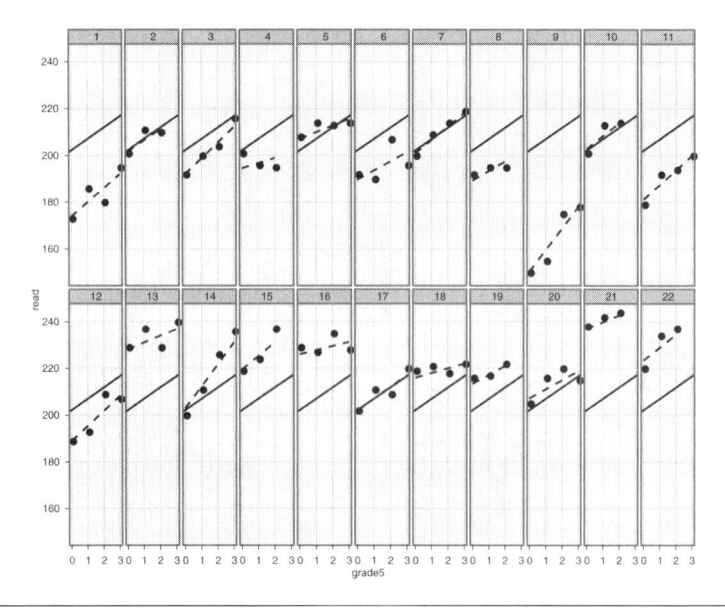

Figure 10.7 Subject facet plots with the fitted group curve (solid line), fitted individual curves (dotted lines), and observed points.

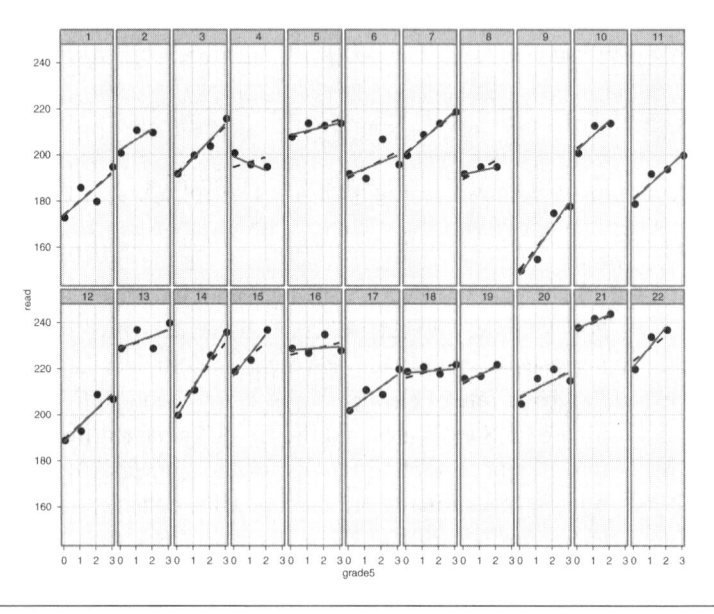

Figure 10.8 Subject facet plots with the OLS fitted individual curves (solid lines), the EBLUP fitted individual curves (dotted lines), and observed points.

and EBLUP curves agree in many cases, but there are some important exceptions. For Subject 4, the EBLUP curve is *increasing*, whereas the OLS curve

10.6 Predicted Random Effects

is *decreasing*. The EBLUP curve illustrates the "borrowing strength" concept. The group curve increases over time, and this group result influences the prediction for all the individuals. Subject 4 has missing data, meaning that the group curve has a greater influence than for a subject with no missing data. The OLS estimates treat Subject 4 in isolation, and the estimates are "unaware" of the group effect. Therefore, the OLS estimates lead to a fitted curve that decreases over time.

If aggregate information is applicable to individuals, then the EBLUP fitted curve is favored over the OLS curve. For example, when there is a shared classroom environment for all the subjects, the group solution indexes this common global effect, at least in part. A researcher probably wants the common environment to inform the predictions for each individual. This is especially so for a subject with missing data, as there is relatively little individual-specific information. In such cases, borrowing information from other subjects in the common environment is an appealing idea.

Extending Linear Mixed Effects Regression 11

This chapter elaborates on several topics previously discussed. Earlier chapters dealt with quantitative and binary categorical static predictors, with focus on intercept and slope effects. These topics are broadened to include categorical static predictors with more than two groups and additional static predictor effects, such as interactions among the static predictors. A key to understanding more complex effects is to graph fitted curves. Therefore, the first part of the chapter is devoted to this topic.

The issue of effect size is revisited. Chapters 7 and 8 dealt with the topic of relative effect size measures, in the form of the AICc (Chapter 7), and the LRT-p calibrated with predictive accuracy (Chapter 8). Relative effect size is important for rank-ordering models, but relative effect size does not indicate whether any of the models in the set are "good" in an absolute sense. Measures of absolute effect size are considered, with emphasis on R^2 based on a fitted LMER model.

Finally, additional issues regarding transformations of the data are discussed. These include transformations of the time predictor to address estimation problems, and transformations of the response variable for describing standardized change.

11.1 Graphing Fitted Curves

Prior to launching into more complex LMER models, the topic of graphing fitted curves is discussed. The reason is that interpretation of effects in LMER models with many parameters is facilitated by graphs of the fitted values. This is similar to the clarity that is gained by graphing group means for interactions in traditional ANOVA.

The graphing of fitted curves is based on a fitted `lmer()` model object. These curves can be a helpful addition to the graphs of observed means. Fitted curves are always smooth, whereas means curves might not be, especially when the observations are not balanced on time (see Chapter 4).

In Chapter 10, the `fitted()` function was used to compute fitted values and graph individual curves. These fitted values were based on the fixed effects and random effects (i.e., the EBLUPs), which means the fitted curves were subject-specific. Such curves are appropriate when individual-level information is of interest.

When the focus is on aggregate effects, as it often is, the fitted curves should be based only on the estimated fixed effects. In this approach, the LMER model is first estimated, and then the fixed effects estimates are used to compute fitted response values based on the observed predictors. Suppose that grade is the only predictor in a LMER model. Then the fitted values are computed as

$$\hat{y}_{ij} = \hat{\beta}_0 + \hat{\beta}_1(\text{grade}_{ij}), \quad (11.1.1)$$

where $\hat{\beta}_0$, $\hat{\beta}_1$ are the maximum likelihood (ML) estimates obtained with `lmer()`.

Unfortunately, there is no function in `lme4` for automatically computing the fitted values of Equation 11.1.1. Therefore, the `FittedFE()` user-defined function is introduced below. The function uses matrix algebra to postmultiply the model matrix by the fixed effects estimates (see the Appendix). The model matrix consists of the multipliers of the fixed effects in the LMER model. This includes a column of 1s for the intercept, the time transformations, and values of the static predictors, including dummy variables if applicable. The following syntax is evaluated, so that the `FittedFE()` function can be used.

```
> FittedFE  <-  function(x) model.matrix(x) %*% fixef(x)
```

After submitting the syntax, the function is executed by supplying the name of a `lmer()` fitted output object. The result is a matrix object of fitted values, based on the fixed effects. In the syntax below, only the head of the resulting data frame is printed for brevity.

```
> lmer.1  <-  lmer(read ~ grade5 + (grade5 | subid), MPLS.LS, REML = FALSE)
> head(FittedFE(lmer.1))
```

```
           [,1]
[1,]   202.1442
[2,]   206.9734
[3,]   211.8026
[4,]   216.6318
[5,]   202.1442
[6,]   206.9734
```

11.1 Graphing Fitted Curves

To better understand the fitted values and to use them in graphing, they are saved as a column in a data frame along with other scores from the output object. In the `lmer()` fitted model object, the `@frame` slot contains the actual scores of the variables used in the analysis. It is important to use these scores rather than the ones from the original data frame because of the possibility of missing data.

In the syntax below, the `frame` variables are saved along with the fitted values based on the fixed effects. Since `grade5` is used in the estimated model, a `grade` variable is created, so that the graphs to follow will have the appropriate *x*-axis metric.

```
> plotdata <- data.frame(lmer.1@frame, fitted = FittedFE(lmer.1))
> plotdata$grade <- plotdata$grade5 + 5
> head(plotdata, n = 11)
    read grade5 subid   fitted grade
1.5  172      0     1 202.1442     5
1.6  185      1     1 206.9734     6
1.7  179      2     1 211.8026     7
1.8  194      3     1 216.6318     8
2.5  200      0     2 202.1442     5
2.6  210      1     2 206.9734     6
2.7  209      2     2 211.8026     7
3.5  191      0     3 202.1442     5
3.6  199      1     3 206.9734     6
3.7  203      2     3 211.8026     7
3.8  215      3     3 216.6318     8
```

The output shows the variables in the `@frame` slot are `read`, `grade5`, and `subid`. The fitted values and the original time predictor appear in the last two columns.

Perusing the `fitted` column of the output, it can be seen that the fitted value for a time point is the same for the three subjects listed above. Using the row labels to the extreme left, it can be seen, for example, that the fitted value in rows 1.5, 2.5, and 3.5 is 202.14. A full listing will reveal that the fitted value for a time point is the same for all subjects. Since the fixed effects are common to all the subjects, the fitted curve is constant among subjects. This is in contrast to the fitted curves based on the fixed effects and random effects considered in Chapter 10.

The constant curve among subjects means that `geom_line()` can be used to draw the fitted group curve. In the syntax below, the observed points and observed mean values are also drawn, and some formatting options are set for future use.

```
> theme_set(theme_bw())
> myx <- scale_x_continuous(breaks = 5:8)
> g1 <- ggplot(plotdata, aes(x = grade, y = read)) + geom_point(shape = 19)
> g2 <- g1 + stat_summary(fun.y = mean, geom = "point", size = 5, shape = 1)
> g3 <- g2 + geom_line(aes(y = fitted), lwd = 1.5) + myx + opts(aspect.ratio = 1)
> print(g3)
```

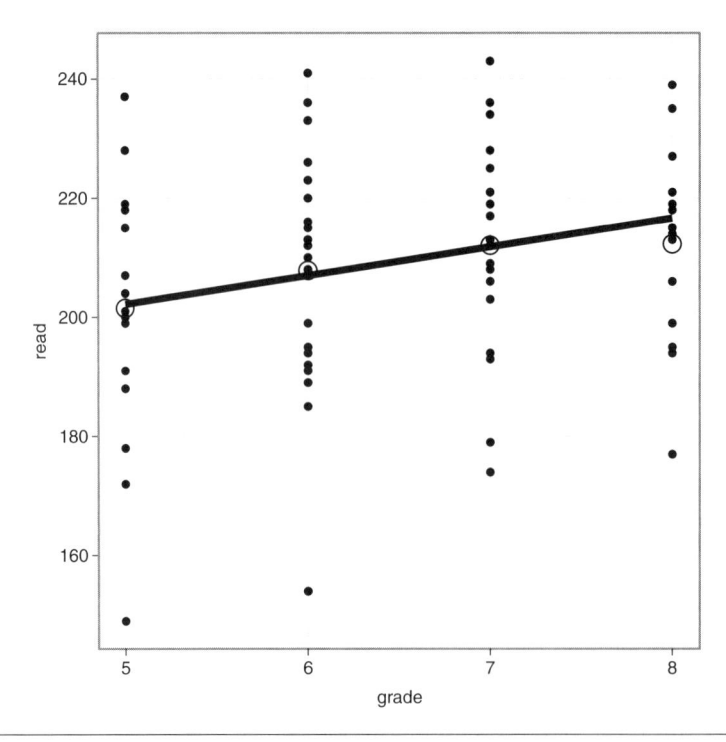

Figure 11.1 Observed points (filled circles), mean values (open circles), and fitted group curve.

The graph is shown in Figure 11.1. The group curve is linear, whereas the observed means have a slight nonlinear trend. As illustrated in Chapter 9, there is little statistical evidence that a nonlinear group curve is needed. Thus, the fitted curve is perhaps preferred, as it is consistent with the statistical results.

As another illustration, consider the model with the predictors grade5, risk2, and eth2. In the syntax below, the model is estimated, the fitted values are computed, and a data frame for graphing is constructed.

```
> lmer.2 <- lmer(read ~ grade5 * risk2 + grade5 * eth2 + (grade5 | subid),
+       MPLS.LS, REML = FALSE)
> plotdata <- data.frame(lmer.2@frame, fitted = FittedFE(lmer.2))
> plotdata$grade <- plotdata$grade5 + 5
> head(plotdata)
```

	read	grade5	risk2	eth2	subid	fitted	grade
1.5	172	0	DADV	NW	1	188.7648	5
1.6	185	1	DADV	NW	1	194.1419	6
1.7	179	2	DADV	NW	1	199.5190	7
1.8	194	3	DADV	NW	1	204.8961	8
2.5	200	0	DADV	NW	2	188.7648	5
2.6	210	1	DADV	NW	2	194.1419	6

The goal in this case is to depict the fitted curve for risk2 and eth2. The static predictors appear as single effect (main effects) in the model. Therefore,

11.2 Static Predictors With Multiple Levels

the goal is to depict the curve for one static predictor, holding the other predictor constant. For example, the curves for advantaged and disadvantaged students might be drawn holding `eth2` constant. This is accomplished by averaging the fitted values for each group of `eth2`. To illustrate, consider the following mean fitted values produced with `ddply()`.

```
> my.m <- ddply(data.frame(plotdata$fitted), .(plotdata$risk2, plotdata$grade), mean)
> colnames(my.m) <- c("risk2", "grade", "mfitted")
> my.m
```

```
  risk2 grade  mfitted
1   ADV     5 217.5279
2   ADV     6 221.9361
3   ADV     7 226.3442
4   ADV     8 230.7901
5  DADV     5 189.3693
6  DADV     6 194.4820
7  DADV     7 199.5948
8  DADV     8 204.6133
```

The output shows the mean fitted values, `mfitted`, over grade for each risk group. Each fitted value is computed by averaging over the subjects within the `eth2` groups.

The averaged fitted values are graphed using `stat_summary()`. In the syntax below, the means for `risk2` are also computed and plotted as points. This helps assess the extent of correspondence between the observed means and the fitted curves.

```
> g1 <- ggplot(plotdata, aes(x = grade, y = read, shape = risk2))
> g2 <- g1 + stat_summary(fun.y = mean, geom = "point")
> g3 <- g2 + stat_summary(fun.y = mean, geom = "line", aes(y = fitted, linetype = risk2))
> g4 <- g3 + opts("aspect.ratio" = 1) + myx
> print(g4)
```

The graph is shown in Figure 11.2. The risk group curves are nearly parallel, with the advantaged group having a higher intercept. A similar graph can be made for the ethnicity groups, averaging over risk.

In the following sections, fitted curves are used for more complex situations than the main effects models considered thus far. It is often easier to interpret complex effects by a visual inspection of the fitted curves rather than by an inspection of `lmer()` output.

11.2 Static Predictors With Multiple Levels

Past chapters considered the case of categorical static predictors with two groups. In this section, models are analyzed that have predictors with more than two groups.

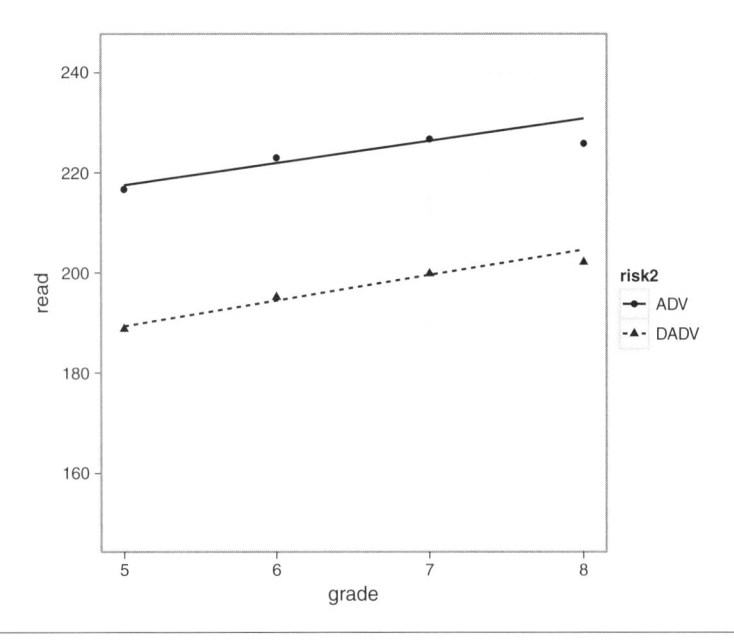

Figure 11.2 Observed means (shapes) and fitted group curves by risk group.

As an example, consider the risk variable in the MPLS data set. The original predictor has three groups: ADV, POV, and HHM. Previously, the last two categories were collapsed into a DADV group for a two-category analysis. Now a three-group analysis will be performed.

Recall that categorical predictors require dummy variables. As seen in Chapter 5 with the two-group case, the value of 0 is assigned for one group, and the value of 1 is assigned for the other group. The binary dummy coding produces parameters representing group differences. In the case of more than two groups, multiple dummy variables are required. The total number of dummy variables is one minus the number of groups.

Most regression-type functions in R, including lmer(), will automatically construct dummy variables when a predictor is a factor variable. One group is designated the *reference group* or *base group*, and all the other groups are compared to it. The reference group has the smallest numeric factor value. This can be determined by examining which group label is printed first with the levels() function. Consider the following.

```
> levels(MPLS.LS$risk)
[1] "ADV"  "HHM"  "POV"
```

The output indicates that for the risk variable, ADV is the reference group. In construction of the dummy variables, ADV is never assigned 1. Each of the other groups receives 1 for a single dummy variable.

11.2 Static Predictors With Multiple Levels

An illustration will help clarify. For the risk variable, two dummy variables must be constructed. These are denoted as riskPOV and riskHHM, which are the variable names that will appear in the lmer() output. The variable names are constructed by concatenating the original factor variable name with the label level assigned 1.

The definition of riskPOV is

$$\text{riskPOV}_i = \begin{cases} 1 & \text{if risk}_i = \text{POV}, \\ 0 & \text{if risk}_i \neq \text{POV}. \end{cases} \quad (11.2.1)$$

The definition of riskHHM is

$$\text{riskHHM}_i = \begin{cases} 1 & \text{if risk}_i = \text{HHM}, \\ 0 & \text{if risk}_i \neq \text{HHM}. \end{cases} \quad (11.2.2)$$

The ADV level is never assigned 1, and thus, is the reference category. That is, a dummy variable is not constructed for ADV. In whatever is being compared (e.g., mean slopes), *the reference group is always subtracted from each other group*. For this example, this means that the two differences will be POV minus ADV, and HHM minus ADV.

Consider a linear change curve model, with risk effects for intercept and slope. Using the names of the dummy variables, the LMER model is

$$\begin{aligned} y_{ij} &= \beta_0 + \beta_1(\text{grade5}_{ij}) \\ &\quad + \beta_2(\text{riskPOV}_i) + \beta_3(\text{riskHHM}_i) \\ &\quad + \beta_4(\text{grade5}_{ij} \cdot \text{riskPOV}_i) \\ &\quad + \beta_5(\text{grade5}_{ij} \cdot \text{riskHHM}_i) + \varepsilon_{ij}^*, \end{aligned} \quad (11.2.3)$$

where $\varepsilon_{ij}^* = b_{0i} + b_{1i}(\text{grade5}_{ij}) + \varepsilon_{ij}$. In Equation 11.2.3, β_2 is the intercept difference between POV and ADV (POV minus ADV), and β_3 is the intercept difference between HHM and ADV (HHM minus ADV). Similar group differences for the slope are represented by β_4 and β_5.

The equation for each group is obtained by substituting the appropriate 0 and 1 for the dummy variables. Doing so for Equation 11.2.3 yields the following three equations.

$$\begin{aligned} \text{ADV:} \quad & y_{ij} = \beta_0 + \beta_1(\text{grade5}_{ij}) + \varepsilon_{ij}^*, \\ \text{POV:} \quad & y_{ij} = (\beta_0 + \beta_2) + (\beta_1 + \beta_4)(\text{grade5}_{ij}) + \varepsilon_{ij}^*, \quad (11.2.4) \\ \text{HHM:} \quad & y_{ij} = (\beta_0 + \beta_3) + (\beta_1 + \beta_5)(\text{grade5}_{ij}) + \varepsilon_{ij}^*. \end{aligned}$$

Inspection of Equation 11.2.4 reveals that the change curve for POV will differ from ADV when either $\beta_2 \neq 0$ (for the intercept) or $\beta_4 \neq 0$ (for the slope). Similarly, the change curve for HHM will differ from ADV when $\beta_3 \neq 0$ or $\beta_5 \neq 0$.

The contrast of POV and HHM is not represented by a dummy variable. If interest is in this comparison, a new set of dummy variables must be constructed using either POV or HHM as the base group. When the specific nature of differences among the groups is not a concern, then the dummy variables defined above will suffice. Simultaneous evaluation of both dummy variables will reveal any type of difference among the groups. This is true regardless of the reference group. Therefore, the only reason for redefining the dummy variables is to provide parameters representing different group comparisons.

As an illustration, consider estimation of the Equation 11.2.3 model.

```
> lmer.3 <- lmer(read ~ grade5 * risk + (grade5 | subid), MPLS.LS, REML = FALSE)
> print(lmer.3, cor = FALSE)
```

```
Linear mixed model fit by maximum likelihood
Formula: read ~ grade5 * risk + (grade5 | subid)
   Data: MPLS.LS
   AIC   BIC  logLik deviance REMLdev
  567.3 591.1 -273.6   547.3   526.2
Random effects:
 Groups   Name        Variance Std.Dev. Corr
 subid    (Intercept) 172.8714 13.1481
          grade5        5.3795  2.3194  -0.610
 Residual              18.5426  4.3061
Number of obs: 80, groups: subid, 22

Fixed effects:
                Estimate Std. Error t value
(Intercept)     217.5155     4.3188   50.36
grade5            4.4268     1.0294    4.30
riskHHM         -23.6003     7.0510   -3.35
riskPOV         -32.6636     7.0510   -4.63
grade5:riskHHM   -0.7995     1.6663   -0.48
grade5:riskPOV    2.1288     1.6663    1.28
```

The last portion of the output shows the fixed effects estimates. The labeling in the first column corresponds to Equation 11.2.3. The ADV group label does not appear, meaning it is the reference group. The ADV intercept and slope estimates are in the first two rows, respectively, of Estimate. In this case, the estimated ADV intercept is $\hat{\beta}_0 = 217.52$, and the estimated ADV slope is $\hat{\beta}_1 = 4.43$.

The intercept *differences* are listed in rows riskHHM and riskPOV. The HHM group has an intercept that is $\hat{\beta}_2 = -23.6$ less than that of the ADV group, and the POV group has an intercept that is $\hat{\beta}_3 = -32.66$ less.

Similarly, the slope *differences* are listed in rows grade5:riskHHM and grade5:riskPOV. The HHM group has a slope that is $\hat{\beta}_4 = -0.8$ less than the ADV group, and the POV group has a slope that is $\hat{\beta}_5 = 2.13$ *greater* than the ADV group.

11.2 Static Predictors With Multiple Levels

The estimated intercepts and slopes for the POV and HHM groups are computed by addition. For example, the estimated POV intercept is $\hat{\beta}_0 + \hat{\beta}_3 = 217.52 + (-32.66) = 184.85$. The estimated POV slope is $\hat{\beta}_1 + \hat{\beta}_5 = 4.43 + 2.13 = 6.56$.

In fitting LMER models, the dummy variables may be redefined to provide all pairwise estimates of differences. If, for example, the difference between the HHM and POV groups is the focus, then either group must be designated as the reference group. The reference group can be changed with the `relevel()` function in the data frame, or by using the `C()` function in the `lmer()` syntax (the `C()` and `c()` functions are distinct). Consider the first approach, in which a new risk factor variable is created, `rrisk`. The variable uses HHM as the reference category.

```
> rrisk <- relevel(MPLS.LS$risk, ref = "HHM")
> lmer.3A <- lmer(read ~ grade5 * rrisk + (grade5 | subid), MPLS.LS, REML = FALSE)
> print(lmer.3A, corr = FALSE)
```

```
Linear mixed model fit by maximum likelihood
Formula: read ~ grade5 * rrisk + (grade5 | subid)
   Data: MPLS.LS
   AIC   BIC  logLik  deviance  REMLdev
  567.3 591.1 -273.6   547.3     526.2
Random effects:
 Groups   Name        Variance  Std.Dev. Corr
 subid    (Intercept) 172.8714  13.1481
          grade5        5.3795   2.3194  -0.610
 Residual              18.5426   4.3061
Number of obs: 80, groups: subid, 22

Fixed effects:
                  Estimate Std. Error t value
(Intercept)       193.9152     5.5736   34.79
grade5              3.6273     1.3103    2.77
rriskADV           23.6003     7.0510    3.35
rriskPOV           -9.0633     7.8823   -1.15
grade5:rriskADV     0.7995     1.6662    0.48
grade5:rriskPOV     2.9283     1.8530    1.58
```

The fixed effects table reflects the change in the reference category. The dummy variable `rriskADV` represents the difference between the ADV and HHM groups (ADV minus HHM). The dummy variable `rriskPOV` represents the difference between the POV and HHM groups (POV minus HHM).

The same effect is accomplished using `C()`. The base category is changed using the `base=` argument. The levels are numbered alphabetically, indicating that HHM is the second level. Thus, HHM is set to the reference category using `base=2`.

```
> lmer.3AA ← lmer(read ~ grade5 * C(risk, base = 2) + (grade5 | subid),
+               MPLS.LS, REML = FALSE)
> summary(lmer.3AA)@coefs
```

	Estimate	Std. Error	t value
(Intercept)	193.9151502	5.573600	34.7917253
grade5	3.6272748	1.310277	2.7683269
C(risk, base = 2)1	23.6003250	7.051037	3.3470717
C(risk, base = 2)3	-9.0633132	7.882260	-1.1498368
grade5:C(risk, base = 2)1	0.7995125	1.666249	0.4798277
grade5:C(risk, base = 2)3	2.9283032	1.853011	1.5802943

The fixed effects table is shown above. The labeling reflects the syntax used to redefine the reference group. Since the labeling is rather cryptic, it is preferable to use `rrisk` as shown above.

It is crucial to note that the overall fit of the model does not change based on which set of dummy variable is used. This can be verified by inspecting the deviance and information criteria. Here the `@AICtab` slot of the `summary()` object is printed for the two types of dummy coding.

```
> summary(lmer.3)@AICtab
```

AIC	BIC	logLik	deviance	REMLdev
567.2603	591.0806	-273.6301	547.2603	526.2388

```
> summary(lmer.3A)@AICtab
```

AIC	BIC	logLik	deviance	REMLdev
567.2603	591.0806	-273.6301	547.2603	526.2388

As the output shows, all the values are identical for the two models. This illustrates the earlier statement that any set of properly constructed dummy variables can be used to detect any type of overall difference among the groups.

It is helpful to plot the observed means for the groups along with their fitted curves. This provides a visual indication of the group differences. The process is the same as in the last section. The first step is to construct a data frame that contains the variables from the analysis and the fitted values.

```
> plotdata ← data.frame(lmer.3@frame, fitted = FittedFE(lmer.3))
> plotdata$grade ← plotdata$grade5 + 5
```

A graph is constructed using `stat_summary()`. The component is used two times, once for the observed mean points and again for the fitted curves.

```
> g1 ← ggplot(plotdata, aes(x = grade, y = read, shape = risk))
> g2 ← g1 + stat_summary(fun.y = mean, geom = "point")
> g3 ← g2 + stat_summary(fun.y = mean, geom = "line", aes(y = fitted, linetype = risk))
> g4 ← g3 + myx + opts("aspect.ratio" = 1) + scale_shape(solid = FALSE)
> print(g4)
```

11.2 Static Predictors With Multiple Levels

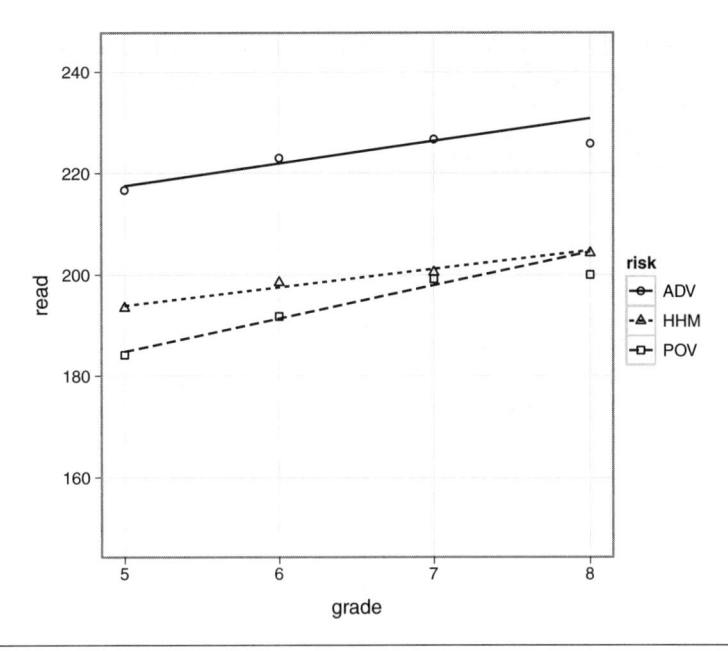

Figure 11.3 Observed means (shapes) and fitted group curves by risk group.

The graph is shown in Figure 11.3. Consistent with the statistical results, the graph shows that the ADV group is consistently higher than the other groups. The HHM group starts a bit higher than the POV group, but their curves converge at the last time point.

11.2.1 EVALUATING SETS OF DUMMY VARIABLES

In the analysis above, the group sample differences were presented without regard to statistical reliability. If the goal is to make inferences about group differences, then the LRT or AICc can be used, as discussed in previous chapters.

There are two common goals of inference with multiple groups, *omnibus* and *specific*.

- Omnibus inference: assess if there is statistical evidence for *any type of difference among the groups*.
- Specific inference: assess if there are *specific differences between pairs of groups*.

The omnibus evaluation is accomplished by considering dummy variables as a set. The set of dummy variables is evaluated by comparing a full model that includes the variables to a reduced model that omits the variables. This comparison can be performed separately for trajectory effects and intercept effects. Alternatively, all effects can be evaluated simultaneously. This latter approach is taken next.

Consider the LRT and AIC for evaluating both intercept and slope effects for all the groups. (The AICc and associated statistics could also be used.)

```
> reduced <- lmer(read ~ grade5 + (grade5 | subid), MPLS.LS, REML = FALSE)
> full <- lmer(read ~ grade5 * risk + (grade5 | subid), MPLS.LS, REML = FALSE)
> anova(reduced, full)
```

```
Data: MPLS.LS
Models:
reduced: read ~ grade5 + (grade5 | subid)
full: read ~ grade5 * risk + (grade5 | subid)
        Df    AIC     BIC    logLik   Chisq Chi Df Pr(>Chisq)
reduced  6 580.96  595.25  -284.48
full    10 567.26  591.08  -273.63  21.699      4   0.0002301 ***
---
Signif. codes:  0 '***' 0.001 '**' 0.01 '*' 0.05 '.' 0.1 ' ' 1
```

The output shows the LRT-p is very small, and the AIC value is much smaller for the full model. There is evidence of an intercept effect difference, a slope difference, or both.

To sort out the intercept and slope omnibus effects, consider the next serious of tests. The `full.1` fitted model object has intercept effects, and the `full.2` fitted model object adds slope effects.

```
> full.1 <- lmer(read ~ grade5 + risk + (grade5 | subid), MPLS.LS, REML = FALSE)
> full.2 <- lmer(read ~ grade5 * risk + (grade5 | subid), MPLS.LS, REML = FALSE)
> anova(reduced, full.1, full.2)
```

```
Data: MPLS.LS
Models:
reduced: read ~ grade5 + (grade5 | subid)
full.1: read ~ grade5 + risk + (grade5 | subid)
full.2: read ~ grade5 * risk + (grade5 | subid)
        Df    AIC     BIC    logLik   Chisq Chi Df Pr(>Chisq)
reduced  6 580.96  595.25  -284.48
full.1   8 565.80  584.85  -274.90  19.1607      2   6.907e-05 ***
full.2  10 567.26  591.08  -273.63   2.5381      2      0.2811
---
Signif. codes:  0 '***' 0.001 '**' 0.01 '*' 0.05 '.' 0.1 ' ' 1
```

LRT-p and the AIC suggest intercept effects are needed, but not slope effects. It should be mentioned that an alternative to the use of the LRT above is to consider the simultaneous fit of all the models with the AICc, as shown in Chapter 7.

11.2.2 EVALUATING INDIVIDUAL DUMMY VARIABLES

For evaluation of specific group differences, results for the individual dummy variables must be considered. The evaluation of group differences

11.2 Static Predictors With Multiple Levels

need not be exhaustive, but it usually is. The reason is that researchers often spend considerable resources on the collection of data. There is usually a desire to know about all possible differences among the groups, so that nothing is overlooked. Such an examination involves all pairwise comparisons.

All pairwise comparisons require that a comparison omitted from the initial dummy coding, such as HHM versus POV, also be evaluated. This requires that the reference group be changed, which was achieved in the analysis above using two different approaches, relevel() and C(). After redefining the reference group, the model was reestimated to obtain the initially omitted comparison.

An alternative to recoding the dummy variables is to use *general linear hypotheses* (GLH). GLH allows contrasts among the parameters in a model to represent all the pairwise differences between the groups. These contrasts can be differences in intercepts, trajectories, or both.

To illustrate, consider the intercept differences among the groups. The formulas in Equation 11.2.4 show that the intercept is β_0 for ADV, $\beta_0 + \beta_2$ for POV, and $\beta_0 + \beta_3$ for HHM. To find the difference between two groups, their intercepts are subtracted.

$$
\begin{aligned}
\text{POV} - \text{ADV}: & \quad (\beta_0 + \beta_2) - \beta_0 & = & \quad \beta_2, \\
\text{HHM} - \text{ADV}: & \quad (\beta_0 + \beta_3) - \beta_0 & = & \quad \beta_3, \\
\text{POV} - \text{HHM}: & \quad (\beta_0 + \beta_2) - (\beta_0 + \beta_3) & = & \quad \beta_2 - \beta_3.
\end{aligned}
\quad (11.2.5)
$$

The first two contrasts occur in Equation 11.2.3 and are estimated when fitting the model. The third contrast must be specified and estimated separately.

A similar set of contrasts for the slopes can be computed. In this case, the slope is β_1 for ADV, $\beta_1 + \beta_4$ for POV, and $\beta_1 + \beta_5$ for HHM. The slope contrasts are the following.

$$
\begin{aligned}
\text{POV} - \text{ADV}: & \quad (\beta_1 + \beta_4) - \beta_1 & = & \quad \beta_2, \\
\text{HHM} - \text{ADV}: & \quad (\beta_1 + \beta_5) - \beta_1 & = & \quad \beta_3, \\
\text{POV} - \text{HHM}: & \quad (\beta_1 + \beta_4) - (\beta_1 + \beta_5) & = & \quad \beta_4 - \beta_5.
\end{aligned}
\quad (11.2.6)
$$

The first two contrasts are in Equation 11.2.3, but the third is not.

To estimate the six parameters[1] in Equations 11.2.5 and 11.2.6, a *contrast matrix* must be constructed. The matrix consists of numbers chosen by the researcher to produce the six contrasts in Equations 11.2.5 and 11.2.6, based on the original six parameters in Equation 11.2.3. The contrast matrix is shown in Table 11.1.

The contrasts of Table 11.1 are specified with the multcomp package, written by Frank Bretz, Torsten Hothorn, Peter Westfall, Richard Heiberger, and Andre Schuetzenmeister (Bretz, Hothorn, & Westfall, 2011). SEs for the parameter estimates are computed with the glht() function. Then *z*-ratios or CIs can be computed to evaluate specific contrasts. The glht() function

---
[1] A difference of parameters is a parameter itself.

Table 11.1 Contrast matrix for six comparisons.

Label	β_0	β_1	β_2	β_3	β_4	β_5	Contrast Parameter
Intercept: POV-ADV	0	0	1	0	0	0	β_2
Intercept: HHM-ADV	0	0	0	1	0	0	β_3
Intercept: POV-HHM	0	0	1	−1	0	0	$\beta_2 - \beta_3$
Slope: POV-ADV	0	0	0	0	1	0	β_4
Slope: HHM-ADV	0	0	0	0	0	1	β_5
Slope: POV-HHM	0	0	0	0	1	−1	$\beta_4 - \beta_5$

requires that the labels for the contrasts and the contrast coefficients be saved as an object. Consider the following syntax related to Table 11.1.

```
> require(multcomp)
> ## Create contrast coefficients.
> K <- rbind("Int: POV-ADV" = c(0,0,1,0,0,0),
+            "Int: HHM-ADV" = c(0,0,0,1,0,0),
+            "Int: HHM-POV" = c(0,0,1,-1,0,0),
+            "Slo: POV-ADV" = c(0,0,0,0,1,0),
+            "Slo: HHM-ADV" = c(0,0,0,0,0,1),
+            "Slo: HHM-POV" = c(0,0,0,0,1,-1))
> ## Save glht() output object.
> glht.3 <- glht(lmer.3, K)
```

Having saved the `glht.3` output object, the `summary()` function is used to compute z-ratios, and the `confint()` function is used to compute CIs. First consider the z-ratios. The `adjusted=` argument is discussed in a moment.

```
> summary(glht.3, test = adjusted(type = "none"))

         Simultaneous Tests for General Linear Hypotheses

Fit: lmer(formula = read ~ grade5 * risk + (grade5 | subid), data = MPLS.LS,
    REML = FALSE)

Linear Hypotheses:
                   Estimate Std. Error z value Pr(>|z|)
Int: POV-ADV == 0  -23.6003     7.0510  -3.347 0.000817 ***
Int: HHM-ADV == 0  -32.6636     7.0510  -4.632 3.61e-06 ***
Int: HHM-POV == 0    9.0633     7.8823   1.150 0.250211
Slo: POV-ADV == 0   -0.7995     1.6663  -0.480 0.631351
Slo: HHM-ADV == 0    2.1288     1.6663   1.278 0.201394
Slo: HHM-POV == 0   -2.9283     1.8530  -1.580 0.114040
---
Signif. codes:  0 '***' 0.001 '**' 0.01 '*' 0.05 '.' 0.1 ' ' 1
(Adjusted p values reported -- none method)
```

11.2 Static Predictors With Multiple Levels

Output lines 8 to 10 show the results for the intercept comparisons. Lines 11 to 13 show the results for the slope comparisons. Lines 8 and 9 indicate that the difference between ADV and each of the other groups is relatively large. The differences are also statistically reliable, using the traditional approach of $p \leq 0.05$. None of the slope differences among the groups is particularly substantial, with HHM versus POV (i.e., HHM-POV) being the largest.

CIs are computed using the `confint()` function. In the syntax below, the request is for CIs with a half-length of 1.96 times the estimated SE.

```
> confint(glht.3, calpha = 1.96)
```

```
            Simultaneous Confidence Intervals

Fit: lmer(formula = read ~ grade5 * risk + (grade5 | subid), data = MPLS.LS,
    REML = FALSE)

Quantile = 1.96
95% confidence level


Linear Hypotheses:
                     Estimate    lwr        upr
Int: POV-ADV == 0    -23.6003   -37.4204   -9.7803
Int: HHM-ADV == 0    -32.6636   -46.4837   -18.8436
Int: HHM-POV == 0      9.0633    -6.3859   24.5125
Slo: POV-ADV == 0     -0.7995    -4.0654    2.4663
Slo: HHM-ADV == 0      2.1288    -1.1371    5.3946
Slo: HHM-POV == 0     -2.9283    -6.5602    0.7036
```

Output line 6 shows that the 1.96 quantile value is used in the calculation. Line 7 indicates these are 0.95 confidence intervals. In line 11, `lwr` refers to the lower bound, and `upr` refers to the upper bound. The CIs agree with the z-ratios in that only the intercept differences for POV-ADV and HHM-ADV do not contain 0 (lines 12 and 13). However, for the slope comparison of HHM-POV, the upper CI limit just barely covers 0 (line 17).

If the researcher wishes to adjust for multiple significance tests or multiple CIs, then simultaneous inference procedures can be used (see, e.g., Bretz et al., 2011; Hsu, 1996). These methods make adjustments aimed at limiting the overall Type I error rate.

In light of the discussions in Chapters 7 and 8, a researcher probably has to be at least a "quasi-Neyman-Pearsonist" for multiple testing to be a concern. Recall that inflation of the Type I error rate is irrelevant in the multimodel inference and the Fisherian framework. To reiterate an earlier point, ML estimation methods are approximate. Therefore, a hypervigilant concern with Type I error rate is probably not justified, as the control will be only approximate. Furthermore, it has been argued that multiple comparison adjustments are most appropriate when there is a possibility that all differences could be negligible (Gelman, 2004). This assumption seems implausible for much applied work, and certainly so for the MPLS data set. Such concerns have led to severe criticism of multiple comparison adjustments (Nelder, 1999; Tukey, 1991).

There are numerous simultaneous inference procedures, and a detailed discussion is beyond our scope. In the `summary()` function used above with `glht.3`, the optional argument `test = adjusted(type = "none")` was added to specify no adjustment. There are many quoted key words that can be used in place of `"none"` for various adjustments. For example, `"bonferroni"` will enact the Bonferroni adjustment (Hsu, 1996, chap. 1). For additional key words, see `?p.adjust` and `?summary.glht`. Adjustments can also be made to confidence intervals; see `?confint.glht`.

As a final comment for this section, by no means is it necessary that one use null hypotheses for evaluating the group effects. In fact, it might be desirable to interpret the z-ratios as indexes of effect size and simply rank-order the group differences. It is acknowledged that tradition and convention sometimes seem to dictate that every effect be evaluated with an inferential statistic, but this need not be the case.

11.3 Interactions Among Static Predictors

In previous chapters, interactions among time variables and static predictors were considered. Recall such interactions are slope effects in longitudinal LMER models. The product term, (`grade5`$_{ij}$ · `riskADV`$_i$) in Equation 11.2.3, is one example. In this section, *interactions among static predictors* are considered.

Interactions among static predictors are considered when the goal is to assess the effects of the combination of the predictors. Consider the binary versions of risk and ethnicity, `risk2` and `eth2`. It might be the case that intercepts and slopes are different for non-White advantaged students and non-White disadvantaged students.

Recall that random effects are indifferent to static predictors, and the maximum number of random effects is determined by the number of time predictors (e.g., polynomials). To keep things simple in this section, each model has a linear change curve, and models will have random intercepts and random slopes.

In previous chapters, `risk2` and `eth2` have been considered main effects, meaning they were never multipliers of each other. As a reminder, consider the LMER model corresponding to the fitted model object `lmer.2`, considered in Section 11.1.

$$\begin{aligned}E(y_{ij}) = &\beta_0 + \beta_1(\text{grade5}_{ij}) + \beta_2(\text{risk2ADV}_i) \\ &+ \beta_2(\text{eth2NW}_i) + \beta_3(\text{grade5}_{ij} \cdot \text{risk2ADV}_i) \\ &+ \beta_4(\text{grade5}_{ij} \cdot \text{eth2NW}_i),\end{aligned} \quad (11.3.1)$$

where `risk2ADV` and `eth2NW` are dummy variables as previously discussed. In Equation 11.3.1, the intercept or slope effect of one dummy variable is

11.3 Interactions Among Static Predictors

considered, holding the other dummy variable constant. The intercept effect of, say, ethnicity, represented by β_2, does not depend on the level of risk.

An interaction among two static predictors means the effect of one predictor depends on the levels of the other. The following model has a static predictor interaction for the intercept effect.

$$\begin{aligned}E(y_{ij}) = {} & \beta_0 + \beta_1(\texttt{risk2ADV}_i) + \beta_2(\texttt{eth2NW}_i) \\ & + \beta_3(\texttt{risk2ADV}_i \cdot \texttt{eth2NW}_i) + \beta_4(\texttt{grade5}_{ij}).\end{aligned} \quad (11.3.2)$$

The nature of the interaction is illustrated by factoring out one of the dummy variables, such as `risk2ADV`. Doing so yields the following:

$$\begin{aligned}E(y_{ij}) = {} & \beta_0 + \beta_2(\texttt{eth2NW}_i) + \Big[\beta_1 + \beta_3(\texttt{eth2NW}_i)\Big](\texttt{risk2ADV}_i) \\ & + \beta_4(\texttt{grade5}_{ij})\end{aligned} \quad (11.3.3)$$

In Equation 11.3.3, the intercept of the risk group depends on the ethnic group. That is, the intercept effect of `risk2ADV` is the sum, $\beta_1 + \beta_3(\texttt{eth2NW}_i)$, which can change as `eth2NW` changes. The formula can be expressed in a similar way, factoring out `eth2NW`, meaning the intercept effect of ethnicity is also dependent on risk.

Equation 11.3.3 has a static predictor interaction effect for the intercept. To include an interaction effect for the slope, the time predictor is multiplied by each of the dummy variables and their product. The latter is the triple product of risk, ethnicity, and the time predictor. Consider the following LMER model.

$$\begin{aligned}E(y_{ij}) = {} & \beta_0 + \beta_1(\texttt{risk2ADV}_i) + \beta_2(\texttt{eth2NW}_i) \\ & + \beta_3(\texttt{risk2ADV}_i \cdot \texttt{eth2NW}_i) + \beta_4(\texttt{grade5}_{ij}) \\ & + \beta_5(\texttt{grade5}_{ij} \cdot \texttt{risk2ADV}_i) \\ & + \beta_6(\texttt{grade5}_{ij} \cdot \texttt{eth2NW}_i) \\ & + \beta_7(\texttt{grade5}_{ij} \cdot \texttt{risk2ADV}_i \cdot \texttt{eth2NW}_i).\end{aligned} \quad (11.3.4)$$

The last expression is the static predictor interaction for the slope. Equation 11.3.4 is expressed in a similar fashion as Equation 11.3.3, by factoring out one of the dummy variables. Factoring out `risk2ADV` yields the following:

$$\begin{aligned}E(y_{ij}) = {} & \beta_0 + \beta_2(\texttt{eth2NW}_i) \\ & + \Big[\beta_1 + \beta_3(\texttt{eth2NW}_i)\Big](\texttt{risk2ADV}_i) \\ & + \beta_4(\texttt{grade5}_{ij}) + \beta_6(\texttt{grade5}_{ij} \cdot \texttt{eth2NW}_i) \\ & + \Big[\beta_5 + \beta_7(\texttt{eth2NW}_i)\Big](\texttt{grade5}_{ij} \cdot \texttt{risk2ADV}_i).\end{aligned} \quad (11.3.5)$$

The last expression in Equation 11.3.5 indicates that the slope effect of `risk2ADV` depends on `eth2NW`. The reason is the risk-by-time interaction effect is $\beta_5 + \beta_7(\texttt{eth2NW}_i)$, which can change as levels of ethnicity change. A similar formulation factoring out `eth2NW` can also be written.

When multimodel inference is used, the above models are included in the model set (see Chapter 7). When the LRT/NHST approach is used, a stepwise analysis is usually carried out (see Chapter 8).

A static predictor interaction increases the complexity of the LMER model. For this reason, it is common to begin with evaluation of the interaction terms when using NHST. If there is evidence that one or more of these terms can be removed, then it is common to adopt a simpler model. Care must be taken in the evaluation of interactions and main effects.

If z-ratios or CIs of specific parameters are evaluated, it is important to remember that main effects and their inferential statistics cannot be interpreted when interactions are in the model. *Therefore, interaction terms should be evaluated first when assessing the need for model simplification.*

11.3.1 STATIC PREDICTOR INTERACTIONS WITH lmer()

Equations such as 11.3.4 are relatively complex because of the number of terms. Fortunately, shorthand notation can be used with lmer() to specify interactions and main effects. For example, the lmer() model formula corresponding to the fixed effects structure of Equation 11.3.4 is

$$\text{read} \sim \text{grade5} * \text{risk2} * \text{eth2}.$$

The asterisks (*) will automatically cause the inclusion of all lower order interactions and main effects. In the model formula syntax, the following predictor effects will be included.

- Triple interaction: grade5:risk2:eth2
- Double interactions: grade5:risk2, grade5:eth2, risk2:eth2
- Main effects: grade5, risk2, eth2
- Intercept: 1

Recall that the difference between the asterisk and the colon (:) is that the latter does not expand to include any lower order effects.

Prior to estimating the static predictor interaction model, it is desirable to examine the counts of subjects for each combination of the variables. Counts of 0 indicate that parameters for certain combinations of the predictors cannot be estimated. The syntax below is used to examine the cross-tabulation of eth2 and risk2 at the first time point (Grade 5).

```
> with(MPLS.LS[MPLS.LS$grade == 5, ], table(risk2, eth2))
```

	eth2	
risk2	NW	W
ADV	3	7
DADV	10	2

11.3 Interactions Among Static Predictors

The output shows there are no cells with 0 counts, but the combination of White and disadvantaged has only two subjects, and the combination of non-White and advantaged has three subjects. These counts are too few to make serious conclusions, but we proceed with estimation for purposes of illustration.

Having verified nonzero counts for combinations of the static predictor levels, the model is now estimated. In addition to the fixed effects structure, two random effects are included. Consider the following.

```
> lmer.4 ← lmer(read ~ grade5 * risk2 * eth2 + (grade5 | subid),
+              MPLS.LS, REML = FALSE)
> print(lmer.4, cor = FALSE)
```

```
Linear mixed model fit by maximum likelihood
Formula: read ~ grade5 * risk2 * eth2 + (grade5 | subid)
   Data: MPLS.LS
   AIC    BIC  logLik deviance REMLdev
  568.1  596.7 -272.1   544.1   513.2
Random effects:
 Groups   Name        Variance Std.Dev. Corr
 subid    (Intercept) 168.2295 12.9703
          grade5        3.7788  1.9439  -0.632
 Residual              18.8277  4.3391
Number of obs: 80, groups: subid, 22

Fixed effects:
                        Estimate Std. Error t value
(Intercept)              209.401      7.787  26.891
grade5                     7.731      1.701   4.544
risk2DADV                -18.993      8.879  -2.139
eth2W                     11.678      9.309   1.254
grade5:risk2DADV          -2.968      1.947  -1.524
grade5:eth2W              -4.850      2.048  -2.368
risk2DADV:eth2W          -17.836     13.984  -1.275
grade5:risk2DADV:eth2W     6.837      2.977   2.296
```

The second to last row of output (risk2DADV:eth2W) shows the interaction intercept effect, and the last row (grade5:risk2DADV:eth2W) shows the interaction slope effect. The *t*-ratio for the interaction slope effect is relatively large, suggesting it is important to retain in the model. Less so for the interaction of the intercept.

As a check on the need for the interaction terms, consider comparison of lmer.4 to a model that omits the static predictor interaction terms. As discussed in Chapter 7, the interaction model might be part of a set of models evaluated with multimodel inference using the AICc. Here the LRT is considered.

```
> lmer.0 ← lmer(read ~ grade5 * eth2 + grade5 * risk2 + (grade5 | subid),
+              MPLS.LS, REML = FALSE)
> anova(lmer.0, lmer.4)
```

```
Data: MPLS.LS
Models:
lmer.0: read ~ grade5 * eth2 + grade5 * risk2 + (grade5 | subid)
lmer.4: read ~ grade5 * risk2 * eth2 + (grade5 | subid)
        Df    AIC    BIC   logLik  Chisq Chi Df Pr(>Chisq)
lmer.0  10 568.82 592.64 -274.41
lmer.4  12 568.14 596.72 -272.07 4.6843      2    0.09612 .
---
Signif. codes:  0 '***' 0.001 '**' 0.01 '*' 0.05 '.' 0.1 ' ' 1
```

The static predictor interaction for the intercept and slope is omitted from the reduced model, `model.0`. Therefore, the LRT has $df = 2$.

The output shows the LRT-p is relatively large, suggesting the interaction terms might not be retained. The AIC for `lmer.4` is slightly smaller than that for `lmer.0`. This indicates a weak preference for the full model. Echoing the discussions in Chapters 7 and 8, the decisions regarding the model to retain here might depend on the values of the researcher. If *any* evidence for the full model is sufficient, then `lmer.4` is adopted. However, if evidence stronger than "weak" is required, then `lmer.0` is adopted. In addition, if parsimony is an issue, then `lmer.0` is preferred.

11.3.2 INTERPRETING INTERACTIONS

Similar to traditional ANOVA, an aid to interpreting interactions is to graph the fitted curves for combinations of levels of variables. For the example above, the goal is to graph fitted values for combinations of W/ADV, NW/ADV, W/DADV, and NW/DADV. It is convenient to create a variable having labels pertaining to these levels.

The first step is to construct the data frame used for the graphs. Variables from the `@frame` slot and the fitted values are saved. Then the `interaction()` function is used to create a new factor variable, `group4`, representing the interaction among `risk2` and `eth2`. Levels of `group4` are the labels resulting from concatenating the level values of `risk2` and `eth2`, that is, NW.ADV, NW.DADV, W.ADV, W.DADV.

```
> plotdata <- data.frame(lmer.4@frame, fitted = FittedFE(lmer.4))
> plotdata$group4 <- with(plotdata, interaction(eth2, risk2))
> plotdata$grade <- plotdata$grade5 + 5
> head(plotdata)
```

```
    read grade5 risk2 eth2 subid   fitted   group4 grade
1.5  172      0  DADV   NW     1 190.4081 NW.DADV     5
1.6  185      1  DADV   NW     1 195.1709 NW.DADV     6
1.7  179      2  DADV   NW     1 199.9337 NW.DADV     7
1.8  194      3  DADV   NW     1 204.6965 NW.DADV     8
2.5  200      0  DADV   NW     2 190.4081 NW.DADV     5
2.6  210      1  DADV   NW     2 195.1709 NW.DADV     6
```

```
> levels(plotdata$group4)
```

11.3 Interactions Among Static Predictors

```
[1]  "NW.ADV"    "W.ADV"    "NW.DADV"   "W.DADV"
```

The `group4` variable is convenient when superimposing the fitted groups curves in a single panel. Having the separate `risk2` and `eth2` is useful for creating graphs with faceting. Both types of graphs are considered below.

First consider the facet graph. The advantage of the graph is that each combination of the variables is displayed in a separate panel. This makes it convenient to include additional quantities, such as the observed means, without too much clutter. In the syntax below, faceting is by combinations of `risk2` and `eth2`. In each panel, the observed subject curves are drawn, along with the observed means and the fitted curve.

```
> g1 <- ggplot(plotdata, aes(x = grade, y = read))
> g2 <- g1 + geom_line(aes(groups = subid), colour = "grey80")
> g3 <- g2 + stat_summary(fun.y = mean, geom = "point", aes(groups = 1))
> g4 <- g3 + stat_summary(fun.y = mean, geom = "line", aes(y = fitted))
> g5 <- g4 + facet_grid(eth2 ~ risk2) + myx
> print(g5)
```

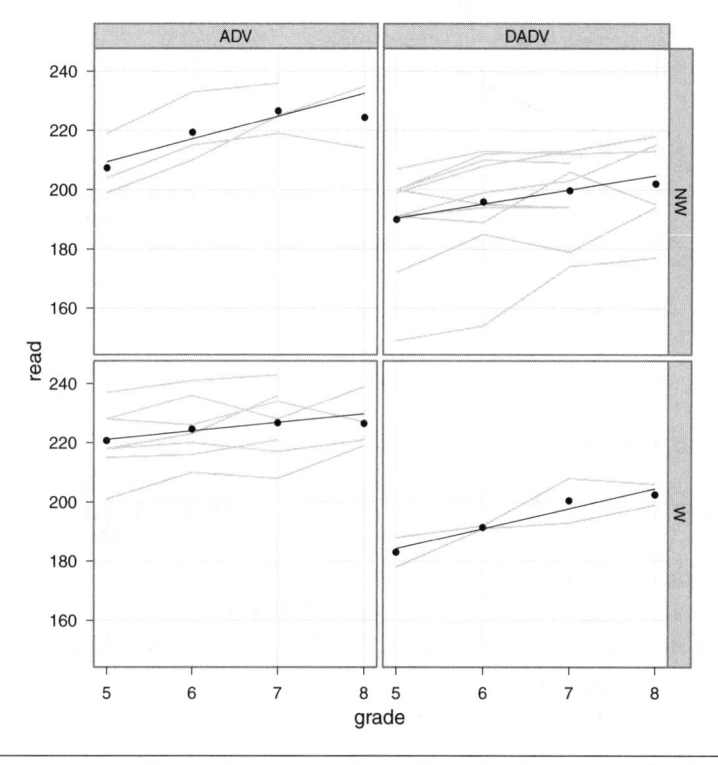

Figure 11.4 Reading achievement by risk and ethnicity, with observed subject curves (light lines), observed means (filled circles), and fitted mean curves (solid line).

The graph is shown in Figure 11.4. The slope interaction of the statistical results is evident in the graph. The slopes of the ethnic groups are close to parallel for the disadvantaged students, but not so for the advantaged students. The non-White advantaged students have a steeper group slope than the White advantaged students.

Rather than faceting, the group curves can be superimposed on the same graph. This may provide easier comparisons, but it probably precludes the drawing of additional quantities. When subject curves along with observed means are drawn, the resulting graph can be considerably cluttered. To create superimposed curves, the `group4` variable previously constructed is used. The group lines are distinguished by both shape and line type.

```
> g1 <- ggplot(plotdata, aes(x = grade, y = fitted, shape = group4, linetype = group4))
> g2 <- g1 + stat_summary(fun.y = mean, geom = "point", size = 2.5) + myx
> g3 <- g2 + stat_summary(fun.y = mean, geom = "line") + opts("aspect.ratio" = 1)
> g4 <- g3 + scale_shape(solid = FALSE)
> print(g4)
```

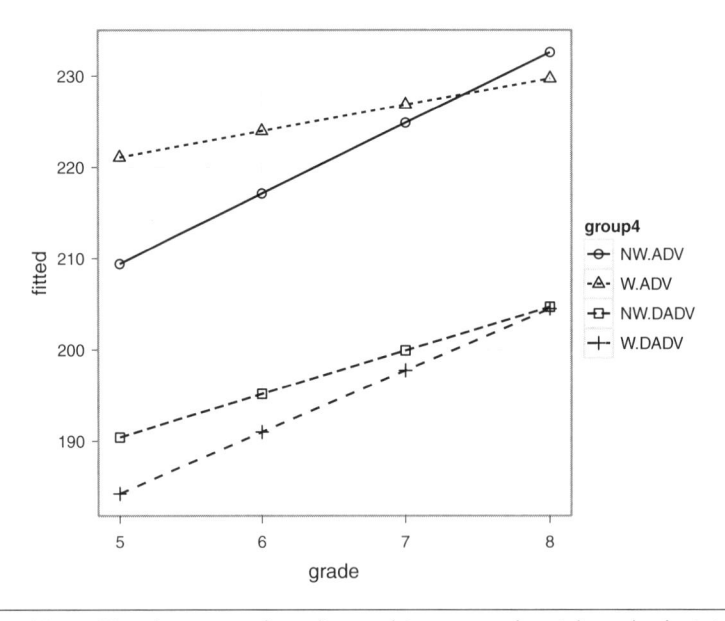

Figure 11.5 Fitted curves of reading achievement by risk and ethnicity.

The superimposed graph is shown in Figure 11.5. There are a number of possible customizations for the legend (see Chapter 4). As shown in the graph, the crossing lines are indicative of the slope interaction, and this effect is perhaps more apparent in this graph than the faceted graph. It is now clear that the curves of the ethnic groups cross for students at both levels of risk.

11.3.3 NONLINEAR STATIC PREDICTOR EFFECTS

In addition to interactions among static predictors, it is possible for a static predictor to have a nonlinear relationship with one or more of the change curve components. For example, attendance might have a quadratic relationship with initial status. Such effects should be dictated by theory, but data-driven approaches might also suggest such effects. As an example of the latter, a scatterplot of the estimated random slopes and a static predictor might reveal a nonlinear pattern.

11.4 Indexes of Absolute Effect Size in LMER

It is well known that a small *p*-value does not necessarily mean the size of an effect has any practical merit (Tatsuoka, 1993). A similar concept applies in multimodel inference, as the size of a weight of evidence only conveys relative fit information (see Chapter 7).

Context for interpreting the size of an effect is usually based on the substance of the area of research. For example, based on the past research with the NALT reading measure (Northwest Evaluation Association, 2003), the 9-point intercept difference between the POV and HHM groups found in the pairwise comparisons of Section 11.2.2 does not represent a particularly meaningful difference. Performance on other reading task, for instance, may be statistically equivalent for the groups. On the other hand, the 32-point difference between the ADV and HHM groups does represent a meaningful difference. It is expected that such a difference would be accompanied by statistically reliable differences on other measures.

The effect size measures previously introduced have weaknesses regarding the representation of substantive importance. The main issue is that the effect sizes of Chapters 7 and 8 are indexes of relative effects and not absolute effects. Consider the weight of evidence in multimodel inference. The weight of evidence can be used to rank-order models, but it does not indicate the worthiness of any one model in isolation. It is certainly possible that the separation between the best-fitting model and the remaining models can be substantial. Yet, the best-fitting model may not represent very important real-world effects. The same idea holds for the LRT methods of Chapter 7, as the LRT is also based on model comparison.

To help clarify the importance of the best-fitting model, it is useful to compute an absolute effect size. As discussed in previous chapters, an effect size can be computed for individual parameter estimates, or the global model. An example of the former is the *t*-ratio (*z*-ratio) found in the standard `lmer()` output. The focus here is on indexes for absolute global effect size.

A number of absolute effect size indexes have been proposed for LMER (Vonesh, Chinchilli, & Pu, 1996; Vonesh & Chinchilli, 1997; Xu, 2003; Zheng, 2000), and multilevel models in general (Kreft & De Leeuw, 1998; Singer, 1998; Snijders & Bosker, 1999). Of these indexes, focus is on the R^2 statistic for LMER proposed by Vonesh and Chinchilli (1997). This is simply the R^2 from traditional regression applied to LMER. Specifically,

$$R^2 = \left[cor(y_{ij}, \hat{y}_{ij})\right]^2, \qquad (11.4.1)$$

where *cor* indicates the Pearson correlation, and the $\hat{y}_{ij}$ are the fitted values based on the fixed effects (only). In terms of actual data, the scores for y_{ij} and

$\hat{y}_{ij}$ reside in a long-format data frame, and the squared Pearson correlation is computed for the two columns containing the scores. Details are provided below.

As an illustration, suppose the LMER model is

$$E(y_{ij}) = \beta_0 + \beta_1(\text{grade5}_{ij}) + \beta_2(\text{risk2DADV}_i).$$

Then the fitted values would be computed as

$$\hat{y}_{ij} = \hat{\beta}_0 + \hat{\beta}_1(\text{grade5}_{ij}) + \hat{\beta}_2(\text{risk2DADV}_i),$$

where the $\hat{\beta}_k$ are the fixed effects estimates in the lmer() output. The fitted values are computed using the FittedFE() function. R^2 is computed with cor(), using the responses from @frame (to account for missing values) and the fitted values.

The main advantage of R^2 is that it has the same interpretation as in traditional regression. R^2 is the proportion of variance of the response accounted for by the predictors. The range of possible values is $0 \leq R^2 \leq 1$, with 0 indicating no variance accounted for, and 1 indicating all the response variance is accounted for. Although R^2 is a measure of absolute effect size, standards for evaluating its magnitude are typically tied to the relevant substantive research area for the analysis. For example, $R^2 = 0.50$ may be "large" for one research discipline, but "small" for another.

Three additional characteristics of R^2 should be kept in mind. First, the fitted values, $\hat{y}_{ij}$, are based only on the fixed effects, which indicates that R^2 is not appropriate for indexing the importance of the random effects.

Second, R^2 is not a penalized index and will increase with the addition of predictors, even if some or all of the additional predictors are worthless. For this reason, R^2 should not be used in model selection. ($\bar{R}^2$ also should not be used in model selection, as the AIC is superior for this purpose.)

Third, R^2 does not distinguish within-subjects and between-subjects variance. Therefore, R^2 will increase when an additional time variable is added to the model, and it will increase when an additional static predictor is added. To observe the effect of adding a static predictor, the number of time variables should be held constant and vice versa.

As an example, consider the computation of R^2 for three models previously considered. The first model has grade5 as a predictor, the second adds risk2, and the third adds eth2. There are intercept and slope effects in the second two models, and all models include two random effects. Consider the syntax below.

```
> ## Estimate models.
> lmer.1 <- lmer(read ~ grade5 + (grade5 | subid), MPLS.LS, REML = FALSE)
> lmer.2 <- lmer(read ~ grade5 * risk2 + (grade5 | subid), MPLS.LS, REML = FALSE)
> lmer.3 <- lmer(read ~ grade5 * risk2 + grade5 * eth2 + (grade5 | subid),
+        MPLS.LS, REML = FALSE)
> ## Compute R-squared.
> my.rsq <- c(cor(y = lmer.1@frame$read, x = FittedFE(lmer.1)) ^ 2,
+        cor(y = lmer.2@frame$read, x = FittedFE(lmer.2)) ^ 2,
+        cor(y = lmer.3@frame$read, x = FittedFE(lmer.3)) ^ 2)
> data.frame(model = c("lmer.1", "lmer.2", "lmer.3"), rsq = my.rsq)
```

11.4 Indexes of Absolute Effect Size in LMER

```
    model       rsq
1  lmer.1  0.0476228
2  lmer.2  0.5457375
3  lmer.3  0.5477809
```

The output shows that when the only predictor is grade5, 4.76% of the response variance is accounted for. When risk2 is added, 54.57% is accounted for, and when eth2 is added, the total variance accounted for is 54.78%. There is a substantial increase in variance accounted for when risk2 is added to the model, but only a modest increase when eht2 is added. Whether $R^2 = 0.55$ is impressive or not depends on values that are found in similar studies. However, the absolute statement can be made that with the latter two models, a slight majority of the response variance is accounted for by the predictors.

As mentioned, R^2 is not a penalized index. $\bar{R}^2$ can be used as a penalized index, but it seem most useful to consider the AICc with R^2. In the syntax below, the AICc and related quantities are computed for the three models. R^2 is computed and attached to the AICc output object.

```
> ## aictab().
> myaicc <- as.data.frame(aictab(list(lmer.1, lmer.2, lmer.3), sort = FALSE,
+                  c("lmer.1", "lmer.2", "lmer.3"))[ ,-c(5,7)])
> ## Compute R-squared.
> myaicc$rsq <- c(cor(y = lmer.1@frame$read, x = FittedFE(lmer.1)) ^ 2,
+                 cor(y = lmer.2@frame$read, x = FittedFE(lmer.2)) ^ 2,
+                 cor(y = lmer.3@frame$read, x = FittedFE(lmer.3)) ^ 2)
> myaicc
```

```
   Modnames  K    AICc  Delta_AICc      AICcWt       rsq
1    lmer.1  6  582.1098  14.378559  0.0006747264  0.0476228
2    lmer.2  8  567.7313   0.000000  0.8941124915  0.5457375
3    lmer.3 10  572.0110   4.279694  0.1052127820  0.5477809
```

The output shows that the second model has the largest weight of evidence, but not the largest value of R^2. The variance accounted for is almost as large as that for the third model. Given these two pieces of information, there appears to be evidence in favor of the second model.

11.4.1 ALTERNATIVE INDEXES

As seen in the preceding section, R^2 can be used as a descriptive measure to index changes when predictors are added to the model. When interest is in static predictor effects, the t-ratio can be used as a relative effect size measure. An absolute effect size measure for static predictor effects can also be computed, based on the proportion reduction in the variance (PRV) of the random effects (Kreft & De Leeuw, 1998; Singer, 1998). The idea behind the PRV measure is to quantify the reduction in the between-subjects variance when a static predictor (or set) is added to the model. This involves the comparison of one or more of the variances of the random effects under a reduced and full model.

Suppose that $Var(b_{ki})_R$ is the variance of a random effect under the reduced model, and $Var(b_{ki})_F$ is that under the full model. The full model adds at least one static predictor effect. Then the PRV is the following:

$$PRV = \frac{Var(b_{ki})_R - Var(b_{ki})_F}{Var(b_{ki})_R}. \tag{11.4.2}$$

The idea behind the PRV measure is that if a static predictor or set of predictors accounts for between-subjects variance of, say, the intercepts, then the variance under the full model should be less than the variance under the reduced model. PRV is an R^2-like measure, as in principle, $0 \leq PRV \leq 1$.

The main weakness of the PRV measure is that it is not always the case the full-model variance will be smaller than the reduced-model variance. Similar to $\bar{R}^2$, the PRV measure sometimes can be a negative value. For this reason, the R^2 measure discussed in the last section is recommended over the PRV measure. An example of a negative PRV value is provided below.

To fix ideas, consider the PRV of the random intercepts. Suppose the reduced model has only grade5 as a predictor, and the full model adds a risk2 intercept effect. In the syntax below, the variance of the intercepts is computed for each model and the results are printed.

```
> reduced <- lmer(read ~ grade5 + (1 | subid), MPLS.LS, REML = FALSE)
> full    <- lmer(read ~ grade5 + risk2 + (1 | subid), MPLS.LS, REML = FALSE)
> v.r <- attr(VarCorr(reduced)$subid, "stddev")^2
> v.f <- attr(VarCorr(full)$subid, "stddev")^2
> v.r; v.f
```

```
(Intercept)
   312.3151
```

```
(Intercept)
   131.1138
```

As seen in the output, the variance under the full model is much smaller than that under the reduced model. Having saved the estimated variance, the PRV measure is computed.

```
> PRV <- (v.r - v.f) / v.r
> PRV
```

```
(Intercept)
  0.5801875
```

The output shows there is a 58.02% decrease in the variance of the intercepts when risk2 is added to the model. Thus, the between-subjects variance of the intercepts is cut by more than half when the static predictor intercept effect is added to the model.

11.4 Indexes of Absolute Effect Size in LMER

A similar PRV measure is computed for the random slopes. In the syntax below, models with two random effects are estimated, but focus is only on the second random effect. The full model includes an intercept and a slope effect for `risk2`. The reduced model includes only a `risk2` intercept effect.

```
> reduced  ← lmer(read ~ grade5 + risk2 + (grade5 | subid), MPLS.LS, REML = FALSE)
> full     ← lmer(read ~ grade5 * risk2 + (grade5 | subid), MPLS.LS, REML = FALSE)
> v.r  ← attr(VarCorr(reduced)$subid, "stddev")[2]^2
> v.f  ← attr(VarCorr(full)$subid, "stddev")[2]^2
> PRV  ← (v.r - v.f) / v.r
> PRV
```

```
         grade5
0.03691316
```

The output shows there is a reduction of 3.69% when the `risk2` slope effect is added to the model. This result, taken with the preceding one, suggests that `risk2` is important for predicting the random intercepts, but not the random slopes. This conclusion is consistent with the model comparison results of Chapters 7 and 8.

If the researcher does not care about the distinction between random intercepts and slopes, then a type of omnibus PRV measure can be computed. This measure is based on the entire G matrix under the reduced and full models (see Chapter 10 for a discussion of G). The idea is to use the *determinant* of the G matrix in the PRV equation. The determinant is a single number (scalar) that summarizes the information about variability in the entire G matrix, and it is similar to a generalized variance (see the Appendix).

The algebraic details of the determinant are not discussed. Rather, focus is on computing the determinant using the `det()` function. The `det()` function requires the name of the estimated G object, which must be a matrix object. The full model has intercept and slope effects for `risk2`, but the reduced model omits `risk2` entirely. Consider the following.

```
> reduced ← lmer(read~grade5+(grade5|subid), MPLS.LS, REML=FALSE)
> full    ← lmer(read~grade5*risk2+(grade5|subid), MPLS.LS, REML=FALSE)
> ## Determinant.
> v.r  ← det(as.matrix(VarCorr(reduced)$subid))
> v.f  ← det(as.matrix(VarCorr(full)$subid))
> v.r; v.f
```

```
[1] 1774.172
```

```
[1] 702.0381
```

```
> ## PRV.
> PRV  ← (v.r - v.f) / v.r
> PRV
```

```
[1] 0.604301
```

The determinant for the full model is 702.04, which is much smaller than that for the reduced model (1774.17). More specifically, the PRV measure indicates there is a reduction of 60.43% in the generalized variance when `risk2` is added to the model. Since the generalized variance makes no distinction between random intercepts variance and random slopes variance, the PRV measure is a type of omnibus, or overall, effect index.

Things do not always work out. As mentioned, a weakness of the PRV measure, as opposed to R^2, is that the former can sometimes be a negative value. The reason is that `lmer()` uses a type of penalized least squares (see Chapter 6). The penalty changes based on what effects are in the model, and there is no guarantee that adding an additional static predictor will reduce the variance of the random effects.

As an example, consider what happens when a static predictor is randomly generated and used in the LMER analysis. In the syntax below, a wide-format data frame is created, and then `rnorm()` is used to create a worthless static predictor, X1. By *worthless*, it is meant that the static predictor is randomly generated, representing no population relationship with the random intercepts or slopes.

```
> mywide <- reshape(MPLS.LS, v.names = "read", timevar = "grade",
+                  idvar = "subid", direction = "wide", drop = "grade5")
> set.seed(1234)        # Use to reproduce this example.
> mywide$X1 <- round(rnorm(nrow(mywide), mean = 100, sd = 15), 0)
> mylong <- reshape(mywide, direction = "long")
> mylong <- mylong[order(mylong$subid),]
> head(mylong)
```

	subid	risk	gen	eth	ell	sped	att	riskC	risk2	ethC	eth2	X1	grade	read
1.5	1	1	HHM	F	Afr	0	N	0.94	DADV	DADV	NW	NW	82	5	172
1.6	1	1	HHM	F	Afr	0	N	0.94	DADV	DADV	NW	NW	82	6	185
1.7	1	1	HHM	F	Afr	0	N	0.94	DADV	DADV	NW	NW	82	7	179
1.8	1	1	HHM	F	Afr	0	N	0.94	DADV	DADV	NW	NW	82	8	194
2.5	2	2	HHM	F	Afr	0	N	0.91	DADV	DADV	NW	NW	104	5	200
2.6	2	2	HHM	F	Afr	0	N	0.91	DADV	DADV	NW	NW	104	6	210

Having created the worthless static predictor, various models are fit. Focus is on changes in the variance components and R^2. The three models from the last examples are refit, and an additional model is estimated adding X1. Two random effects are included for each model, and `grade` is the time predictor rather than `grade5`.

```
> ## Estimate the models.
> sim.1 <- lmer(read ~ grade + (grade | subid), MPLS.LS, REML = FALSE)
> sim.2 <- lmer(read ~ grade * risk2 + (grade | subid), MPLS.LS, REML = FALSE)
> sim.3 <- lmer(read ~ grade * risk2 + grade * eth2 + (grade | subid),
+               MPLS.LS, REML = FALSE)
> sim.4 <- lmer(read ~ grade * risk2 + grade * eth2 + grade * X1 + (grade | subid),
+               mylong, REML = FALSE)
> ## Extract the variances.
> myvar <- data.frame(rbind(attr(VarCorr(sim.1)$subid,"stddev") ^ 2,
+                            attr(VarCorr(sim.2)$subid,"stddev") ^ 2,
+                            attr(VarCorr(sim.3)$subid,"stddev") ^ 2,
+                            attr(VarCorr(sim.4)$subid,"stddev") ^ 2))
```

11.5 Additional Transformations

```
> rownames(myvar) <- c("(none) ", "risk2", "risk2.eth2", "risk2.eth2.X1")
> ## Compute the determinant of G.
> myvar$det <- c(det(as.matrix(VarCorr(sim.1)$subid)),
+               det(as.matrix(VarCorr(sim.2)$subid)),
+               det(as.matrix(VarCorr(sim.3)$subid)),
+               det(as.matrix(VarCorr(sim.4)$subid)))
> ## Compute R-squared.
> myvar$rsq <- c(cor(x = sim.1@frame$read, y = FittedFE(sim.1))^2,
+               cor(x = sim.2@frame$read, y = FittedFE(sim.2))^2,
+               cor(x = sim.3@frame$read, y = FittedFE(sim.3))^2,
+               cor(x = sim.4@frame$read, y = FittedFE(sim.4))^2)
> ## Deviance.
> myvar$deviance <- c(deviance(sim.1),deviance(sim.2),deviance(sim.3),deviance(sim.4))
> ## AIC.
> myvar$AIC <- c(AIC(sim.1), AIC(sim.2), AIC(sim.3), AIC(sim.4))
> ## Print the results.
> colnames(myvar)[1:2] <- c("Var(int)", "Var(slopes)")
> myvar
```

	Var(int)	Var(slopes)	det	rsq	deviance	AIC
(none)	812.3325	6.558031	1774.1694	0.0476228	568.9591	580.9591
risk2	569.3635	6.505265	702.0393	0.5457374	549.7031	565.7031
risk2.eth2	541.2523	5.964526	639.7391	0.5477809	548.8226	568.8226
risk2.eth2.X1	554.1327	6.216351	660.7895	0.5504032	548.2405	572.2405

The row names indicate the static predictors in the model. The estimated variance of the intercepts is in the first numeric column (Var(int)), the variance of the slopes is in the second (Var(slopes)), the generalized variance is in the third, followed by R^2, deviance, and AIC.

As the output shows, both variances decrease when risk2 is added and also when eth2 is added. However, when X1 is added, the variances *increase*.

The importance of the result is that if a PRV measure is computed based on the last two models (with and without X1), its value will be negative regardless of the variance used. For example, it can be verified that the PRV measure based on the variance of the intercepts is -0.02. A negative PRV result is counterintuitive at best, and nonsensible at worst.

On the other hand, the values of R^2 and deviance increase, but the AIC decreases. Perhaps the change in AIC (or AICc) should be inspected prior to computing PRV, as an increase in the AIC is an indication that no PRV measure is needed.

11.5 Additional Transformations

In Chapter 5, linear transformations of the time predictor were discussed with the goal of anchoring the intercept. In Chapter 9, there was a discussion of polynomial transformations of the time predictor for modeling nonlinear trends. In this section, additional transformations of both the time predictor and the response variable are considered.

The additional transformations are important for addressing issues that sometimes arise in applied analysis. One issue is that small (near 0) estimates of variance components can cause interpretation problems and estimation problems. A judicious transformation of the time predictor can often help solve the problems.

Another issue is transforming the response variable. Applied researchers in the behavioral sciences are well acquainted with standardizing variables for various purposes, such as facilitating interpretation, or accounting for differences in variability when compositing. Standardizing can be used in longitudinal analysis for the same purposes.

11.5.1 TIME UNITS AND VARIANCES

The unit of the time predictor in LMER is important, as it influences the rate of change and the variance of the rate of change. The finer the unit, the smaller the change per unit will be, and the smaller the variability of the rate of change. Conversely, the coarser the unit, the larger the change per unit will be, and the larger the variance.

For example, suppose observations are collected on a yearly basis, and there is a steady increase over time. The per day or per month increase will be smaller than the per year increase, as there is a shorter time span over which the increase is recorded. A 10-point reading achievement increase per year is equivalent to a $\frac{10}{12} = 0.8333$ increase per month, and a $\frac{10}{365} = 0.0274$ increase per day.

As the example above hints, time units are largely arbitrary, in the respect that one linear transformation is just as valid as any other. However, certain linear transformations might be advantageous for interpretation and also for purposes of estimation. If a linear transformation produces very small change over time, then small fixed effects estimates and small variance estimates may be spuriously interpreted as negligible effects.

Judgments of worth of variance components are difficult in standard lmer() output, as estimates of SEs are not printed along with the variance components estimates. The SE facilitates the assessment of estimates because the *t*-ratio (*z*-ratio) can be inspected to see if an estimate is particularly large or small in relation to its SE. This provides a scale-independent indication of effect size. Very small estimates can represent strong effects if the estimated SEs are even smaller. On the other hand, very large estimates can represent weak or even negligible effects if the SEs approach or exceed the size of the estimates themselves.

As an illustration, consider the evaluation of the fixed effect estimate for various transformations of the time predictor. Recall that grade5 in the MPLS.LS data frame represents the year of the study (0, 1, 2, 3). Suppose a researcher wants to reexpress this in terms of months, and then in terms of days. Below the year variable is created and then multiplied by 12 to reexpress time in months, and then multiplied by 360 to reexpress time in days.

```
> year   <- MPLS.LS$grade5
> month  <- year * 12
> day    <- year * 360
> head(data.frame(year, month, day), n = 4)
```

11.5 Additional Transformations

	year	month	day
1	0	0	0
2	1	12	360
3	2	24	720
4	3	36	1080

Suppose that three models are estimated using the different units. The slope row of the fixed effects table for each model is concatenated and printed. REML is used for estimation, as the variance components are the focus of the illustration.

```
> ## Estimate models.
> year.out  <- lmer(read ~ year + (year | subid), MPLS.LS, REML = TRUE)
> month.out <- lmer(read ~ month + (month | subid), MPLS.LS, REML = TRUE)
> day.out   <- lmer(read ~ day + (day | subid), MPLS.LS, REML = TRUE)
> ## Concatenate and print.
> my.f <- rbind(summary(year.out)@coefs[2, ],
+               summary(month.out)@coefs[2, ],
+               summary(day.out)@coefs[2, ])
> row.names(my.f) <- c("year", "month", "day")
> my.f
```

	Estimate	Std. Error	t value
year	4.82925048	0.748654982	6.450569
month	0.40243724	0.062388326	6.450522
day	0.01341462	0.002079556	6.450713

As the output shows, the size of the fixed effect estimate (`Estimate`) and the SE (`Std. Error`) is a function of the unit, with day having the smallest estimates. Despite the different slope estimates, the *t*-ratio is equivalent within rounding for each. The *t*-ratio helps ensure one will not mistakenly interpret a small value for the slope as a negligible effect.

As discussed in Chapter 6, SEs for variance components are not provided in the `lmer()` output. This may make it difficult to judge the importance of the variance of the slopes (and other curve components). To illustrate, the variance components are extracted for the three models estimated immediately above.

```
> my.v <- data.frame(rbind(attr(VarCorr(year.out)$subid,  "stddev") ^ 2,
+                          attr(VarCorr(month.out)$subid, "stddev") ^ 2,
+                          attr(VarCorr(day.out)$subid,   "stddev") ^ 2),
+                    Cor = rbind(attr(VarCorr(year.out)$subid,  "correlation")[1,2],
+                                attr(VarCorr(month.out)$subid, "correlation")[1,2],
+                                attr(VarCorr(day.out)$subid,   "correlation")[1,2]))
> row.names(my.v) <- c("year", "month", "day")
> colnames(my.v)[1:2] <- c("Var(int)", "Var(slopes)")
> round(my.v, 6)
```

	Var(int)	Var(slopes)	Cor
year	398.6429	7.140641	-0.527848
month	398.6422	0.049588	-0.527847
day	398.6422	0.000055	-0.527847

`Var(int)` lists the variance of the intercepts, and `Var(slopes)` lists the variance of the slopes. The correlation is listed in `Cor`. The estimated variance of the intercepts and the correlation are the same for all models, within rounding error. However, the estimated variance of the slope decreases dramatically as the unit shrinks. When the unit is days, the slope variance estimate is very small (0.000055).

Although the slope of days is small, it is important to retain in the model. The following LRT bears this out.

```
> day.out0 <- lmer(read ~ day + (1 | subid), MPLS.LS)
> anova(day.out0, day.out)
```

```
Data: MPLS.LS
Models:
day.out0: read ~ day + (1 | subid)
day.out:  read ~ day + (day | subid)
         Df    AIC    BIC  logLik  Chisq Chi Df Pr(>Chisq)
day.out0  4 585.82 595.35 -288.91
day.out   6 580.98 595.28 -284.49 8.8375      2    0.01205 *
---
Signif. codes:  0 '***' 0.001 '**' 0.01 '*' 0.05 '.' 0.1 ' ' 1
```

The output shows the LRT-p is 0.012. Recall that the LRT-p in the output is "conservative," meaning the value tends to be larger than it should. With this in mind, there is relatively strong evidence the random slopes should be retained in the model. The reader can verify that the identical results will be retained regardless of the unit that is used.

The above result verifies an earlier point made in Chapter 10: *small values of variance components can be meaningful*. Consequently, a random effect should not be omitted from the model based solely on the size of its variance in the output.

When the units are small, as with days, there are potentially two drawbacks. The first is that the researcher may be misled—at least initially—regarding the importance of the variance (or the fixed effect) because of its small size. Again, this is due to the absence of reporting SEs in the former case. Second, very small variances can cause estimation problems in the `lmer()` algorithm. The reason lies with the matrix algebra underlying the estimation algorithm, a topic that is beyond our scope.

For these reasons, it may be desirable to express the time variable in larger units. As illustrated above, the reexpression does not change the anchoring of the intercept. It can also be shown that the t-ratios of static predictor effects are unaffected by the choice of unit. Since there is little if any negative regarding the reexpression, its use is encouraged when the original units are particularly small.

11.5.2 TRANSFORMING FOR STANDARDIZED CHANGE

In certain studies, it is desirable to transform the response variable so that the LMER parameters reflect change in SD units, known as *standardized change*. Standardized change is examined by centering and scaling the response variable prior to the analysis. For the entire vector of response values, the mean is subtracted out and divided by the SD. The mean and SD might be based on the sample or the population, depending on the situation.

One motivation for standardizing is it allows the researcher to examine how things change relative to a criterion, such as a norm group. For example, with the reading measure in the MPLS data set, the goal might be to see how the starting point of the sample compares to national norms for fifth grade. The progress of the sample can also be tracked relative to norm change. In this case, the response is centered and scaled using the norm mean and norm SD (the norm mean and SD must be available to the researcher).

A second motivation is that some behavioral measures appear to lack a meaningful inherent metric, and standardizing is an attempt to provide one. Composites of ordinal items, for example, do not have definable units, which seems at odds with certain parameter interpretations in regression models (Cliff, 1996; Long, 2005; Long et al., 2003). Recall the linear slope is often interpreted as the *unit* change in the response for a one-unit increase in the time variable. Standardization provides an SD unit interpretation of change. When the response variable is appropriately transformed, then the linear slope, for example, is interpreted as *the change of the response in SD units for a unit increase in time*. Such interpretations seem to be desirable when the response does not have a "natural" measurement unit.

Finally, standardization may be useful when two or more measures are to be composited for the analysis. The researcher might have two measures of reading recorded for each subject at each time point. Suppose the goal is to combine the scores to create a single response. The scores of the measures might be standardized prior to compositing, especially if they are on different scales.

It is important to point out that information criteria, such as the AICc, cannot be used to determine if standardization improves the model. Standardization changes the response variable, and information criteria can only be used to compare models with the same response.

The response is centered and scaled using the `scale()` function. The name of the variable to be scaled must be supplied, and there are two optional arguments, `center=` and `scale=`. If the two optional arguments are omitted, then the sample mean is used for centering, and the sample SD is used for scaling. Supplying numbers (or functions) for the optional arguments provides alternative types of centering and scaling. These are used when scaling is in reference to population parameters.

As an illustration, suppose the goal is to use fifth-grade norms as a touchstone for evaluating initial status and change for the MPLS sample. For the reading measure, the fifth-grade norm group has a mean of 206.7 and an SD of 15.6 (Northwest Evaluation Association, 2003). In the syntax below, a new response variable is created, read.norm, that is centered and scaled using the norm values.

```
> MPLS.LS$read.norm <- scale(MPLS.LS$read, center = 206.7, scale = 15.6)
> with(MPLS.LS, head(data.frame(subid, grade, read, read.norm)))
```

	subid	grade	read	read.norm
1	1	5	172	-2.2243590
2	1	6	185	-1.3910256
3	1	7	179	-1.7756410
4	1	8	194	-0.8141026
5	2	5	200	-0.4294872
6	2	6	210	0.2115385

The read.norm column contains the centered and scaled reading variable. The first subject has standardized reading values that are below the norm mean for all time points.

It should be noted that the centering and scaling are performed on the entire response vector in the long-format data frame. That is, the scores of all the time points are used, as opposed to standardizing within each time point. Standardizing within each time point sets the mean to a constant, which is of no use in studying change.

Now consider a LMER model with the standardized response and grade5 as the sole predictor. Two random effects are included, and ML is used for the estimation.

```
> norm.1 <- lmer(read.norm ~ grade5 + (grade5 | subid), MPLS.LS, REML = FALSE)
> summary(norm.1)@coefs
```

	Estimate	Std. Error	t value
(Intercept)	-0.2920407	0.27125482	-1.076629
grade5	0.3095646	0.04681823	6.612052

The estimated intercept is -0.29, indicating the initial status of the sample is 0.29 SD less than the norm group. The estimated slope indicates there is an increase of 0.31 SD per grade.

For an unstandardized response variable, the statistical test of the intercept is usually not meaningful. The reason is that the null hypothesis, $H_0 : \beta_0 = 0$, contains the often meaningless value of 0. The response scale is such that a value of 0 either cannot occur, or its occurrence would be exceedingly strange. With the NALT reading test of the MPLS data set, the minimum value is not 0, so this is a value that is meaningless for the statistical testing of the intercept in the original metric.

There is an advantage of standardizing in this example, as the value of 0 is a meaningful reference point for the intercept. Zero represents the standardized mean of the norm group, so that if one is inclined to use NHST, the

11.5 Additional Transformations

null hypothesis of $H_0 : \beta_0 = 0$ is an informative test. In the output above, the absolute value *t*-ratio for the intercept is relatively small, indicating that $H_0 : \beta_0 = 0$ is not rejected. The observed deviation of the sample intercept from the group norm is not statistically reliable.

11.5.3 STANDARDIZING AND COMPOSITING

Another use of standardizing is for compositing two or more response variables. Chapter 13 discusses the simultaneous analysis of two response variables without combining them together. Here the focus is on creating a single response out of two or more variables.

In some behavioral research, multiple response measures are administered, and the researcher wants to combine them to analyze a single overall score. Subscales of the same measure might be composited to form a total score, or the composite can consist of completely different measures. The measures to be composited are usually assumed to index the same construct (Long et al., 2007).

When the measures to be combined are on different scales, there are two main approaches to standardization. If equal weight is to be allocated to each measure, then each should be standardized separately, prior to compositing. This accounts for possible differences in the SDs and ensures that the measure with the largest SD will not be more heavily weighted in the composite. On the other hand, if one wants weighting based on SDs, then the measures should be composited first and then standardized.

As an illustration, consider the made-up data in Table 11.2. There are two variables, *A* and *B*, measured at two time points, with time being indexed by the subscript of a variable. An inspection of Table 11.2 reveals that *A* and *B* have quite different scales, with the latter consisting of much smaller numbers.

The data of 11.2 are available from the book website in the file `mytab.txt`. In the syntax below, the text file is read in with `read.table()`, and the top portion of the data frame is printed.

```
> MTWO <- read.table("C:/Mine/mytab.txt", header = TRUE)
> head(MTWO)
```

	a.1	a.2	b.1	b.2
1	103	110	13	19
2	101	109	15	21
3	93	111	14	19
4	100	111	15	23
5	99	96	16	20
6	92	102	12	22

The `MTWO` data frame is in wide format, and it must be reshaped to long format for LMER analysis. As discussed in Chapter 3, the `reshape()` function is used.

Table 11.2 Scores of measures A and B at two time points.

Subject	A_1	A_2	B_1	B_2
1	103	110	13	19
2	101	109	15	21
3	93	111	14	19
4	100	111	15	23
5	99	96	16	20
6	92	102	12	22
7	97	102	14	19
8	106	105	13	19
9	103	101	14	19
10	102	109	15	20

```
> MTWO.L <- reshape(MTWO, varying=1:4, direction="long")
> head(MTWO.L)
    time   a   b id
1.1    1 103  13  1
2.1    1 101  15  2
3.1    1  93  14  3
4.1    1 100  15  4
5.1    1  99  16  5
6.1    1  92  12  6
```

Having reshaped the data, the means and SDs of both the measures are computed. This is performed for both time points.

```
> desc <- ddply(MTWO.L, .(time = MTWO.L$time), function(x)
+           c(Mean.a = mean(x$a), SD.a = sd(x$a),
+             Mean.b = mean(x$b), SD.b = sd(x$b)))
> round(desc, 2)
  time Mean.a  SD.a Mean.b SD.b
1    1   99.6  4.48   14.1 1.20
2    2  105.6  5.17   20.1 1.45
```

As the output shows, the mean difference among the time points of both measures is 6. However, the SDs of measure B are smaller than those of measure A, indicating the mean difference of B constitutes a greater relative magnitude.

11.5 Additional Transformations

If the goal is to equally weight the measures, then the different magnitudes are accounted for by standardizing before compositing. If the goal is to allow measure *B* to be more heavily weighted, the measures are composited and then standardized.

For LMER analysis, standardizing should always be performed with the long-format data frame rather than the wide-format data frame. If the `scale()` function is used with the format of Table 11.2, for example, each column will be corrected by its mean, yielding standardized variables with means of 0 at each time point. Such standardized variables are worthless for studying change in level over time.

In the syntax below, `scale()` is used to compute two different composite variables. For the first variable, `c.z`, a and b are *composited prior to standardizing*. For the second variable, `z.c`, a and b are each *standardized prior to compositing*. The means of the composites are computed, and then the differences between the means at the two times are computed.

```
> # Composite then standardize.
> MTWO.L$c.z <- scale(MTWO.L$a + MTWO.L$b)
> # Standardize then composite.
> MTWO.L$z.c <- scale(MTWO.L$a) + scale(MTWO.L$b)
> # Means.
> desc <- ddply(MTWO.L[ , 5:6], .(time=MTWO.L$time),mean)
> round(desc, 2)
```

```
  time   c.z    z.c
1    1 -0.75  -1.43
2    2  0.75   1.43
```

```
> # Row differences.
> round(data.frame(c.z.diff = diff(desc[, 2]), z.c.diff = diff(desc[ , 3])), 2)
```

```
  c.z.diff z.c.diff
1      1.5     2.86
```

As the output reveals, the standardized difference for `z.c` is almost twice that of `c.z`. The reason is that compositing prior to standardizing weights the variable with the larger variability more heavily in the composite. In the case of the example data, variable *A* has much higher variability and a lower standardized difference, which has the effect of diminishing the overall effect. In contrast, standardizing prior to compositing sets the SDs of the variables equal, so that the effects are equally weighted.

Which method is the "correct" method? It depends on the goals of the compositing. Usually standardizing prior to compositing is performed, as the researcher often wants to adjust for differences in scale, not retain them.

Modeling Nonlinear Change 12

In past chapters, nonlinear change curves were polynomials of the time predictor. This chapter expands on the earlier material in several ways. First, there is a discussion of how polynomials account for nonlinear change. Focus is on the quadratic polynomial, as this is the simplest of nonlinear polynomial models. Additional types of polynomials are introduced, including orthogonal polynomials.

Following the discussion of polynomials, alternative nonlinear change models are presented. Similar to polynomials, the alternatives rely on transformations of the time predictor. However, the transformations are not limited to integer power terms. Three types of alternative transformations are considered: trigonometric functions, fractional polynomials, and splines.

Some of the alternative methods, such as splines, are desirable for specific situations, as when trajectories are expected to change direction at landmark time points. Other methods, such as fractional polynomials, are for more general application, and they can have some advantages over conventional polynomials.

As in previous chapters, examples are based on the MPLS data set. To thoroughly illustrate the nonlinear models, the previous data set is extended to include Grades 2 to 8 (Grades 5–8 have been considered up to now). The response variable is again reading achievement, and the time predictor is grade.

All the transformations discussed in this chapter can be used in confirmatory or exploratory analysis. Entanglements regarding confirmatory/exploratory issues are largely sidestepped in this chapter, as these issues were covered in previous chapters. Some outstanding features of the data analysis strategy are stated when applicable, but the focus is on acquainting the reader with the methods. Similar to previous chapters, attention is aimed at the fixed effects portion of the models. Practical issues are addressed, including the specifics of creating the time transformations necessary for estimating the models.

Some readers will find the material of this chapter to be at a higher level than previous chapters. One reason is that nonlinear change models require explanatory concepts that go beyond those needed to discuss linear change. One such concept is the derivative, introduced in Section 12.3. The intention is to provide sufficient material so that the reader can be an informed user of the models.

12.1 Data Set and Analysis Strategy

The change curves of the reading data considered in previous chapters appear to be well characterized by linear growth. One reason for this is the limited time span, which is Grades 5 to 8. For a sufficiently wide span of time, change curves for reading skills can be similar to developmental curves of height or weight, marked by early rapid development and a plateauing in adolescence (Shin et al., 2009).

There is empirical evidence that many variables in human development have nonlinear trajectories, provided the observed time interval is sufficient (see, e.g., Kuczmarski, Ogden, & Guo, 2002). To the extent that longitudinal behavioral data mimic general human development data, a case can be made for assuming change curves will be nonlinear.

In previous chapters, the MPLS data set was analyzed with reading scores measured over Grades 5 to 8. This chapter considers an augmented data set that includes observations over Grades 2 to 8. The data are shown in Table 12.1 and are available on the book website. Missing values are indicated by −9. The data of Table 12.1 will be the basis of illustrations throughout the chapter. As shown below, when Grades 2 to 4 are included, nonlinear change curves now appear to be required.

The Table 12.1 data set does not have any static predictors. It is desirable to include static predictors in the data set to illustrate nonlinear conditional change curve models. The first order of business, then, is to create a data frame out of the Table 12.1 data and then merge in a static predictor. For purposes of illustration, the risk2 static predictor is merged with the Table 12.1 data.

Suppose the data in Table 12.1 are saved in the text file MPLS2.W.txt, with the column names in the first row. Then the following syntax is used to read in the data set.

```
> MPLS2.W <- read.table("C:/Mine/MPLS2.W.txt", header = TRUE, na.strings = "-9")
```

The goal is to merge the MPLS2.W data frame with the risk2 variable from the original wide data frame, MPLS.W. The merge() function is used to perform this task. The resulting data frame is named MPLS2.WM.

12.1 Data Set and Analysis Strategy

Table 12.1 Nonlinear data.

subid	read.2	read.3	read.4	read.5	read.6	read.7	read.8
1	137	186	192	172	185	179	194
2	154	163	186	200	210	209	−9
3	154	186	181	191	199	203	215
4	166	168	198	200	195	194	−9
5	179	185	183	207	213	212	213
6	156	171	175	191	189	206	195
7	163	177	184	199	208	213	218
8	175	159	185	191	194	194	−9
9	177	159	173	149	154	174	177
10	151	177	177	200	212	213	−9
11	145	168	171	178	191	193	199
12	157	170	172	188	192	208	206
13	181	195	203	228	236	228	239
14	177	185	199	199	210	225	235
15	183	202	204	218	223	236	−9
16	195	192	211	228	226	234	227
17	187	204	206	201	210	208	219
18	185	204	219	218	220	217	221
19	189	200	226	215	216	221	−9
20	203	195	208	204	215	219	214
21	182	194	177	237	241	243	−9
22	174	205	220	219	233	236	−9

```
> ## Read in data, grades 5-8.
> MPLS.W <- read.table("C:/Mine/MPLS.W.txt", header = TRUE, na.strings = "-9")
> ## Define risk2.
> MPLS.W$riskC[MPLS.W$risk == "HHM"] <- "DADV"
> MPLS.W$riskC[MPLS.W$risk == "POV"] <- "DADV"
> MPLS.W$riskC[MPLS.W$risk == "ADV"] <- "ADV"
> MPLS.W$risk2 <- factor(MPLS.W$riskC)
> ## Merge.
> MPLS2.WM <- merge(MPLS2.W, subset(MPLS.W, select = c(subid, risk2)), by = "subid")
> head(MPLS2.WM)
```

	subid	read.2	read.3	read.4	read.5	read.6	read.7	read.8	risk2
1	1	137	186	192	172	185	179	194	DADV
2	2	154	163	186	200	210	209	NA	DADV
3	3	154	186	181	191	199	203	215	DADV
4	4	166	168	198	200	195	194	NA	DADV
5	5	179	185	183	207	213	212	213	DADV
6	6	156	171	175	191	189	206	195	DADV

Having successfully added `risk2`, the wide-format data frame can now be reshaped into the long format necessary for LMER analysis. The final data frame is named `MPLS2.LS` and is sorted by subject identification number (see Chapter 3 for additional details).

```
> MPLS2.L  <- reshape(MPLS2.WM, varying = 2:8, times = 2:8, idvar = "subid",
+                    timevar = "grade", direction = "long")
> MPLS2.LS <- MPLS2.L[order(MPLS2.L$subid), ]
> head(MPLS2.LS, n = 14)
```

	subid	risk2	grade	read
1.2	1	DADV	2	137
1.3	1	DADV	3	186
1.4	1	DADV	4	192
1.5	1	DADV	5	172
1.6	1	DADV	6	185
1.7	1	DADV	7	179
1.8	1	DADV	8	194
2.2	2	DADV	2	154
2.3	2	DADV	3	163
2.4	2	DADV	4	186
2.5	2	DADV	5	200
2.6	2	DADV	6	210
2.7	2	DADV	7	209
2.8	2	DADV	8	NA

It is desirable to construct both group-level and subject-specific graphs of the data. We begin with group-level graphs of the observed means. Detailed explanation of the syntax is found in Chapter 4.

```
> ## Set options for all graphs.
> theme_set(theme_bw())
> myx <- scale_x_continuous(breaks = 2:8)
> ## ggplot().
> g1 <- ggplot(MPLS2.LS, aes(x = grade, y = read, groups = subid)) + myx
> g2 <- g1 + geom_line(colour = "grey80") + facet_grid(. ~ risk2, margins = TRUE)
> g3 <- g2 + stat_summary(aes(group = 1), fun.y = mean, geom = "point", size = 3.5)
> g4 <- g3 + stat_summary(aes(group = 1), fun.y = mean, geom = "line", lwd=1.5)
> print(g4)
```

The graphs of the means are shown in Figure 12.1. The collapsed group (unconditional group) is shown in the last panel on the right and labeled "(all)."[1] The risk groups are shown in the left-hand panels. The individual curves are the thin gray lines; the trend line of the means is the solid line. The curves of the means indicate there is a near-linear increase for the earlier grades (2–5) and then a deceleration beginning at approximately Grade 5.

---

[1] As noted in Chapter 4, `margins=TRUE` was disabled at the time of this writing. An alternative is to copy `MPLS2.LS` and relabel `risk2` to `(all)`, then stack the original data frame and the altered one and run the `ggplot()` syntax on the stacked data frame. In this example, the syntax for stacking is the following:

```
MPLS2.LSa <- MPLS2.LS                      # Copy data frame.
MPLS2.LSa$risk2 <- "(all)"                 # Relabel risk2.
plotdata <- rbind(MPLS2.LS, MPLS2.LSa)     # Stack data frames.
```

12.1 Data Set and Analysis Strategy

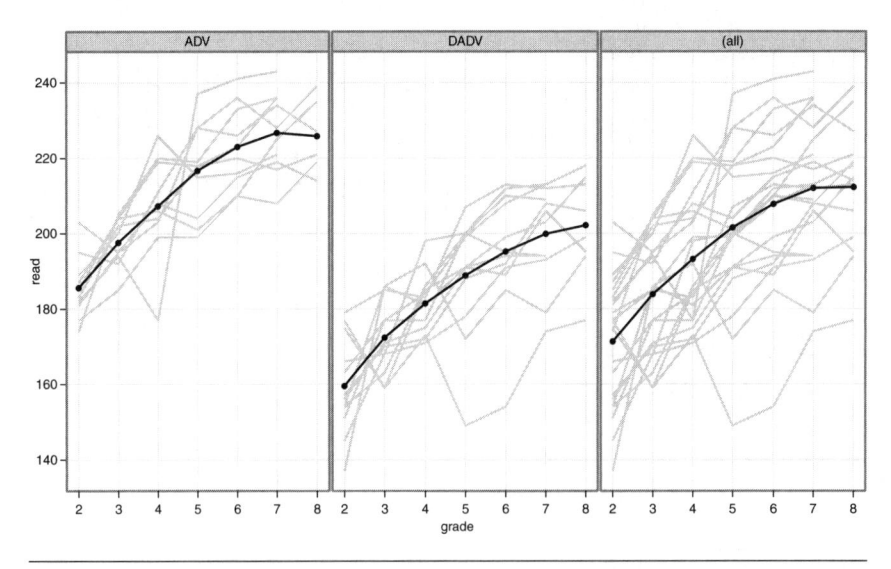

Figure 12.1 Individual curves (thin gray lines) and observed mean curves by risk group.

Next, the individual change curves are drawn with faceting by subject. This is performed separately for each risk group, and the resulting graphs are printed side by side. The reason for doing this separately is to avoid many empty panels that would result from faceting by both subject and group.

In the syntax below, a data frame for each group is created. Then the facet plots are constructed using the same scaling for both groups.

```
> ## Create data frames.
> DADV <- subset(MPLS2.LS, risk2 == "DADV")
> ADV <- subset(MPLS2.LS, risk2 == "ADV")
> ## DAVD group.
> d1 <- ggplot(DADV, aes(x = grade, y = read)) + geom_line()
> d2 <- d1 + facet_wrap( ~ subid) + opts(title = "DADV") + ylim(140, 240)
> ## ADV group.
> a1 <- ggplot(ADV, aes(x = grade, y = read)) + geom_line()
> a2 <- a1 + facet_wrap( ~ subid) + opts(title = "ADV") + ylim(140, 240)
> ## Print graphs to one page.
> grid.newpage()
> pushViewport(viewport(layout = grid.layout(1, 2)))
> vplayout <- function(x,y) viewport(layout.pos.row = x, layout.pos.col = y)
> print(d2, vp = vplayout(1, 1))
> print(a2, vp = vplayout(1, 2))
```

The observed subject curves are shown in Figure 12.2. A majority of the subject curves have nonlinear trends. For clarity of demonstration, some of the methods of this chapter will be illustrated using data from individual subjects in Figure 12.2.

As discussed in Chapter 7, it is not always clear how to handle static predictors in nonlinear models. If different nonlinear trends appear to be required

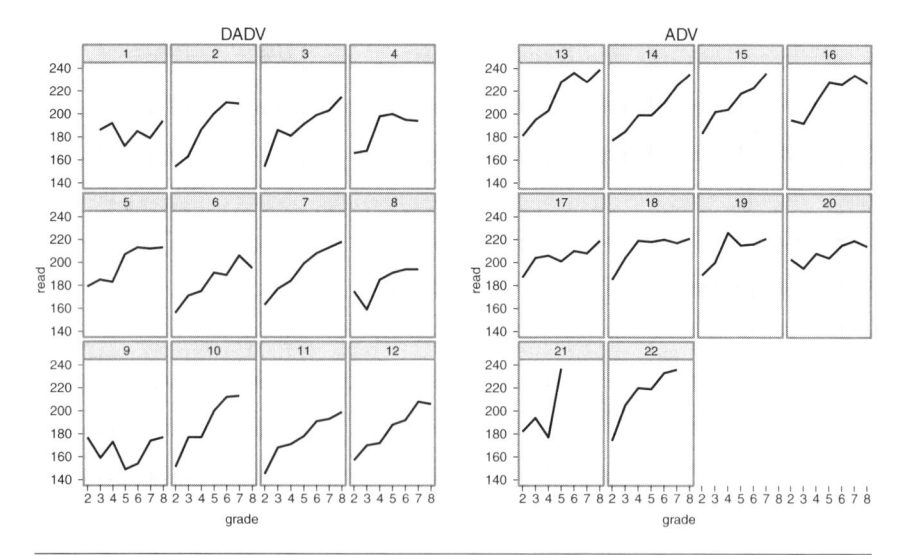

Figure 12.2 Individual observed change curves by risk group.

for different levels of the static predictor(s), then model selection should probably focus on subject-specific fits. Otherwise, group-level fits are used. As discussed in Chapter 9, subject-specific fits are examined using `lm()`, `ldply()`, and `dlply()`. Group-level fits are evaluated using the AICc and/or the LRT.

12.2 Global Versus Local Models

In the discussion of nonlinear models, the distinction is made between a *global model* and a *local model*. For global models, the curve equation applies to the entire observed time interval. This means that the collection of fixed effects determines the shape of the change curve over the entire observed span of time. Global models are the most common type in the behavioral sciences and usually involve polynomials. In this chapter, additional global models are considered that use trigonometric functions and fractional polynomials.

Local models are based on the idea of breaking the observed time period into smaller pieces, or a series of shorter spans of time. Local models have different curve equations for different spans. This means that different fixed effects determine the shape of the curve for different spans, or the fixed effects are "local" to the particular span. A spline model is an example of a local model.

The spline models considered in this chapter require the researcher to define spans of time based on landmark time points, called *knots*. A potential point of confusion is that spline models usually incorporate polynomials. However, unlike global polynomial models, local polynomial models always have different fixed effects for different spans of time.

Other types of local fitting methods are essentially automatic in nature. Examples include the smoothers introduced in Chapter 4. Smoothers use an algorithm to fit a smooth curve to sample data. The algorithms are relatively complex, as they involve overlapping spans and robust fitting techniques (see, e.g., Cleveland, Grosse, & Shyu, 1992). Smoothers can be very useful in suggesting a curve shape for the fixed effects structure, especially when the mean curve is erratic (lots of twists and turns). Smoothers are typically more resistant to outliers and other wrinkles of sample data than mean curves. Thus, smoothers might provide a better basis for constructing a fixed effects structure.

12.3 Polynomials

The most common global models use polynomials, which were discussed in Chapter 9 and previous chapters. In this section, some additional details are provided regarding the interpretation of polynomial terms. Alternate forms of polynomials are also presented, which are sometimes convenient for estimation and interpretation.

Polynomials have the advantage of being flexible, and they are relatively easy to construct and specify. Polynomials are familiar to applied researchers, and they provide an "automatic" means of increasing curve complexity. The power term can always be incremented by 1 to obtain the next highest polynomial.

Because polynomial models have been discussed previously, expected value equations are stressed in this section as they are simpler to depict. The expected value equation for polynomial LMER is written as

$$E(y_{ij}) = \beta_0 + \beta_1(\text{grade}_{ij}) + \beta_2(\text{grade}_{ij}^2) + \beta_3(\text{grade}_{ij}^3) + \cdots + \beta_p(\text{grade}_{ij}^p). \quad (12.3.1)$$

The time transformations in Equation 12.3.1 are referred to as *raw polynomials* to distinguish them from alternatives presented below.

A special case of Equation 12.3.1 is the quadratic polynomial, which is the simplest nonlinear polynomial model,

$$E(y_{ij}) = \beta_0 + \beta_1(\text{grade}_{ij}) + \beta_2(\text{grade}_{ij}^2).$$

To gain insight into the nature of polynomial models, consider rewriting the quadratic polynomial by factoring grade,

$$E(y_{ij}) = \beta_0 + \left[\beta_1 + \beta_2(\text{grade}_{ij})\right](\text{grade}_{ij}). \quad (12.3.2)$$

Equation 12.3.2 indicates that the effect of grade on the response depends on grade itself. The slope term is $\beta_1 + \beta_2(\text{grade}_{ij})$, which means there is a linear change in the slope for grade, as grade itself increases. This illustrates the nonlinear nature of the quadratic polynomial. *The linear relationship between grade and read changes as grade increases.*

The changing linear relationship is quantified by the *derivative*. The derivative is the slope of the linear curve that is tangent to the polynomial curve at a particular value of grade. Using the notation of Equation 12.3.1, it can be shown that the derivative of a polynomial, D, is

$$D\left[E(y_{ij})\right] = \sum_{k=1}^{p}(k)(\beta_k)(\text{grade}_{ij}^{k-1}). \qquad (12.3.3)$$

For example, when $k = 2$, the derivative of the quadratic model is

$$\begin{aligned} D\left[E(y_{ij})\right] &= (1)(\beta_1)(\text{grade}_{ij}^{1-1}) + (2)(\beta_2)(\text{grade}_{ij}^{2-1}) \\ &= \beta_1 + 2\beta_2(\text{grade}_{ij}). \end{aligned} \qquad (12.3.4)$$

The derivative indicates that the slope of the tangent line is a linear function of grade. The slope changes value as grade increases. A visual representation is provided in Figure 12.3. Below it is shown how Figure 12.3 is constructed in R.

The derivative of a function is found using expression() and D(). Within expression() is the polynomial model for which the derivative is to be computed. Since Greek letters cannot be used, let B stand for β. The mathematical operations implied in the model must be explicitly specified using the appropriate symbols—for instance, +, *, and ^. The expression is saved as an object, and then the object name is supplied to D(), along with the quoted time variable ("grade"). Consider the following.

```
> quad <- expression(B0 + B1 * grade+B2 * grade^2)
> dey <- D(quad, "grade")
> dey
```
```
B1 + B2 * (2 * grade)
```

With minor rearranging of terms, the output confirms the derivative is the same as in Equation 12.3.4.

Given values of the coefficients and grade, the derivative output object, dey, can be evaluated using eval() to obtain a numeric solution. This means the slope of the tangent line at each value of grade can be computed. The result provides an indication of how the tangent line changes as grade changes.

As an illustration, consider fitting a quadratic model with two random effects using the MPLS2.LS data frame. The variables B0, B1, and B2 are set to the values of the estimated fixed effects using a for() loop. Then the prediction equation is saved in quad, and dey is evaluated at values of grade.

12.3 Polynomials

```
> ## Estimate model and extract fixed effects.
> myfe <- fixef(lmer(read ~ grade + I(grade ^ 2) + (grade | subid),
+                    MPLS2.LS, REML = FALSE))
> ## Assign values to B0, B1, B2.
> for(i in 1:3){assign(paste("B", i - 1, sep = ""), myfe[i])}
> print(c(B0, B1, B2))
```

```
(Intercept)       grade    I(grade^2)
 143.622847    15.745161     -0.839052
```

```
> ## Compute predicted values and derivatives.
> grade <- 2:8
> myd <- data.frame(grade, fitted = eval(quad), dey = eval(dey))
> myd
```

```
  grade   fitted        dey
1     2 171.7570  12.388953
2     3 183.3069  10.710849
3     4 193.1787   9.032745
4     5 201.3724   7.354642
5     6 207.8879   5.676538
6     7 212.7254   3.998434
7     8 215.8848   2.320330
```

The `fitted` column in the output shows the fitted value for each grade, and the `dey` column shows the derivative. The slope of the tangent line decreases as grade increases. The rate of decrease is linear, with slope $2\hat{\beta}_2 = -1.6781$. The decreasing slope is consistent with the pattern of the observed means in Figure 12.1, as there is a deceleration in the reading means as grade increases.

Using the point-slope formula (Hirst, 2006, chap. 5), it can be shown that the intercept of the tangent line is

$$\hat{y}_{ij} - D\big[E(y_{ij})\big](\text{grade}_{ij}),$$

where $\hat{y}_{ij}$ are the fitted values.

The value of the intercept of the tangent line is added to the data frame. Then `ggplot2` is used in a `for()` loop to create three graphs of the fitted values and tangent lines. The component `geom_abline()` is used to draw the tangent lines in each graph for Grades 4, 6, 8. Note that these values reside in rows 3, 5, 7 of `myd`. Inside the `for()` loop, `assign()` is used to save a `ggplot()` object with a unique name, `g3`, `g5`, and `g7`. The graph objects are then printed on a single page.

```
> ## Intercept of tangent line.
> myd$int <- myd$fitted - myd$dey * myd$grade
> ## Construct separate graphs.
> for(i in c(3, 5, 7)){
+     df <- data.frame(a = myd$int[i], b = myd$dey[i],
+                     y1 = myd$fitted[i], x1 = myd$grade[i])
+     assign(paste("g", i, sep = ""),
+            ggplot(data = myd, aes(x = grade, y = fitted)) + geom_line()
+            + geom_abline(aes(intercept = a,slope = b), data = df,linetype = 2)
+            + geom_point(aes(x = x1, y = y1), data = df, size = 3)
+            + ylab("read") + opts(aspect.ratio = 1))
+ }
> ## Print graphs to one page.
> grid.newpage()
> pushViewport(viewport(layout = grid.layout(1, 3)))
> vplayout <- function(x, y) viewport(layout.pos.row = x, layout.pos.col = y)
> print(g3, vp = vplayout(1, 1))
> print(g5, vp = vplayout(1, 2))
> print(g7, vp = vplayout(1, 3))
```

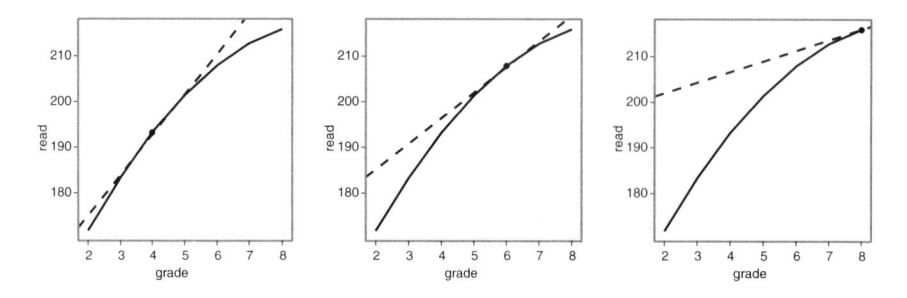

Figure 12.3 Tangent lines for the quadratic polynomial at Grade 4 (left), Grade 6 (middle), and Grade 8 (right).

The graphs are shown in Figure 12.3. The solid line is the fitted curve, and the dashed line is the tangent. The slope of the tangent line decreases as grade increases.

Similar graphs can be constructed for higher order polynomials. Consider the cubic polynomial.

$$E(y_{ij}) = \beta_0 + \beta_1(\text{grade}_{ij}) + \beta_2(\text{grade}_{ij}^2) + \beta_3(\text{grade}_{ij}^3). \quad (12.3.5)$$

If grade_{ij} is factored, the equation is

$$E(y_{ij}) = \beta_0 + \left[\beta_1 + \beta_2(\text{grade}_{ij}) + \beta_3(\text{grade}_{ij}^2)\right](\text{grade}_{ij}). \quad (12.3.6)$$

Equation 12.3.6 indicates the relationship between grade and the response is a nonlinear function of grade.

The derivative of the cubic polynomial is obtained as follows.

```
> cubic <- expression(B0 + B1 * grade + B2 * grade ^ 2 + B3 * grade ^ 3)
> dey <- D(cubic, "grade")
> dey
```

```
B1 + B2 * (2 * grade) + B3 * (3 * grade^2)
```

12.3 Polynomials

The output shows that the derivative is $D\left[E(y_{ij})\right] = \beta_1 + 2\beta_2(\text{grade}_{ij})$ $+ 3\beta_3(\text{grade}_{ij}^2)$. The result shows that the slope of the tangent line is a non-linear function of grade. Therefore, the slope can increase and decrease as grade increases.

As an illustration of computing the derivative for the cubic polynomial based on data, consider the first subject of the data frame, subid = 1 (see Figure 12.2). The subject's curve appears to require at least a cubic polynomial.

Since the data for a single subject are considered, lm() is used for estimation. The goal here is description, with focus on the regression weights. The subset= argument in lm() is used to select only the first subject from the data frame. Once the cubic polynomial model is estimated, the fitted values and derivatives are calculated.

```
> myfe <- coef(lm(read ~ grade + I(grade ^ 2) + I(grade ^ 3),
+                MPLS2.LS, subset = (subid == 1)))
> for(i in 1:4){assign(paste("B", i-1, sep = ""), myfe[i])}
> print(c(B0, B1, B2, B3))
```

```
(Intercept)       grade   I(grade^2)   I(grade^3)
 -67.428571  158.992063   -31.535714     1.972222
```

```
> ## Compute fitted values and derivatives.
> grade <- 2:8
> myd   <- data.frame(grade, fitted = eval(cubic), dey = eval(dey))
> myd
```

```
  grade    fitted        dey
1     2  140.1905  56.515873
2     3  178.9762  23.027778
3     4  190.1905   1.373016
4     5  185.6667  -8.448413
5     6  177.2381  -6.436508
6     7  176.7381   7.408730
7     8  196.0000  33.087302
```

The output shows the slope of the tangent line decreases to Grade 5 and then increases. The next step is to compute the intercept of each tangent line and then graph the result. The tangent is drawn for Grades 4, 6, and 8.

```
> myd$int <- myd$fitted - myd$dey * myd$grade
> for(i in c(3,5,7)){
+   df <- data.frame(a = myd$int[i], b = myd$dey[i], y1 = myd$fitted[i], x1 = myd$grade[i])
+   assign(paste("g", i ,sep = ""),
+          ggplot(data = myd, aes(x = grade, y = fitted)) + geom_line() + ylab("read")
+          + geom_abline(aes(intercept = a, slope = b), data = df, linetype = 2)
+          + geom_point(aes(x = x1, y = y1), data = df, size = 3) + opts(aspect.ratio = 1)
+   )
+ }
> ## Print graphs to one page.
> grid.newpage()
> pushViewport(viewport(layout = grid.layout(1, 3)))
> vplayout <- function(x, y) viewport(layout.pos.row = x, layout.pos.col = y)
> print(g3, vp = vplayout(1, 1))
> print(g5, vp = vplayout(1, 2))
> print(g7, vp = vplayout(1, 3))
```

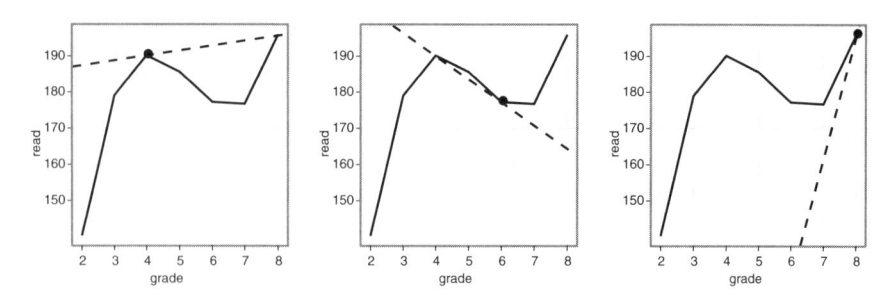

Figure 12.4 Tangent lines for the cubic polynomial at Grade 4 (left), Grade 6 (middle), and Grade 8 (right).

The graphs are shown in Figure 12.4. The solid line is the cubic polynomial, and the dashed line is the tangent. The slope of the tangent changes as grade increases, alternating between a positive slope (Grades 4 and 8) and a negative slope (Grade 6).

12.3.1 MEAN-CORRECTED POLYNOMIALS

A potentially important characteristic of raw polynomials is that they are highly correlated. In addition, as the order increases, the variance of a random effect associated with the polynomial term tends to decrease. For example, the random quadratic term, b_{2i}, can have a very small variance as compared to the lower order terms, b_{1i} and b_{0i}. The random effects can be highly correlated, just like the predictors. Very small variance component estimates along with high correlations among the random effects can lead to estimation problems. In such instances, it is desirable to have predictors with reduced correlations.

One method of lowering the correlations among the polynomials is to subtract out the mean before applying the power transformation, known as *mean correcting* (see the discussion of types of random effects in Chapters 1 and 10). For example, $\text{grade}_{ij} - 5$ can be computed prior to the power transformations, where 5 is the mean of the grades. In this case, the linear mean-corrected polynomial is ($\text{grade}_{ij} - 5$), the quadratic is ($\text{grade}_{ij} - 5)^2$, the cubic is ($\text{grade}_{ij} - 5)^3$, and so on.

Mean correcting anchors the intercept at the mean of the original time predictor. This is important to keep in mind when making inferences about the intercept. The variance of the intercept will reflect variability in the "middle" of the time range.

12.3.2 ORTHOGONAL POLYNOMIALS

Mean correcting will lower the correlation among some terms, but not among others. For instance, the correlation between the linear and quadratic terms can be 0, but the linear and cubic terms can still have a very high correlation.

12.3 Polynomials

An alternative to mean correction is to construct *orthogonal polynomials*. Orthogonal polynomials represent the same effects as raw polynomials, but the correlations among all the predictors are 0 (within computing or machine error). Orthogonal polynomials are constructed by applying a transformation to a set of raw polynomials.

The transformation for orthogonal polynomials is involved, and the details are relegated to the optional Section 12.8.1. Orthogonal polynomials can certainly be used without understanding the details of their construction, which is the approach adopted here.

12.3.3 THE poly() FUNCTION

Raw, mean-corrected, and orthogonal polynomials are constructed using the poly() function. The user provides the name of the time predictor to be transformed, the order of the polynomial, and a logical argument for the raw or orthogonal polynomial.

As an illustration, consider the first subject in the data frame. Raw, mean-corrected, and orthogonal third-order polynomials are computed, and the values are printed.

```
> poly.ex       <- subset(MPLS2.LS, subid < 2, select = -c(read, risk2))
> poly.ex$rawp  <- poly(poly.ex$grade, 3, raw = TRUE)
> poly.ex$mcor  <- poly(poly.ex$grade - mean(poly.ex$grade), 3, raw = TRUE)
> poly.ex$orth  <- poly(poly.ex$grade, 3)
> round(poly.ex[ ,-1], 4)
```

	grade	rawp.1	rawp.2	rawp.3	mcor.1	mcor.2	mcor.3	orth.1	orth.2	orth.3
1.2	2	2	4	8	-3	9	-27	-0.5669	0.5455	-0.4082
1.3	3	3	9	27	-2	4	-8	-0.3780	0.0000	0.4082
1.4	4	4	16	64	-1	1	-1	-0.1890	-0.3273	0.4082
1.5	5	5	25	125	0	0	0	0.0000	-0.4364	0.0000
1.6	6	6	36	216	1	1	1	0.1890	-0.3273	-0.4082
1.7	7	7	49	343	2	4	8	0.3780	0.0000	-0.4082
1.8	8	8	64	512	3	9	27	0.5669	0.5455	0.4082

The output shows the values of the raw polynomials (rawp), the mean-corrected polynomials (mcor), and the orthogonal polynomials (orth). The orthogonal polynomial values are not readily interpretable, requiring more explanation than is provided here. However, they do correspond to linear, quadratic, and cubic transformations.

Consider the correlations among each of the polynomials.

```
> print("- Raw -", quote = FALSE); round(cor(poly.ex$rawp), 2)
```

```
[1]  - Raw -
```

	1	2	3
1	1.00	0.99	0.95
2	0.99	1.00	0.99
3	0.95	0.99	1.00

```
> print("- Mean-Corrected -", quote = FALSE); round(cor(poly.ex$mcor), 2)
```

```
[1] - Mean-Corrected -
```

```
    1 2    3
1 1.00 0 0.93
2 0.00 1 0.00
3 0.93 0 1.00
```

```
> print("- Orthogonal -", quote = FALSE); round(cor(poly.ex$orth), 2)
```

```
[1] - Orthogonal -
```

```
  1 2 3
1 1 0 0
2 0 1 0
3 0 0 1
```

The correlations between the raw polynomials are very high, whereas the correlations between the orthogonal polynomials are 0 within computing error. For the mean-corrected polynomials, the correlation between the linear and quadratic terms is 0, but that for the linear and cubic terms is high.

The `poly()` function is convenient, as it can be used in regression functions such as `lmer()`. One drawback of using `poly()` directly is that the labeling in the output will consist of the syntax used to create the polynomials. This can produce cryptic output, especially for novice users.

As an alternative, the various polynomials can be saved in the data frame. The polynomials are saved as a list object, so a single label can be used to specify the group of polynomials in `lmer()`. Individual polynomials are accessed using the index bracket notation, `[ , ]`.

In the syntax below, three versions of a LMER model are estimated using different types of polynomials. To anchor the intercept at the first time point, the raw polynomials are based on subtracting 2 from each grade value. Each model has two random effects, and the same scaling is used for the random effects as for the fixed effects. To compare the models, the fixed effects tables are printed. The various polynomials are saved in the data frame and accessed using a single variable name.

```
> ## Create polynomials.
> MPLS2.LS$rp  <- poly(MPLS2.LS$grade - 2, degree = 2, raw = TRUE)
> MPLS2.LS$mc  <- poly(MPLS2.LS$grade - mean(MPLS2.LS$grade), degree = 2, raw = TRUE)
> MPLS2.LS$op  <- poly(MPLS2.LS$grade, degree = 2)
> ## Estimate models.
> poly.rawp <- lmer(read ~ rp + (rp[ ,1] | subid), MPLS2.LS, REML = FALSE)
> poly.mcor <- lmer(read ~ mc + (mc[ ,1] | subid), MPLS2.LS, REML = FALSE)
> poly.orth <- lmer(read ~ op + (op[ ,1] | subid), MPLS2.LS, REML = FALSE)
> ## Print fixed effects.
> print("- Raw -", quote = FALSE); round(summary(poly.rawp)@coefs, 4)
```

```
[1] - Raw -
```

12.3 Polynomials

	Estimate	Std. Error	t value
(Intercept)	171.7570	3.3086	51.9130
rp1	12.3890	1.4021	8.8361
rp2	-0.8391	0.2193	-3.8260

```
> print("- Mean-Corrected -", quote = FALSE); round(summary(poly.mcor)@coefs, 4)
```
[1] - Mean-Corrected -

	Estimate	Std. Error	t value
(Intercept)	201.3724	3.3018	60.9891
mc1	7.3546	0.6501	11.3125
mc2	-0.8391	0.2193	-3.8260

```
> print("- Orthogonal -", quote = FALSE); round(summary(poly.orth)@coefs, 4)
```
[1] - Orthogonal -

	Estimate	Std. Error	t value
(Intercept)	198.0161	3.2093	61.7007
op1	182.5371	16.1360	11.3124
op2	-36.0697	9.4275	-3.8260

Comparison of the output for the three models reveals a number of important aspects of polynomial model fitting. First, with one exception, the fixed effects estimates are different for each type of polynomial. The difference in the coefficients reflects the difference in the scale of the predictors. The orthogonal polynomials produce relatively large estimates for the linear and quadratic terms. The other polynomials have much smaller estimates.

Second, the intercept is different for each type of transformation. Computing the fitted values based on the fixed effects, the following can be verified. For the raw polynomial model (poly.rawp), the intercept is the fitted value for Grade 2. For the mean-corrected polynomial model (poly.mcorr), the intercept is the fitted value for the mean of grades, which is Grade 5. For the orthogonal polynomial model, the intercept is the average of the fitted values at all the grades. The different definitions are important if inferences about the intercept or its variance are to be made.

A third issue evident in the fixed effects coefficients tables is that the scaling is compensated for by the SE of the highest order term. This results in the quadratic coefficient having the identical t-ratio in all three cases. The t-ratio for the quadratic coefficient is the only one that does not change under transformation. This will be true of any linear transformation of the time metric and underscores an important point. *Inferential statistics will be identical under linear transformation only for the highest order regression coefficient.* There are some important scientific considerations related to this fact.

Since a linear transformation does not alter the shape of the change curve, it is desirable that the t-ratio of a fixed effect coefficient also not change. As illustrated, such invariance is only true for the fixed effect associated with the highest order polynomial. For this reason, valid inference is only possible for the highest order coefficient when polynomials are considered.

Amplifying this point is the fact that the t-ratios of the lower order coefficients can be made to be any value based on judicious choice of linear transformation (see Section 12.6.4). This arbitrariness implies that all the lower order coefficients should be ignored, as their importance cannot be reliably evaluated.

Ignoring the lower order terms does not mean they are dropped from the model. The lower order terms are needed because they contribute to the overall curve shape, and they allow for proper scaling of the random effects. Therefore, as a general rule, all lower order terms should be included in the model regardless of their t-ratios or any other statistical values (e.g., p-values).

Now consider the variance components for the three different models. Below, the Random Effects table is printed for each of the output objects.

```
> print("- Raw -", quote = FALSE); print(summary(poly.rawp)@REmat, quote = FALSE)
```

```
[1]  - Raw  -
```

Groups	Name	Variance	Std.Dev.	Corr
subid	(Intercept)	184.6118	13.5872	
	rp[, 1]	6.0792	2.4656	-0.121
Residual		72.7715	8.5306	

```
> print("- Mean-Corrected -", quote = FALSE); print(summary(poly.mcor)@REmat, quote = FALSE)
```

```
[1]  - Mean-Corrected  -
```

Groups	Name	Variance	Std.Dev.	Corr
subid	(Intercept)	215.0901	14.6660	
	mc[, 1]	6.0791	2.4656	0.393
Residual		72.7715	8.5306	

```
> print("- Orthogonal -",quote = FALSE);print(summary(poly.orth)@REmat,quote = FALSE)
```

```
[1]  - Orthogonal  -
```

Groups	Name	Variance	Std.Dev.	Corr
subid	(Intercept)	215.091	14.6660	
	op[, 1]	3744.761	61.1945	0.393
Residual		72.772	8.5306	

As the output shows, the variances and covariances (correlations) of the random effects can completely change under transformations of the time predictors. Similar to the fixed effects, the sizes of the variances are partly determined by the scaling of the time metric, yielding relatively small values for the raw and mean-corrected polynomials, and large values for the orthogonal polynomials. Similar to lower order fixed effects, the variance components are always tentative because of their vulnerability to changes in the time scale.

12.3 Polynomials

There is a striking difference in the correlation among the random effects. There is a weak negative correlation between the random effects when raw polynomials are used, and a moderate *positive* correlation when mean-corrected or orthogonal polynomials are used.

The discrepancy in the correlation among the random effects is attributable to the intercept being anchored at different locations. Since the variance of the intercepts is not constant among the grades, neither is its correlation with other random effects. Given the potential change in fixed effects and variance components, the researcher must be careful regarding conclusions about the intercept under transformations of the time metric.

Despite some radical differences in the fixed effects and variance component estimates, the predicted values produced by raw, mean-corrected, and orthogonal polynomials are equal up to computing error. By printing the @AICtab slot of the summary() object, it can be verified that the different polynomials all produce the same AIC.

Because of the equivalence in results, the researcher might want to use raw polynomials initially, and consider mean-corrected and orthogonal polynomials only when interpretation and/or estimation problems are encountered. Raw polynomial values are more readily interpretable than orthogonal polynomials, in the sense that they are simple power transformations. Furthermore, the researcher has direct control over anchoring of the intercept.

12.3.4 POLYNOMIAL EXAMPLE

As discussed in Chapters 7 and 8, selection of a polynomial model depends on the goals of the analysis. If the polynomial is to be preselected, then a variety of descriptive and inferential methods can be used, as discussed in Chapter 9. This section illustrates group-level selection of a polynomial using the AICc and the LRT.

In light of the discussions in previous chapters, selection based on the AICc is straightforward. All the models are fit, and the model with the smallest AICc value is selected. This is the polynomial that is used in any subsequent analysis. The goal is not to create a bouquet of models in this step. Rather, the goal is to a make a preselection decision about the polynomial, which will be used in the subsequent multimodel evaluation.

For the LRT, the common method of selecting an adequate order is to build from the basic to the complex, in a step-up manner (see Chapter 8). One begins by fitting a relatively low-order polynomial model, and then the next most complex polynomial model. If the LRT is significant, then the higher order model is accepted, and then compared to the next highest order model. If the LRT test is not significant, then one reverts to the simpler model. Some authors suggest reverting to the simpler model only when the next *two* more complex models are not statistically significant (e.g., Ryan, 1997, chap. 8).

As an illustration of analysis at the group level, consider three different polynomial models for the data. In the syntax below, the linear, quadratic, and cubic models are estimated with orthogonal polynomials. Fit is examined with the AICc and LRT.

```
> ## Construct orthogonal polynomials.
> op1 <- poly(MPLS2.LS$grade, 1)
> op2 <- poly(MPLS2.LS$grade, 2)
> op3 <- poly(MPLS2.LS$grade, 3)
> ## Estimate the models.
> l.out <- lmer(read ~ op1 + (op1 | subid),      MPLS2.LS, REML = FALSE)
> q.out <- lmer(read ~ op2 + (op2[ ,1] | subid), MPLS2.LS, REML = FALSE)
> c.out <- lmer(read ~ op3 + (op3[ ,1] | subid), MPLS2.LS, REML = FALSE)
> ## Model fit.
> print(aictab(list(l.out, q.out, c.out),c("linear", "quadratic", "cubic")),LL = FALSE)

Model selection based on AICc :

          K    AICc  Delta_AICc  AICcWt  Cum.Wt
quadratic 7  1143.25       0.00    0.73    0.73
cubic     8  1145.22       1.97    0.27    1.00
linear    6  1154.87      11.62    0.00    1.00

> ## LRT.
> anova(l.out, q.out, c.out)

Data: MPLS2.LS
Models:
l.out: read ~ op1 + (op1 | subid)
q.out: read ~ op2 + (op2[, 1] | subid)
c.out: read ~ op3 + (op3[, 1] | subid)
      Df    AIC    BIC   logLik   Chisq Chi Df Pr(>Chisq)
l.out  6 1154.3 1172.2  -571.13
q.out  7 1142.4 1163.3  -564.22 13.8268      1  0.0002005 ***
c.out  8 1144.2 1168.0  -564.08  0.2707      1  0.6028941
---
Signif. codes:  0 '***' 0.001 '**' 0.01 '*' 0.05 '.' 0.1 ' ' 1
```

The output indicates the quadratic polynomial has the best fit based on the AICc. Moreover, the weight of evidence is relatively high, indicating a relatively clear distinction between the quadratic model and the other models.

The LRT shows statistical significance for the quadratic model, but not for the cubic model. Therefore, both methods suggest the quadratic model should be selected.

12.4 Alternatives to Polynomials

As discussed in previous chapters, the most common method of dealing with nonlinearity in the behavioral sciences is to fit smooth curves using polynomials of the time predictor. Polynomials have the advantage of being very flexible, as any nonlinear trend in the observed means can be modeled given enough terms.

However, there are particular cases in which polynomials might not be the best choice. For these cases, the researcher may want to consider alternative transformations. The alternatives considered are trigonometric functions, fractional polynomials, and spline transformations.

Trigonometric functions are useful when there are period effects due to such phenomena as seasonal variation, or more generally, when there is "waviness" in the observed change curves. Fractional polynomials provide similar curve shapes as polynomials, but usually require fewer parameters. This can be helpful when parsimony is a high priority. Spline transformations are useful when the study involves landmark time points that are associated with changes in the direction of the trajectory. Additional details of each approach are provided below.

12.5 Trigonometric Functions

When change curves are wavy or show *oscillation*, trigonometric functions are useful to include in the model. The discussion here focuses on sine and cosine functions, whose trends are shown in Figure 12.5. As the figure shows, the sine and cosine functions are periodic in nature. They can be used with lower order polynomials (e.g., linear or quadratic) to account for waves in the observed trajectory. One advantage of trigonometric functions is they can sometimes account for certain nonlinearity with relatively few terms.

As an example of a trajectory that might require trigonometric terms, consider Subject 13 in Figure 12.2. The observed trend for this subject winds its way up with a number of turns. To model such a trend, a linear polynomial with a trigonometric term might be used, the latter being the cosine transformation.

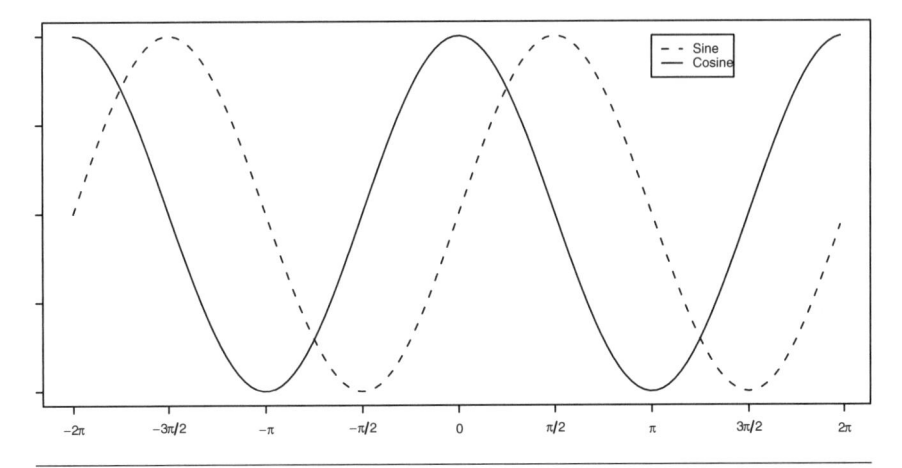

Figure 12.5 Sine function (dashed line) and cosine function (solid line).

Before proceeding, it is important to mention that a researcher needs to think carefully about modeling observed oscillation. If the bends in the curves are considered to be vagaries of sampling, then the inclusion of trigonometric terms might not be justified. In such cases, the scatter about the regression curve would be considered random error, and terms other than polynomials would not be required.

On the other hand, if one believes there are period effects, then it makes sense to include terms of that nature in the model. Periodic terms are preferable to the inclusion of higher order polynomial terms, as the latter may require several predictors to approximate periodic effects. The decision regarding the modeling of oscillation should be based on theory, although fits to the data can also be informative. Often the question of whether oscillation is "real" or not is addressed by using the AICc or LRT.

Trigonometric functions are perhaps best illustrated by considering the multilevel model depiction of LMER (see Chapter 5). The discussion begins with the Level 1 model, and then extensions are made to the Level 2 model. Consider the following Level 1 model with a linear and cosine term:

$$y_{ij} = \beta_{0i}^* + \beta_{1i}^*(\text{c.grade}_{ij}) + \beta_{2i}^*\Big[cos(\text{c.grade}_{ij})\Big] + \varepsilon_{ij}, \quad (12.5.1)$$

where $cos(\cdot)$ is the cosine transformation, and c.grade is a scaled version of grade to be explained in a moment. The sine transformation, $sin(\cdot)$, can be used in place of the cosine transformation in Equation 12.5.1, and the decision between the two is usually based on statistical fit or theoretical considerations.

In Equation 12.5.1, c.grade is used because it is convenient to scale the scores of the time predictor to have certain values. Specifically, it is convenient to have the minimum correspond to the beginning of a single rotation around a circle, and the maximum to correspond to the end of a single rotation. These values correspond to $min = 0°$ and $max = 360°$ or, in radians, $min = 0$ and $max = 2\pi$. Radians are on the horizontal axis of Figure 12.5. The formula for the scaling is

$$\text{c.grade}_{ij} = 2\pi \left\{ \frac{\text{grade}_{ij} - min(\text{grade}_{ij})}{max(\text{grade}_{ij}) - min(\text{grade}_{ij})} \right\}.$$

In the syntax below, c.grade is computed for all the subjects in the data frame. The data frame is printed for the first subject.

```
> MPLS2.LS$c.grade  ←  {2 * pi * (MPLS2.LS$grade - min(MPLS2.LS$grade)) /
+                 max(MPLS2.LS$grade - min(MPLS2.LS$grade))}
> head(data.frame(subid = MPLS2.LS$subid, grade = MPLS2.LS$grade,
+           c.grade = MPLS2.LS$c.grade), n = 7)
```

	subid	grade	c.grade
1	1	2	0.000000
2	1	3	1.047198
3	1	4	2.094395
4	1	5	3.141593
5	1	6	4.188790
6	1	7	5.235988
7	1	8	6.283185

12.5 Trigonometric Functions

As seen in the output, $c.grade_{i1} = 0$, meaning the intercept is anchored at the first time point (Grade 2). The largest value at Grade 8 is $c.grade_{i7} = 2\pi = 6.2832$. Therefore, $c.grade_{ij} \in (0, 2\pi)$.

To gain some insight regarding the linear-cosine model, consider the derivative of Equation 12.5.1. As in previous sections, the symbolic derivative is obtained using expression() and D().

```
> cos  <- expression(B0 + B1 * c.grade + B2 * cos(c.grade))
> dey  <- D(cos, "c.grade")
> dey
```

```
B1 - B2 * sin(c.grade)
```

The output illustrates that the slope of the tangent line is a nonlinear function of c.grade. This means the slope can vary in sign and value as grade increases.

In the following syntax, the model of Equation 12.5.1 is estimated for Subject 13 (i.e., $i = 13$), along with the quadratic polynomial for comparison purposes. A data frame is constructed for the subject, and then lm() is used to estimate the models. Graphs are made with ggplot2, based on the observed and fitted values.

```
> subid13 <- with(MPLS2.LS[MPLS2.LS$subid == 13, ], data.frame(read, grade, c.grade))
> ## Estimate linear-cosine model.
> lm.cos <- lm(read ~ c.grade + I(cos(c.grade)), subid13)
> ## Create data frame for graphing.
> plotdata <- data.frame(read = subid13$read, grade = subid13$grade,
+                       fitted = fitted(lm.cos))
> ## Linear-cosine graph.
> c1 <- ggplot(plotdata, aes(x = grade, y = read)) + geom_point()
> c2 <- c1 + geom_line(aes(y = fitted)) + opts(aspect.ratio = 1)
> ## Quadratic polynomial graph.
> q1 <- ggplot(plotdata, aes(x = grade, y = read)) + geom_point() + opts(aspect.ratio = 1)
> q2 <- q1 + stat_smooth(method = "lm", formula = y ~ poly(x, 2), se = FALSE)
> ## Print to one page.
> grid.newpage()
> pushViewport(viewport(layout = grid.layout(1, 2)))
> vplayout <- function(x, y) viewport(layout.pos.row = x, layout.pos.col = y)
> print(c2, vp = vplayout(1, 1))
> print(q2, vp = vplayout(1, 2))
```

The graphs are shown in Figure 12.6. As the graph on the left shows, the linear-cosine fitted curve is monotonically increasing but wavy. The curve has similar convexity to that of the quadratic polynomial up to Grade 7. However, unlike the quadratic polynomial, the linear-cosine curve continues to increase after Grade 7.

It is preferable to chose between the two models depicted in Figure 12.6 based on theoretical considerations. If there is a substantive reason to believe that the reading scores will continue to increase after Grade 7, then the linear-cosine model is appropriate. Otherwise, the quadratic polynomial is favorable.

In terms of statistical fit, the models can be compared using the AICc. To extend the example a bit, three models are estimated in the syntax below: the

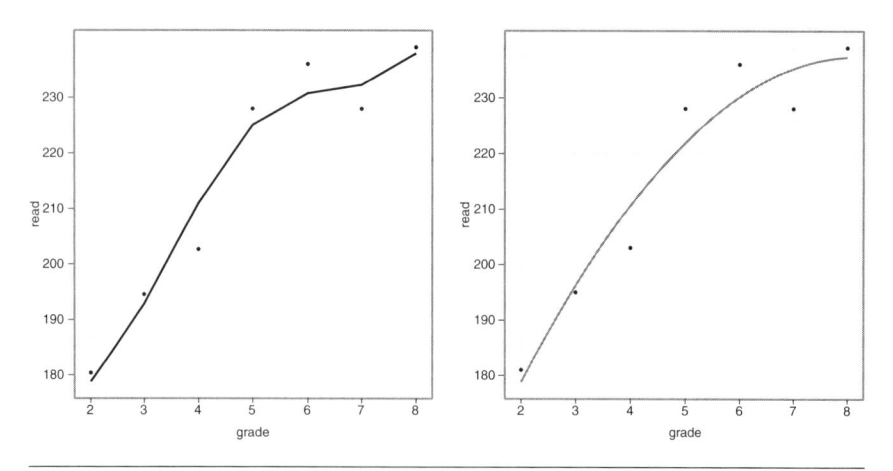

Figure 12.6 Fitted curve of the linear-cosine model (left) and quadratic polynomial (right) to the observed data (points) for Subject 13.

quadratic polynomial, the linear-cosine, and the linear-sine. Note the models are not nested, as they have the same number of fixed effects.

```
> quad   <- lm(read ~ poly(grade, 2), subid13)
> cosine <- lm(read ~ c.grade + I(cos(c.grade)), subid13)
> sine   <- lm(read ~ c.grade + I(sin(c.grade)), subid13)
> print(aictab(list(quad, cosine, sine), c("quad", "cosine", "sine")), LL = FALSE)

Model selection based on AICc :

         K  AICc  Delta_AICc  AICcWt  Cum.Wt
cosine   4  68.26       0.00    0.78    0.78
quad     4  71.03       2.77    0.20    0.98
sine     4  75.62       7.36    0.02    1.00
```

The linear-cosine model is the best-fitting model, followed by the quadratic polynomial. The weight of evidence for the linear-cosine model is relatively high, indicating it is substantially better fitting than the quadratic polynomial. The linear-sine model is substantially worse fitting than the other two.

Now consider a LMER model with a linear polynomial and a cosine term. This is written as

$$y_{ij} = (\beta_0 + b_{0i}) + (\beta_1 + b_{1i})(\text{c.grade}_{ij})$$
$$+ \beta_1\left[cos(\text{c.grade}_{ij})\right] + \varepsilon_{ij}. \quad (12.5.2)$$

Like the higher order polynomial models previously discussed, a random effect is not included for every fixed effect. Rather, a random effect is included only for the polynomial portion of the model, and this need not be exhaustive (but here it is).

In the syntax below, the model of Equation 12.5.2 is estimated using the `MPLS2.LS` data frame. For purposes of comparison, the quadratic

12.5 Trigonometric Functions

polynomial model is also estimated. The AICc and associated indexes are used to compare the models.

```
> quad  <- lmer(read ~ poly(grade,2) + (poly(grade,1) | subid),MPLS2.LS,REML = FALSE)
> lincos <- lmer(read ~ c.grade + I(cos(c.grade)) + (c.grade | subid),
+                MPLS2.LS, REML = FALSE)
> print(aictab(list(quad, lincos), c("Quad", "Linear-Cosine")), LL = FALSE)
```

```
Model selection based on AICc :

                K    AICc  Delta_AICc  AICcWt  Cum.Wt
Quad            7  1143.25        0.0    0.68    0.68
Linear-Cosine   7  1144.75        1.5    0.32    1.00
```

The weight of evidence of the quadratic model is more than twice that of the linear-cosine model. There is evidence that the quadratic model is sufficient for describing group change.

Consider graphs of the fitted values of each model and their correspondence to the observed means. Due to missing values and the use of `poly()`, a "dummy" model is estimated, from which `grade` and `read` are extracted in the `@frame` slot. This makes it much easier to construct the data frame for graphing.

```
> ## Estimate "dummy" model.
> lmer.d <- lmer(read ~ grade + (grade | subid), MPLS2.LS, REML = FALSE)
> ## Create plotting data set.
> plotdata <- data.frame(grade = lmer.d@frame$grade, read = lmer.d@frame$read,
+                q.pred = model.matrix(quad) %*% fixef(quad),
+                c.pred = model.matrix(lincos) %*% fixef(lincos))
> ## ggplot2.
> c1 <- ggplot(plotdata, aes(x = grade, y = read)) + geom_point(colour = "grey60")
> c2 <- c1 + stat_summary(fun.y = mean,geom = "point",size = 3) + opts(aspect.ratio = 1)
> c3 <- c2 + stat_summary(fun.y = mean, geom = "line", lwd = 1.5, aes(y = c.pred))
> c4 <- c3 + opts(title = "linear-cosine")
> ##
> q1 <- ggplot(plotdata, aes(x = grade, y = read)) + geom_point(colour = "grey60")
> q2 <- q1 + stat_summary(fun.y = mean,geom = "point",size = 3) + opts(aspect.ratio = 1)
> q3 <- q2 + stat_summary(fun.y = mean, geom = "line", lwd = 1.5, aes(y = q.pred))
> q4 <- q3 + opts(title = "quadratic")
> ## Print graphs.
> grid.newpage()
> pushViewport(viewport(layout = grid.layout(1, 2)))
> vplayout <- function(x, y) viewport(layout.pos.row = x, layout.pos.col = y)
> print(c4, vp = vplayout(1, 1))
> print(q4, vp = vplayout(1, 2))
```

The graphs are shown in Figure 12.7. The linear-cosine fitted curve is more wavy than the quadratic curve. The linear-cosine curve shows greater distance from the observed means than for the quadratic polynomial, most notably at Grades 2, 3, and 8. In addition, beginning at Grade 7, the linear-cosine curve increases at a faster rate than the polynomial curve, which appears less consistent with the deceleration of the observed means.

Models more complex than the linear-cosine may be constructed by adding additional polynomial terms and/or the sine function. Eubank and Speckman (1990) present a general form of a regression model that can be used as the basis for including additional terms. Two examples are provided.

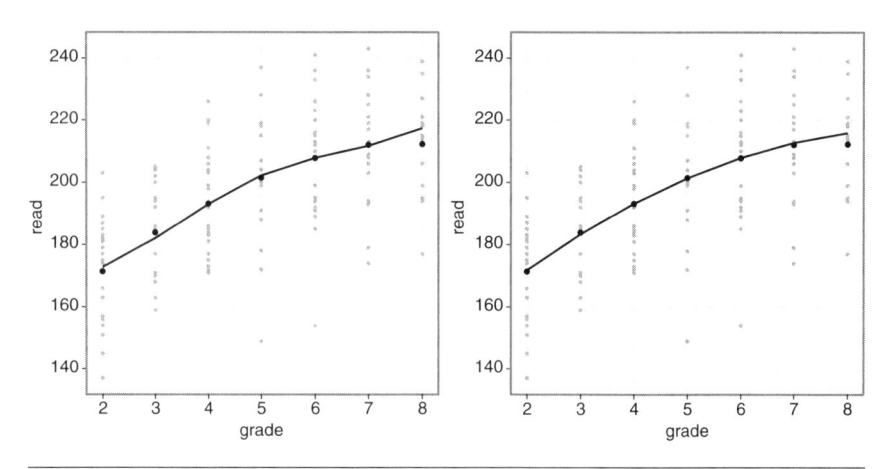

Figure 12.7 Fitted curves for the linear-cosine model (left) and quadratic polynomial (right).

Additional polynomial terms can affect the global behavior of the curve. For instance, a quadratic polynomial along with the cosine term can produce a curve with global concavity or convexity that also has local oscillation. This model is the following:

$$y_{ij} = (\beta_0 + b_{0i}) + (\beta_1 + b_{1i})(\texttt{c.grade}_{ij}) + \beta_2(\texttt{c.grade}_{ij}^2) \\ + \beta_3\Big[cos(\texttt{c.grade}_{ij})\Big] + \varepsilon_{ij}. \quad (12.5.3)$$

The model might be appropriate for Subject 1 in Figure 12.2. This subject's trend appears to have a global convexity relative to the time axis, with oscillation for Grades 3 through 8.

Finally, when the amount of short-term oscillation is relatively large, the sine and cosine terms can be used together. Consider a model with a linear polynomial and the two trigonometric terms:

$$y_{ij} = (\beta_0 + b_{0i}) + (\beta_1 + b_{1i})(\texttt{c.grade}_{ij}) + \beta_2\Big[cos(\texttt{c.grade}_{ij})\Big] \\ + \beta_3\Big[sin(\texttt{c.grade}_{ij})\Big] + \varepsilon_{ij}. \quad (12.5.4)$$

The model is useful when there is a global tendency to increase or decrease, and the oscillation is particularly strong.

12.6 Fractional Polynomials

To expand the repertoire of methods, consider another class of transformations known as *fractional polynomials* (FPs; Royston & Altman, 1994; Royston & Sauerbrei, 2008). FPs are similar to the raw polynomials previously

12.6 Fractional Polynomials

discussed, in that, transformations of the time metric are used to account for nonlinear change. However, the FP power terms need not be the counting numbers, 1, 2, 3, ... This means other types of transformations are considered, such as the square root of time, the log of time, and so on. The counting numbers are among the possible power transformations, so raw polynomials are special cases of FPs.

FPs are useful because they provide additional curve shapes and often provide similar fit as polynomials but with fewer terms. This is advantageous when the number of time points is limited and theory suggests nonlinear trends. For example, if there are three time points, the quadratic polynomial will produce a perfect-fitting change curve, as the number of fixed effects is equal to the number of time points. Such saturated models should be avoided, as they are unrealistic. They do not allow individual random error, as there is no scatter of points about an individual regression line. As discussed below, the first-order FP model is not saturated with three time points. Therefore, it can be used to model monotonic but nonlinear trends. For an applied example, see Zeller, Modi, Noll, Long, and Inge (2009).

FPs are also useful when a curve appears to plateau, meaning the rate of change becomes 0 or nearly so. Although FPs, like polynomials, do not have asymptotes, the former tend to be able to better approximate them. In addition, FPs can also have less extreme behavior at the edges of the observed time span, making them more attractive for extrapolation (extrapolation should always be used with caution; see Donnelly, Laird, and Ware (1995)).

The discussion will be limited to first-order and second-order FPs, as these will probably suffice for a majority of situations in the behavioral sciences. Higher order FPs are constructed based on the general formulas presented in the optional Section 12.8.2. The term *order* is used in a general sense with FPs. It refers to the number of time transformations in the model. This does not count the intercept, which is always included in the model. The first-order FP has one time transformation, and the second-order FP has two time transformations.

12.6.1 FIRST-ORDER FRACTIONAL POLYNOMIALS

The first-order FP model consists of monotonic change curves, with the linear curve being a special case. *Monotonic* refers to curves that are constantly increasing or decreasing, but not necessarily at a constant rate (i.e., not necessarily linear). First-order FP models have a single time transformation, which is either a power transformation, or the natural log transformation. Suppose the power value (or exponent) is denoted by a. Then the first-order FP for LMER is defined as

$$y_{ij} = (\beta_0 + b_{0i}) + (\beta_1 + b_{1i})(\texttt{grade}_{ij}^a) + \varepsilon_{ij}. \qquad (12.6.1)$$

The same transformation is used in the fixed and random effects portions of the model. A simplification is to drop the random slope term, yielding the random intercepts model. But this should be determined by the data or theoretical considerations.

The power value, a, is limited to one of the elements in the set:

$$\Gamma = (-3, -2, -1, -0.5, 0, 0.5, 1, 2, 3), \qquad (12.6.2)$$

where 0 indicates the natural log transformation. The elements in Γ constitute the main values of Tukey's *ladder of reexpressions*, used for general curve-fitting problems (Mosteller & Tukey, 1977, chap. 4). Table 12.2 shows the transformation represented by each value in Γ, along with its verbal description.

To ensure the FPs are defined, there is a requirement that the minimum score of the time predictor be greater than 0. If this is not the case, then the researcher must add a constant to the time variable prior to constructing and examining the FP models. Additional details are presented below.

Table 12.2 First-order fractional polynomials.

Transformation	Description
$\frac{1}{\text{grade}_{ij}^3}$	Inverse cube
$\frac{1}{\text{grade}_{ij}^2}$	Inverse square
$\frac{1}{\text{grade}_{ij}}$	Inverse
$\frac{1}{\sqrt{\text{grade}_{ij}}}$	Inverse square root
$log(\text{grade}_{ij})$	Log
$\sqrt{\text{grade}_{ij}}$	Square root
grade_{ij}	Linear (no transformation)
grade_{ij}^2	Square
grade_{ij}^3	Cube

Figure 12.8 shows examples of first-order FP curves. Figure 12.8a shows curves for $\beta_1 < 0$ and Figure 12.8b shows curves for $\beta_1 > 0$. As shown in the figure, first-order FPs are monotonic. The curves in Figure 12.8 are continually increasing over time, but each curve has a decreasing mirror image created when the sign of β_1 is reversed.

12.6.1.1 FIXED EFFECTS INTERPRETATION

The intercept term, β_0, in Equation 12.6.1 has the same interpretation as in the polynomial model. Namely, it is the predicted mean value when the time score is 0. An important feature of FPs is that different transformations (controlled by a) result in the anchoring of the intercept at different time points. To see this, suppose a subject's grade values are $1, 2, 3, 4$. If $a = 0$, then $log(\text{grade}_{i1}) = log(1) = 0$, and β_0 is anchored at the first time point.

12.6 Fractional Polynomials

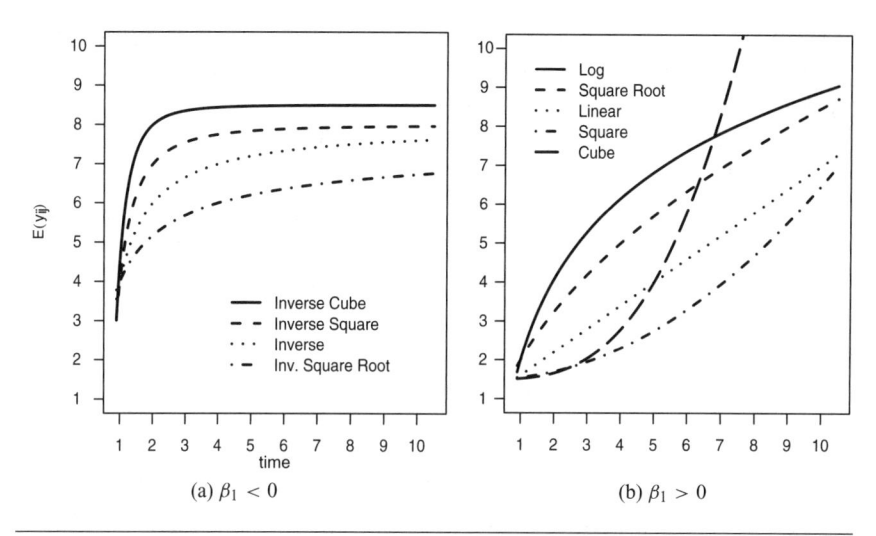

Figure 12.8 First-order fractional polynomial curves.

However, if $a = 0.5$, then $\sqrt{\text{grade}_{i1}} = \sqrt{1} = 1$, and β_0 is anchored at the unobserved time point previous to the first.

The main point is that the intercept is not consistently anchored for the various FPs. Thus, the values of β_0 and $Var(b_{0i})$ are not consistent among FP models. A researcher must be cognizant of this, if inferences regarding the intercept are to be made.

Although similar in form to the linear polynomial model, the β_1 parameter of Equation 12.6.1 is not the linear slope, except when $a = 1$. To see this, consider the symbolic derivative for the models with $a = 1, -1, 0$.

```
> D(expression(B0 + B1 * grade), "grade")
```
```
B1
```

```
> D(expression(B0 + B1 * grade ^ -1), "grade")
```
```
-(B1 * grade^-(1 + 1))
```

```
> D(expression(B0 + B1 * log(grade)), "grade")
```
```
B1 * (1/grade)
```

The output indicates that the derivatives for the linear, inverse, and log model are, respectively, β_1, $\frac{-\beta_1}{\text{grade}_{ij}^2}$, and $\frac{\beta_1}{\text{grade}_{ij}}$. For the linear model, the tangent line is identical to the regression line. The derivative for the linear model is β_1 and does not include grade. Thus, the slope of the tangent line is constant for all grades.

For the other two transformations, the derivative is a function of grade. This means the slope of the tangent is not constant over time, and the trend lines for the original functions are nonlinear.

Rather than attempt to interpret β_1 directly when $a \neq 1$, it is perhaps more useful to discuss the slope of the tangent. As an illustration, consider the derivative for the log model. When $\beta_1 > 0$, the curve is monotonically increasing, but the slope of the tangent decreases as grade increases. When $\beta_1 < 0$, the curve is monotonically decreasing, but the slope of the tangent increases as grade increases.

12.6.1.2 SELECTION OF FPS

With the possibility of nine first-order FPs, the question of which one to use naturally arises. A particular transformation might be chosen based on past research, because its curve appears appropriate for the data at hand, or because it is considered a good general-purpose tool. Selection of a transformation can also be data driven.

Data-driven selection proceeds by fitting all nine models, identifying the best-fitting model, and determining if it has substantially better fit than the linear model. If no nonlinear model has substantially better fit than the linear model, then the simpler linear model is selected. The best-fitting first-order FP might also be compared to the quadratic polynomial. The reason is that the quadratic model can account for monotonic change over the observed time period, much like a first-order FP.

Consider the fit of the nine FP models to the data, along with the fit of the quadratic polynomial. The AICc and associated criteria are used. Note that the FP models are not nested, so the LRT cannot be used for general model comparison.

```
> ## Quadratic Model.
> quad  <-   lmer(read ~ poly(grade, 2, raw = TRUE) + (grade | subid),
+                MPLS2.LS, REML = FALSE)
> ## 1st Order FP models.
> n3   <- lmer(read ~ I(grade ^  -3)  + (I(grade ^  -3) | subid),MPLS2.LS,REML = FALSE)
> n2   <- lmer(read ~ I(grade ^  -2)  + (I(grade ^  -2) | subid),MPLS2.LS,REML = FALSE)
> n1   <- lmer(read ~ I(grade ^  -1)  + (I(grade ^  -1) | subid),MPLS2.LS,REML = FALSE)
> n05  <- lmer(read ~ I(grade ^ -.5)  + (I(grade ^ -.5) | subid),MPLS2.LS,REML = FALSE)
> ze   <- lmer(read ~ I(log(grade))   + (I(log(grade))  | subid),MPLS2.LS,REML = FALSE)
> p05  <- lmer(read ~ I(grade ^  .5)  + (I(grade ^  .5) | subid),MPLS2.LS,REML = FALSE)
> p1   <- lmer(read ~ grade           + (grade          | subid),MPLS2.LS,REML = FALSE)
> p2   <- lmer(read ~ I(grade ^   2)  + (I(grade ^   2) | subid),MPLS2.LS,REML = FALSE)
> p3   <- lmer(read ~ I(grade ^   3)  + (I(grade ^   3) | subid),MPLS2.LS,REML = FALSE)
> ## Fit.
> mymods   <- list(n3, n2, n1, n05, ze, p05, p1, p2, p3, quad)
> mynames  <- c("-3", "-2", "-1", "-.5", "0", ".5", "1", "2", "3", "Quad")
> print(aictab(mymods, mynames), LL = FALSE)
```

```
Model selection based on AICc :

        K     AICc   Delta_AICc   AICcWt   Cum.Wt
0       6   1138.88        0.00     0.76     0.76
.5      6   1143.04        4.16     0.09     0.85
```

12.6 Fractional Polynomials

```
Quad  7  1143.25         4.37     0.09    0.94
-.5   6  1143.85         4.97     0.06    1.00
1     6  1154.87        15.99     0.00    1.00
-1    6  1155.69        16.81     0.00    1.00
-2    6  1184.87        45.99     0.00    1.00
2     6  1186.93        48.06     0.00    1.00
-3    6  1208.05        69.17     0.00    1.00
3     6  1215.00        76.12     0.00    1.00
```

The output indicates the best-fitting model has the natural log transformation ($a = 0$), with a weight of evidence equal to 0.76. The weight of the linear model ($a = 1$) is negligible, and the weight of the quadratic model is relatively low (0.09).

For additional insight, consider plots of the fitted curves for the log model and quadratic model, along with the observed means.

```
> ## Graph data.
> graphdata <- data.frame(read = p1@frame$read, grade = p1@frame$grade,
+                         ze.pred = model.matrix(ze) %*% fixef(ze),
+                         quad.pred = model.matrix(quad) %*% fixef(quad))
> ## ggplot().
> l1 <- ggplot(graphdata, aes(x = grade, y = read)) + geom_point(colour = "grey80")
> l2 <- l1 + geom_line(aes(y = ze.pred), size = 1.5)
> l3 <- l2 + stat_summary(aes(y = read), fun.y = mean, geom = "point", size = 4)
> l4 <- l3 + opts(aspect.ratio = 1)
> ##
> q1 <- ggplot(graphdata, aes(x = grade, y = read)) + geom_point(colour="grey80")
> q2 <- q1 + geom_line(aes(y = quad.pred), size=1.5)
> q3 <- q2 + stat_summary(aes(y = read), fun.y = mean, geom = "point", size = 4)
> q4 <- q3 + opts(aspect.ratio = 1)
> ## Print graphs.
> grid.newpage()
> pushViewport(viewport(layout = grid.layout(1, 2)))
> vplayout <- function(x, y) viewport(layout.pos.row = x, layout.pos.col = y)
> print(l4, vp = vplayout(1, 1))
> print(q4, vp = vplayout(1, 2))
```

A graph of the fitted curves is shown in Figure 12.9. The curves are similar, but the one based on the log transformation overestimates the observed mean at the last time point a bit more than the quadratic curve. Since the overfit of the log model is slight, and it has one less parameter than the quadratic model, a case could be made for selecting the log model.

12.6.2 SECOND-ORDER FRACTIONAL POLYNOMIALS

First-order FPs are helpful when the researcher wants to fit monotonic curves. For more complex patterns, higher order FPs are used. The next most complex FP model considered is the second-order model. Second-order FPs are similar to the quadratic polynomial in that their curves all have a single extreme point. This means they are either concave or convex with respect to the time axis. Unlike the quadratic polynomial, second-order FPs are asymmetric about their extreme point. For this reason, second-order FPs are more flexible while having the same number of fixed effects as the quadratic polynomial.

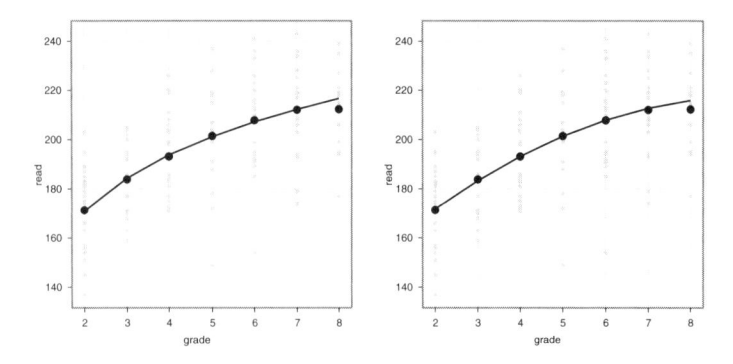

Figure 12.9 Fitted curve for the log transformation (left) and quadratic polynomial (right).

Second-order FPs have two power terms, a and b. The constraint is imposed that $a \leq b$. The form of the model depends on whether $a < b$ or $a = b$. When $a < b$, the second-order model is

$$y_{ij} = (\beta_0 + b_{0i}) + (\beta_1 + b_{1i})(\text{grade}_{ij}^a) + \beta_2(\text{grade}_{ij}^b) + \varepsilon_{ij}. \quad (12.6.3)$$

The values of a and b are chosen from Γ in Equation 12.6.2. Two random effects appear in Equation 12.6.3, but a different number might also be considered.

When $a = b$, the second-order model is

$$\begin{aligned} y_{ij} &= (\beta_0 + b_{0i}) + (\beta_1 + b_{1i})(\text{grade}_{ij}^a) \\ &\quad + \beta_2(\text{grade}_{ij}^a)\left[log(\text{grade}_{ij})\right] + \varepsilon_{ij}. \end{aligned} \quad (12.6.4)$$

Based on set Γ, 36 second-order models are possible. The quadratic polynomial is the special case of $a = 1$, $b = 2$. Curve shapes for a number of second-order FPs are shown in Figure 12.10, with the values of a and b listed. As the figure shows, the quadratic polynomial is symmetric about its extreme value, whereas the other second-order FPs are not. The extent of asymmetry varies based on the combination of transformations, and the values of the fixed effects.

Similar to first-order FPs, a particular second-order FP might be chosen because its curve shape is appropriate for the data at hand. Another possibility is to routinely fit both the quadratic and the general-purpose log-log square curve ($a = 0$, $b = 0$), and compare their fits as a check on symmetry. A fully data-driven analysis involves the fitting and evaluation of all 36 possible models. A researcher might have discomfort in fitting 36 (or more) models to the same data set, but the level of discomfort depends on one's statistical strategy. All models need not be examined, and if the AICc is used, there are no multiple testing issues (see Chapters 7 and 8).

12.6 Fractional Polynomials

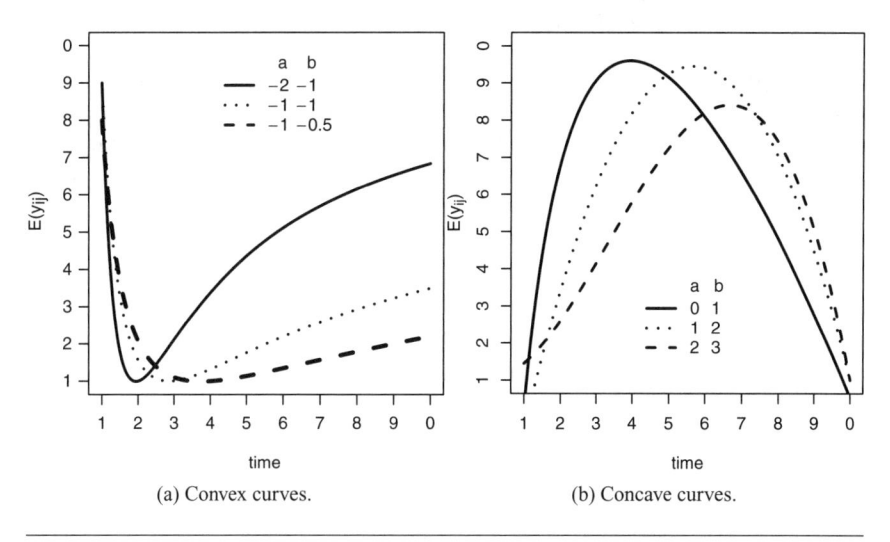

Figure 12.10 Second-order fractional polynomial curves.

For simplicity of illustration, the fits of three FP models are considered, with the models having power values of $(a, b) = (-2, -1), (0, 0), (1, 2)$. These models are the inverse quadratic, the log-log square, and the quadratic polynomial, respectively. Each model fit below has two random effects, consisting of random intercepts and random slopes, which are based on the first type of FP transformation (i.e., based on a). For comparison purposes, the first-order log model from the last section is also included.

```
> n2n1 <- lmer(read ~ I(grade ^ -2) + I(grade ^ -1) + (I(grade ^ -2) | subid),
+              MPLS2.LS, REML = FALSE)
> zeze <- lmer(read ~ I(log(grade)) + I(log(grade) ^ 2) + (I(log(grade)) | subid),
+              MPLS2.LS, REML = FALSE)
> mymods <- list(ze, n2n1, zeze, quad)
> mynames <- c("( 0,    )", "(-2, -1)", "( 0,  0)", "( 1,  2)")
> print(aictab(mymods, mynames), LL = FALSE)
```

```
Model selection based on AICc :

          K     AICc  Delta_AICc  AICcWt  Cum.Wt
( 0,   )  6  1138.88        0.00    0.65    0.65
( 0,  0)  7  1141.05        2.17    0.22    0.87
( 1,  2)  7  1143.25        4.37    0.07    0.95
(-2, -1)  7  1143.90        5.02    0.05    1.00
```

The output indicates the first-order log model ($a = 0$) has the best fit, and the second-order log-log model ($a = 0, b = 0$) has the second best fit. The weight of evidence of the first-order log model is relatively large. In this situation, it appears that none of the second-order models is an improvement over the best first-order FP model.

12.6.3 STATIC PREDICTORS

Static predictors can be included in models with FPs. The method of inclusion is the same as with conventional polynomials. Static predictors are included alone for intercept effects, and as multipliers of the FPs for trajectory effects. As an example, consider the following multilevel model depiction, with a first-order FP and the risk static predictor.

$$y_{ij} = \beta_{0i}^* + \beta_{2i}^*\left[log(\text{grade}_{ij})\right] + \varepsilon_{ij},$$
$$\beta_{0i}^* = \beta_0 + \beta_2(\text{risk2ADV}_i) + b_{0i},$$
$$\beta_{1i}^* = \beta_1 + \beta_3(\text{risk2ADV}_i) + b_{1i}.$$

Recall that risk2ADV is a dummy predictor with ADV = 1 and DADV = 0. By substitution, the LMER model is obtained:

$$y_{ij} = (\beta_0 + b_{0i}) + (\beta_1 + b_{1i})\left[log(\text{grade}_{ij})\right] + \beta_2(\text{risk2ADV}_i) \quad (12.6.5)$$
$$+ \beta_3\left[log(\text{grade}_{ij})\right](\text{risk2ADV}_i) + \varepsilon_{ij}.$$

Interpretations of the parameters are similar to polynomial models, with β_2 representing intercept differences, and β_3 representing differences in trajectory. The caveat here is that when $a = 1$, the change curve is not linear. Furthermore, when $\beta_3 = 0$, the change curves of the groups are not parallel, differing in their nonlinear monotonic patterns.

Consider estimation of the model of Equation 12.6.5. The quadratic polynomial version is also estimated for comparison purposes. Relative fit is evaluated using the AICc.

```
> quadrisk  <- lmer(read ~ poly(grade, 2) * risk2 + (poly(grade, 1) | subid),
+             MPLS2.LS, REML = FALSE)
> logrisk   <- lmer(read ~ I(log(grade)) * risk2 + (I(log(grade)) | subid),
+             MPLS2.LS, REML = FALSE)
> print(aictab(list(quadrisk, logrisk), c("Quad", "Log")), LL = FALSE)

      Model selection based on AICc :

             K    AICc   Delta_AICc  AICcWt  Cum.Wt
      Log    8   1101.45      0.00     0.98    0.98
      Quad  10   1108.91      7.45     0.02    1.00
```

The output shows the weight of evidence for the log model is very large (0.98). Based on this result, a case can be made for adopting the log model rather than the quadratic model.

To provide visual information about the two models, the fitted curves are graphed, along with the observed means and individual data points.

```
> plotdata <- data.frame(read = logrisk@frame$read, grade = exp(logrisk@frame[ ,2]),
+                        risk2 = logrisk@frame$risk2,
+                        q.pred = model.matrix(quadrisk) %*% fixef(quadrisk),
+                        l.pred = model.matrix(logrisk) %*% fixef(logrisk))
> ##
> 11 <- ggplot(plotdata, aes(x = grade, y = read)) + geom_point(color = "grey80")
> 12 <- 11 + stat_summary(fun.y = mean, geom = "point", size = 4)
> 13 <- 12 + geom_line(aes(y = l.pred), lwd = 1.5) + facet_grid(. ~ risk2)
> 14 <- 13 + opts(aspect.ratio = 1, title = "Log")
> ##
> q1 <- ggplot(plotdata, aes(x = grade, y = read)) + geom_point(color = "grey80")
> q2 <- q1 + stat_summary(fun.y = mean, geom = "point", size = 4)
> q3 <- q2 + geom_line(aes(y = q.pred), lwd = 1.5) + facet_grid(. ~ risk2)
> q4 <- q3 + opts(aspect.ratio = 1, title = "Quadratic")
> ##
> grid.newpage()
> pushViewport(viewport(layout = grid.layout(2, 1)))
> vplayout <- function(x, y) viewport(layout.pos.row = x, layout.pos.col = y)
> print(14, vp = vplayout(1, 1))
> print(q4, vp = vplayout(2, 1))
```

The graphs are shown in Figure 12.11. The log transformation provides fitted curves similar to the quadratic polynomial, especially for the disadvantaged group. Similar to the unconditional case of Figure 12.9, the log curve overestimates the observed mean at the last time point for the advantaged group, as compared to the quadratic polynomial.

12.6.4 CAVEATS REGARDING THE USE OF FRACTIONAL POLYNOMIALS

There are some caveats concerning the use of FPs relative to conventional polynomials (i.e., raw polynomials). The two issues on which we focus involve the effects of applying a linear transformation prior to considering FPs. An example of such a transformation is adding a constant to each subject's grade score before computing the log transformation.

From the perspective of conventional polynomial modeling, FP models are not well formulated (Peixoto, 1987). This means that lower order polynomials may be "hidden" in FPs, and can make the interpretation of the fixed effects difficult.

Consider the expected value square model, $a = 2$, when the initial time metric is altered by adding a constant, c.

$$\begin{aligned} E(y_{ij}) &= \beta_0 + \beta_1(\text{grade}_{ij} + c)^2 \\ &= (\beta_0 + c^2\beta_1) + 2c\beta_1(\text{grade}_{ij}) + \beta_1(\text{grade}_{ij}^2). \end{aligned}$$

The last equation shows that a linear polynomial is embedded in the FP model, and thus, the model has the form of a quadratic polynomial. However, the quadratic polynomial is strange because β_1 acts as both the linear coefficient and the quadratic coefficient.

The double duty of β_1 is not a problem from a purely curve-fitting perspective, as a monotonic curve is defined. But the fact that β_1 serves two purposes might appear strange to some researchers. This is especially so in light of

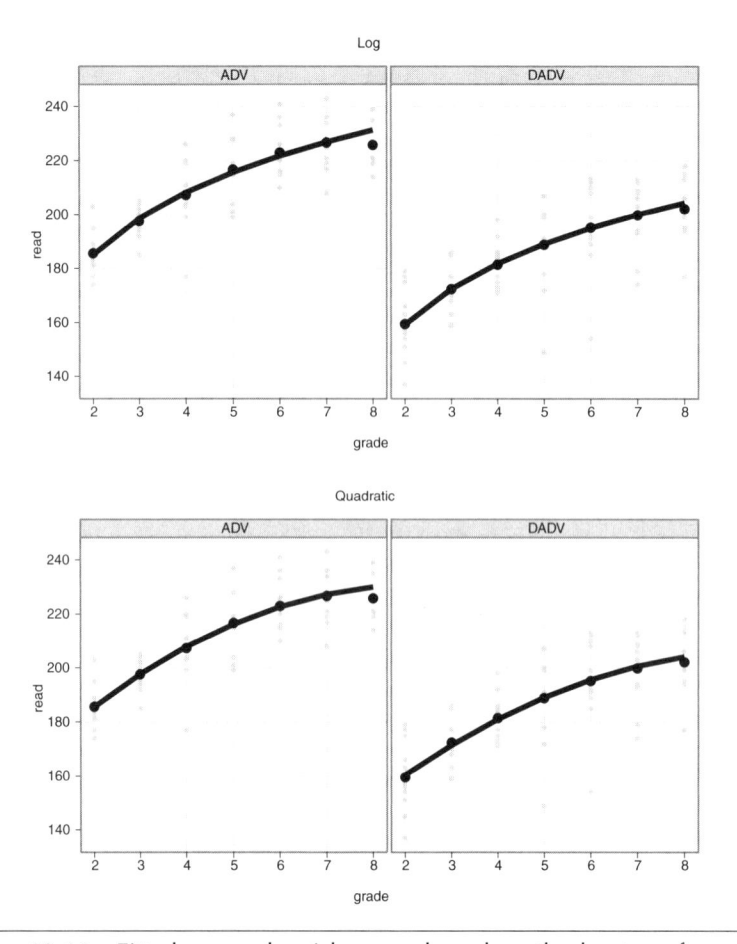

Figure 12.11 Fitted curves by risk group based on the log transformation (upper) and quadratic polynomial (lower).

the fact that the conventional quadratic polynomial has unique coefficients for each power term under the same type of initial time transformation. Consider the following:

$$E(y_{ij}) = \beta_0 + \beta_1(\text{grade}_{ij} + c) + \beta_2(\text{grade}_{ij} + c)^2$$
$$= \left[\beta_0 + c\beta_1 + c^2\beta_2\right] + \left[\beta_1 + 2c\beta_2\right](\text{grade}_{ij}) + \beta_2(\text{grade}_{ij}^2).$$

The last equation indicates that the linear and quadratic terms have unique coefficients. Although β_2 appears in the linear coefficient term, so does β_1, meaning the linear and quadratic coefficients do not simply differ by a constant. Harking back to an earlier theme, the last equation illustrates why only the highest order polynomial term is unaffected by the linear transformation. As the equation shows, c appears in both the intercept term and the linear term but not the quadratic term. Since c can be any value, the intercept and the linear term can also be any value.

12.6 Fractional Polynomials

Perhaps more important than the interpretation issue is the fact that the FP model fit changes under linear transformations of the original time metric. This does not occur with the conventional polynomial model. As an illustration, consider again the analysis using first-order FPs. Suppose grade1 = grade − 1 is computed *before any of the models are fit*. The syntax below fits the quadratic polynomial and the nine first-order FPs using the scaled variable.

```
> grade1 <- MPLS2.LS$grade-1
> cquad <- lmer(read ~ poly(grade1, 2, raw=T) + (grade1 | subid),
+               data = MPLS2.LS, REML = FALSE)
> cn3  <- lmer(read ~ I(grade1 ^ -3)   + (I(grade1 ^ -3)   | subid), MPLS2.LS, REML = FALSE)
> cn2  <- lmer(read ~ I(grade1 ^ -2)   + (I(grade1 ^ -2)   | subid), MPLS2.LS, REML = FALSE)
> cn1  <- lmer(read ~ I(grade1 ^ -1)   + (I(grade1 ^ -1)   | subid), MPLS2.LS, REML = FALSE)
> cn05 <- lmer(read ~ I(grade1 ^ -.5)  + (I(grade1 ^ -.5)  | subid), MPLS2.LS, REML = FALSE)
> cze  <- lmer(read ~ I(log(grade1))   + (I(log(grade1))   | subid), MPLS2.LS, REML = FALSE)
> cp05 <- lmer(read ~ I(grade1 ^ .5)   + (I(grade1 ^ .5)   | subid), MPLS2.LS, REML = FALSE)
> cp1  <- lmer(read ~ grade1           + (grade1           | subid), MPLS2.LS, REML = FALSE)
> cp2  <- lmer(read ~ I(grade1 ^ 2)    + (I(grade1 ^ 2)    | subid), MPLS2.LS, REML = FALSE)
> cp3  <- lmer(read ~ I(grade1 ^ 3)    + (I(grade1 ^ 3)    | subid), MPLS2.LS, REML = FALSE)
> mymods <- list(cn3, cn2, cn1, cn05, cze, cp05, cp1, cp2, cp3, cquad)
> mynames <- c("-3", "-2", "-1", "-.5", "0", "0.5", "1", "2", "3", "quad")
> print(aictab(mymods, mynames), LL = FALSE)
```

```
Model selection based on AICc :

       K    AICc  Delta_AICc  AICcWt  Cum.Wt
0.5    6  1140.70       0.00    0.59    0.59
0      6  1142.44       1.74    0.25    0.83
quad   7  1143.25       2.55    0.16    1.00
1      6  1154.87      14.16    0.00    1.00
-.5    6  1159.62      18.92    0.00    1.00
-1     6  1181.90      41.20    0.00    1.00
2      6  1195.78      55.07    0.00    1.00
-2     6  1216.05      75.35    0.00    1.00
3      6  1226.00      85.30    0.00    1.00
-3     6  1233.43      92.73    0.00    1.00
```

The output reveals that the best-fitting model is now the square root model, with $a = 0.5$ and $\sqrt{\text{grade}_{ij}}$. The quadratic polynomial is still the third best-fitting model. If a different constant is subtracted out, say 1.5, then the fits of all the FP models will again change.

The changes illustrated above must be carefully considered if the analysis will involve different initial alterations of the time metric. The key word here is *initial*, as the crucial issue is altering the time metric before any of the FPs are considered. The most common reason for such alterations is to anchor the intercept at a particular time point of interest. In contrast to analysis with polynomials, transforming to anchor the intercept is not recommended in FP analysis. As previously mentioned, the intercept is not consistently anchored among FPs for a fixed time metric.

It is assumed that in most situations, FP models will be fit to the natural time metric without alteration. However, if the natural time metric involves 0 and/or negative values, then a shift in origin prior to fitting FP models is essential so that the transformations are defined. Suppose that $time_{ij}$ stands for an arbitrary time variable that has as its smallest value $min(time_{ij})$. Following Royston and Altman (1997), a useful transformation is to add a constant, c, that is the smallest positive increment in successive values of the original time metric. For example, if $time_{ij} = 0, 1, 2, 2.5, 3.5$, the smallest successive increment is $2.5 - 2.0 = 0.5$, and the change in origin is $time_{ij} + 0.5$.

If $min(time_{ij}) < 0$, then the change of origin is $time_{ij} + (c - min(time_{ij}))$. For example, if $time_{ij} = -1, 0, 1, 2, 3$, then $min(time_{ij}) = -1$, $c = 1$, and the change in origin is $time_{ij} + 1 - (-1) = time_{ij} + 2$. It is also possible to standardize the time metric to the interval $(\delta, 1)$, where δ is some small value such as 0.2 (Royston & Sauerbrei, 2007). Such standardization is desirable when results based on two different ranges of time will be compared.

If the lack of invariance under change of origin needs to be defended, then consider the following. Although the fits of FP models change when the origin is altered, their fits relative to polynomial models may change little, or not at all. In the example above, when `grade1` was used, the best-fitting FP model had approximately the same superior fit to the quadratic polynomial for the original and altered initial time metric, `grade`. Thus, one may view the *class* of FP models as having favorable properties relative to polynomials, rather than any one FP model having such properties (Long & Ryoo, 2010).

12.7 Spline Models

The preceding sections focused on global models whose time transformations, fixed effects, and random effects apply to the entire observed time span. Local models are useful for situations in which the researcher wants to have different curve equations for different spans of time. For example, one might want a particular model for the span of time prior to administering a treatment, and a different model after the treatment commences. In such situations, the local behavior of the curve varies based on the span of time.

Local fit methods were previously encountered in the form of smoothers, used in the `stat_smooth()` component of `ggplot2` (see Chapter 4). A disadvantage of smoothers is they do not produce a readily interpretable change curve equation. In addition, they provide only indirect user control in the form of the smoothing parameter. These drawbacks can be largely avoided by using spline transformations.

The spline transformations considered in this chapter are piecewise polynomials, also known as *regression splines*. The idea behind regression splines is to break up the observed time span into two or more pieces and fit

12.7 Spline Models

a different polynomial model to each piece. This is most easily accomplished by constructing spline transformations in the data frame, and then including them as additional predictors in lmer(). The transformations are chosen so that the fitted curve is smooth and continuous.

Regression splines are an alternative to polynomials, trigonometric functions, and FPs. Regression splines can have better fits to the data than the aforementioned curves, but the demand on the user is usually greater. In most applications in the behavioral sciences, the user specifies the knots, which are the landmark time points used to define the pieces. Regression splines are perhaps most natural when the research design dictates the landmark time point(s), as in the pretreatment/posttreatment example mentioned above. However, knots can be specified in an exploratory manner based on plots of the means or smoothed curves.

Focus is on regression splines that use low-order polynomials—that is, linear or quadratic models for the pieces. The presentation begins with unconditional models not having static predictors. Static predictor models are considered in a later section.

12.7.1 LINEAR SPLINE MODELS

Linear spline models fit a different straight line for each time span defined by the researcher. The simplest linear spline breaks the time span into two pieces, defined by the split point of a single knot. The knot is constant among the subjects and is denoted as κ. In the context of LMER, the linear spline with a single knot is

$$y_{ij} = (\beta_0 + b_{0i}) + (\beta_1 + b_{1i})(\text{grade}_{ij}) + \beta_2(\text{grade}_{ij} - \kappa)_+ + \varepsilon_{ij}, \quad (12.7.1)$$

where the spline transformation is

$$(\text{grade}_{ij} - \kappa)_+ = \begin{cases} 0 & \text{if } \text{grade}_{ij} \leq \kappa, \\ \text{grade}_{ij} - \kappa & \text{if } \text{grade}_{ij} > \kappa. \end{cases}$$

In Equation 12.7.1, β_2 is the regression coefficient for the spline term. If $\beta_2 \neq 0$, then the slope over the interval for which $\text{grade}_{ij} > \kappa$ is different from the slope over the interval for which $\text{grade}_{ij} \leq \kappa$.

Equation 12.7.1 has two random effects, but a different number might be considered. If the variability is expected to be very different for the pieces, a third random effect term may be added. A practical reason for omitting the third random effect is that it is usually highly correlated with the second random effect, and this can lead to estimation problems. The high correlation results from the spline transformation being a linear transformation of the original time variable over the span defined by $\text{grade}_{ij} > \kappa$. Furthermore, omitting the third random effect allows one to unambiguously compare the spline model with the simpler linear model. In the analysis examples below, two random effects are included in the models.

An example will help to clarify the concepts. Suppose the researcher locates the knot at Grade 6, based on a visual inspection of the last panel of Figure 12.1. It is best to select the knot based on theory, as visual inspection can be biased by subjectivity, and thus, may not hold up under replication. Nevertheless, $\kappa = 6$ is selected to illustrate the ideas. In this case, the linear spline model is

$$y_{ij} = (\beta_0 + b_{0i}) + (\beta_1 + b_{1i})(\text{grade}_{ij}) + \beta_2(\text{grade}_{ij} - 6)_+ + \varepsilon_{ij}. \quad (12.7.2)$$

Based on Equation 12.7.2, the regression formula at each time interval is the following:

$$y_{ij} = \begin{cases} (\beta_0 + b_{0i}) \\ \quad + (\beta_1 + b_{1i})(\text{grade}_{ij}) + \varepsilon_{ij} & \text{if grade}_{ij} \leq 6, \\ (\beta_0 - 6\beta_2 + b_{0i} - 6b_{2i}) \\ \quad + (\beta_1 + b_{1i} + \beta_2)(\text{grade}_{ij}) + \varepsilon_{ij} & \text{if grade}_{ij} > 6. \end{cases} \quad (12.7.3)$$

Equation 12.7.3 indicates that when $\beta_2 \neq 0$, the slope over the interval 2, 6 will be different from the slope over the interval (6, 8). If $\beta_2 = 0$, then the lower order β terms are sufficient, and the spline is not needed. Thus, an evaluation of the estimate of β_2 is usually of prime interest.

As an example analysis, the model of Equation 12.7.2 is estimated with the MPLS data. Linear splines can be specified directly in lmer() by providing the spline transformation formula within the insulate function, I(). An alternative is to create the splines in the data frame, and then include them within lmer() as additional predictors.

In the syntax below, a spline term is created in the data frame for a knot at year 6, using the ifelse() function. The spline transformation is included as an additional predictor in the lmer() syntax.

```
> ## Create spline terms within the data frame.
> MPLS2.LS$spline1 <- ifelse(test = MPLS2.LS$grade > 6,
+                            yes = MPLS2.LS$grade - 6, no = 0)
> head(data.frame(grade = MPLS2.LS$grade, spline1 = MPLS2.LS$spline1), n = 7)
```

	grade	spline1
1	2	0
2	3	0
3	4	0
4	5	0
5	6	0
6	7	1
7	8	2

```
> ## Run lmer() with spline term as second predictor.
> sp1 <- lmer(read ~ grade + spline1 + (grade | subid), data = MPLS2.LS, REML = FALSE)
> sp1
```

12.7 Spline Models

```
Linear mixed model fit by maximum likelihood
Formula: read ~ grade + spline1 + (grade | subid)
   Data: MPLS2.LS
  AIC  BIC  logLik  deviance  REMLdev
 1146 1167  -566.1    1132      1124
Random effects:
 Groups   Name         Variance  Std.Dev. Corr
 subid    (Intercept)  222.1986  14.9063
          grade          5.9856   2.4465  -0.431
 Residual               75.4386   8.6855
Number of obs: 146, groups: subid, 22

Fixed effects:
             Estimate  Std. Error  t value
(Intercept)  155.5373     4.0103    38.78
grade          8.9845     0.7706    11.66
spline1       -5.6834     1.7505    -3.25

Correlation of Fixed Effects:
         (Intr) grade
grade    -0.654
spline1   0.362 -0.544
```

The absolute *t*-ratio for the spline predictor (spline1) is large, indicating the need for two different linear regressions for the pieces. The sign of $\hat{\beta}_2$ is negative, meaning the slope of the second piece is less than that for the first piece.

The fixed effect of the spline transformation is tested by comparing this model to a reduced model that omits spline1. Alternatively, the AICc can be used for the evaluation. Below, both approaches are considered.

```
> ## Reduced model.
> sp0 <- lmer(read ~ grade + (grade | subid),data = MPLS2.LS, REML = FALSE)
> ## LRT.
> anova(sp0, sp1)
```

```
Data: MPLS2.LS
Models:
sp0: read ~ grade + (grade | subid)
sp1: read ~ grade + spline1 + (grade | subid)
    Df   AIC    BIC   logLik  Chisq Chi Df Pr(>Chisq)
sp0  6 1154.3 1172.2 -571.13
sp1  7 1146.2 1167.0 -566.08 10.108      1   0.001476 **
---
Signif. codes:  0 '***' 0.001 '**' 0.01 '*' 0.05 '.' 0.1 ' ' 1
```

```
> ## AICc.
> print(aictab(list(sp1, sp0), c("Spline","Linear")), LL = FALSE)
```

```
Model selection based on AICc :

        K     AICc  Delta_AICc  AICcWt  Cum.Wt
Spline  7  1146.97         0.0    0.98    0.98
Linear  6  1154.87         7.9    0.02    1.00
```

The LRT-*p* is very small (< 0.001), and the AICc indicates substantially better fit for the model with the spline transformation. There is evidence the spline model should be retained.

To better understand the spline model, fitted values are computed and graphed. The observed means are included in the graph.

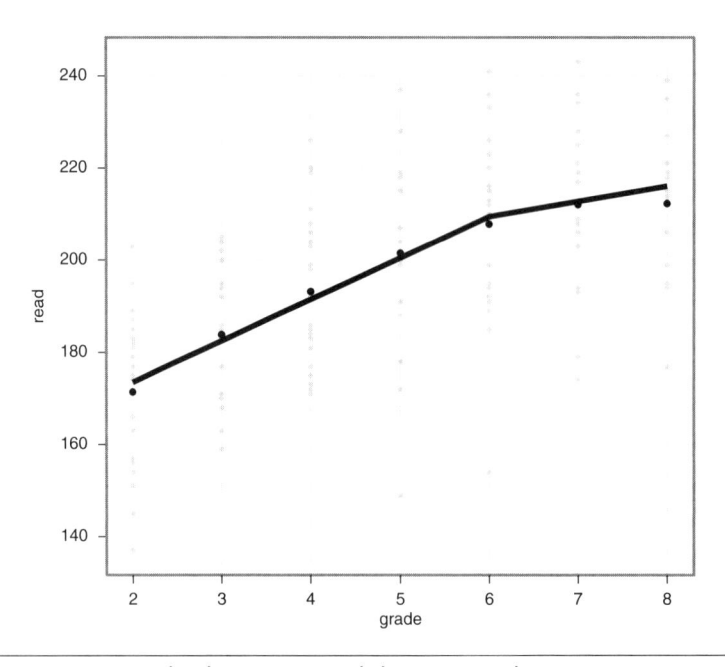

```
> graphdata <- data.frame(read = sp1@frame$read, grade = sp1@frame$grade,
+                         pred = model.matrix(sp1) %*% fixef(sp1))
> g1 <- ggplot(graphdata, aes(x = grade, y = read)) + geom_point(colour = "grey80")
> g2 <- g1 + stat_summary(fun.y = mean, geom = "point", size = 3)
> g3 <- g2 + geom_line(aes(y = pred), size = 1.5)
> print(g3)
```

Figure 12.12 Fitted spline curve with knot at Grade 6.

Figure 12.12 shows the fitted curve and observed means. The fitted spline curve has a linear increase for the first piece (up to Grade 6), and a smaller rate of increase for the second piece. The overall pattern is similar to the convexity of the quadratic model in Figure 12.9. However, the splines are constrained to be straight lines.

12.7 Spline Models

12.7.1.1 LINEAR SPLINE WITH MULTIPLE KNOTS

Knots can occur at more than one time point. For example, there might be knots at two time points, denoted as κ_1 and κ_2, with $\kappa_1 < \kappa_2$. In this case, the expected value LMER model is

$$E(y_{ij}) = \beta_0 + \beta_1(\text{grade}_{ij}) + \beta_2(\text{grade}_{ij} - \kappa_1)_+ \\ + \beta_3(\text{grade}_{ij} - \kappa_2)_+. \quad (12.7.4)$$

Similar to the last section, a random effect can be associated with each fixed effect, but two random effects are favored for the reasons previously given.

The spline transformations are the following:

$$(\text{grade}_{ij} - \kappa_1)_+ = \begin{cases} 0 & \text{if grade}_{ij} \leq \kappa_1, \\ \text{grade}_{ij} - \kappa_1 & \text{if grade}_{ij} > \kappa_1; \end{cases}$$

$$(\text{grade}_{ij} - \kappa_2)_+ = \begin{cases} 0 & \text{if grade}_{ij} \leq \kappa_2, \\ \text{grade}_{ij} - \kappa_2 & \text{if grade}_{ij} > \kappa_2. \end{cases}$$

Suppose the knots are at Grades 4 and 6. Then $\kappa_1 = 4$ and $\kappa_2 = 6$, and the linear spline is

$$E(y_{ij}) = \beta_0 + \beta_1(\text{grade}_{ij}) + \beta_2(\text{grade}_{ij} - 4)_+ \\ + \beta_3(\text{grade}_{ij} - 6)_+. \quad (12.7.5)$$

Based on Equation 12.7.5, the change curve equations are the following:

$$E(y_{ij}) = \begin{cases} \beta_0 + (\beta_1)(\text{grade}_{ij}) & \text{if grade}_{ij} \leq 4, \\ (\beta_0 - 4\beta_2) \\ \quad + (\beta_1 + \beta_2)(\text{grade}_{ij}) & \text{if } 4 < \text{grade}_{ij} \leq 6, \\ (\beta_0 - 4\beta_2 - 6\beta_3) \\ \quad + (\beta_1 + \beta_2 + \beta_3)(\text{grade}_{ij}) & \text{if grade}_{ij} > 6. \end{cases}$$
$$(12.7.6)$$

Equation 12.7.6 indicates that when $\beta_2 = \beta_3 = 0$, there is no difference in the change curve for the different pieces. For this reason, β_3 and β_4 are usually the focus of inference.

To estimate the model of Equation 12.7.5, two spline transformations are constructed, which are defined by the two knots. Both transformations are used as additional predictors in `lmer()`. Consider the following.

```
> MPLS2.LS$spline1 <- ifelse(test = MPLS2.LS$grade > 4,
+                            yes = MPLS2.LS$grade - 4, no = 0)
> MPLS2.LS$spline2 <- ifelse(test = MPLS2.LS$grade > 6,
+                            yes = MPLS2.LS$grade - 6, no = 0)
> ## Use spline terms in lmer().
> sp2 <- lmer(read ~ grade + spline1 + spline2 + (grade | subid),
+             MPLS2.LS, REML = FALSE)
> sp2
```

```
Linear mixed model fit by maximum likelihood
Formula: read ~ grade + spline1 + spline2 + (grade | subid)
   Data: MPLS2.LS
  AIC  BIC logLik deviance REMLdev
 1145 1169 -564.3     1129    1117
Random effects:
 Groups   Name        Variance Std.Dev. Corr
 subid    (Intercept) 225.7414 15.0247
          grade         6.1857  2.4871  -0.441
```

```
 Residual                         72.7652   8.5303
Number of obs: 146, groups: subid, 22

Fixed effects:
            Estimate Std. Error t value
(Intercept)  149.760      5.045  29.683
grade         11.045      1.338   8.256
spline1       -4.024      2.136  -1.884
spline2       -2.732      2.319  -1.178

Correlation of Fixed Effects:
        (Intr) grade  splin1
grade   -0.796
spline1  0.608 -0.818
spline2 -0.198  0.321 -0.671
```

The fixed effects associated with the spline predictors both have reasonably large absolute *t*-ratios. Model comparison for a single transformation, or the group, can also be performed. The details are left to the reader.

To see the nature of the model, the fitted values are computed and graphed, along with the mean curve and the observed points.

```
> graphdata <- data.frame(read = sp2@frame$read, grade = sp2@frame$grade,
+                         sp2.pred = model.matrix(sp2) %*% fixef(sp2))
> g1 <- ggplot(graphdata, aes(x = grade, y = read)) + geom_point(colour = "grey80")
> g2 <- g1 + stat_summary(fun.y = mean,geom = "point",size = 4)+ opts(aspect.ratio= 1)
> g3 <- g2 + geom_line(aes( y = sp2.pred), size = 1.5)
> print(g3)
```

Figure 12.13 shows the fitted curve. The graph indicates the segments $(2, 4)$, $(4, 6)$, and $(6, 8)$, have straight lines with different slopes. The first two segments correspond rather closely with the observed means, but the last segment overestimates the final mean in a similar manner as the quadratic model (see Figure 12.9).

12.7.1.2 STATIC PREDICTORS AND SPLINES

Static predictors can be included in spline models. To illustrate, consider the multilevel depiction of a model with a single knot and the `risk2` static predictor.

12.7 Spline Models

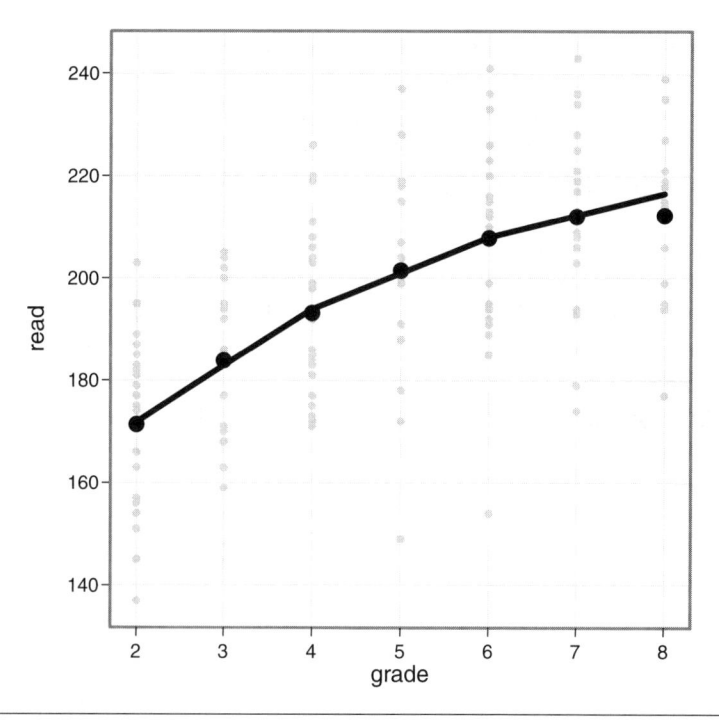

Figure 12.13 Fitted spline curve with knots at Grades 4 and 6.

$$y_{ij} = \beta^*_{0i} + \beta^*_{1i}(\text{grade}_{ij}) + \beta^*_{2i}(\text{grade}_{ij} - \kappa)_+ + \varepsilon_{ij},$$
$$\beta^*_{0i} = \beta_0 + \beta_3(\text{riskAVD}_i) + b_{0i},$$
$$\beta^*_{1i} = \beta_1 + \beta_4(\text{riskAVD}_i) + b_{1i},$$
$$\beta^*_{2i} = \beta_2 + \beta_5(\text{riskAVD}_i).$$

In the equations, $\beta_3, \beta_4, \beta_5$ index the static predictor effects. More specifically, β_3 is the group intercept difference, β_4 is the group slope difference for the first piece, and β_5 is the group slope difference for the second piece.

12.7.2 HIGHER ORDER REGRESSION SPLINES

In both spline examples above, the variation evident in the mean curve for each span probably can be accounted for by more complex models for the pieces. For example, the fit for the latter grades in Figure 12.13 can be improved by increasing the complexity of the polynomial. Similar to the comments regarding oscillation with trigonometric functions, the goal is not necessarily to approximate perfect fit. If the researcher believes that observed variation is due to sampling vagaries, then some degree of misfit is expected. However, in the case where one wants to account for additional variation within a span of time, the spline model can be based on higher order polynomials.

Similar to the linear spline model, higher order spline models consist of a polynomial portion and spline transformations, with the latter being based on the number of knots. The spline transformations always have the same power coefficient as the highest order polynomial. For example, consider the quadratic spline with a single knot:

$$E(y_{ij}) = \beta_0 + \beta_1(\text{grade}_{ij}) + \beta_2(\text{grade}_{ij}^2) + \beta_3(\text{grade}_{ij} - \kappa)_+^2. \quad (12.7.7)$$

Unlike the polynomial portion of the model, there is a single spline transformation whose power coefficient is the same as the highest order polynomial.

To illustrate the single-knot model for the two spans of time, assume the knot is located at Grade 6. Then Equation 12.7.7 defines the following change curves:

$$E(y_{ij}) = \begin{cases} \beta_1 + \beta_2(\text{grade}_{ij}) + \beta_3(\text{grade}_{ij}^2) & \text{if grade}_{ij} \leq 3; \\ (\beta_1 + 9\beta_4) + (\beta_2 - 6\beta_4)(\text{grade}_{ij}) \\ + (\beta_3 + \beta_4)(\text{grade}_{ij}^2) & \text{if grade}_{ij} > 6. \end{cases}$$
$$(12.7.8)$$

Equation 12.7.8 shows that the model for the pieces is now a quadratic polynomial, which will provide better fit than the linear model for each span of time. Using even higher order polynomials will further increase the fit for each span. A qualification here, as always, is that the researcher should consider the trade-off between fit and parsimony. Increasing fit for each span of time may come at the cost of a relatively large number of parameters.

12.8 Additional Details*

This optional section covers the details of constructing orthogonal polynomials. As discussed above, poly() can be used to compute orthogonal polynomials. The following discussion illustrates how the function works.

There is also a subsection discussing the general form of FPs. This is provided for researchers who want to investigate curves based on more complex functions than first-order and second-order FPs. FPs of any order can be constructed based on the general formulas.

12.8.1 COMPUTING ORTHOGONAL POLYNOMIALS*

Orthogonal polynomials are computed by transforming the original design matrix of the analysis, symbolized as X_i (see Chapter 5). The first column of the design matrix is a vector of 1s, and the remaining columns consist of the raw polynomials. Suppose the following matrix is defined:

$$T_i = X_i^T X_i,$$

12.8 Additional Details*

where X_i^T is the transpose of the design matrix. The orthogonal polynomial transformation involves the Cholesky decomposition of T_i. The Cholesky decomposition is an upper triangular matrix, C_i, with positive diagonal entries, where

$$T_i = C_i^T C_i.$$

The orthogonal polynomial design matrix, X_i^*, is computed as

$$X_i^* = X_i C_i^{-1},$$

where C_i^{-1} denotes the inverse (see the Appendix).

As an illustration, consider a design matrix with original time values, 1, 2, 3, 4, and up to a cubic polynomial transformation. Computing the orthogonal polynomials requires the matrix functions for the transpose, `t()`; matrix multiplication, `%*%`; the Cholesky decomposition, `chol()`; and the inverse, `solve()`. As a check on the work, the results of the `poly()` function are printed. Consider the syntax and output below.

```
> X <- matrix(c(rep(1,4), 1:4, (1:4) ^ 2, (1:4) ^ 3), ncol = 4)
> X
```

	[,1]	[,2]	[,3]	[,4]
[1,]	1	1	1	1
[2,]	1	2	4	8
[3,]	1	3	9	27
[4,]	1	4	16	64

```
> T <- t(X) %*% X
> C <- chol(T)
> C
```

	[,1]	[,2]	[,3]	[,4]
[1,]	2	5.000000	15.00000	50.000000
[2,]	0	2.236068	11.18034	46.510214
[3,]	0	0.000000	2.00000	15.000000
[4,]	0	0.000000	0.00000	1.341641

```
> X.star <- X %*% solve(C)
> X.star
```

	[,1]	[,2]	[,3]	[,4]
[1,]	0.5	-0.6708204	0.5	-0.2236068
[2,]	0.5	-0.2236068	-0.5	0.6708204
[3,]	0.5	0.2236068	-0.5	-0.6708204
[4,]	0.5	0.6708204	0.5	0.2236068

```
> ## poly() output.
> poly(1:4, 3)
```

```
                1          2          3
[1,]   -0.6708204    0.5   -0.2236068
[2,]   -0.2236068   -0.5    0.6708204
[3,]    0.2236068   -0.5   -0.6708204
[4,]    0.6708204    0.5    0.2236068
attr(,"degree")
[1] 1 2 3
attr(,"coefs")
attr(,"coefs")$alpha
[1] 2.5 2.5 2.5

attr(,"coefs")$norm2
[1] 1.0 4.0 5.0 4.0 1.8

attr(,"class")
[1] "poly"     "matrix"
```

The `poly()` function omits the first column of the design matrix, which is always a vector of constant values. The columns of the `poly()` output agree with the last three columns of X.star. Additional details can be found in Rencher (2000, chap. 12) and similar sources.

12.8.2 GENERAL FORM OF FRACTIONAL POLYNOMIALS*

Earlier in this chapter, first-order and second-order FPs were presented. Higher order FPs may be constructed from general formulas. To write the general formulas, it is necessary to alter the notation for the power coefficients. Suppose a power coefficient is now denoted as m_h, $h = 1, 2, \ldots, p$. For the discussion earlier in the chapter, $a = m_1$, $b = m_2$.

Let t_{ij} stand for the generic time variable (e.g., grade). Then the general form of the FP is

$$f_h(t_{ij}) = \begin{cases} t_{ij}^{(m_h)} & \text{if } m_h \neq m_{h-1}; \\ f_{h-1}(t_{ij}) \cdot log(t_{ij}) & \text{if } m_h = m_{h-1}, \end{cases} \quad (12.8.1)$$

with $m_1 \leq m_2 \leq \ldots \leq m_p$, and $log(t_{ij})$ indicates the natural log of t_{ij}. The round bracket notation, $t_{ij}^{(m_h)}$, represents the Box and Tidwell transformation (G. E. P. Box & Tidwell, 1962),

$$t_{ij}^{(m_h)} = \begin{cases} t_{ij}^{m_h} & \text{if } m_h \neq 0; \\ log(t_{ij}) & \text{if } m_h = 0, \end{cases} \quad (12.8.2)$$

with the constraint, $t_{ij} > 0$, so that all transformations are defined. Based on Equations 12.8.1 and 12.8.2, FPs of any order can be constructed.

Advanced Topics 13

The LMER models in the previous chapters were characterized by the inclusion of a single response variable, at least one time predictor, and at least one static predictor. There are situations in which the research questions or the data structure require more advanced models. This final chapter discusses three advanced topics.

1. Dynamic predictors
2. Multiple response variables
3. Additional levels of nesting

The first topic concerns the situation in which there is a least one time-varying (i.e., dynamic) predictor that is *not* a time predictor. The second topic is concerned with the simultaneous analysis of more than one response variable. The last topic involves the case of a nesting structure that requires more than the two levels previously considered. Static predictors can be included in all of these models, and the specifics of their inclusion are discussed for each topic.

The first two topics have the common feature that the data set includes at least two dynamic variables. In dynamic predictor models, one time-varying variable is the response, and the other is the predictor. A time predictor might also be included in a dynamic predictor model, but focus is on the dynamic predictor effects. For this scenario, the researcher usually wants to know if changes in the response are associated with changes in the dynamic predictor. Models for addressing this type of question are discussed in Section 13.1.

In the case of multiple response variables, the dynamic variables are treated as distinct responses. The goal is usually to determine the form the change curves for the responses, and if the change curves are distinct. Additional questions regarding differences in intercepts and the relationship among, say, the random intercepts of two responses can also be addressed. Models of this type are discussed in Section 13.2.

The third topic is distinct from the first two, as there is at least one additional level of nesting beyond the two levels already discussed. For example, suppose that in addition to the repeated reading measurements considered in the previous chapters, the subjects are nested within classrooms. In this case, the dependency due to the common classroom environment may be important to account for, in addition to the dependency due to repeated measures. Models for this nesting structure are presented in Section 13.3.

13.1 Dynamic Predictors

A dynamic predictor is any predictor other than a time predictor that changes over time. Recall that a time predictor is an index of duration, and as such, its scores always increase as time elapses. This concept can be depicted symbolically. Assume time stands for the time variable. Then it is always the case that $time_{ij-1} < time_{ij}$.

A dynamic predictor is assumed to be more than just a proxy for time. A dynamic predictor, in principle, can have values that either increase or decrease as time elapses. If dyn stands for the dynamic predictor, then it is possible that $dyn_{ij-1} < dyn_{ij}$, $dyn_{ij-1} = dyn_{ij}$, or $dyn_{ij-1} > dyn_{ij}$.

Dynamic predictors and time predictors can be included in the same LMER model. Because of this, it is important that the dynamic predictor not be redundant with the time predictor. If the dynamic predictor is simply a proxy for time, this can lead to conceptual problems as well as estimation problems. In the MPLS data set, the time predictor is grade, having values $grade_{ij} = 5, 6, 7, 8$. Suppose age in years is another time-varying predictor—a dynamic predictor—with values of $age_{ij} = 10, 11, 13, 14$. Grade and age should not both be used as predictors because one is just a linear transformation of the other, $grade_{ij} = age_{ij} - 5$. The predictors are completely redundant, and the inclusion of both seems unjustified from a scientific point of view. The inclusion is also unjustified from a statistical point of view because no meaningful improvement in fit can be gained by having both predictors rather than one.

If the researcher is convinced that a dynamic predictor is not a proxy for time, then a second question is whether it is better to treat the predictor as dynamic or static. Ideally, the answer to this question should be based on theory, but in some cases empirical justification is warranted. The issue here is that static predictors *only* account for between-subject variability, whereas dynamic predictors can account for between-subject and within-subject variability. Between-subjects variance exists if the overall level varies among the subjects, and within-subjects variance exists if there is variability over time. Because of this possibility, the interpretation of dynamic predictor effects can be more involved than that of static predictors.

As an illustration of the problem, consider the risk variable in the MPLS data set. The school district originally measured risk as a dynamic variable. However, risk was treated as a static predictor in the previous chapters. The MPLS school district has a yearly evaluation for each student that is used for risk classification into the three groups: ADV, POV, or HHM (see Chapters 1

13.1 Dynamic Predictors

and 3). Based on theory and past research, it was hypothesized that subjects experiencing even a single year in either of the two disadvantaged groups (POV, HHM) should be denoted the particular status throughout the duration of the study (Masten et al., 2008; Obradović et al., 2009). In this case, it is believed that between-subject differences are most important, and within-subject effects are trifling for the time period considered. This has empirical justification, as membership in the risk groups tends to be steady for students in the MPLS school district, and the within-subjects variance is considered negligible (Mizerek & Hinz, 2004).

When the researcher is convinced that important within-subject variability will be accounted for by a dynamic predictor, or when one wants to investigate the possibility, a number of models can be considered. Putting aside the issue of static predictors for the moment, the primary concern is whether a time predictor will be included along with the dynamic predictor. The choice of model depends on the research question(s) to be addressed by the analysis. Three options are considered here.

1. Including only the dynamic predictor (excluding time predictors).

2. Including the dynamic predictor and time predictor(s) as main effects (single effects).

3. Including a dynamic predictor by time predictor interaction along with the main effects.

To better understand each of these, a dynamic predictor is introduced to the MPLS data set.

Dynamic predictors can be quantitative or categorical, and a categorical variable is considered in this chapter. It is hoped that a generalization to a quantitative predictor is straightforward for the reader.

For purposes of explication, assume the dynamic predictor is based on a hypothetical study of the effect of financial incentives on student achievement. There is evidence that financial incentives improve academic achievement and related factors, such as school attendance (Henry & Rubinstein, 2002). An important question in the study of incentives is what occurs when incentives are discontinued.

To study the introduction and withdrawal of financial incentives, suppose a researcher carries out the following study. Over 4 years (grades), each student is assigned two instances of financial incentive and two instances of no incentive. To control for order effects, the order of the conditions is randomized. At the beginning of each year of the study, the students are told they will either receive a cash payment at the end of the year to motivate improved performance, or told they will not receive a cash payment at the end of the year. In the data frame, the dynamic predictor is coded as $1 =$ received cash payment and $0 =$ did not receive cash payment.

Table 13.1 Financial incentive (0 = no incentive, 1 = incentive).

subid	incent.5	incent.6	incent.7	incent.8
1	0	1	0	1
2	0	1	1	0
3	0	1	1	0
4	1	0	0	1
5	1	1	0	0
6	1	0	1	0
7	0	1	1	0
8	1	0	0	1
9	0	0	1	1
10	0	1	0	1
11	1	1	0	0
12	0	0	1	1
13	0	1	0	1
14	1	1	0	0
15	0	0	1	1
16	1	0	1	0
17	1	0	0	1
18	0	1	0	1
19	1	1	0	0
20	0	1	1	0
21	1	0	1	0
22	0	1	1	0

The hypothetical incentive scores for the $N = 22$ subjects are shown in Table 13.1. The table is in wide format with repeated measures represented by different columns. Each repeated measures column has the abbreviated label incent, and the number in the label corresponds to grade.

Suppose the data in Table 13.1 are saved as a comma-separated values (CSV) file named incentive.csv, with the variable names in the first row of the file. The data are available on the book website. In the syntax below, the CSV file is read in, and the data frame is named incentive. The Rdata file with the MPLS.LS data frame is also loaded. The incentive data frame is reshaped to long format and merged with MPLS.LS based on subject identification numbers and grade. The resulting data frame is named MPLS.LS.IN.

```
> incentive <- read.csv("C:/Mine/incentive.csv", header = TRUE)
> load("C:/Mine/MPLS.LS.Rdata")
> ## Show objects.
> objects()
```

```
[1] "incentive" "MPLS.LS"
```

13.1 Dynamic Predictors

```
> ## Reshape.
> incentive.1 <- reshape(incentive, varying = c("incent.5", "incent.6",
+                                                "incent.7", "incent.8"),
+                        timevar = "grade", times = 5:8,
+                        idvar = "subid", direction = "long")
> MPLS.LS.IN <- merge(MPLS.LS, incentive.1, by = c("subid", "grade"))
> ## Sort by id.
> MPLS.LS.IN <- MPLS.LS.IN[order(MPLS.LS.IN$subid), ]
> head(MPLS.LS.IN, n = 8)
```

	subid	grade	risk	gen	eth	ell	sped	att	read	incent
1	1	5	HHM	F	Afr	0	N	0.94	172	0
2	1	6	HHM	F	Afr	0	N	0.94	185	1
3	1	7	HHM	F	Afr	0	N	0.94	179	0
4	1	8	HHM	F	Afr	0	N	0.94	194	1
45	2	5	HHM	F	Afr	0	N	0.91	200	0
46	2	6	HHM	F	Afr	0	N	0.91	210	1
47	2	7	HHM	F	Afr	0	N	0.91	209	1
48	2	8	HHM	F	Afr	0	N	0.91	NA	0

The output shows that the incentive variable, incent, is the last column in the data frame. It is important to note that the values of incent change over time. In addition, the pattern of 0s and 1s is not the same for the two subjects depicted in the output. A listing of the entire data frame will confirm that there are various patterns for the subjects.

To better understand the incentive variable and the research questions related to reading, consider a graph of read and incent as a function of grade. For brevity, only the first six subjects are graphed.

```
> ## Save some settings.
> theme_set(theme_bw())
> myx <- scale_x_continuous(breaks = 5:8)
> myy <- scale_y_continuous(breaks = 0:1)
> ## Select the first 6 subjects.
> graphdata <- na.omit(MPLS.LS.IN[MPLS.LS.IN$subid < 7, ])
> ## Create the graphs.
> g1 <- ggplot(graphdata, aes(x = grade, y = read, group = subid))
> g2 <- g1 + geom_line() + geom_point() + facet_wrap(~ subid, ncol = 2) + myx
> q1 <- ggplot(graphdata, aes(x = grade, y = incent, group = subid))
> q2 <- q1 + geom_line() + geom_point() + facet_wrap(~ subid, ncol = 2) + myx + myy
> ## Print graphs side-by-side.
> grid.newpage()
> pushViewport(viewport(layout = grid.layout(1, 2)))
> vplayout <- function(x, y) viewport(layout.pos.row = x, layout.pos.col = y)
> print(g2, vp = vplayout(1, 1))
> print(q2, vp = vplayout(1, 2))
```

The graphs are shown in Figure 13.1. There are some missing data values, as the panels for Subjects 2 and 4 reveal. Due to the nature of the research design, each subject has a nonlinear trend for financial incentive. The trends perhaps appear odd, as the values of the variable alternate between 0 and 1.

13.1.1 DYNAMIC PREDICTOR AS A SINGLE EFFECT

The type of dynamic predictor model to be used depends on the research question one wants to address. The simplest model includes the dynamic

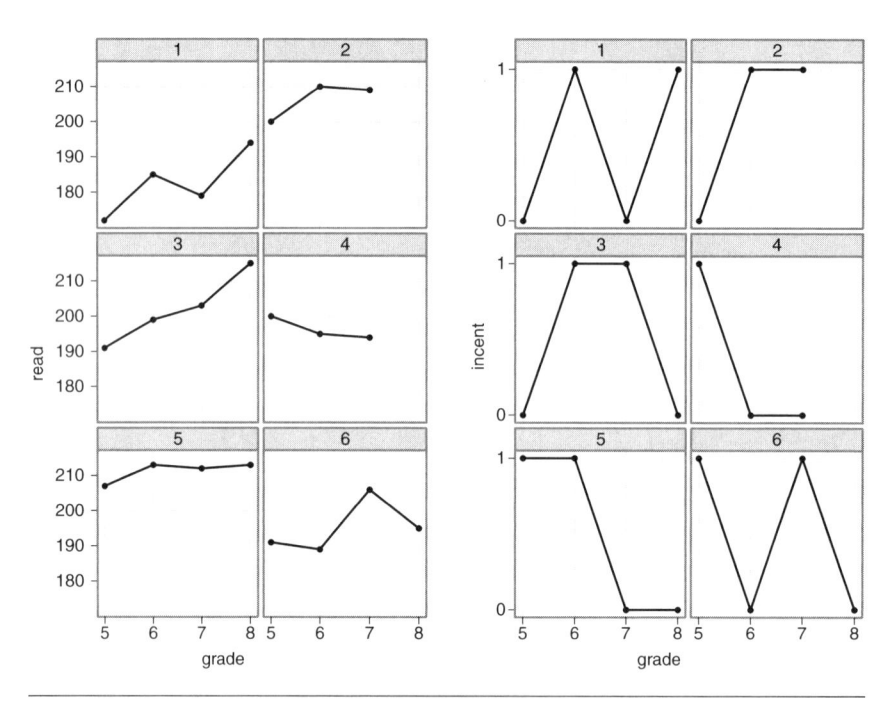

Figure 13.1 Observed curves of reading (left) and financial incentive (right) for six subjects.

predictor as a main effect, or as the single predictor in the LMER model. In terms of the expected value model, this is

$$E(y_{ij}) = \beta_0 + \beta_1(\text{incent}_{ij}). \tag{13.1.1}$$

At each time point, mean reading is predicted by financial incentive measured at the same time point. The goal of this model is to study how the two variables covary over time, which is referred to as their *longitudinal covariation*.

To gain additional insight, consider expressing change in the expected response from wave $j-1$ to wave j. The expected value equations are the following:

$$E(y_{ij}) - E(y_{ij-1}) = \beta_0 + \beta_1(\text{incent}_{ij}) - [\beta_0 + \beta_1(\text{incent}_{ij-1})]$$
$$E(y_{ij}) - E(y_{ij-1}) = \beta_1(\text{incent}_{ij} - \text{incent}_{ij-1}).$$

The last equation shows that β_1 indexes the relation between the change in the mean response and the change in the dynamic predictor. In terms of Figure 13.1, Equation 13.1.1 allows the researcher to investigate if the changes in the right-hand graphs are associated with the average changes in the corresponding left-hand graphs—that is, whether change in financial incentive is associated with mean change in reading scores.

13.1 Dynamic Predictors

Inspection of the individual curves in Figure 13.1 suggests that for at least some subjects, change in the two variables might be related. For the first subject, a change from 0 to 1 in `incent` is associated with an increase in `read`, and a change from 1 to 0 in `incent` is associated with a decrease in `read`. Similar consistency appears for some of the other subjects.

If β_1 is positive, then the direction of change in the response is the same as in the predictor. This can be either an increase or decrease, and the change can be linear or nonlinear. Conversely, if β_1 is negative, then the direction of change in the response is the opposite of the predictor, as when the response increases but the predictor decreases.

As shown above, dynamic predictors are included in `lmer()` just like any other predictor. Similar to time predictors, random effects can be associated with dynamic predictors. The inclusion of a random effect for a dynamic predictor is desirable when one wants to allow for individual differences in the longitudinal covariation of the two variables.

Consider estimating the model of Equation 13.1.1 using a single random effect. For comparison, an intercept-only model is also estimated.

```
> ## Intercept-only.
> dyn.0 <- lmer(read ~ 1 + (1 | subid), MPLS.LS.IN, REML = FALSE)
> ## Dynamic predictor.
> dyn.1 <- lmer(read ~ incent + (1 | subid), MPLS.LS.IN, REML = FALSE)
> ## Comparison of fit.
> anova(dyn.0, dyn.1)
```

```
Data: MPLS.LS.IN
Models:
dyn.0: read ~ 1 + (1 | subid)
dyn.1: read ~ incent + (1 | subid)
      Df    AIC    BIC  logLik Chisq Chi Df Pr(>Chisq)
dyn.0  3 630.53 637.68 -312.26
dyn.1  4 627.55 637.07 -309.77 4.985      1    0.02557 *
---
Signif. codes:  0 '***' 0.001 '**' 0.01 '*' 0.05 '.' 0.1 ' ' 1
```

```
> print(aictab(list(dyn.0, dyn.1), c("Intercept", "Dynamic")), LL = FALSE)
```

```
Model selection based on AICc :

          K   AICc Delta_AICc AICcWt Cum.Wt
Dynamic   4 628.08       0.00    0.8    0.8
Intercept 3 630.85       2.77    0.2    1.0
```

The output indicates LRT-p is relatively small (< 0.03), and the weight of evidence of the model with `incent` is relatively large ($W_2 = 0.8$). A case can be made for the model with `incent`.

Equation 13.1.1 makes no statement about the nature of the longitudinal trajectories of reading or financial incentive. Time is expressed completely through the dynamic predictor. In the case of incent, this is perhaps a bit awkward, as the dynamic predictor is a binary variable, allowing only a coarse type of change curve (see Figure 13.1). The effect of duration on the response variable shows up completely through its association with the dynamic predictor. The shape of the trajectories of the variables can be inferred from graphs as in Figure 13.1, but there are no terms in the model that are informative in this regard. The next section considers models that explicitly represent the trend of the response.

13.1.2 DYNAMIC PREDICTOR WITH A TIME VARIABLE

A dynamic predictor is used alone when the shape of the response trajectory is not of interest. When the shape of the response trajectory is of interest, then a time predictor can be included along with the dynamic predictor.

In addition to main effects, the interaction among the time predictor and dynamic predictor can be included in the model. This interaction model is similar to what was encountered with time predictors and static predictors in past chapters. The fundamental difference is that the effects have a within-subjects interpretation rather than a between-subjects interpretation. Illustrations are presented below.

As a first step, consider the interaction model using grade and incent as predictors. This is written as

$$y_{ij} = (\beta_0 + b_{0i}) + (\beta_1 + b_{1i})(\text{grade}_{ij}) + \beta_2(\text{incent}_{ij}) \\ + \beta_3(\text{grade}_{ij} \cdot \text{incent}_{ij}) + \varepsilon_{ij}. \quad (13.1.2)$$

Equation 13.1.2 has two random effects, but a different number may be used.

Similar to static predictor models, the interaction allows one to examine if linear change in reading depends on financial incentive. Because incent is a binary predictor, this is made explicit by substituting the values of 0 and 1 in Equation 13.1.2. For simplicity, consider the expected value equations:

$$E(y_{ij}) = \begin{cases} \beta_0 + \beta_1(\text{grade}_{ij}) & \text{if incent}_{ij} = 0, \\ (\beta_0 + \beta_2) + (\beta_1 + \beta_3)(\text{grade}_{ij}) & \text{if incent}_{ij} = 1. \end{cases} \quad (13.1.3)$$

The result is an equation for reading by grade, for each level of financial incentive. If financial incentive was a static predictor, then the equations would reflect between-group differences. That is, students in the no-incentive group would have a mean predicted curve with intercept β_0 and slope β_1; students in the incentive group would have a mean predicted curve with intercept $\beta_0 + \beta_2$ and slope $\beta_1 + \beta_3$. The between-subjects interpretation focuses on the contrast between different groups of students.

But financial incentive is a dynamic predictor, and here there is a within-subjects interpretation. This means that as the *same* students change from no incentive ($\text{incent}_{ij} = 0$) to incentive ($\text{incent}_{ij} = 1$), the linear curve of reading changes its intercept by β_2, and its slope by β_3. The within-subjects

13.1 Dynamic Predictors

interpretation focuses on the average change in reading trajectory, for changes in incentive levels experienced by all the students.

The lmer() syntax for Equation 13.1.2 is identical to the case when the predictor is static. Consider the following.

```
> dyn.int <- lmer(read ~ grade * incent + (grade | subid), MPLS.LS.IN, REML = FALSE)
> print(dyn.int, corr = FALSE)
```

```
Linear mixed model fit by maximum likelihood
Formula: read ~ grade * incent + (grade | subid)
   Data: MPLS.LS.IN
   AIC   BIC  logLik deviance REMLdev
  560.7 579.7 -272.3   544.7   535.7
Random effects:
 Groups   Name        Variance Std.Dev. Corr
 subid    (Intercept) 861.2544 29.3471
          grade         8.4000  2.8983  -0.816
 Residual               9.8854  3.1441
Number of obs: 80, groups: subid, 22

Fixed effects:
             Estimate Std. Error t value
(Intercept)  177.8611    7.2279   24.608
grade          4.4689    0.8372    5.338
incent        -0.7439    6.0771   -0.122
grade:incent   0.8810    0.9472    0.930
```

Consider the estimates from the fixed effects table in the output, substituted in the fitted value equations (see Equation 13.1.3).

$$\text{No incentive: } \hat{y}_{ij} = 177.86 + 4.47(\text{grade}_{ij}), \qquad (13.1.4)$$

$$\text{Incentive: } \hat{y}_{ij} = 177.12 + 5.35(\text{grade}_{ij}). \qquad (13.1.5)$$

For the sample, the reading slope increases by 0.88, when the incentive is introduced. Likewise, the reading slope decreases by 0.88, when the incentive is withdrawn. The t-ratio for the interaction is rather small ($t = 0.93$), meaning the change in the slope may not be statistically reliable.

Consider comparison of the interaction model with a model that has grade and incent as main effects.

```
> dyn.main <- lmer(read ~ grade + incent + (grade | subid), MPLS.LS.IN, REML = FALSE)
> anova(dyn.main, dyn.int)
```

```
Data: MPLS.LS.IN
Models:
dyn.main: read ~ grade + incent + (grade | subid)
dyn.int:  read ~ grade * incent + (grade | subid)
         Df    AIC    BIC  logLik  Chisq Chi Df Pr(>Chisq)
dyn.main  7 559.48 576.15 -272.74
dyn.int   8 560.66 579.72 -272.33 0.8184      1     0.3657
```

```
> print(aictab(list(dyn.main, dyn.int), c("Main Effects", "Interaction")), LL = FALSE)
```
```
Model selection based on AICc :

              K    AICc  Delta_AICc  AICcWt  Cum.Wt
Main Effects  7  561.03        0.00     0.7     0.7
Interaction   8  562.69        1.65     0.3     1.0
```

According to the LRT and the AICc, the interaction is not statistically reliable. The output for the main effects model is printed.

```
> print(dyn.main, cor = FALSE)
```
```
Linear mixed model fit by maximum likelihood
Formula: read ~ grade + incent + (grade | subid)
   Data: MPLS.LS.IN
   AIC    BIC  logLik  deviance  REMLdev
 559.5  576.2  -272.7     545.5    538.3
Random effects:
 Groups   Name        Variance  Std.Dev.  Corr
 subid    (Intercept) 846.6802  29.0978
          grade         7.9918   2.8270   -0.816
 Residual              10.3160   3.2118
Number of obs: 80, groups: subid, 22

Fixed effects:
            Estimate  Std. Error  t value
(Intercept) 175.2881      6.6435   26.385
grade         4.8740      0.7062    6.902
incent        4.8391      0.8663    5.586
```

Similar to a main effects model with a static predictor (see Chapter 5), the linear curves for the levels of financial incentive are parallel, with an estimated vertical shift of $\hat{\beta}_2 = 4.84$. Since financial incentive is a dynamic predictor, there is a within-subjects interpretation. As financial incentive increases, there is a predicted intercept increase of $\hat{\beta}_2 = 4.84$, and as financial incentive decreases, there is a predicted decrease of the same amount. The t-ratio for incent is almost as large as that for grade, meaning the incentive effect is about as strong as the duration effect.

To this point, the discussion has focused on a categorical dynamic predictor, but the same ideas generalize to quantitative dynamic predictors. Conditioning on a quantitative dynamic predictor is similar to a categorical predictor, except the number of levels can be numerous and perhaps unique. Thus, with quantitative dynamic predictors, it is often impractical to write conditional equations, such as Equation 13.1.3. As an alternative, one can estimate the parameters and produce fitted equations as in Equation 13.1.4 using, say, the empirical quartiles of the quantitative dynamic predictor.

Static predictors can be introduced along with dynamic predictors and time predictors. The models can be relatively complex, especially if an interaction

13.1 Dynamic Predictors

among the time predictor, dynamic predictor, and static predictor is included. An example of such a model is the following:

$$\begin{aligned}
y_{ij} = &(\beta_0 + b_{0i}) + (\beta_1 + b_{1i})(\text{grade}_{ij}) + \beta_2(\text{incent}_{ij}) \\
&+ \beta_3(\text{grade}_{ij} \cdot \text{incent}_{ij}) \\
&+ \beta_4(\text{risk2DADV}_i) + \beta_5(\text{grade}_{ij} \cdot \text{risk2DADV}_i) \quad (13.1.6)\\
&+ \beta_6(\text{incent}_{ij} \cdot \text{risk2DADV}_i) \\
&+ \beta_7(\text{grade}_{ij} \cdot \text{incent}_{ij} \cdot \text{risk2DADV}_i) + \varepsilon_{ij}.
\end{aligned}$$

The triple interaction in the last line of the equation warrants further comment.

One means of interpreting the triple interaction is to express Equation 13.1.6 conditional on risk2DADV and discuss the multiple equations for each level. Using Equation 13.1.6, it can be shown that for the advantaged group, $\text{risk2DADV}_i = 0$, and

$$E(y_{ij}) = \begin{cases} \beta_0 + \beta_1(\text{grade}_{ij}) & \text{if incent}_{ij} = 0, \\ (\beta_0 + \beta_2) + (\beta_1 + \beta_3)(\text{grade}_{ij}) & \text{if incent}_{ij} = 1. \end{cases} \quad (13.1.7)$$

The equations show that as the subjects in the advantaged group increase from no incentive to incentive, there is a change in the intercept of the reading curve of β_2 and a change in the slope of β_3. This is a within-subjects interpretation, as focus is on the change of incentive status for the same subjects over time.

For the disadvantaged group, $\text{risk2DADV}_i = 1$, and the equation is

$$E(y_{ij}) = \begin{cases} (\beta_0 + \beta_4) + (\beta_1 + \beta_5)(\text{grade}_{ij}) & \text{if incent}_{ij} = 0, \\ (\beta_0 + \beta_2 + \beta_4 + \beta_6) \\ \quad + (\beta_1 + \beta_3 + \beta_5 + \beta_7)(\text{grade}_{ij}) & \text{if incent}_{ij} = 1. \end{cases}$$
$$(13.1.8)$$

The equations show that as the subjects in the advantaged group increase from no incentive to incentive, there is a change in the intercept of the reading curve of $\beta_2 + \beta_6$ and a change in the slope of $\beta_3 + \beta_7$. Again, this is a within-subjects interpretation.

Statements regarding between-group differences are also possible. Equations 13.1.7 and 13.1.8 indicate the risk groups have different parameters for levels of incentive. For no incentive, the difference in the mean intercept of the risk groups is β_4. Similar between-groups comparisons for the slope can be made but are left to the reader.

Finally, it should be noted that a limited number of the possible dynamic predictor models were presented. Alternatives might be considered when required by the research questions or subject matter. For example, a class of models popular in some areas of research, such as business and economics, are lagged models that essentially use earlier dynamic scores to predict later response scores (Diggle et al., 2002, chap. 12).

13.2 Multiple Response Variables

In some research situations, several dynamic variables are collected and the investigator wishes to treat them as response variables. One approach is to consider each response variable in isolation and perform a separate analysis. This approach is acceptable, provided the investigator does not want to make direct statistical comparisons among the response variables. An example of a direct statistical comparison is a test of the equality of linear slopes of two or more response variables. In isolated analyses, direct comparisons cannot be made because covariances among the parameters related to the responses are not modeled. For instance, the covariance of the linear slopes is not estimated, making it impossible to compute a SE for slope differences.

When direct comparisons are of interest, it is advantageous to consider two or more response variables in the same LMER model. In such models, the variance-covariance matrix among the fixed effects is estimated. This provides a basis for direct statistical comparisons among the change curves. The estimated SE for the difference in linear slopes, for example, can be computed. SEs for other potentially important differences can also be computed.

13.2.1 READING AND MATHEMATICS

As motivation for the discussion, consider the two responses of reading scores and mathematics scores. The data set is the same as discussed in Section 3.9.1 and is available on the book website. Suppose the researcher is interested in examining whether the change curves for the two variables have statistically equivalent intercepts and linear slopes. The analysis will involve a linear curve for reading and a linear curve for mathematics. The covariances among the parameters of the curves will need to be estimated to allow for inferences about the curve differences. These considerations require the two response variables be modeled simultaneously in `lmer()`.

The text file, `math.txt`, contains the math data in wide format, along with the subject identification numbers. The column labels are included in the file, and missing values are coded as −99. In the syntax below, the math data file is read in, the wide data frame is reshaped to long format, and then it is merged with the reading data.

```
> ## Read in the data.
> MATH.W <- read.table("C:/Mine/math.txt", header = TRUE, na.strings = "-99")
> head(MATH.W)
```

	subid	math.5	math.6	math.7	math.8
1	1	175	172	169	185
2	2	201	192	178	195
3	3	182	202	192	218
4	4	196	161	210	NA
5	5	192	218	174	NA
6	6	184	178	209	232

13.2 Multiple Response Variables

```
> ## Reshape
> MATH.L  <-  reshape(MATH.W, varying = 2:5, idvar= "subid",
+                    direction = "long", timevar = "grade")
> MATH.LS  <-  MATH.L[order(MATH.L$subid), ]
> ## Merge
> READ.MATH  <-  merge(MPLS.LS, MATH.LS, by = c("subid", "grade"))
> head(READ.MATH)
```

	subid	grade	risk	gen	eth	ell	sped	att	read	math
1	1	5	HHM	F	Afr	0	N	0.94	172	175
2	1	6	HHM	F	Afr	0	N	0.94	185	172
3	1	7	HHM	F	Afr	0	N	0.94	179	169
4	1	8	HHM	F	Afr	0	N	0.94	194	185
5	10	5	POV	F	Afr	0	N	0.96	200	181
6	10	6	POV	F	Afr	0	N	0.96	212	203

The data are stacked to facilitate constructing a facet graph by type of response. Then ggplot2 is used to plot observed curves for individuals and connected means curves.

```
> ## Stack the data.
> plotdata  <-  with(READ.MATH, data.frame(response = c(read, math),
+                grade= c(grade, grade), subid = c(subid, subid),
+                label= c(rep("read",nrow(READ.MATH)),rep("math",nrow(READ.MATH)))))
> ## ggplot2.
> g1  <-  ggplot(plotdata, aes(x = grade, y = response, group = subid))
> g2  <-  g1 + geom_line(colour = "grey80") + facet_grid(.~ label) + myx
> g3  <-  g2 + stat_summary(aes(group = 1), fun.y = mean, geom = "point", size = 3)
> g4  <-  g3 + stat_summary(aes(group = 1), fun.y = mean, geom = "line", lwd = 1.5)
> print(g4)
```

The graphs are shown in Figure 13.2. Since both the reading measure and the mathematics measure are from the NALT (see Chapter 1), their scores can be compared directly. The reading mean is slightly greater than the mathematics mean at the first time point. Both mean curves show a monotonic increase over time, but the reading curve flattens out at the latter grades, whereas the mathematics mean curve does not.

13.2.2 ANALYZING TWO RESPONSES WITH lmer()

The key to modeling two or more response variables in LMER is to stack the response vectors for each subject, and then create predictor variables similar to those used in the spline models in Chapter 12. For two response variables and linear change curves, four predictors are required. These are listed below along with the names of the variables to be created in the data frame.

1. An intercept predictor for reading (read.int).

2. An intercept predictor for mathematics (math.int).

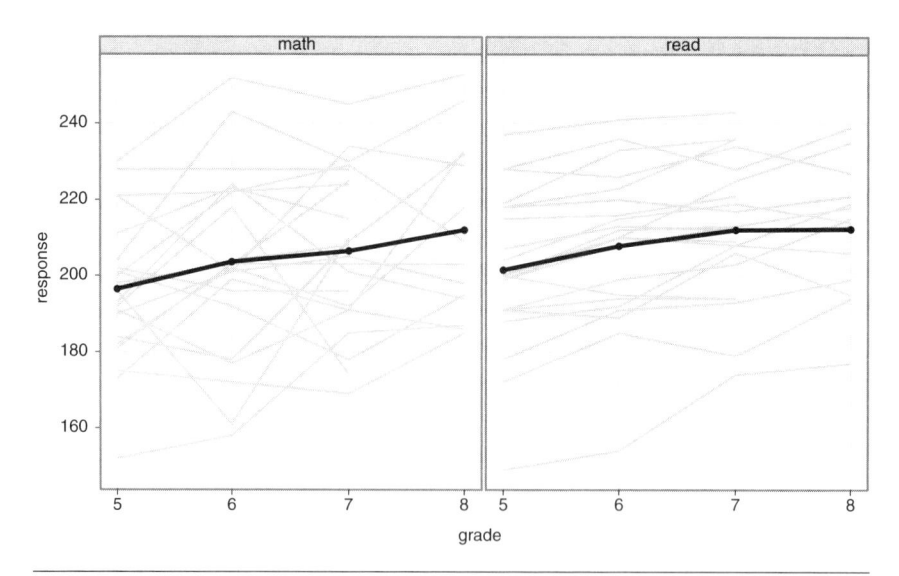

Figure 13.2 Individual curves (thin) and mean curves (thick) for mathematics (left) and reading (right).

3. A grade predictor for reading (read.grade).

4. A grade predictor for mathematics (math.grade).

These four predictors are used in LMER to specify change curves for the two response variables. Constraints on the predictors are used to address particular research questions. The constraints can be used to form nested models that can be evaluated with the LRT or the AICc.

Table 13.2 illustrates the type of data structure required for a single subject. The table shows the stacked response vector, response, and the four predictors listed above. The response vector depicts the repeated measurements for reading and mathematics. The symbol, read$_{i1}$, stands for the reading score of the ith subject at the first time point (Grade 5) and similarly for the other values in the column. For read.int, a value of 1 is assigned if the response is reading and a value of 0 otherwise; math.int is similarly constructed. For read.grade, the appropriate value of grade is assigned if the response is reading and a value of 0 otherwise; math.grade is constructed in a similar fashion. (In this example, grade is considered, but grade5 may also be used.)

Stacking similar to Table 13.2 must be performed for all the subjects in the data frame. Once this is performed for each subject, the data array for the individual subjects is stacked to form the data structure for the analysis. Thus, the data frame is "double-stacked" in the sense that reading and mathematics are stacked within subjects, and subject blocks are then stacked one atop another.

The syntax for creating the appropriate double-stacked data set is shown below. There is stacking of subid, grade, and the response variables. A character variable with string labels is created to denote the type of response. The four predictors are constructed using ifelse().

13.2 Multiple Response Variables

```
> ## Double stack.
> stackdata <- with(READ.MATH, data.frame(subid = c(subid, subid),
+                  grade = c(grade, grade), response = c(read, math),
+                  label = c(rep("read", nrow(READ.MATH)), rep("math", nrow(READ.MATH)))))
> ## Create predictors.
> stackdata$read.int <- ifelse(test = (stackdata$label == "read"), yes = 1, no = 0)
> stackdata$math.int <- ifelse(stackdata$label== "math", yes = 1, no = 0)
> stackdata$read.grade <- ifelse(stackdata$label == "read", yes = stackdata$grade, no = 0)
> stackdata$math.grade <- ifelse(stackdata$label == "math", yes = stackdata$grade, no = 0)
> ## Sort and print.
> stackdata2 <- stackdata[order(stackdata$subid), ]
> head(stackdata2, n = 8)
```

	subid	grade	response	label	read.int	math.int	read.grade	math.grade
1	1	5	172	read	1	0	5	0
2	1	6	185	read	1	0	6	0
3	1	7	179	read	1	0	7	0
4	1	8	194	read	1	0	8	0
89	1	5	175	math	0	1	0	5
90	1	6	172	math	0	1	0	6
91	1	7	169	math	0	1	0	7
92	1	8	185	math	0	1	0	8

Table 13.2 Schematic of two-response data for a single subject.

grade	response	read.int	math.int	read.grade	math.grade
5	$read_{i1}$	1	0	5	0
6	$read_{i2}$	1	0	6	0
7	$read_{i3}$	1	0	7	0
8	$read_{i4}$	1	0	8	0
5	$math_{i1}$	0	1	0	5
6	$math_{i2}$	0	1	0	6
7	$math_{i3}$	0	1	0	7
8	$math_{i4}$	0	1	0	8

Having created the appropriate double-stacked data set, the model can now be estimated. The expected value form of the two-response model is written as

$$E(y_{ij}^{(k)}) = \beta_1(\text{read.int}_{ij}) + \beta_2(\text{math.int}_{ij}) + \beta_3(\text{read.grade}_{ij}) + \beta_4(\text{math.grade}_{ij}), \quad (13.2.1)$$

where $y^{(k)}$ is a vector of stacked response values, as in Table 13.2. The first elements are the vector of reading scores, denoted as $y_{ij}^{(1)}$, and the remaining elements are the vector of mathematics scores, denoted as $y_{ij}^{(2)}$. Equation 13.2.1 is distinct in the sense that there is no intercept parameter, β_0. This feature requires special consideration when using lmer(), as shown below.

The key to understanding the fixed effects of Equation 13.2.1 is to consider the data structure of Table 13.2. A portion of each predictor vector in Equation 13.2.1 consists of 0s (see Table 13.2). This leads to the selective elimination of parameters in Equation 13.2.1, conditional on the response. The conditional representation is

$$E(y_{ij}^{(1)}) = \beta_1 + \beta_3(\text{read.grade}_{ij}) \quad \text{if response = read,}$$
$$E(y_{ij}^{(2)}) = \beta_2 + \beta_4(\text{math.grade}_{ij}) \quad \text{if response = math.} \quad (13.2.2)$$

Equation 13.2.2 shows that β_1 is the intercept for the reading curve, and β_3 is the slope. Similarly, β_2 is the intercept for the math curve, and β_4 is the slope. From these definitions, it can be seen that the model allows the two response variables to have different change curves.

An advantage of estimating the parameters in Equation 13.2.1 is that the variance-covariance matrix among the fixed effects can be used as a basis for inference. As explained in previous chapters, the variance-covariance matrix among the fixed effects is necessary to test fixed effects. In this case, the LRT can be used to test for equality of intercepts, $H_0 : \beta_1 = \beta_2$, or equality of slopes, $H_0 : \beta_3 = \beta_4$; a similar comparison can be performed with the AICc. It is reiterated that such hypotheses cannot be evaluated directly when the change curves for the response variables are estimated in separate models.

In the lmer() syntax for estimating the model of Equation 13.2.1, 0 is used to denote that β_0 is to be omitted in the fixed effects portion. The 0 appears immediately after the tilde ($\sim$) in the formula syntax. Zero must also be used to request that a random effect for b_{0i} be omitted from the model.

In the code below, the model is estimated using two random effects: a random intercept term for reading, and a random intercept term for mathematics. A different number of random effects is possible, but the structure here is used in anticipation of the model comparison to be discussed later.

```
> twodvs.1 <- lmer(response ~ 0 + read.int + math.int + read.grade + math.grade +
+                   (0 + read.int + math.int | subid), data = stackdata, REML = FALSE)
> twodvs.1
```

```
 1 Linear mixed model fit by maximum likelihood
 2 Formula:response ~ 0 + read.int + math.int + read.grade + math.grade+(0 + read.int + math.int|subid)
 3    Data: stackdata
 4    AIC   BIC  logLik deviance REMLdev
 5   1293  1318  -638.5    1277    1265
 6 Random effects:
 7  Groups    Name     Variance Std.Dev. Corr
 8  subid     read.int 291.31   17.068
 9            math.int 290.56   17.046   0.872
10  Residual          100.56   10.028
11 Number of obs: 160, groups: subid, 22
12
13 Fixed effects:
14            Estimate Std. Error t value
15 read.int   178.047      7.794  22.844
16 math.int   168.354      7.792  21.607
17 read.grade   4.821      1.075   4.485
18 math.grade   5.673      1.075   5.278
19
20 Correlation of Fixed Effects:
21            red.nt mth.nt rd.grd
22 math.int    0.194
23 read.grade -0.872 -0.006
24 math.grade -0.006 -0.873  0.008
```

Lines 8 to 9 of the output list the variances of the random intercepts of the two responses. In this case, the variances are similar and the random effects are highly correlated. The correlation matrix among the fixed effects

13.2 Multiple Response Variables

is shown in lines 20 to 24, which is based on a corresponding variance-covariance matrix.

Lines 13 to 18 contain the fixed effects output, which reveals a linear increase for both response variables. Lines 15 to 16 indicate that the estimated intercept for reading ($\hat{\beta}_1 = 178.05$) is larger than that for mathematics ($\hat{\beta}_1 = 168.35$). Lines 17 to 18 show that the estimated slope for mathematics ($\hat{\beta}_1 = 5.67$) is larger than that for reading ($\hat{\beta}_1 = 4.82$). The *t*-ratios for the slopes are relatively large, providing evidence that the linear growth is statistically reliable for each response.

To examine if the slopes of the responses are statistically equivalent, the insulate function is used to impose a constraint. When $\beta_3 = \beta_4$, the model simplifies to

$$E(y_{ij}^{(k)}) = \beta_1(\text{read.int}_{ij}) + \beta_2(\text{math.int}_{ij})$$
$$+ \beta_3\Big[(\text{read.grade}_{ij}) + (\text{math.grade}_{ij})\Big]. \qquad (13.2.3)$$

That is, reading and mathematics have a common slope, β_3.

The insulate function is used to specify the sum in the last predictor term. Consider the following.

```
> twodvs.2 <- lmer(response ~ 0 + read.int + math.int + I(read.grade + math.grade) +
+                 (0 + read.int + math.int | subid), data = stackdata, REML = FALSE)
> summary(twodvs.2)@coefs
```

	Estimate	Std. Error	t value
read.int	175.348798	6.1522934	28.501371
math.int	171.049498	6.1428959	27.845091
I(read.grade + math.grade)	5.246942	0.7633638	6.873449

The output shows that two fixed intercepts are estimated, $\hat{\beta}_1$ and $\hat{\beta}_2$, but there is a single common slope, $\hat{\beta}_3$. To provide statistical evidence that this simplification is warranted, the simpler model (twodvs.2) is compared with the more complex one (twodvs.1). Both the LRT and the AICc are used in the comparison.

```
> anova(twodvs.2, twodvs.1)
```

```
Data: stackdata
Models:
twodvs.2: response~0 + read.int + math.int + I(read.grade+math.grade)+
twodvs.2:          (0 + read.int + math.int | subid)
twodvs.1: response ~ 0 + read.int + math.int + read.grade + math.grade +
twodvs.1:          (0 + read.int + math.int | subid)
         Df    AIC    BIC  logLik  Chisq Chi Df Pr(>Chisq)
twodvs.2  7 1291.3 1312.8 -638.66
twodvs.1  8 1293.0 1317.6 -638.50 0.3155      1     0.5743
```

```
> print(aictab(list(twodvs.1, twodvs.2), c("Two slopes", "One slope")), LL = FALSE)
```

```
Model selection based on AICc :

              K    AICc  Delta_AICc  AICcWt  Cum.Wt
One slope     7  1292.05         0.0    0.72    0.72
Two slopes    8  1293.95         1.9    0.28    1.00
```

As seen in the output, the LRT-*p* is relatively large. The weight of evidence of the model with one slope is larger than that of the model with two slopes. There is statistical evidence that the population reading and mathematics linear slopes might be equal.

The same type of comparison can be performed for the intercepts. However, a complication is that the model cannot have separate random effects for the responses when there is a common intercept. Therefore, for model comparison purposes, the number of random effects is reduced to one for the following evaluation.

```
> twodvs.1 <- lmer(response ~ 0 + read.int + math.int + I(read.grade + math.grade) +
+                  (0 + I(read.int + math.int) | subid), data = stackdata, REML = FALSE)
> twodvs.2 <- lmer(response ~ 0 + I(read.int + math.int) + I(read.grade + math.grade) +
+                  (0 + I(read.int + math.int) | subid), data = stackdata, REML = FALSE)
> anova(twodvs.1, twodvs.2)
```

```
Data: stackdata
Models:
twodvs.2:  response~0+I(read.int + math.int)+I(read.grade + math.grade) +
twodvs.2:             (0 + I(read.int + math.int) | subid)
twodvs.1:  response ~ 0 + read.int + math.int + I(read.grade + math.grade) +
twodvs.1:             (0 + I(read.int + math.int) | subid)
         Df    AIC     BIC   logLik  Chisq Chi Df Pr(>Chisq)
twodvs.2  4 1299.4  1311.7  -645.71
twodvs.1  5 1296.1  1311.5  -643.07 5.2759      1    0.02162 *
---
Signif. codes:  0 '***' 0.001 '**' 0.01 '*' 0.05 '.' 0.1 ' ' 1
```

```
>print(aictab(list(twodvs.1,twodvs.2),c("Two intercepts","One intercept")),LL = FALSE)
```

```
Model selection based on AICc :

                 K    AICc  Delta_AICc  AICcWt  Cum.Wt
Two intercepts   5  1296.53        0.00    0.83    0.83
One intercept    4  1299.67        3.14    0.17    1.00
```

The output reveals that the LRT-*p* for the LRT is relatively small, and the weight of evidence for the model with two separate intercepts is large. There is evidence that a model with separate intercepts and a common slope is warranted. On the basis of the above results, we would revert to the model that had separate random intercepts for the response with a single random slope.

Additional research questions can be addressed with two-response models (Fieuws & Verbeke, 2004). By including random intercepts and slopes for each response, various types of correlations may be examined. These include the correlation between individual slopes of the two responses, and correlations between intercepts of one response and slopes of the other. The variance component of interest can be tested using the bootstrap methods discussed in Chapter 10.

Static predictors can be included in multiple response models. Static predictor variables must be constructed similar to the intercept and grade variables in Table 13.2. There must be one new static predictor per response. Each new predictor will have the static values for the response in question, and 0 otherwise. Once these new static predictors are constructed, they are used in lmer() in a similar manner as single-response models. The new static predictors can appear alone as intercept effects, or as interactions with the time predictors. One can test to see, among other things, if the size of a static predictor effect is statistically equivalent for the two responses.

13.3 Additional Levels of Nesting

The final topic is additional levels of nesting. As discussed in Chapter 5, given some mild assumptions, LMER can be expressed as a multilevel model. The preceding chapters dealt with a two-level model, in which repeated measures were nested within subjects. The within-subjects repeated measures portion is the Level 1 model, and Level 2 is the between-subjects model. A key assumption in the two-level model is that the repeated measures are correlated, but the subjects are not.

There are situations in which an additional level of nesting occurs in the research design. There may be repeated measures nested within subjects, but also subjects nested within classrooms, or siblings nested within families. For these scenarios, the subjects' scores are expected to be correlated due to the shared environment. Students in the same classroom are expected to have scores that are more highly correlated than students among different classrooms. This is due to the shared experience of the same teacher, the same classroom facilities, and so on. Siblings in the same family share the same parents, housing, and so forth.

When the correlation due to nesting is appreciable, it should be accounted for in the statistical analysis. Just as one would not be inclined to use traditional regression for longitudinal analysis, one would not want to use a two-level model when there is additional nesting.

Regardless of the levels of the model, a key assumption is that there is dependency for the lower levels, but not for the highest level. With the two-level model considered in past chapters, there is dependency among the repeated measures, but independence among the subjects due to random sampling. When the highest level is groups of subjects (e.g., classrooms), there is still a random sampling assumption. For example, it is assumed that repeated measures within subjects are correlated, subjects within classrooms are correlated, but the classrooms themselves are not correlated.

13.3.1 THREE-LEVEL MODEL

This section considers a three-level model, and extensions to more levels are possible. In previous chapters, the response variable notation, y_{ij}, was used to denote the score for the ith person at the jth time point. The order of the subscripts signifies nesting, as the outer subscript, j, depicts nesting within the inner subscript, i. Another way of saying this is when the data frame is sorted by the highest level, which is subjects (i), then the time subscript (j) changes faster than the subject subscript.

In a three-level model, there is an additional level of nesting, such that the subjects are nested within a higher level unit, which is taken to be classrooms for the examples. To be consistent with what was stated in the last paragraph, the additional level subscript should be innermost, as time is nested within subjects, who are nested within classrooms. Therefore, the response notation is augmented as y_{hij}, which refers to the jth time point, for the ith subject, in the hth classroom. The range for each subscript is $j = 1, \ldots, n_i$, $i = 1, \ldots, N_h$, and $h = 1, \ldots, N^*$. It follows that when the data are sorted by the highest level, classrooms, the time subscript (j) changes faster than the subject subscript (i), which changes faster than the classroom subscript (h).

The changes in values of the nesting variables are the key to specifying the LMER model. To be explicit, suppose that the students in the data set are nested within classrooms A, B, ..., G. Suppose information about classrooms is contained in the text file classroom.txt, which is available on the book website. The file contains the subject identification number, the classroom letter (A–G), and the column labels. In the syntax below, the data are read in, and the top portion of the data frame is printed.

```
> classroom <- read.table("C:/Mine/classroom.txt", header = TRUE)
> head(classroom)
```

	subid	classr
1	1	A
2	2	A
3	3	A
4	4	B
5	5	B
6	6	B

The classroom information is merged with the MPLS.LS data frame. This is a one-to-many merge, as the classroom data frame is in wide format and MPLS.LS is in long format.

```
> ## Merge.
> MPLS.LS.CL <- merge(MPLS.LS, classroom, by = c("subid"))
> ## Print header of nesting variables.
> with(MPLS.LS.CL, head(data.frame(classr, subid, grade), n = 24))
```

13.3 Additional Levels of Nesting

```
   classr subid grade
1       A     1     5
2       A     1     6
3       A     1     7
4       A     1     8
5       A     2     5
6       A     2     6
7       A     2     7
8       A     2     8
9       A     3     5
10      A     3     6
11      A     3     7
12      A     3     8
13      B     4     5
14      B     4     6
15      B     4     7
16      B     4     8
17      B     5     5
18      B     5     6
19      B     5     7
20      B     5     8
21      B     6     5
22      B     6     6
23      B     6     7
24      B     6     8
```

The output reveals the nested structure of the data frame. It can be seen that `grade` changes faster than `subid`, which in turn changes faster than `classr`. Independence among units is assumed only for the highest level. In this case, it is assumed that classrooms are independent, but not subjects or repeated measures.

To get a sense of the possible variability among classrooms and subjects within classrooms, graphs are constructed. In the syntax below, individual observed reading curves are graphed over grade and faceted by classroom. Linear regression lines are plotted in each panel using `lm()`.

```
> g1 <- ggplot(MPLS.LS.CL, aes(x = grade, y = read, group = subid))
> g2 <- g1 + geom_line(colour = "grey60") + myx
> g3 <- g2 + facet_grid(. ~ classr) + opts(aspect.ratio = 2)
> g4 <- g3 + stat_smooth(aes(group = 1), method = "lm", se = F, lwd = 1.5)
> print(g4)
```

The graphs are shown in Figure 13.3. The vertical scatter within each panel illustrates the variability of subjects nested within classrooms. The horizontal scatter among panels represents variability among classrooms. There appears to be nontrivial variability among classrooms, at least with respect to the intercepts of the regression curves.

Similar to the two-level case, random effects are used to account for the dependency due to the nested structure of the data. The caveat here is that

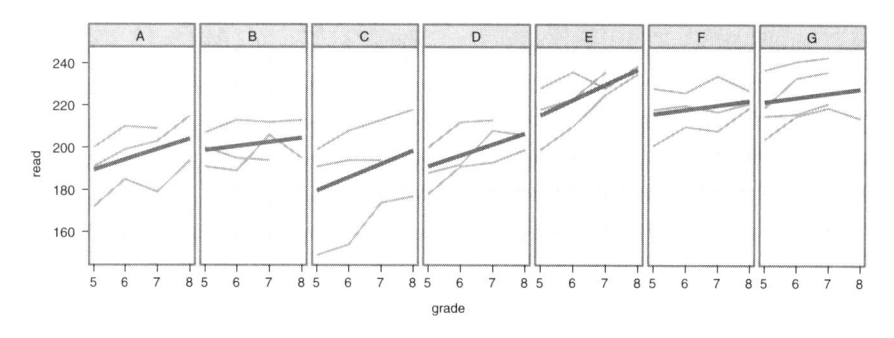

Figure 13.3 Individual curves (thin) and regression curves (thick) for reading by classroom.

random effects at multiple levels must be considered. In the two-level model, random effects are included at the second level. In the three-level model, random effects are included at the second and third levels.

In the three-level model, Level 1 is for the longitudinal data, Level 2 is for subjects, and Level 3 is for classrooms. The three levels are depicted in the following manner:

$$
\begin{aligned}
&\text{Level 1:} \quad \left\{ y_{hij} = \beta^*_{0hi} + \beta^*_{1hi}(\texttt{grade5}_{hij}) + \varepsilon_{hij}. \right. \\
&\text{Level 2:} \quad \begin{cases} \beta^*_{0hi} = \beta^{\dagger}_{0h} + b_{0hi} \\ \beta^*_{1hi} = \beta^{\dagger}_{1h} + b_{1hi}. \end{cases} \\
&\text{Level 3:} \quad \begin{cases} \beta^{\dagger}_{0h} = \beta_0 + b_{0h} \\ \beta^{\dagger}_{1h} = \beta_1 + b_{1h}. \end{cases}
\end{aligned}
\tag{13.3.1}
$$

Level 1 is a longitudinal model for the repeated measures nested within subjects, nested within classrooms. β^*_{0hi} is the random intercept of the ith subject, nested in the hth classroom, and similarly for the slope, β^*_{1hi}. The random error term, ε_{hij}, is assumed to be independent and normally distributed, with mean of 0 and constant variance.

Level 2 is a model for subjects nested within classrooms. The repeated measures have been summarized in the Level 1 regression coefficients, β^*_{0hi} and β^*_{1hi}. Thus, the time subscript does not appear at Level 2. $\beta^{\dagger}_{0h}$ is the average intercept of the subjects, and $\beta^{\dagger}_{1h}$ is the average slope of the subjects. The Level 2 random effects, b_{0hi} and b_{1hi}, represent the deviation of each subject from the subject average intercept and slope, respectively. The Level 2 random effects are assumed to be normally distributed with mean of 0 and variance-covariance matrix, $\boldsymbol{G}$.

Level 3 is the classroom model, with β_0 being the average intercept of classrooms and β_1 being the average slope. The subject subscript, i, does not appear at Level 3, as the subject information is summarized in the Level 2 parameters, $\beta^{\dagger}_{0h}$ and $\beta^{\dagger}_{1h}$. The Level 3 random effects, b_{0h} and b_{1h}, represent

13.3 Additional Levels of Nesting

the deviation of each classroom from the average classroom intercept and slope, respectively. The Level 3 random effects are assumed to be normally distributed, with mean of 0 and variance-covariance matrix, H. The interlevel random effects are assumed to be completely uncorrelated, and uncorrelated with the Level 1 random error.

Substituting higher level terms into the lower level equations yields the LMER model,

$$y_{hij} = (\beta_0 + b_{0h} + b_{0hi}) + (\beta_1 + b_{1h} + b_{1hi})(\texttt{grade5}_{hij}) + \varepsilon_{hij}. \quad (13.3.2)$$

Equation 13.3.2 is perhaps easier to deal with than the multilevel model because there are fewer terms. It is easier to see that β_0 is the mean intercept among subjects and classrooms, and there are two deviation terms, one for subjects (b_{0hi}) and one for classrooms (b_{0h}). Likewise, β_1 is the mean slope among subjects and classrooms, with individual deviations for subjects (b_{1hi}) and for classrooms (b_{1h}). The assumptions of the model can be written in the following manner: $b_{khi} \sim \mathcal{N}(\mathbf{0}, G) \perp b_{kh} \sim \mathcal{N}(\mathbf{0}, H) \perp \varepsilon_{hij} \sim \mathcal{N}(\mathbf{0}, \sigma_e^2 I_{hi})$, where $\perp$ indicates orthogonality.

The goals of the analysis are usually the same as with a two-level model—namely, to make inferences about β_1 and possibly β_0. The random effects are handmaidens to these goals, being included to account for dependency due to nesting.

Unlike the two-level model, there are a relatively large number of variance components. There are three unique elements in G, three in H, and the random error variance, σ_ε^2, for a total of seven. It may not always be the case that all the random effects are required, and the methods discussed in Chapter 10 can be used to evaluate this possibility. Because of the number of parameters in Equation 13.3.2, serious inferences cannot be made based on the toy data frame of this example. Nevertheless, the model is estimated to illustrate how a serious analysis might be performed.

The lmer() syntax for a three-level model requires a term for the additional level of random effects. To appreciate the syntax, note that the random effects portion of Equation 13.3.2 can be written as

$$\left[b_{0hi}(1) + b_{1hi}(\texttt{grade5}_{hij})\right] + \left[b_{0h}(1) + b_{1h}(\texttt{grade5}_{hij})\right]. \quad (13.3.3)$$

Each random intercept term appears as a single effect, and each random slope term is multiplied by the time predictor (grade5 is used here, but grade can also be used). The first bracketed part is for subjects, and the second is for classrooms. The subject random effects must be pinned to the subject identification number, and the classroom random effects must be pinned to the classroom identification letter. The random effects syntax, then, is

```
(1 + grade5 | subid) + (1 + grade5 | classr)
```

The 1 is optional and included here for clarity.

In the syntax below, the model of Equation 13.3.2 is estimated, and the results are printed. The reader is again cautioned that the data set is not large enough to make serious inferences for this model.

```
> MPLS.LS.CL$grade5 <- MPLS.LS.CL$grade - 5
> thrlvl.1 <- lmer(read ~ grade5 + (1 + grade5 | subid) + (1 + grade5 | classr),
+                  MPLS.LS.CL, REML = FALSE)
> print(thrlvl.1, cor = FALSE)
```

```
 1 Linear mixed model fit by maximum likelihood
 2 Formula: read ~ grade5 + (1 + grade5 | subid) + (1 + grade5 | classr)
 3    Data: MPLS.LS.CL
 4    AIC   BIC  logLik  deviance  REMLdev
 5   580.4 601.8 -281.2    562.4    555.7
 6 Random effects:
 7  Groups   Name        Variance  Std.Dev. Corr
 8  subid    (Intercept) 232.1735  15.2372
 9           grade5        4.2698   2.0663  -0.748
10  classr   (Intercept) 145.2937  12.0538
11           grade5        2.2691   1.5063  -0.178
12  Residual              18.5997   4.3127
13 Number of obs: 80, groups: subid, 22; classr, 7
14
15 Fixed effects:
16             Estimate Std. Error t value
17 (Intercept) 201.5319    5.6570   35.63
18 grade5        4.8454    0.8627    5.62
```

In output lines 15 to 18, it is seen that the fixed effects table is identical in form to that of the two-level model. What is distinct in the output is the variance components table, lines 6 to 12. Lines 8 to 9 show the variances for the subject intercepts and slopes, and lines 10 to 11 show the same for classrooms. The variability due to subjects is greater than that due to classrooms, and the correlation between the subject random effects is also greater in absolute value. Line 13 indicates there are 80 total rows of the data frame used in the analysis, 22 subjects, and 7 classrooms.

The fixed effects estimates in lines 17 to 18 show that the estimated mean reading score at Grade 5 is 201.53, and the estimated mean increase per grade is 4.85. The objects of inference in this case are the subjects. After all, it is subjects that are measured repeatedly, not classrooms. Inferences regarding subjects should take into account the nesting within classrooms, as we expect the intra-classroom correlation to be higher than the inter-classroom correlation.

The influence of classrooms is reflected in the estimated H matrix. The estimated variance components are considered when computing the deviance and when computing the SEs of the fixed effects. It can be verified in Section 5.4.1 that when a two-level model is fit ignoring classrooms, the SEs are *smaller* than seen above. Thus, the adjustment for the nesting within classrooms results in wider CIs and smaller t-values for the fixed effects. The tendency for overly optimistic SEs to occur is the primary motivation for including additional levels of nesting.

13.3.2 STATIC PREDICTORS IN THREE-LEVEL MODELS

Static predictors may be included in three-level models. A complication is that static predictors can be specified at different levels depending on the type of between-unit contrast they represent. For the example above, there might be static predictors that represent between-subject differences, or between-classroom differences. The former vary among subjects with no regard for classrooms, or at least not explicitly so. Classroom-level predictors vary among classrooms, and they only vary among subjects because of the nesting within classrooms.

An example of a classroom-level static predictor might be the presence or absence of a student teacher. If some classrooms are assigned a student teacher over the duration of the study and others are not, this will be a dichotomous classroom-level predictor. In this scenario, the student teachers are assigned to classrooms and not subjects. The variability in subjects is due entirely to the variability in classrooms. Such static predictors are included in the Level 3 model.

An example of a subject-level static predictor is `risk2`. Values of this categorical predictor are assigned to subjects, not classrooms. For this reason, `risk2` is included in the Level 2 model. The level at which the static predictor is included is denoted by its subscript. The model with `risk2` uses the Level 2 subscript, *hi*:

$$y_{hij} = (\beta_0 + b_{0h} + b_{0hi}) + (\beta_1 + b_{1h} + b_{1hi})(\text{grade5}_{hij})$$
$$+ \beta_2(\text{risk2DADV}_{hi}) + \beta_3(\text{grade5}_{hij} \cdot \text{risk2DADV}_{hi}) + \varepsilon_{hij}.$$
(13.3.4)

In `lmer()`, static predictors are specified as previously discussed, with nothing in the syntax to distinguish their level. The level must be inferred from the nature of the static predictor, or by examination of the data frame. Consider the estimation of the model of Equation 13.3.4 after the `risk2` variable is constructed.

```
> ## Create risk2.
> MPLS.LS.CL$riskC[MPLS.LS.CL$risk == "HHM"] <- "DADV"
> MPLS.LS.CL$riskC[MPLS.LS.CL$risk == "POV"] <- "DADV"
> MPLS.LS.CL$riskC[MPLS.LS.CL$risk == "ADV"] <- "ADV"
> MPLS.LS.CL$risk2 <- factor(MPLS.LS.CL$riskC)
> ## Estimate model.
> thrlvl.2 <- lmer(read ~ grade5 * risk2+ (1 + grade5 | subid) + (1 + grade5 | classr),
+                 MPLS.LS.CL, REML = FALSE)
> print(thrlvl.2, cor = FALSE)
```

```
Linear mixed model fit by maximum likelihood
Formula: read ~ grade5 * risk2 + (1 + grade5 | subid) + (1 + grade5 |     classr)
   Data: MPLS.LS.CL
   AIC   BIC logLik deviance REMLdev
 570.2 596.4 -274.1    548.2   534.9
Random effects:
 Groups   Name        Variance Std.Dev. Corr
 subid    (Intercept) 179.8901 13.4123
          grade5        3.8154  1.9533  -0.721
 classr   (Intercept)   4.1809  2.0447
          grade5        2.6355  1.6234  -1.000
```

```
 Residual                     18.6114   4.3141
Number of obs: 80, groups: subid, 22; classr, 7

Fixed effects:
                  Estimate Std. Error t value
(Intercept)       217.4972     4.5550   47.75
grade5              4.4400     1.3309    3.34
risk2DADV         -28.1467     6.1571   -4.57
grade5:risk2DADV    0.7009     1.7746    0.39
```

The random effects table in the output suggests some problems. The perfect correlation among the Level 3 random effects for classroom indicates that not all elements of *H* need be estimated. It is also odd that the variance of the classrooms random intercepts has decreased so much as compared to the model without the static predictor. This is due to the way the classroom variable was generated, and it should not be taken as regular.

The fixed effects table suggests there might be a population intercept difference among the risk groups, but not a slope difference. The estimated fixed effect for riskDADV is −28.15, indicating that the disadvantaged group curve has an intercept that is below that of the advantaged group.

The object of inference is again subjects, as a risk group status is assigned to a subject and not to a classroom. Although between-subject differences are the primary focus, the three-level model is important here because it accounts for the dependency associated with nesting within classrooms.

As a final word, there are many varieties of nesting and crossing that can be handled by LMER. A number of these cases are discussed in Pinheiro and Bates (2000) and Bates (2011).

Appendix
Soft Introduction to Matrix Algebra

Comprehension of many of the optional sections of this book is facilitated with some knowledge of matrix algebra. A major reason for using matrix algebra is that summation notation using $\sum$ can be very cumbersome for expressing the general details of linear mixed effects regression (LMER). This is especially true for the formula of the variances and covariances among the responses in Chapter 5 and the formula for the fixed effects estimator in Chapter 6.

The treatment here is "soft" in the respect that few general formulas are presented. Rather, the focus is mostly on special cases. This should be adequate to facilitate an understanding of the matrix algebra material in the optional sections of this book. The reader desiring a general and more rigorous treatment of matrix algebra is referred to Schott (1997) or similar resources.

A.1 Matrices

A matrix is a rectangular array consisting of numbers, letters, symbols, or a mixture of these. A matrix is distinguished by its rows, which count from top to bottom, and by its columns, which count from left to right. Square brackets or round brackets are used to enclose a matrix when it is typeset, but not so when a matrix is printed in the R terminal window (see Chapter 2). Here are some examples of matrices:

$$\begin{bmatrix} 10 & 4 & .5 \\ 6 & 1 & 25 \\ 0.1 & 17 & 2 \end{bmatrix}, \begin{bmatrix} a & b \\ b & c \end{bmatrix}, \begin{pmatrix} 1 & 5 \\ 1 & 6 \\ 1 & 7 \\ 1 & 8 \end{pmatrix}. \qquad (A.1.1)$$

It is customary to use an italicized, boldface, Roman letter (e.g., *A*), to stand for a matrix. This facilities the depiction of certain matrix operations, as discussed in a moment. Suppose the third matrix in Equation A.1.1 is labeled as *Z*, so that

$$Z = \begin{bmatrix} 1 & 5 \\ 1 & 6 \\ 1 & 7 \\ 1 & 8 \end{bmatrix}. \quad\quad (A.1.2)$$

It is important to keep track of the number of rows and columns of a matrix, as this has implications for matrix operations. In Equation A.1.2, *Z* has four rows and two columns. This is referred to as a "four-by-two" matrix and is denoted as 4×2. The number of rows and columns are known as the *dimensions* of the matrix. The dimensions sometimes appear as a subscript to the matrix symbol, $Z_{4\times 2}$. In this appendix, the dimensions are made explicit by putting them in subscripts, but this is not done in the optional sections of the chapters.

When the number of rows and columns is equal, this is the special case of a *square matrix*. An example of a 2×2 square matrix is the variance-covariance matrix of the random effects, discussed in Chapters 5 and 10:

$$G_{2\times 2} = \begin{bmatrix} Var(b_{0i}) & Cov(b_{0i}, b_{1i}) \\ Cov(b_{0i}, b_{1i}) & Var(b_{0i}) \end{bmatrix}.$$

In addition to being square, *G* is also *symmetric*, as the upper right element is equal to the lower left element. The equal elements reside in the *off-diagonal*, and the other variance elements reside in the *diagonal*.

For a larger matrix, symmetry means the elements in the upper right off-diagonal are a mirror image of the elements in the lower left off-diagonal. Consider the following.

$$H_{3\times 3} = \begin{bmatrix} 10 & a & b \\ a & 11 & c \\ b & c & 12 \end{bmatrix}.$$

The elements, a, b, c, are a mirror image on either side of the diagonal elements of $10, 11, 12$.

When a matrix has only one row or only one column, this is the special case known as a *vector*. A row vector is a matrix with one row, and a column vector is a matrix with one column. The following are examples of each type.

$$x_{1\times 2} = \begin{bmatrix} 10 & 7 \end{bmatrix}, \quad \beta_{2\times 1} = \begin{bmatrix} \beta_1 \\ \beta_2 \end{bmatrix}.$$

Often a lowercase, italicized, boldface letter is used for a vector, as with *x* above. However, an uppercase letter or symbol (e.g., *β*) can also be used.

A.2 Transpose

Another special case is a matrix that has only one row and only one column. This is a 1×1 matrix known as a *scalar*. It may sound funny, but every number is a scalar matrix.

When introducing the concept of a matrix, it is helpful to use particular symbols to accentuate the row and column concepts. This can be done by using two subscripts, the first for the row and the second for the column.

$$Z_{4\times 2} = \begin{bmatrix} z_{11} & z_{12} \\ z_{21} & z_{22} \\ z_{31} & z_{32} \\ z_{41} & z_{42} \end{bmatrix}. \qquad (A.1.3)$$

Each symbol indexes the element's location in the matrix. For instance, z_{21} resides in the second row and first column; z_{42} is in the fourth row and second column.

Another special case is a *diagonal matrix*, which has nonzero diagonal elements and 0s on the off-diagonal. An even more special case is a diagonal matrix that has 1s on the diagonal, which is known as an *identity matrix*. A diagonal matrix and an identity matrix can have any symbol, but in the example below, we use D and I, respectively.

$$D_{3\times 3} = \begin{bmatrix} 10 & 0 & 0 \\ 0 & 5 & 0 \\ 0 & 0 & 15 \end{bmatrix}, \quad I_{3\times 3} = \begin{bmatrix} 1 & 0 & 0 \\ 0 & 1 & 0 \\ 0 & 0 & 1 \end{bmatrix}.$$

A.2 Transpose

Transposing a matrix means exchanging the rows and columns. The first row of the matrix becomes the first column in the transpose of the matrix, the first column becomes the first row, and so on. The result is that the number of columns of the original matrix becomes the number of rows of the transposed matrix, and the number of rows of the original matrix becomes the number of columns in the transposed matrix. In terms of symbols, a superscript T is used with the matrix letter to denote the transposed matrix, for example, Z^T.

The following is an illustration of transposing a 4×2 matrix into a 2×4 matrix. The same element subscripts are used to keep track of what happens in transposing.

$$Z_{4\times 2} = \begin{bmatrix} z_{11} & z_{12} \\ z_{21} & z_{22} \\ z_{31} & z_{32} \\ z_{41} & z_{42} \end{bmatrix}, \quad Z^T_{2\times 4} = \begin{bmatrix} z_{11} & z_{21} & z_{31} & z_{41} \\ z_{12} & z_{22} & z_{32} & z_{42} \end{bmatrix} \qquad (A.2.1)$$

The transposed matrix swaps rows for columns and vice versa. The dimensions of the transposed matrix are defined by a swap of the rows and columns as well.

A.3 Matrix Addition

Matrix addition requires that two matrices have the same number of rows and columns. Addition is performed for each matrix location using the corresponding elements from both matrices.

$$A_{2\times 2} + B_{2\times 2} = \begin{bmatrix} a_{11} & a_{12} \\ a_{21} & a_{22} \end{bmatrix} + \begin{bmatrix} b_{11} & b_{12} \\ b_{21} & b_{22} \end{bmatrix} = \begin{bmatrix} a_{11}+b_{11} & a_{12}+b_{12} \\ a_{21}+b_{21} & a_{22}+b_{21} \end{bmatrix}.$$
(A.3.1)

In may be easier to see this using numbers.

$$A_{2\times 2} + B_{2\times 2} = \begin{bmatrix} 5 & 7 \\ 9 & 11 \end{bmatrix} + \begin{bmatrix} 1 & 2 \\ 3 & 4 \end{bmatrix} = \begin{bmatrix} 5+1 & 7+2 \\ 9+3 & 11+4 \end{bmatrix} = \begin{bmatrix} 6 & 9 \\ 12 & 15 \end{bmatrix}.$$
(A.3.2)

Matrix subtraction works in a similar way.

A.4 Multiplication of a Matrix by a Scalar

Matrix addition is relatively clear, as the sum is performed on an element-by-element basis. A simple form of matrix multiplication also works in the same manner. This is the multiplication of a matrix by a scalar.

$$2 \cdot A_{2\times 2} = 2 \begin{bmatrix} a & b \\ b & c \end{bmatrix} = \begin{bmatrix} 2a & 2b \\ 2b & 2c \end{bmatrix}.$$
(A.4.1)

Each element in the nonscalar matrix is multiplied by the scalar. The dimensions of the resulting matrix are the same as the original nonscalar matrix. It does not matter if the scalar appears before the matrix, as in $2 \cdot A$, or after the matrix, as in $A \cdot 2$.

A.5 Matrix Multiplication

General matrix multiplication is very different from the scalar multiplication described above. Matrix multiplication is symbolized by two matrices being listed next to each other. For example, $C = AB$, or with dimension subscripts,

$$C_{2\times 3} = A_{2\times 2} B_{2\times 3}.$$
(A.5.1)

A.5 Matrix Multiplication

The dimensions are important because they provide the key to the operations defining matrix multiplication.

The first important point is that *two matrices can be multiplied only if their inner dimensions agree*. This means the number of columns of the first matrix must be equal to the number of rows of the second matrix. This requirement is met in Equation A.5.1, as A has two columns and B has two rows. Because of this requirement, matrix multiplication is sometimes referred to as the *inner product*.

The second important point is that *the resulting matrix has dimensions that are the outer dimensions of the two matrices being multiplied*. This means the product matrix (i.e., C) has the same number of rows as the first matrix and the same number of column as the second matrix. In Equation A.5.1, A has two rows and B has three columns. The product matrix, C, has dimensions 2×3.

The third important point is that *to compute an element in the resulting product matrix, you work with the row of the first matrix and the column of the second matrix*. By "work with," it is meant that multiplication *and* addition occur at the element level with matrix multiplication.

It is perhaps best to use a concrete example to illustrate the procedures. Suppose the goal is to multiply the following two matrices:

$$A_{2 \times 2} = \begin{bmatrix} a_{11} & a_{12} \\ a_{21} & a_{22} \end{bmatrix}, \quad B_{2 \times 2} = \begin{bmatrix} b_{11} & b_{12} \\ b_{21} & b_{22} \end{bmatrix}.$$

The resulting product matrix will be symbolized as C. That is, $C = AB$.

It is best to begin by listing the elements of C using the subscripts for rows and columns, as was done immediately above:

$$C_{2 \times 2} = \begin{bmatrix} c_{11} & c_{12} \\ c_{21} & c_{22} \end{bmatrix}.$$

The subscripts of each element dictate which row and column of A and B are involved in the calculation.

The first subscript of a c element indicates what row of A is used, and the second subscript indicates what column of B is used. For example, c_{12} indicates the first row of A with elements a_{11}, a_{12} and the second column of B with elements b_{12}, b_{22}.

The formulas for each element of C are listed below. The genesis of these formulas is explained in a moment.

$$\begin{aligned} c_{11} &= a_{11} \cdot b_{11} + a_{12} \cdot b_{21}, \\ c_{12} &= a_{11} \cdot b_{12} + a_{12} \cdot b_{22}, \\ c_{21} &= a_{21} \cdot b_{11} + a_{22} \cdot b_{21}, \\ c_{22} &= a_{21} \cdot b_{12} + a_{22} \cdot b_{22}. \end{aligned} \quad (A.5.2)$$

The formulas illustrate a number of conventions. The first a subscript is always the same as the first subscript of c, and the second b subscript is always the same as the second subscript of c. When a row of A is chosen by the first subscript of the c element, the products are summed until all elements in a row are exhausted, which also exhausts all the elements in the column of B. When the inner dimensions of a and b agree, the elements are multiplied. Summation is over product terms that have different inner dimensions.

For those who prefer a detailed formula, the element c_{ij} in C is computed as the following:

$$c_{ij} = \sum_{k=1}^{K} a_{ik} b_{kj}. \tag{A.5.3}$$

In the examples, $K = 2$, but the formula holds for matrices of any size. The subscripts and superscript here should be interpreted in isolation and not confused with uses in the chapters of the book.

A graphical representation of matrix multiplication for the 2×2 matrices is shown in Figure A.4. The figure is based on an illustration provided by Matthes (2010). The four panels of the figure each illustrate how one element of C is computed. In each panel, the A matrix is at the lower left, the B matrix is at the upper right, and the C matrix is at the lower right. The arcs indicate what elements of A and B are multiplied. The plus sign ($+$) between the boxes in each arc indicates the products that are summed. Finally, an arrow points to the resulting element in the product matrix, C.

A.6 Determinant

The *determinant* of a matrix is useful when one wants to summarize the information with a single number. The determinant also plays an important role in the operation described in the next section. *The determinant is only defined for a square matrix.* Thus, the matrix must have the same number of rows and columns.

The determinant is illustrated for a 2×2 matrix, as the calculations are cumbersome for larger matrices. The determinant is denoted by vertical bars on either side of the matrix symbol, for example, $|A|$. Consider the following illustration.

$$\begin{aligned}|G| &= \left| \begin{pmatrix} Var(b_{0i}) & Cov(b_{0i}, b_{1i}) \\ Cov(b_{0i}, b_{1i}) & Var(b_{1i}) \end{pmatrix} \right| \\ &= Var(b_{0i}) \cdot Var(b_{1i}) - Cov(b_{0i}, b_{1i}) \cdot Cov(b_{0i}, b_{1i}) \\ &= Var(b_{0i}) \cdot Var(b_{1i}) - \left[Cov(b_{0i}, b_{1i}) \right]^2. \end{aligned}$$

As the equations show, the determinate of a 2×2 matrix is the product of the diagonal elements minus the product of the off-diagonal elements. The result

A.7 Inverse   521

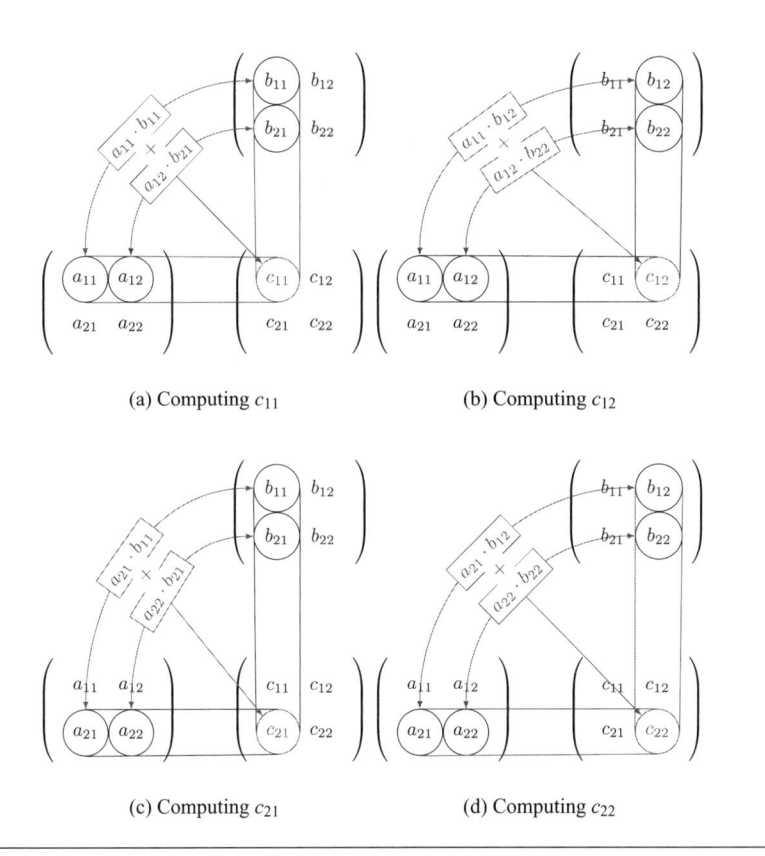

Figure A.4 Computing elements of $C = AB$.

(a) Computing c_{11}
(b) Computing c_{12}
(c) Computing c_{21}
(d) Computing c_{22}

is a scalar that summarizes the information contained in the matrix. When the determinant is computed for a variance-covariance matrix as is done above, the scalar is sometimes referred to as a *generalized variance* (see Chapter 10 for a usage of the generalized variance).

A.7 Inverse

Matrix *inversion* is analogous to division in scalar algebra. Recall in scalar algebra that $\frac{1}{a} = a^{-1}$. This same notation is used to denote the inverse of a matrix, for example, A^{-1}. *Similar to the determinant, the inverse can only be computed for a square matrix.*[1]

---
[1] The *generalized inverse* can be used for matrices that are not square (see Schott, 1997, chap. 5).

Table A.3 R functions for matrix algebra.

Operation	R Function	Example	Result
Define a matrix	`matrix()`	`A <- matrix(c(10, 15), ncol = 1)`	$\begin{bmatrix} 10 \\ 15 \end{bmatrix}$
Diagonal matrix	`diag()`	`B <- diag(c(10, 15))`	$\begin{bmatrix} 10 & 0 \\ 0 & 15 \end{bmatrix}$
Identity matrix	`diag()`	`diag(rep(1, times = 2))`	$\begin{bmatrix} 1 & 0 \\ 0 & 1 \end{bmatrix}$
Transpose	`t()`	`t(A)`	$\begin{bmatrix} 10 & 15 \end{bmatrix}$
Addition	`+`	`A + A`	$\begin{bmatrix} 20 \\ 30 \end{bmatrix}$
Subtraction	`-`	`A - A`	$\begin{bmatrix} 0 \\ 0 \end{bmatrix}$
Scalar multiplication	`*`	`3 * A`	$\begin{bmatrix} 30 \\ 45 \end{bmatrix}$
Matrix multiplication	`%*%`	`B %*% A`	$\begin{bmatrix} 100 \\ 225 \end{bmatrix}$
Determinant	`det()`	`det(B)`	150
Inverse	`solve()`	`solve(B)`	$\begin{bmatrix} \frac{10}{150} & \frac{-0}{150} \\ \frac{-0}{150} & \frac{15}{150} \end{bmatrix}$

Inversion is illustrated for a 2 × 2 matrix, as the calculations are cumbersome for larger matrices. The determinant from the last section plays a role in the computation of the inverse. Here is an example of the inverse of a square and symmetric matrix.

$$A^{-1} = \begin{bmatrix} a & b \\ b & c \end{bmatrix}^{-1}$$
$$= \frac{1}{|A|} \begin{bmatrix} c & -b \\ -b & a \end{bmatrix}$$
$$= \frac{1}{a \cdot c - b^2} \begin{bmatrix} c & -b \\ -b & a \end{bmatrix}$$
$$= \begin{bmatrix} \frac{c}{a \cdot c - b^2} & \frac{-b}{a \cdot c - b^2} \\ \frac{-b}{a \cdot c - b^2} & \frac{a}{a \cdot c - b^2} \end{bmatrix}.$$

It is not always the case that a square matrix will have an inverse. In such cases, the matrix is known as *singular* or, more pejoratively, *degenerate*.

A.8 Matrix Algebra and R Functions

Functions such as lmer() incorporate many of the matrix operations discussed in this appendix. The operations are largely invisible to the user. Matrix operations can be explicitly performed in R using particular functions or operators. Table A.3 lists the operations discussed in this appendix and the R functions used to perform the operations. Examples of R syntax are provided for each function.

References

Abelson, R. P. (1997). A retrospective on the significance test ban of 1999 (If there were no significance tests, they would be invented). In L. L. Harlow, S. A. Mulaik, & J. H. Steiger (Eds.), *What if there were no significance tests?* (p. 117–141). Mahwah, NJ: Erlbaum.

Akaike, H. (1973). Information theory as an extension of the maximum likelihood principle. In B. N. Petrov & F. Csaki (Eds.), *Second international symposium on information theory* (p. 267–281). Budapest, Hungary: Akademiai Kiado.

Akaike, H. (1974). A new look at the statistical model identification. *IEEE Transactions on Automatic Control, AC-19*, 716–723.

Akaike, H. (1981). Likelihood of a model and information criteria. *Journal of Econometrics, 16*, 3–14.

Allison, P. D. (2009). Missing data. In R. E. Millsap & A. Maydeu-Olivares (Eds.), *The SAGE handbook of quantitative methods in psychology* (p. 72–89). Thousand Oaks, CA: Sage Publications Inc.

American Educational Research Association. (2006). Standards for reporting on empirical social science research in AREA publications. *Educational Researcher, 35*, 33–40.

American Psychological Association. (2010). *Publication manual of the American Psychological Association* (6th ed.). Washington, DC: Author.

Anderson, D. R. (2008). *Model based inference in the life sciences: A primer on evidence.* New York: Springer.

Anderson, D. R., & Burnham, K. P. (2002). Avoiding pitfalls when using information-theoretic methods. *Journal of Wildlife Management, 66*, 912–918.

Anderson, D. R., Burnham, K. P., Gould, W. R., & Cherry, S. (2001). Concerns about finding effects that are actually spurious. *Wildlife Society Bulletin, 29*, 311–316.

Anderson, D. R., Burnham, K. P., & Thompson, W. L. (2000). Null hypothesis testing: Problems, prevalence, and an alternative. *Journal of Wildlife Management, 64*, 912–923.

Applebee, A. N., & Langer, J. A. (2006). *The state of writing instruction in America's schools: What existing data tell us.* Albany, NY: Center on English Learning and Achievement University at SUNY, Albany.

Arnold, D. H., & Doctoroff, G. L. (2003). The early education of socioeconomically disadvantaged children. *Annual Review of Psychology, 54*, 517–545.

Azari, R., Li, L., & Tsai, C. L. (2006). Longitudinal data model selection. *Computational Statistics and Data Analysis, 50*, 3053–3066.

Azzalini, A. (1996). *Statistical inference based on the likelihood.* Boca Raton, FL: Chapman & Hall/CRC.

Baayen, R. H., Davidson, D. J., & Bates, D. M. (2008). Mixed-effects modeling with crossed random effects for subjects and items. *Journal of Memory and Language, 59*, 390–412.

Bates, D. M. (2005). Fitting linear mixed models in R. *R News, 5*, 27–30.

Bates, D. M. (2009, July). *Mixed models in R using the lme4 package*. Seewiesen, Germany. Available from http://lme4.r-forge.r-project.org/slides/2009-07-21-Seewiesen/1Intro-4a4.pdf

Bates, D. M. (2011). *lme4: Mixed-effects modeling with R*. New York: Springer.

Berger, J. O. (2003). Could Fisher, Jeffreys and Neyman have agreed on testing? *Statistical Science, 18*, 1–12.

Berger, J. O., & Pericchi, L. R. (1996). The intrinsic bayes factor for model selection and prediction. *Journal of the American Statistical Association, 91*, 109–122.

Berger, J. O., & Wolpert, R. L. (1988). *The likelihood principle: A review, generalizations, and statistical implications* (2nd ed.). Hayward, CA: Institute of Mathematical Statistics.

Berkson, J. (1942). Tests of significance considered as evidence. *Journal of the American Statistical Association, 37*, 325–335.

Blume, J. D. (2002). Likelihood methods for measuring statistical evidence. *Statistics in Medicine, 21*, 2563–2599.

Bolker, B. M. (2008). *Ecological models and data in R*. Princeton, NJ: Princeton University Press.

Boos, D. D. (2003). Introduction to the bootstrap world. *Statistical Science, 18*, 168–174.

Box, G. (1979). Robustness in the strategy of scientific model building. In R. Launer & G. Wilkinson (Eds.), *Robustness in statistics* (p. 201–236). New York: Academic Press.

Box, G. E. P., & Tidwell, P. W. (1962). Transformation of the independent variables. *Technometrics, 4*, 531–550.

Bretz, F., Hothorn, T., & Westfall, P. (2011). *Multiple comparisons using R*. Boca Raton, FL: CRC Press.

Burnham, K. P., & Anderson, D. R. (2002). *Model selection and multimodel inference*. New York: Springer.

Burnham, K. P., & Anderson, D. R. (2004). Multimodel inference: Understanding AIC and BIC in model selection. *Sociological Methods and Research, 33*, 261–304.

Burt, K. B., Obradović, J., Long, J. D., & Masten, A. S. (2008). The interplay of social competence and psychopathology over 20 years: Testing transactual and cascade models. *Child Development, 79*, 359–374.

Buyske, S. (2006). *mmlcr: Mixed-mode latent class regression* (Tech. Rep.). Boston, MA: Free Software Foundation, Inc. Available from http://cran.r-project.org/web/packages/mmlcr/index.html

Calinski, T., & Harabasz, J. (1974). A dendrite method for cluster analysis. *Communications in Statistics, 3*, 1–27.

Campbell, J. R., Hombo, C. M., & Mazzeo, J. (2000). *NAEP 1999 trends in academic progress: Three decades of student performance*. Washington, DC: OERI, U.S. Department of Education.

Caro, D. H., McDonald, J. T., & Willms, J. D. (2009). Socio-economic status and academic achievement trajectories from childhood to adolescence. *Canadian Journal of Education, 32*, 558–590.

Carroll, R. J. (2003). Variances are not always nuisance parameters. *Biometrics, 59*, 211–220.

Chamberlain, T. C. (1890). The method of multiple working hypotheses. *Science, 15*, 92–96.

Chatfield, C. (1995). Model uncertainty, data mining and statistical inference. *Journal of the Royal Statistical Society. Series A (Statistics in Society), 158*, 419–466.

Chatterji, M. (2006). Reading achievement gaps, correlates, and moderators of early reading achievement: Evidence from the Early Childhood Longitudinal Study (ECLS) kindergarten to first grade sample. *Journal of Educational Psychology, 98*, 489–507.

Christensen, R. (2003). Significantly insignificant F tests. *American Statistician, 57*, 27–32.

Christensen, R. (2005). Testing Fisher, Neyman, Pearson, and Bayes. *American Statistician, 59*, 121–126.

Cleveland, W. S. (1993). *Visualizing data*. Summit, NJ: Hobart Press.

Cleveland, W. S., Grosse, E., & Shyu, W. M. (1992). Local regression models. In *Statistical models in S*. New York: Wadsworth & Brooks/Cole.

Cliff, N. (1996). *Ordinal methods for behavioral data analysis*. Mahwah, NJ: Erlbaum.

References

Cnaan, A., Laird, N. M., & Slasor, P. (1997). Using the general linear mixed model to analyse unbalanced repeated measures and longitudinal data. *Statistics in Medicine, 16,* 2349–2380.

Cohen, J. (1988). *Statistical power analysis for the behavioral sciences* (2nd ed.). Hillsday, NJ: Lawrence Erlbaum.

Cohen, J. (1994). The earth is round ($p < 0.5$). *American Psychologist, 49,* 997–1003.

Cohen, J., Cohen, P., West, S. G., & Aiken, L. S. (2003). *Applied multiple regression/correlation analysis for the behavioral sciences.* Mahwah, NJ: Lawrence Erlbaum Associates.

Cox, D. R. (1990). Role of models in statistical analysis. *Statistical Science, 5,* 169–174.

Cox, D. R. (1995). The relation between theory and application in statistics. *Test, 4,* 207–261.

Cox, D. R. (1999). Discussion of "Some statistical heresies" by J. K. Lindsey. *Journal of the Royal Statistical Society. Series D (The Statistician), 48,* 30–31.

Crainiceanu, C., & Ruppert, D. (2004). Likelihood ratio tests in linear mixed models with one variance component. *Journal of the Royal Statistical Society, Series B, 66,* 165–185.

Davison, A. C., Hinkley, D. V., & Young, G. A. (2003). Recent developments in bootstrap methodology. *Statistical Science, 18,* 141–157.

Dearing, E., Kreider, H., Simkins, S., & Weiss, H. B. (2006). Family involvement in school and low-income children's literacy: Longitudinal associations between and within families. *Journal of Educational Psychology, 98,* 653–664.

DeLeeuw, J. (1988). Model selection in multinomial experiments. In T. K. Dijkstra (Ed.), *On model uncertainty and its statistical implications* (p. 118–138). New York: Springer-Verlag.

Diggle, P. J., Heagerty, P., Liang, K. Y., & Zeger, S. L. (2002). *Analysis of longitudinal data, 2nd ed.* New York: Oxford.

Ding, C. S., Davison, M. L., & Petersen, A. C. (2005). Multidimensional scaling analysis of growth and change. *Journal of Educational Measurement, 42,* 171–191.

Donnelly, C. A., Laird, N. M., & Ware, J. H. (1995). Prediction and creation of smooth curves for temporally correlated longitudinal data. *Journal of the American Statistical Association, 90,* 984–989.

Eamon, M. K. (2002). Effects of poverty on mathematics and reading achievement of young adolescents. *Journal of Early Adolescence, 22,* 49–74.

Edwards, A. W. (1992). *Likelihood* (2nd ed.). Baltimore: Johns Hopkins University Press.

Efron, B., & Gous, A. (2001). Scales of evidence for model selection: Fisher versus Jeffreys. In P. Lahiri (Ed.), *Model selection* (Vol. 38, p. 210–246). Beachwood, OH: Institute of Mathematical Statistics.

Efron, B., & Tibshirani, R. J. (1993). *An introduction to the boostrap.* New York: Chapman & Hall.

Eubank, R. L., & Speckman, P. (1990). Curve fitting by polynomial-trigonometric regression. *Biometrika, 77,* 1–9.

Faraway, J. J. (1992). On the cost of data analysis. *Journal of Computational and Graphical Statistics, 1,* 213–229.

Faraway, J. J. (2005). *Linear models with R.* Boca Raton, FL: Chapman & Hall / CRC Press.

Feyerabend, P. (1968). How to be a good empiricist -a plea for tolerance in matters epistemological. In P. H. Nidditch (Ed.), *The philosophy of science* (p. 12–39). Oxford: Oxford University Press.

Fidler, F. (2002). The fifth edition of the APA publication manual: Why its statistics recommendations are so controversial. *Educational and Psychological Measurement, 62,* 749–770.

Fieuws, S., & Verbeke, G. (2004). Joint modelling of multivariate longitudinal profiles: pitfalls of the random-effects approach. *Statistics in Medicine, 23,* 3093–3104.

Finch, S., Thomason, N., & Cumming, G. (2002). Past and future American Psychological Association guidelines for statistical practice. *Theory and Psychology, 12,* 825–853.

Fisher, R. A. (1922). On the mathematical foundations of theoretical statistics. *Philosophical Transactions of the Royal Society of London, Series A, 22,* 309–368.

Fisher, R. A. (1925). *Statistical methods for research workers* (1st ed.). Edinburgh: Oliver and Boyd.

Fisher, R. A. (1954). *Statistical methods for research workers* (12th ed.). New York: Haffner.

Fisher, R. A. (1960). Scientific thought and the refinement of human reasoning. *Journal of the Operations Research Society of Japan, 3*, 1–10.

Fisher, R. A. (1991). The design of experiments, 8th edition. In J. H. Bennett (Ed.), *Statistical methods, experimental design, and scientific inference*. Oxford: Oxford University Press.

Fitzmaurice, G. M., Laird, N. M., & Ware, J. H. (2004). *Applied longitudinal analysis*. New York: Wiley.

Forster, M. R. (1999). Model selection in science: The problem of language variance. *British Journal of the Philosophy of Science, 50*, 83–102.

Forster, M. R. (2000). Key concepts in model selection: Performance and generalizability. *Journal of Mathematical Psychology, 44*, 205–231.

Forster, M. R. (2002). Predictive accuracy as an achievable goal of science. *Philosophy of Science, 69*, S124–S134.

Forster, M. R., & Sober, E. (1994). How to tell when simpler, more united, or less ad hoc theories will provide more accurate predictions. *British Journal for the Philosophy of Science, 45*, 1–35.

Forster, M. R., & Sober, E. (2004). Why likelihood? In M. L. Taper & S. R. Lele (Eds.), *The nature of scientific evidence* (p. 153–165). Chicago, IL: University of Chicago Press.

Forster, M. R., & Sober, E. (2011). AIC scores as evidence—a Bayesian interpretation. In M. R. Forster & P. Bandyopadhyay (Eds.), *The philosophy of statistics* (p. 1–25). New York: Kluwer.

Free Software Foundation. (2007). *Gnu general public license* (Tech. Rep.). Boston, MA: Free Software Foundation, Inc. Available from http://fsf.org

Freedman, D. (1983). A note on screening regression models. *American Statistician, 37*, 152–255.

Gelman, A. (2004). Exploratory data analysis for complex models. *Journal of Computational and Graphical Statistics, 13*, 755–779.

Gelman, A., & Park, D. K. (2008). Splitting a predictor at the upper quarter or third and the lower quarter or third. *American Statistician, 62*, 1–8.

Gelman, A., & Stern, H. (2006). The difference between "significant" and "not significant" is not itself statistically significant. *The American Statistician, 60*, 328–331.

Genolini, C., & Falissard, B. (2010). Kml: k-means for longitudinal data. *Computational Statistics, 25*, 317–328.

Gigerenzer, G., Krauss, S., & Vitouch, O. (2004). The null ritual: What you always wanted to know about significance testing but were afraid to ask. In D. Kaplan (Ed.), *The Sage handbook of quantitative methodology for the social sciences* (p. 391–408). Thousand Oaks, CA: Sage.

Godfrey, L. G. (1998). Test of non-nested regression models: Some results on small sample behavior and the bootstrap. *Journal of Econometrics, 84*, 59–74.

Golden, R. M. (2000). Statistical tests for comparing possibly misspecified and nonnested models. *Journal of Mathematical Psychology, 44*, 153–170.

Goodman, S. N. (1993). P values, hypothesis tests, and likelihood: Implications for epidemiology of a neglected historical debate. *American Journal of Epidemiology, 137*, 485–496.

Goodman, S. N. (1999). Toward evidence-based medical statistics. 1: The P value fallacy. *Annals of Internal Medicine, 130*, 995–1004.

Goodman, S. N., & Royall, R. M. (1988). Evidence and scientific research. *American journal of public health, 78*, 1568–1574.

Greene, W. (2008). *Econometric analysis* (6th ed.). Upper Saddle River, NJ: Prentice Hall.

Greenland, S. (1998). Induction versus Popper: substance versus semantics. *International Journal of Epidemiology, 27*, 543–548.

Greven, S., & Kneib, T. (2010). On the behaviour of marginal and conditional Akaike information criteria in linear mixed models. *Biometrika, 97*, 773–789.

Griepentrog, G. L., Ryan, J. M., & Smith, L. D. (1982). Linear transformations of polynomial regression models. *American Statistician, 36*, 171–174.

References

Hacking, I. (1972). Review: Likelihood. *British Journal for the Philosophy of Science, 23*, 132–137.

Hand, D. J. (1996). Statistical strategy: Step 1. In P. Cheeseman & R. W. Oldford (Eds.), *Selecting models from data: Artificial intelligence and statistics iv* (p. 3–9). New York: Springer-Verlag.

Hardy, A. (1996). On the number of clusters. *Computational Statistics & Data Analysis, 23*, 83–96.

Harrell, F. E. (2001). *Regression modeling strategies*. New York: Springer.

Harwell, M., & LeBeau, B. (2010). Student eligibility for a free lunch as an SES measure in education research. *Educational Researcher, 39*, 120–131.

Hedges, L. V., & Nowell, A. (1999). Black-white test score convergence since 1965. In C. Jencks & M. Phillips (Eds.), *The black-white test score gap* (p. 149–181). Washington, DC: Brookings Institution Press.

Hedges, L. V., & Olkin, I. (1985). *Statistical methods for meta-analysis*. Orlando, FL: Academic Press.

Henry, G. T., & Rubinstein, R. (2002). Paying for grades: Impact of merit-based financial aid on educational quality. *Journal of Policy Analysis and Management, 21*, 93–109.

Hirst, K. E. (2006). *Calculus of one variable*. New York: Springer.

Hogan, T. P. (2010). *Bare-bones R*. Thousand Oaks, CA: Sage.

Hornik, K. (2010). *The R FAQ*. Available from http://CRAN.R-project.org/doc/FAQ/R-FAQ.html (ISBN 3-900051-08-9)

Howell, D. C. (2010). *Statistical methods in psychology* (7th ed.). Belmont, CA: Cengage Wadsworth.

Hsu, J. C. (1996). *Multiple comparisons: Theory and methods*. London: CRC Press, Chapman & Hall.

Hubbard, R., & Bayarri, M. J. (2003). Confusion over measures of evidence (p's) versus errors (α's) in classical statistical testing. *American Statistician, 57*, 171–182.

Hubbard, R., & Lindsay, R. M. (2008). Why P values are not a useful measure of evidence in statistical significance testing. *Theory & Psychology, 18*, 69–88.

Hurvich, C. M., & Tsai, C.-L. (1989). Regression and time series model selection in small samples. *Biometrika, 76*, 297–307.

Jaeger, A., & Kramer, W. (1998). A final twist on the equality of OLS and GLS. *Statistical Papers, 39*, 321–324.

Johnstone, D. J. (1986). Tests of significance in theory and practice. *Journal of the Royal Statistical Society, Series D, 35*, 491–504.

Johstone, D. J. (1987). Tests of significance following R. A. Fisher. *British Journal for the Philosophy of Science, 38*, 481–499.

Kadane, J. B., & Lazar, N. A. (2004). Methods and criteria for model selection. *Journal of the American Statistical Association, 99*, 279–290.

Keppel, G. (1991). *Design and analysis: A researcher's handbook*. Englewood Cliffs, NJ: Prentice Hall.

Kieseppä, I. A. (2001). Statistical model selection criteria and the philosophical problem of underdetermination. *British Journal of the Philosophy of Science, 52*, 761–794.

Kleinbaum, D. G., Kupper, L. L., Muller, K. E., & Nizam, A. (1998). *Applied regression analysis and other multivariable methods*. Pacific Grove, CA: Brooks/Cole Publishing Company.

Klimes-Dougan, B. K., Long, J. D., Lee, C. Y. S., Ronsaville, D., Gold, P., & Martinez, P. P. (2010). Continuity and cascades in offspring of bipolar parents: A longitudinal study of externalizing, internalizing, and thought problems. *Development and Psychopathology, 22*, 851–868.

Kolen, M. J., & Brennan, R. L. (2004). *Test equating, scaling, and linking*. New York: Springer.

Krantz, D. H. (1999). The null hypothesis testing controversy in psychology. *Journal of the American Statistical Association, 94*, 1372–1381.

Kreft, I., & De Leeuw, J. (1998). *Introducing multilevel modeling*. London: Sage Publications.

Kuczmarski, R. J., Ogden, C. L., & Guo, S. S. (2002, May). *2000 CDC growth charts for the united states: Methods and development*. (Tech. Rep. No. 111). Hyattsville, Maryland:

National Center for Health Statistics. Available from http://www.cdc.gov/nchs

Kuha, J. (2004). AIC and BIC: Comparisons of assumptions and performance. *Sociological Methods and Research, 33*, 188–229.

Kullback, S., & Leibler, R. A. (1951). On information and sufficiency. *Annals of Mathematical Statistics, 22*, 79–86.

Laird, N. M., & Ware, J. H. (1982). Random-effects models for longitudinal data. *Biometrics, 38*, 963–974.

Lee, J. (2002). Racial and ethnic achievement gap trends: Reversing the progress toward equity? *Educational Researcher, 31*, 3–12.

Leisch, F. (2002). Sweave user manual (2.7.1 ed.) [Computer software manual]. Technische Universitat Wien, Vienna, Austria. Available from http://www.stat.uni-muenchen.de/leisch/Sweave/Sweave-manual.pdf

Liang, H., Wu, H., & Zou, G. (2008). A note on conditional AIC for linear mixed-effects models. *Biometrika, 95*, 773–778.

Lindquist, M. A., & Gelman, A. (2009). Correlations and multiple comparisons in functional imaging: A statistical perspective. *Perspectives on Psychological Science, 4*, 310–313.

Lindsey, J. K. (1999). Some statistical heresies. *Journal of the Royal Statistical Society. Series D (The Statistician), 48*, 1–40.

Link, W. A., & Barker, R. J. (2006). Model weights and the foundations of multimodel inference. *Ecology, 87*, 2626–2635.

Littell, R. C., Milliken, G. A., Stroup, W. W., Wolfinger, R. D., & Schabenberger, O. (2006). *SAS for mixed models*. Cary, NC: SAS Institute Inc.

Long, J. D. (2005). Omnibus hypothesis testing in dominance-based ordinal multiple regression. *Psychological Methods, 10*, 329–351.

Long, J. D., Feng, D., & Cliff, N. (2003). Ordinal analysis of behavioral data. In J. Schinka & W. F. Velicer (Eds.), *Research methods in psychology. Volume 2 of the handbook of psychology (I. B. Weiner, Editor-in-Chief)* (p. 635–662). New York, NY: John Wiley.

Long, J. D., Herring, J. R., Brekke, J. S., Test, M. A., & Greenberg, J. (2007). Longitudinal construct validity of Brief Symptom Inventory subscales in schizophrenia. *Psychological Assessment, 19*, 298–308.

Long, J. D., & Ryoo, J. (2010). Using fractional polynomials to model non-linear trends in longitudinal data. *British Journal of Mathematical and Statistical Psychology, 63*, 177–203.

Lovell, M. C. (1983). Data mining. *Review of Economics and Statistics, 65*, 1–12.

Magee, L. (1998). Nonlocal behavior in polynomial regressions. *American Statistician, 52*, 20–22.

Mallows, C. (1998). The zeroth problem. *American Statistician, 52*, 1–9.

Masten, A. S., Heistad, D., Cutuli, J. J., Herbers, J. E., Obradovic, J., Chan, C. K., et al. (2008). School success in motion: Protective factors for academic achievement in homeless and highly mobile children in Minneapolis. *CURA Reporter, 38*, 3–12.

Masten, A. S., Roisman, G. I., Long, J. D., Burt, K. B., Obradović, J., Riley, J. R., et al. (2005). Developmental cascades: Linking academic achievement and externalizing and internalizing symptoms over 20 years. *Developmental Psychology, 41*, 733–746.

Matthes, A. (2010). *TikZ examples*. Available from http://www.texample.net/tikz/examples/author/alain-matthes/

Mayo, D. G. (1992). Did Pearson reject the Neyman-Pearson philosophy of statistics? *Synthese, 90*, 233–262.

Mazerolle, M. J. (2010). AICcmodavg: Model selection and multimodel inference based on (Q)AIC(c). [Computer software manual]. (R package version 1.07)

McClelland, G., & Irwin, J. R. (2003). Negative consequences of dichotomizing continuous predictor variables. *Journal of Marketing Research, 40*, 366–371.

McDonald, R. P. (1999). *Test theory: A unified treatment*. Mahwah, NJ: Lawrence Erlbaum.

McLoyd, V. C. (1998). Socioeconomic disadvantage and child development. *American Psychologist, 53*, 185–204.

Meehl, P. E. (1978). Theoretical risks and tabular asterisks: Sir Karl, Sir Ronald, and the slow progress of soft psychology. *Journal of Consulting and Clinical Psychology, 46*, 806–834.

References

Meehl, P. E. (1997). The problem is epistemology, not statistics. replace significance tests by confidence intervals and quantify accuracy of risky numerical predictions. In L. L. Harlow, S. A. Mulaik, & J. H. Steiger (Eds.), *What if there were no significance tests?* (p. 393–426). Mahwah, NJ: Lawrence Erlbaum Associates.

Miller, A. (2002). *Subset selection in regression, 2nd edition*. Boca Raton, FL: Chapman & Hall/CRC.

Mizerek, E. A., & Hinz, E. E. (2004, May). Helping homeless students. *Principal Leadership Magazine, 4*(8).

Molenberghs, G., & Fitzmaurice, G. M. (2009). Incomplete data: Introduction and overview. In G. M. Fitzmaurice, M. Davidian, G. Verbeke, & G. Molenberghs (Eds.), *Longitudinal data analysis* (p. 395–408). Boca Raton, FL: CRC Press.

Molenberghs, G., & Kenward, M. G. (2007). *Missing data in clinical studies*. West Sussex, England: Wiley.

Molenberghs, G., & Verbeke, G. (2004). Meaningful statistical model formulations for repeated measures. *Statistica Sinica, 14*, 989–1020.

Morrell, C. H., Pearson, J. D., & Brant, L. J. (1997). Linear transformations of linear mixed-effects models. *American Statistician, 51*, 338–343.

Mosteller, F., & Tukey, J. (1977). *Data analysis and regression: A second course*. New York: Addison-Wesley.

Murdoch, D. J., Tsai, Y. L., & Adcock, J. (2008). P-values are random variables. *American Statistician, 62*, 242–245.

Muthén, B. O., & Christoffersson, A. (1981). Simultaneous factor analysis of dichotomous variables in several groups. *Psychometrika, 46*, 407–419.

Nagin, D. S. (1999). Analyzing developmental trajectories: A semiparametric, group-based approach. *Psychological Methods, 4*, 139–157.

Nelder, J. A. (1971). Discussion on the papers by Wynn and Bloomfield, and O'Neill and Wetherill. *Journal of the Royal Statistical Society, Series B, 33*, 244–246.

Nelder, J. A. (1999). From statistics to statistical science. *Statistician, 48*, 257–269.

Neuwirth, E. (2007). Rcolorbrewer: Colorbrewer palettes [Computer software manual]. (R package version 1.0-2)

Neyman, J., & Pearson, E. S. (1928a). On the use and interpretation of certain test criteria for purposes of statistical inference. Part I. *Biometrika, 20A*, 175–240.

Neyman, J., & Pearson, E. S. (1928b). On the use and interpretation of certain test criteria for purposes of statistical inference. Part II. *Biometrika, 20A*, 263–294.

Neyman, J., & Pearson, E. S. (1933). On the problem of the most efficient tests of statistical hypotheses. *Philosophical Transactions of the Royal Society, Series A*(231), 289–337.

No Child Left Behind Act of 2001. (2002). *20 U.S.C. § 6301 et seq.* Available from http://www.gpo.gov/fdsys/pkg/PLAW-107publ110/content-detail.html

Northwest Evaluation Association. (2003). Technical manual for the NWEA measures of academic progress and achievement level tests. [Computer software manual]. Portland, OR.

Obradović, J., Long, J. D., Cutuli, J. J., Chan, C. K., Hinz, E., Heistad, D., et al. (2009). Academic achievement of homeless and highly mobile children in an urban school district: Longitudinal evidence on risk, growth, and resilience. *Development and Psychopathology, 21*, 493–518.

Obradović, J., Pardini, D. A., Long, J. D., & Loeber, R. (2007). Measuring interpersonal callousness in boys from childhood to adolescence: An examination of longitudinal invariance and temporal stability. *Journal of Clinical Child and Adolescent Psychology, 36*, 276–292.

Peirce, C. S. (1903). On selecting hypotheses. In *Collected papers of Charles Sander Peirce* (p. 413–422). Cambridge, MA: Harvard University Press.

Peixoto, J. L. (1987). Hierarchical variable selection in polynomial regression models. *The American Statistician, 41*, 311–313.

Pinheiro, J. C., & Bates, D. M. (2000). *Mixed-effects models in S and S-PLUS*. New York: Springer.

Pitts, S. C., West, S. G., & Tein, J. Y. (1996). Longitudinal measurement models in evaluation research:

Examining stability and change. *Evaluation and Program Planning, 19*, 333–350.

Platt, J. R. (1964). Strong inference. *Science, 146*, 347–353.

Popper, K. R. (1959). *The logic of scientific discovery*. New York: Basic Books.

Pungello, E. P., Kupersmidt, J. B., Burchinal, M. R., & Patterson, C. J. (1996). Environmental risk factors and children's achievement from middle childhood to early adolescence. *Developmental Psychology, 32*, 755–767.

Rao, C. R. (1992). R. A. Fisher: The founder of modern statistics. *Statistical Science, 7*, 34–48.

Rao, C. R., & Wu, Y. (2001). On model selection. In P. Lahiri (Ed.), *Model selection* (Vol. 38, p. 1–57). Beachwood, OH: Institute of Mathematical Statistics.

R Development Core Team. (2010). R: A language and environment for statistical computing [Computer software manual]. Vienna, Austria. Available from http://www.R-project.org (ISBN 3-900051-07-0)

Rencher, A. C. (2000). *Linear models in statistics*. New York: Wiley.

Richards, S. A. (2005). Testing ecological theory using the information-theoretic approach: Examples and cautionary results. *Ecology, 86*, 2805–2814.

Rossini, A. J., Heiberger, R. M., Hornik, K., Maechler, M., Sparapani, R. A., & Eglen, S. J. (2010). ESS —Emacs Speaks Statistics [Computer software manual]. Boston, MA. Available from http://ess.r-project.org/index.php?Section=home

Royall, R. M. (1996). *Statistical evidence: A likelihood paradigm*. Boca Raton, FL: Chapman & Hall/CRC.

Royall, R. M. (2000). On the probability of observing misleading statistical evidence. *Journal of the American Statistical Association, 95*, 760–768.

Royston, P., & Altman, D. G. (1994). Regression using fractional polynomials of continuous covariates: Parsimonious parametric modeling. *Applied Statistics, 43*, 429–467.

Royston, P., & Altman, D. G. (1997). Approximating statistical functions by using fractional polynomial regression. *Statistician, 46*, 411–422.

Royston, P., & Sauerbrei, W. (2007). Improving the robustness of fractional polynomial models by preliminary covariate transformation: A pragmatic approach. *Computational Statistics & Data Analysis, 51*, 4240–4253.

Royston, P., & Sauerbrei, W. (2008). *Multivariate model-building*. New York: Wiley.

Rubin, D. B. (1976). Inference and missing data. *Biometrika, 63*, 581–592.

Russell, B. (1966). *The Viking book of aphorisms* (W. H. Auden & L. Kronenberger, Eds.). New York: Viking.

Ryan, T. P. (1997). *Modern regression methods*. New York: Wiley.

Sakamoto, Y., Ishiguro, M., & Kitagawa, G. (1986). *Akaike Information Criterion Statistics*. Dordrecht/Boston/Lancaster/Tokyo: D. Reidel.

Sarkar, D. (2007). *Lattice: Multivariate data visualization with R*. New York: Springer.

Scheipl, F., Greven, S., & Küchenhoff, H. (2008). Size and power of tests for a zero random effect variance or polynomial regression in additive and linear mixed models. *Computational Statistics and Data Analysis, 52*, 3283–3299.

Schenk, C. (2009). MikTex 2.8 Manual [Computer software manual]. Boston, MA. Available from http://miktex.org/

Schervish, M. J. (1996). P values: What they are and what they are not. *American Statistician, 50*, 203–206.

Schott, J. R. (1997). *Matrix analysis for statistics*. New York: Wiley.

Schwarz, G. (1978). Estimating the dimension of a model. *Annals of Statistics, 6*, 461–464.

Self, S., & Liang, K. (1987). Asymptotic properties of maximum likelihood estimators and likelihood-ratio test under nonstandard conditions. *Journal of the American Statistical Association, 82*, 605–610.

Shin, T., Davison, M. L., & Long, J. D. (2009). Effects of missing data methods in structural equation modeling with nonnormal longitudinal data. *Structural Equation Modeling, 16*, 70–98.

Singer, J. D. (1998). Using SAS PROC MIXED to fit multilevel models, hierarchical models, and individual growth models. *Journal *of Educational and Behavioral Statistics*, *24*, 323–355.

Smedslund, G. (2006). All bachelors are unmarried men ($p < 0.05$). *Quality and Quantity*, *42*, 53–73.

Snijders, T., & Bosker, R. (1999). *Multilevel analysis: An introduction to basic and advanced multilevel modeling*. London: Sage.

Sober, E. (2002). Instrumentalism, parsimony, and the Akaike framework. *Philosophy of Science*, *69*, S112–S123.

Sober, E. (2006). Parsimony. In S. Sarkar & J. Pfeifer (Eds.), *The philosophy of science: An encyclopedia* (Vol. 2, p. 531–538). New York: Routledge.

Sprott, D. A. (2000). *Statistical inference in science*. New York: Springer.

Stallman, R. (2010). GNU Emacs Manual 23.2 [Computer software manual]. Boston, MA. Available from http://www.gnu.org/software/emacs/

Stram, D. O., & Lee, J. W. (1994). Variance components testing in the longitudinal mixed effects model. *Biometrics*, *50*, 1171–1177.

Taper, M. L. (2004). Model identification from many candidates. In M. L. Taper & S. R. Lele (Eds.), *The nature of scientific evidence* (p. 488–500). Chicago, IL: University of Chicago Press.

Tatsuoka, M. (1993). A handbook for data analysis in the behavioral sciences: Methodological issues. In G. Keren & C. Lewis (Eds.), (p. 461–480). Hillsdale, NJ: Lawrence Erlbaum.

Thompson, B. (2002). What future quantitative social science research could look like: Confidence intervals for effect sizes. *Educational Researcher*, *31*, 24–31.

Thompson, B. (2007). *The nature of statistical evidence*. New York: Springer.

Tukey, J. W. (1977). *Exploratory data analysis*. New York: Addison-Wesley.

Tukey, J. W. (1991). The philosophy of multiple comparisons. *Statistical Science*, *6*, 100–116.

Tukey, J. W. (1995). Discussion of "Assessment and propagation of model uncertainty" by D. Draper. *Journal of the Royal Statistical Society, Series B*, *57*, 45–70.

Ugarte, M. D. (2009). Comments on: Missing data methods in longitudinal studies: a review. *Test*, *18*, 44–46.

Vaida, F., & Blanchard, S. (2005). Conditional Akaike information for mixed-effects models. *Biometrika*, *92*, 351–370.

Vandenberg, R. J., & Lance, C. E. (2000). A review and synthesis of the measurement invariance literature: Suggestions, practices, and recommendations for organizational research. *Organizational Research Methods*, *3*, 4–70.

Verbeke, G., & Molenberghs, G. (2000). *Linear mixed models for longitudinal data*. New York: Springer-Verlag.

Verzani, J. (2005). *Using R for introductory statistics*. Boca Raton, FL: Chapman & Hall / CRC Press.

Vonesh, E. F., Chinchilli, V., & Pu, K. (1996). Goodness-of-fit in generalized nonlinear mixed-effects models. *Biometrics*, *52*, 572–587.

Vonesh, E. F., & Chinchilli, V. M. (1997). *Linear and nonlinear models for the analysis of repeated measurements*. New York: Marcel Dekker.

Ward, E. J. (2008). A review and comparison of four commonly used bayesian and maximum likelihood model selection tools. *Ecological Modeling*, *211*, 1–10.

Ware, J. H. (1985). Linear models for the analysis of longitudinal studies. *American Statistician*, *39*, 95–101.

Wasserman, L. (2000). Bayesian model selection and model averaging. *Journal of Mathematical Psychology*, *44*, 92–107.

Weakliem, D. L. (2004). Introduction to the special issue on model selection. *Sociological Methods and Research*, *33*, 167–187.

Weisberg, S. (2005). *Applied linear regression* (3rd ed.). New York: John Wiley & Sons.

Wickham, H. (2009a). plyr: Tools for splitting, applying and combining data [Computer software manual]. Available from http://CRAN.R-project.org/package=plyr (R package version 0.1.9)

Wickham, H. (2009b). *ggplot2: Elegant graphics for data analysis*. New York: Springer.

Wilk, M. B., & Gnanadesikan, R. (1968). Probability plotting methods for the analysis of data. *Biometrika*, *55*, 1–17.

Wilkinson, L., & APA Task Force on Statistical Inference. (1999). Statistical methods in psychology journals: Guidelines and explanations. *American Psychologist, 54*, 594–604.

Xu, R. (2003). Measuring explained variation in linear mixed effects models. *Statistics in Medicine, 22*, 3527–3541.

Xue, Y., & Meisels, S. J. (2004). Early literacy instruction and learning in kindergarten: Evidence from the early childhood longitudinal study—kindergarten class of 1998-99. *American Educational Research Journal, 41*, 191–229.

Zeller, M. H., Modi, A. C., Noll, J. G., Long, J. D., & Inge, T. H. (2009). Psychosocial functioning improves following adolescent bariatric surgery. *Obesity, 17*, 985–990.

Zhang, D., & Davidian, M. (2001). Linear mixed models with flexible distributions of random effects for longitudinal data. *Biometrics, 57*, 795–802.

Zheng, B. (2000). Summarizing the goodness of fit of generalized linear models for longitudinal data. *Statistics in Medicine, 19*, 1265–1275.

Zill, N., & West, J. (2001). *Entering kindergarten: Findings from the Condition of Education 2000*. Washington, DC: U.S. Department of Education/OERI.

Author Index

Abelson, R.P., 235
Adcock, J., 290
Akaike, H., xviii, 23, 210, 228, 235
Allison, P.D., 89
Altman, D.G., 466, 478
American Educational Research Association, 288
American Psychological Association, 275, 287, 288, 290
Anderson, D.R., xviii, 25, 235, 243, 247, 248, 254–256, 281, 287, 299, 311
Applebee, A.N., 27, 262
Arnold, D.H., 27
Azzalini, A., 191, 193

Baayen, R.H., 222
Barker, R.J., 283
Bates, D.M., xvii, xviii, 170, 189, 207, 223, 224, 299, 312, 355, 360, 383–385, 514
Bayarri, M.J., 218, 294
Berger, J.O., 202, 218, 234, 283, 289
Berkson, J., 259, 287, 288
Blume, J.D., 234
Bolker, B.M., 202, 205
Boos, D.D., 282
Bosker, R., 427
Box, G.E.P., 100, 258, 488
Bretz, F., 418, 419
Burnham, K.P., xviii, 25, 210, 235, 254, 287, 311
Burt, K.B., 4
Buyske, S., 355

Calinski, T., 352
Campbell, J.R., 262
Caro, D.H., 27, 262
Carroll, R.J., 387
Chamberlain, T.C., 25, 233
Chatfield, C., 25, 106, 231, 301
Chatterji, M., 27, 261
Chinchilli, V.M., 427

Christensen, R., 218, 219, 234, 256, 259, 289, 294
Cleveland, W.S., 321, 448
Cliff, N., 437
Cnaan, A., 29
Cohen, J., 29, 235, 258, 259, 287, 316
Cox, D.R., 232, 254, 290, 311, 312
Crainiceanu, C., 384

Davison, A.C., 282
Davison, M.L., 27, 262, 444
Dearing, E., 27, 262
DeLeeuw, J., 258, 427, 429
Diggle, P.J., 98, 168, 189, 320, 500
Ding, C.S., 27
Donnelly, C.A., 467

Eamon, M.K., 27
Edwards, A.W.F., 191, 202
Efron, B., 277, 294
Eubank, R.L., 465

Falissard, B., 351
Faraway, J.J., 25, 106, 231
Feyerabend, P., 25, 233
Fidler, F., 288, 290
Fieuws, S., 506
Finch, S., 256
Fisher, R.A., 27, 191, 234, 256, 257, 259, 288, 294, 419
Fitzmaurice, G.M., xviii, 8, 89, 189, 224, 384
Forster, M.R., xviii, 232, 235, 242, 258, 285, 290, 292
Free Software Foundation, 33
Freedman, D., 25, 26

Gelman, A., 75, 132, 256, 257, 290, 419
Genolini, C., 351
Gigerenzer, G., 235
Godfrey, L.G., 315
Golden, R.M., 255

Goodman, S.N., 24, 256, 257, 288, 289, 294
Greene, W., 220
Greenland, S., 289
Greven, S., 311, 393
Griepentrog, G.L., 302

Hacking, I., 288, 292
Hand, D.J., 23
Harabasz, J., 352
Hardy, A., 351, 352
Harrell, F.E., xxi, 308
Harwell, M., 27, 261
Hedges, L.V., 262, 299
Henry, G.T., 491
Hinz, E.E., 491
Hirst, K.E., 451
Hogan, T.P., xviii
Hornik, K., xvii, 33
Hothorn, T., 418, 419
Howell, D.C., 57
Hsu, J.C., 419
Hubbard, R., 29, 218, 235, 256, 287–290, 294
Hurvich, C.M., 245

Jaeger, A., 163, 174
Johnstone, D.J., 287, 290

Kadane, J.B., 282
Keppel, G., 19
Kieseppä, I.A., 232
Kleinbaum, D.G., 158
Klimes-Dougan, B.K., 6, 255
Kneib, T., 311, 393
Kolen, M.J., 7, 21
Krantz, D.H., 235, 255, 287
Kreft, I., 427, 429
Kuczmarski, R.J., 444
Kuha, J., 210
Kullback, S., 235

Laird, N.M., xviii, 185, 467
Lee, J., 261
Lee, J.W., 384
Leibler, R.A., 235
Leisch, F., xxi
Liang, H., 244
Liang, K., 384
Lindquist, M.A., 290

Lindsey, J.K., 202, 258, 292
Link, W.A., 283
Littell, R.C., 222
Long, J.D., 7, 22, 27, 262, 437, 439, 444, 467, 478
Lovell, M.C., 25, 301

Magee, L., 302
Mallows, C., 23
Masten, A.S., 4, 491
Matthes, A., 520
Mayo, D.G., 289, 294
Mazerolle, M.J., 244
McClelland, G., 75, 132
McDonald, B.W., 4, 7
McLoyd, V.C., 27
Meehl, P.E., 29
Miller, A., 26, 301
Mizerek, E.A., 491
Molenberghs, G., 18, 89, 92, 99, 164, 223, 347, 366
Morrell, C.H., 302
Mosteller, F., 468
Murdoch, D.J., 290
Muthén, B.O., 7

Nagin, D.S., 350
Nelder, J.A., 287, 290, 419
Neyman, J., 234, 256, 288, 290, 419
Northwest Evaluation Association, 21, 427, 437

Obradović, J., 7, 21, 261, 491
Olkin, I., 299

Pearson, E.S., 234, 256, 288, 290
Peirce, C.S., 25, 233
Pericchi, L.R., 283
Pinheiro, J.C., xvii, 189, 207, 224, 299, 300, 312, 355, 360, 384, 514
Pitts, S.C., 7
Platt, J.R., 25, 233
Popper, K.R., 289
Pu, K.W., 427
Pungello, E.P., 27

R Development Core Team, xvii, 3
Rao, C.R., 292, 294
Rencher, A.C., 488

Author Index

Richards, S.A., 255
Royall, R.M., 191, 202, 288, 292, 311
Royston, P., 466, 478, 488
Rubin, D.B., 89
Rubinstein, R., 491
Ruppert, D., 384
Russell, B., 193
Ryan, T.P., 334, 459

Sarkar, D., 203
Sauerbrei, W., 466, 478
Scheipl, F., 385, 389
Schervish, M.J., 259
Schott, J.R., 515
Schwartz, G., 210, 282
Self, S., 223, 384
Shin, T., 27, 262, 444
Singer, J.D., 427, 429
Smedslund, G., 287
Snijders, T., 427
Sober, E., xviii, 235, 242, 268
Speckman, P., 465
Sprott, D.A., 27, 191, 193, 195, 211, 259
Stram, D.O., 384

Taper, M.L., 258
Tatsuoka, M., 427
Thompson, B., 259, 288
Tidwell, P.W., 488

Tsai, C.L., 245
Tsai, Y.L., 290
Tukey, J.W., 26, 29, 105, 254, 260, 419, 468

Ugarte, M.D., 98, 223

Vaida, F., 244
Vandenberg, R.J., 7
Verbeke, G., 18, 171, 211, 223, 347, 366, 506
Verzani, J., 151
Vonesh, E.F., 427

Ward, E.J., 283
Ware, J.H., xviii, 29, 467
Wasserman, L., 282
Weakliem, D.L., 258, 291
Weisberg, S., 152
Westfall, P., 418, 419
Wickham, H., 55, 107, 145
Wilkinson, L., 255, 256, 288
Wu, Y., 294

Xu, R., 427
Xue, Y., 261

Zeller, M.H., 467
Zhang, D., 168
Zheng, B., 427
Zill, N., 261

Subject Index

AICcmodavg, 244
Akaike information criterion (AIC),
  23, 30, 171, 173, 191, 208, 210,
  212, 213, 228, 235, 241,
  245–246, 286, 326, 393
  corrected, see AIC
analysis comprehension, 34
anchoring intercept, 12, 175–177,
  385, 386, 433, 478
ANCOVA, 2, 149, 154–157,
  159, 160
ANOVA/MANOVA, 19, 64, 102, 149,
  308, 366, 405
approximating model, 238, 242, 243,
  246, 268, 277, 295
ASCII file, see text file
assignment, 38

backward elmination, see top-down
Bayesian information criterion (BIC),
  171, 210, 212, 213, 282
best linear unbiased predictor
  (BLUP), 395
  empirical (EBLUP),
  395–403, 406
between-subjects variability, 10, 184,
  364, 376, 429
bootstrap, 268, 277–282, 312–316,
  384–392
bouquet of models,
  26, 254

candidate model, 237
change curve, 4, 11,
  336, 446
character vector, 40
clustering, 322, 325, 336,
  350–355
compound symmetry, 366
concatenation, 39, 67, 378
conditional model, 75, 82,
  130, 335
confidence set, 248

contrast matrix, 417–420
convergence failure, 359
correlation
  fixed effects, 173, 220, 500,
    504–506
  random effects, 18, 31, 165, 167,
    168, 172, 176, 185, 188, 215,
    216, 220, 225, 229, 358, 360,
    362, 389, 505, 510, 512
  responses, 4, 73, 80, 169, 184,
    214, 220, 224, 337, 358,
    363–371, 507
covariance, see correlation
covariate, 2, 100

data frame, 45–51, 70
  creating, 65–68, 100
  displaying, 68–70
  merging, 121, 180
data structure, 44–49, 63
  balanced, 84, 85, 100, 102, 104,
    125, 128
  long format, 9, 64–65, 76, 79, 80,
    84–86, 100, 104, 150, 151, 161
  reshaping, 64, 76, 79, 100, 104
  wide format, 64, 72, 76, 79, 84,
    85, 100, 104, 351
data type, 41, 70
decay pattern, 74, 189, 368
derivative, 449–454, 463
design matrix, 182, 187, 270, 384,
  406, 486, 488
deviance, 171, 192, 198–201, 203,
  208–212, 214–238
  predictive, 239, 241, 243
dummy coding, 155, 271, 409–420
dynamic predictor, 11, 100, 489–500

effect size
  absolute, 427–433
  AIC, 30, 246, 254, 272
  delta, 246–248, 292

539

evidence ratio, 247, 252–253, 265, 277–281
weight of evidence, 30, 247–251, 256, 265
error, 17, 116, 152, 161, 162, 164, 165, 167, 168, 171, 174, 182, 195, 196, 214, 215, 229, 321, 360, 362, 376, 395, 461
variance, 17, 153, 168, 174, 185, 188, 363, 376
estimators, 193

F-test, 60, 153
faceting, 446
factor variable, 41
false model, 238
fitted model object, 151, 263, 269, 278, 334
fitted values, 116, 126, 153, 165, 239, 270, 405–409, 414, 424, 475, 482, 484
fixed effects, 9, 18, 29, 31, 123, 149, 150, 162–165, 171, 173, 182, 214, 229, 406, 468
forward selection, *see* step-up
functions, 61–63
statistical, 40–41
user-defined, 54–59, 278, 313, 317, 338, 349, 364, 365, 388, 406, 450

general linear hypothesis, 417
generalized least squares (GLS), 215, 224
ggplot2, 106, 145, 154, 197, 200, 297, 451
global model, 448, 478
graph
bar, 264
boxplot, 342, 343, 345, 373, 378, 380, 397
customizing, 143–145
density plot, 57, 397
facet, 112, 136, 138
means, 123, 125, 132, 141
Q-Q plot, 382, 397
saving, 112
spaghetti plot, 109
growth curve, *see* change curve

hierarchical model, *see* multilevel model
hypothesis
alternative, 28, 29, 233
nil, 259
null, 28, 233, 258, 260
statistical, 27–32
working, 25, 28, 232, 258, 260

identifiability, 216
indexing, 38, 49–52, 71, 87, 456
inference
multimodel, xviii, 25–32, 191, 228, 254–277, 326–327, 419, 421, 427
omnibus, 60, 415
specific, 415
statistical, 230
information criterion, 235
information theory, 23, 26, 210
initial status, 179
interaction, 12, 149, 158, 307, 308, 507
among dynamic predictors, 491, 495, 496
among static predictors, 420–426
as slope effect, 158, 420
intercept effect, 156, 160, 177–179, 181, 227, 271, 408
item response theory (IRT), 7, 21

jittering, 125, 343

large-sample, 193
likelihood ratio test (LRT), 26, 191, 208, 211, 213, 218, 228, 234, 257, 333–335, 383
linear mixed effects regression (LMER), xviii, 2, 9, 14, 63, 85, 97, 147, 160–189, 191, 243
linear model (LM), 14, 59–60, 116, 126, 148–160, 167, 168, 173, 194, 236
lme4, 170, 171, 181, 222
lmer(), 170, 171, 181, 222
local model, 448, 478
log-likelihood, 171, 197, 208, 212
longitudinal covariation, 493, 495

main effect, 156, 307, 308, 491
as intercept effect, 156, 408, 420

Subject Index 541

matrix algebra, 181, 187, 270, 365, 406, 431, 486, 515–523
maximum likelihood (ML), 27, 163, 171, 228
mean change, 4, 73, 75, 123, 125, 132, 141, 153, 216, 409, 414, 446, 484
missing data, 20, 43, 63, 67, 74, 79, 82, 85–100, 104, 109, 119, 121, 150, 153, 162, 163, 172, 222, 223, 291, 337, 344, 351, 363, 493
    concepts, 89–92
model evaluation uncertainty, 248, 252, 302, 305
model matrix, *see* design matrix
monotonic curve, 467, 468, 471, 474
MPLS data set, 21, 63, 260, 261, 444, 490
multilevel model, 147, 163, 177, 178, 229, 322, 336, 395, 462, 474, 484, 490, 507, 510
multiple regression, *see* linear model (LM)

NA, *see* missing data
nested models, 84, 211, 228, 245, 262, 285, 288, 291–294, 316, 390, 464, 489, 507–514
nonlinear curves, 117, 119, 122, 150, 212, 493
normality, 17, 152, 168, 195–197, 214, 360, 382, 397
null hypothesis statistical testing (NHST), 24, 26, 28, 191, 228, 234, 235, 255–260, 285, 294, 421
numerical methods, 201–207

object, 38
ordinary least squares (OLS), 14, 192, 195, 198, 209, 337, 339, 346, 348, 357, 371–376, 400
outlier, 109, 110, 355
over-fit, 25
overfit, 238, 239

parsimony, 268, 285, 288, 295, 324, 333, 486
penalized index, 210, 239, 348

periodic effects, 461
plausible model, 246, 254, 268, 273
polynomials, 12, 117, 118, 123, 126, 127, 180, 212, 230, 322–326, 340, 433, 443
    fractional, 443, 466–478, 488
    mean-corrected, 454–460
    orthogonal, 20, 118, 454–460, 486–488
    raw, 449–460
predictive accuracy, 235–243, 295–301
proportion reduction in error (PRE), 377, 380
proportion reduction in variance (PRV), 429

quit, 37

R^2
    Level 1 model, 336, 338–346, 375
    LM, 60, 153, 200, 210, 235, 273, 322
    LMER, 250, 273, 405, 427–429
    pooled (meta), 346–350
random effects, 9, 13–19, 31, 147, 149, 162–171, 182, 184, 186–187, 214, 229, 324, 339, 395, 420
    predicted, 14, 394–403
random intercept, 16
random slope, 16
randomization, 491
Rdata file, 37, 53, 78, 109, 150
recoding, 70
relative fit, 273
required sample size, 287, 288, 316–320
residual, 60, 152, 376, 378, 382
    variance, 377
residual standard error (RSE), 60, 207
    pooled (meta), 347
response variable, 8
    multiple, 489, 500–507
restricted maximum likelihood (REML), 171, 207, 212, 225, 361–363, 385, 386, 388
R software, xvii, 3, 33, 34

saturated model, 119, 323, 340, 344
script file, 34, 36
slope effect, 158, 160, 177–179, 181, 227, 272, 420
smoothers, 116, 122, 126–128
sorting, 78
splines, 443, 448, 478–486
　piecewise polynomials, 478, 479, 481, 483, 486
　regression, 478, 479
stability coefficient, 4
standard error of regression, 116
standard errors, 60, 216–223
standardized change, 405, 433, 437–441
static predictor, 11, 82, 130–143, 156, 164, 177–180, 227, 262, 322, 324, 329, 394, 409–427, 474, 484, 507, 513
statistical computing, 3
statistical efficiency, 359
statistical model, 232
statistical power, 311, 316, 317, 319
statistical strategy, 23, 105–106, 115, 148, 227–235, 472
　confirmatory, 23, 25, 105, 227, 273, 286, 301, 324, 325, 443
　exploratory, 25, 105, 115, 123, 227, 273, 286, 301, 324, 325, 327, 335, 350, 443, 472

statistics
　descriptive, 72, 74, 80, 82, 93, 336, 346, 348, 357, 371, 376
step-up, 301–307, 333, 459
sum of squared error (SSE), 192, 215
sum of squared residuals (SSR), 209, 240
sums of squares (SS), 346, 347

text file
　comma-delimited, 65, 68
　space-delimited, 65, 68
time predictor, 9, 170, 490
top-down, 301, 307–310, 333
t-ratio, *see* z-ratio
trigonometric functions, 443, 461–466
true model, 236, 277, 278, 283, 285, 295

unconditional model, 12, 150, 160, 181, 327–329, 333, 336, 475, 479

variance component, 229, 359–363, 394

Wald test, 218
within-subjects variability, 10, 17, 174–175, 184, 364
workspace image, 37

z-ratio, 60, 152, 159, 173, 217, 218

SAGE Research Methods Online
The essential tool for researchers

Sign up now at www.sagepub.com/srmo for more information.

An expert research tool
- An **expertly designed taxonomy** with more than 1,400 unique terms for social and behavioral science research methods
- **Visual and hierarchical search tools** to help you discover material and link to related methods

- Easy-to-use navigation tools
- Content organized by complexity
- Tools for citing, printing, and downloading content with ease
- Regularly updated content and features

A wealth of essential content
- The most comprehensive picture of quantitative, qualitative, and mixed methods available today
- More than **100,000 pages of SAGE book and reference material** on research methods as well as editorially selected material from SAGE journals
- More than **600 books** available in their entirety online

Launching 2011!

$SAGE research methods online